Exotic Preferences

Exotic Preferences

Behavioral Economics and Human Motivation

Edited by
George Loewenstein

OXFORD
UNIVERSITY PRESS

OXFORD
UNIVERSITY PRESS

Great Clarendon Street, Oxford ox2 6DP

Oxford University Press is a department of the University of Oxford.
It furthers the University's objective of excellence in research, scholarship,
and education by publishing worldwide in

Oxford New York

Auckland Cape Town Dar es Salaam Hong Kong Karachi
Kuala Lumpur Madrid Melbourne Mexico City Nairobi
New Delhi Shanghai Taipei Toronto

With offices in

Argentina Austria Brazil Chile Czech Republic France Greece
Guatemala Hungary Italy Japan Poland Portugal Singapore
South Korea Switzerland Thailand Turkey Ukraine Vietnam

Oxford is a registered trade mark of Oxford University Press
in the UK and in certain other countries

Published in the United States
by Oxford University Press Inc., New York

First published 2007

First published in paperback 2008

British Library Cataloguing in Publication Data
Data available

Library of Congress Cataloging in Publication Data
Data available

Typeset by SPI Publisher Services, Pondicherry, India
Printed in Great Britain
on acid-free paper by
CPI Antony Rowe, Chippenham, Wiltshire

ISBN 978-0-19-925707-2 (Hbk.)
       978-0-19-925708-9 (Pbk.)

1 3 5 7 9 10 8 6 4 2

This book is dedicated to my collaborators and friends, without whom it truly would not have been possible. Exotic or not, they have turned work into its antithesis.

Acknowledgments

I thank Roland Benabou, Sarah Caro, Donna Harsch, Jules Lobel, Terry Vaughn, and especially Nina Pillard for helpful comments on this introduction. I am also grateful to Rosa Stipanovic, who provided diverse forms of assistant that enabled the project to move forward, and Julie Wade, who copyedited the manuscript.

Contents

Contents

Introduction

George Loewenstein

While many things diminish with advancing age, at least two tend to increase: the ratio of funerals to weddings that one attends and the average age of the celebrant at birthday parties one is invited to. And, although funerals and late-age birthdays are generally gloomier affairs than celebrations for those who still have the 'best years' of their lives ahead of them, there are compensations. Chief among these is the opportunity that such occasions afford for reflection. Viewing a life in retrospect (or at least that part which can be gleaned from oratories, eulogies, and conversations about the celebrant with other attendees), one naturally makes judgments about the quality of the life being celebrated, with inevitable spillover into evaluations of one's own. In fact, if the celebrated individual is sufficiently more advanced in age than oneself, and provides either positive or negative 'object lessons', one can even contemplate course corrections—for example, the inevitable "I need to spend more time with my family!" However, much like the tendency to slow down immediately after witnessing a car crash, such fleeting resolutions rarely produce sustained change.

Publishing a collection of one's own past work is a bit like attending one's own late birthday or funeral. Although there is a natural tendency to not judge one's own life and works as critically as one judges others', it is difficult to completely turn off critical faculties that have been honed over one's entire academic career, in contentious academic seminars, referee reports, and grading student work. When all of your training has turned you into the neural equivalent of an attacking dog, even one's own tail becomes an attractive target. It is therefore with some squeamishness that I offer these papers for public perusal. Perhaps in part out of insecurity about the quality of the papers themselves, I have preceded each with some informal comments intended to provide a flavor of when, how, and why I wrote the paper and, more importantly, a sense of the eccentricities and endearing qualities of some of the researchers I have had the good fortune to work with.

My colleague and sometimes collaborator Roberto Weber read several of my vignettes about coauthors and cautioned me that I should share them with their subjects because, he believed, several would be unlikely to be pleased. Insightful as always, he further suggested that I should try to imagine how I would feel if someone wrote in a similar fashion about me, a prospect that, as he intended it to, filled me with horror. Hopefully, therefore, this won't be the first of a series of tell-all book introductions by behavioral economists, or at least not by any who work with me. To preempt such an outcome, however, let me admit to a few of the negative characteristics I'm least ashamed to acknowledge.

Generic Man

Like many of my friends, I often feel out of step with the world around me. Ninety percent of Americans believe in God, but even on the verge of death (at times when I overestimated my prowess at various outdoor activities) I haven't been able to summon even a ray of hope that I would eventually meet my 'loved ones' in some 'better place'. I wouldn't describe myself as Generic Man 'spiritual'; Expensive fast cars leave me cold, as does cheap fast food. I don't watch sports on TV (except when the Steelers are on a roll); in fact, I barely watch TV at all. Count me lucky to have never wished to run for public office.

Although out of step with the vast majority of the population, I've made a career of assuming the opposite—that if I am feeling something or do something, most people are probably feeling and doing the same. And, if I notice that I'm responding to a particular situation in a way that strikes me as inconsistent with the assumptions and predictions of economics, it's likely that I have a new project on my hands. In other words, despite an acute awareness of my own idiosyncrasies, when it comes to research my working assumption is that my own reactions, feelings, or behavior are typical.

For example, the standard assumption in economics is that people care more about the present than the future, which implies that they should put off unpleasant tasks and overindulge their immediate appetites. I notice, however, that my own distaste for having unpleasant things hanging over me motivates me to do away with them quickly. Likewise, I often have to precommit to doing fun stuff like taking a vacation or buying something I want. These self-reflections have led to a variety of research projects which challenge the standard assumption that people steeply 'discount' (i.e. care less about) the future.

Mainstream economists sometimes refer to the type of work I do as the study of 'exotic preferences' (with the implication that such preferences are unusual and not worthy of study). But the preferences that conventional economists view as exotic shed light on important aspects of what is actually very ordinary behavior. It is, after all, hardly exotic that people derive current pleasure and pain from thinking about what might happen in the future, and, as a result, often expedite negative experiences to 'get them over with quickly' or 'save the best for last'. Faced with fuller explication and data, only Vulcans (a category within which I would include a rather large fraction of fellow economists) would fail to appreciate the reality and significance of the common, and not at all exotic, desire for things to get better over time.

But, enough attacks on conventional economics. Twenty years ago, behavioral economists might reasonably have felt like an embattled minority, and felt self-righteous about lashing out at those too ignorant to see the light. Such a posture has come to seem somewhat paranoid, however, given the great success of behavioral economics over the last few decades. Behavioral economics is still being attacked, but the attackers, who of late seem to consist mainly of hard-line theorists, have less the quality of defenders of the faith and more that of desperados who fear that their own perspective is in decline.

Paranoid Loner

Having cast myself as generic man, it may seem somewhat contradictory that I am also something of a loner. Even when one occupies the favorable ground of an academic specialty that happens to be in favor at a particular moment,[1] academia is a nasty environment, strewn with hidden traps and populated by hostile, territorial tribes protecting their ideas with a ferocity akin to what one would expect a parent to direct at someone trying to steal his baby.[2] In part because I don't want to deal with reviewers who view me as a baby-stealer, and in part because I can't trust myself not to take a similar posture when evaluating others' work, I have always tried, as much as possible, to

[1] Alain De Bottom (2004: 88–9) in his characteristically brilliant treatise *Status Anxiety*, writes: "Our status also depends on a range of favourable conditions that could be loosely defined by the word *luck*. It may be merely good luck that places us in the right occupation, with the right skills at the right time, and little more than bad luck that denies us the selfsame advantages. But, pointing to luck as an explanation for for what happens in our lives has, regrettably, become effectively unacceptable.... While few would deny outright that luck retains a theoretical role in mapping the course of careers, the evaluation of individuals proceeds, in practical terms, on the assumption that they may fairly be held responsible for their own biographies. It would sound to our ears unduly (and even suspiciously) modest for someone to ascribe a personal or professional triumph to 'good luck',.... Winners make their own luck, so goes the modern mantra."

[2] One of my graduate advisers, Bob Abelson, wrote a paper titled "Beliefs as Possessions" which we argued that people treat their beliefs as they do possessions—e.g. defending them from attack or theft. Given the heat of the emotion behind the protectiveness, "Beliefs as Babies" strikes me as more on-target.

work on subjects to which other people aren't paying much attention—to slip by the legions of possessive idea-parents unnoticed.

Hannah Arendt captured my own feelings perfectly when she commented on the feeling of isolation she experienced as the people around her got swept up by social or national movements that left her cold. As she expressed it, "I have never in my life 'loved' any people or collective—neither the German people, nor the French, nor the American, nor the working class or anything of that sort." Like Arendt, I've never been much of a team player, perhaps as a result of always having been the last person chosen for athletic teams when I was growing up.[3] And I feel the most freakish and out of step with my environment when the people around me are motivated by group spirit. If Tajfel's famous 'minimal group' experiments had been populated by people like Arendt and me, he probably would have come up with the opposite theory of the one he is known for.[4]

The closest thing I've experienced to a feeling of group identity happens when a group that I'm a member of comes under attack. I've never felt as much a Jew as the year my family and I spent in Berlin, confronted wherever I wandered with memorials to atrocities against Jews. When I travel abroad and people verbally attack the United States I used to occasionally experience a weak stirring of patriotism that is noticeably absent when I am home.

A similar thing happens to me with respect to my disciplinary (as opposed to religious or national) identity. When I'm in the company of psychologists, I often find myself identifying with economists, and the reverse is true when I'm in the company of economists.

Psychologists often view economics as a branch of mathematics, and they have a point. Economists claim that mathematics 'disciplines' their thinking, which may have a germ of truth, but the reality is that very little of that fancy math is ever used in empirical research or in guiding policy. And a downside of the math is that economists have made their work inaccessible to those outside the profession—even to the mathematically unsophisticated *within* the profession. Whereas economics used to boast public thinkers, such as John Kenneth Galbraith, who brought economic ideas to the populace, with a few exceptions (notably Robert Frank, Paul Krugman, and most recently Steve Leavitt), journalists, such as Malcom Gladwell, are currently the main people bringing economists' ideas to the public.

---

[3] It was once widely believed that personality is formed in the first three years of life, but I believe it is formed in junior high school. I know that *I've* spent my adult years trying unsuccessfully to live down the trauma of those years.

[4] In his 'minimal groups' paradigm Tajfel found that forming people into a group on the flimsiest basis—e.g., their preference for different colors—was sufficient to create loyalty such that people liked, and thought highly of, others in their own group and had opposite feelings toward those in other groups.

Economists, on their side, often view psychology as ad hoc. For better or for worse, economists have a unified theoretical framework that they apply to all types of problems.[5] Psychologists, economists sometimes charge (again with some validity), have a different 'theory' to account for every observation. Much of psychology seems to consist of proving the obvious or playing what I call the 'name game': In psychology the person who comes up with the label for a phenomenon in some sense 'owns it', which leads to a proliferation of different labels for barely differentiated concepts.

I've generally dealt with my identity crisis by trying to write papers that either group can understand and appreciate. But, I haven't been all that successful. Most psychologists who don't know me assume that I'm an economist, and most economists I know assume that I'm a psychologist. Fortunately, up to this point, neither clan has asked me to sign an oath of loyalty.

A Note on the Choice of Chapters

The overwhelming desire to include everything is one of the most destructive motivations in academia, and it applies not only to seminars, but to the choice of chapters for a book of collected works like this one. As an imperfect solution to the problem of self-censorship, I decided to limit the number of papers by limiting the topics included in the book. Not included are papers dealing with policy issues which fall under the main headings of (1) law, (2) medicine, or (3) accounting. With a few exceptions, I also decided to exclude unrefereed book chapters and review papers.[6] Within the categories of papers that I did not exclude, I selected papers based on quality and quirkiness. In some cases, such as the second chapter, I decided to reprint papers in this volume as a way of, in effect, resurrecting them—because I felt that they had not received the degree of attention I had hoped. If you don't like the papers included in this volume, I can assure you that you would *love* the papers that didn't make it.

[5] For a discussion of the pros and cons of a unified perspective, See Sanfrey, A., Loewenstein, G., Cohen, J. D., and McClure, S. M. (2006). 'Neuroeconomics: Integrating the disparate approaches of neuroscience and economics. *Trends in Cognitive Science*, 10(3): 108–16.

[6] That editorial decision left on the cutting room floor two papers that I am particularly fond of: Frederick, S., Loewenstein, G., and O'Donoghue, T. (2002). 'Time Discounting and Time Preference A Critical Review', *Journal of Economic Literature*, 40(2): 351–401; Camerer, C., Loewenstein, G., and Prelec, D. (2005). 'Neuroeconomics: How Neuroscience Can Inform Economics', *Journal of Economic Literature*, 43(1): 9–64.

Part I

General Perspectives, History, and Methods

1

Because It Is There: The Challenge of Mountaineering . . . for Utility Theory

George Loewenstein

This paper began as the solution to a self-control problem. I wrote it during the year that I spent at the Center for Advanced Study in the Behavioral Sciences at Stanford along with Colin Camerer, Drazen Prelec, Matthew Rabin, and Dick Thaler. Although I think it's often difficult to assess how much one enjoys experiences (see Chapter 10), without a doubt this was the best year of my life. I was living in a place that offered all the things I love most: a supportive research environment where I could live with my family and near several of my closest friends and without any teaching responsibilities—all in an outdoor enthusiast's paradise.

The administration of the Center, knowing that they were dealing with a bunch of over-ambitious compulsive workaholics, intervened periodically to get us to relax—for example, by encouraging attendance at the daily post-lunch volleyball game, and hosting wine tasting parties. Relaxing, however, just isn't me; I was, and had been for along time, working too hard. I would often arrive at my cubicle at the Center before the sun rose over the San Francisco Bay and long before any other souls showed up at the Center. I could see the illogic of my ways. I knew that when my children (a second, Rosa, came along a few years later) had left home I would wish I had spent more time with them, and that, at the moment I retire, all the long hours and professional accomplishments wouldn't, as the saying goes, amount to a 'hill of beans'. I knew all that, but I just couldn't act on the knowledge.

For years I had wanted to read the literature on mountaineering, having done some amateur mountaineering myself, but I couldn't find the time—even at the Center. The opportunity arrived in the form of an invitation—to give one of two keynote addresses at a conference on economics and psychology at Oxford that was scheduled for that July. To force myself to do what I really wanted to do anyway, I agreed to present a paper at the conference on the subject of mountaineering.

What I came to realize when I read the mountaineering literature (and in fact already knew from my own, albeit much tamer, experiences) was that mountaineering is an activity that doesn't fit the standard economic model of individual behavior. Serious mountaineering exposes one to a relentless alternation of boredom, exhaustion, discomfort, and terror. Why, then, do people do it? In the paper, I discuss four different motives (of which the most important is self-esteem) which, I believe, have not been adequately treated by economics. Moreover, as I argue at the end of the paper, mountaineering is not unusual in being driven by these noneconomic motives; much if not most human activity, including academic enterprise, is driven by motives that are rarely discussed by economists.

The paper was well received at the conference and, even better, my fellow keynote speaker, Bruno Frey, liked the paper sufficiently to volunteer to publish it in his house journal, *Kyklos*—the International Zeitshift for the Social Sciences. The paper also caught the attention of the organizers of a conference on Extreme Sports in Geneva, and got me invited to that conference, where it received a much less positive reception than it had at Oxford. At that conference, I had the opportunity to meet several extreme athletes[1] and to make myself *extremely* unpopular, in part due to my inability to speak French, but far more due to the cynical central message of my paper—that the motivations for doing extreme sports are far less lofty than the extreme athletes at the conference professed to believe. In response to my assertion that mountaineering is driven largely by ego, and is in reality a matter of almost unremitting misery, one French skier (who, among other amazing accomplishments, had climbed Mount Everest and then skied down) took me aside to tell me "no no, you have it all wrong. Eet ees not miserable, eet is wonderful—like making luuv to a beautiful woman." I had no doubt that he spoke from experience. However, no one is going to persuade me that climbing into the "death zone" holds a candle to some of the other pleasures that life has to offer.

---

[1] Some of my friends consider me a lunatic outdoorsman, but here were some real extremists. One invented a sport of swimming down waterfalls, holding a rubberized protector in front of him that looked like the prow of a boat. (At the conference, they showed a movie of him doing that.) Another showed a film of himself taking off in a small float-plane in the Chugach range of Alaska, jumping off the plane's pontoon onto the cornice of a mountain, and skiing down the ensuing avalanche.

Because It Is There: The Challenge of Mountaineering ... for Utility Theory*

*George Loewenstein***

> *If the old question, the one that Mallory tried to answer is a valid one, I have given up trying to meet it rationally.*
>
> David Roberts, Mountain of My Fear

1.1. Introduction

Among recent contributions of psychology to economics, perhaps the most compelling and influential have been those that have enriched the economic concept of utility. In its early incarnations, utility was a robustly psychological construct. In the century following Bentham's (1789) conception of utility, economists and moral philosophers devoted considerable discussion to its characteristics and determinants. The evolution of the utility concept during our century, however, has been characterized by a progressive stripping away of psychology, culminating in notions of ordinal utility and revealed preference that encompass little more psychological insight than the observation that people choose what they prefer.

In the last few decades, however, some of the original richness and complexity of the utility concept has been restored. This restoration has involved,

* This chapter was originally published as Loewenstein, G. (1999) 'Because It Is There', Kyklos, 52: 315–344. It has been reproduced here by kind permission of Blackwell Publishing.

** I am grateful for comments from Iris Bohnet, Colin Camerer, Shane Frederick, Donna Harsch, Tim Heath, Kalle Moene, Kathleen Much, Drazen Prelec, Daniel Read, Michal Strahilevitz, James Thompson, Chuck Tilly and George Wu. This paper was written for the Conference on Decision-Making in Theory and Practice at University College, Oxford, July 1 & 2, 1998, which was sponsored by the Economic Beliefs and Behavior Programme in the Economic and Social Research Council of Great Britain. The paper was written during my sabbatical at the Center for Advanced Study in the Behavioral Sciences, which was supported by NSF grant # SBR – 960123 to the Center.

in part, a rediscovery of the benefits of the hedonic, Benthamite, notion of utility, which Daniel Kahneman has resurrected as 'experience utility' (Kahneman and Snell 1990, Kahneman, Wakker and Sarin 1997; for a history see Loewenstein 1992). When we deal with experience utility, it is meaningful to ask questions that make no sense with ordinal utility, such as whether people correctly predict the utility they will experience from a particular activity, or whether they successfully maximize experienced utility.

These refinements of the utility concept have been accompanied by efforts to derive empirically some of the specific properties of representative utility functions. One of the most important advances along this line has been the discovery of 'loss aversion' – the tendency to weight losses much more heavily than gains of equal absolute value (Tversky and Kahneman 1991). Recognition of loss aversion has led to advances in modeling a wide range of behaviors, including behavior under risk and uncertainty (Kahneman and Tversky 1979), intertemporal choice (Loewenstein and Prelec 1992), labor supply (Camerer et al. 1997), investment behavior (Bernartzi and Thaler 1995), and consumer behavior (Hardie, Johnson and Fader 1993).

Other refinements of utility have entailed an expansion of the arguments of the utility function to incorporate motives involving other people, such as social comparison (Loewenstein, Thompson and Bazerman 1989), reciprocity (Fehr and Gächter 1998), and fairness (Rabin 1993). In addition, psychologically minded economists have begun to recognize the importance of *intrapersonal* comparisons. Utility functions have been proposed and tested that incorporate the effect of past consumption on current utility, via either memory (Wolfe 1970) or level of adaptation (e.g. Clark 1998). Other formulations incorporate utility from anticipation (Loewenstein 1987) or from disappointment or regret arising from a comparison of realized outcomes against those that could have happened but did not (Loomes 1987, Sugden 1994). Many of these developments were anticipated by Bentham, who included in his rather short list of pleasures and pains, those arising from memory, expectation, imagination, disapointment, and regret.

Despite the blossoming of the utility concept and expanding appreciation for the diverse determinants of utility, the list of human motives that have been codified in utility functions, and hence incorporated into economic analyses, remains seriously incomplete. All of the ingredients of utility that are commonly rendered in utility functions share an important feature: they involve consumption, broadly construed (or in some cases leisure and wealth). The consumption may not be one's own. It may be planned for the future or have happened in the past. It may *never* happen (but could have happened if events had unfolded differently). But even when all of these complexities are incorporated, the resultant utility function is still based on *consumption*.

How important is consumption as an input into experienced utility? Even Bentham did not view consumption as all-important. Although the first two sources of utility in his list – pleasures of sense and pleasures of wealth – *do* seem to fit into an inclusive conception of consumption, the seven that follow do not. These are the pleasures of skill, self-recommendation, a good name, power, piety, benevolence, and malevolence. My central argument in this essay is that several of these non-consumption-related sources of utility are powerful and important motivators of human behavior. In the classic case of searching for the wallet under the lamp-post, these motives have been left out of most economists' utility functions, not because their importance is denied, but because they are difficult to formalize in decision-theoretic terms.

To illustrate the importance of motives that are unconnected to consumption, I will focus on personal accounts of a specific activity: *mountaineering*. Why mountaineering? Admittedly, I examine mountaineering in part because it so obviously is *not* about pleasure from consumption. Serious mountaineering – which I define broadly to include polar exploration[1] – tends to be one unrelenting misery from beginning to end. The reason why mountaineers are so often asked why they climb mountains, and the reason why their explicit answers are so often unilluminating (e.g. Mallory's 'because it is there') is precisely that their reasons don't fit neatly into materialistic notions of human motivation. Dentists, investment bankers, and real estate brokers are rarely asked why they are engaged in these activities (though I suspect that the extent to which they are motivated by material considerations is exaggerated).

Although mountaineering is ideal for illustrating these non-consumption-related motives, it could be argued that, as a pathological activity engaged in by a small number of unusual people, it has little relevance to economics. The descriptions of mountaineering included in this essay will do nothing to dispel such opinions. But, as I argue in the conclusion, the motives that drive mountaineers are also pervasive in the general population in diverse domains of behavior.

If mountaineers aren't very good at answering the 'why' question when it is posed *directly*, a close reading of the mountaineering literature reveals myriad clues about their motives. In this essay I draw on works by and about mountaineers to illustrate the importance for human behavior of motives that don't *directly* involve pleasure from consumption.

---

[1] The conditions experienced in mountaineering and polar exploration – e.g. cold, hunger, and exhaustion – are similar. Moreover, there is some overlap in central figures. For example, Reinhold Messner – arguably the greatest living mountaineer – made a solo trip across Antarctica.

1.2. The Miseries of Mountaineering

To understand why mountaineering cannot be interpreted as a pleasurable consumption experience, one needs to have some appreciation of its hardships, which are amply catalogued in the mountaineering literature. They include relentless cold (often leading to frostbite and loss of extremities, or death), exhaustion, snow-blindness, sunburn, altitude sickness, sleeplessness, squalid conditions, hunger, fear, and realization of that fear (in the form of accidents). Mountaineering death rates are mind-boggling. Approximately one person has died for every four who have successfully ascended Everest; in 1996, seven lost their lives in a single day. Ten years earlier 27 men and women reached the top of K2 during the climbing season, but 13 died, several while descending after summiting. On smaller mountains such as Denali (aka, Mount McKinley), and even on the tourist route of the Matterhorn, death rates are also shockingly high.

Despite the tremendous literary talents revealed in the mountaineering literature, an appreciation for these hardships is almost impossible to achieve from the typical reader's vantage point of warmth, rest, comfort, and satiety.[2] In a recent paper (Loewenstein 1996), I have argued that people who are not experiencing 'visceral' states such as cold, exhaustion, pain, or hunger are bad at imagining how they would feel or behave when experiencing one of these sensations. When you are warm it is virtually impossible to empathize with the miseries of cold; when rested to understand exhaustion; or when satiated to appreciate the intensity of hunger pangs. Mountaineering writers are exquisitely aware of this problem. Thus, for example, Joe Simpson (1997, p. 206), who, after escaping from the crevasse which he fell into when his partner cut the climbing rope with a knife, dragged himself with a broken leg through a giant ice-field, expressed frustration at his inability to convey the true misery of the experience:

'however painful readers may think our experiences were, for me this book still falls short of articulating just how dreadful were some of those lonely days. I simply could not find the words to express the utter desolation of the experience'.

This 'empathy gap' is not only a problem for readers of mountaineering literature; mountaineers themselves can't remember the miseries of climbing, which helps to explain why they keep returning for more. In his account of an earlier climb in the Alps, Simpson (1993, p. 137) described conditions as

---

[2] The same is true of battle, as Michael Norman (1996) commented in a *New York Times* article about war movies: No war film has ever or will ever, capture the fierce savagery, the ineffable suffering and the galling waste of combat. Samuel Fuller, a combat veteran of World War II and the director of "The Steel Helmet", "The Big Red One" and other war films, once told an interviewer that the only way to recapture the reality of war on film was to put a machine gun behind the screen and gun down the audience. I'd amend that with: then prop up the wounded and cut their hearts out'.

'harshly uncomfortable, miserable and exhausting',

and also admitted to experiencing near-debilitating fear both before and during the climb. However, he reports, his perspective changed almost instantly after he and his partner had achieved the summit:

'On the summit my memory edited out the anxiety and tension and fed me happy recollections of the superb climbing, the spectacular positions we had been in, feeling confident and safe, knowing we were going to succeed'.

Mike Stroud (1993, p. 178), in his brilliant account of the first unassisted crossing of Antarctica, noted that

'Even though I can clearly remember saying to myself every day of the journey 'I must never do this again', I don't feel now as I did then. The memory deficit is playing its tricks already'.

The strange thing about both Simpson's and Stroud's recollections is that they recognize that their memories are faulty, but don't make the obvious adjustments to their behavior. It is as if, though they can remember the misery at an abstract level, it has no real meaning to them when it comes to deciding whether to expose themselves to the misery again.

If the physical sensations of mountaineering are distinctly aversive, one might hope to discover the answer to the 'why' question in the interpersonal realm. The older mountaineering literature did, in fact, emphasize the solidarity of the assault team and the depth of interpersonal relations forged by hardship. But more recent accounts tell a different story, whether because human solidarity has broken down or (as I believe) because the new generation is more honest. The new literature conveys the tremendous loneliness and isolation of mountaineering, and profound separation even from one's climbing partners. Being roped to another person, and dependent on him or her for one's safety is not, as one might think, a 'bonding' experience, but one that fosters supreme alienation, and far from forging deep and lasting friendships, mountaineering often creates enemies out of friends. Thus, in the course of a two month ordeal that ended in a failed attempt on Alaska's Mount Debora, Roberts (1991, p. 224) writes,

'Because of the intensity of being forced together for so long (for more than a month, we never got farther than a rope-length apart), we began to antagonize each other. We spent much of the trip in silent anger and parted at the end of the summer with harsh words'.

Mike Stroud similarly describes one horrible disagreement after another with his partner Ranulph Fiennes, culminating in a bitter feud when it was over that they aired over the media and in the books that each wrote about the expedition (for the opposing view, see Fiennes 1995). Jim Curran (1987), in *K2: Triumph and Tragedy*, reports that during the 1996 climbing season on K2, intense squabbling broke out in the British expedition even before the climbers had left base camp, and that two members of a small French expedition lugged an extra tent up the mountain (in a situation where every ounce counts) so they wouldn't have to sleep in the same tent.

The isolation of mountaineering is exacerbated by the hot/cold empathy-gap which renders mountaineers unable to truly appreciate their partners' miseries. As Stroud (1993, p. 109) recounts,

'Ran's foot was much worse. Ever since the graft had broken down it had been getting worse and a deep ulcer was now eroding his forefoot. In the mornings it gave him hell, particularly when we had just started, and although he would generally steel himself and say nothing, occasionally even he would have to say something about the pain – try to share a part of it. Then he would be ashamed of himself, and call himself a wimp. I could do nothing but reassure him that I understood, though I didn't really. *Pain is a problem that cannot be shared*' (italics added).

What about the thrill? Mountaineering does have its thrilling moments, but they are rare. In fact, mountaineering suffers from the worst possible combination of long periods of stultifying boredom punctuated by brief periods of terror. On a typical ascent, the vast majority of time is spent in mind-bogglingly monotonous activities – for example, 'weathered out' in a cramped, squalid, tent, or 'ferrying' crushingly heavy packs up endless snow-slopes with fixed ropes. The monotony of endless plodding combined with constant exhaustion produces a kind of catatonia that many climbers allude to. Mike Stroud (1993, p. 108), for example, reports that

'when not gloating over Ran's difficulties (his aforementioned foot-wound), I occupied my head with inanities. This consisted chiefly of silly songs, such as 'The Teddy Bear's Picnic''.

Joe Simpson (1997, p. 161) was similarly tormented not only by hunger, thirst, and pain from his broken leg but also by his inability to silence a song

'that I hated. Somehow I couldn't get its insistent chant out of my mind, . . . "Brown girl in the ring . . . Tra la la la la . . . " '.

Even the much-vaunted beauty of the mountains is overplayed. Aside from subtle distinctions between, say, limestone and granite, one glacier, couloir, corniced ridge, or jagged peak looks much like another. Base camps of major peaks tend to be squalid shanty-towns overflowing with human excrement. And the view from the top often isn't much better. According to Beck Weathers (1998), who was lucky to survive his 1996 trip to Everest with his life, albeit minus all of his left and much of his right hand as well as several large chunks of his face, the major navigational landmarks on the higher reaches of Everest consist of 'the discarded oxygen tank canisters of the prior expeditions and the scattered bodies of the climbers who preceded you'.

Why, then, do people do it? This question preoccupies many climbers, particularly in times of hardship. The answer to the why question constitutes a – perhaps *the* – central theme in the climbing literature.

1.3. Self-Signaling

Clearly, recognition, prestige, or as Bentham expressed it, 'the pleasure of a good name' is an important motive. Jon Elster (forthcoming) quotes John Adams to the effect that

'The desire of esteem is as real a want of nature as hunger: and the neglect and contempt of the world as severe a pain as gout and stone'.

Mountaineering is a prestigious activity, at least in some social circles. Almost anyone will be wowed by the first ascent of a major peak or by the first unassisted crossing of Antarctica. Although loath to admit that they care about public acclaim, mountaineers are forced to confront the reality. As Mike Stroud (1993, p. 27) writes,

'There was one less acceptable motivation – ego. How much of me wanted to go out and prove myself...to others? How much of me wanted to revel in admiration and praise? They were difficult questions and although I liked to think they were unimportant, I sometimes wondered whether I was fooling myself and just not admitting that it was the achievement in the eyes of others that mattered. After all, everything we tried was an attempt to be 'first', and if it had been done before, I doubt that we would have bothered with it. This...would seem to hint at a need to impress'.

Expressing similar doubts, Joe Simpson (1993, p. 87) grappled with his own motives for climbing:

'The truth seemed uncomfortably egoistical. I wanted to do only hard climbs, great north faces, impressive and daunting rock routes. I wanted a 'tick list' of hard routes under my belt...It seemed wrong to want such things, shallow and superficial'.

Incorporating a desire to impress into a utility function is complicated, but possible. In fact, many economic analyses have incorporated the desire to impress others with one's consumption (Leibenstein 1976), as well as more general positional concerns (Frank 1985).

More complicated to formally model than the desire to impress would be the desire to impress without appearing that one is trying to impress. These dual motives have influenced the configuration of many mountaineering expeditions. To avoid the appearance of being motivated by a desire for public acclaim, many expeditions that seek to accomplish 'firsts' disguise their true purpose by including a 'scientific' or 'humanitarian' component. For example, the French expedition to climb an 8.000-meter peak, which is documented in Herzog's classic *Annapurna*, included a doctor who ministered to the poor of Nepal. Shackleton's ill-fated attempt to cross Antarctica required

'the blessings of the government and of various scientific societies ... to justify the expedition as a serious scientific endeavor' (Lansing 1959, p. 15).

Stroud's Antarctic expedition incorporated medical research (the men collected daily urine samples) as well as a philanthropic component (they raised money for muscular sclerosis though they never explained why they had chosen this particular cause). These scientific or humanitarian goals not only help to disguise the mountaineers' obsessive drive for fame, but also provide at least one goal that, by nature of its ambiguity, is almost certain to be achieved. Thus, when Mike Stroud and Ranulph Fiennes finally reached the limit of their endurance and terminated their Antarctic crossing in the middle of the Ross ice-shelf, Fiennes attempted to comfort his partner by noting that

'we ... have raised millions for charity, and your scientific programme is a success. All we haven't achieved is to cross the ice-shelf, the ice shelf that isn't part of the continent' (Stroud 1993, p. 167).

Closely related to, but more difficult to model formally than the need to impress *others*, is the need to impress *oneself* – what Bentham referred to as 'pleasures of self-recommendation'. Deferring again to Stroud,

'the need to impress ... does not altogether exclude self-satisfaction as a motive. Doing something first or best can still be for oneself' (p. 27).

Although pride is one of the 'deadly sins', most mountaineers view ego as a much more acceptable motive for their endeavours than impressing others.

Like the desire to impress, people's concern about their own motives can be translated into utility terms, though the complexities that are introduced are significant. In an insightful paper titled 'The Diagnostic Value of Actions in a Self-signaling Model', Ronit Bodner and Drazen Prelec (1996, see also Akerlof and Kranton 1998) show how it can be done. They distinguish between 'outcome utility', which corresponds to the usual notion of utility from consumption, and a new type of utility, 'diagnostic utility', which stems from an

'estimate of one's disposition' (p. 2).

If one knew one's own disposition, diagnostic utility would be fixed and would have few implications for behavior. But people are, in fact, unsure of their own dispositions.[3] To resolve this uncertainty in a manner favorable to themselves – that is, to boost their own diagnostic utility – people attempt to signal to themselves that they have desirable attributes by taking actions that they believe are consistent with those attributes. Thus, for example, people give to charity in part so that they can perceive themselves as generous.

As Bodner and Prelec (1996) discuss, however, such attempts at self-signaling are inherently problematic because the recognition that our actions are motivated by self-signaling should, logically, undermine the signaling value of those actions. Thus, for example, the diagnostic utility benefit derived from giving to charity should be undermined by the awareness that we are doing it for that reason.

Part of the appeal of mountaineering is that it avoids this problem to a great extent. One aspect of self-signaling that remains undeveloped is the idea that different situations provide differential scope for self-signaling. The daily commute, for example, may provide some opportunities for revealing oneself to be an inconsiderate jerk, but few opportunities for revealing truly exceptional qualities.

'In ordinary situations',

Lansing (1959, p. 13) writes,

'Shackleton's tremendous capacity for boldness and daring found almost nothing worthy of its pulling power; he was a Percheron draft horse harnessed to a child's wagon cart. But in the Antarctic – here was a burden which challenged every atom of his strength'.

The same point can be seen in Potterfield's (1996, p. 103) description of Colby Coombs as

'a gifted mountaineer and ice climber. But . . . you don't really find out about him until things get hard – until he's at altitude, or climbing in bad weather high on the mountain'.

It can also be seen in Beck Weather's account of the motives of the helicopter pilot who rescued him on Everest in an unprecedented high-altitude flight. The pilot, Weathers said, believed that he

'had a brave heart but he had never been sufficiently tested to know whether this is true'.

Mountaineering provides an ideal venue for self-signaling because it is largely impossible to 'fake it'. As the polar explorer Robert Scott noted in his Antarctic diary (cited in Cherry-Gerrard 1922, p. lxiii),

---

[3] This is undoubtedly part of the reason for the popularity of self-administered personality tests, such as those in magazines, self-help books, and now on the World Wide Web.

'I do not think there can be any life quite so demonstrative of character as that we had on these expeditions . . . Here the outward show is nothing . . . Pretence is useless'.

From observing people in daily life it is completely impossible to predict how they will act under the duress of mountaineering. Indeed, I believe, people cannot predict how they themselves will behave. Some people who appear tough in daily life fall to pieces at the first hardship encountered on a mountain; others – seeming 'wimps' – discover, and reveal to those around them, unrecognized reserves of strength in the face of harsh conditions. Recognizing that mountaineering has such self-signaling value, Roberts (1968, p. 282) comments that

'mountaineers have claimed that the only discovery one can make by climbing is that of oneself',

though, he ponders,

'there must be easier ways'.

In fact, there may not be easier ways; mountaineering reveals character only because it is not easy.[4] A big part of the purpose of a trip is to test one's own mettle, and pain and discomfort provide the grist for such tests. This desire for a harsh test of one's own fortitude, along with poor memory for misery, may help to explain why the most miserable trips often produce the best memories; pain and discomfort are, to some degree, the *point* of the trip.

1.4. Goal Completion

Fame, self-esteem, and the desire for mastery may bring people to the mountains, but other forces keep them at it when conditions get miserable. One such force is the almost obsessive human need to fulfill self-set goals. This compulsion seems to be particularly refined in mountaineers, and especially in successful ones – at least as long as they survive. Thus, for example, after dislocating his shoulder and almost dying in an accident on K2 – the second highest mountain in the world and one of the most technically difficult – Scott Fischer went on to climb the peak. Potterfield (1997, p. 129) writes that

'most people in his situation probably would have bagged it and gone home. But Fischer possessed an almost irrational drive to get to the top of the mountains he climbed'.

---

[4] Milan Kundera (1998) argues that friendship, like self-signaling, requires adversity: 'How is friendship born?' Jean Marc asks Chantal. 'Certainly as an alliance against adversity', he continues. But 'maybe there's no longer a vital need for such alliance'. 'There will always be enemies', rejoins Chantal. 'Yes, but they're invisible and anonymous. Bureaucracies, laws', responds Jean-Marc. 'Friendship can no longer be proved by some exploit'. He concludes, 'We go through our lives without great perils, but also without friendship'.

Fischer may have been lucky on K2; as documented in Jon Krakauer's best-seller *Into Thin Air*, his need for completion did him in on Everest a few years later.

The intensity of the drive for goal completion is evident not only in mountaineers' Herculean efforts to make the peak, but also in the torment they experience when they fail. Doug Hansen, who died on Everest in 1996 after summiting at 4 pm (two hours after the prespecified turn-back time), had attempted to climb the mountain one year earlier, coming within 300 vertical feet of the summit when he had to turn back. According to Beck Weathers (1998), his earlier failure

'had come to possess him, take hold of his life, and control his every waking moment. And he came back this year vowing that under no circumstance was he going to allow himself to be turned around again'.

Mike Stroud, in his account of the first unassisted 900-mile crossing of Antarctica, displayed a similar obsession:

'To the vast majority of people who had heard that we had crossed the Antarctic, going on to finish the ice-shelf would seem pointless, but we were not the vast majority of people. We knew in our hearts, or at least I did in mine, that we had not completed what we set out to do. For me it would probably be difficult to live with, and much more so since a possibility remained that it was still achievable'.

David Roberts (1968, p. 332), in his epic tale of the first ascent of the west rib of Alaska's Mount Huntington, lamented that an unstable cornice prevented his team from standing on top of the highest point of the peak. He reassured himself, however, that he had achieved his goal because, as he precisely noted, 'our heads stood higher' than the peak.

The motive to complete goals may result partly from self-signaling. Repeated deviations from one's plans – particularly when those plans call for some type of virtuous behavior – signal undesirable traits such as a weak will and impulsiveness. I suspect, however, that more than self-signaling is involved, in part because the need for goal completion *feels* so visceral. Krakauer (1997, p. 234), for example, refers to a 'summit fever' that consumes mountaineers when they are within striking distance of the peak.

The urge to complete a goal is important for decision making because it is an antidote to time-inconsistent behavior. Time inconsistency occurs when one makes plans for the future, then systematically departs from them. As Strotz (1955) pointed out, any time discount function other than the exponential (with a constant rate of time discounting) implies that behavior will be time-inconsistent. In fact, empirical studies of time discounting have revealed that time discounting is not exponential, but hyperbolic (see, e.g., Ainslie 1975). Interpreted loosely, this means that people place disproportionate weight on immediate pleasures and pains relative to those that are delayed even only slightly. Hyperbolic time discounting has been used to explain why people often resolve to start dieting, save money, or quit smoking beginning *tomorrow*, but fail to execute their plans when tomorrow becomes today.

Hyperbolic time discounting predicts, however, that people will be *consistently* time inconsistent – that they will display the same impulsive pattern frequently and in all domains of behavior – but that is by no means the case. Many people have self-control problems in a few specific domains of behavior but, for the most part, exhibit a high degree of time consistency in their daily behavior. The need for goal completion may help to explain why hyperbolic time discounters typically behave in a time-consistent fashion. Most people are uncomfortable with deviations from their own plans, whether they call for climbing a mountain, jogging five miles, or eschewing dessert after dinner.

In a clever study, Christensen-Szalanski (1984) asked women whether they wanted anesthesia during childbirth. Most said that they did not, but changed their minds when they went into labor. It would be easy to imagine that mountaineers would exhibit a similar pattern – discount future discomfort when planning a climb, but 'bag it' when the discomfort is actually experienced. Successful mountaineers, as Potterfield's description of Scott Fischer hints, may be a self-selected group for whom the completion drive is particularly strong.

Goal completion is, however, not only an antidote to time inconsistency, but also a source of it. The visceral need to complete a self-determined goal often takes on a life of its own and becomes divorced from changing material incentives. Once a mountaineer has set his sights on a peak, the goal of making the summit becomes detached from rational calculations about the cost of achieving the goal. Mountaineers are well aware of the difficulty of relinquishing their summit ambitions even when abandonment of the goal is strongly merited. At the beginning of the day on which an assault on the peak takes place, most climbers – knowing of the hazards posed by 'summit fever' – designate a turnback time, typically around mid-day, that will permit a return to the tent site before nightfall. When the appointed time arrives, however, and the day still seems young, many find it difficult or impossible to adhere to their earlier resolution. The failure to adhere to self-established turn-back times has led to innumerable deaths in the mountains, including seven mountaineers on Everest in 1996.

A strange aspect of goal completion, from a decision-making perspective, is why people set goals in the first place and why they subsequently adhere to them when they no longer make sense. Given that people choose their own goals, one might think they would find it easy to abandon them. Any theory of rational goal setting will need to explain not only what purpose goals serve, but also why, if the goals represent the output of a rational calculation, people don't drop them when they become patently counterproductive.

My own suspicion is that the drive toward goal establishment and goal completion is 'hard-wired'. Humans, like most animals and even plants, are maintained by complex arrays of homeostatic mechanisms that keep the body's systems in equilibrium. Many of the miseries of mountaineering, such as hunger, thirst, and pain, are manifestations of homeostatic mechanisms that motivate people to do what they need to do to survive, such as taking in calories (hunger) and liquids (thirst) and avoiding tissue damage (pain). Although we think of ourselves as eating because we are hungry, this account of eating begins in the middle of the causal chain. We become hungry when our brain receives information from the body that it interprets as signals that our body needs food, and, when we are hungry, food seems more appealing, through a process that Cabanac (1979) calls 'aliesthesia'.[5] Even frostbite, one of the major banes of mountaineering, results from the body's attempt to maintain core body temperature at the expense of extremities. The visceral need for goal completion, then, may be simply another manifestation of the organism's tendency to deal with problems – in this case the problem of executing motivated actions – homeostatically. As proposed in Miller, Gallanter and Pribram's (1960) classic *Plans and the Structure of Behavior*, most human volitional behavior takes the same form of goal setting and goal seeking. The only difference between the visceral need for goal completion and visceral feeling of hunger is that the former goal state is, in some sense, self-chosen.[6]

Another anomalous feature of the drive for goal completion is the striking disparity between the motivation to complete a goal and the weakness of the satisfaction that typically results from doing so. As Roberts (1968, p. 312) writes,

[5] Mountaineers, and even more so polar explorers, suffer from almost constant hunger (except at high altitudes, where people lose their appetites and starve even faster) which produces an obsession with food. The diary entry of one member of Shackleton's crew commented that 'it is scandalous – all we seem to live for and think of now is food'. Mike Stroud wrote that his partner, Ran, 'in his diary . . . wrote of food and little else. Day after day, he would expand a massively imaginative menu he planned to sit down and eat with Ginny when he got back to his farm on Exmoor' (1993, p. 152). The constant hunger not only makes people obsessed with food, but changes one's tastes dramatically. Before leaving on the climb that killed Colby Coombs's two partners and broke his neck (among other body parts), 'the three climbers had made a big pot of spaghetti, but they had not consumed it all'. When Colby stumbled into base camp days after the accident, the pot 'was buried in the snow next to the tent. Colby dug up the old spaghetti. He was so hungry he didn't bother to start the stove. He ate hungrily and fast. To Colby, the congealed spaghetti was delicious, one of the best meals he had ever eaten'.

[6] Goal-driven behavior may increase efficiency by focussing scarce cognitive and physical capabilities on specific problems. The pitfall of such focusing is that the individual could be oblivious to unexpected dangers. Thus, for example, a cave-person who focused all his mental energy on making an arrowhead might be oblivious to the approach of a hungry bear. Simon (1967) and more recently Armony et al. (1995, 1997) and DeBecker (1997), speculate that emotions such as fear serve as interrupt mechanisms to refocus attention and motivation to unexpected environmental threats. The drive for goal completion and fear, therefore, may perform antagonistic functions.

'climbing is defined by a purposed completion, the summit; yet the best of it is never that final victory'.

Joe Simpson (1993, p. 101) wrote that, after a major climb in the French Alps,

'It was strange to be filled so soon with a sense of anti-climax, now that it was finished. All the glory with which I had invested the route had vanished the moment I had climbed it'.

In decision-theoretic accounts of motivation, it is usually assumed that one's motivation to achieve a goal bears some relationship to the pleasure one will derive from achieving it (see Heath, Larrick and Wu 1998), but this does not seem to be the case for mountaineering. The discrepancy between desire and satisfaction is also characteristic of other motives such as curiosity (see Loewenstein 1994, p. 86), envy, and some forms of drug addiction (Berridge 1995).

1.5. Mastery

In a once-influential, now largely forgotten, article, Robert White (1959) argued that humans are powerfully motivated by the desire to master their environments, a tendency that he dubbed 'effectance' motivation and that Bentham referred to as 'pleasures of skill'. It is generally pleasant to engage in an activity you are good at, no matter how useless it might be. By the same token, it is typically aversive to do something you are incompetent at, no matter how instrumental the activity.

Part of the reason for why mountaineers climb mountains is that they *can* do it – they are good at it. Writing of a brief pleasurable period of climbing, lamentably cut short by his partner's fatal plunge over a 5.000-foot cliff, Roberts (1968, pp. 308–309) relates,

'At times like those, the mind does not wander, nor does it really think, except to make the almost automatic judgments of route, piton, and rope the climbing calls for... The touch and strain of ice and rock under my hands (send) pleasure as well as blood surging through my veins'.

Simpson (1993, p. 119) remarks (somewhat unrealistically, given his own uniquely gruesome history of accidents) that

'there is a perverse delight in putting oneself in a potentially dangerous situation, knowing that your experience and skill make you quite safe'.

The concept of mastery actually blends together a number of more specific motives. It is almost certainly associated with self-esteem or 'self-recommendation', and it also often involves a feeling of total absorption in an activity – that is, 'flow' (Csikszentmihalyi 1991) – and an easing of the burdens and complexities of everyday life. Potterfield (1996, p. 173) refers to mountaineering as

'the best foil I've found for the onerous realistics of the twentieth century'.

Simpson (1993, p. 276) writes that the climber

'steps out of the living world of anxiety into a world where there is no room, no time, for ... distractions. All that concerns him is surviving the present. Any thoughts of gas bills and mortgages, loved ones and enemies, evaporate under the absolute necessity for concentration on the task in hand. He leads a separate life of uncomplicated black and white decisions – *stay warm, feed yourself, be careful, take proper rest, look after yourself and your partner, be aware*'.

And Lansing (1959, p. 22) writes that Shackleton, within a few hours of leaving the last outpost of civilization on his way to Antarctica, felt that

'life had been reduced from a highly complex existence, with a thousand petty problems, to one of the barest simplicity in which only one real task remained – the achievement of his goal'.

Perhaps most important, however, mastery involves a feeling of control over one's environment. Control is, in and of itself, powerfully reinforcing (Langer 1975), and the absence of control is commensurately aversive (Brehm 1966). Kornetsky et al. found that rats who self-administered alcohol had lower thresholds for brain stimulation reward (suggesting greater ability to obtain pleasure from the environment) than yoked rats who received the same alcohol at identical times but had no control over its intake. Perceived control also seems to render aversive stimuli more tolerable. Seligman and Maier (1967), for example, found that dogs who were given shocks that they could terminate by making body motions got fewer ulcers than 'yoked' dogs who received identical, but uncontrollable, sequences of shock. Glass and Singer (1972), found that the debilitating effects of an uncontrollable loud noise on performance of a cognitive task were virtually eliminated when subjects believed they could terminate the noise by pressing a button.

Perceived control also seems to reduce fear, even when probabilities and consequences are held constant. Mineka et al. (1984), for example, found that the effectiveness of fear conditioning in rats was cut in half when a bell that could be terminated by lever-press preceded electric shock, holding constant the actual shock intensity and duration. In an experiment with humans, Sanderson et al. (1988) administered a known panic-provoking agent (5.5% carbon dioxide, CD) to panic-prone patients. Half of the participants were told that they could reduce the concentration of carbon dioxide by turning a dial when a light was illuminated. This group reported fewer and less severe panic symptoms, had fewer catastrophic thoughts, and reported less distress, even though the dial was actually inoperative.

The dislike of uncontrolled risks can be seen in mountaineers, who draw a sharp distinction between 'objective risks', which include events that are completely uncontrollable and unavoidable, such as falling rocks and collapsing seracs (ice towers), and risks that can be mitigated by skill or caution. Whereas they are relatively unperturbed by hazards that are seen as potentially controllable, however severe, mountaineers do fear objective risks. As Roberts (1968, p. 225) comments,

'When the risks depend solely on chance, not skill, the mountaineer enjoys them as little as anyone'.

Perhaps because they have an illusion of control, mountaineers tend to be remarkably unfazed by the astronomical risks they face. It is as if, at the level of fear, the risks have no reality. The feeling of control, however, often disappears after a serious accident, at which point fear enters the picture. As Potterfield (1996, p. 234) notes,

'the terror of a bad fall . . . never really goes away'.

In the same way that people may require a near-death experience to truly recognize their own mortality, it often takes an accident for a mountaineer to appreciate the danger of mountaineering at the level of experiencing fear. The ironic consequence is that mountaineers often 'discover' fear *after* an accident, when they are in a position of safety. Maurice Herzog (1952, p. 264), for example, after becoming lost, snowblind, and severely frostbitten on his descent from Annapurna, did not report experiencing fear during the ordeal. Days later, however, when he was in a safe position being carted out of the mountain region on the back of a porter, he was

'haunted by anxiety and a shameful fear',

and later

'I no longer had the strength to fight my fears, and I knew now what fear really was. Lachenal (his climbing partner) also was petrified by fright' (p. 271).

Similarly, after Shackleton's ship was trapped in polar ice and then splintered and sunk by it, the crew drifted on the ice for *nearly a year* and then endured a harrowing trip across icy, stormy, seas in life-boats to an island – their first land after 497 days. As the boats were being pulled to safety, Lansing reports, a member of the crew named Rickenson suddenly turned pale, and a minute later collapsed of a heart attack (Lansing 1959).

1.6. Meaning

Just as people aren't certain about *who* they are (and so attempt to signal, both to themselves and to others that they have desirable traits), many people also don't have a good understanding of what they want out of life and what they value. One commonly vaunted benefit of mountaineering and wilderness travel is that it offers a new perspective on life.

The cost of such perspective, however, tends to be high. Simple discomfort rarely produces new insights into life, or a greater appreciation of it; that typically requires a near-death experience. Reminiscent of the Joni Mitchell song, 'You don't know what you've got till it's gone', it requires an impending loss of one's life to appreciate what one is about to lose. As Joe Simpson (1993, p. 119) wrote of his near-death in an avalanche,

'Maybe for the first time I learned in the avalanche exactly what it was to be alive, how precious, and how fragile. There was so much to be lost from a moment's careless mistake but so much more to be gained by knowing the value of life'.

Meaning-making may also be enhanced by the loss of body parts. The first man to climb an 8.000-meter peak, Maurice Herzog, lost several fingers and parts of his feet to gangrene. But he gained an appreciation for

'the deep significance of existence of which till then I had been unaware'.

The ordeal, he reported,

'has given me the assurance and serenity of a man who has fulfilled himself. It has given me the rare joy of loving that which I used to despise. A new and splendid life has opened out before me' (1952, p. 12).

Beck Weathers (1998), who in 1996 was abandoned overnight in a blizzard on Mount Everest and lost his hands and much of his face, reports that 'I traded my hands for my family and my future, and it is a bargain I readily accept'.[7]

Adherents of rational expectations assume that new information or insights should be unpredictable. They may be disturbed to learn that such changes in perspective are actually quite predictable. Almost invariably, they involve an enhanced appreciation of human relationships and a demotion of professional and material ambitions. Peter Potterfield (1996, p. 233), who suffered a bone-shattering fall during an ascent of Chimney Rock in the Cascades and then barely survived an excruciating 24-hour wait for rescue, reported that

---

[7] One may suspect that there is an element of cognitive dissonance in the common discovery of a self-insight 'silver lining' following the loss of body parts.

'the air time on Chimney Rock changed the way I thought about everything, including marriage'.

Beck Weathers stated that when he gained consciousness after his exposed night on Everest,

'I saw my own future and I didn't like it . . . The relentless pursuit of success and goals and ambition without balance was pushing out of my life that which was most precious to me . . . In the final analysis that which matters, really the only thing that matters, are the people you hold in your heart and the people who hold you in theirs'.

Roberts (1968, p. 234) comments,

'Nobody on his death bed ever said, "I wish I had spent more time at the office" '.

These shifts in perspective raise some important issues for decision theory. First, what is it about almost dying that produces such shifts in perspectives? Second, why are the insights gained almost always the same; why don't some people come to recognize that they should apply themselves more assiduously to achieving professional ambitions before leaving the earth? And finally, are these new priorities more valid than the old ones they replace?

One reason why nearly dying may be important is that dying is an emotional experience (if one has time to think about it). Beck Weathers, for example, reports that when he realized he was going to die he did not experience the terror that he would have expected, but rather

'an enormous, encompassing, sense of melancholy'.

If emotions provide an important input into decision making, as much recent work suggests (e.g. Damasio 1994, Zajonc 1980, 1984), then this input is about as powerful as one could imagine receiving.

Damasio (1994), in his provocative book *Descartes' Error*, argues that emotions are crucial in decision making because they provide a crude but quick and automatic summary of the costs and benefits associated with alternative courses of action. In support of this idea, he cites the behavioral impact of certain types of frontal lobe brain lesions that have no measurable effect on cognition but that block emotional reactions associated with mental imagery, which he labels 'somatic markers'. Consistent with the idea that emotions are critical in decision making, people with such frontal lesions are pathologically indecisive and can spend hours making the most trivial decision – such as whether to schedule the next doctor's appointment for 10 or 11 am on the following day. Timothy Wilson, Jonathan Schooler, and colleagues (Wilson and Schooler 1991, Wilson et al. 1993), reached a similar conclusion in their work on 'verbal overshadowing' of emotion. Their studies show that people who verbalized pros and cons made worse decisions because doing so prevents them from gaining access to their 'gut reactions' to the alternatives.

How can somatic markers help to explain near-death shifts in priorities? If emotional reactions that are subtle enough to be overshadowed by verbalizing are important inputs into decision making, think about how much more influential the feelings that accompany the prospect of imminent death must be. The prospect of death produces a powerful form of attention focusing; it is as if the brain realizes that it has limited computation time left, and spends it thinking about things that are important. Later, in a process akin to the notion of 'flash-bulb memories' (Brown and Kulik 1977), whatever one thought about during this period is retained in memory and infused with significance.

It is also possible that these changes in values are illusory. Perhaps the people who report changes of perspective had recognized the importance of family all along but had put off acting on this awareness. Ted O'Donoghue and Matthew Rabin (forthcoming) have developed a theoretical account of procrastination that seems to be particularly applicable to this situation. The model applies to situations in which people have the opportunity to take an action that would expose them to an immediate small cost but produce a delayed larger benefit. The critical feature of their model is that people recognize that a particular action is worth taking, but naively anticipate that they will take the action in the future, which helps them to rationalize why they do not have to do it today. When the future becomes the present, however, the same logic applies once again. An important prediction of the model is that if people were given one last opportunity to take the action they would do so; procrastination is encouraged by awareness that there will be future opportunities to take the action, coupled with a naive prediction of one's own future behavior in the absence of such deadlines.

O'Donoghue and Rabin's theory could explain why perspective change, whether real or illusory, requires a near-death experience. Perhaps most people actually recognize the importance of family, and plan to spend time with them in the future, but are distracted from doing so by the immediate lure of career ambitions, mountains, or golf. The effect of almost losing your life is to make you realize that if you don't spend time with your family *now* you may not have a chance to do so in the future. Today may in fact be your last opportunity to go out to dinner with your spouse, call your parents, or take your child to the zoo. As Potter commented,

'After Chimney Rock, there was a strong sense that life is uncertain, highly so' (1996, p. 233).

The procrastination account of perspective shifts could explain why the insights gained are always the same. What we gain, it suggests, is not actually a greater appreciation for the importance of human relationships, but an awareness that if we continue to defer investing in personal relationships we may well depart from the world having missed our opportunity to do so.

Are post-near-death priorities more valid than pre-near-death priorities? If neglect of friends and family is due to procrastination, the answer may be yes. But if it is due to somatic markers, the answer is likely to be no. Being close to death is a relatively unusual state. Just as the insights gained during an LSD trip are inherently suspect, it is questionable whether the pre-death perspective provides a clear view of one's 'true' values. Whether the newly found priorities survive the complexities of real life, therefore, is open to question. During the worst moments of his Antarctic bid, Mike Stroud lamented his detachment from his children and vowed, on his return, to become a model father and to cease his quest for 'firsts'. In the epilogue to his book, however, he reports that he never quite got around to building the doll house that he had resolved to construct for his daughter and that, within weeks of his return to daily life, the *wanderlust* had him in its grip once again.

1.7. Concluding Comments

Behavioral economics – the application of psychological insights to economic problems – has gained increasing acceptance among mainstream economists. Nevertheless, some holdouts in the profession persist in the desire to strip economics of underlying psychology. The point that they fail to understand is that psychology and economics are inextricably linked. Utility maximization, which lies at the heart of neoclassical economics, is a *psychological* theory of behavior. It states that human behavior can be explained as an attempt to achieve a certain goal, whether it be happiness (in the Benthamite account) or satisfaction of preferences (from the ordinal utility perspective). The ordinal utility/revealed preference approach does not divorce economics from psychology, but builds economics up from a hollow foundation. The issue is not whether economics will be based on psychology or not, but whether it will be grounded in good psychology or bad psychology.

Recent developments in the field of behavioral economics have substantially enriched the utility concept and increased the explanatory power of utility maximization, in many cases with changes that are highly tractable. Ironically, as I pointed out in the introduction, many of these advances involve a rediscovery of insights that were present at the very birth of the utility concept. These advances in formulating utility – in elaborating on the specific character of *economic man* – however, have run up against the inherent limitations of trying to model human behavior purely as a function of consumption.

Economists since Bentham's time have periodically paid tribute to the importance of non-consumption-related motives. Adam Smith (cited in Offer 1997, p. 451), for example, not only recognized the importance of the desire for regard (Bentham's pleasures of a good name, and self-recommendation), but believed that the drive for material improvement (i.e. for consumption) was actually *derivative of* the desire for such regard:

'What is the end of avarice and ambition, of the pursuit of wealth, of power, and preheminance? ... To be observed, to be attended to, to be taken notice of with sympathy, complacency, and approbation, are all the advantages which we can propose to derive from it'.

Alfred Marshall (1898), in a passage in his *Principles of Economics*, attributed great importance to what could be interpreted as a mastery motive:

'A large part of the demand for the highly skilled professional services and the best work of the mechanical artisan arises from the delight people have in the training of their faculties and in exercising them'.

And Keynes (1936), in *The General Theory of Employment, Interest and Money* argued:

'If human nature felt no ... satisfaction (profit apart) in constructing a factory, a railway, a mine or a farm, there might not be much investment as a result of cold calculation ... Enterprise only pretends to itself to be mainly motivated by the statement in its own prospectus ... *Only a little more than an expedition to the South Pole is it based on an exact calculation of benefits to come*' (emphasis added).

But despite the occasional display of appreciation for non-consumption-related motives by psychologically astute economists, there have been very few attempts to integrate such motives into a systematic analysis of economic behavior.

Consumption has great advantages as an input into utility. It is measurable, and it generally enters monotonically into the utility function. Consumption also bears a simple, logical relationship to other important economic variables, such as income, wealth, prices, wages, and labor supply. None of this is true of the desire to impress, self-signaling, goal completion, mastery and meaning-seeking.

Self-signaling is probably the easiest non-consumption motive to model and, of the four non-consumption motives I discuss, has received the most attention from economists and decision theorists. Significant advances have already been made in modeling people's desire for the respect and admiration of *others* (e.g. Duesenberry 1952, Frank 1985, Bernheim 1994), and in measuring its impact on economic behavior (e.g. Chao and Schor 1998). *Self*-esteem has also received limited attention from economists (e.g. Khalil 1996, Lea and Webley 1997), although there has been inadequate attention to the problems raised by Bodner and Prelec (1996). Despite some advances, therefore, we remain a long way from understanding, let alone formally modeling, the determinants of self-esteem and its role in behavior.

The need for goal completion remains similarly unintegrated into decision theory. One specific aspect of goal completion – the effect of externally set goals on effort and performance – has received considerable attention from experimental psychologists (e.g. Locke and Latham 1990), and more recently decision theorists (Heath, Larrick and Wu 1998). However, other important issues remain largely unaddressed. Thus, currently we have little understanding of why people set goals for themselves, of the amount of control that people have over their own goals, and, to the degree that people do have control over their own goals, whether goal-setting can be described as the outcome of a decision that weighs the costs and benefits of alternative goals. We are also far from possessing satisfactory explanations for the two anomalous properties of goals that are salient in the mountaineering literature: the difficulty of relinquishing counterproductive self-set goals, and the disparity between the power of the motivation to achieve goals and (lack of) pleasure experienced when goals are achieved.

The mastery motive similarly remains largely unaddressed by decision theory, although again there are fragments of research that could be built upon. Heath and Tversky (1991), for example, show that people prefer to bet on their own judgment over an equiprobable chance event when they consider themselves knowledgeable, but not otherwise. It seems that mountaineers are not the only people who like to exert control in domains in which they feel competent. Loewenstein and Issacharoff (1994) show that people's valuations of objects depends on how the objects were obtained, a phenomenon we label 'source-dependence'. When people feel that they earned an object, as a result of their performance on a task, they are much less willing to give up the object (i.e. they state higher selling prices) than when they received the same object as a gift. This research suggests that mastery is not only desirable in and of itself, but also has secondary effects on preferences.

Of the four nonconsumption motives, meaning is certainly the furthest from being integrated into economics or decision theory. That economists are leery of introducing anything that resembles meaning into their models is apparent in a recent paper by Ed Glaeser and Spencer Glendon – two economists who are quite open to psychology – on 'The Demand for Religion' (1997). The authors investigate three theories about why people 'demand' religion: (1) religion provides social connections, (2) it provides rewards after death or (3) it provides moral instruction. Notable for its absence from the paper is any mention of the possibility that religion may provide people with some type of meaning. The reluctance to introduce meaning-seeking as a motive in economic models is perfectly understandable. Until we have a much better understanding of its determinants and consequences, meaning will continue to elude formalization in decision-theoretic terms.

Each of these non-consumption motives poses severe challenges to would-be modelers. Thus, there may be good reasons for halting progress short of the consumption barrier. The decision about whether to model non-consumption-related motives should not, however, depend only on tractability, but also on the *importance* of these motives for economic behavior. If they are critical for daily economic behavior, as I have attempted to show is true for mountaineering, then there is no excuse for not trying to model them, at least. The question, then, is whether mountaineers and mountaineering are unusual in the degree to which they are motivated by non-consumption-related motives. The answer, I believe, is that they are not. Although these non-consumption motives may be more important in mountaineering than in other activities, and better developed in mountaineers than other people, the same motives can also be seen in most people's daily behavior.

Consider, for example, academia – a domain with which most readers of this paper will have personal familiarity. Self- and other-signaling may well be one of the most important motives driving academic achievement and is probably much more important for understanding decisions to enter the profession, choices between jobs, and the persistence of work effort following tenure (even in institutions with rigid pay scales) than are pecuniary motives such as salary. Academics care about how other academics perceive them, and many are powerfully driven by the desire to maintain self-esteem. Many academics have faced a choice between a low-paying job at a high-prestige university or a high-paying job at a low-prestige university; my own casual observation is that few have opted for the latter. Although it could be argued that academics, too, are an unrepresentative group, it would be easy to make a similar case for almost any profession. Self-signaling may also help to explain the prevalence of another common but anomalous activity that has had momentous consequences for human history and which bears a resemblance to mountaineering in its distinctively negative consumption aspect. I'm referring to the willingness and even eagerness of generations of insecure young men to risk 'the ultimate sacrifice' in battle.

Goal completion is also important in academia in part because academic accomplishments, such as getting a PhD, landing a job, getting tenure, and publishing articles, tend to be naturally discrete (though academia is by no means unique in this respect). Academics can become extraordinarily obsessed with achieving these goals. Indeed, many academics require elaborate self-control strategies to take a break from their work, such as booking expensive, nonrefundable vacations. On the face of it, such a pattern is strange because we usually think of people as requiring self-control to work rather than to play.

Mastery is also a vastly underappreciated motive, especially prominent among academics. Three categories of activities are highly valued in the social sciences, and perhaps other academic domains: research, teaching, and grants-manship. Many people enter the profession with some degree of talent in all three areas but a slight comparative advantage in one. As time passes, however, many academics tend to specialize excessively in one area. Good teachers, for example, find teaching highly rewarding and, instead of cutting back on preparation time to further develop areas of comparative weakness, respond to the students' accolades by allocating even more time to teaching. This response increases their success at teaching at the expense of other activities and lures them into even more lopsided use of their time. It is probably not a coincidence that winning a teaching award is frequently a leading indicator of denial of tenure.

Finally, I have no idea if academics are unusual in their search for meaning in life. Like the rest of the population, academics are no strangers to self-help books, religion, and psychotherapy. I have noticed, however, that an amazing profusion of academics (particularly in the humanities) are writing memoirs, including some who have not lived particularly exciting or unusual lives. My guess is that memoirs give expression to people's need to make meaning out of the sequence of events that compose their lives. Jerome Bruner (1998) argues that, whether or not they record it on paper, people naturally construct autobiographical accounts of their lives that put their lives into context and invest them with meaning.

Is it possible to incorporate non-consumption-related motives into formal models of economic behavior? I am not at all sure. But the chances of it happening will certainly be improved if a competent economic modeler, perhaps to signal her modeling acumen to the world or to herself, sets such a goal for herself.

References

Ainslie, George (1975). Specious Reward: A Behavioral Theory of Impulsiveness and Impulse Control, *Psychological Bulletin*. 82: 463–496.

Akerlof, George A. and Rachel E. Kranton (1998). Economics and Identity, Working paper, Department of Economics, University of California, Berkeley.

Armony, Jorge L., David Servan-Schreiber, Jonathan D. Cohen, and Joseph E. LeDoux (1995). An Anatomically-constrained Neural Network Model of Fear Conditioning, *Behavioral Neuroscience*. 109: 246–256.

Armony, Jorge L., David Servan-Schreiber, Jonathan D. Cohen and Joseph E. LeDoux (1997). Computational Modeling of Emotion: Explorations Through the Anatomy and Physiology of Fear Conditioning, *Trends in Cognitive Sciences*. 1: 28–34.

Babcock, Linda, and George Loewenstein (1997). Explaining Bargaining Impasse: The Role of Self-serving Biases, *Journal of Economic Perspectives*. 11: 109–126.

Bentham, Jeremy (1948/1789). *The Principles of Morals and Legislation*. New York: Macmillan.

Bernartzi, Shlomo and Richard H. Thaler (1995). Myopic Loss Aversion and the Equity Premium Puzzle, *Quarterly Journal of Economics*. CXII: 73–92.

Bernheim, Douglas (1994). A Theory of Conformity, *Journal of Political Economy*. 102: 841–877.

Berridge, Kent C. (1995). Food Reward: Brain Substrates of Wanting and Liking, *Neuroscience and Biobehavioral Reviews*. 20: 1–25.

Bodner, Ronit and Drazen Prelec (1996). The Diagnostic Value of Actions in a Self-signaling Model, MIT working paper.

Bouton, Mark E. (1994). Conditioning, Remembering, and Forgetting, *Journal of Experimental Psychology*. 20: 219–231.

Brehm, Jack (1966). *A Theory of Psychological Reactance*. New York: Academic Press.

Brown, Roger and J. Kulik (1977). Flashbulb Memories, *Cognition*. 5: 73–99.

Bruner, Jerome (1998). Composing Protoselves Through Improvisation The Remembering Self, in: Ulric Neisser and Robyn Fivush (eds.), *Construction and Accuracy in the Self-narrative: The Sixth Emory Symposium on Cognition*. Cambridge (England): Cambridge University Press.

Cabanac, Michel (1979). Sensory Pleasure, *Quarterly Review of Biology*. 54: 1–29.

Camerer, Colin, Linda Babcock, George Loewenstein and Richard Thaler (1997). Labor Supply of New York City Cab Drivers: One Day at a Time, *Quarterly Journal of Economics*. CXII: 407–441.

Chao, Angela and Juliet B. Schor (1998). Empirical tests of status consumption: Evidence from women's cosmetics, *Journal of Economic Psychology*. 19:107–131.

Cherry-Gerrard, Apsley (1922). *The Worst Journey in the World*. London: Constable.

Christensen, Szalanski and J. J. Jay (1984). Discount Functions and the Measurement of Patients' Values: Women's Decisions During Childbirth, *Medical Decision Making*. 4: 47–58.

Clark, Andrew (1998). *Are Wages Habit-forming? Evidence from Micro Data*, Working paper, Centre de Recherche Sur l'Emploi et la Production, Laboratoire d'Économie d'Orléans.

Csikszentmihalyi, Mihaly (1991). *Flow: The Psychology of Optimal Experience*. New York: HarperCollins.

Curran, Jim (1987). *K2: Triumph and Tragedy*. Seattle: The Mountaineers.

Damasio, Antonio R. (1994). *Descartes' Error: Emotion, Reason, and the Human Brain*. New York: Putnam.

DeBecker, Gavin (1997). *The Gift of Fear: Survival Signals that Protect Us from Violence*. Boston: Little, Brown, and Company.

Duesenberry, James S. (1952). *Income, Saving, and the Theory of Consumer Behavior*. Cambridge: Harvard University Press.

Elster, Jon (forthcoming). *Strong Feelings: Emotion, Addiction, and Human Behavior*. Cambridge, MA: MIT Press.

Fehr, Ernst and Simon Gächter (1998). *Reciprocity and Economics: The Economic Implications of Homo Reciprocans*, Working Paper, University of Zurich.

Fiennes, Ranulph (1995). *Mind Over Matter: The Epic Crossing of the Antarctic Continent*. London: Delta.

Frank, Robert (1985). *Choosing the Right Pond*. New York: Oxford University Press.

Glaeser, Edward L. and Spencer Glendon (1997). The Demand for Religion, Working paper, Harvard University, Department of Economics.

Glass, David C. and Jerome E. Singer (1972). *Urban Stress: Experiments on Noise and Social Stressors.* New York: Academic Press.

Hardie, Bruce G. S., Eric J. Johnson and Peter S. Fader (1993). Modeling Loss Aversion and Reference Dependence Effects on Brand Choice, *Marketing Science.* 12: 378–394.

Heath, Chip, Richard Larrick and George Wu (1998). Goals as Reference Points, Working paper, Fuqua School of Business, Duke University.

Heath, Chip and Amos Tversky (1991). Preference and Belief: Ambiguity and Competence in Choice Under Uncertainty, *Journal of Risk and Uncertainty.* 4: 5–28.

Herzog, Maurice (1952/1997). *Annapurna.* New York: Lyons Press.

Kahneman, Daniel and Jackie S. Snell (1990). Predicting Utility, in: R.M. Hogarth (ed.), *Insights in Decision Making: A Tribute to Hillel J. Einhorn.* Chicago: University of Chicago Press.

Kahneman, Daniel and Amos Tversky (1979). Prospect Theory: An Analysis of Decision Under Risk, *Econometrica.* 47: 263–291.

Kahneman, Daniel, Peter Wakker and Rakesh Sarin (1997). Back to Bentham? Explorations of Experienced Utility, *Quarterly Journal of Economics.* CXII: 375–406.

Keynes, John Maynard (1936). *The General Theory of Employment, Interest and Money.* London: Macmillan.

Khalil, Elias L. (1996). Respect, admiration, aggrandizement: Adam Smith as economic psychologist, *Journal of Economic Psychology.* 14: 555–577.

Krakauer, Jon (1997). *Into Thin Air: A Personal Account of the Mount Everest Disaster.* New York: Doubleday.

Kundera, Milan (1998). *Identity.* New York: Harper Flamingo.

Langer, Ellen J. (1975). The Illusion of Control, *Journal of Personality and Social Psychology.* 32: 311–328.

Lansing, Alfred (1959). *Endurance: Shackleton's Incredible Voyage.* New York: Carroll & Graf.

Lea, Stephen and Paul Webley (1997). Pride in economic psychology, *Journal of Economic Psychology.* 18: 323–340.

Leibenstein, Harvey (1976). Bandwagon, Snob and Veblen Effects, in: *Beyond Economic Man: A New Foundation for Microeconomics.* Cambridge (Mass.): Harvard University Press.

Locke, Edwin A. and Gary P. Latham (1990). *A Theory of Goal Setting & Task Performance.* Englewood Cliffs, N.J.: Prentice Hall.

Loewenstein, George (1987). Anticipation and the Valuation of Delayed Consumption, *Economic Journal.* 97: 666–684.

Loewenstein, George (1992). The Fall and Rise of Psychological Explanation in the Economics of Intertemporal Choice, in: George Loewenstein and Jon Elster (eds.), *Choice Over Time.* New York (NY): Russell Sage: 3–34.

Loewenstein, George (1994). The Psychology of Curiosity: A Review and Reinterpretation, *Psychological Bulletin.* 116: 75–98.

Loewenstein, George (1996). Out of Control: Visceral Influences on Behavior, *Organizational Behavior and Human Decision Processes.* 65: 272–292.

Loewenstein, George and San Issacharoff (1994). Source-dependence in the Valuation of Objects, *Journal of Behavioral Decision Making.* 7: 157–168.

Loewenstein, George and Drazen Prelec (1992). Anomalies in Intertemporal Choice: Evidence and an Interpretation, *Quarterly Journal of Economics*. May: 573–597.

Loewenstein, George, Leigh Thompson and Max Bazerman (1989). Social Utility and Decision Making in Interpersonal Contexts, *Journal of Personality and Social Psychology*. 57: 426–441.

Loomes, Graham (1987). Some Implications of a More General Form of Regret Theory, *Journal of Economic Theory*. 41: 270–287.

MacCrimmon, Kenneth R. and Donald A. Wehrung (1986). *Taking Risks: The Management of Uncertainty*. New York: The Free Press.

Marshall, Alfred (1898). *Principles of Economics*. London: MacMillan.

Miller, George A., Eugene Galanter and Karl H. Pribram (1960). *Plans and the Structure of Behavior*. New York: Holt.

Mineka, Susan, Michael Cook and S. Miller (1984). Fear Conditioned with Escapable and Inescapable Shock: The Effects of a Feedback Stimulus, *Journal of Experimental Psychology Animal Behavior Processes*. 10: 307–323.

Norman, Michael (1996, July 7). Truth? *Sunday New York Times, Arts and Leisure Section*. p. 19.

O'Donoghue, Ted and Matthew Rabin (forthcoming). Doing it Now or Later, *American Economic Review*.

Offer, Avner (1997). Between the Gift and the Market: the Economy of Regard, *Economic History Review*. 3: 450–476.

Potterfield, Peter (1996). *In the Zone: Epic Survival Stories from the Mountaineering World*. Seattle: The Mountaineers.

Rabin, Matthew (1993). Incorporating Fairness into Game Theory and Economics, *American Economic Review*. 83: 1281–1302.

Roberts, David (1991/1968). *The Mountain of My Fear*. Seattle, WA: The Mountaineers.

Sanderson, W. C., Ronald M. Rapee and David H. Barlow (1988). The Influence of Illusion of Control on Panic Attacks Induced via Inhalation of 5.5% CO_2 Enriched Air, Manuscript submitted for publication.

Scott, Robert Falcon (1996). *Scott's Last Expedition: The Journals*. New York: Caroll & Graf.

Seligman, Martin E. P. and Steven F. Maier (1967). Failure to Escape Traumatic Shock, *Journal of Experimental Psychology*. 74: 1–9.

Simon, Herb (1967). Motivational and Emotional Controls of Cognition, *Psychological Review*. 57: 386–420.

Simpson, Joe (1993). *This Game of Ghosts*. Seattle: Mountaineers.

Simpson, Joe (1997). *Touching the Void*. London: Random House.

Strotz, Robert H. (1955). Myopia and Inconsistency in Dynamic Utility Maximization, *Review of Economic Studies*. 23: 165–180.

Stroud, Mike (1993). *Shadows on the Wasteland: Crossing Antarctica with Ranulph Fiennes*. Woodstock, NY: Overlook Press.

Sugden, Robert (1994). *Regret and Recrimination*.

Tversky, Amos and Daniel Kahneman (1991). Loss Aversion in Riskless Choice: A Reference-dependent Model, *Quarterly Journal of Economics*. 106: 1039–1061.

Weathers, Beck (1998). Verbal address delivered to conference of physicians.

White, Robert W. (1959). Motivation Reconsidered: The Concept of Competence, *Psychological Review*. 66: 297–333.

Wilson, Timothy D., D. J. Lisle, J. W. Schooler, S. D. Hodges, K. J. Klaaren and S. J. LaFleur (1993). Introspecting About Reasons can Reduce Post-choice Satisfaction, *Personality and Social Psychology Bulletin*. 19: 331–339.

Wilson, Timothy D. and Jonathan W. Schooler (1991). Thinking too Much: Introspection can Reduce the Quality of Preferences and Decisions, *Journal of Personality and Social Psychology*. 60: 181–192.

Wolfe, C., Jr. (1970). The Present Value of the Past, *Journal of Political Economy*. 78: 783–792.

Zajonc, Robert B. (1980). Feeling and Thinking: Preferences Need no Inference, *American Psychologist*. 35: 151–175.

Zajonc, Robert B. (1984). On Primacy of Affect, *American Psychologist*. 39: 117–123.

2

The Economics of Meaning

Niklas Karlsson, George Loewenstein, and Jane McCafferty

One important recent development in economics is a new interest in happiness research. This research, I believe, is at least partly motivated by two concerns: a questioning of whether people know what is best for them (see Chapter 13 on projection bias) and a questioning of whether, due to self-control problems, people are able to act in their own self-interest even when they do know what's best for them (see Chapters 18–22). To the extent that people don't know what's good for them, or can't pursue it successfully on their own, it may be useful to attempt to determine what in fact makes people happy and to think about ways to help people achieve happiness.

Despite having contributed to this general line of research, I've long had misgivings about whether people generally do attempt to maximize their happiness and, moreover, whether they *should* attempt to do so. Happiness researchers, beginning with Bentham, take it as a matter of faith that happiness is not *a* goal of human existence, but is *the* single correct goal that humans should have. To me, this seems to be a rather arbitrary value judgment. Unless happiness is defined so broadly as to include the achievement of anything one values, it strikes me as more correct to view happiness and unhappiness simply as motivational mechanisms—a carrot on the one hand and a stick on the other—that evolution has devised to get us to do what we need to do to survive and reproduce. Whether we want to be slaves to those signals is up to us.

Philosophers, of course, have registered numerous objections to the idea that happiness should be the goal, from John Stuart Mill's rhetorical question of whether it is better to be an unhappy Socrates or a happy pig to Nozick's implicit indictment of an imaginary "experience machine" which would "simulate your brain so that you would think and feel you were writing a great novel, or making a friend, or reading an interesting book".[1] Although

---

[1] Nozick, R. (1974). *Anarchy, State and Utopia*. Blackwell: Oxford.

Nozick and I differ in the applications of the experience machine that first comes to mind (mine, I must admit, are somewhat more porcine), like Nozick and Mill, I have serious reservations about the idea that the purpose of life is, or should be, to maximize happiness.

To me, part of the purpose of being alive is to be *alive*, which means having a range of emotions.[2] This is what I sometimes say to people who are trying to decide whether to have children but are disturbed by the research showing that people with children tend to be less happy, on average. Having experienced parenthood myself, I don't feel ready to question that empirical finding. If parenting does lower the mean, however, it also radically increases the variance. There are few things more agonizing than vicariously living out one's children's problems while being helpless to do anything about them. But there are also few things more wonderful than your child leaping into your arms when you return from a trip, watching your older child take care of the younger, or witnessing the first time they walk, talk, ride a bike, and so on. There is also pleasure from the feeling of caring deeply about someone or something outside of yourself—the liberation of not being only obsessed with your own happiness, and relatedly, the deep experience of human interconnection. Robert Sugden, in a brilliant essay on Adam Smith, refers to this sense of connection as "fellow feeling", and argues that experiencing what another person experiences can be satisfying in and of itself, even if the feelings or emotions that are shared are negative.[3]

In this paper, I focus on yet another motivation driving human behavior that is relatively disconnected from happiness and that has received little if any treatment by economists: the seeking of meaning. What does it mean to seek out meaning? And can the different possible interpretations of meaning-seeking be incorporated into economics? Read the paper and decide for yourself. Here, I'd like to make two points; the first is that humans are,

---

[2] In a remarkable short story that illustrates the importance of emotional vitality much more eloquently than our academic paper could hope to do, Stefan Zweig writes about a man who, as he puts it was "suffering from emotional impotence, an inability to take passionate control of life". In the story, a woman he has been seeing for years gets engaged to another man and, breaking off the relationship, sends him a consolatory letter, "begging me not to be angry with her, not to feel too much pain at her sudden termination of our relationship." But, instead he feels nothing. "At that moment," he writes, "I was fully aware for the first time how far advanced the process of paralysis already was in me—it was as if I were moving through flowing, bright water without being halted or taking root anywhere, and I knew very well that this chill was something dead and corpse-like, not yet surrounded by the foul break of decomposition but already numbed beyond recovery, a grimly cold lack of emotion."

[3] Sugden, R. (2002). 'Beyond Sympathy and Empathy: Adam Smith's Concept of Fellow Feeling', *Economics and Philosophy*, 18(1): 63–87. This idea has recently received empirical support from Rajagopal Raghunathan and Kim Corfman in their paper 'Is Happiness Shared Doubled and Sadness Shared Halved? Social Influence on Enjoyment of Hedonic Experiences', *Journal of Marketing Research*, 43(3): 386–394.

in effect, meaning-making machines. Even when we are asleep, our brains are busy constructing a narrative that makes sense of the random firings of our neurons. The second is that people are often willing to sacrifice other goals, such as wealth and time, for meaning. In fact, I suppose that a part of the purpose of writing this chapter was to find meaning—which, happily, remains unfinished business.

The Economics of Meaning[*]

Niklas Karlsson, George Loewenstein, and Jane McCafferty

One of the ways in which behavioral economics – the application of insights from psychology to economics – has extended the scope of economic analysis has been by expanding the range of human motives taken into account to explain economic behavior. Neoclassical economic theory rests on an updated notion of the utility concept first proposed by Bentham, but only recently have economists begun to explore the full range of determinants of utility that Bentham enumerated over 200 years ago. For example, Loomes and Sugden (1982, 1987; Loomes, 1988) have explored the economic consequences of avoidance of regret and disappointment, both of which Bentham included in his short list of pains. Caplin and Leahy (1997) discuss implications that follow from the idea that people derive utility not only from immediate experiences, but also from anticipation – what Bentham called "pleasures and pains of expectation and imagination" (see also, Loewenstein, 1987; Brunnermeier and Parker, 2002). And game theory has been similarly enriched by the expanded recognition of motives such as altruism, fairness and reciprocity, all closely related to what Bentham referred to as "pleasures of benevolence or good will" and "pains of enmity." Most recently, economists have taken account of even more exotic motives such as ego (Koszegi, 2000; Prelec and Bodner, 2003) – the "pleasures of a good name," as Bentham expressed it – and identity (Akerlof and Kranton, 2000).

One important motive that was not recognized by Bentham (or at least not included in his list of pleasures and pains), and which has also not found its way into contemporary economics is *meaning*. Among those with an interest in understanding human behavior, economists are unusual in their

* This chapter was originally published as Karlsson, N., Loewenstein, G. and McCafferty, J. (2004), 'The Economics of Meaning', Nordic Journal of Political Economy. 30(1), 61–75. Reproduced with permission.

We thank Eli Finkel, George Akerlof, Botond Koszegi and Jennifer Lerner for helpful comments, and the Swedish Foundation for International Cooperation in Research and Higher Education (STINT) for financial support to Karlsson and Loewenstein.

neglect of meaning. Philosophers since Plato have viewed search for meaning as *the* activity which brings value to human life. And many psychologists (e.g. Bruner, 2002; Kegan, 1982) see meaning-making as the fundamental activity of human existence. Perhaps even more than among philosophers and psychologists, believers in the importance of meaning can be found in the ranks of writers, critics, and purveyors of literature. In literature, human experiences are organized and assembled to bring meaning to what would otherwise be inchoate experiences and events. Literature, therefore, may be the most important arena in which people express their desire for meaning and reveal different avenues toward attaining it. In writing this paper on the economics of meaning, therefore, we experimented with an unusual combination of collaborators: an economist, psychologist, and writer. When we explore the potential role of meaning in economics, we therefore draw not only on psychological research, but also on ideas about meaning revealed in literature.

Economists should be interested in meaning not because others are, but because meaning has direct significance for economics. First and most obviously, considerable economic activity is devoted to meaning-making. Besides religion,[1] which is a huge source of economic activity, there are self-help books, insight therapies, various types of volunteer activities and a wide range of other activities including, for some, work, that offer meaning as at least one important benefit.

Second, meaning is important because it is an extremely important determinant of well-being. Without meaning, psychologists and philosophers argue, even the most prosperous existence isn't worth living. People need to feel they have a purpose in their life in order to function and feel well psychologically as well as physically (Emmons, 1996). And, the capacity to find meaning can attenuate even the most severe hardships (Taylor, 1983). Victor Frankl (1963) is especially associated with meaning as a result of his popular book *Man's Search for Meaning*. Frankl formulated a therapy based on the will to meaning in the 1930s that he was forced to personally put to test in German concentration camps. To Frankl it is people's innate will to find meaning, and not their striving for pleasure, power, or wealth, that is the strongest motivation for living. To the extent that economics is the science of promoting well-being with constrained resources, then, meaning should be part of the equation.

Third, as we attempt to demonstrate, an exploration of the role of meaning in economics can help to illuminate both some of the strengths and

---

[1] An early version of a paper by Ed Glaeser and Spencer Glendon on "The Demand for Religion" (1997) is indicative of the neglect of meaning by economists, and provides a stark illustration of the pitfalls of doing so. The authors investigate three theories of why people demand religion: (1) religion provides social connections, (2) it provides rewards after death or (3) it provides moral instruction. It seems somewhat striking that the possibility that religion may provide people with meaning is not considered.

limitations of the assumptions incumbent in the economic interpretation of behavior as an attempt to maximize utility.

2.1. Four Interpretations of Meaning

Although meaning is sometimes treated as a generic concept, we find it useful to distinguish between four different interpretations of the concept. The first one, we show, is quite amenable to analysis with the standard economic tool of utility maximization, but as one goes down the list, successive concepts of meaning pose an ever-greater challenge to the traditional economic model of human behavior. The four interpretations are:

- *Meaning as a resolution of uncertainty about preferences*: People are often uncertain about what they want from life. Finding meaning, in some cases, can entail learning about what one values or cares about.

- *Meaning as an extension of self either socially or temporally*: One's life can often seem insignificant and inconsequential when viewed in the context of the span of human (or even natural) history or of the vast numbers of people alive in the world. The quest for higher meaning may serve the function of expanding the self through time and across persons.

- *Meaning as an act of sense-making*: The brain is a sense-making organ, and one of its most important tasks is to make sense of the life of its owner. Such sense-making typically takes the form of a narrative – a "life story."

- *Meaning as an assertion of free will*: People derive personal meaning from the act of making autonomic choices. Hence, meaning-making can involve the assertion of free will.

In the remainder of the paper, we elaborate on these four concepts of meaning and discuss their potential connection to economics.

2.2. Meaning as a Resolution of Uncertainty about Preferences

Standard economics, at least in its most stripped-down form, assumes that people come to the world with well-defined preferences then seek to satisfy those preferences maximally given the objective constraints that they face. The reality, of course, is somewhat different. As decision research on preference uncertainty (Payne, Bettman, and Johnson, 1992, 1993; Slovic 1995; Ariely, Loewenstein, and Prelec, 2003) recognizes, people do not always know what they want. Such lack of information is not at all surprising when it comes to things that one hasn't actually experienced – e.g. items on the menu of a restaurant one hasn't visited previously – but it can also extend to much larger aspects of life. The resolution of uncertainty about higher level preferences – about what's important in life – is without doubt one goal that people often want to attain when they say that they are seeking meaning.

Many self-help books and personal growth programs appear to be focused on meaning-making of this kind. For example, 'Lifespring' – one of a large number of popular programs that seems to be aimed precisely at resolving this type of uncertainty – promises to help enrollees discover "what is so vitally important to you . . . so that the choices in your life are truly aligned with your purposes." And among the best selling self-help books are titles such as "The life you were born to live: A guide to finding your life purpose", and "Finding your own north star: Claiming the life you were meant to live." Such self-help books can be seen as popularized offshoots of certain classic texts of literature and philosophy. The American Transcendentalists, for example, were fully focused on what it meant to live an honorable or meaningful life, and how dependent such a life was on finding one's own path to walk. "You think me the child of circumstance; I make my circumstance," wrote Emerson. Thoreau, who at the very least wrote like a man who knew what he wanted, remains popular today, and one reason for his popularity must rest in people's hunger and appreciation for written enactments of other people resolving their preferences. Thoreau lived a life both of renunciation and appreciation. The great poet, Whitman, offers the same written resolution of preferences in his classic poem "Song of Myself" that celebrates his love of nature, culture, people, and his own self. It's a poem where the poet's passionate and varied preferences in this life are named specifically.

If having purposes and goals, and gaining a sense of what one "really" wants ultimately enhances happiness, then this kind of meaning-making is easily reconciled with utility maximization. Meaning-making can be interpreted as the act of reducing preference uncertainty, which, by providing insights into what brings utility, allows one to do a better job of maximizing it.[2]

2.3. Meaning as an Extension of Self Either Socially or Temporally

Another way in which people seek meaning, which points to an alternative interpretation of the concept, is by seeking to put their lives into some kind of larger perspective. Viewed against the backdrop of human history or against the multitudes of people currently alive, one's own life can easily seem

---

[2] There is some question about whether people even have underlying preferences that they could potentially discover. Plott (1996) has been the most prominent advocate of the idea that people do have underlying preferences which they discover through experience and economic activity, but others (e.g. Ariely, Loewenstein and Prelec, 2003) have questioned whether this is in fact the case.

inconsequential. To allay such feelings of inconsequentiality, people may seek to extend their own being either socially or temporally. The journalist and activist Dorothy Day was said to be successful because she had "a knack for situating herself and her story into a larger story." Day herself wrote about watching the crisis of a serious San Francisco earthquake unfold, and how, while the crisis lasted, "people loved each other." Certainly this "love" is the result of a sense of an expanded or extended self most easily experienced in times of shared jeopardy.

Social Extension involves ameliorating feelings of inconsequentiality by viewing oneself in a broader social context, such as a family, profession, nation or religion. By identifying oneself with some larger organization, one can, in effect, leverage one's identity. An American can think, "I'm a citizen of the most powerful nation in the world," a Moslem's identity can include being a member of the most widespread religion, and a union member can view himself as part of a significant social movement. Indeed, nationalism, religious identification, and social class are all sources of identification that have had enormous consequences for human society.

As social identity theory highlights, people's definitions of themselves as being part of a group – their social identities – have important implications for the behaviors of individuals as well as the functioning of groups and organizations (Haslam, 2000). As demonstrated in minimal group studies (e.g. Tajfel et al., 1971; Turner, 1982), even when people are assigned to a group based on some irrelevant, arbitrary, criterion, such as their preference between the abstract painters Klee and Kandinsky, they come to powerfully identify with their group; they tend to view their group as superior to other groups on measurable, valued, dimensions, and are willing to contribute to their group to promote its competition with other groups. Other research has shown that it is possible to activate either people's personal or social identities. When people's personal identities are made salient to them, they are motivated to enhance themselves as individuals, but when their social identities are salient they are motivated less by personal gains and more by working for the collective interest of the group (Haslam, 2000). Hence, if people try to escape the perceived futility of their own personal existence by perceiving themselves as part of a larger social context, such a search for meaning through social extension can have important consequences for behavior.

Temporal extension is a second important means by which people combat feelings of inconsequentiality. The fact that we all have to die is an important source of feelings of insignificance and hence meaninglessness, perhaps particularly in Western societies, where people often want to avoid the very idea of it (Ariès, 1981). It has frequently been observed that when people are exposed to thoughts about dying, as in war, in the presence of a life threatening disease or in the death of a loved one, beliefs in a higher meaning and religiosity increase (Baumeister, 1991). One thing that is offered by religion is ideas and assurances about a life after death. In times of war, it has been noted that rates of suicide goes down – presumably because war gives people's lives meaning in terms of a broader context, and also because it causes people to focus their attention outward rather than inward. "The rush of battle is a potent and often lethal addiction," writes Chris Hedges, in *War Is a Force That Gives Us Meaning*. War, he continues, "can give us what we long for in life."

In by far the most extensive and far-reaching line of research on effects of mortality salience, Greenberg, Solomon and Pyszczynski (1997) produced direct experimental evidence of a causal link between worries about mortality and seeking meaning through the extension of self. In tests of what they call "terror management theory" (the source of terror being recognition of one's own mortality), they show that reminding people of their own mortality causes people to embrace more strongly the beliefs and values of the groups to which they belong. Furthermore, when exposed to the threat of death, people show a greater appreciation for being a part of a broader social context with a past and a future, such as family (Taylor, 1983) or culture (Rosenblatt et al., 1989).

On the other hand, such beliefs and values, however, might be exactly what is transcended when mortality becomes more than an idea and closer to an actuality. In Flannery O'Connor's most famous story, "A Good Man Is Hard To Find", a dying middle-class character recognizes her "white trash" murderer known only as "the misfit" as "one of her own." In the moments that precede her death, she extends herself by identifying not just with her own group, not just with her culture's set of beliefs, but rather with all of humanity. The murderer recognizes the woman's extension of self and comments, "She would have been a good woman if there'd been someone there to kill her all the time," a line famous not just for its humor but for its wise commentary on death's impact on character. The woman's social extension ultimately transcends social category in this case, and the story can be read not as a tragedy but as a depiction of a woman who finally understands ultimate meaning of "better late than never".

The desire to extend oneself in time, like the desire to be part of a larger social entity, has momentous consequences for individual behavior and societal outcomes. Thus, for example, the desire for posterity is undoubtedly an important motive underlying religious beliefs. Most religions embody beliefs about life after death. In the US, more than 80% of adults believe that life continues in some way after death (Greeley and Hout, 1999).[3] Needless to say,

---

[3] A March 1997 Yankelovich Partners survey of 1,018 adults in the United States found that 81% of Americans agreed with the question "Do you believe in the existence of heaven, where people live forever with God after they die?"

religion has been a powerful force in human affairs. But, not only for religious people can the idea of life ending completely at death render the experience of living meaningless. This sense of meaninglessness often confronts even the most stubborn of atheists on their death-beds, which is why "death-bed conversions" are cliché.

The desire to extend oneself in time may also underlie the common obsession with fame. Fame has been described as a secular religion (Baumeister, 1991), and like beliefs in the afterlife, fame can provide at least the illusion that one will not be ignored and forgotten once one is dead. The idea that fame confers a type of immortality has been expressed in a wide range of contexts, from the song lyrics of Irene Cara, "Remember my name! Fame! I wanna live forever!," to the writings of William Shakespeare:

> "Let fame, that all hunt after in their lives,
> Live registered upon our brazen tombs,
> And then grace us in the disgrace of death"
>
> —The King, in Love's Labor's Lost,
> act 1, sc. 1, l. 1-7

Closely related to fame is the desire to leave some kind of mark on history, a motivation that has almost certainly played an important role in the behavior of many politicians, business-leaders, writers, artists, and other public figures. It is even possible that much academic output is motivated by thoughts of posterity (over optimism may be another important ingredient). Similar motives may help to explain the prevalence of child-bearing in the face of evidence that children tend to decrease happiness (again, another possible explanation is people's over optimism that this pattern won't apply to them personally). A poignant example of a father's sense of defeat when his own sense of self cannot be expanded in time through his schizophrenic son can be read in "Drummond and Son" by Charles D'Ambrosio. The character Drummond has a powerful sense of carrying his own father into the future, and feels keenly that his son, due to mental illness, cannot extend his own sense of self through time; the son feels no link to posterity or to his ancestors.

The desperate desire for a few moments of fame or notoriety, which seem to have increased in the twentieth century with the rise of visual media, appears to have been a significant motive in the recent spate of "school shootings." In a television interview, one of the pre-Columbine school shooters was asked whether he regretted his actions. His response revealed that his big regret was that people had forgotten about him because Columbine had overshadowed him. It may not be a coincidence that many of the school shootings involve adolescents (as opposed to, for example, college students). Adolescence is a time of life that is notoriously fraught with questions about meaning (Fry, 1998). Adolescence also seems to be a period in life in which a search for identity and fame are especially salient, and in which these motives often lead to self-destructive and shortsighted behavior.

To accommodate meaning as an expansion of the self through time and across persons, the standard framework of utility maximization would require some modification, although not a major renovation. Most easily, one could make utility a function of identity, as have, in fact, Akerlof and Kranton (2000). More drastically, one may 'extend time' (in the standard utility maximization problem) to include the generations before and after an individual's life and expand 'utility' to include abstract entities such as an individual's nation, religion, or social group.

2.4. Meaning as an Act of Sense-Making

Yet another way to interpret meaning is as the act of making sense of one's life as a whole. Without meaning of this kind, experiences, life and the world is perceived as chaotic. We want to make sense of our experiences for very much the same reasons that Graham Greene gave for why he decided to write an autobiography, which he believed was "much the same motive that has made me a novelist: a desire to reduce a chaos of experience to some sort of order...". A.S. Byatt takes this further when she writes of narration as "as much a part of human nature as breath and the circulation of blood," continuing more in line with the idea of meaning as an effort to achieve posterity: "Our stories are like genes, they keep part of us alive after the end of our story."

According to many psychologists (e.g. Bruner, 1990; Frankl, 1963; Kegan, 1982) meaning-making is the most fundamental of all human mental activities. As noted by Gilovich (1991), "We are predisposed to see order, pattern, and meaning in the world, and we find randomness, chaos, and meaninglessness unsatisfying. Human nature abhors a lack of predictability and the absence of meaning" (p. 9). People seem to need to make sense of their experiences and life in order to function and feel well (Baumeister and Vohs, 2002; McAdams et al., 1997), and the positive effects of meaning-making seem to be especially pronounced when it comes to coping with negative life events (Davis, Nolen-Hoeksema, and Larson, 1998).

Sense-making seems to be a critically important way that people deal with negative life outcomes. This is apparent in literature, where so many memoirs, indeed, focus on tragic, premature losses or "dysfunction." There is also substantial evidence that finding meaning in emotional or traumatic life events promotes health (e.g. Scheier and Carver, 2001; Ryff and Singer, 1998; Taylor and Brown, 1988). Some research supports the not-all-that-surprising conclusion that finding meaning in response to stressful life events is associated with better *psychological* health outcomes (e.g. Davis et al., 1998;

Mendola et al., 1990; Tait and Silver, 1989). More surprisingly, at least two studies have found a positive connection between meaning-making and *physical* health outcomes. The first of these studies was an 8-year study of heart attack victims (Affleck et al., 1987). At both 7 weeks and 8 years following infarction, participants responded to the following questions: "Despite all the problems and worries which your illness has involved, do you see any possible benefits, gains or advantages in this experience? If so, what are they?" Almost 60% answered the first question in the affirmative at both time points, with typical responses to the second question falling into categories such as "change in philosophy of life / values / religious views," "change in mode of life to increase enjoyment," and "learn value of healthy behavior" (Affleck et al., 1987:31). Results revealed that participants who cited benefits from their misfortune 7 weeks after the first myocardial infarction were less likely to have another attack and had lower levels of morbidity 8 years later. The second study examined the effects of finding meaning on the physical health outcomes of HIV-seropositive men who had recently experienced an AIDS-related bereavement (Bower et al., 1998). Participants were classified as having "discovered meaning" if they manifested a major shift in values, priorities, or perspectives in response to the bereavement in an open-ended interview. Statements indicative of finding meaning included, "I certainly appreciated more the friends that I have and became much closer with them" and "I would say that (his) death lit up my faith" (Bower et al., 1998: 981). Whereas men who failed to discover meaning exhibited substantial drops in CD4 cell counts (a key immunological marker of HIV progression) over a 2- 3-year follow-up period, those who managed to find meaning showed no reduction in CD4 cell counts over the same time period. Even more remarkably, the discovery of meaning was associated with a lower rate of AIDS-related mortality over a 4- to 9-year follow-up period.

More generally, sense-making seems to be a common and effective method by which people blunt diverse forms of setbacks and disappointments. In a recent paper on affective forecasting Wilson and Gilbert (2003) argue that people's inclination to make sense of their experiences is a way to temper emotional reactions. Making sense of affective experiences decreases the intensity and duration of affect. In several studies Wilson and Gilbert show that for groups of subjects for whom it is made easier to make sense of an event, both positive and negative emotional reactions are weaker than for groups of subjects for whom it is made harder to make sense. For instance, in one study Gilbert et al. (1998) showed that students that were interviewed and rejected for a desirable job differed in their unhappiness depending on how easy it was to rationalize the rejection.

How do people make sense of the events of their lives? In part, they make up stories or 'scripts' (Bruner, 2002; Schank, 1990; Schank and Abelson, 1995). During the bombardment of Sarajevo in 1994 a group of theatre workers in

Amsterdam commissioned tales from different European writers to be read aloud in theatres in Sarajevo and all over Europe, every Friday until the fighting ended. "This project," wrote A.S. Byatt, "pitted storytelling against destruction, imaginative life against real death." In virtually all cultures and historical periods, people have communicated their experiences and under-standings of the world by telling stories. Schank and Abelson (1995) argue that virtually all human knowledge is based on stories about past experiences. Even if this is an overstatement, there is research showing the stories help people to integrate knowledge, such as demonstrations that subjects are much more successful in learning a list of words if they are instructed to make up a story using the words (Bower and Clark, 1969). Narrative-based representations of knowledge have also been shown to underlie some types of judgment and decision making (Wyer, Adaval, and Colcombe, 2002). For instance, studies by Pennington and Hastie (1986, 1992) demonstrated that information conveyed in the form of a narrative has a greater impact on jury decision-making than information conveyed in other formats. In one study (Pennington and Hastie, 1992), participants read transcripts of a court trial, including testimonies of both prosecution witnesses and defense witnesses. These were either conveyed in the order provided by the witnesses (witness-order condition) or in the order it became relevant in the sequence of events leading to the crime (story-order condition). When participants read defense and prosecution testimonies from different conditions – e.g. the defense position in witness order and the prosecution position in story order – 73% of the participants favored the testimony conveyed in the story order in their verdicts.

The stories that people tell about themselves rarely follow the utilitarian theme "I was happy as much of the time as I possibly could have been given the opportunities that I faced." Rather, people spontaneously adopt classic narrative structures, such as, an innocent person is beset by crises and setbacks, but her struggles are finally crowned with happiness or, at least, wisdom (McAdams et al., 1997; Wilson and Ross; 2001). People tend to focus on and construct stories of experiences that revolve around specific common aspects of the experiences. According to Baumeister and Newman (1994) people tell stories that revolve around the extent to which the experiences of the person or persons that the story is about had a purpose, were justifiable, were carried out efficiently and increased or decreased self-worth. They further argue for a polarization in the sense that they don't make good stories if they are not towards the end continuum of those aspects of the experiences. That is, people tend to exaggerate the ups and downs, successes and failures of experiences. Experiences are either successes or break-downs in achieving or fulfilling goals; actions are either morally right or wrong; situations are either highly controllable or out of control; and experiences put oneself either in a good light or a bad light. Literature both complies with and complicates such rules of story-telling. While a good story or novel must have a distinct "conflict" and must attempt to make some kind of sense of that conflict in a given character's life, moral ambiguities in both situation and character are not only acceptable, but necessary, if literature is to be judged as "true." And yet certainly literature falls flat when nothing is as stake for a character's sense of self-worth, or when stories unfold without seeming purpose. Only in 'meta-fiction' do you find writers making arguments against narrative and "sense-making," and these arguments by now are a bit stale.

The propensity to make sense of experiences by telling stories has profound implications not only for happiness, but also for behavior. People don't just retrospectively reconstruct their lives; the stories they tell about themselves profoundly affect how they live. As Bruner (1987) expresses it, "eventually the culturally shaped cognitive and linguistic processes that guide the self-telling of life narratives achieve the power to structure perceptual experience, to organize memory, to segment and purpose-build the very 'events' of a life. In the end, we become the autobiographical narratives by which we 'tell about' our lives" (p. 15). The implications of this are profound; perhaps we should be more careful in choosing the stories we tell about ourselves. Story-telling matters because the types of actions and sequences of outcomes that make us happiest are unlikely to be the same as those that make for a good story. Perhaps the most dramatic example of this is serious mountaineering or polar exploration which tends to involve virtually unremitting misery (Loewenstein, 1999). At least one important benefit brought at the expense of this misery, however, is meaning. Staying home may be the most fun and relaxing way to spend one's summer vacation, but enduring the miseries of altitude, fear, cold and hunger makes for a far better narrative. This may be one reason why people return again and again to such misery; the actual experience of misery itself fades and is usurped and transformed by the retrospective pleasures of having shaped it into a story to share with others, and with oneself.

As noted, good stories tend to follow certain natural trajectories. The high school basketball star makes for an interesting story, but not one that most people would like to tell about themselves. In contrast, a story that involves an eventual triumph over initial hardships and setbacks is one that is not only interesting but socially desirable. Story-telling, hence, introduces a 'path-dependence' to preferences, with some paths being more desirable than others, even, often, at the expense of the integral of total utility. The propensity for story-telling may well contribute to the recent finding that people tend to represent certain kinds of past affective experiences in terms of their most intense part (the peak) and their ending. According to Frederickson (2000) these moments carry more weight in retrospective judgments because they carry more personal meaning than other moments. Peaks provide personal meaning in the sense that it gives the individual information about ones resources or capacities of experiencing certain events or episodes. Ends give personal meaning in terms of certainty, that is, the certainty about what an experience contained.

On the face of it, one might conclude that the importance of story-telling is antithetical to economic accounts of utility maximization, but a more accurate assessment might be that story-telling can be construed as a case of intertemporal choice – early sacrifice made for a life enriched by meaning. On the other hand, it isn't clear if people are really gaining happiness per se from such meaning, or whether meaning is an end in itself. Even if the quantity of pleasure would have been the same, people may prefer being happy on love than happy on pills. Or, as John Stuart Mill puts it "It is better to be Socrates dissatisfied than a fool satisfied." Consistent with utility-maximization theory, meaning may be seen as providing utility. However, it may not be a utility that is evaluated only in terms of amounts of pleasure and pain, but could even be a type of utility that is enhanced by the introduction of pain – albeit at the right moments.

2.5. Meaning as an Assertion of Free Will

A final interpretation of meaning involves the expression of free will. People want to believe that they have some control over their behavior and hence their destiny – they want to feel as if they are more than the sum of nerve firings happening in obscure parts of their brain. In line with this, one of the key assumptions in existential psychology is that people derive personal meaning from the individual decisions that they make (Frankl, 1963; Maddi, 1998). However, long before Newton uncovered the iron-clad regularity of physical laws, humans struggled with the knotty problem of free will. Are we free agents or preprogrammed by Nature or God?

Dostoyevsky articulated this dilemma in a scene from *Notes from the underground* in which his protagonist explicitly articulates to an assembled audience of scientists that there is one thing that is always left out in models of choice,

"But, after all, here is something amazing: why does it happen that all these statisticians, sages and lovers of humanity, when they calculate human advantages invariably leave one out?" (p. 19)

and a few pages later he declares what is missing

"One's own free unfettered choice, one's own fancy, however wild it may be . . . What man needs is simply independent choice, whatever that independence may cost and wherever it may lead." (p. 23)

Echoing the same theme, the contemporary novelist Don DeLillo asks in his novel *White Noise*, "How do you know whether something is really what you want to do or just some kind of nerve impulse in the brain? Some minor little activity takes place somewhere in this unimportant place in one of the brain hemispheres and suddenly I want to go to Montana or I don't want to go to Montana."

The act of making autonomous choices generates utility. It was identified by J. S. Mill as "one of the principal ingredients of human happiness" (1859/1974: 172). Mill's assertion has since been bolstered by diverse lines of research. For instance, studies find that one's perceived autonomy and extent to which one sees one's actions and life to be self determined is positively related to psychological and physiological well-being (e.g. Ryan and Deci, 2001). Efforts to achieve goals, and satisfaction with achieving those goals, are greater if those are intrinsically – i.e. internally – rather than extrinsically motivated (Deci, 1975). Hence, people appear to derive both meaning and utility from making autonomous choices.

On the face of it one might conclude, contrary to our initial assertion that this fourth motive is the most difficult of the four to assimilate to economics, that in fact it is the easiest. What contradiction could there be between utility maximization and the assertion of free will? The problem is, people do not only want to exercise their free will, but they want to *feel* that they are exercising it, and utility maximization in and of itself provides few clues about the involvement of will. A hedonistic interpretation of human behavior leaves little room for the assertion of free will.

How, then, is it possible to *know* that one is exercising free will? The answer, according to Dostoyevsky is that one can only be certain one is exercising free will if one does precisely the opposite of what one wants to do – of what would make us well off:

"But I repeat for the hundredth time, there is one case, one only, when man may purposely, consciously, desire what is injurious for himself, what is stupid, very stupid – simply in order to have the right to desire for himself even what is very stupid and not to be bound by any obligation to desire what is only rational." (p. 26)

Ironically, then, if we accept Dostoyevsky's argument, the motive to make autonomous choices may actually contribute to self-destructive behavior. Of course, if we assume that people derive pleasure from the assertion of their free will, then voluntary misery might be assimilated into a model of utility maximization. But this paradox only reveals the skeleton in the closet: the concept of utility is irrefutable and, hence, vacuous.

2.6. Conclusions

Economists have probably steered clear of meaning, not based on a denial of its importance, but from fear that modeling meaning, and its role in economic behavior, is likely to be difficult. In this paper, we argue that such fears are largely unjustified. Not only are most conceptions of meaning possible to model (indeed, some already have been – e.g. Akerlof and Kranton, 2000), but, we believe, doing so can shed light on a wide range of behaviors that seem otherwise incompatible with standard theory. The significance of meaning-making extends far beyond such obvious activities as religion and self-help media; the search for meaning has consequences that extend into all domains of life, including virtually all domains of economic behavior.

Turning to the first motive we discussed, the attempt to resolve uncertainty about preferences drives a tremendous amount of behavior. There is a market for resolving preference uncertainty, which is discernible not only by the presence of self-help counseling on bookshelves and in media. People also pay to take personality tests and tests such as the Myers–Briggs test of occupational interests. And in magazines and on the web there are plenty of tests offered to find out your preferences for how your partner should look like and be, and even to help you discover if you truly love your partner. Even if these behaviors do not seem to be accord with the assumption in economics about stable and coherent preferences, if reducing uncertainty provide insights to what brings utility, then this interpretation of meaning-making is in line with the notion of utility maximization.

What needs to be added to standard economic views, however, are accounts of how and why people actively want to manipulate their own preferences, and how not only fulfillment of goals but also having and striving towards goals brings utility. Such accounts would, for instance, be likely to contribute to models of labor economics. For many people work – even in occupations that many academics would consider mundane – is not just a mean to an end, it is not only a job but a 'career' or a 'calling' (Baumeister, 1991; Wrzesniewski et al., 1997). Personal development is not something that people engage in on their leisure time, people also strive for personal development and self-actualization through their work.

The desire to extend oneself either socially or temporally likewise has far-reaching consequences for individuals and society. For example, economists have a difficult time explaining common behaviors, such as voting, fighting in wars, and participation in outlawed political movements, that occur despite the existence of severe free-rider problems. Why do people expose themselves to the costs and risks associated with these activities when their individual participation is unlikely to make a difference? Part of the answer may be that synchronizing their own activities with those of larger collectives helps them to feel an integral part of those collectives, and hence decrease feelings of insignificance.

By enlarging the scope of "us" in the dichotomy between "us" and "them," the social extension of self may change people's behavior in significant ways. In social contexts, the choices we make may actually be more guided by what is appropriate to do and which rules to follow than by the utility of consequences (March, 1994; Messick, 1999). And our happiness as part of a collective may depend as much as the successes or failures of the collective rather than our own private successes and failures. For instance, we may find great pleasure in the successes for our favorite soccer or baseball team, the victories of our countrymen in the Olympics, the triumph of our supported presidential candidate, or the high rankings of our own university.

Meaning as an act of sense-making also has far reaching consequences for behavior. Consider the case of John D. Rockefeller who spent half his life making money, then, after recovering from a severe and life threatening disease, spent the rest of his life involved in philanthropy. While economics is well suited to account for his behavior the first part of his life, the second part of his life seems to be more driven by meaning-making than money-making. Even if sense-making ultimately brings utility, there seems to be a demand for making sense of the world and one's life that is not that obviously related to pleasures and pains. For instance, when a public figure is murdered (as was recently the Swedish foreign minister) people spend an enormous amount of time reading and watching news about the event, presumably driven by a wish to make sense of what has happened. Likewise, it seems that the large industry for story telling that exists in literature and on the screen is not only driven by peoples' search for happiness but also by a wish to make sense of experiences and events that also have bearings on their own lives.

Finally, turning to the interpretation of meaning as an assertion of free will, is the potential contradiction between utility maximization and the assertion of free will utterly a philosophical query with no real relevance for human behavior and economics? People may not scrutinize in each and every situation whether they choose freely or not, but may still abhor the idea that they are not the head of their own decisions. This abhorrence is depicted by Naomi Klein who in her best-selling book *No Logo* describes a movement, especially among young people, that take action against how companies through their ubiquitous brands try to make people buy their products. And there are various other cases in which people rather seem to be driven by a wish to make autonomous choices than by maximizing utility, such as, youth rebellion and protest voting.

We have discussed four different interpretations of meaning that pose different, and more or less fundamental, challenges to standard economic models of human behavior. Although the human quest for meaning is not captured in standard economic models, each of the different interpretations of meaning we discussed, with the possible exception of meaning as an exertion of free will, is in fact amenable to interpretation in economic terms. If economics do not take into account meaning, it runs the risk of missing something important in the understanding of human behavior. This suspicion we share with John Stuart Mill who in his autobiography asked himself: "Suppose that all your objects in life were realized; that all the changes in institutions and opinions you are looking forward to, could be completely effected at this very instant: would this be a great joy and happiness to you?" Recognizing that the answer was unambiguously negative, he reports that "my heart sank within me and the whole foundation on which my life was constructed fell down."

References

Affleck, G., H. Tennen, S. Croog, and S. Levine, 1987. Casual attribution, perceived benifit, and morbidity after a heart attack: An 8-year study. *Journal of Consulting and Clinical Psychology*, 55: 29–35.

Akerlof, G. A. and R. E. Kranton, 2000. Economics and identity. *Quarterly Journal of Economics*, 115: 715–753.

Ariely, D., G. Loewenstein, and D. Prelec, 2003. Coherent arbitrariness: Stable demand curves without stable preferences. *Quarterly Journal of Economics*, 118: 73–106.

Ariès, P. 1981. *The hour of our death*. New York: Knopf.

Baumeister, R. F. 1991. *Meanings of life*. New York: The Guilford Press.

Baumeister, R. F. and L. S. Newman, 1994. How stories make sense of personal experiences: Motives that shape autobiographical narratives. *Personality and Social Psychology Bulletin*, 20: 676–690.

Baumeister, R. F. and K. D. Vohs, 2002. The pursuit of meaningfulness in life. In C. R. Snyder and S. J. Lopez (eds). *Handbook of Positive Psychology*. (pp. 608–618). London, Oxford University Press.

Bower G. H. and M. C. Clark, 1969. Narrative stories as mediators for serial learning. *Psychonomic Science*, 14: 181–182.

Bower, J. M. E. Kemeny, S. E. Taylor, and J. L. Fahey, 1998. Cognitive processing, discovery of meaning, CD4 decline, and AIDS-related mortality among bereaved HIV-seropositive men. *Journal of Consulting and Clinical Psychology*, 66: 979–986.

Bruner, J. 1987. Life as narrative. *Social Research*, 54: 11–32.

Bruner, J. 1990. *Acts of meaning*. Cambridge, MA: Harvard University Press.

Bruner, J. 2002. *Making stories: Law, literature, life*. New York: Farrar, Straus and Giroux.

Brunnermeier, M. K. and J. A. Parker, 2002. Optimal Expectations. *Princeton University Economics Department Working Paper*. Princeton, NJ.

Caplin, A. and J. Leahy, 1997. Psychological expected theory and anticipatory feelings, *NYU Working Paper 4766*.

Davis, C. G., S. Nolen-Hoeksema, and J. Larson, 1998. Making sense of loss and benefiting from the experience: Two construals of meaning. *Journal of Personality and Social Psychology*, 75: 561–574.

Deci, E. 1975. *Intrinsic motivation*. New York: Plenum.

Emmons, R. A. 1996. Striving and feeling: Personal goals and subjective well-being. In J. A. Bargh and P. M. Gollwitzer (eds). *Psychology and action: Linking cognition and motivation to behavior* (pp. 314–337). New York: Guilford Press.

Frankl, V. E. 1963. *Man's search for meaning*. New York: Pocket Books.

Fredrickson, B. 2000. Extracting meaning from past affective experiences: The importance of peaks, ends, and specific emotions. *Cognition and Emotion*, 14: 577–606.

Fry, P. S. 1998. The development of personal meaning and wisdom in adolescence: A reexamination of moderating and consolidating factors and influences. In P. T. P. Wong and P. S. Fry (eds). *The human quest for meaning* (pp. 91–110). Mahwah, NJ: Erlbaum.

Gilbert, D. T., E. C. Pinel, T. D. Wilson, S. J. Blumberg, and T. P. Wheatley, 1998. Immune neglect: A source of durability bias in affective forecasting. *Journal of Personality and Social Psychology*, 75: 617–638.

Gilovich, T. 1991. *How we know what isn't so: The fallibility of human reason in everyday life*. New York: The Free Press.

Greeley, A. M. and M. Hout, 1999. American's increasing belief in life after death: Religious competition and acculturation. *American Sociological Review*, 64: 813–835.

Greenberg, J., S. Solomon, and T. Pyszczynski, 1997. Terror management theory of self-esteem and social behavior: Empirical assessments and conceptual refinements. In M. P. Zanna (ed.) *Advances in Experimental and Social Psychology* (Vol. 29, pp. 61–139). New York: Academic Press.

Haslam, A. S. 2000. *Psychology in organizations: The social identity approach*. London: Sage Publications Ltd.

Kegan, R. 1982. *The evolving self*. Cambridge: Harvard University Press.

Koszegi, B. 2000. Ego utility, overconfidence, and task choice. *UC Berkeley Working Paper*.

Loewenstein, G. 1987. Anticipation and the Valuation of Delayed Consumption. *Economic Journal*, 97: 666–684.

Loewenstein, G. 1999. Because it is there: The challenge of mountaineering . . . For utility theory. *Kyklos*, 52: 315–344.

Loomes, G. 1988. Further Evidence of the Impact of Regret and Disappointment in Choice under Uncertainty. *Economica*, 55: 47–62.

Loomes, G. and R. Sugden, 1982. Regret theory: An alternative theory of rational choice under uncertainty. *Economic Journal*, 92: 805–824.

Loomes, G. and R. Sugden, 1987. Testing For Regret And Disappointment In Choice Under Uncertainty. *The Economic Journal*, 97: 118–129.

McAdams, D. P., A. Diamond, E. de St. Aubin, and E. Mansfield, 1997. Stories of commitment: The psychological construction of generative lives. *Journal of Personality and Social Psychology*, 72: 678–694.

Maddi, S. R. 1998. Creating meaning through making decisions. In P. T. P. Wong and P. S. Fry (eds). *The human quest for meaning* (pp. 3–26). Mahwah, NJ: Erlbaum.

March, J. G. 1994. *A primer on decision making*. New York: Free Press.

Mendola, R. H., Tennen, G. Affleck, L. McCann, and T. Fitzgerald, 1990. Appraisal and adaptation among women with impaired fertility. *Cognitive Therapy and Research*, 14: 79–93.

Messick, D. 1999. Alternative logics for decision making in social settings. *Journal of Economic Behavior and Organization*, 39: 11–28.

Payne, J. W., J. R. Bettman, and E. J. Johnson, 1992. Behavioral decision research: A constructive processing perspective. *Annual Review of Psychology*, 43: 87–131.

Payne, J. W., J. R. Bettman, and E. J. Johnson, 1993. *The adaptive decision maker*. Cambridge, England, Cambridge University Press.

Pennington, N. and R. Hastie, 1986. Evidence evaluation in complex decision making. *Journal of Personality and Social Psychology*, 51: 242–258.

Pennington, N. and R. Hastie, 1992. Explaining the evidence: Tests of the story model for juror decision making. *Journal of Personality and Social Psychology*, 62: 189–206.

Plott, C. R. 1996. Rational Individual Behaviour in Markets and Social Choice Processes: The Discovered Preference Hypothesis. In Arrow, Kenneth J., et al. (eds). *The rational foundations of economic behaviour: Proceedings of the IEA Conference held in Turin, Italy. IEA Conference Volume, no. 114*. London: Macmillan Press in association with the International Economic Association, 225–50.

Prelec, D. and R. Bodner, 2003. Self-signaling and self-control. In G. Loewenstein, D. Read, and R. F. Baumeister (eds). *Time and Decision: Economic and Psychological Perspectives on Intertemporal Choice* (pp. 277–300). New York: Russel Sage Foundation.

Rosenblatt, A., J. Greenberg, S. Solomon, T. Pyszczynski, and D. Lyon, 1989. Evidence for terror management theory I: The effects of mortality salience on reactions to those who violate or uphold cultural values. *Journal of Personality and Social Psychology*, 57: 681–690.

Ryan, R. M. and E. L. Deci, 2001. On happiness and human potentials: A review of research on hedonic and eudaimonic well-being. *Annual Review of Psychology*, 52: 141–166.

Ryff, C. D. and B. Singer, 1998. The role of purpose in life and personal growth in positive human health. In P. T. P. Wong and P. S. Fry (eds). *The human quest for meaning* (pp. 213–236). Mahwah, NJ: Erlbaum.

Schank, R. C. 1990. *Tell me a story: A new look at real and artificial memory*. New York: Scribner.

Schank, R. C. and R. P. Abelson, 1995. Knowledge and memory: The real story. In R. S. Wyer (ed.) *Advances in Social Cognition* (Vol. 8, pp. 1–85). Hillsdale, NJ: Lawrence Erlbaum Associates.

Scheier, M. F. and C. S. Carver, 2001. Adapting to cancer: The importance of hope and purpose. In A. Baum and B. L. Andersen (eds). *Psychosocial interventions for cancer* (pp. 15–36). Washington, DC: American Psychological Association.

Slovic, P. 1995. The construction of preferences. *American Psychologists*, 50: 364–371.

Tait, R. and R. C. Silver, 1989. Coming to terms with major negative life events. In J. S. Uleman and J. A. Bargh (eds). *Unintended thought* (pp. 351–382). New York, NY, US: Guilford Press.

Tajfel, H., C. Flament, M. Billig, and R. P. Bundy, 1971. *European Journal of Social Psychology*, 1: 149–177.

Taylor, S. E. 1983. Adjustment to threatening events: A theory of cognitive adaptation. *American Psychologist*, 38: 1161–1173.

Taylor, S. E. and J. D. Brown, 1988. Illusion and well-being: A social psychological perspective on mental health. *Psychological Bulletin*, 103: 193–210.

Turner, J. C. 1982. Towards a cognitive redefinition of the social group. In H. Tajfel (ed.) *Social identity and intergroup relations* (pp. 15–40). Cambridge: Cambridge University Press.

Wilson, A. E. and M. Ross, 2001. From chump to champ: People's Appraisals of their earlier and present selves. *Journal of Personality and Social Psychology*, 80: 572–584.

Wilson, T. D. and D. T. Gilbert, 2003. Affective forecasting. In M. Zanna (ed.) *Advances in experimental social psychology* (Vol. 35, pp. 345–411). New York: Elsevier.

Wrzesniewski, A., C. McCauley, P. Rozin, and B. Schwartz, 1997. Jobs, careers, and callings: People's relations to their work. *Journal of Research in Personality*, 31: 21–33.

Wyer, R. S., R. Adaval, and S. J. Colcombe, 2002. Narrative based representations of social knowledge: Their construction and use in comprehension, memory, and judgment. *Advances in Experimental Social Psychology*, 34: 131–197.

3

The Fall and Rise of Psychological Explanations in the Economics of Intertemporal Choice

George Loewenstein

This chapter was first published in a volume, titled *Choice Over Time* that I coedited with Jon Elster. The paper covers the historical evolution of the 'utility' concept in economics and the consequences of the evolving interpretation of utility for the economic analyses of intertemporal choice. A subsidiary, but more general purpose of the paper is to trace the history of how psychology, though once integral to economics, was expunged from economics during the first half of the twentieth century and then subsequently became rediscovered.

Unlike the other chapters in this book, this paper never appeared in a refereed journal, and not for lack of trying. I think part of the reason that it kept getting rejected at journals was that I missed some of the stylistic elements of papers on the history of economic thought. Subtle, and to my view generally arbitrary, stylistic differences across fields constitute one of the most impenetrable barriers to interdisciplinary work. Like regional dialects, each discipline and even subdiscipline has its own myriad unwritten rules of discourse; violate any one of them and you're instantly branded an outsider deserving of extra scrutiny and skepticism.

Another, somewhat less excusable, reason for the paper's repeated rejection may have been its looseness with historical details. I am not aware of any outright inaccuracies, but I have always loved a good story, so it is quite likely that I played up the bits and pieces of evidence that supported my story and downplayed the inconvenient ones that didn't. For the record, I can report that so far no one has refuted the story that the paper tells, but that could mean, not that it is correct, but simply that it has fallen into the all-too-well populated academic purgatory and been ignored.

Writing about this chapter gives me the opportunity to provide a long-overdue acknowledgment of the amazing fortune I have had to be associated with a man named Jim Thompson, who, last time I communicated with him, was a teacher in a private school in LA. This is a great job for him because Jim is a born teacher. When I was a graduate student at Yale, he was working for an organization called the Vera Institute of Justice, in midtown Manhattan, and hired me as a research assistant. I did assist him in research, but most of the gains flowed in the other direction. Not only did the job (along with my father) subsidize my graduate education, but Jim gave me all sorts of other help and advice, including on the writing of this chapter. I had a vague idea of what I wanted to say, but whatever I put down on paper seemed wrong or trite, so I couldn't make any progress on it. Seeing my frustration, Jim sat down at the computer (or perhaps it was a typewriter back then), asked me what it was that I wanted to say, and then typed it in coherent, beautiful sentences. Seeing my thoughts turned into sentences somehow jump-started my own writing abilities, and, since then, I have made a habit of doing the same for my own graduate students who have difficulty writing. One of the strange things for me is to pick up an element of style in their subsequent writing that I can trace to myself and know that I picked up from Jim. Much like biological progeny, teaching can produce benefits (as well as verbal tics) that echo through successive generations.

The Fall and Rise of Psychological Explanations in the Economics of Intertemporal Choice*

George Loewenstein

In recent years, despite lingering skepticism, the influence of psychology on economics has steadily expanded. Challenged by the discovery of individual and market level phenomena that contradict fundamental economic assumptions, and impressed by theoretical and methodological advances, economists have begun to import insights from psychology into their work on diverse topics. This influence has been most pronounced in the area of decision making under uncertainty, but recently it has extended to the cognate topic of intertemporal choice.

Economists have joined psychologists in using experimental methods to address fundamental questions about time preference. Moving beyond the usual attempts to measure discount rates, this research seeks to test critically the predictions and assumptions of the discounted utility model (DU), the most widely employed model of intertemporal choice. These studies have generally not affirmed the descriptive validity of DU; observed patterns of choice violate virtually every one of the model's basic assumptions and, therefore, its implications.

The exchange between psychology and economics has also occurred at a theoretical level. The descriptive inadequacies of DU have led economists and other social scientists to develop alternative theoretical models that incorporate psychological insights. Some of these retain DU's multiplicative formulation, introducing specialized discount or utility functions. But others adopt

* This chapter was originally published as Loewenstein, G. "The Fall and Rise of Psychological Explanations in the Economics of Intertemporal Choice". In *Choice Over Time*, edited by George Loewenstein and Jon Elster. © 1992 Russell Sage Foundation, 112 East 64th Street, New York, NY 10021. Reprinted with permission.

radically different frameworks, modeling intertemporal choice as a collective action or principal-agent problem between temporally situated "selves."

Although commonly credited to psychology, many of the insights currently enriching the economics of intertemporal choice were pre-figured in the work of nineteenth- and early twentieth-century economists. In a period when the border between psychology and economics was less sharply defined, economists like Rae, Senior, Jevons, and Böhm-Bawerk addressed such fundamental questions as "Why do people discount the future?" In some cases their answers reveal a sophisticated grasp of psychology.

It is possible to discern four basic historical stages in the evolution of the economics of intertemporal choice. In the first stage, nineteenth-century economists such as Senior and Jevons explained time discounting in terms of what psychologists now label *motivational effects;* these refer to emotional and/or hedonic influences on behavior. Both Senior and Jevons believed that willingness to defer gratification depended on immediate emotions experienced by decision makers.

In the second stage, which was dominated by contributions from Böhm-Bawerk and Fisher at the turn of the century, intertemporal choice was viewed in cognitive terms, as a tradeoff between present and future satisfactions. Discounting was attributed mainly to inadequacies in the decision maker's ability to imagine the future.

The third stage entailed an attempt to eliminate psychological content from the economics of intertemporal choice. In the first decades of the twentieth century, a distaste for psychology became wide-spread among economists. In part because of their dismay over new developments in psychology that did not seem amenable to interpretation as utility maximization (e.g. Freud's theory of unconscious motivations), economists sought to stake out the independence of their profession.[1] The psychological richness that characterized early discussions of intertemporal choice was supplanted by mathematical and graphical analyses that seemed to render psychology superfluous. Psychological concepts reflecting motivational and cognitive influences—*willpower* and *imagination*—gave way to nonevocative terms such as *time preference* that were deliberately agnostic about underlying causes.

Finally, in the last few decades, a fourth stage has emerged characterized by a renewed interest in psychology by economists interested in intertemporal choice. The shift in perspective has benefited from research by contemporary psychologists. Much of this work is represented in the chapters of this book.

This chapter follows the economics of intertemporal choice from its infancy to the present. The first section discusses the nineteenth-century contributions of Rae, Senior, and Jevons. The second examines the pivotal work

---

[1] See, for example, Davenport (1901).

of Böhm-Bawerk and Fisher at the turn of the century. Section 3 examines the ordinal utility revolution and its consequences for intertemporal choice.

3.1. Rae, Senior, and Jevons: Three Early Perspectives

John Rae, an obscure and tragic economist of Scottish descent,[2] provided the first in-depth treatment of intertemporal choice. Rae's interest in the topic, like that of other economists of the period, arose from his desire to understand changes in the standard of living over time and differences across countries. Earlier economists such as Smith had argued that such discrepancies derived from differences in the accumulation of capital. They believed that such differences depended on the proportion of the surplus product of labor devoted to production of *capital* as opposed to *consumption* goods. Rae recognized that such accounts, although not inaccurate, were incomplete. If capital accumulation depended on the allocation of surplus product between consumption and production, on what did that allocation depend?

Rae argued in the 1834 volume, *Statement of Some New Principles on the Subject of Political Economy*,[3] that the allocation of the surplus product depended on the public's willingness to defer gratification—on the "effective desire of accumulation." If this desire for accumulation were high, then people would be willing to allocate the surplus product to capital rather than consumption. Rae identified four major determinants of the effective desire of accumulation, the first two limiting the desire for accumulation, and the second two promoting it. First, he cited the brevity and uncertainty of human life:

Were life to endure for ever, were the capacity to enjoy in perfection all its goods, both mental and corporeal, to be prolonged with it, and were we guided solely by the dictates of reason, there could be no limit to the formation of means of future gratification, till

---

[2] The exceptionally creative Rae was repeatedly undermined by a chain of misfortunes. At 20 he dropped out of Edinburgh University, where he was studying medicine, disappointed with his professors' response to his thesis topic, and convinced (correctly, as it turned out) that it was ahead of its time. Five years later, disillusioned, impoverished by his father's bankruptcy, and ostracized for marrying the daughter of a shepherd, he emigrated to Quebec, where he taught school and established himself in Montreal's Scottish expatriate community. During this period he published his magnum opus, *Statement of Some New Principles on the Subject of Political Economy*. His book was initially poorly received, in large part because of its vitriolic attacks on the inviolable Adam Smith. Having failed to establish his intellectual credentials, he was forced to take a job as headmaster in Hamilton, Ontario, at that time a rural outpost. Later dismissed in a power struggle, he drifted to California, where he took part in the 1848 gold rush, and then to Hawaii. In the last year of this life, he moved to Staten Island, New York, to live with a former student from Hamilton. He appears to have died unaware that his work was already widely cited and praised by the major economists of his time. For a superb account of Rae's life and works, see James (1965).

[3] Later renamed *Sociological Theory of Capital*.

our utmost wishes were satisfied. A pleasure to be enjoyed, or a pain to be endured, fifty or a hundred years hence would be considered deserving the same attention as if it were to befall us fifty or a hundred minutes hence. (1834, p. 119)

In support of this argument, he cited numerous examples:

When engaged in safe occupations, and living in healthy countries, men are much more apt to be frugal, than in unhealthy, or hazardous occupations, and in climates pernicious to human life. Sailors and soldiers are prodigals. In the West Indies, New Orleans, the East Indies, the expenditure of the inhabitants is profuse. The same people, coming to reside in the healthy parts of Europe, and not getting into the vortex of extravagant fashion, live economically. Wars and pestilence, have always waste and luxury, among the other evils that follow in their train. (1834, p. 57)

Rae's second factor limiting the effective desire for accumulation was the psychological discomfort of deferring gratification—what Senior was to call *abstinence:*

Such pleasures as may now be enjoyed generally awaken a passion strongly prompting to the partaking of them. The actual presence of the immediate object of desire in the mind by exciting the attention, seems to rouse all the faculties, as it were to fix their view on it, and leads them to a very lively conception of the enjoyments which it offers to their instant possession. The prospects of future good, which future years may hold out to us, seem at such a moment dull and dubious, and are apt to be slighted, for objects on which the daylight is falling strongly, and showing us in all their freshness just within our grasp.... Everywhere we see, that to spend is easy, to spare, hard. (1834, p. 120)

Counterpoised against the brevity of life and the psychological discomfort of deferral were two factors contributing to the effective desire of accumulation: "the prevalence throughout the society of the social and benevolent affections" (in contemporary parlance, the "bequest motive"), and "the extent of the intellectual powers, and the consequent prevalence of habits of reflection, and prudence, in the minds of the members of society" (1834, p. 58). It was to this last factor that Rae devoted most of his book. Perhaps because of his personal experience with different cultures, Rae saw culture as the critical determinant of differences in the effective desire of accumulation: "The mass of the individuals composing any society, being operated on by the same causes, and having similar manners, habits, and to a great extent feelings also, must approximate to each other, in the strength of their effective desires of accumulation" (1834, p. 198). As a result, much of his book is devoted to anecdotes about different countries, social classes, and historical epochs, all illustrating a simple point: that in early times, more primitive societies, and "lower" orders of society, intellectual powers, habits of reflection, prudence, and, hence, the effective desire of accumulation were less well developed.

Although cited cursorily by Senior, Rae first gained prominence in 1848 with the publication of J. S. Mill's *Principles of Political Economy*.[4] Mill devoted an entire chapter titled "Of the Law of the Increase of Capital" to Rae's work, in the process citing vast passages verbatim. Indeed Mill's coverage of Rae was so extensive that it may have discouraged people from examining the original work; later commentators tended to cite the passages that were presented in Mill's book. This is unfortunate because Mill focused almost exclusively on Rae's sensational sociological observations—in the process neglecting to credit him for his fundamental insights into the determinants of time preference.

3.1.1. *Senior*

Two years after Rae published his book, the English economist N. W. Senior came out with his influential *Outline of the Science of Political Economy*, in which he expounded a new theory of capital that, like Rae's, emphasized the psychological element. Senior's analysis of intertemporal choice (like much recent work) was motivated by a paradox: Why should interest be paid on a capital sum? As expressed by Smart (1891, p. 675):

The striking aspect which interest presents when one's critical attention is first drawn to it is, that it is an income got apparently from simple possession of wealth. There seems some reason why *rent* should be paid:—is it not the price of the original and indestructible powers of the soil, from whence must come all food and raw material? There is even stronger ground for paying wage:—does not labor involve sacrifice of time, brain, and body, and is there not a visible return to the labor of every man who can put a spade into the earth? But [why should] the owner of wealth, whose tangible property, perhaps, consists in a few securities locked away in a safe, be able for all time to draw income without work and, practically, without risk?

Early treatments of capital had skirted this problem by noting that most loans went to capital creation and that capital generally provided a positive rate of return; it seemed natural that those who provided funds for the capital would earn a return. However, as Senior recognized, this perspective did not explain why the rate of interest was positive. Why didn't investors continue to invest in increasingly low-yield investments until the rate of return fell to zero?

Senior was the first to provide a psychological explanation for interest. In Senior's "abstinence theory," interest was viewed as compensation to the holder of capital for enduring the pain of abstaining from consumption, which he viewed as "among the most painful exertions of the human will"

---

[4] Mill credited Senior for having brought Rae to his attention.

(1836, p. 60).[5] In this view new investment ceased when, at the margin, its return could no longer compensate for the pain of deferring consumption.

However, Senior went further, when perhaps he should have quit while he was ahead; he actually defined abstinence as an input into production rather than a determinant of the supply of loanable funds: "By the word Abstinence, we wish to express that agent, distinct from labor and the agency of nature, the concurrence of which is necessary to the existence of Capital" (1836, p. 49).

The notion of abstinence as a factor of production later came under blistering attack from Irving Fisher and Böhm-Bawerk, both of whom were inclined to separate the production side of capital from the psychological side. Senior's inclusion of abstinence as a factor of production was distasteful to them because it assimilated the psychological element into the production perspective.

Senior's abstinence perspective remained popular during the remainder of the century, but there were few efforts to develop further his scant psychology. Besides the observation that the pain of abstinence is inversely related to wealth, debate among subscribers to the abstinence view was confined to an often tedious back-and-forth about whether *abstinence* was the best term for the concept it represented. Cairnes (1874) suggested the term *postponement*, Macvane (1887) proposed *waiting*, while others insisted on the superiority of expressions such as *forbearance* and *frugality*.

3.1.2. Jevons

Thirty years after Senior proposed his abstinence theory, Jevons advanced a characterization of intertemporal choice that turned Senior's perspective on its head. Whereas Senior had viewed equal treatment of present and future as the baseline and asked why people commonly deviated from that baseline, Jevons implicitly asked a more fundamental question: Why do people take the future into account at all?

Jevons' answer can be understood only in the context of a paradox bequeathed him by Bentham. Benthamite man, as interpreted by later commentators such as James Mill, was highly self-centered with respect to other individuals and centered in the present with respect to himself at other points in time. This characteristic presented Jevons, a Benthamite who sought to develop a theoretical account of intertemporal choice, with a problem: Why

[5] This view of the agonies of deferral was attacked by socialists such as Lassalle, who noted the evident absurdity of the notion that wealthy investors suffer great privation while they forestall from consuming their entire income at once. But, as Cassel (1903) later rebutted, this criticism fails to draw the appropriate distinction between total and marginal privation. In fact, the wealthy are prone to abstention precisely because they suffer, on average, little privation in doing so.

should such a myopic decision maker ever defer consumption into the future? His solution was to identify specific presently felt pleasures and pains that resulted from contemplating future consumption:

Bentham has stated, that one of the main elements in estimating the force of a pleasure or pain is its *propinquity* or *remoteness*. It is certain that a large part of what we experience in life depends not on the actual circumstances of the moment so much as on the anticipation of future events. As Mr. Bain says, "the foretaste of pleasure is pleasure begun." (1871, p. 40)

Pleasures and pains associated with the future, but realized in the present rescued the Benthamite decision maker from total myopia. In Jevons's view, the decision maker who deferred consumption did not defer pleasure but substituted pleasure from anticipation—what Bentham had referred to as "pleasures of expectation"—for pleasure from current consumption.

Jevons was convinced that his theory was not qualitatively different from Senior's, and argued that Senior's abstinence was simply the inverse of his pleasures of expectation. And the two perspectives do indeed share important commonalities. Unlike later perspectives, which were to view intertemporal choice as a tradeoff between utility at different points in time, Senior and Jevons saw decision makers as highly anchored in present and influenced by immediately experienced emotions. The theories are, however, strikingly different in the way that they characterize these emotions; Senior focused exclusively on the immediate pain of deferral, Jevons on the immediate pleasure of deferral.

Jevons, like Senior, viewed equal treatment of present and future as a norm of behavior, and wanted to understand why human behavior deviated from the norm. But, whereas Senior's explanation for discounting centered on the pain of abstinence, Jevons' hinged on imperfections in the translation of future events into present utility. In his framework, the ideal would only be realized if "all future pleasures or pains should act upon us with the same force as if they were present" (1871, p. 76). But he recognized that "no human mind is constituted in this perfect way."

Jevons went to great lengths to describe the mechanics of pleasure and pain from anticipation. For example, he noted that rate of devaluation of the future relative to the present would likely be greater for short time delays than for long ones,[6] an insight taken up a century later by Strotz (1955) and Ainslie (1975): "The intensity of present feeling must, to use a mathematical expression, be some function of the future feeling, and it must increase as we approach the moment of realization. The change, again, must be less rapid

[6] This does not mean that the distant future is devalued less than the immediate future, but rather that the amount of devaluation *per unit of time delay* is smaller.

63

the further we are from the moment, and more rapid as we come nearer to it" (1871, p. 41).

Although Jevons's conceptualization of intertemporal choice was rapidly displaced by newer contributions, elements of his perspective can be discerned in the work of later economists. For example, although Marshall's views on intertemporal choice were very close to those of Böhm-Bawerk, his writings contain passages that sound distinctly Jevonian. In a chapter of his *Principles* titled "Choices Between Different Uses of the Same Thing: Immediate and Deferred Uses," he states, somewhat ambiguously, "When a person postpones a pleasure-giving event he does not postpone the pleasure; but he gives up a present pleasure and takes in its place another, or an expectation of another at a future date" (1898, p. 121). In this passage it is unclear whether the tradeoff is between present utility from present consumption and present utility from future consumption (as Jevons saw it), or between present utility from present consumption and future utility from future consumption (Böhm-Bawerk's perspective, which is discussed in the next section). The first part of the statement—that deferral of consumption does not involve postponement of pleasure—is clearly Jevonian; the second part, where it is acknowledged that the substitute pleasure could occur at another date is more in line with Böhm-Bawerk.

Noting this inconsistency, Böhm-Bawerk, in a late edition of *Capital and Interest*, classified Marshall as an "eclectic" who, "unable to make one of his own [theories], or equally unable or unwilling to align himself completely with one of the available theories, selected from two or three or even a greater number of heterogeneous theories such features as appealed to him, and wove them together into a whole that was for the most part lacking in unity" (1914, p. 322).

Pareto, too, in spite of his central role in the depsychologizing of the utility concept, evinced a Jevonian perspective in his discussion of intertemporal choice. For example, in considering the problem of why seldom used goods may nevertheless fetch high prices, Pareto noted:

If a woman has ten dresses, she need not wear them all at once; also it is not customary to wear all the gowns one possesses.... But granted that, the meaning of the quantities regarding goods which enter into the formulas of pure economics changes somewhat. They are no longer quantities consumed, but quantities which are at the individual's disposal.... For the sensation of present consumption we substitute, as the cause of the actions of the individual, the *present sensation of the future consumption* of the goods which are at his disposal (italics added). (1909, p. 181)

Finally, the contemporary economist Shackle adopts a pure neo-Jevonian perspective in his book *Time in Economics*. In a section titled "Enjoyment by Imaginative Anticipation," he writes, "The enjoyment or satisfaction which the decision-maker seeks to maximize by his choice of one action-scheme rather than others is a pleasure of the imagination" (1958, p. 41).

3.2. Böhm-Bawerk, Fisher, and the Discounted Utility Model

The second stage in the evolution of the economics of intertemporal choice witnessed an Indian summer of psychological insight. Böhm-Bawerk and Fisher's accounts of intertemporal choice were profoundly psychological and illustrate the potential for fruitful interaction between economics and psychology. Böhm-Bawerk introduced a radically new, cognitively based theory of intertemporal choice, while at the same time assimilating the psychological observations of his predecessors.

Nevertheless, specific features of their contributions—Böhm-Bawerk's view of intertemporal choice as essentially comparable to atemporal choice, and Fisher's indifference curve analysis—paved the way for the subsequent stripping away of psychology. Böhm-Bawerk and Fisher, therefore, occupied pivotal positions in the history of the economics of intertemporal choice.

3.2.1. Böhm-Bawerk

Until Böhm-Bawerk turned his attention to the problem, all treatments of intertemporal choice were subsidiary to discussions of capital and interest. This tie hindered progress on intertemporal choice because the psychological determinants of time preference were always discussed in connection with the productivity of capital. Böhm-Bawerk eliminated this connection by observing, in *Capital and Interest*, that the interest rate could be viewed entirely independent of capital—as the relative price of current as compared with future consumption. It followed logically that this single price could play the role of equilibrating the demand for capital (determined by willingness to delay gratification) and its supply (determined by technical factors). Böhm-Bawerk assailed Senior and others who had attempted to incorporate the psychological factor into the supply side:[7] "Nothing is further from my thoughts than to follow the example of Senior and attempt to claim that saving constitutes a third factor of production arrayed beside nature and labor. It does not stand beside them, but in the background behind them . . . saving does not belong among the *means* of production but among the *motives* which determine the direction that production shall take (1889, p. 117).

---

[7] Böhm-Bawerk was a victim of his own personality; he lacked the willpower to resist denigrating all previous intellectual contributions. This enraged his contemporaries and inspired countless efforts to demonstrate that *his* views were derivative. The most common charge was that Böhm-Bawerk had gleaned most of his insights from Rae, whose work he denigrated in the later editions of *Capital and Interest*. Böhm-Bawerk took pains to note, in later editions, that "when the first edition of Capital and Interest appeared, his [Rae's] book was completely unknown to me" (1889, p. 209).

Böhm-Bawerk's second major contribution was to provide a new account of intertemporal choice based on what would now be considered a "cognitive" perspective. Like Senior and Jevons, Böhm-Bawerk believed that interest resulted from a difference in the evaluation of present and future consumption. However, his psychological analysis was radically different. Senior's and Jevons' decision makers were intrinsically oriented to the present; their deficient evaluation of the future resulted from presently experienced emotions—in the one case deprivation, in the other, the insufficient potency of immediate utility from anticipation. Böhm-Bawerk envisioned a much more even-handed choice between present and future. Instead of maximizing immediate well-being, his decision makers traded off satisfactions at different points in time. He attacked the Jevonian notion that intertemporal choice actually involved a maximization of current utility: "It can hardly be maintained, as some of our older economists and psychologists used to be fond of assuming, that we possess the gift of literally *feeling in advance* the emotions we shall experience in the future" (1889, p. 260).

In Böhm-Bawerk's writings, the distinction between utility from immediate sensation and from anticipation disappears; rather, gratifications stemming from all points in time are thought to be comparable because placed on a cognitive plane: "*These imagined future emotions are comparable.* Indeed, they are comparable not only with present emotions experienced at the moment, but also with each other; and that comparability, furthermore, obtains irrespective of whether they belong to the same or different future periods of time" (1889, p. 261).

Böhm-Bawerk, like Senior and Jevons, viewed equal treatment of present and future as an ideal: "What is going to happen to us in a week or in a year is no less something touching *us*, than what happens to us today. It is therefore equally entitled to be considered in our own economy, for the object of that economy is to provide for *our well-being*" (1889, p. 262). But, like his predecessors, he acknowledged, "Whether this equality of rights as a matter of principle is matched by a full equality of rights as a matter of practice is another question" (1889, p. 262).

Böhm-Bawerk provided a list of the determinants of time preference, which he divided into two categories. The first was "the relation of supply and demand as it exists at one point in time and that relation of supply and demand as it exists at another point in time" (1889, p. 266). This is simply the impact of the temporal distribution of consumption on marginal utility at different points in time. Because people tend to become wealthier over time, Böhm-Bawerk believed that the marginal utility of wealth would be lower in the future than in the present, leading to a disproportionate valuation of current wealth. He saw this factor as one that would decrease effective impatience. This factor is, however, in some ways uninteresting, because the distribution of consumption over time is largely a matter of choice—of individual decisions to borrow and save. The argument that time preference depends on the marginal utility of consumption, which in turn depends on the outcome of a decision that depends on time preference, has a certain circularity.

Far more interesting was Böhm-Bawerk's second set of causes, which encompassed several distinct psychological determinants including those mentioned by Rae, Senior, and Jevons, plus one of his own.

Böhm-Bawerk's original contribution was a "systematic tendency to underestimate future wants" based on a rather sophisticated cognitive psychology similar to modern concepts such as "availability" (Tversky and Kahneman, 1973):

> We feel less concerned about future sensations of joy and sorrow simply because they do lie in the future, and lessening of concern is in proportion to the remoteness of that future. Consequently we accord to goods which are intended to serve future ends a value which falls short of the true intensity of their future marginal utility. *We systematically undervalue our future wants and also the means which serve to satisfy them....* It may be that we possess inadequate power to imagine and to abstract, or that we are not willing to put forth the necessary effort, but in any event we limn a more or less incomplete picture of our future wants and especially of the remotely distant ones. And then there are all those wants that never come to mind at all. (1889, pp. 268–269)

A final cause of discounting was a failure of willpower, in effect the obverse of Rae's "reflection and prudence":

> It occurs frequently, I believe, that a person is faced with a choice between a present and a future satisfaction or dissatisfaction and that he decides in favor of lesser present pleasure even though he knows perfectly well, and is even explicitly aware at the moment he makes his choice, that the future disadvantage is the greater and that therefore his well-being, on the whole, suffers by reason of his choice ... how often does each of us "give in to weakness" and allow himself to be swept along into acquiescence or action which he knows immediately he is going to regret on the morrow.

In introducing willpower—a psychological element that implies that deferring gratification requires effort—Böhm-Bawerk clearly deviated from his intention to depict intertemporal choice in purely cognitive terms. If time preference arose solely from a tendency to undervalue future satisfactions, there would be no need for willpower because discounting would reflect what appeared to be a rational tradeoff. If they mobilize willpower ("moral effort") to defer consumption, people must want, at some level, to delay consumption but find it difficult to implement that preference. Inclusion of the willpower element implicitly acknowledges that intertemporal choice does involve an emotional element.

Later writers have sometimes mistakenly attributed to Böhm-Bawerk the belief that people tend to view time itself in distorted terms. This view, in fact, comes from Pigou. In a frequently cited passage in his *Economics of*

Welfare, Pigou referred to time discounting as a perspective phenomenon analogous to an optical illusion: "Our telescopic faculty is defective, and … we, therefore, see future pleasures, as it were, on a diminished scale." The difference between this and Böhm-Bawerk's failure of imagination can be seen by analogy between time perspective and a driver's view of objects on the road. On the one hand, analogous to Böhm-Bawerk's failure of imagination, objects in the distance may seem blurry, or not be visible at all. On the other hand, and in line with Pigou, we may actually misestimate the distance of remote objects; objects may appear to be more distant than they actually are.

3.2.2. Fisher

Irving Fisher's main contribution was to clarify and formalize Böhm-Bawerk's analysis. Fisher was the first to apply the indifference curve apparatus to intertemporal choice and to express Böhm-Bawerk's theory in mathematical terms. Figure 3.1 reproduces a temporal indifference diagram of the type first presented by Fisher in *The Theory of Interest*. Consumption in the current year is represented on the abscissa, and consumption in the following year is represented on the ordinate. A series of indifference curves or "willingness lines" (as Fisher called them) for a single person are depicted in the figure. Each curve represents different levels of current and future consumption that the individual is indifferent between. Lines lying to the northeast are preferable to those to the southwest.

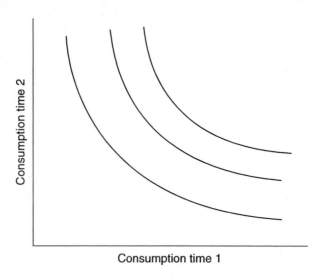

Figure 3.1.

The slope of the tangent to any indifference curve corresponds to time-preference or "impatience";[8] it represents the individual's willingness to give up current consumption in exchange for future consumption. The steeper the curve, the less the willingness to sacrifice current for future consumption and, hence, the greater the rate of time preference.

The lines become steeper toward the northwest because time preference becomes more pronounced, the greater is consumption in the future relative to consumption in the present. This curvature reflects Böhm-Bawerk's first cause of time discounting. The slope of the tangent at points intersecting the 45° line emanating from the origin represents the individual's rate of time preference when consumption is equal in the present and future. This can be seen as a proxy for the "pure rate of time preference" and corresponds to Böhm-Bawerk's second set of causes.

Fisher's exposition then introduced "investment opportunity" lines into the graphical analysis. These lines represented the economy's ability to transform consumption physically in one period into consumption in the other. The forces of supply and demand would then equate the average of individuals' marginal tradeoffs between current and future consumption to the economy's ability to transform one type of consumption into the other at the margin.

Expressing intertemporal choice in terms of indifference curves had two consequences. First, it suggested that intertemporal choice was not qualitatively different from atemporal choice, because the graphical representations of choice in the two domains were virtually indistinguishable before one labeled the axes. Second, Fisher's analytical separation of "willingness" (time preference) and "investment opportunity" lines made crystal-clear the separation of the supply and demand for capital and the role of interest in equilibrating supply and demand. Fisher denounced those who persisted in emphasizing one at the expense of the other:

Any attempt to solve the problem of the rate of interest exclusively as one of productivity or exclusively as one of psychology is necessarily futile. The fact that there are still two schools, the productivity school and the psychological school, constantly crossing swords on this subject is a scandal in economic science and a reflection on the inadequate methods employed by these would-be destroyers of each other. (1930, p. 312)

Fisher's writings included extensive discussions of the determinants of time preference. Like Böhm-Bawerk he divided his list of determinants into two major categories: objective factors, and psychological determinants that

---

[8] Fisher used "impatience" interchangeably with "time preference," an unfortunate practice that continues to the present. This definition of impatience created semantic problems when he discussed the various determinants of impatience. Fisher wished to state that self-control is one factor that determines time preference. However, because of his equating of impatience with time preference, he was forced to speak of self-control as a determinant of impatience rather than, as is conventional, the act of resisting impatience.

he called "the personal factor." Objective factors included the time path of income, which he acknowledged to be identical to Böhm-Bawerk's "first cause," and the influence of risk, a factor not discussed by Böhm-Bawerk. Fisher's view was that

"the risk of losing the income in a particular period of time operates, in the eyes of most people, as a virtual impoverishment of the income in that period, and hence increases the estimation in which a unit of certain income in that particular period is held. If that period is a remote one, the risk to which it is subject makes for a high regard for remote income; if it is the present (immediate future), the risk makes for a high regard for immediate income" (1930, pp. 78–79).

The impact of risk on time preference, therefore, could not be determined a priori, because it depended on its incidence over time. However, Fisher believed that in general, the future tends to be riskier than the present and the distant future riskier than the near future. As a result, he thought, the overall impact of risk would be to increase appreciation for the future and therefore to reduce time preference.

Fisher's list of "personal" determinants of time preference included foresight (the inverse of Böhm-Bawerk's "systematic tendency to underestimate future wants"), and four factors first mentioned by Rae: (1) self-control, (2) habit, (3) life expectancy, and (4) concern for the lives of other persons. Fisher's new contribution was what he called *fashion*, which he believed to be "of vast importance to a community, in its influence both on the rate of interest and on the distribution of wealth itself" (1930, p. 88):

The most fitful of the causes at work is probably fashion. This at the present time acts, on the one hand, to stimulate men to save and become millionaires, and, on the other hand, to stimulate millionaires to live in an ostentatious manner.... In whatever direction the leaders of fashion first chance to move, the crowd will follow in mad pursuit until almost the whole social body will be moving in that direction. (1930, p. 87)

Despite evident similarities, Fisher's view of psychological factors differs in one important respect from those of Rae and Böhm-Bawerk. They had viewed culture, social class, and racial differences as the most important determinants of the psychological factors responsible for time preference. Fisher, in contrast, paid much greater heed to situational factors. For example, whereas Rae and Böhm-Bawerk saw poverty mainly as the *product* of high time preference,[9] Fisher recognized that causality might run in the opposite direction. While "poverty bears down heavily on all portions of a man's expected life," Fisher wrote, "it increases the want for immediate income *even more* than it increases

[9] In one of many passages to this effect, Rae commented that "all members of any society, whose accumulative principle is lower than the average, are gradually reduced to poverty" (1834, p. 199).

the want for future income" (1930, p. 72). To illustrate the lack of class-based inborn impatience, Fisher cited the example of the English poor, who had been widely viewed as spendthrifts, but who had rapidly developed the habit of saving following the introduction of postal savings banks. And he wryly commented that the English upper class could be induced to display extremes of self-denial or profligacy, depending on the vicissitudes of fashion. He also attacked Rae's imputation of Chinese improvidence based on the flimsiness of their housing, noting the "large accumulations of capital made by Chinese living abroad where they are freed from the exactions of arbitrary governors and from the tyranny of the clan-family system" (1930, p. 378).

Despite the sophistication of his psychological reflections, Fisher had difficulty integrating the psychology with his analytical and graphical analysis. The value of the psychological insights are not dependent on the validity of the analytics, and the implication of the psychology for his equations or graphs is unclear. The two contributions are segregated into separate chapters in his book with little cross-referencing.

This bifurcation turned out to be convenient in the next phase in the development of the economics of intertemporal choice, with its antagonism toward psychology. Fisher's analytical contributions were adopted and further developed in the decades following the publication of *Theory of Interest*, but his psychological insights were all but forgotten.

3.3. The Discounted Utility Model and the Ordinal Utility Revolution

The next critical step in the economics of intertemporal choice was the formulation of the discounted utility model by Samuelson in 1937. In its most restrictive form, the discounted utility model states that consumption sequence $(c_1, c_2, \ldots c_n)$ is preferred to sequence $(d_1, d_2, \ldots d_n)$ if and only if,

$$\sum U(c_t)\delta^t > \sum U(d_t)\delta^t,$$

where U is a "ratio scale" utility function with positive first and negative second derivative, and δ' is the discount function with $0 < \delta < 1$. The discounted utility model, in effect, partitions Böhm-Bawerk's first and second causes of time discounting. His first cause—variations in marginal utility arising from differences in level of consumption at different points in time—is captured in the utility function. His second set of causes leading to a systematic tendency to undervalue the future are captured in the discount function, which is independent of consumption plans. The discount rate is sometimes referred to as the "pure rate of time preference," indicating that it is invariant with respect to a person's immediate wealth or consumption plans.

Samuelson was very cautious in presenting his new model, pointing to potential problems at every step of his exposition, and stressing the arbitrariness of the underlying assumptions: "It is completely arbitrary to assume that the individual behaves so as to maximize an integral of the form envisaged in [DU]. This involves the assumption that at every instant in time the individual's satisfaction depends only upon consumption at that time, and that furthermore, the individual tries to maximize the sum of instantaneous satisfactions reduced to some comparable base by time discount" (1937, p. 159). But despite its arbitrariness, the simplicity and elegance of his apparatus were irresistible. The discounted utility model was rapidly established as the framework of choice for analyzing decisions with a temporal component.

Almost as soon as it was proposed, however, DU confronted a serious challenge to its scientific status. The concept of utility maximization in economics had undergone a transformation during the past half century, which culminated in the so-called ordinal utility revolution that swept the field of economics in the early 1940s. DU relies on a strongly cardinal (ratio-scale) form of utility of a type inimical to the ordinal perspective.[10] The ordinalists proposed replacing DU with the more general assumption that decision makers maximize some arbitrary function of current and future consumption— $U(c_1, \ldots c_n)$—which was a generalization of Fisher's two-period indifference curve formulation. However, this formulation proved insufficiently restrictive in practice, and has enjoyed little popularity outside of advanced microeconomic textbooks.

The work of Koopmans (1960) can be viewed, in part, as an attempt to restore DU to its former stature. Following von Neumann and Morgenstern's (1949) similar efforts in decision making under uncertainty, Koopmans formulated a set of axioms governing the manner in which people rank temporal sequences of consumption that, taken together, are logically equivalent to the DU model. Restricted in this manner, the DU framework can be shown to be compatible with the ordinal approach. The rehabilitation of DU, however, was not completely successful. As both Samuelson and Koopmans recognized, DU and its axioms are deficient either as normative standards or positive descriptions of choice.

At the core of the discounted utility model are two basic assumptions—a strong form of preferential independence, and a property called *stationarity*.[11]

[10] The ordinal utility revolution reflected the belief that motivational concepts could be dispensed with to explain individual behavior. In the ordinalists' view it was only necessary to know an agent's preference ranking of alternative consumption bundles in order to explain her behavior. Ordinal utility constituted a repudiation of theories of behavior based on psychological concepts such as maximization of well-being or satisfaction of desires. Ironically, Samuelson, whose discounted utility model was thrown into scientific limbo by ordinal utility, was one of the triumvirate who initiated the revolution.

[11] This discussion is adapted from an early draft of Prelec and Loewenstein (1990).

The independence property states that if two temporal prospects, $X \equiv (x_1, \ldots x_n)$ and $Y \equiv (y_1, \ldots y_n)$, share a common outcome at a given point in time, then preference between them is determined solely by the remaining $(n - 1)$ outcomes. In combination with a series of technical axioms collectively referred to as "completeness," outcome separability implies that preferences can be represented by the *general additively separable* (GAS) formula:

$$U(X) = \sum u_t(x_t).$$

The stationarity condition states that if the first outcome in both X and Y is the same, $x_1 = y_1$, then preference between X and Y will be preserved by dropping the first outcome and shifting the remaining outcomes by one period.

Stationarity and intertemporal independence (along with the technical axioms) imply that any representation of preferences over temporal prospects can be monotonically transformed into a discounted-utility representation.

At a normative level, DU has many appealing features. Stationarity, which implies logarithmic discounting at a constant rate, is attractive in the sense that it implies a neutral attitude toward time delay; a given time delay has the same impact on preferences, regardless of when it occurs. The additive separable form implied by independence has, from a normative perspective, one desirable and one undesirable consequence. The desirable consequence is that it implies that different outcomes are discounted at the same rate; time preference is independent of atemporal preference. To see why this is desirable, imagine the intertemporal allocation problem of an individual for whom this is not the case. Imagine a person who must allocate a fixed bundle of apples and oranges between present and future. Suppose she prefers apples to oranges in the present and in the future, but prefers oranges in the present to oranges in the future and apples in the future to apples in the present. The person's time preferences would lead her to delay apple consumption and speed up orange consumption, which would conflict with atemporal preference for apples.

The undesirable consequence of preferential independence is the implication that consumption in one period has no effect on preferences in other periods. It is easy to construct counter-examples that are normatively compelling. For example, consider a gastronome who is indifferent between chicken and beef. Independence implies that such a person would be indifferent between beef today, beef tomorrow, and beef the day after, on the one hand, and beef today, chicken the day after, and beef on the third day. There is no good reason, besides analytical simplicity, to assume that such indifference would hold.

At a descriptive level, DU's problems are far more striking. Numerous behavioral tendencies have been observed that are incompatible with DU. There

73

is a common tendency to bite the bullet, to get unpleasant outcomes over with quickly rather than to defer them as predicted by DU (Loewenstein, 1987) (see Chapter 9). Losses are generally discounted at a lower rate than gains (Thaler, 1981). People have asymmetric preferences for the speedup and delay of consumption (Loewenstein, 1988) when, according to DU, these preferences should be symmetrical. A list of discounted utility "anomalies" has been enumerated, including these and a variety of other phenomena (Loewenstein and Thaler, 1989; Prelec and Loewenstein, 1991; Loewenstein and Prelec, Chapter 5 and 1991). Recognition of these anomalies has been one of the factors stimulating the reintroduction of psychology into the economics of intertemporal choice.

3.4. New Evidence for Old Theories

Although the psychological analyses of nineteenth- and early twentieth-century economists were derived from introspection or casual empiricism, many of the insights of these economists have been confirmed in recent research. Psychologists since the early 1960s and, more recently, economists, have conducted empirical research addressing basic issues of time preference. Most of the speculations of Rae, Senior, Jevons, Böhm-Bawerk, and Fisher have been evaluated empirically.

3.4.1. *Rae and Senior*

All four of the determinants of time preference cited by Rae—the brevity and uncertainty of life, the bequest motive, the painfulness of deferring gratification, and the impact of socioeconomic and cultural factors—have been examined in empirical research.

   It is difficult to test for the effect of life expectancy on time preference cross-sectionally, because people who differ in life expectancy often differ in other respects that may be associated with attitude toward the future. However, one empirical analysis has avoided this pitfall by employing a time-series approach. Slemrod (1984, 1986) found a small but systematic relationship between changes in the threat of nuclear war as measured by the setting of the "doomsday" clock published monthly in the *Bulletin of the Atomic Scientists* and changes in the national savings rate—a proxy for time perspective; the savings rate tends to drop when the clock setting approaches zero. He has also found an inverse relationship, cross-sectionally, between saving rates in different countries and fear of nuclear war. Although only suggestive, these results are consistent with the notion that life expectancy influences time preference.

Evidence concerning the bequest motive is mixed. Some economists have argued that bequests play a key role in saving behavior (Kotlikoff and Summers, 1981), at least among those at the upper levels of income (Moore, 1978). The bequest motive has been used to explain why the elderly continue to save after retirement rather than dissaving as predicted by a stripped-down life-cycle model (Danziger, v.d. Gaag, Smolensky, and Taussig, 1982). But others have argued that observed dissaving is illusory (Diamond and Hausman, 1984), and one empirical study that compared savings by those with and without living children found no difference (Hurd, 1987). Although Rae's assertion that the benevolent affections influence time preference seems intuitively plausible, the effect is remarkably difficult to demonstrate.

Numerous articles in the 1960s and early 1970s examined the relationship between some of the socioeconomic characteristics discussed by Rae—social class, wealth, and ethnicity—and time discounting. However, most of these analyses were severely flawed methodologically and suffered from what modern cognitive psychologists term *confirmation bias*. Studies correlating time perspective with demographic characteristics almost disappeared from mainstream journals after Mischel (1968) demonstrated that differences in situations have a greater effect on willingness to delay gratification than differences between persons. However, Mischel's more recent work—mainly his finding of strong continuity in delay of gratification over a person's lifetime (Mischel, Shoda, and Peake, 1988)—once again highlights the importance of individual differences.

Whether there are strong socioeconomic correlates of time preference, and the cause of such differences if they exist, has not been addressed satisfactorily. Hausman (1979) did find a striking negative relationship between income and discounting, as measured by the tradeoff between immediate purchase price of air conditioners and delayed energy payments. But his results could plausibly be explained by liquidity constraints at low income levels or simple ignorance of the tradeoff rather than discounting per se.

Finally, Rae's notion that people find it painful to defer consumption, which also underlay Senior's abstinence perspective, has received considerable support. Social psychologist Mischel and his colleagues view delay of consumption in much the same way as Senior did: as a cause of frustration. Their aim is to understand the conditions that intensify or attenuate that frustration. In Mischel's two-stage theory of intertemporal choice (or "delay of gratification"), the first step is reminiscent of Böhm-Bawerk, the second of Senior. The first stage consists of the decision to defer, and depends on a relatively dispassionate assessment of costs and benefits. The second stage entails the implementation of the decision to defer during which the decision maker must actually endure the pain of abstinence.

In a series of experiments using children as subjects, Mischel (1974) focused on the implementation stage. In a typical experiment, a child is placed in a room and learns that he or she can summon the experimenter by ringing a bell. The experimenter then shows the child an inferior and a superior object and explains that the child will receive the superior object if he or she can wait for the experimenter to return, but that he or she can obtain the inferior object at any time by ringing the bell. The dependent variable in these experiments is the length of time the child is able to wait, limited by a fixed interval (typically 15 minutes) after which the experimenter returns with the promised reward. [12]

In his early work, Mischel examined the effect of the visible presence or absence of the immediate and deferred rewards on waiting times. These experiments demonstrated that children wait less in the physical presence of either reward than when the rewards are absent. In later experiments, children were instructed to distract themselves while waiting or to transform the rewards cognitively (e.g. to think of marshmallows as little white clouds or chocolate bars as logs). Mischel found that both distraction and cognitive transformation lengthened waiting times.

These results can be easily assimilated into the abstinence perspective. Factors that increase privation during waiting, such as the presence of the reward, appear to decrease the ability to wait. However, when subjects are distracted from the privation of waiting, or when privation is reduced by denigration of the reward, ability to delay is enhanced.

3.4.2. Jevons

Perhaps even more than the abstinence perspective, the Jevonian view has many connections to current theories and observations. To the modern economist, Jevons' views on intertemporal choice seem rather extreme. Clearly, we often defer consumption without immediate compensation in the form of pleasure from anticipation. Our conception of self extends forward in time so that we do not perceive deferral as a sacrifice to an alien other, and do not require immediate compensation (in the form of pleasure from anticipation) for such deferral. Nevertheless, there is considerable truth in Jevons' perspective. Much of our pleasure and pain in life *does* stem from expectations of the future as Bentham and Jevons argued, and these pleasures and pains have profound implications for behavior.

One of the most persuasive modern arguments in favor of the Jevonian perspective is presented by Cottle and Klineberg (1974) in *The Present of Things Future*. They argue that the ability to imagine the future is not sufficient

---

[12] In earlier experiments subjects were not informed of the exact duration of the delay period. Recently, however, Mischel has run several experiments in which children are informed of the delay period, and has not observed any substantial differences in behavior under the two conditions.

for voluntary deferral and that, as Jevons argued, deferral will only occur if such imagery is associated with immediately experienced emotions. They cite evidence ranging from animal behavior to the myopic behavior of people who have had frontal lobotomies in support of their claim.

The so-called immediacy effect (Prelec and Loewenstein, 1991)—the finding that people give far greater weight to current consumption than to consumption delayed for any length of time—is also congruent with Jevonian perspective. While emphasizing the importance of pleasure and pain from anticipation, Jevons keenly recognized the greater power of immediate experience over anticipation of the future. The former is immediate and highly salient; the latter is hypothetical. This difference is analogous to that between actual and "statistical" accident victims. It has been observed that people are willing to expend large amounts to save the life of an identifiable accident victim, such as a child who has fallen into a well, but resist expending resources on preventive measures that benefit statistical victims.

Substantial evidence bolsters the notion of an immediacy effect.[13] Consumption items that are immediately available seem to exert a disproportionate pull; similarly, it is very difficult to impose pain on oneself, even when it is known that the pain will be short-lived and the beneficial consequences prolonged. Witness, for example, the difficulty of plunging into a swimming pool even when other swimmers can be seen paddling about with no apparent discomfort. In a study that illustrates this point, Christensen-Szalanski (1984) elicited expectant mothers' preferences for anesthesia during childbirth. When asked at various intervals leading up to labor, a sizable majority stated a preference for childbirth without medication. However, preferences shifted abruptly following the onset of labor. Christensen-Szalanski explained these reversals by the tendency for discounting to increase as time delay diminishes (Ainslie, 1975). However, a simpler explanation follows from the distinction between pleasure and pain from anticipation and that arising from current sensation.[14]

---

[13] A similar point has been made by Phelps and Pollak (1968) in an intergenerational context. In their intergenerational welfare analysis, they use two distinct discount factors to balance the competing utility of successive generations: the first a conventional discount rate that simply refers to a generation's distance from the present, and a second that overweights the utility of the current generation relative to all other generations. The latter, which suggests that the current generation does not put the consumption of hypothetical future generations on an equal footing with its own immediate consumption, is analogous to the notion that people are unable to treat their own immediate and hypothetical future consumption as perfectly commensurable. This analogy between the intergenerational and intraindividual cases was proposed by Elster (1985).

[14] The preference shift does not appear to be due to the decrease in time delay prior to labor per se, as suggested by the standard account of time inconsistency but rather to the actual experience of pain. If the declining discounting explanation was correct, we would expect to observe some women reversing their preference at intermediate points prior to the onset of labor. But as noted, virtually all shifts occurred only after Labor had begun. It also can't be argued that the preference reversal observed by Christensen-Szalanski was caused

This same logic also provides a simpler explanation for various other examples of time inconsistency. For example, Schelling notes the difficulty of responding to the alarm clock, cavalierly set to an early hour the night before. When set, the pain of waking and the benefits of early rising were both on the same cognitive plane. But when the alarm drones, the pain of waking is immediate and real, while the benefits of early rising remain abstract and in the future.

A second phenomenon that resists interpretation by DU, while easily explicable in Jevons' terms, concerns time preferences for undesirable outcomes (Loewenstein, 1987). DU, with positive discounting, predicts that people should always prefer to defer undesirable outcomes, because doing so moves the negative impact on utility to a time that is less heavily weighted. However, considerable evidence suggests that the opposite—a preference for getting losses over with quickly—is a common, perhaps even typical, pattern of preference. For example, Thaler (1981) found that an unexpectedly high proportion of respondents to a hypothetical choice questionnaire preferred to pay parking tickets immediately rather than defer payment, despite considerations of interest. Carlsmith (1962) and others (Barnes and Barnes, 1964; Knapp, Krause, and Perkins, 1959; Mischel and Grusec, 1967) discovered that subjects, given a choice, prefer to experience aversive stimuli, such as an unavoidable electric shock, sooner rather than later. The usual explanation for such behavior is that waiting for unpleasant outcomes induces anxiety that can be avoided by getting the outcomes over with quickly. Such an explanation is consistent with a Jevonian tradeoff between reduced pain from anticipation and increased immediate pain.

Recent advertising, in which "peace of mind" allegedly flows from the purchases of automobile maintenance contracts,[15] universal life insurance, and other current expenditures, also attests to the significance of pain deriving from anticipation. Similarly, lottery ticket purchases may be viewed not simply as uncertain investments yielding high potential payoffs, but as a certain investment—in pleasurable anticipation. As M. Landau, the former director of the Israeli lottery, commented, "In spite of the great unlikelihood of winning the desirable sum of money, an individual may still be willing to

by unfamiliarity with and, thus, an underestimation of future pain. The effect was observed equally often in women giving birth for a second or subsequent time, when women should be familiar with the pain and when, in fact, labor is typically less painful than initial childbirth.

[15] For example, a recent advertisement for an automobile maintenance contract read, "Backed by GM and honored at GM dealerships throughout the US and Canada, the protection plan gives you added convenience and peace of mind." GM's competitor in this area, USAA, advertised, "Only you can decide if a service contract is worth the price to you, but if peace of mind is what you need, an extended warranty is a wise investment." A variant of this is the slogan of the French insurance conglomerate GAN on cartoon posters that juxtapose the potential chaos of an accident with the smug satisfaction of a man who has anticipated it: "Un homme assuré est un homme tranquille."

pay a relatively high price for a lottery ticket because of the satisfaction he is deriving from the thrill of anticipation" (1968, p. 36). The common "buy a dream" sales pitch reinforces such nonpecuniary motivations for buying lottery tickets.

3.4.3. *Böhm-Bawerk and Fisher*

The psychology underlying the second phase of the economics of intertemporal choice, epitomized by Böhm-Bawerk and Fisher, was predominantly cognitive. Although there was lingering discussion of motivational elements such as willpower, Böhm-Bawerk and Fisher believed that cognitive limitations were predominantly responsible for time discounting. Such a perspective is well represented in modern work on intertemporal choice and in the various chapters of this book.

Mischel, Ebbesen, and Zeiss (1972) found that, while actual presence of a desired reward decreased waiting time, viewing a photograph of the reward actually enhanced deferral of gratification. Apparently the photograph increases the reality of the reward for delaying without increasing frustration to the same extent as the sight (and perhaps smell) of the actual object.

Research on intertemporal framing (Loewenstein, 1988) also corroborates the cognitive perspective in the sense of demonstrating that how a person internally represents (frames) a choice can have a major impact on willingness to delay. For example, people dislike delaying scheduled consumption but are relatively indifferent to speedup. As a result, when deciding between an inferior immediate and superior delayed consumption objects, they may select the immediate object if the alternative is expressed as delayed, but later object if the immediate object is described as having been sped up. The theory of melioration (Herrnstein and Prelec, Chapter 13) is also reminiscent of Böhm-Bawerk's perspective in its assertion that people tend to ignore (or at least underweigh) information about the future consequences of decisions.

Although difficult to evaluate empirically, the concept of willpower, which appeared in Böhm-Bawerk and Fisher's work, and the idea that deferral of gratification involves as Schelling (1984) expresses it, an "internal struggle for self-command," has received empirical support. For example, Sjöberg and Johnson (1978) repeatedly interviewed smokers who attempted to quit (see, also, Sjöberg, 1980). They found that subjects who resumed smoking often were aware of "cognitive distortions of reality"—rationalizations—that occurred prior to the resumption of smoking. According to Sjöberg and Johnson, the stress engendered by quitting smoking "may leave the door open for a corrupt, twisted, and shortsighted reasoning which generates excuses for changing the initial decision" (1978, p. 151). Rook and Hoch (1985), in interviewing consumers who purchase on impulse, obtained numerous testaments to inner conflict: "The pants were shrieking 'buy me,' so I knew right then that I better walk away and get something else done." "It gnaws at me until I buy it. If I want to get it I keep thinking about it. It won't get out of my mind until I buy it." Ainslie (1987) elicited college students' and prisoners' endorsement of various types of self-control tactics. These included extrapsychic devices (e.g. taking pills to change appetite), attention control (distraction), emotional control, and private rules (e.g. a rigid diet). He found that all four of the self-control devices were approximately equally endorsed, but that the types of strategies endorsed by a particular individual correlated in an intuitively sensible way, with measured personality traits.

There is also some evidence supporting Pigou's notion that people view time in a distorted fashion. Ekman and Lundberg (1971) asked people to rate the "subjective temporal distance" of a range of different objective time delays and to also rate their emotional involvement with different periods. From both of these judgments they estimated psychophysical time functions that were not linear, but conformed closely to a power function of the form $t_s = t_o^a$, with $0 < a < 1$, where the subscripts s and o stand for "subjective" and "objective."

3.4.4. *The Ordinalists*

Even the third stage in the economics of intertemporal choice, despite its antagonism toward psychology, makes connections to modern psychology. Among contemporary psychologists, there are those who adhere to a perspective that is closely analogous to the ordinal approach. Behavioral psychologists such as Herrnstein and Rachlin (in their earlier work) and, more recently, Mazur (1987), Logue (1987), and many others, eschew cognitive and motivational psychology, restricting themselves to encoding behavior mathematically. These psychologists have sought to estimate mathematical functions representing the desirability of rewards as a function of time delay. The research has generally involved animals instead of humans, presumably with the goal of avoiding the idiosyncratic concerns that inevitably come into play with human subjects. Interestingly, even the animal work has tended to reinforce some of the observations made by early economists. For example, in line with Jevons' observations, neither animals nor people discount the future at a constant rate; most species are disproportionately sensitive to short as opposed to long time delays. As Strotz (1955) demonstrated, such a discount function implies time inconsistent behavior; we always plan to be more farsighted in our future behavior than we are in the present. In confronting the problem of how people deal with the problem posed by time consistency, behavioral psychologists have fallen into the same trap as Böhm-Bawerk in his attempt to reduce intertemporal choice to a cognitive plane. Concepts such as "self-control" (Rachlin and Green, 1972) are not easily reduced to equation form.

3.5. Concluding Remarks

In his essays on the history of economic thought, Stigler (1965) argues that, to take root, an economic theory must meet the triple criteria of generality, manageability, and congruence with reality. Because, in his view, ideas compete with one another in the intellectual market-place, the most general, manageable, and realistic must inevitably triumph. The case of intertemporal choice chronicled here points to a more cyclical pattern of scientific progress.

The early history of intertemporal choice demonstrates a relatively unselfconscious cooperation between psychology and economics, which was followed by a century of work that attempted—never with full success—to expunge the psychological content from the economics. In recent decades, however, economists have begun to reawaken to the possibility that the discarded psychology was not quite as superfluous as had been supposed.

Rather than an evenhanded balancing of Stigler's three criteria, the economics of intertemporal choice has bounced between the three extreme points on the triangle. In the first critical transition, from the psychological perspectives of Senior, Jevons, and Böhm-Bawerk to the formulation of DU by Samuelson, realism was sacrificed for manageability; in the second, albeit only partially successful transition from DU to the ordinal approach, manageability was sacrificed for generality. Thus, the economics of intertemporal choice has not evolved toward Stigler's ideal.

Until recently, economists who sought a descriptive theory of intertemporal choice were caught in an uncomfortable dilemma. On the one hand, they could plead ignorance of the intricacies of intertemporal choice and treat time simply as an additional dimension of choice over which preferences are defined, an approach compatible with the ordinalist perspective. The problem is that the ordinalist alternative suffers from excessive generality and ignores what is known about the economics and psychology of intertemporal choice. As Samuelson notes, "functions that allow unlimited interrelationships become so general as to be almost vacuous" (1937, p. 155). Another problem is its intractability, which probably explains the infrequent appearance of the generalized formulation in economic modeling.

Alternatively, economists could rely on the discounted utility framework. However, DU's psychology is dubious: Few people are willing to accept the axioms of Koopmans either as descriptions of, or as prescriptions for, intertemporal choice behavior. DU is not an explanatory theory; it cannot explain why objects lose or gain in value when delayed. It is simply a way of summarizing and encoding intertemporal preference. But as a method of encoding preferences, it is also deficient. Its behavioral implications are contradicted by empirical research and common experience.

The new borrowings from psychology offer the possibility to transcend the conflict between tractability and realism. Economists need a more refined model of intertemporal choice than that offered by the ordinalist approach. But they want a restrictive model that is realistic. This is where modern psychology can play a constructive role. The speculations of Freud and LeBon have been largely displaced by a contemporary academic psychology that is much closer to economics, both theoretically, and in terms of research methods. During much of the time that economics was purging itself of psychological content, these psychologists have been studying empirically, and in many cases validating, the very insights discarded by economists.

In order to formulate a more realistic theory of intertemporal choice, economists must grapple with the problems confronted by their predecessors and by modern psychologists. Why do individuals take account of the future? How is utility from future consumption experienced in the present? What are the determinants of pleasure from anticipation and privation? They must become aware of the distinction between cognitive and motivational determinants of time preference and of their implications for intertemporal choice.

This book provides a sample of work from a group of psychologists and economists who have met annually to discuss issues relating to intertemporal choice. It is one example of the growing number of exchanges between the two disciplines (see, e.g., Hogarth and Reder, 1987). If the exchange, so far, has tended to be unidirectional, economists can take comfort in the observation that, in borrowing from psychology, they are, in effect, rediscovering their own past.

•

I thank Nora Bartlett, John Campbell, Donna Harsch, Steve Hoch, Joshua Klayman, Marilyn Quadrel, George Stigler, and especially James Thompson for invaluable comments and suggestions. The Russell Sage Foundation and the Alfred P. Sloan Foundation provided support for this research.

References

Ainslie, G. "Specious Reward: A Behavioral Theory of Impulsiveness and Impulse Control." *Psychological Bulletin* 82 (1975): 463–509.

——. "Self-reported Tactics of Impulse Control." *International Journal of Addictions* 22 (1987): 167–179.

Barnes, O., and L.W. Barnes. "Choice of Delay of Inevitable Shock." *Journal of Abnormal Social Psychology* 68 (1964): 669–672.

Böhm-Bawerk, E.v. *Capital and Interest*. South Holland, IL: Libertarian Press (1889), 1970.

——. *History and Critique of Interest Theories*. South Holland, IL: Libertarian Press (1914), 1970.

Cairnes, J. H. *Some Leading Principles of Political Economy Newly Expounded*. New York: Harper, 1874.

Carlsmith, J. M. *Strength of Expectancy: Its Determinants and Effects*. Unpublished doctoral dissertation, Harvard University, 1962.

Cassel, G. *The Nature and Necessity of Interest*. New York: Macmillan, 1903.

Christensen, Szalanski, and J. J. Jay. "Discount Functions and the Measurement of Patients' Values: Women's Decisions During Childbirth." *Medical Decision Making* 4 (1984): 47–58.

Cottle, T. J., and S. L. Klineberg. *The Present of Things Future: Explorations of Time in Human Experience*. New York: Free Press, 1974.

Danziger, S., J.v.d. Gaag, E. Smolensky, and M. K. Taussig. "The Life-Cycle Hypothesis and the Consumption Behavior of the Elderly." *Journal of Post-Keynesian Economics* 5 (1982): 208–227.

Davenport, H. S. "Proposed Modifications in Austrian Theory and Terminology." *Quarterly Journal of Economics* 16 (1901): 355–383.

Diamond, P., and J. Hausman. "Individual Retirement and Savings Behavior." *Journal of Public Economics* 23 (1984): 81–114.

Ekman, G., and U. Lundberg. "Emotional Reaction to Past and Future Events as a Function of Temporal Distance." *Acta Psychologica* 35 (1971): 430–441.

Elster, J. "Weakness of Will and the Free-Rider Problem." *Economics and Philosophy* 1 (1985): 231–265.

Fisher, I. *The Theory of Interest*. New York: Macmillan, 1930.

Hausman, J. "Individual Discount Rates and the Purchase and Utilization of Energy-Using Durables." *Bell Journal of Economics* 10 (1979): 33–54.

Hogarth, R. M., and M. W. Reder. *Rationale Choice: The Contrast Between Economics and Psychology*. Chicago: University of Chicago Press, 1987.

Hurd, M. D. "Savings of the Elderly and Desired Bequests." *American Economic Review* 77 (1987): 298–312.

James, R. W. *John Rae, Political Economist*. Toronto: University of Toronto Press, 1965.

Jevons, W. S. *Theory of Political Economy*. London: Macmillan, 1871.

Knapp, R. K., R. H. Kause, and C. C. Perkins. "Immediate versus Delayed Shock in T-Maze Performance." *journal of Experimental Psychology* 58 (1959): 357–362.

Koopmans, T. C. "Stationary Ordinal Utility and Impatience." *Econometrica* 28 (1960): 287–309.

Kotlikoff, L. J., and L. H. Summers. "The Role of Intergenerational Transfers in Aggregate Capital Accumulation." *Journal of Political Economy* 89 (1981): 706–732.

Landau, M. *A Manual on Lotteries*. Israel: Massada Publishing, 1968.

Loewenstein, G. "Anticipation and the Valuation of Delayed Consumption." *Economic Journal* 97 (1987): 666–684.

——. "Frames of Mind in Intertemporal Choice." *Management Science* 34 (1988): 200–214.

——, and D. Prelec. "Negative Time Preference." *American Economic Review* 81 (1991): 347–352.

——, and R. Thaler. "Anomalies: Intertemporal Choice." *Journal of Economic Perspectives* 3 (1989): 181–193.

Macvane, S. M. "Analysis of Cost of Production." *Quarterly Journal of Economics* 1 (1887): 481–487.

Marshall, A. *Principles of Economics*. London: Macmillan, 1898.

Mazur, J. E. "An Adjustment Procedure for Studying Delayed Reinforcement," Chap. 2 in M. L. Commons, J. E. Mazur, J. A. Nevins, and H. Rachlin (eds.). *Quantitative Analysis of Behavior: The Effect of Delay and of Intervening Events on Reinforcement Value*. Hillsdale, NJ: Erlbaum, 1987.

Mill, J. S. *Principles of Political Economy*, 5th edn. New York: D. Appleton, 1864.

Mischel, W. *Personality and Assessment*. New York: Wiley, 1968.

——. "Processes in Delay of Gratification," in D. Berkowitz (ed.). *Advances in Experimental Social Psychology*, vol. 7. 1974, pp. 249–292.

——, E. B. Ebbesen, and A. Zeis. "Cognitive and Attentional Mechanisms in Delay of Gratification." *Journal of Personality and Social Psychology* 21 (1972): 204–218.

——, and J. Grusec. "Waiting for Rewards and Punishments: Effects of Time and Probability on Choice." *Journal of Personality and Social Psychology* 5 (1967): 24–31.

——, Y. Shoda, and P. K. Peake. "The Nature of Adolescent Competencies Predicted by Preschool Delay of Gratification." *Journal of Personality and Social Psychology* 54 (1988): 687–696.

Moore, B. J. "Life-cycle Saving and Bequest Behavior." *Journal of Post Keynesian Economics* 1 (1978): 79–99.

Pareto, V. *Manuel D'Économie politique* (Alfred Bonnet trans.). Paris: Giard & Briétr, 1909.

Phelps, E. S., and R. A. Pollak. "On Second-best National Saving and Game-theoretic Equilibrium Growth." *Review of Economic Studies* 35 (1968): 185–199.

Pigou, A. C. *The Economics of Welfare*. London: Macmillan, 1920.

Prelec, D., and G. Loewenstein. "Decision Making over Time and Under Uncertainty: A Common Approach." *Management Science* 37 (1991): 770–776.

Rachlin, H., and L. Green. "Commitment, Choice and Self-Control." *Journal of the Experimental Analysis of Behavior* 17 (1972): 15–22.

Rae, J. *The Sociological Theory of Capital* (reprint of original 1834 edition) London: Macmillan, 1905.

Rook, D., and S. Hoch. "Consuming Impulses." In E. C. Hirschman and M. B. Holbrook (eds.). *Advances in Consumer Research*, vol. 12, Provo, UT: Association for Consumer Research, 1985, pp. 23–27.

Samuelson, P. "A Note on Measurement of Utility." *Review of Economic Studies* 4 (1937): 155–161.

Senior, N. W. *An Outline of the Science of Political Economy*. London: Clowes & Sons, 1836.

Shackle, G. L. S. *Time in Economics*. Amsterdam: North Holland, 1958.

Sjöberg, L. "Volitional Problems in Carrying Through a Difficult Decision." *Acta Psychologica* 45 (1980): 123–132.

——, and T. Johnson. "Trying to Give up Smoking: A Study of Volitional Breakdowns." *Addictive Behaviors* 3 (1978): 149–164.

Slemrod, J. "The Economic Impact of Nuclear Fear." *Bulletin of the Atomic Scientists* 40 (1984): 42–43.

Slemrod, J. "Saving and the Fear of Nuclear War." *Journal of Conflict Resolution* 30 (1986): 403–419.

Smart, W. "The New Theory of Interest." *Economic Journal* (1891): 675–687.

Stigler, G. "The Development of Utility Theory," Chap. 5. *Essays in the History of Economics*. Chicago: University of Chicago Press, 1965.

Strotz, R. H. "Myopia and Inconsistency in Dynamic Utility Maximization." *Review of Economic Studies* 23 (1955): 165–180.

Thaler, R. "Some Empirical Evidence on Dynamic Inconsistency." *Economic Letters* 8 (1981): 201–207.

Tversky, A., and D. Kahneman. "Availability: A Heuristic for Judging Frequency and Probability." *Cognitive Psychology* 5 (1973): 207–232.

von Neumann, J., and O. Morgenstern. *Theory of Games and Economic Behavior*. Princeton: Princeton University Press, 1949.

4

Adam Smith, Behavioral Economist

Nava Ashraf, Colin F. Camerer, and George Loewenstein

The genesis of this paper is a typical story in academia. Nava Ashraf was a graduate student at Harvard, and had participated in the biennial Russell Sage Foundation Summer Institute in Behavioral Economics that Colin Camerer and I co-organized at different times. She wrote a paper for a class on Adam Smith, and it caught the attention of one of her advisers at Harvard, an editor at the *Journal of Economic Perspectives*, who asked her to write a longer piece on Adam Smith for the journal. Nava enlisted the help of Colin, and Colin, knowing of my obsession with Smith, enlisted me.

Smith fascinates me not only for what he wrote, but for the different ways that people use his work. He is, of course, a darling of the political right, which has not moved much beyond the concept of the invisible hand discussed in the *Wealth of Nations* whereby people pursuing their own self-interest, through their market interactions with other self-interested individuals, inadvertently promote the public good. For conservatives, Smith is the champion of the market.

In our paper, we focus on Smith's other famous volume, *The Theory of Moral Sentiments*, which is becoming as much a manifesto for behavioral economists as the *Wealth of Nations* has long been for free-market economists. In the paper, we show that many of the most important ideas in behavioral economics, such as loss aversion, hyperbolic time discounting, and the concern for fairness, were anticipated by Smith and, moreover, that he laid out these ideas in the context of a unified theoretical framework that is very similar to many 'dual process' theories that are popular in psychology (and starting to be in economics as well). Given Smith's use by the political right, however, to me the most eye-opening aspect of *TOMS* is Smith's view—seemingly totally contradictory to the notion of the invisible hand—that capitalism is based on an enormous illusion: that wealth will buy happiness.[1]

---

[1] There is a deep paradox in the *Theory of Moral Sentiments*. Smith claims that wealth does not bring happiness and that those who pursue it are chasing after an illusion. But, he also

Since this is the only paper in this book that I coauthored with Colin Camerer, who is in fact one of my most frequent collaborators, let me say a few words about him. Colin is, most famously, a certifiable "genius". He began college (Johns Hopkins) at the age of 14, graduated at age 18, and got his PhD from the University of Chicago at the ripe age of 21, at which point he taught at Northwestern for two years before moving to the Wharton School at the University of Pennsylvania. That's where I met him, in 1985. His senior colleague there, Howard Kunreuther, playing matchmaker, invited me to visit Penn for a day, then left the two of us to our own devices.

Colin, at the time, was managing punk bands, with names like "the Dead Milkmen" and the "Bonemen of Barumba." In the buttoned-down atmosphere of Wharton, a steady stream of dissolute looking punk rockers walked through the office suite where his department was housed, and from Colin's office there emanated a mixture of pulsing music and diverse types of smoke. Although I never shared Colin's love of punk music, the two of us share the bond of a deep appreciation for the music of Barry White. During an overnight drive on one of the hiking trips we took together, we challenged ourselves by testing how many times in a row we could listen to his smash hit *"Can't Get Enough of Your Love"* without going crazy. And, on a sea kayaking trip in Alaska, following White's untimely death, we became convinced that a certain sea lion that wouldn't leave us alone, was the reincarnation of our R&B hero. We still have plans for a paper, much in the vein of the current one on Adam Smith, drawing insights from *The Man's* lyrics for behavioral economics.

---

believes that the pursuit of wealth is a good thing because it stimulates economic activity. What he doesn't explain is why so much economic activity is such a good thing if it doesn't bring happiness. Perhaps he has a kind of trickle-down perspective—that wealth does not bring happiness to the capitalists who amass great quantities of it, but it does help to alleviate the material misery of the masses.

Adam Smith, Behavioral Economist*

Nava Ashraf, Colin F. Camerer, and George Loewenstein

In *The Wealth of Nations*, published in 1776, Adam Smith famously argued that economic behavior was motivated by self-interest. But 17 years earlier in 1759, Smith had proposed a theory of human behavior that looked anything but self-interested. In his first book, *The Theory of Moral Sentiments*, Smith argued that behavior was determined by the struggle between what Smith termed the "passions" and the "impartial spectator." The passions included drives such as hunger and sex, emotions such as fear and anger, and motivational feeling states such as pain. Smith viewed behavior as under the direct control of the passions, but believed that people could override passion-driven behavior by viewing their own behavior from the perspective of an outsider—the impartial spectator—a "moral hector who, looking over the shoulder of the economic man, scrutinizes every move he makes" (Grampp, 1948, p. 317).[1]

The "impartial spectator" plays many roles in *The Theory of Moral Sentiments*. When it comes to choices that involve short-term gratification but long-term costs, the impartial spectator serves as the source of "self-denial, of self-government, of that command of the passions which subjects all the movements of our nature to what our own dignity and honour, and the

* This chapter was originally published as Ashraf, N., Camerer, C. and Loewenstein, G. (2005). "Adam Smith, Behavioral Economist" *Journal of Economic Perspectives* 19(3): 131–145. Reproduced with permission.
[1] A long-standing dispute has raged over whether Adam Smith's view of human motivation as expressed in *The Theory of Moral Sentiments* complements or contradicts the view of human motivation expressed in *The Wealth of Nations*. Although much has been written about "das Adam Smith problem" of reconciling these texts, most modern Smith scholarship asserts that there is no essential contradiction between the texts. As the editors of the Glasgow Edition of the Works and Correspondence of Adam Smith edition of *The Theory of Moral Sentiments* write (Raphael and Macfie, 1976, p. 20), "the so called 'Adam Smith problem' was a pseudo-problem based on ignorance and misunderstanding. Anybody who reads *The Theory of Moral Sentiments*, first in one of the earlier editions and then in edition six, will not have the slightest inclination to be puzzled that the same man wrote this book and *The Wealth of Nations*, nor to suppose that he underwent any radical change of view about human conduct."

propriety of our own conduct, require" (Smith, 1759 [1981], I, i, *v*, 26), much like a farsighted "planner" entering into conflict with short-sighted "doers" (Shefrin and Thaler, 1981; Meardon and Ortmann, 1996). In social situations, the impartial spectator plays the role of a conscience, dispassionately weighing the conflicting needs of different persons. Smith (I, i, *v*, 29) recognized, however, that the impartial spectator could be led astray or rendered impotent by sufficiently intense passions: "There are some situations which bear so hard upon human nature that the greatest degree of self-government ... is not able to stifle, altogether, the voice of human weakness, or reduce the violence of the passions to that pitch of moderation, in which the impartial spectator can entirely enter into them."

Adam Smith's psychological perspective in *The Theory of Moral Sentiments* is remarkably similar to "dual-process" frameworks advanced by psychologists (for example, Kirkpatrick and Epstein, 1992; Sloman, 1996; Metcalf and Mischel, 1999), neuroscientists (Damasio, 1994; LeDoux, 1996; Panksepp, 1998) and more recently by behavioral economists, based on behavioral data and detailed observations of brain functioning (Bernheim and Rangel, 2004; Benhabib and Bisin, 2004; Fudenberg and Levine, 2004; Loewenstein and O'Donoghue, 2004). It also anticipates a wide range of insights regarding phenomena such as loss aversion, willpower and fairness (V. Smith, 1998) that have been the focus of modern behavioral economics (see Camerer and Loewenstein, 2004, for a recent review). The purpose of this essay is to draw attention to some of these connections. Indeed, as we propose at the end of the paper, *The Theory of Moral Sentiments* suggests promising directions for economic research that have not yet been exploited.

4.1. Preferences and the Dual-Process Perspective

The Theory of Moral Sentiments is packed with insights about preferences, using the dual-process framework of the passions and the impartial spectator. Some of the discussion relates to aspects of individual preference and judgment: what we would today call loss aversion, intertemporal choice and overconfidence. Other parts of the discussion focus on preferences that arise in social contexts: altruism, fairness and how they together generate trust in markets.

4.1.1. *Loss Aversion*

Approximately 200 years before Kahneman and Tversky (1979) identified the regularity in choices that has come to be known as "loss aversion," Adam Smith (1759 [1981], III, *ii*, 176–177) displayed an acute awareness of loss-aversion as an experiential phenomenon: "Pain...is, in almost all cases, a more pungent sensation than the opposite and correspondent pleasure. The one almost always depresses us much more below the ordinary, or what may be called the natural state of our happiness, than the other ever raises us above it." Smith also drew attention to what behavioral economists would now refer to as the *underweighting of opportunity costs relative to out-of-pocket costs*. Smith (II, ii, *ii*, 121) notes that "breach of property, therefore, theft and robbery, which take from us what we are possessed of, are greater crimes than breach of contract, which only disappoints us of what we expected."[2]

Modern research has produced a wealth of evidence from human behavior supporting both of these effects, and Capuchin monkeys also exhibit loss-aversion (Chen, Lakshminarayanan and Santos, 2005). Brain imaging technology has shown that that losses and gains are processed in different regions of the brain (O'Doherty, Kringelback, Rolls, Hornak and Andrews, 2001), suggesting that gains and losses may be processed in qualitatively different ways. Moreover, a body of literature has shown that when loss aversion is combined with narrow bracketing of decisions—the tendency to take decisions one at a time without considering the big picture—its effects are evident in asset returns (Benartzi and Thaler, 1997), labor supply (Camerer, Babcock, Loewenstein and Thaler, 1997), the reluctance to sell losing stocks and houses (Odean, 1998; Genesove and Mayer, 2001) and large gaps between buying and selling prices (Kahneman, Knetsch and Thaler, 1990).

4.1.2. *Intertemporal Choice and Self-Control*

Intertemporal choice offers a straightforward application of Smith's dual process model. Smith (1759 [1981], IV, *ii*, 273) viewed the passions as largely myopic: "The pleasure which we are to enjoy ten years hence, interests us so little in comparison with that which we may enjoy to-day, the passion which the first excites, is naturally so weak in comparison with that violent emotion which the second is apt to give occasion to, that the one could never be any balance to the other, unless it was supported by the sense of propriety." "The spectator," in contrast, "does not feel the solicitations of our present appetites. To him the pleasure which we are to enjoy a week hence, or a year hence, is just as interesting as that which we are to enjoy this moment" (IV, *ii*, 272).

The struggle between the myopic passions and farsighted impartial spectator appears later in behavioral economics in the form of a "doer" and "planner" in Shefrin and Thaler (1981; see also Benabou and Pyciak, 2002;

---

[2] Thaler (1980), who first drew attention to the underweighting of opportunity costs relative to out-of-pocket costs, attributes it to loss aversion; opportunity costs are treated as foregone gains, rather than as losses.

Bernheim and Rangel, 2002). What are now called "quasi-hyperbolic discounting models" (Laibson, 1997), in a similar spirit, have also been used by Angeletos, Laibson, Tobacman, Repetto and Weinberg (2001) to study life cycle saving, by O'Donoghue and Rabin (1999) to study life cycle temptation and by Ashraf, Karlan and Yin (2004) to study demand for committed savings in the Philippines.[3] Moreover, recent research in which decisionmakers' brains were scanned while they made intertemporal choices vindicates Smith's view that decisions that provide the potential for pleasures that we may enjoy today activate emotional regions of the brain in a way that decisions involving only delayed outcomes do not (McClure, Laibson, Loewenstein and Cohen, 2004).

4.1.3. Overconfidence

Adam Smith (1776, I, x, 1) wrote about the "over-weening conceit which the greater part of men have of their own abilities," a pattern of judgment that influences preferences over risky choices. According to Smith, "the chance of gain is by every man more or less over-valued, and the chance of loss is by most men under-valued, and by scarce any man, who is in tolerable health and spirits, valued more than it is worth."

Smith's "overweening conceit" reappears in modern behavioral economics in the form of executive "hubris" that motivates the failure of so many mergers (Roll, 1986) and other business failures (Camerer and Lovallo, 1999) and can be derived theoretically from evolutionary considerations (Waldman, 1993; Compte and Postelwaite, 2005). Moreover, Smith's caveat that overconfidence only applies to those in "tolerable health and spirits" anticipates modern studies showing that people who are *not* in tolerable health and spirits—specifically, the clinically depressed—are the exceptional ones among us who are *not* optimistic wishful thinkers (for example, Taylor and Brown, 1994).

4.1.4. Altruism

Judging from the extensive treatment that Adam Smith gave to sympathy in *The Theory of Moral Sentiments*, he viewed it as one of the more important passions. However, he also viewed sympathy as an extremely unreliable guide to moral behavior, sometimes falling short and sometimes exceeding what is morally required.

---

[3] Using the terms of Laibson (1997), these are sometimes called $\beta - \delta$ discounting models. Mapped roughly onto Smith's terms, β is the weight on all future outcomes, so that $1/\beta$ represents the relative strength of the passions that prefer immediate rewards, and δ is a conventional discount rate. Smith's passage above suggests that the impartial spectator uses $\delta = 1$.

Smith argued that natural sympathy often falls short of what is morally justified by mass misery. In one evocative passage he noted the striking lack of sympathy that a resident of Europe would be likely to experience if an earthquake eliminated the population of China. After expressing "very strongly his sorrow for the misfortune of that unhappy people," Smith (1759 [1981], III, *iii*, 192–193) commented, such an individual would likely "pursue his business or his pleasure, take his repose or his diversion, with the same ease and tranquility as if no such accident had happened. . . . If he was to lose his little finger to morrow, he would not sleep to-night; but, provided he never saw them, he will snore with the most profound security over the ruin of a hundred millions of his brethren." Although modern media may help to bring vivid images of distant tragedies into people's homes (like the 2004 Indian Ocean tsunami), thus reducing social distance, such imagery does so in a highly selective fashion that only amplifies Smith's concerns. Recent incidents caught on videotape capture the public's sympathies, but more serious problems that society may have adapted to, or that don't lend themselves to vivid imagery, are as likely as they were in Smith's time to elicit a paucity of sympathy.

In other cases, Smith believed that people experience sympathy that is completely out of proportion to the plight of the individual one feels sympathetic toward. "We sometimes feel for another, a passion of which he himself seems to be altogether incapable," Smith (1759 [1981], I, i, *i*, 7–8) wrote. "What are the pangs of a mother, when she hears the moanings of her infant, that, during the agony of disease, cannot express what it feels? In her idea of what it suffers, she joins, to its real helplessness, her own consciousness of that helplessness, and her own terrors for the unknown consequences of its disorder; and out of all these, forms, for her own sorrow, the most complete image of misery and distress. The infant, however, feels only the uneasiness of the present instant, which can never be great." Smith adds dryly that "we sympathize even with the dead," who themselves experience nothing.

If humans were under the control of their passions, one could expect to observe extreme callousness alternating with remarkable generosity, with little logic or consistency governing the transitions. This tendency is manifested in the "identifiable victim effect," in which people sympathize more with a known victim than with a statistical likelihood that a not-yet-known person is likely to become a victim (Schelling, 1984; Small and Loewenstein, 2003). In the political economy, fluctuations in sympathy probably influence public policies, creating huge inconsistencies in the implicit value that different policies place on saving a human life (Tengs and Graham, 1996).

Controlled economics experiments show some fluctuations in expressed sympathy, too. For example, in "dictator game" experiments, people simply divide a known sum of money between themselves and another person.

Absent any knowledge about the target recipient, people offer an average of 20 percent (offers of nothing and half are most common; Camerer, 2003, chapter 2). When dictators know the recipient is the Red Cross, rather than a fellow student, the average allocation doubles (Eckel and Grossman, 1996). When the recipient stands up and gives a few facts about him- or herself, the average amount given goes up to half and the variance increases—as if dictator givers generally sympathize when they know a little about somebody, but also make snap character judgments of who is deserving and who is not (Bohnet and Frey, 1999).

These fluctuations in sympathy are moderated, according to Smith, by the impartial spectator. Returning to the case of devastation in China, Smith (1759 [1981], III, *iii*, 192) asks whether his representative European would be willing to "sacrifice the lives of a hundred millions of his brethren" to save the injury to his little finger. Smith concludes that the answer is "No": "Human nature startles with horror at the thought, and the world, in its greatest depravity and corruption, never produced such a villain as could be capable of entertaining it." The impartial spectator recognizes (194) that "we are but one of the multitude, in no respect better than any other in it."

4.1.5. *Fairness*

Although Smith viewed altruism as a somewhat erratic force, he believed that other motivations played a more reliable civilizing role. Chief among these was fairness. Smith (1759 [1981], II, ii, *iii*, 125) writes: "Nature has implanted in the human breast, that consciousness of ill-desert, those terrors of merited punishment which attend upon its violation, as the great safe-guards of the association of mankind, to protect the weak, to curb the violent, and to chastise the guilty." Smith believed this natural sentiment toward fairness was the source of the virtue of justice, which he saw as the "main pillar that upholds the whole edifice. If it is removed, the great, the immense fabric of human society . . . must in a moment crumble to atoms." Moreover, Smith (129) viewed the desire for justice as something primal: "All men, even the most stupid and unthinking, abhor fraud, perfidy, and injustice, and delight to see them punished. But few men have reflected upon the necessity of justice to the existence of society, how obvious soever that necessity may appear to be."

Modern research suggests that an innate concern for fairness extends even beyond humans to other primates. Capuchin monkeys will reject small rewards when they see other monkeys they perceive as undeserving getting more than they do (Brosnan and de Waal, 2002). Cotton-top tamarins will pull a lever to give marshmallows (which tamarins love) to other tamirins who have altruistically rewarded them with marshmallows in earlier lever-pulls more often then they will pull levers to tamarins who were not previously altruistic (Hauser, Chen, Chen and Chang, 2003).

The impartial spectator plays an essential role in fairness, by causing individuals to internalize other people's sense of fairness. Smith (1759 [1981], III, iii, 195) argues: "There is no commonly honest man who does not dread the inward disgrace of such an action."

4.1.6. *Altruism, Fairness and Market Interactions*

Market interactions require, as Boulding (1969, p. 5) points out, "a minimum degree of benevolence, even in exchange, without which it cannot be legitimated and cannot operate as a social organizer." Arrow (1974) also notes the importance of trust as a lubricant of exchange, economizing on the costs of gathering information about trading partners. For Adam Smith, a mixture of concern about fairness (enforced by the fear of negative appraisal by the impartial spectator) and altruism played an essential role in market interactions, allowing trust, repeated transactions and material gains to occur.

Smith described the beginnings of market exchange thus: "in a nation of hunters, if any one has a talent for making bows and arrows better than his neighbours he will at first make presents of them, and in return get presents of their game. By continuing this practice he will live better than before and will have no occasion to provide for himself, as the surplus of his own labor does it more effectually" (Smith, 1762–1763 [1976a], p. 220).

As Jeffrey Young (1997, p. 62) remarks, "[T]he other regarding principles of human nature which bind people together in society are a necessary condition for the emergence of the exchange of surplus produce amongst neighbours. Smith uses the moral side of human nature to help him explain why voluntary agreement and not violence takes place when these two hunters meet."

In experiments, norms of positive reciprocity often create trust where it has no business flourishing (according to the textbook view that emphasizes moral hazard when contracts are incomplete)—among strangers in one-shot transactions. For example, in simple "trust game" experiments, subjects decide how much money to put in a mailbox, and their investment is tripled (representing a socially productive return). A second subject takes the tripled money out and can keep it all, or repay some to the original investor. Most experiments show that the second subject *does* repay money, even in one-shot games that control for anonymity, and they typically repay just enough to make the investment worthwhile (Berg, Dickhaut and McCabe, 1995; Camerer, 2003, chapter 2). Experiments run in Russia, South Africa and the United States showed that many trustors do not even expect to make money, but are motivated to "invest" by pure "warm-glow" altruism (Ashraf, Bohnet and Piankov, 2003). Simple models that incorporate a preference for fairness

95

or equality have been developed and applied to a broad range of games (Rabin, 1993; in this journal, Fehr and Gächter, 2000).

Furthermore, trust, as measured in simple surveys, is strongly correlated with economic growth (Knack and Keefer, 1997) (though the direction of causality is unknown). An anthropology experiment involving 15 small-scale societies found that in societies in which people buy and sell more often in markets, offers in ultimatum bargaining games are, perhaps surprisingly, closer to equal sharing than in less market intensive societies (Henrich, Boyd, Bowles, Gintis, Fehr and Camerer, 2004).[4] Adam Smith would not be surprised by the finding that markets are often built on motivations of fairness, altruism and trust—rather than on self-interest alone—yet this mixture of motivations remains a challenge to the modern economics profession.

4.2. Consumption and Its Discontents

In *The Theory of Moral Sentiments*, Smith argues that much economic activity is the product of a forecasting error—people's illusion that acquiring wealth, possessions and status will make them permanently happy. In fact, Smith (1759 [1981], III, *iii*, 209) argued, both pleasure and pain are often transient: "By the constitution of human nature, agony can never be permanent." Following a calamity, he noted, a person "soon comes, without any effort, to enjoy his ordinary tranquility." Smith further observed that people not only adapt quickly to circumstances, but underestimate such adaptation and, as a result, often overestimate the duration of happy and sad feelings:

A man with a wooden leg suffers, no doubt, and foresees that he must continue to suffer during the remainder of his life, a very considerable inconveniency. He soon comes to view it, however, exactly as every impartial spectator views it; as an inconveniency under which he can enjoy all the ordinary pleasures both of solitude and of society. . . . He no longer weeps, he no longer laments, he no longer grieves over it, as a weak man may sometimes do in the beginning.

Considerable modern research backs up Smith's contentions. For example, Frederick and Loewenstein (1999) review diverse lines of research showing that ongoing conditions, such as health problems, incarceration, poverty

---

[4] An "ultimatum game" has two players. The first player is given a sum of money. The player is instructed to offer some share of that money to the second player. If the second player accepts the division, then both players keep the money. If the second player rejects the division, both players receive zero. In a one-shot play of the game, if players are rational and self-interested, then the first player should offer the second player only a minimal amount, which the second player will accept because it is better than nothing. But when the game is actually played, small offers are commonly rejected (even for high stakes), and even in a one-shot game, it is common for the first player to offer a 50:50 split of the original stake. For expositions of the ultimatum game in this journal, see Thaler (1988) and Camerer and Thaler (1995).

and wealth have little long-term impact on subjective well-being. Indeed, Smith's example of the man with a wooden leg foreshadows a classic study by Brickman, Coates and Janoff-Bulman (1978) showing that the happiness of paraplegics and lottery winners tends to revert surprisingly close to a normal baseline after their respectively tragic and wonderful life-changing events.

Perhaps even more important for economics than the fact that people adapt to ongoing conditions is the equally well documented finding that people are generally unaware of the extent to which they will adapt. A large body of contemporary psychological research suggests that people typically believe that pleasure and pain will last longer than they actually do (for example, Wilson and Gilbert, 2003; and Loewenstein, O'Donoghue and Rabin, 2003, for a summary of research on this point and discussion of implications for economics). Smith (1759 [1981], IV, I, 259) anticipated both points in *The Theory of Moral Sentiments*. Anticipating later findings documenting adaptation to material conditions, he expresses skepticism about the pleasure derived from possessions: "How many people ruin themselves by laying out money on trinkets of frivolous utility?" And he also devotes numerous pages of *The Theory of Moral Sentiments* to describing ways in which the anticipation of status gained was much better than the realization. Only at the end of life, when it was too late to remedy the situation, did Smith believe that the wealthy come to recognize the folly of their ways—the paucity of pleasure they derive from all the goods they struggled so hard to procure (1759 [1981], IV, *i*, 260–261):

Through the whole of his life he pursues the idea of a certain artificial and elegant repose which he may never arrive at, for which he sacrifices a real tranquility that is at all times in his power, and which, if in the extremity of old age he should at last attain to it, he will find to be in no respect preferable to that humble security and contentment which he had abandoned for it. It is then, in the last dregs of life, his body wasted with toil and disease, his mind galled and ruffled by the memory of a thousand injuries and disappointments which he imagines he has met with from the injustice of his enemies, or from the perfidy and ingratitude of his friends, that he begins at last to find that wealth and greatness are mere trinkets of frivolous utility, no more adapted for procuring ease of body or tranquility of mind, than the tweezer-cases of the lover of toys.

Smith would have done well to heed his own advice. He worked himself so sick in drafting *The Wealth of Nations* that in 1773, he sent David Hume a letter making Hume his literary executor in case he should die before publishing his manuscripts (though as it turned out, Smith outlived Hume by 14 years).

Because the rich pursue ends that fail to make them happy, Smith (1759 [1981], IV, *i*, 265) believed that they end up being no more happy than the poor: "In ease of body and peace of mind, all the different ranks of life are really upon a level, and the beggar, who suns himself by the side of the highway, possesses that security which kings are fighting for" and "in what constitutes the real happiness of human life, [the poor] are in no respect inferior to those who would seem so much above them." Indeed, a large body of modern research on the determinants of happiness has quite consistently found surprisingly weak connections between happiness and wealth or income, especially over time or across countries (Easterlin, 1974; Diener, and Biswas-Diener, 2002; Frey and Stutzer, 2002).

Yet while believing that consumption of goods, as well as wealth and greatness, all provide only "frivolous utility," Smith believed that the productivity of market economy is driven by this "deception"—the misguided belief that wealth brings happiness. As Smith (1759 [1981], IV, i, 263–264) notes, "[I]t is this deception which rouses and keeps in continual motion the industry of mankind. It is this which first prompted them to cultivate the ground, to build houses, to found cities and commonwealths, and to invent and improve all the sciences and arts, which ennoble and embellish human life; which have entirely changed the whole face of the globe."

Indeed, Adam Smith even invokes the "invisible hand"—a term that may be the the most prominent legacy of his work, although it occurs only once in *The Wealth of Nations* and only once in *The Theory of Moral Sentiments*— to argue that as the wealthy seek out goods and status that ultimately bring them little pleasure, they inadvertently end up promoting the good of the poor.[5] Here is Smith's invisible hand (1759 [1981], IV, i, 264) in *The Theory of Moral Sentiments*:

In spite of their natural selfishness and rapacity, though they mean only their own conveniency, though the sole end which they propose from the labours of all the thousands whom they employ be the gratification of their own vain and insatiable desires, they divide with the poor the produce of all their improvements. They are led by an invisible hand to make nearly the same distribution of the necessities of life which would have been made had the earth been divided into equal portions among all inhabitants; and thus, without intending it, without knowing it, advance the interest of the society.

While perhaps overstating the case, when Smith refers to the equitable distribution of the necessities of life he is arguing that the distribution of things that actually bring happiness to people is far more equitable than the distribution of tweezer-cases and other "trinkets of frivolous utility." That the things that really matter for happiness are more equitably distributed than those that don't may help to explain why cross-sectional differences in income seem to bring such small increments in happiness.

---

[5] For discussion in this journal of the context for the "invisible hand" in *The Wealth of Nations*, see Persky (1989). For a discussion in this journal of the "invisible hand" in the context of *The Theory of Moral Sentiments* and Adam Smith's ethical system, see Evensky (1993).

4.3. Unexploited Ideas

Adam Smith's *Theory of Moral Sentiments* is not only packed with insights that presage developments in contemporary behavioral economics, but also with promising leads that have yet to be pursued. Here we enumerate four of them: (1) the desire to be well-regarded by posterity; (2) negative reactions to being misjudged; (3) mistaken belief in the objectivity of tastes; and (4) sympathy for the great and rich.

A *desire to be well regarded by posterity* certainly drives the efforts of many creative professionals—artists, writers, architects and academic economists. As Smith (1759 [1981], I, *ii*, 169) comments, "Men have voluntarily thrown away life to acquire after death a renown which they could no longer enjoy. Their imagination, in the meantime, anticipated that fame which was in future times to be bestowed upon them." A concern for one's reputation to posterity might be thought of as reserved for the richest and most powerful members of society, such as those whose names adorn buildings in universities and hospitals, but it is not limited to the rich. Economists have studied the bequest motive, which is no doubt partly fueled by this motive, but they have not yet explored what may be more potent effects of posterity on current decisions.

Economics generally assumes that people care about outcomes, not about the source of outcomes. However, Adam Smith pointed out that people have *negative reactions to being misjudged* that go beyond the outcome. Smith (1759 [1981], III, *ii*, 174) drew special attention to one particular situation—that of "unmerited reproach," which, he noted, "is frequently capable of mortifying very severely even men of more than ordinary constancy.... An innocent man, brought to the scaffold by the false imputation of an infamous or odious crime, suffers the most cruel misfortune which it is possible for innocence to suffer." Research on "procedural justice" shows a substantial concern for whether a trial was fair, for example, as well as for the outcome of the trial (Lind and Tyler, 1988). One study showed that the propensity to file wrongful-termination lawsuits after firing is correlated with workers' perceptions of whether their firing was just (controlling for expected payoffs from litigation; Lind, Greenberg, Scott and Welchans, 2000). This insight has interesting implications for principal-agent theory. Smith's insights suggest that goodwill could be seriously eroded if a principal penalizes an agent who produced a low level of output due to bad luck rather than poor effort.

Ample evidence—beginning with the huge cross-cultural differences in tastes for food—suggests that tastes are subjective, based on culture, familiarity and so on. However, Smith argued that people underestimate such influences, having instead a *mistaken belief in objectivity of tastes*. Smith (1759 [1981], V, *i*) commented, "[F]ew men...are willing to allow, that custom or fashion have much influence upon their judgments concerning what is beautiful," and they "imagine that all the rules which they think ought to be observed in each of them are founded upon reason and nature, not upon habit or prejudice." Ross and Ward (1996) refer to the tendency for people to think their own tastes and beliefs are more legitimate and more widely shared than they really are as naive realism. Naive realism has potentially important implications for a variety of economic issues: gift-giving; negotiations in which both parties are likely to think that their own preferences are shared by the other side more than they are; principal-agent situations in which the principal has to set rewards for the agent; and sales and marketing (Davis, Hoch and Ragsdale, 1986). It can also lead to cultural conflict. If those in one society believe that eating monkey is *inherently* disgusting, then we are likely to disparage monkey-eaters, rather than treating the tastes of those who disagree as akin to tastes for opera or smelly cheese.

Finally, contrary to the sensible notion that one should sympathize with those less fortunate than oneself, Smith (1759 [1981], iii, *ii*, 72–73) argued that there is a natural tendency to experience *sympathy for the great and rich*:

When we consider the condition of the great, in those delusive colours in which the imagination is apt to paint it, it seems to be almost the abstract idea of a perfect and happy state. It is the very state which, in all our waking dreams and idle reveries, we had sketched out to ourselves as the final object of all our desires. We feel, therefore, a peculiar sympathy with the satisfaction of those who are in it. We favour all their inclinations, and forward all their wishes. What pity, we think, that any thing should spoil and corrupt so agreeable a situation! It is the misfortunes of kings only which afford the proper subjects for tragedy.

Smith's description recalls the outpouring of grief after the accidental deaths of Princess Diana and John F. Kennedy Jr. Popular Magazines like *People* and *US*, and similar highly rated TV shows, are filled with stories about where athletes and stars shop, what they eat and wear and the ups and downs of their love lives. Fascination with celebrity of this sort also has a direct economic effect through the use of celebrities as marketing vehicles.

Smith believed both that this sympathy for the rich was a form of corruption based on a moral mistake, and also that it provided an important underpinning for social stability. Smith (1759 [1981], I, iii, *iii*, 84) described the moral mistake in this way: "[T]hat wealth and greatness are often regarded with the respect and admiration which are due only to wisdom and virtue; and that the contempt, of which vice and folly are the only proper objects, is most unjustly bestowed upon poverty and weaknesses, has been the complaint of moralists in all ages." Indeed, Smith further argued that the "disposition to admire, and almost to worship, the rich and the powerful, and to despise, or at least, to neglect, persons of poor and mean condition ... is ... the great and most universal cause of the corruption of our moral sentiments." However, Smith also held that this sympathy was "necessary both to establish and to maintain the distinction of ranks and the order of society." This sympathy for the rich may help to explain one of the puzzles of capitalism: the failure of the majority democratic societies to impose extremely high taxes on the richest members. Smith's perspective suggests the possibility that people don't want to tax the rich not because they expect to become rich themselves, as some have suggested, but because average citizens don't want to "spoil and corrupt" what they perceive as the "agreeable situation" of the rich!

4.4. Conclusion

Adam Smith's actors in *The Theory of Moral Sentiments* are driven by an internal struggle between their impulsive, fickle and indispensable passions, and the impartial spectator. They weigh out-of-pocket costs more than opportunity costs, have self-control problems and are overconfident. They display erratic patterns of sympathy, but are consistently concerned about fairness and justice. They are motivated more by ego than by any kind of direct pleasure from consumption and, though they don't anticipate it, ultimately derive little pleasure from either. In short, Adam Smith's world is not inhabited by dispassionate rational purely self-interested agents, but rather by multidimensional and realistic human beings.

■ *Thanks to Kim Border for an apt Adam Smith quotation; to Eric Angner, James Hines, Jesse Shapiro, Jeremy Tobacman, Timothy Taylor and Michael Waldman for helpful comments; and to Ed Glaeser and Andrei Shleifer for encouragement.*

References

Angeletos, George-Marios, David Laibson, Jeremy Tobacman, Andrea Repetto and Stephen Weinberg. 2001. "The Hyperbolic Consumption Model: Calibration, Simulation, and Empirical Evaluation." *Journal of Economic Perspective*. 15:3, pp. 47–68.

Arrow, Kenneth. 1974. *The Limits of Organisation*. New York: Norton.

Ashraf, Nava, Iris Bohnet and Nikita Piankov. 2003. "Is Trust a Bad Investment?" Kennedy School of Government Working Paper No. 03-047, November.

Ashraf, Nava, Dean Karlan and Wesley Yin. 2004. "Tying Odysseus to the Mast: Evidence from a Commitment Savings Product in the Philippines." Mimeo.

Bénabou, Roland and Marek Pyciak. 2002. "Dynamic Inconsistency and Self-Control: A Planner-Doer Interpretation." *Economics Letters*. 77:3, pp. 419–424.

Benartzi Shlomo and Richard Thaler. 1997. "Myopic Loss Aversion and the Equity Premium Puzzle." *Quarterly Journal of Economics.* 110:1, pp. 73–92.

Benhabib, Jess and Alberto Bisin. Forthcoming. "Self-Control and Consumption-Savings Decisions: Cognitive Perspectives." *Games and Economic Behavior.*

Berg, Joyce, John Dickhaut and Kevin A. McCabe. 1995. "Trust, Reciprocity, and Social History." *Games and Economic Behavior.* 10:1, pp. 290–307.

Bernheim, Douglas and Antonio Rangel. 2004. "Addiction and Cue-Triggered Decision Processes." *American Economic Review.* 94:5, pp. 1558–1590.

Bohnet, Iris and Bruno Frey. 1999. "The Sound of Silence in Prisoner's Dilemma and Dictator Games." *Journal of Economic Behavior and Organization.* 38:1, pp. 43–57.

Boulding, Kenneth E. 1969. "Economics as a Moral Science." *American Economic Review.* 59:1, pp. 1–12.

Brickman, Philip, Dan Coates and Ronnie Janoff-Bulman. 1978. "Lottery Winners and Accident Victims: Is Happiness Relative?" *Journal of Personality and Social Psychology.* 36:8, pp. 917–927.

Brosnan, Sarah F. and Frans B. M. de Waal. 2002. "A Proximate Perspective on Reciprocal Altruism." *Human Nature.* 13:1, pp. 129–152.

Camerer, Colin F. 2003. *Behavioral Game Theory: Experiments on Strategic Interaction.* Princeton: Princeton University Press.

Camerer, Colin F. and George Loewenstein. 2004. "Behavioral Economics: Past, Present, Future," in *Advances in Behavioral Economics.* Colin F. Camerer, George Loewenstein and Mathew Rabin, eds. New York: Russell Sage, pp. 3–51.

Camerer, Colin and Dan Lovallo. 1999. "Over-Confidence and Excess Entry: An Experimental Approach." *American Economic Review.* 89:1, pp. 306–318.

Camerer, Colin and Richard Thaler. 1995. "More Dictator and Ultimatum Games." *Journal of Economic Perspectives.* 9:2, pp. 209–219.

Camerer, Colin F., Linda Babcock, George Loewenstein and Richard Thaler. 1997. "Labor Supply of New York City Cab Drivers: One Day at a Time." *Quarterly Journal of Economics.* May, 111, pp. 408–441.

Chen, M. Keith, Venkat Lakshminarayanan and Laurie Santos. 2005. "The Evolution of Our Preferences: Evidence from Capuchin Monkey Trading Behavior." Working paper, Yale; Available at ⟨http://www.som.yale.edu/Faculty/keith.chen/papers/LossAversionDraft.pdf⟩.

Damasio, Antonio R. 1994. *Descartes' Error: Emotion, Reason, and the Human Brain.* New York: Putnam.

Davis, Harry L., Steven J. Hoch and E. K. Easton Ragsdale. 1986. "An Anchoring and Adjustment Model of Spousal Predictions." *Journal of Consumer Research.* 13:1, pp. 25–37.

Diener, Edward and R. Biswas-Diener. 2002. "Will Money Increase Subjective Well-Being?" *Social Indicators Research.* 57:2, pp. 119–169.

Easterlin, Richard. 1974. "Does Economic Growth Improve the Human Lot?" in *Nations and Households in Economic Growth: Essays in Honor of Moses Abramovitz.* Paul A. David and Melvin W. Reder, eds. New York: Academic Press, pp. 89–125.

Eckel, Catherine and Philip Grossman. 1996. "Altruism in Anonymous Dictator Games." *Games and Economic Behavior.* 16:2, pp. 181–191.

Evensky, Jerry. 1993. "Retrospectives: Ethics and the Invisible Hand." Spring, 7:2, pp. 197–205.

Fehr, Ernst and Simon Gächter. 2000. "Fairness and Retaliation: The Economics of Reciprocity." *Journal of Economic Perspectives*. 14:3, pp. 159–181.

Frey, Bruno and Alois Stutzer. 2002. "What Can Economists Learn from Happiness Research?" *Journal of Economic Literature*. 40:2, pp. 402–435.

Fudenberg, Drew and David Levine. 2004. "A Dual Self Model of Impulse Control." Working paper, February.

Genesove, David and Christopher Mayer. 2001. "Loss Aversion and Seller Behavior: Evidence from the Housing Market. *Quarterly Journal of Economics*. 116:4, pp. 1233–1260.

Grampp, William. 1948. "Adam Smith and the Economic Man." *Journal of Political Economy*. 56:4, pp. 315–336.

Heifetz, A. and Yossi Spiegel. 2000. "On the Evolutionary Emergence of Optimism." Discussion Paper No. 1304, Northwestern University, Center for Mathematical Studies in Economics and Management Science.

Henrich, Joseph, Robert Boyd, Samuel Bowles, Herbert Gintis, Ernst Fehr and Colin Camerer. 2004. *Foundations of Human Sociality: Ethnography and Experiments in 15 Small-Scale Societies*. Oxford University Press.

Hauser, Marc D., M. Keith Chen, Frances Chen and Emmeline Chang. 2003. "Give Unto Others: Genetically Unrelated Cotton-Top Tamarin Monkeys Preferentially Give Food to Those Who Altruistically Give Food Back." *Proceedings of the Royal Society B*. 270, pp. 2363–2370.

Kahneman, Daniel and Amos Tversky. 1979. "Prospect Theory: An Analysis of Decision Under Risk." *Econometrica*. 47:2, pp. 263–291.

Kahneman, Daniel, Jack L. Knetsch and Richard Thaler. 1990. "Experimental Tests of the Endowment Effect and the Coase Theorem. *Journal of Political Economy*. 98:6, pp. 1325–1348.

Kirkpatrick, Lee A. and Seymour Epstein. 1992. "Cognitive-Experiential Self-Theory and Subjective Probability: Further Evidence for Two Conceptual Systems." *Journal of Personality and Social Psychology*. 63:4, pp. 534–544.

Knack, Stephen and Philip Keefer. 1997. "Does Social Capital Have an Economic Payoff? A Cross-Country Investigation." *Quarterly Journal of Economics*. 112:4, pp. 1251–1288.

Laibson, David. 1997. "Golden Eggs and Hyperbolic Discounting." *Quarterly Journal of Economics*. 112:2, pp. 443–477.

LeDoux, Joseph E. 1996. *The Emotional Brain: The Mysterious Underpinnings of Emotional Life*. New York, N.Y.: Simon & Schuster.

Lind, E. Allen and Thomas R. Tyler. 1988. *The Social Psychology of Procedural Justice*. New York: Plenum Press.

Lind, E. Allen, Jerald Greenberg, Kimberly Scott and Thomas Welchans. 2000. "The Winding Road from Employee to Complainant: Situational and Psychological Determinants of Wrongful-Termination Claims." *Administrative Science Quarterly*. 45:3, pp. 557–590.

Loewenstein, George, Ted O'Donoghue and Matthew Rabin. 2003. "Projection Bias in Predicting Future Utility." *Quarterly Journal of Economics*. 118, pp. 1209–1248.

Loewenstein, George and Ted O'Donoghue. 2004. "Animal Spirits: Affective and Deliberative Influences on Economic Behavior." Working paper, Department of Social and Decision Sciences, Carnegie Mellon University; Available at ⟨http://papers. ssrn.com/sol3/papers.cfm?abstract_id=539843⟩.

McClure, Sam, David Laibson, George Loewenstein and Jonathan Cohen. 2004. "Separate Neural Systems Value Immediate and Delayed Monetary Rewards." *Science.* 304:5695, pp. 503–507.

Meardon, Stephen and Andreas Ortmann. 1996. "Self-Command in Adam Smith's *Theory of Moral Sentiments:* A Game-Theoretic Re-Interpretation." *Rationality and Society.* 8:1, pp. 57–80.

Metcalf, Janet and Walter Mischel. 1999. "A Hot/Cool-System Analysis of Delay of Gratification: Dynamics of Willpower." *Psychological Review.* 106:1, pp. 3–19.

Odean, Terrance. 1998. "Are Investors Reluctant to Realize their Losses?" *Journal of Finance.* 53:5, pp. 1775–1798.

O'Doherty J., M. L. Kringelbach, E. T. Rolls, J. Hornak and C. Andrews. 2001. "Abstract Reward and Punishment Representations in the Human Orbitofrontal Cortex." *Nature Neuroscience.* 4:1, pp. 95–102.

O'Donoghue, Ted and Matthew Rabin. 1999. "Doing It Now or Doing It Later." *American Economic Review.* 89:1, pp. 103–121.

Panksepp, Jaak. 1998. *Affective Neuroscience.* Oxford: Oxford University Press.

Persky, Joseph. 1989. "Retrospectives: Adam Smith's Invisible Hands." *Journal of Economic Perspectives.* Fall, 3:4, pp. 195–201.

Postlewaite, Andrew and Olivier Compte. 2005. "Confidence Enhanced Performance." *American Economic Review.* 94:5, pp. 1536–1557.

Rabin, Matthew. 1993. "Incorporating Fairness into Game Theory and Economics." *American Economic Review.* 83:5, pp. 1281–1302.

Raphael, David D. and Alec Macfie. 1976. "Introduction," in their edition of Adam Smith, *The Theory of Moral Sentiments.* London: Oxford University Press.

Roll, Richard. 1986. "The Hubris Hypothesis of Corporate Takeovers." *Journal of Business.* 59:2, pp. 197–216.

Ross, Lee and Andrew Ward. 1996. "Naive Realism in Everyday Life: Implications for Social Conflict and Misunderstanding," in *Values and Knowledge.* T. Brown, E. Reed and E. Turiel, eds. Mahwah, N.J.: Lawrence Erlbaum Associates, Inc., pp. 103–136.

Shane, Frederick and George Loewenstein. 1999. "Hedonic Adaptation," in *Well-Being: The Foundations of Hedonic Psychology.* Daniel Kahneman, Edward Diener and Norbert Schwarz, eds. New York: Russell Sage Foundation Press, pp. 302–329.

Shefrin, Hersh M. and Richard H. Thaler. 1981. "An Economic Theory of Self-Control." *Journal of Political Economy.* April, 89:2, pp. 392–406.

Sloman, Steven A. 1996. "The Empirical Case for Two Systems of Reasoning." *Psychological Bulletin.* 119:1, pp. 3–22.

Small, Deborah A. and George Loewenstein. 2003. "Helping *a* Victim or Helping *the* Victim: Altruism and Identifiability." *Journal of Risk and Uncertainty.* 26:1, pp. 5–16.

Smith, Adam. 1759 [1981]. *The Theory of Moral Sentiments.* D. D. Raphael and A. L. Macfie, eds. Liberty Fund: Indianapolis.

Smith, Adam. 1762–1763 [1976a]. *Lectures on Jurisprudence.* R. L. Meek, D. D. Raphael and A. L. Macfie, eds. Oxford: Clarendon Press.

Smith, Adam. 1776 [1981]. *An Inquiry into the Nature and Causes of the Wealth of Nations, Volumes I and II*. R. H. Campbell and A. S. Skinner, eds. Liberty Fund: Indianopolis.

Smith, Vernon L. 1998. "The Two Faces of Adam Smith." *Southern Economic Journal*. 65:1, pp. 2–19.

Taylor, Shelly E. and Jonathon D. Brown. 1994. "Positive Illusions and Well-Being Revisited: Separating Fact from Fiction." *Psychological Bulletin*. 116, pp. 21–27.

Tengs, Tammy O. and John D. Graham. 1996. "The Opportunity Costs of Haphazard Social Investments in Life-Saving," in *Risks, Costs and Lives Saved*. Robert W. Hahn, ed. New York: Oxford University Press, pp. 167–179.

Thaler, Richard. 1980. "Toward a Positive Theory of Consumer Choice." *Journal of Economic Behavior and Organization*. 1:1, pp. 39–60.

Thaler, Richard. 1988. "The Ultimatum Game." *Journal of Economic Perspectives*. Fall, 2:4, pp. 195–206.

Waldman, Michael. 1994. "Systematic Errors and the Theory of Natural Selection." *American Economic Review*. 84:3, pp. 482–497.

Wilson, Timothy D. and Daniel T. Gilbert. 2003. "Affective Forecasting," in *Advances in Experimental Social Psychology*. Mark Zanna, ed. New York: Elsevier, pp. 345–411.

Young, Jeffrey T. 1997. *Economics as a Moral Science: The Political Economy of Adam Smith*. Cheltenham: Edward Elgar.

5

Experimental Economics from the Vantage-Point of Behavioural Economics

George Loewenstein

This paper was published in 1999, a few years before Daniel Kahneman and Vernon Smith won the 2002 Nobel Prize in economics. Many of us in the field of behavioral economics suspected that a Nobel Prize was in the works for our field, and we worried that it would be jointly conferred on behavioral economics and experimental economics by people who couldn't tell the difference between them. The paper starts by pointing out that behavioral economics and experimental economics are entirely different enterprises. Behavioral economics is the application of insights from psychology (and sometimes other disciplines) to economics. Experimental economics is the application of experimental methods to economics. There is nothing inherent in behavioral economics that favors any particular methodology, and in recent work behavioral economists have employed the full diversity of methods. Similarly, nothing in experimental economics dictates that experiments should be applied to phenomena of interest to behavioral economists, and most experimental economics does not focus on behavioral phenomena. Indeed, among the few experimental economics papers that do focus on behavioral phenomena many are implicitly or even explicitly antagonistic toward behavioral economics. There is actually a long history in experimental economics of designing experiments designed to make inconvenient behavioral effects disappear through the introduction of, for example, market forces, feedback and stationary replication over large numbers of trials. Notwithstanding that some behavioral economists also practice experimental economics, and that both are on the fringe of the discipline, the two fields are wholly distinct. But that—and this paper—didn't prevent the Nobel committee from granting experimental and behavioral economics a joint prize.

Besides the illogical combination of recipients, the Nobel prize that year had other surprising features. Specifically, most people probably don't realize that, on occasion, there are *auditions* for the prize. One such audition is reported in Silvia Nassar's brilliant book *A Beautiful Mind*, about John Nash, who won the Nobel prize in 1994. I had the fortune to attend the audition that took place the year before the prize was awarded to Daniel Kahneman and Vernon Smith. The audition was held at a wonderful old-world hotel located on the Swedish coast near Stockholm (though the beauty of the spot was somewhat lost on us in the almost constant darkness of December).

Besides its very occurrence, the conference had many strange dimensions. First, somehow the idea of the Nobel prize seemed to produce performance anxiety even in many who were obviously not contenders, but only, like myself, supporting cast. I knew that this conference was different from others when a close friend and colleague who is universally known as a brilliant public speaker and whom I have never known to prepare for a speaking engagement more than a few days ahead of time, telephoned months before the meeting to ask if I had begun preparing my presentation. Moreover, despite the long period of preparation, he was only one of several who, it seemed to me, did not give the best performances of their careers. The standard economic theory of labor supply assumes that when the incentives are greater people work harder, and when they work harder, they perform better, but there are many patterns of behavior that violate both of these assumptions.[1] In my own experience, if I really care about a public presentation, I get dry mouth and say "um" every other word. If I run into trouble when I'm rock climbing, the fear causes my leg to wobble violently, as if it's powering a manual sewing machine. When I really need to sleep, because I have to be 'on' the following day, I might as well give up before I even start. Not only are we 'strangers to ourselves'—the apt title of a recent book by Timothy Wilson—in many ways we are at war with ourselves.

As I write this, seven years after the original paper was published, the uneasy relationship between behavioral and experimental economics continues. On

---

[1] The assumption that greater incentives produce greater effort is violated in at least three situations. One is when people are already intrinsically motivated to do a task, and the introduction of new incentives 'crowds out' existing incentives (see Gneezy, U. and Rustichini, A. (2003). 'Incentives, Punishment and Behavior', in C. Camerer, G. Loewenstein, and M. Rabin, (eds.), *Advances in Behavioral Economics*. Princeton, NJ: Princeton University Press, NY: Russell Sage Foundation Press. A second is when people have a short-term earnings target, in which case increasing the wage rate can result in a reduction of effort (see Camerer, C., Babcock, L., Loewenstein, G., and Thaler, R. (1997). 'Labor Supply of New York City Taxi Drivers: One Day at a time, *Quarterly Journal of Economics*, 112: 407–41.) A third situation is when people engage in a pattern of behavior that psychologists call 'self-handicapping'; they fail to put in effort when they really care about a task because it enables them to attribute failure to lack of trying rather than to their own incompetence. The assumption that greater effort leads to improved performance, while often valid, is contradicted by research on 'choking under pressure', much of which is reviewed in Ariely, D., Gneezy, U., Loewenstein, G., and Mazar, N. (2005). 'Large Stakes and Big Mistakes'. Available at SSRN: http://ssrn.com/abstract=774986

the one hand, there are new avenues of cooperation: Experimental and behavioral economists have become the main players in the new field of Neuroeconomics (see Chapters 20 and 22). However, some experimentalists have kept behavioral economics in their sights. For example, in a recent paper Charlie Plott reports on an elaborate experiment in which he managed to make the endowment effect—the tendency for people to become attached to, and hence reluctant to part with, objects in their possession—disappear.[2] Although the endowment effect is a robust behavioral phenomenon that has been documented not only in myriad laboratory studies, but in financial and real estate markets and many other real-world settings, Plott concludes from his study that "WTA–WTP gaps do not reflect a fundamental feature of human preferences."

However frustrating and unpleasant such controversies can be, I believe that they often lead to scientific progress. Researchers rarely expose their own findings and ideas to the same critical scrutiny that they expose those of their colleagues to, even when they consciously attempt to do so.[3] Often, it seems to require a researcher who is motivated to discredit an idea—that is, who has an 'ax to grind'—to subject a theory or finding to real critical scrutiny. And my own rule of thumb is to try to retain a skeptical attitude toward theories and findings until they have experienced, and withstood, such an attack. So, while I strongly disagree with Plott's blanket dismissal of the endowment effect, I do think his research may eventually help to identify some, albeit rarified, conditions in which the endowment effect may not occur.[4]

---

[2] Plott, C. R. and Zeiler, K. (2005). 'The Willingness to Pay-Willingness to Accept Gap, the "Endowment Effect," Subject Misconceptions, and Experimental Procedures for Eliciting Valuations', *American Economic Review*, 95(3): 530–45. I speculate that an important reason that he did not observe the effect was that he placed the focal object (a coffee mug) in front of each subjects, giving all subjects the subjective feeling of being endowed.

[3] A useful habit for researchers, and one which I often urge graduate students to adopt, is to attempt to think about whether it would be possible to devise an experiment that would produce results that are opposite to what one's theory predicts. This is a habit that needs to be inculcated because it is not a practice that occurs naturally for most researchers. And, even when one deliberately sets out to do it, coming up with ways to discredit one's own theories is an unpleasant and unnatural mental task.

[4] One interesting situation in which the reverse of the endowment effect may occur is with housing, a phenomenon I observed firsthand. Though I taught negotiations for years, I've always been the world's most pathetic negotiator, and buying our last house was no exception. After making some kind of feeble counteroffer to the seller's asking price, and having it rejected, I rapidly moved up toward the asking price, eventually clinching it in a much shorter interval than would have been the case had I adopted a more dispassionate attitude toward the deal. I should have been aware of what was going on, because Sam Issacharoff had alerted me to it years earlier. When you sell a house, Sam pointed out, not only do you become rapidly reconciled to losing it, but you have an active desire to get it off your hands. When you are in the market for a house, on the other hand, the moment you make an offer you become effectively endowed with the house, and, if the offer is rejected, you feel as if you have lost what's yours. The same effect seems to occur in what is sometimes referred to as "buying fever" in auctions, including internet auctions.

Experimental Economics from the Vantage-Point of Behavioural Economics*

George Loewenstein

As a behavioural economist (an economist who brings psychological insights to bear on economic phenomena), preparing a controversy corner piece criticising experimental economics (the use of experimentation to address economic questions) is like working yourself up to enter the boxing ring against a friend. Experimental economics and behavioural economics have much in common.

Both groups can trace their origins to psychology – psychological theory in one case and experimentation in the other. Both subfields came of age in the last quarter of this century, and have gained growing acceptance within the discipline of economics as measured by almost any criterion: publications in mainstream journals, academic positions in top departments, prominence at meetings, etc. In the current climate it is easy to forget that only 20 years ago the simple fact that an article reported experiments or discussed psychology was regarded by many editors as grounds for summary rejection.

Perhaps more importantly, many behavioural economists (BEs) use economics-style experiments, and some experimental economists (EEs) embrace psychology. Indeed, some researchers would find it difficult to classify themselves into one group or the other, and would be embraced by both groups as one of their own. There is, therefore no *inherent* conflict between the two approaches; indeed, there is good cause for synergistic coexistence. Nevertheless, there is often value in obtaining another field's perspective on

* Thanks to Iris Bohnet, Colin Camerer, Graham Loomes, Drazen Prelec, Matthew Rabin, and Richard Thaler for helpful comments. This comment was completed while the author was visiting the Center for Advanced Study in the Behavioural Sciences, which was supported by NSF grant no. SBR - 960123.

This chapter was originally published as Loewenstein, G. (1999) "Experimental Economics from the Vantage-Point of Behavioural Economics". The Ecomic Journal 109: F25–F34. Reproduced by kind permission of Blackwell Publishing.

what one does. Some EEs have not been particularly reticent about providing BEs with such input (see, e.g., Smith, 1991). In this essay I attempt to return the favour in a small way.

There are, in fact, many differences between the two subfields, the most important of which is one of basic orientation. BEs are methodological eclectics. They define themselves, not on the basis of the research methods that they employ, but rather their application of psychological insights to economics. In recent published research, BEs are as likely to use field research as experimentation (see, e.g., Camerer *et al.*, 1997; Babcock *et al.*, 1996). EEs on the other hand, define themselves on the basis of their endorsement and use of experimentation as a research tool. Consistent with this orientation, EEs have made a major investment in developing novel experimental methods that are suitable for addressing economic issues, and have achieved a virtual consensus among themselves on a number of important methodological issues. As a result, EE experiments share methodological features to a much greater extent than is true of experiments conducted by psychologists. My goal in this essay is to provide some reflections, from the perspective of a psychologically minded economist, on some of these features of EE experiments.

5.1. External Validity

Most empirical research methods textbooks written by psychologists begin with a discussion of the tension between internal and external validity.[1] Internal validity refers to the ability to draw confident causal conclusions from one's research. External validity refers to the ability to generalise from the research context to the settings that the research is intended to approximate. Among psychologists, experiments have the reputation of being high in internal validity but low in external validity, whereas field studies are seen as embodying the opposite characteristics. Field experiments and the quasi-experimental methods developed by psychologists are designed to increase external validity with a minimal sacrifice of the internal validity that is usually associated with experimentation.

My focus in this commentary is on external validity – the dimension on which I believe EE experiments are particularly vulnerable. Many EEs seem to believe that certain features of their experiments, such as the incorporation of market institutions, stationary replication, and carefully controlled incentives, make their experiments immune to the problems of external validity

---

[1] It is a curious fact that undergraduate economics majors, unlike psychology majors, rarely take courses in empirical research methods. As a result, while they may be well-tooled in regression techniques, they are typically at a complete loss when it comes to other aspects of empirical research.

that psychologists lament in their own studies. Indeed, by naming their professional society the "Economic *Science* Association" EEs (deliberately, I believe) make the implicit claim that experimentation is superior on both dimensions – internal *and* external validity – to the field methods that are still more commonly employed by economists.

If the goal of EEs is to represent the behaviour of certain highly structured market settings, such as stock exchanges or auction houses, then EEs are probably justified in holding such a view. The situation is quite different, however, if one defines external validity more broadly, as I believe most EEs would like to do. The same features that make EE experiments predictive of behaviour in one class of formal markets, I would argue, actually limit their applicability to the types of economic settings that play a more prominent role in daily economic life. In the remainder of the essay, I elaborate on this point by focusing on a small number of features that are common elements of EE experiments.

5.2. Auctions and Markets

Many, if not most, experiments conducted by EEs incorporate market mechanisms such as double oral auctions, short-selling, etc.. Such markets have remarkable efficiency properties; they even converge to equilibrium when participants are 'zero intelligence' traders (Gode and Sunder, 1993). They do so, in part, by 'disciplining' suboptimal behaviour – i.e. by reducing the wealth, and eliminating the influence, of participants who behave in a suboptimal fashion.

Efficiency, however, is not the same as high external validity. Double oral auctions or even one-sided auctions, not to mention short-selling, are rare in daily life. I do not think I have ever encountered a double oral auction outside of participating in an experiment, and the last time I participated in *any* type of auction was as a teenager when I bought a broken washing machine motor for $0.25. Most of the economic transactions that I, and probably most people, participate in, whether large or small, are notable for the lack of disciplining mechanisms. For example, if I pay too much for a car or invest my retirement savings foolishly my influence on the economy barely changes. And, unlike the stock market, in which I may be able to rely on the 'smart money' to ensure that I pay a fair price, I have no such protection when it comes to buying or selling my car or house.

The issue of external validity is of particular interest to BEs because EEs have examined the robustness, in EE markets, of many of the phenomena that BEs have identified, such as expected utility anomalies, preference reversals, non-constant time discounting, the willingness to accept/willingness to pay discrepancy (the endowment effect), fairness effects, and the winner's curse.

If the patterns of behaviour observed by BEs disappeared in experimental markets – which they do not – many EEs would undoubtedly conclude that they must not be very important in the real world. However, such a conclusion would be unfounded. One could perhaps surmise that they would not be displayed by currency traders, or others who engage in repetitive transaction in a market with massive rapid feedback and short-selling. But only a small fraction of economic transactions take place in settings that have these informational or incentive features.

5.3. Repetition

Among EEs there is a strong, and seemingly growing, belief in the importance of repetition. Experiments often consist of a series of 'periods' in which individuals engage in the same activity repeatedly, sometimes 10 to 20 times in a row. Although such 'stationary replication' severely limits the duration and maximum complexity of tasks that can be examined, it is unquestionably a useful tool for studying the important question of how people learn in highly repetitive situations. Many EEs, however, view stationary replication not as a tool for studying learning, but as a technique for increasing external validity. The view of most advocates of stationary replication seems to be that people's behaviour at the end of a series of stationary repetitions is more representative of their behaviour in economic settings than their behaviour at the beginning.

Consider an experiment conducted by Coursey *et al.* (1987). The experiment was intended as a criticism of earlier research by Knetsch and Sinden showing a disparity between willingness to pay for a good (a lottery) and willingness to accept compensation for giving up the same good. Some participants in Coursey *et al.*'s experiment were told they would have to taste a spoonful of a bitter substance (SOA) and an auction was conducted to elicit willingness to pay to avoid tasting the SOA. Willingness to accept compensation for tasting the substance was elicited from other subjects who were not initially made to expect that they would have to taste the SOA. The disparity between WTA and WTP began at a ratio of approximately 5, but by the end of 10 market sessions had diminished to approximately 1.6 which was not statistically significant, albeit using a low-power rank-sum test with a small number of subjects and a 0.01 significance level. The authors conclude that 'the divergence obtained in early trials of the experiment . . . may result mainly from a lack of market experience' and that 'individuals may well learn to become more rational under the pressure of a competitive market' (p. 688).

As Camerer (1996) notes, the situation that participants face in experiments of this type is somewhat akin to that of the protagonist in the film 'Groundhog Day', who repeatedly relives the same day until he 'gets it right'. Outside of this fictional film, how many people are exposed to the situation of repeatedly, and in close succession, bidding on the same good (or a bad)? Stationary replication is simply not a common feature of economic life. There are a few settings, such as working in a highway tollbooth or perhaps trading options, in which people face many highly repetitive situations in close succession, but these are probably not the most interesting or important when it come to understanding human (or market) behaviour. And they certainly are not the *uniquely* interesting case.

According to Ledyard (1995), the benefit of repetition is that it allows the experimenter 'to discover whether the data are simply the result of confusion and inexperience.' He is clearly correct that it is bad for subjects to be confused about the mechanics of the experiment. However, when the confusion reflects a lack of understanding about how to behave in a particular situation, perhaps due to the lack of relevant experience, it is by no means clear that behaviour at the end of the repetitions is more representative of actual economic behaviour than behaviour at the beginning. People may be confused about whether to obtain an advanced degree and what type of degree to obtain, about what type of job will advance their career goals, or even what those goals are. They might eventually behave optimally if they faced these decisions repeatedly and received feedback about the consequences of their choices. But they do not.

Defenders of stationary replication could argue that, although people rarely face the type of unchanging situation characterised by stationary replication, they can apply what they learn in one situation to their behaviour in other situations. For example, if one blunders in bargaining over the price of a used car it is possible that one will be less likely to blunder subsequently when bargaining over the purchase of a house. But if people are so successful at what psychologists call 'transfer of learning' across situations, it is surprising that they do not transfer such insights to experimental settings.

In fact, psychological research suggests that transfer of learning across situations is surprisingly weak. Even when subjects are explicitly informed that their experience on one task is relevant to a second task, they often learn the wrong lesson from the first task. Thus, for example, Bassok *et al.* (1995) trained subjects on a problem in which the manager of a country club randomly assigned caddies to golfers. Their task was to compute the probability that the three most experienced caddies would be assigned to the three newest members. The essential insight to solving the problem is that the answer depends on the size of the 'assigned' set (caddies) and not on the size of the 'receiving' set (golfers). Subjects were able to learn the rule that enabled them to provide relatively accurate answers to the problem. However, when the problem was changed superficially so that subjects were asked to assigning caddies to golf carts instead of golfers, 76% gave wrong answers which indicated that they had learned the wrong rule – one based on superordinate and subordinate relations (golfers are superior to caddies and caddies are superior to carts) rather than one based correctly on the assigned/received distinction.

Analogous results have been obtained by experimental economists. Consider, for example, an auction experiment conducted by Kagel and Levin (1986). Subjects who bid on an asset in a 3-person auction initially exhibited the winner's curse (by overbidding) but, after several repetitions, dropped their bids to the point where they no longer lost money. One interpretation is that subjects dropped their bids because they had learned about the winner's curse. However, when they were subsequently placed in a 6-person auction, instead of lowering their bids, as they would have done if they had learned the essential principle behind the winner's curse, they raised them. Subjects learned a rule in the first situation that reduced their losses in that situation, but did not generalize to even a subtly different situation.

Besides exaggerating the degree of learning that takes place in real-world settings, stationary replication can also affect people's preferences in a way that may or may not enhance external validity. Repetition tends to repress certain types of psychological motives, such as fairness, that may play a prominent role in early-period play. How many times can a subject get angry about someone splitting a pie unevenly? It must be acknowledged, however, that similar factors may be operative in daily life: how many trips to the wine store does it take before one forgets one's resolution to punish the French for violating the nuclear test ban treaty?

5.4. Context

Many experimental economists seem to view their enterprise as akin to silicon chip production. Subjects are removed from all familiar contextual cues. Like the characters 'thing one' and 'thing two' in *Dr. Suess' Cat in the Hat*, buyers and sellers become 'persons *A* and *B*', and all other information that might make the situation familiar and provide a clue about how to behave is removed. The desire to expunge context is reminiscent of a movement among behaviourist psychologists in the middle of this century, at the peak of which some researchers conducted experiments in 'context free' temperature and sound-regulated white egg-shaped enclosures. The context-free experiment is, of course, an elusive goal. An egg-shaped cage provides the same amount of context, albeit somewhat more alien, as any other environment.

Nor would a context-free experiment necessarily be a good thing if it were possible. A major discovery of cognitive psychology is the degree to which all forms of thinking and problem solving are context-dependent, including such seemingly straightforward tasks as language-comprehension. For an example in the domain of problem-solving, consider the 'Wason four-card problem'.

There are four cards, each with a letter on one side and a number on the other. The exposed faces read 'X', 'Y', '1', and '2'. Subjects are asked which cards would need to be turned over to test the rule: 'If there is an X on one side there is a 2 on the other.' Very few subjects give the right answer, which is X and 1. However, when the problem is put into a more familiar context (for example, there are 4 children from two different towns and two school districts and the rule is 'If a child lives in Concord he goes to Concord High'), a much higher fraction of subjects give the right answer. Subjects may seem like zero intelligence agents when they are placed in the unfamiliar and abstract context of an experiment, even if they function quite adequately in familiar settings. Indeed, the pervasive confusion on the basis of which Ledyard justifies the need for repetition may stem, in part, from the difficulty of explaining the experiment to subjects in the absence of any familiar contextual cues.

In addition to context effects, social psychologists have documented social contagion effects, as well as pressures to conform, than can exert a powerful influence in experimental settings. In social encounters, including laboratory experiments, most people are engaged in a constant search for cues about how they are supposed to behave. These cues can trigger off complex inferences. For example, in a study of dictator game behaviour conducted by Hoffman *et al.* (1994), dictators who made decisions behind a cardboard partition and were given detailed instructions about the elaborate measures that had been taken to ensure anonymity gave away less money than in conditions that did not ensure anonymity. The authors conclude that 'people act as if they are other regarding because they are better off with the resulting reputation. Only under conditions of social isolation are these reputation concerns of little force' (page 659). Although the effects of anonymity may result, in part, from concerns about reputation, it seems likely that what psychologists refer to as 'demand effects' also played a role. It is natural for subjects to infer from the elaborate measures taken to ensure anonymity that they are supposed to behave in a way that they would not like others to observe.

As a result of their experience with experimental games, EEs are beginning to gain an appreciation of the importance of context effects. For example, in investigations of the 'ultimatum game', fairly subtle experimental manipulations (such as whether the game is posed a matter of selling and buying or of division of a resource, and whether money offers are actually presented in cash) can have large effects on the behaviour of the players. Similarly, defection rates in the prisoners' dilemma game are dramatically different if subjects are told they are playing the 'Wall Street Game' or the 'Community Game' (Ross and Ward, 1996). It could be argued that such results indicate that the game should be played without labels, but in such a situation subjects will inevitably apply their own labels. Unfortunately, there is no 'neutral' presentation of these games, simply a variety of alternatives, so there is no way to remove the context.[2] The goal of external validity is served by creating a context that is similar to the one in which economic agents will actually operate, not by engaging in futile attempts to eliminate context.

5.5. Incentives

Of all the 'rules' of EE experiments, perhaps the most stringently enforced is the use of monetery payments that are contingent on behaviour, which is seen as a means of maintaining strict control over incentives. It is difficult to think of any economics experiment published in a major journal that did not incorporate such contingent payments.

Although the use of contingent financial rewards makes good sense, EEs should not deceive themselves that the use of such rewards allows them to control the incentives operating in their experiments. Even with monetary rewards in place, subjects are likely to be influenced powerfully by motives other than profit maximization. Such motives include the desire to behave in an appropriate fashion, conform to the expectations of the experimenter, appear to be a smart (or at least not stupid), a good person, a winner, etc.

Some EEs seem to believe that some of these motives can be eliminated through procedures that assure anonymity. For example, Hoffman *et al.* (1994), articulating such a view, state that 'it seems unreasonable to believe that people directly consume their reputations in isolation' (p. 659). Quite to the contrary, from a psychological perspective the idea that people directly 'consume' (that is, care about) their reputations is not only eminently reasonable, but consistent with a myriad of studies (see Bodner and Prelec, 1996). For example, people behave very differently in the presence of a mirror, even when they believe that no one is observing them (Duval and Wicklund, 1972). Certainly, people do behave differently when they believe they are being watched, but how much this is due to reputation effects is unclear. Most people will not pick their nose while a car is passing them on the freeway, even in

[2] Because context cannot be eliminated, experiments should never be used for the purpose of measuring individual propensities. It is tempting, but a big mistake, to think that behaviour in dictator games measures an individual's altruism, that responders' behaviour in ultimatum games measures their taste for fairness, or that behaviour in the trust game measures trustworthiness. I am aware of no evidence showing that people who give more money in dictator games contribute more to charities, are more likely to put themselves at risk to rescue a drowning stranger, or give their subway seat to the elderly or infirm. But, even if such data are collected and the correlations prove to be positive, the fact remains that it would be easy, through a suitable manipulation of context, to design a dictator study in which people would give none of their money to a stranger, or one in which most people would give all of their money away. Which of these contexts uncovers people's 'true' level of altruism? Some EEs seem to believe that they know the answer: whatever context gives results that are closest to the standard economic model.

a foreign country. Moreover, people may be almost as concerned about maintaining a particular *self-image* as they are about maintaining an external image.

Even if experimenters were able to eliminate motives other than profit maximisation from their experiments, it would not necessarily be a good thing insofar as external validity is concerned. Profit maximization may be an important incentive in economic transactions, but it probably is not the most important. Anyone working in a business setting, for example, can attest to the power of social comparison. Most academics seem to be motivated more by ego than by the size of their salary, and academics probably are not exceptional in this regard. Even when people do care about money, their degree of concern is often remarkably unrelated to the amount of money involved. Small amounts of money can gain momentous significance under certain circumstances – for example, if one gets an undeserved speeding or parking ticket, or if one is unfairly denied a small year-end bonus. Much larger changes in wealth, such as those which result from a change in stock prices, can leave one remarkably unmoved.

Moreover, monetary incentives interact with nonpecuniary incentives in ways that are poorly understood. For example, in a tournament situation, there is likely to be an extreme discontinuity between no difference between the winning and losing prizes and even trivially small differences. Any difference in prizes that tips players off as to who won and who lost is likely to unleash a tremendous amount of motivation that will be relatively insensitive to further increases in the difference. Although the use of monetary incentives in an experiment probably rarely decreases external validity, given that they are probably not the most important source of motivation in daily economic life, their contribution to external validity is likely to be minimal.

5.6. Internal Validity

Although my focus has been on the issue of external validity, it is worth noting that EE experiments, like all empirical research, also face threats to internal validity. Many of these threats to internal validity result from a common failure by EEs to assign subjects randomly to different treatments. For psychologists and BEs, random assignment to treatment groups is *the* single most critical measure for achieving high internal validity. As a BE, I have been repeatedly shocked by EEs who, unapologetically, make direct comparisons between treatment groups run at different times (even sometimes in different years) and with different populations of subjects. The problem is exacerbated by the fact that observations are often not independent of one-another because subjects provide multiple observations and interact with one-another.

As virtually all introductory empirical research textbooks discuss, random assignment eliminates, in one fell swoop, a long list of threats to internal validity such as, selection, maturation, history and regression to the mean. If an experimenter conducts a study of behaviour in dictator games and compares one treatment collected in one class on Monday with another collected in a different class on Friday, any observed difference may be due to the experimental treatment, but it is equally plausible that it resulted from differences in the composition of the two classes, important news events that took place during the week, or course materials that subjects were exposed to during the week. For the BE, running an experiment without random assignment defeats the whole purpose of the enterprise.

5.7. Concluding Comments

In more than thirty years of productive research, EEs have developed some extremely compelling experimental conventions. For example, EE methods of ensuring incentive compatibility, the discouragement of deception, and the practice of reporting methods in sufficient detail to allow for replication, are all worthy of broad emulation. However, despite (or even partly as a result of) their incorporation of markets, repetition, and incentives, EEs have not, in my opinion, been able to avoid the problem of low external validity that is the Achilles heel of all laboratory experimentation. EE experiments have high external validity if they are intended to represent the behaviour, and consequences of that behaviour, of people operating in highly structured markets. They are much less well suited for testing predictions about the economic consequences of individual behaviour in the 'real world,' including the real world of decentralised markets.

Whatever the external validity of their experiments, EE-style experiments are ideal for examining individual behaviour under conditions of varying incentives, opportunities for learning, interpersonal interactions, etc.. Given that BEs have proposed some of the most novel and provocative hypotheses about individual behavior, BE may well be the single best application of EE methods.

Carnegie Mellon University, Pittsburgh

References

Babcock, L., Wang, X., and Loewenstein, G. (1996). 'Choosing the wrong pond: social comparisons that reflect a self-serving bias.' *Quarterly Journal of Economics*, vol. 111, pp. 1–19.

Bassok, M., Wu, L. L. and Olseth, K. L. (1995). 'Judging a book by its cover: interpretative effects of content on problem-solving transfer.' *Memory and Cognition*, vol. 23, pp. 354–367.

Bodner, R. and Prelec, D. (1996). 'The diagnostic value of actions in a self-signaling model,' MIT working paper.

Camerer, C. F. (1996). 'Rules for experimenting in psychology and economics, and why they differ.' In (W. Albers, W. Guth, and E. Van Damme) *Experimental Studies of Strategic Interaction: Essays in Honor of Reinhard Selten*. Berlin: Springer-Verlag.

Camerer, C., Babcock, L., Loewenstein, G. and Thaler, R. (1997). 'Labor supply of New York City taxi drivers: one day at a time'. *Quarterly Journal of Economics*, vol. 112, pp. 407–441.

Coursey, D. L., Hovis, J. L. and Schulze, W. D. (1987). 'The disparity between willingness to accept and willingness to pay measures of value.' *Quarterly Journal of Economics*, vol. 102, pp. 679–690.

Duval, S. and Wicklund, R. A. (1972). *A Theory of Objective Self-awareness*. New York: Academic Press.

Gode, D. K. and Sunder, S. (1993). 'Allocative efficiency of markets with zero-intelligence traders: market as a partial substance for individual rationality.' *Journal of Political Economy*, vol. 101, pp. 119–137.

Hoffman, E., McCabe, K., Shachat, K., and Smith, V. (1994). 'Preferences, property rights, and anonymity in bargaining games,' *Games and Economic Behaviour*, vol. 7, pp. 346–380.

Kagel, J. and Levin, D. (1986). 'The winner's curse and public information in common value auctions,' *American Economic Review*, vol. 76, pp. 894–920.

Ledyard, J. O. (1995). 'Public goods: a survey of experimental research.' In (J. H. Kagel and A. E. Roth, eds.) *Handbook of Experimental Economics*. Princeton: Princeton University Press, pp. 111–194.

Ross, L. and Ward, A. (1996). 'Naive realism: implications for social-conflict and misunderstanding.' In (E. S. Reed, E. Turiel and T. Brown). *Values and Knowledge*, Mahwah, NJ: Lawrence Erlbaum Associates.

Smith, V. (1991). 'Rational choice – the contrast between economics and psychology.' *Journal of Political Economy*, vol 99, pp. 877–897.

6

The Psychology of Curiosity: A Review and Reinterpretation

George Loewenstein

The genesis of this paper was a gripe.[1] A few years before writing it I had become interested in the phenomenon of curiosity. I read all the literature on curiosity that I could get my hands on, came up with my own "information gap" theory, and ran a series of studies to test the theory. I then submitted the resulting paper for publication, with disastrous results. Curiosity as a topic of study was 'off the map' in psychology at that point, and had been for decades, so the editor must have had trouble identifying appropriate reviewers. He must have decided that 'intrinsic motivation' was the closest topic to curiosity that people were actively researching. At least that was my inference, based on a series of reviews, the main gist of which seemed to be that my theory was crap, that the right theory was based on the concept of intrinsic motivation, and that I obviously didn't know anything about the topic of curiosity. Given all the time I had put into reading the literature on curiosity, the charge of heedlessness really got to me, and I decided to write a review of curiosity so that no one could charge me with ignorance about the topic. Having established my credentials, my plan was to then resubmit the original paper.

The main thing that I find so fascinating about curiosity is a property that, since this paper was published, the neuroscientist Kent Berridge has come to refer to as the difference between 'wanting' and 'liking'. Wanting represents how motivated you are to take an action. Liking represents how much pleasure you can expect to get from doing it. Rational choice theories of behavior assume that we want things because we anticipate that we will like them. However, Berridge argues that the brain has separate neural systems for

[1] Resentment can be a powerful and often productive motivator. My mother, who was also an academic, told me about a student who, years after graduating, visited her in her office to inform her about what a success he had become despite the fact that she had not appreciated his talents. She had the strong sense that part of the drive that had contributed to his success was the desire to prove her wrong.

wanting and liking, which points to the possibility that the two can diverge. He finds evidence of such divergences in the behavior of rats (which often vigorously approach a reward but then don't show the facial signs of enjoying it), and argues that the same is true for humans, and that drug addiction presents the best example of the phenomenon. Addicts, Berridge points out, often exhibit overwhelming motivation to take a drug, but report deriving very little pleasure from actually consuming it. While suspecting that Berridge is right about wanting being disproportionate to liking for drug addicts, I don't find the example very compelling, because it doesn't take into account the negative state of the addict if he or she *doesn't* take the drug; maybe the addict wants to take the drug, not because he or she likes taking it, but because he or she *dis*likes not taking it.

Curiosity, I believe, poses a more clear-cut example of wanting without liking. In the most extreme cases, people cannot resist perusing information that they know with virtual certainty will make them miserable. True, unsatisfied curiosity can make you miserable, much like not taking a drug one is addicted to, but the misery of unmet curiosity is usually far more transient than the misery of drug withdrawal. In fact (and this is another point I discuss in the paper), it is remarkable how quickly curiosity can spike and then dissipate, as occurs when you are walking behind someone and get curious about what they look like from the front. However intense the curiosity of the moment (and it can be remarkably intense), inevitably it disappears within moments if they turn a corner and disappear from sight.

The other obvious drive for which wanting can often far outstrip liking (although the opposite can also happen) is the sex drive. In fact, maybe the similarity isn't coincidental; Sigmund Freud, perhaps not surprisingly, believed that curiosity was derivative of the sex drive. Although this seems unlikely to me (in fact, I'm not even exactly sure what it means), curiosity and sex certainly do have striking similarities even beyond the frequent mismatch between wanting and liking. Both are highly stimulus bound—they can reach very intense levels very quickly given the right stimuli,[2] and can also dissipate

---

[2] For curiosity, it doesn't seem to take much. For example, in a recent study, we produced several paragraphs, each describing a year in the life of a lottery winner, based loosely on facts about an actual lottery winner. We wanted to test whether people would be more motivated to read about the third year when the package was presented to them as "three years in the life of a lottery winner" as opposed to "ten years in the life of a lottery winner," and we measured their motivation by testing whether they preferred to read the final (third) paragraph or receive a fixed amount of money. We observed the predicted effect; those who believed they could read about the third year of three were willing to pay more to read it than those who believed it was the third year out of ten. But, an even more interesting finding was the willingness to pay of both groups. We started by asking subjects if they would prefer to receive $0.25 or to read about the lottery winner's third year, reasoning that people's valuation of the information was unlikely to be much higher than that. However, given a choice between reading the paragraph or getting $0.25, virtually all the subjects in both conditions chose to read the paragraph, a ceiling effect which precluded observing any

very quickly when the stimulus is removed. Both can also be satisfied very abruptly, although the pleasure from satisfying the drive often seems paltry relative to the motivation to satisfy it.

What about the original paper the rejection of which spawned this one? Twelve years later, I have finally returned to doing empirical research on curiosity. With Colin Camerer and a team from Cal Tech, we have been scanning subjects using fMRI in an attempt to discover the neural underpinnings of curiosity. And, with the addition of new collaborators, I have returned to the original paper that empirically tested the information gap theory. The essence of the information gap theory is that curiosity occurs when there is a gap in one's information and that gap becomes salient for some reason or one senses the possibility of closing the gap. In one of the new studies, we have people take a personality test and then inform them that the computer *has* scored it or that the computer *can* score it, in both cases eliciting their curiosity to get feedback (it is greater when the test is scored than when it can be scored); in another, we find that people are more curious about information when they know that someone else possesses it. Perhaps this is why, on public transportation, other people's newspapers and magazines always seem so interesting and enticing.

difference between the experimental conditions. So, we upped the amount to $0.50, then to $0.75, and finally to a dollar. At a dollar, a sufficient number of subjects chose to take the money so we could observe a difference between the conditions (which emerged in the predicted direction). However, even at a dollar, the majority of subjects chose to read the paragraph over taking the money.

The Psychology of Curiosity: A Review and Reinterpretation[*]

George Loewenstein

Curiosity is the most superficial of all the affections; it changes its object perpetually; it has an appetite which is very sharp, but very easily satisfied; and it has always an appearance of giddiness, restlessness and anxiety. (Edmund Burke, 1757/1958, p. 31)

Curiosity has been consistently recognized as a critical motive that influences human behavior in both positive and negative ways at all stages of the life cycle. It has been identified as a driving force in child development (e.g. Stern, 1973, p. 33; Wohlwill, 1987) and as one of the most important spurs to educational attainment (Day, 1982). The pedagogical literature encourages teachers to stimulate curiosity (e.g. McNay, 1985), provides practical guidelines for doing so (e.g. Tomkins & Tway, 1985; Vidler, 1974), and decries the educational system's tendency to quell it (Torrance, 1965). Curiosity has also been cited as a major impetus behind scientific discovery, possibly eclipsing even the drive for economic gain (e.g. see Koestler, 1973; Simon, 1992). Furthermore, curiosity is seen as a significant response evoked by literature and art (H. Kreitler & Kreitler, 1972) and has recently been exploited in the commercial realm. Advertisers have begun to harness the power of curiosity in "mystery" ads that reveal the identity of the product only at the end of the advertisement (King, 1991).[1] Less happily, curiosity is associated with behavior disorders such as voyeurism and has been blamed for nonsanctioned

[*] This chapter was originally published as George Loewenstein (1994) 'The Psychology of Curiosity', Psychological Bulletin, 116(1): 75–98. Published by APA and reprinted with permission.

I thank Baruch Fischhoff, Colin Camerer, Linda Babcock, Donna Harsch, Sophie Freud, Daniel Kahneman, Richard Goodkin, Dan Adler, Jodi Gillis, and Dean Behrens for helpful comments and suggestions; three anonymous referees for highly constructive comments; and Jill Shapiro for editorial advice.

[1] Researchers have found that such advertisements produce greater subsequent brand recognition than matched nonmystery ads that reveal the product's identity from the start (Fazio, Herr, & Powell, 1992).

behaviors such as drug and alcohol use (Green, 1990), early sexual experimentation (Cullari & Mikus, 1990), and certain types of crime such as arson (Kolko & Kazdin, 1989).

Yet our fascination with curiosity does not derive from its practical significance alone. Curiosity poses an anomaly for rational-choice analyses of behavior that assume that the value of information stems solely from its ability to promote goals more basic than the satisfaction of curiosity. Such analyses assume that "the utility of information to the agents...is indirect and not direct like the utility derived from consuming goods" (Laffont, 1989, p. 54). However, there is considerable research documenting situations in which people demand more information than would be predicted by "value of information analyses"—as if they value the information for its own sake. For example, managers "systematically gather more information than they use, yet continue to ask for more" (Feldman & March, 1981, p. 171). Patients want more information about their medical conditions than they typically receive but do not want more control over decisions (Strull, Lo, & Charles, 1984). Asch, Patton, and Hershey (1990) described this as a paradox because the decision-theoretic view is that patients should only want to know something if it helps them to make a more informed decision. The theoretical puzzle posed by curiosity is why people are so strongly attracted to information that, by the definition of curiosity, confers no extrinsic benefit.

This combination of practical importance and theoretical puzzle has stimulated psychologists' interest in various aspects of curiosity. Rather than producing an ever-growing mountain of research, however, the interest in curiosity has surged in two major "waves," divided from each other not only by an intervening trough of publications but by a focus on different issues.

The first wave, which crested in the early 1960s, focused on three basic issues. Foremost was the question of curiosity's underlying cause. Psychologists representing diverse intellectual perspectives speculated about the cause of curiosity and invariably concluded that curiosity could be explained in terms of their own preexisting theoretical frameworks. Secondarily, curiosity researchers pondered why people voluntarily seek out situations that they know will induce curiosity, such as mysteries and puzzles. Curiosity seeking posed a paradox for those early theorists who interpreted curiosity as a drive, because drive-based accounts viewed curiosity as aversive and, hence, seemed to predict that people would want to minimize curiosity rather than seek it out. Finally, a very limited body of research examined the situational determinants of curiosity, but the first wave of curiosity research subsided without experiencing the full influence of the situationalist revolution in psychology.

The second wave of curiosity research began in the mid-1970s and ebbed a decade later. It concentrated almost exclusively on the problem of measuring curiosity, a task that has proven to be extraordinarily difficult. Attempts to cross-validate curiosity scales have typically produced low intercorrelations, and efforts to correlate scales with behavior or with individual characteristics such as age, gender, and IQ have produced contradictory findings. Nevertheless, despite its failure to produce a reliable and valid curiosity scale, the measurement research has shed light on the important question of curiosity's definition and dimensionality.

This article reviews the literature on curiosity with a focus on the four central issues that were investigated in the two waves of research: curiosity's *definition and dimensionality*, its underlying *cause*, the explanation for *voluntary exposure to curiosity*, and curiosity's *situational determinants*. In addition to reviewing past efforts to address these issues. I offer some ideas of my own. In the second part of the article. I propose a new theoretical account of curiosity that integrates insights from existing perspectives with ideas from Gestalt psychology, behavioral decision theory, and social psychology. The new account views curiosity as a form of cognitively induced deprivation that results from the perception of a gap in one's knowledge. It points to a number of situational variables that stimulate curiosity and offers a new explanation for voluntary exposure to curiosity.

In addition to discussing the four issues that have occupied previous research, I raise a fifth that has not been discussed by psychologists but finds ample expression in fiction, philosophy, and theology. It is the question of what causes curiosity's peculiar combination of *superficiality* and *intensity* so eloquently described by Burke in the quote opening the article. Curiosity is superficial in the sense that it can arise, change focus, or end abruptly. For example, at the supermarket, the intense desire to learn the latest news of a movie star's marital woes typically vanishes immediately after one leaves the tabloids behind. Despite its transience, however, curiosity can exert a powerful motivational force. Like sexual attraction, curiosity often produces impulsive behavior and attempts at self-control. The stories of Pandora. Eve, and Lot's wife, in which curiosity causes people (frequently young women) to expose themselves knowingly to terrible consequences, pay tribute to curiosity's motivational power. These characteristics of curiosity have not been discussed in the psychological literature, although they are prominent in religious writing and fiction. To ignore these characteristics, however, is to lose sight of the very features that induce "curiosity about curiosity."

6.1. Curiosity's Definition and Dimensionality

The earliest discussions of curiosity, predating the emergence of the field of psychology, were conducted by philosophers and religious thinkers and centered on the question of curiosity's moral status rather than on its psychological underpinnings. These discussions gave expression to epochal attitude swings when the assumption that curiosity is a virtue was periodically super-seded by the tendency to condemn it as a vice.[2] Although there was little explicit discussion of curiosity's definition, it is evident that a common under-standing of curiosity remained remarkably uniform across writers and over many centuries.

First, curiosity was seen as an intrinsically motivated desire for informa-tion. Aristotle, for example, commented that men study science for intrinsic reasons and "not for any utilitarian end" (Posnock, 1991, p. 40), and Cicero referred to curiosity as an "innate love of learning and of knowledge ... *without the lure of any profit* [italics added]" (1914, p. 48). Although they acknowledged that information was also desired for extrinsic reasons, these early thinkers drew a sharp distinction between such an extrinsically motivated desire for information and curiosity.[3]

Second, curiosity was viewed as a passion, with the motivational intensity implied by the term. Cicero referred to curiosity as a "passion for learning" and argued that the story of Ulysses and the Sirens was really a parable about curiosity. "It was the passion for learning that kept men rooted to the Siren's rocky shores" (1914, p. 48). St. Augustine described curiosity as a "certain vain and curious longing for knowledge" (1943, p. 54) that he referred to as "ocular lust" to emphasize its frequent although not exclusive connection to visual perception. Hume (1777/1888) expressed an ambivalent attitude toward curiosity, but one respectful of its power, by subdividing it into two distinct motives: a good variety, which he called "love of knowledge," (p. 453) and a bad type, which he saw as a "passion deriv'd from a quite different principle" (p. 453). Good curiosity was exemplified by scientific inquiry; bad

[2] Harold Blumenberg (1966/1983) traced shifts in an ongoing "trial of curiosity," beginning with the ancient Greeks' embracing of curiosity as a virtue to be nurtured, a subsequent indictment of curiosity as a vice during the Middle Ages, and a somewhat ambivalent "rehabilitation" of curiosity during the Enlightenment. Blumenberg argued that such shifts resulted from the actions of identifiable historical events and personalities. He attributed the initial reaction against curiosity to the influence of St. Augustine and specifically to the diatribe against curiosity in his influential *Confessions*. Curiosity's rehabilitation in the 17th century was traced to the dissemination of Galileo's discoveries. According to Blumenberg (1966/1983), Galileo's discoveries with the telescope produced an appreciation of the knowledge-enhancing potential of scientific exploration, an awareness that " 'curiosity is rewarded'—the weighty significance of what had hitherto been withheld from man is confirmed and thus the morality of self-restriction is disabused and put in the wrong" (p. 369).

Other writers have identified more recent fluctuations in the regard for curiosity. For example, Berlyne (1978) reported that "since about 1950, there has been a reversal. Curiosity has been lauded as a virtue and as one of the prime aims of education" (p. 99). He held this upsurge in regard for curiosity responsible for the coincident increase in interest in the topic. Holmes and Holmes (1991) found that the proportion of negative portrayals of curiosity in children's literature, which had always been higher than that of positive portrayals, showed, after 1969, a clear shift toward portraying curiosity in a negative light.

[3] Such a division is clearly evident in the assertion of an 18th-century physics handbook that "necessity and curiosity have perhaps made equal contributions to the discovery and further elaboration of the science of nature" (Blumenberg, 1966/1983, p. 233).

curiosity was exemplified by "an insatiable desire for knowing the actions and circumstances of [one's] neighbors" (p. 453).

Third, curiosity was seen as appetitive. Bentham (1789/1948, p. 34) referred to the "appetite of curiosity," Burke (1757/1958, p. 31) observed that curiosity "has an appetite which is very sharp," Kant referred to an "appetite for knowledge" (Blumenberg, 1966/1983, p. 430), and St. Augustine used the term *appetite for knowledge* interchangeably with *ocular lust*. As late as the 19th century, Feuerbach referred to the "pains [resulting from an] unsatisfied knowledge drive" (Blumenberg, 1966/1983, p. 445), suggesting that, analogous to physiological appetites, he viewed curiosity as producing painful feelings of deprivation if not satisfied. In sum, curiosity was viewed by premodern writers as an intense, intrinsically motivated appetite for information.

Early discussions by psychologists adhered to the premodern view of curiosity. For example, Freud referred to curiosity as a "thirst for knowledge" (1915, p. 153) or as "Schaulust," which, translated, approximates St. Augustine's ocular lust. James distinguished between two varieties of curiosity: a more common but unnamed type that was characterized by a "susceptibility for being excited and irritated by the mere novelty of...the environment" (James, 1890/1950, p. 430) and a second category referred to as "scientific curiosity" that was directed toward specific items of information. Although the exact distinction between the two types was described cursorily, both appear to be roughly consistent with the historically prevailing definition of curiosity.

The consensus definition of curiosity disintegrated early in the century when behavioristically oriented psychologists began to examine a wide range of behaviors that they referred to collectively as "curiosity" or "exploratory behavior." For example, Pavlov (1927), in the course of his research on conditioned responses, found that dogs would turn toward any unusual sight or sound and attributed the phenomenon to an investigatory reflex. Bühler and her colleagues (Bühler, Hetzer, & Mabel, 1928) referred to the same tendency observed in babies as curiosity. Such orienting reflexes have more in common with the modern term *attention* than with curiosity as defined in the premodern period. They are not necessarily intrinsically motivated, are unemotional in character, and lack the drive properties associated with a cognitive appetite.

Other researchers found that animals and humans seek out environmental variability. For example, a large number of studies showed that rats would explore the less familiar of two arms of a maze (e.g. Dember, 1956; Kivy, Earl, & Walker, 1956; Williams & Kuchta, 1957) or that they would learn a bar-press response when it was followed by either weak light onset or offset, as if they found any change in illumination reinforcing (for a summary, see Fowler, 1965, p. 36). Parallel findings were obtained with human subjects, who, when kept in darkness, repeatedly pressed a button to produce a quasi-random pattern of illumination (A. Jones, Wilkinson, & Braden, 1961).

Although these studies differed in terms of subjects and specific research questions, there was a consensus that the observed behavior could be labeled curiosity.

When D. E. Berlyne began his path-breaking research on curiosity in the early 1950s, he recognized that the concept had become fragmented and proposed a categorization of different types of curiosity. He located curiosity on two dimensions: one extending between perceptual and epistemic curiosity and the other spanning specific and diversive curiosity. Perceptual curiosity referred to "a drive which is aroused by novel stimuli and reduced by continued exposure to these stimuli" (Berlyne, 1954a, p. 180). It was intended to describe the exploratory behavior of the animals in the studies just cited. Epistemic curiosity referred to a desire for knowledge and applied mainly to humans. Specific curiosity referred to the desire for a particular piece of information, as epitomized by the attempt to solve a puzzle. Finally, diversive curiosity referred to a more general seeking of stimulation that is closely related to boredom. In the four-way categorization produced by these two dimensions, specific perceptual curiosity is exemplified by a monkey's efforts to solve a puzzle, diversive perceptual curiosity is exemplified by a rat's exploration of a maze (in both cases with no contingent rewards or punishments), specific epistemic curiosity is exemplified by the scientist's search for the solution to a problem, and diversive epistemic curiosity is exemplified by a bored teenager's flipping among television channels.

Berlyne sided with the premodern writers by excluding extrinsically motivated exploratory behavior from his concept of curiosity. Thus, "orienting reflexes" (Pavlov, 1927) for which the biological significance is obvious would not be classified in Berlyne's taxonomy as curiosity. However, by including diversive and perceptual curiosity in his fourfold classification, Berlyne effectively institutionalized the tendency to classify the desire for change and novelty as curiosity.[4]

Although Berlyne's distinction between perceptual and epistemic curiosity has not been investigated, perhaps because doing so would require an awkward comparison of human with animal data, his specific–diversive distinction became a central focus of the second wave of research. For example,

---

[4] In addition to the division proposed by Berlyne, numerous other classifications of curiosity have been proposed. For example, S. Kreitler, Zigler, and Kreitler (1984) distinguished among manipulated curiosity, conceptual curiosity, and curiosity about the complex or the ambiguous and proposed novel measurement methods for each that involve observing children playing with toys and interacting with the researcher. Langevin (1971) suggested a division of curiosity into breadth and depth dimensions. Breadth curiosity reflects the number of different interests a person has, whereas depth curiosity indicates the extent to which a person pursues a single area of interest. Although the breadth–depth distinction might appear similar to that between diversive and specific curiosity, it actually subdivides the category of specific curiosity. Pursuing an interest, whether there be one or many, reflects a desire for specific information rather than a desire for stimulation in general. High breadth curiosity therefore simply signifies a diversity of interests.

Day's (1971) Ontario Test of Intrinsic Motivation (OTIM) consists of 110 trait-oriented true–false items that measure areas of interest such as "I try to think of answers to the problems of international social relationships" and includes both diversive and specific curiosity subscales. The validity of the diversive–specific division was supported by a factor analysis of the scale demonstrating that the two subscales loaded on separate quasi-independent factors. However, Day himself raised the question of whether diversive curiosity should be classified as curiosity, or whether it was more closely related to boredom and to the sensation seeking and stimulus seeking that boredom evoked. Supporting Day's doubts, a subsequent factor analysis of the OTIM and a variety of other scales (Olson & Camp, 1984a) indicated that the Specific Curiosity subscale of the OTIM loaded on a factor labeled General Curiosity whereas the Diversive Curiosity subscale loaded on a separate factor, along with Zuckerman's (1971) sensation seeking scale.

Furthermore, in a factor analysis of two curiosity scales—the Melbourne Curiosity Inventory (MCI) and the State Epistemic Curiosity Scale (SECS)—conducted with 300 secondary school students in Australia, Boyle (1989) found that negatively worded items tend to load together in a common factor that is independent of positively worded items. The MCI, developed by Naylor (1981), includes 40 items, half positively worded (e.g. "I feel absorbed in things I do") and half negatively worded (e.g. "I am not interested in what I am doing"); the items are rated on a 4-point scale ranging from *almost never* to *almost always*. The SECS, developed by Leherissey-McCombs (1971; Leherissey, 1972), includes 14 positively worded self-report items (e.g. "When I read a sentence that puzzles me, I will keep reading it until I understand it") and 6 reversed items (e.g. "I will find myself getting bored when the material is redundant"). One plausible interpretation of Boyle's finding is that the negatively worded items measure boredom, which is largely independent of specific curiosity. In other words, people answer positively worded items affirmatively when they are curious and answer negatively worded questions affirmatively when they are bored, and each of these states is relatively independent of the other.

These findings suggest that researchers may have included behaviors under the heading of curiosity that are only distantly related to one another. The curiosity that produces a preference for changing levels of illumination and a distaste for sensory deprivation may have little in common with the curiosity that motivates educational attainment and scientific achievement. Diversive curiosity appears to be more closely related to sensation seeking or novelty seeking than to curiosity as the term has been used historically. Interestingly, the posthumously published fragments of a book by Berlyne (1974, p. 144) suggest that he eventually regretted having classified the diversive type as curiosity, referring to it as "the other, rather odd, technical sense that some psychologists give to the term."

Other than Berlyne's distinction between diversive and specific curiosity, the most commonly studied division of curiosity has been that between state and trait curiosity. State curiosity refers to curiosity in a particular situation, whereas trait curiosity refers to a general capacity or propensity to experience curiosity. For example. Naylor's MCI includes trait and state subscales that are very similar in the items they contain. The trait scale asks subjects to rate how they generally feel and includes items such as "I feel absorbed in things I do," whereas the state scale asks respondents whether they feel absorbed in what they are doing "at this particular moment." The state scale must be administered in the context of an activity such as a career seminar or math lesson. Naylor tested his scales on 10th-grade students through college graduates and found, supportive of a meaningful state–trait distinction, that the trait scale had high test–retest validity and the state scale varied across situations. The items from the two scales also clustered neatly into two separate factors. Similar results were obtained by Boyle (1983, 1989).

However, perhaps not too much should be made of these results. For almost any construct, one could generate trait and state measures that would load on quasi-independent factors. For example, illumination preference could be measured in its trait and state versions, respectively, by asking "Do you generally find the rooms you are in to be too bright?" and "Is the room you are in too bright?" Questions of these two types would probably also load on independent factors. The presence of quasi-independent trait and state factors seems to reflect, at best, the fact that curiosity is influenced by both situation and disposition.

Besides the use of multi-item scales, other techniques have been used to estimate trait curiosity. Most significant, W. H. Maw, E. W. Maw, and occasional colleagues conducted a series of studies involving fifth-grade subjects (e.g. Maw & Magoon, 1971; Maw & Maw, 1964, 1968, 1972) in which they evaluated the reliability and validity of measures of curiosity derived from teacher evaluations, peer evaluations, and self-evaluations. Teacher ratings were obtained by having teachers rank their pupils in terms of relative curiosity on the basis of a four-part definition of curiosity.[5] To aid in the ranking process, teachers were also provided with specific examples of behavior exemplifying curiosity. Peer ratings were obtained by having children name classmates whose behavior most resembled that of the characters in eight written scenarios. Four of the scenarios described the behavior of children who displayed high levels of curiosity, and the remaining four described the behavior

---

[5] The definition they used was as follows. An elementary school child demonstrates curiosity when "he (a) reacts positively to new, strange, incongruous, or mysterious elements in his environment by moving toward them, exploring them, or manipulating them; (b) exhibits a need or a desire to know more about himself and/or his environment; (c) scans his surroundings seeking new expences; and/or (d) peruses in examining and/or exploring stimuli in order to know more about them" (Maw & Maw, 1968, p. 462).

of children with low curiosity. The peer score was equal to the number of times a student was named in connection with the high-curiosity sketches minus the number of times the student was named in association with the low-curiosity sketches. The self-rating scale asked students to evaluate a series of items on a 4-point scale ranging from *never* to *always*. Items included "I like to explore strange places," "I ask questions in school," and "I keep my hands clean." (On the last item, for some reason, the two extreme responses *never* and *always* were considered indicative of low curiosity.) Although the correlations among all three measures were not reported, a later study reported that the self-rating scale correlated .25 with a composite measure based on peer and teacher ratings (Maw & Magoon, 1971). However, the same study found a correlation of 0.61 between the same composite curiosity index and measured intelligence, raising the possibility—corroborated by subsequent research (Coie, 1974)—that the observed correlation between the curiosity measures resulted from their common relationship to IQ. Maw and Magoon also examined the correlation of the composite measure of curiosity with 26 different individual characteristics and traits elicited from a battery of personality sub-scales. They found that curiosity was significantly correlated with (in order of importance) effectiveness, loyalty, reliability, accountability, intelligence, creativity, degree of socialization, tolerance for ambiguity, sense of personal worth, and responsibility. In yet another study, Maw and Maw (1972) found that a composite measure of curiosity correlated significantly with students' ability to recognize verbal absurdities such as "Give me my glasses and turn out the light so I can read the newspaper," even after matching subjects by IQ. However, the authors failed to provide an adequate explanation for why they anticipated such an association.

One particularly innovative study of curiosity was conducted by Coie (1974), in part to test the validity of Maw and Maw's teacher-rating method of curiosity measurement. Coie presented 120 schoolchildren of varying ages with four situations designed to gauge their levels of curiosity. In each, children were placed in the presence of a powerfully curiosity-evoking stimulus item such as a box with windows, lights, and protruding knobs. For two of the stimulus items (the "sanctioned" items), the children were encouraged to explore the item, establishing a setting in which failure to explore was unlikely to result from a fear of disobeying authority. The children were neither encouraged nor discouraged from exploring the other two stimulus items. Coie also administered two tests of intellectual ability, obtained the students' grade point averages, and elicited teacher ratings of curiosity in the manner prescribed by Maw and Maw. He found that behavioral measures of curiosity (e.g., approach latencies) toward the two sanctioned stimulus items were inter-correlated, as were those for the two nonsanctioned items. However, measures of curiosity toward the sanctioned items were not significantly correlated with measures of curiosity toward the nonsanctioned items. The behavioral measures of curiosity were also correlated with teacher ratings of curiosity, but that relationship vanished once Coie controlled for intelligence. Coie concluded that teacher ratings of curiosity actually measure intelligence.

The main use of trait curiosity scales and other types of measures has been to compare the curiosity of individuals who differ demographically. However, such investigations have produced a highly contradictory pattern of findings. Although many studies have detected significant relationships between curiosity and variables such as age (Vidler, 1977), gender (Stoner & Spencer, 1986) and socioeconomic status (S. Kreitler, Zigler, & Kreitler, 1984), other studies have yielded null results for the same variables (e.g. Camp, Rodrigue, & Olson, 1984; Engelhard & Monsaas, 1988), and statistically significant findings often differ in sign.

The inconsistent results obtained in analyses of group differences in curiosity may reflect a fundamental problem associated with efforts to measure interpersonal differences in trait curiosity. Curiosity scales almost inevitably measure curiosity toward particular topics or objects. Thus, Engelhard and Monsaas's (1988) School Related Curiosity scale consists of 10 yes–no statements including "I get excited about topics discussed in my classroom," "I am always asking questions and trying to find out more about my classwork," and "Being curious about my classwork is important to me." Langevin's Experimental Curiosity Measure (1971) provides subjects with a list of 40 "things" they might like to experience, which they rate on a 3-point scale for "wanting to experience." Clearly, an individual's or group's measured level of curiosity on these scales depends on the match between their own areas of curiosity and those included in the scale. For example, if younger students are curious about different topics than older students, the group that is more curious about the specific items included in the scales will score higher in curiosity. Thus, Engelhard and Monsaas's finding, in one of the schools they investigated, that school-related curiosity declined with age is as likely to be due to differences in the curriculum for those age groups as to an actual decline in trait curiosity. Other than asking "Are you a curious person?" which many scales in fact do, it may be impossible to create curiosity items that are not vulnerable to this problem. However, asking people how curious they are (and most of the other items included in curiosity scales) makes the purpose of the scale obvious to subjects. This is a serious deficiency when one is measuring a trait that is widely recognized as socially desirable.

Researchers have also examined the correlation between curiosity and traits such as IQ and creativity. Such analyses reflect, in part, efforts to test the convergent validity of curiosity scales, because there are good reasons to expect a positive relationship between curiosity and these traits. As Voss and Keller noted, "exploratory behavior is a major determinant for the development of intelligence," and "exploration is a form of intelligent behavior" (1983, p. 122). The same argument can be made for curiosity and creativity.

Therefore, it would be disturbing *not to* find a positive interrelationship among these three constructs. There are also empirical findings that should lead one to anticipate a positive interrelationship among curiosity, intelligence, and creativity. The response to novelty by infants has been found to be correlated with later intelligence (Berg & Sternberg, 1985), and the desire for novelty by adults has been consistently linked to creativity (see Voss & Keller, 1983, p. 123). Because, as I discuss later, novelty plays a central role in several theories of curiosity, such results also suggest a positive relationship between curiosity, on the one hand, and creativity and intelligence, on the other.

However, studies that have examined the interrelationship among scales measuring curiosity, IQ, and creativity have not consistently observed the expected positive correlations. For example, Langevin (1971) found a range of correlations, from negative to small but significantly positive, between IQ (measured by the Otis Quick-Scoring Mental Abilities Test and the Ravens Progressive Matrix Test) and seven different measures of curiosity, and Penney and McCann (1964) found no relationship between IQ and curiosity. Similarly, mixed findings have been obtained for the relationship between measures of creativity and various curiosity scales (Voss & Keller, 1983). These mixed results may reflect the curiosity scales' lack of validity, but a more radical conclusion is also possible. As Coie (1974) speculated, perhaps curiosity simply does not exist as a stable, generalized trait.

In conclusion, the study of specific state curiosity seems to hold greater promise than a focus on either diversive curiosity or trait curiosity. Diversive curiosity is more closely related to boredom and sensation seeking than to curiosity as the term is conventionally understood, and the deficiencies of existing trait scales may point to fundamental problems associated with the measurement of trait curiosity or even with the existence of such a trait. Even if trait curiosity were measurable, the practical benefits of such a scale are questionable. Although individuals with high trait curiosity probably make superior students and scientists, the ability to measure such differences would, at best, aid in sorting or tracking students or scientists on the basis of their curiosity. An improved understanding of state curiosity, in contrast, has the potential to suggest practical methods of stimulating curiosity in the broader population. Moreover, if trait differences reflect the cumulative effect of situational factors, effective situational interventions to stimulate state curiosity might ultimately serve to enhance trait curiosity.

6.2. The Underlying Cause of Curiosity

The most basic problem that has occupied curiosity researchers and theorists is the underlying cause of curiosity. Psychologists representing diverse intellectual perspectives have debated whether curiosity is a primary or secondary drive or motive and, if secondary, from what more basic drive or motive it derives.

6.2.1. Early Accounts

An early account of curiosity, articulated by William James and then extended slightly by McDougall, viewed curiosity as an emotion closely related to fear in the sense that it is produced by the same stimuli. To illustrate the close connection between curiosity and fear, James cited the behavior of an alligator he had observed swimming gradually toward a man seated on the beach, "gradually drawing near as long as he kept still, [but] frantically careering back as soon as he made a movement" (James, 1890/1950, p. 429). In keeping with his functionalist approach. James believed that curiosity had evolved to motivate organisms to explore their environments, whereas fear had evolved, in part, to temper the risks posed by such exploration. McDougall (1918) proposed an almost identical perspective, complete with a description of a horse displaying the same behavior as James's alligator. McDougall's innovation was to include curiosity in his list of basic instincts.

6.2.2. Drive Theories

In the first half of this century, the most common response to the question of curiosity's cause was to postulate the existence of a curiosity drive. The defining feature of such accounts is their assumption that curiosity produces an unpleasant sensation (usually labeled *arousal*) that is reduced by exploratory behavior. Drive-based accounts differ from each other in whether they view curiosity as primary or secondary (i.e. derivative of other more basic drives) and in whether they view curiosity as a homeostatic drive or one that is stimulus induced. Homeostatic drives, such as hunger and thirst, are internally stimulated and generally intensify over time if not satisfied, whereas stimulus-induced drives such as fear are triggered by environmental cues. However, it is generally acknowledged that no drive fits squarely into either of these categories; all drives are influenced by both external stimuli and internal states.[6]

Freud: Curiosity and sex. From passages scattered through several of his essays, one can piece together Freud's interpretation of curiosity. Freud viewed

---

[6] Another difference between drive theorists is largely semantic. Most drive theorists have referred to the aversive state that produces exploration as curiosity, but a small group of dissenters have substituted other terms, such as stimulus hunger (Glanzer, 1953) or boredom (Fowler, 1965; Myers & Miller, 1954), while retaining an otherwise virtually identical theoretical outlook.

curiosity as derivative of the sex drive.[7] He believed that curiosity was the product of sublimated infantile sexual exploration that arises between 3 and 5 years of age when the child begins to associate the pleasure evoked by genital manipulation with the looking impulse. When, under social pressure, sexual exploration is later abandoned, it becomes sublimated in one of three ways. In neurotic inhibition, the individual's thought processes become generally blocked by the act of repression, one consequence of which is that curiosity is stymied. Alternatively, residual sexual curiosity can manifest itself as compulsive brooding, which is also antithetical to curiosity. Finally, sexual curiosity can be sublimated directly into a generalized curiosity about the world. Although Freud saw this last case as the "rarest and most perfect" type of sublimation, he noted that "the research becomes to some extent compulsive and a substitute for sexual activity" (Freud, cited in Posnock, 1991, p. 46). Thus, one implication of Freud's account is that curiosity, in those rare cases when it develops, should exhibit some of the characteristics typically ascribed to the sex drive.

Perhaps because it is virtually nonfalsifiable, Freud's interpretation of curiosity persists in the psychiatric literature, which remains largely unaware of psychological research on the topic. As recently as 1984, the president of the American Academy of Child Psychiatry wrote (without citing supporting evidence) that "puberty marks a period of enormous upsurge of curiosity" (Beiser, 1984, p. 519). Again without citing any relevant research, she then cautioned parents against stiffing curiosity in their children: "Some may go too far, and satisfy sexual curiosity with direct knowledge of their own sexual life. This can interfere with the development of a broader curiosity" (Beiser, 1984, p. 518).

Behaviorist accounts. Freud's account was unusual among drive theories, in part because it viewed curiosity as a personality trait and in part because it saw curiosity as derivative of the sex drive rather than as primary. Other early drive theorists such as Thorndike (see Hunt, 1963, p. 41) and Dashiell (1925), as behaviorists, were uninterested in individual differences and viewed curiosity as a primary drive.

Although drive theorists have often been criticized for inventing a new drive for every type of behavior—a tendency pejoratively labeled *drive naming*—such a criticism is misplaced in the case of curiosity. Beyond postulating the existence of a curiosity drive, behaviorists conducted numerous experiments to test whether curiosity, in fact, possesses the basic characteristics of a primary drive.

To demonstrate curiosity's status as a primary drive, it is first necessary to show that curiosity is not derivative of other, more basic drives. However,

[7] See Aronoff (1962) and Voss and Keller (1983) for detailed analyses of Freud's views on curiosity.

like the proposition that all swans are white, such primacy is impossible to demonstrate. Just as it is always possible that a swan hidden in some backwater is black, one can never rule out the possibility that curiosity derives from an as yet unidentified but more fundamental drive. Nevertheless, researchers attempted to exclude the possibility that curiosity depends on core drives such as hunger, thirst, and fear.

These efforts took two directions. In some cases (e.g. Harlow, Harlow, & Meyer, 1950), researchers sought to demonstrate that animals whose physiological needs were completely satisfied (they could eat and drink at will) nonetheless displayed exploratory behavior. However, such demonstrations are inconclusive because, as Brown (1953) pointed out, it is impossible to rule out the existence of very low levels of hunger, fear, thirst, and other drives. An alternative procedure induced different levels of biological drives in animals and monitored the effect on exploration. Although such studies produced a wide range of both negative and positive correlations between exploration and different forms of physiological deprivation, they, too, are inherently inconclusive. If animals search more when they are hungry, it suggests that hunger influences exploration but not that exploration is influenced only by hunger.

A second, more fruitful set of studies sought to demonstrate that curiosity, like drives such as hunger and fear, possesses motivational force. Early on, Dashiell (1925) and Nissen (1930) demonstrated that rats were willing to endure electrical shock to explore novel stimuli with no apparent connection to food or water. Later, Harlow and various coauthors (Harlow et al., 1950) showed that monkeys would attempt to solve a puzzle with no external incentive for doing so, and Butler (1953) found that monkeys kept in a shielded cage learned to discriminate the color of the window that would afford them a glimpse of the experimental room. Monkeys were placed in a bland covered cage with two opaque windows that looked out on the experimental laboratory. In each of a series of periods, one window would be covered with a panel of a specific color and then unlocked, and the other window would be covered with a different-colored panel and locked. Monkeys rapidly learned to discriminate the color that was associated with the unlocked window and would rush to open it and peer out, even though the only reward was a glimpse of the experimental laboratory. Subsequent experiments by Butler and Alexander (1955) introduced physical barriers to opening the windows. The fact that monkeys will hold a window open for long periods even though it requires physical dexterity and effort suggests that the animals are powerfully motivated to look out the window.

Similar results have been obtained with human subjects. Studies conducted mainly at McGill University in the 1950s and 1960s found that sensorially deprived human subjects will ask repeatedly to listen to numbingly boring material such as old stock market reports (Hebb, 1958). Although significant questions have been raised about the implementation and interpretation of the sensory deprivation studies (e.g. Zubek, 1973), it remains widely accepted that prolonged sensory deprivation is aversive.

A third line of research showed that unsatisfied curiosity tends to intensify over some interval, as do other drives such as hunger and thirst. For example, a second follow-up study by Butler (1957) found that the rate at which monkeys opened windows increased, at least initially, as a function of how long the monkeys spent in the box without visual stimulation. Other studies observed a similar pattern of behavior with subjects as varied as cockroaches (Darchen, 1957) and humans. For example, in the study by A. Jones et al. (1961), the frequency of button pushes to produce flashes of light first increased and then decreased as a function of the time that subjects spent in the darkened room (see also A. Jones, 1966). The authors noted that such an inverted U-shaped pattern of motivation is analogous to that observed with food deprivation and concluded that "information deprivation functions as a drive variable in the same sense as the well-studied homeostatic drives of hunger, pain, and thirst" (A. Jones *et al.*, 1961, p. 135).

Still other research demonstrated that curiosity, like standard drives, could be seemingly "satisfied" by repeated exposure to stimulus materials (Glanzer, 1961; Montgomery, 1952). For example, Berlyne (1955) demonstrated that rats initially explored but later showed little interest in a novel stimulus item. As Woodworth noted, however, the decline of interest tends to be object specific in the case of curiosity, in contrast to other drives in which satiation is more generalized (cited in Fowler, 1965, p. 193). After one consumes a large restaurant meal, any additional food seems unappealing; however, even after a dinner companion has regaled one with the latest gossip about mutual friends, the muffled conversation at the next table retains its distractive potency.

Perhaps most telling, researchers have uncovered evidence of the link between curiosity and arousal that is the sine qua non of the drive perspective. Smith, Malmo, and Shagass (1954) had subjects listen to a recording of an article that was periodically made inaudible. They observed an initial increase in the tension of the arm muscles when the tape became inaudible. Wallerstein (1954) obtained a similar result with subjects who listened to a garbled reading of a philosophical essay: There was an initial rise in muscular tension followed by a fall after the first few minutes.

D. E. Berlyne. Whereas drive-theoretic accounts of curiosity generally assumed that curiosity is a homeostatic drive (i.e. internally stimulated), an alternative drive-based perspective advanced by D. E. Berlyne viewed curiosity as externally stimulated. Berlyne's theory also differed from those proposed by other behaviorists in that it cast cognitive variables in a central role. According to Berlyne, the curiosity drive is aroused by external stimuli, specifically "stimulus conflict" or, "incongruity." This construct encompasses properties such as complexity, novelty, and surprisingness. Berlyne believed that stimuli embodying these properties activate the curiosity drive and raise the organism's level of arousal.

Berlyne's view of curiosity as stimulus evoked was attacked by Fowler (1965), whose boredom-based perspective interpreted curiosity as a homeostatic (i.e., internally stimulated) drive. Fowler noted the apparent contradiction inherent in the view that the curiosity drive was both evoked and satisfied by the same stimuli. He argued that theorists such as Berlyne who viewed curiosity as externally stimulated were "forced to ascribe both drive-eliciting and reinforcing properties to the *same* stimuli—namely the novel stimuli for which the animal responded" (Fowler, 1965, p. 38). In many experiments, Fowler noted, animals produced the exploration-initiating response *before*, rather than after, exposure to the stimulus. For example, in Butler's studies, apes would open the window to see outside the cage, not in response to a view of the outside of the cage. Examined superficially, the temporal pattern of events seemed inconsistent with Berlyne's notion that curiosity was evoked by novel stimuli.

As is often the case in such disputes, both positions have merit. On the one hand, novelty, or the awareness that novel stimuli are available for inspection, can induce curiosity, just as the sight of food or the awareness that it is available can stimulate hunger. On the other hand, studies that found that the degree of exploration increases with the duration of sensory deprivation (e.g. Darchen, 1957; Premack, Collier, & Roberts, 1957) are consistent with the idea that exploration is in part internally stimulated.

Whether curiosity is or is not a drive is probably neither answerable nor particularly important. What is important is that curiosity possesses many of the features commonly associated with primary drives: It does not appear to be derivative of the other basic drives, it can be satisfied by an appropriate response, it does intensify if not satisfied (at least in some situations), and it seems to be aversive. Moreover, regardless of its status as a drive, it appears to be influenced by external and (to a lesser extent) internal factors.

6.2.3. *Incongruity Theories*

In the 1950s, a rather different account of curiosity was developed independently by Hebb, Piaget, and Hunt, who each reached the same conclusion from very different starting points. This account can be summarized by three basic propositions. First, curiosity reflects a natural human tendency to try to make sense of the world. Second, this need is not constant but is evoked by violated expectations. Third, there is an inverted U-shaped relationship between evoked curiosity and the extremity of such expectation violations.

Like Berlyne, therefore, these theorists saw curiosity as evoked by incongruity. However, their focus was on only one of the categories of incongruities mentioned by Berlyne: violations of expectations. Also, most incongruity theories dropped Berlyne's assumption that curiosity is a drive.

Hebb (1955) arrived at this tripartite view of curiosity from his research on the connection between neurology and psychology. He noted that both neurological investigations and sensory deprivation studies contradicted the drive theorists' assumption that organisms seek to achieve a state of quiescence: "The nerve cell is not physiologically inert, does not have to be excited from outside in order to discharge. The nervous system is alive, and living things by their nature are active" (Hebb, 1955, p. 246).[8] Consistent with this perspective, Hebb saw curiosity as a manifestation of the organism's natural tendency toward cognitive processing.

He argued, further, that there is an optimal level of incongruity at which people function most effectively and that they find states of incongruity either above or below this point aversive: "Up to a certain point, lack of correspondence between expectancy and perception may simply have a stimulating (or 'pleasurable') effect; beyond this point, a disruptive (or unpleasant) effect" (Hebb, 1949, p. 149). Thus Hebb, like James, believed that minor violations of expectations induced curiosity but that major violations produced a fearlike aversive reaction.

Piaget arrived at a strikingly similar view of curiosity on the basis of his research on cognitive development. First, he saw curiosity as inextricably linked to the child's need to make sense of the world. According to Kakar (1976, p. 192), curiosity for Piaget "plays a part in the search for coherence and organization. It is a motive force in the need to order reality." Second, Piaget viewed curiosity as the product of cognitive disequilibrium evoked by the child's attempt to assimilate new information into existing cognitive structures. Such a need would naturally arise when reality diverged from expectations, pointing to the inadequacy of existing cognitive structures. Finally, Piaget also postulated an inverted U-shaped discrepancy–motivation relationship. At very low levels of discrepancy, he believed that new information would be assimilated effortlessly and automatically without requiring much attention or motivation. At very high levels of discrepancy, new information would be ignored because the infant would be unable to relate the new stimuli to existing cognitive structures (McCall & McGhee, 1977, p. 193).

---

[8] This view was echoed in even more radical form by Nissen (1954), who believed that the brain and other organs carried with them their own source of motivation: "Among the requirements of all tissues is that they perform their normal functions. An unused muscle atrophies, and so does an unused gland. It is positively painful to deny any organ the exercise of its usual function.... The sense organs 'want to' see and hear and feel just as much as the mouth or stomach or blood-stream 'want to' eat or contract or maintain a certain nutrient balance. It is the function of the brain to perceive and to know" (p. 300).

Hunt arrived at a virtually identical position from his research on intrinsic motivation (1963, 1965). His theory of intrinsic motivation drew on diverse developments in psychology, each of which emphasized the importance of violated expectations as interrupters or motivators of behavior. These developments were McClelland's model of motivation (McClelland, Atkinson, Clark, & Lowell, 1953); G. A. Miller, Galanter, and Pribram's (1960) test–operate–test–exit (TOTE) analysis of behavior, and Helson's adaptation-level theory (Helson, 1947, 1948). On the basis of G. A. Miller et al. (1960), Hunt postulated that curiosity was triggered by violated expectations. On the basis of McClelland et al.'s theory of affect, he, too, postulated an inverted U-shaped function relating affect to the magnitude of such cognitive discrepancies. For Hunt, curiosity reflected a search for an intermediate level of cognitive incongruity that, in turn, was motivated by a desire for positive affect.

Hunt's incongruity account of curiosity was further refined by Kagan (1972) in a classic article on motivation. According to Kagan, there are four basic human motives: the motive to resolve uncertainty, sensory motives, anger and hostility, and the motive for mastery. The first, in his view, is synonymous with curiosity: "The motive to resolve uncertainty might be renamed the motive for cognitive harmony, consonance, equilibrium, or simply the motive to know, which Berlyne calls epistemic curiosity" (Kagan, 1972, p. 54). However, whereas Hebb, Piaget, and Hunt each believed that curiosity results from violations of expectations, Kagan (1972) argued that "Hunt ignored three other sources of uncertainty with motivational significance": incompatibility between ideas, incompatibility between ideas and behavior—both based on cognitive dissonance theory (Festinger, 1957)—and the inability to predict the future. Thus, Kagan, too, viewed curiosity as a response to incongruity but expanded the list of incongruities postulated to give rise to curiosity. In effect, Kagan's perspective can be viewed as a modern version of Berlyne's without the complicating baggage of behaviorism.

Incongruity theories express the intuition—supported by recent research— that people tend to be curious about events that are unexpected or that they cannot explain. Research examining when people make causal attributions (when they ask "why" questions) demonstrates that violated expectations do, in fact, often stimulate a search for an explanation (Hastie, 1984; Psyszcynski & Greenberg, 1981; Wong & Weiner, 1981). The notion of an optimal level of incongruity also seems highly intuitive, although it has received less empirical support. Some researchers have obtained weak supportive evidence (e.g. Miyake & Norman, 1979), including one study particularly relevant to curiosity that found that frequency of question asking depends on the match between the difficulty of the question and the expertise of the respondent (McCall & McGhee, 1977). But one systematic review found, at best, mixed support for the hypothesis and discussed numerous difficulties inherent in measuring the relevant constructs and their relationship to one another (Wachs, 1977).

Finally, the incongruity theorists' notion that there is a natural human need for sense making has received broad support from diverse areas of research, although little of it was cited by incongruity theorists. As Gilovich (1991, p. 9) wrote, "We are predisposed to see order, pattern, and meaning in the world, and we find randomness, chaos, and meaninglessness unsatisfying. Human nature abhors a lack of predictability and the absence of meaning."

Gestalt psychologists have been some of the most persistent advocates of the view that there is a human need for sense making. Indeed, the very notion of a gestalt reflects the fundamental human tendency to make sense of information by organizing it into coherent "wholes." More important, Gestalt psychologists have argued that the drive toward gestalt creation has motivational force (Heider, 1960; see also Suchman, 1971). As H. Kreitler and Kreitler (1972) wrote in their book on aesthetics, the "pressure to straighten out, to improve, or to perfect... perceived figures may be so potent that it can be neither disregarded nor withstood by the spectator and is accompanied by tension and discomfort until it is resolved by a proper perceptual act" (pp. 86–87).[9] An analogous observation in the epistemic realm was made by Reiser (1931, p. 361), who noted that "a problem presents itself as an open Gestalt which 'yearns' for a solution, and it is the function of thought to find the solution by transforming the open Gestalt into a closed one." Although Gestalt psychologists have not discussed curiosity explicitly, Malone (1981) proposed—but did not further develop—an account of "cognitive curiosity" based on gestalt concepts. Cognitive curiosity "is evoked by the prospect of modifying higher level cognitive structures...[and] can be thought of as a desire to bring better 'form' to one's knowledge structures" (Malone, 1981, p. 363).

A need for sense making is reflected in other diverse areas of research. For example, the need for cognition (Cohen, Stotland, & Wolfe, 1955, p. 291) is defined as "a need to structure relevant situations in meaningful, integrated ways...to understand and make reasonable the experiential world." The original article laying out the need for cognition hypothesis further proposed that "feelings of tension and deprivation arise from its [the need for cognition's] frustration (Cohen et al., 1955, p. 291), a proposition that is consistent with the idea that sense making has motivational force. Supportive of a link between need for cognition and curiosity is the high correlation between need for cognition and various specific curiosity scales (mean $r = .57$) found in one study (Olson & Camp, 1984b). Clearly, need for cognition is closely related

---

[9] Kreitler and Kreitler also conducted extensive research on curiosity (e.g. S. Kreitler, Kreitler, & Zigler, 1974; S. Kreitler, Zigler, & Kreitler, 1984) but, surprisingly, failed to apply the insights from their work on aesthetics to that on curiosity.

to specific curiosity. However, as it has evolved, the research on the need for cognition provides few insights applicable to specific epistemic state curiosity because of its focus on trait differences and their consequences (e.g. Cacioppo & Petty, 1982). Need for cognition has become widely viewed as a personality trait rather than a psychological state subject to situational influences.

Also closely related to the need for sense making is the concept of ambiguity aversion (Ellsberg, 1961; Frenkel-Brunswik, 1949). Ambiguity refers to the absence of a single coherent interpretation of a situation or, obversely, the presence of more than one plausible interpretation. Recently, Frisch and Baron (1988) have characterized ambiguity aversion as the avoidance of situations in which one believes that there is a lack of information relevant to making a decision (Frisch & Baron, 1988). The main difference between the literature on ambiguity aversion and that on curiosity is their focus. The ambiguity literature examines how people avoid ambiguity by not making decisions when information is missing or by avoiding alternatives with ambiguous attributes, whereas curiosity research tends to focus on the desire for information itself.

Although the various components of the incongruity approach have generally been supported by empirical research, it is questionable whether incongruity provides a sufficiently comprehensive account of curiosity or even of its specific epistemic state variant. Although incongruity is an important instigator of curiosity, it is not the only instigator of curiosity, even using Kagan's broad definition of the concept. In many cases, such as in straining to overhear a conversation taking place at an adjoining table in a restaurant, in the desire to solve a puzzle, or in the compulsion to read another person's diary, curiosity does not seem to result from incongruity but from other factors such as the salience of specific missing information or understanding.

6.2.4. Competence and Intrinsic Motivation

Diametrically opposed to both the drive-based and incongruity-based accounts of curiosity is a theoretical perspective articulated by White (1959). According to White, curiosity results from a motivation to master one's environment that he called the "competence" or "effectance" motive. White denied the existence of a curiosity drive, arguing that curiosity has none of the characteristics usually associated with such physiological drives as hunger. First, he noted that unlike hunger, curiosity does not involve "a tissue need or deficit external to the nervous system" (White, 1959, p. 301), and he attacked Hebb's contention that curiosity could originate spontaneously in the nervous system. Second, White (1959) asserted that curiosity "cannot be regarded as leading to any kind of consummatory response" (p. 301). Responding to the natural objection that obtaining information often leads to a sudden reduction in curiosity. White (1959) stated that "if the animal at some point turns away and leaves the once novel object we may say that its curiosity is 'satisfied,' but we do not mean by this that the equivalent of a consummatory response has just taken place" (p. 301). White argued that curiosity is derivative of the competence motive so that the former could be subsumed under the latter without causing great theoretical damage.

White's analysis was later extended by Deci (1975), who embraced White's competence notion and, like White, proposed to subsume curiosity into "the more general realm of all intrinsically motivated behaviors" (p. 53). In support of a link between curiosity and competence, Deci (1975) noted that competence, like curiosity, "is not intense and immediate in the sense that thirst, fear, etc. are, but rather it is an ongoing process which is periodically interrupted by tissue needs" (p. 55). In other words, Deci viewed curiosity as a mild motivational state that is easily overwhelmed by even weak physiological drives.

Just as the incongruity perspective was inspired by the observation that violated expectations trigger curiosity, the competence perspective reflects the well-established observation that people are curious about their own abilities (e.g. Festinger, 1954). The competence perspective has received some empirical support (although not intended as such) in research by Swann, Stephenson, and Pittman (1981). They found that the tendency to ask diagnostic questions during an interview (a measure of curiosity) was greater for subjects who had earlier been deprived of control (presumably undermining their feelings of mastery over their environment). However, the competence account suffers from the same deficiency as the incongruity perspective in that it fails to offer a comprehensive account of curiosity. *Competence* is not synonymous with *curiosity*. On the one hand, the effort to learn how to pitch a baseball is likely to be motivated by a desire for mastery but not by curiosity. On the other, the desire to overhear a conversation at the next table in a restaurant seems to reflect curiosity but not a desire to achieve competence, except in the most remote sense of the term. Furthermore, contrary to Deci's assumption that curiosity is overwhelmed by even weak physiological drives, most people can recall times in their lives when curiosity was extremely intense, even to the point of interfering with "tissue needs" such as hunger and thirst. Interestingly, although Kagan (1972) included mastery in his list of four fundamental motives, he explicitly disavowed a connection between mastery and curiosity.

6.2.5. *Summary*

Each of the theoretical perspectives discussed here—the drive theories, the incongruity perspective, and the competence approach—gives expression to one or more of curiosity's salient characteristics. Drive theories reflect the observation that curiosity is aversive, has motivational force, and can be stimulated internally (by boredom) or by external stimuli Incongruity theories point to the importance of violated expectations as instigators of curiosity, and the competence perspective highlights the fact that curiosity is pronounced toward topics that involve one's self-concept. However, none of these theories offers a comprehensive account of curiosity that can explain the wide range of circumstances in which it arises. Furthermore, the question of curiosity's underlying cause is inherently unanswerable because it is always possible that curiosity stems from some as yet unidentified, more basic drive or motive. Perhaps the best one can do is to note the similarity between curiosity and a wide range of information-seeking phenomena that all seem to reflect a human need for sense making or, as Kagan called it, a "need to know."

6.3. Voluntary Exposure to Curiosity

Drive-based accounts of curiosity assume that unsatisfied curiosity produces aversive arousal. The desire to reduce such arousal produces the information-seeking that is curiosity's most basic behavioral manifestation. The assumption that curiosity is aversive, however, seems to imply, less plausibly, that people will avoid exposing themselves to curiosity in the first place. But, in fact, people frequently expose themselves intentionally to situations that they know will make them curious. As Hebb (1955) commented,

It is nothing short of extraordinary what trouble people will go to in order to get into more trouble at the bridge table, or on the golf course; and the fascination of the murder story, or thriller, and the newspaper accounts of real-life adventure or tragedy, is no less extraordinary. (p. 250)

Such curiosity-seeking behavior, Hebb noted, posed a paradox for drive-based accounts of curiosity.

Hebb believed that his own account of curiosity, which assumed that people actually like limited levels of arousal, was not vulnerable to this paradox because it predicted curiosity seeking: "It appears that, up to a certain point, threat and puzzle have positive motivating value, beyond that point negative value" (1955, p. 250). Stated simply, Hebb's argument is that people seek out moderate amounts of curiosity because they find moderate levels more pleasurable or less aversive than low or high levels.

When Berlyne became aware of Hebb's challenge to his drive-based account of curiosity, he modified his theory in a manner that, although very similar to Hebb's, adhered to the behaviorist view of arousal as uniformly aversive. Berlyne drew a distinction between *arousal*, which referred to the individual's internal state, and *arousal potential* or *stimulus intensity*, which referred to the degree of stimulus complexity of the environment. He argued that low as well as high levels of stimulus intensity—very undifferentiated or highly complex environments—produced high levels of arousal. In other words, he postulated that boredom produces high levels of arousal. In an impoverished environment, stimulus intensity would be low and arousal high, and the individual would attempt to increase arousal by seeking curiosity-inducing stimuli. In a highly complex environment, both stimulus intensity and arousal would be high, and the individual would attempt to decrease them through curiosity-reducing exploration. Thus, Berlyne, too, predicted that organisms should be attracted to stimuli that have moderate arousal potential corresponding to moderate levels of curiosity. Berlyne, however, did not seem particularly convinced by his own account and defended it against Hebb's with little more than the argument that he did not want to change his mind.[10]

Hebb's and Berlyne's accounts of curiosity seeking are very similar because both postulate an inverted U-shaped curiosity preference function. Both infer from curiosity seeking that people must like curiosity. It might appear somewhat circular and therefore uninteresting to explain curiosity-seeking by arguing that people like curiosity. However, such an account of curiosity seeking is not boring; it is wrong because it is inconsistent with commonly observed behavior. If people like positive levels of curiosity, why do they attempt to resolve the curiosity? Why do they not put mystery novels down before the last chapter or turn off the television before the final inning of a close ball game? Arguing that people seek curiosity because they like it simply shifts attention back to the original question of why people attempt to satisfy it. Thus, neither the drive nor the incongruity theories provide a viable account of curiosity seeking.

Advocates of the competence perspective have not grappled with the problem of curiosity seeking because they do not assume that curiosity is aversive and therefore do not view curiosity seeking as a paradox. Nevertheless, it is not difficult to imagine how competence theorists would account for curiosity seeking; they would argue that people seek out curiosity-inducing problems both to develop and demonstrate their competence.

6.4. Situational Determinants of Curiosity

Most of the theories reviewed earlier point to specific situational determinants of curiosity. Drive theories, for example, predict that curiosity will intensify if left unsatisfied and that curiosity can be "satisfied" and thus eliminated

---

[10] "It is tempting to suppose that the conditions that make for boredom will produce exceptionally low arousal, and that low arousal, as well as high arousal, must therefore be aversive. Such a hypothesis has been put forward by several writers (e.g. Hebb, 1955). Nevertheless, we shall stand firm against the temptation and refrain from adopting this hypothesis. Instead, we shall suggest, though with even more diffidence than accompanies our other theoretical suggestions, that boredom works through a *rise in arousal*" (Berlyne, 1954a, p. 188).

by exposure to suitable stimuli. Incongruity theories draw attention to the importance of violated expectations as a source of curiosity and postulate an inverted U-shaped relationship between curiosity and the extremity of expectation violations. The competence interpretation suggests that people should be curious about information that pertains to their competence. Most of these observations have been supported by empirical research. However, no theory provides a broad account of situational determinants, because few theorists have specified testable implications of their theories beyond the observations that originally motivated them. Thus, Hebb (1955), after laying out his own account of curiosity, acknowledged that "I know this leaves problems. It is not *any*... form of problem that is rewarding; we still have to work out the rules for this formulation" (p. 250). However, Hebb, and most other curiosity theorists, never got around to working out such rules.

Berlyne presents one major exception to this pattern. He conducted numerous empirical studies addressing the question of what stimulus properties are associated with high levels of arousal potential and thus induce curiosity. He identified a number of "collative" variables that, he predicted, would arouse cognitive conflict, stimulating curiosity. As noted previously, these included stimulus characteristics such as novelty, complexity, and surprise.

Berlyne tested several elements of his theory in one of the first experiments on curiosity involving human subjects. His experiment was fabulously complicated, involving three groups of subjects, a seven-stage procedure, and an endless series of ratings by subjects (Berlyne, 1954b). Distilled to its essentials, subjects were given questions about invertebrates, indicated which they found most curiosity evoking and surprising,[11] were presented with a randomly ordered list of answers, and then completed the initial questionnaire about invertebrates a second time.

Berlyne's main prediction was borne out. Questions rated as eliciting greater curiosity in the first questionnaire were more likely to be answered correctly in the second. The underlying logic was that the original questions that generated curiosity increased the individual's arousal level. As subjects heard the answers to these questions in the second stage of the study, their curiosity would be satisfied, and arousal would be successively reduced. The temporal association of arousal reduction with learning the answer to the questions that had piqued their curiosity would reinforce learning those particular answers. As Berlyne (1954b) expressed it, "the rehearsal of the answer would reduce the curiosity drive to a subliminal value, and this drive-reduction would

---

[11] The idea of a question being surprising is somewhat confusing, and Berlyne's (1954b) failure to report any of the specific questions that he asked subjects, surprising or not surprising, does not help to clarify the matter. The article stated that "incompatibility was judged by having subjects mark those questions in the fore-questionnaire which surprised them, and also by using a group of judges, who indicated which predicates seemed to them least applicable to animals" (p. 258).

reinforce the learning of the answer" (p. 257). Also as predicted, questions that were designated as surprising in the first questionnaire were more likely to be rated as evoking curiosity, thus supporting Berlyne's hypothesized link between conflict (approximated here by surprise) and curiosity. Numerous other predictions were also supported, although most, including those just discussed, have alternative interpretations that are simpler than those proposed by Berlyne (Cofer & Appley, 1964, p. 298).

One of the predictions examined in the study by Berlyne—that conceptual controversy produces curiosity—was examined in a classroom setting by Lowry and Johnson (1981). The study was innovative in many respects, particularly the diversity of dependent measures used. Fifth and sixth graders working on class projects were randomly assigned to interact in groups in a manner intended either to foster intellectual consensus or to produce argument and epistemic conflict. The prediction was that conflictual group interactions would stimulate curiosity. Dependent measures of curiosity included achievement tests that measured the subjects' eventual mastery of the topic areas, scales measuring subjects' self-rated interest in the topics, and behavioral measures of information search including study time, use of information from special sources (e.g. the library), and attendance at an optional film shown during recess. All of these measures were affected significantly by the controversy manipulation. Indeed, 45% of controversy subjects gave up their recess to view the film, whereas only 18% of the noncontroversy group did so.

After publishing the experiment discussed above. Berlyne continued to test his own theory. However, after this experiment, which used self-reports of curiosity, he seemed to rediscover the behaviorist's aversion to subjective measures. In subsequent research, he switched from verbal to visual stimuli and measured curiosity not by asking subjects which stimuli evoked curiosity but by monitoring subjects' focus of attention. In numerous studies (e.g. Berlyne & Parham, 1968), which were followed by a flood of similar experiments by other researchers (e.g. S. Kreitler, Zigler, & Kreitler, 1975; Munsinger & Kessen, 1964; Nunnally, 1971), Berlyne presented subjects with geometric shapes that varied in complexity or novelty and measured curiosity by recording the amount of time subjects spent looking at them. In such experiments, there was no cost to subjects for looking at one stimulus item rather than another, they were expected to examine at least one. It is therefore possible that subjects were not curious about any of the stimuli but found one marginally less boring than the others. Such experiments provided no outlet for the expression of a positive motivation for looking at a particular stimulus. The *Random House Dictionary* defines curiosity as "the desire to learn or know about anything"; in these studies, however, subjects could learn little by selecting one stimulus item over another because no information was hidden. In this case, it seems natural that aesthetic considerations would influence subjects' allocation of attention to stimuli at least as much as curiosity.

Perhaps because attention to geometric shapes has little to do with curiosity, efforts to measure individual differences in curiosity using a similar setup (e.g. by examining the level of complexity of shapes that people attend to) have not proven reliable and do not correlate reliably with other measures of curiosity (S. Kreitler, Zigler, & Kreitler, 1974; Munsinger & Kessen, 1964; Munsinger, Kessen, & Kessen, 1964; Voss & Keller, 1983). Berlyne himself eventually seemed to recognize this problem because he subsequently repackaged this line of research as an investigation of aesthetics (Berlyne, 1974). Thus, although Berlyne set out to delineate situational (stimulus) determinants, he failed to achieve this goal as a result of his shift to a research paradigm that measured attention and aesthetic appreciation rather than curiosity.

6.5. Curiosity's Combination of Transience and Intensity

The final question that was not raised or addressed in either wave of curiosity research—but that is fundamental to achieving a comprehensive understanding of the phenomenon—concerns why curiosity possesses the curious combination of qualities described by Edmund Burke in the quote opening this article. First, curiosity tends to be highly transient but, at the same time, quite intense. Consider the curiosity one occasionally experiences about the facial features of a person seen from the back. In such cases, it is remarkable how quickly curiosity dissipates after one loses sight of the person. Likewise, the office—and hence telephone—of a colleague of mine is located adjacent to the departmental conference room. When his phone rings during a conference or seminar, he becomes curious about who is calling, often to the extent that he actually walks out of a seminar to take the call. However, when his phone is not ringing, he has no qualms about leaving his office for other parts of the building, and, out of hearing range from his phone, he is not distracted by the possibility that he may be receiving calls, nor does he wonder who might be calling. This latter observation reflects a closely related characteristic of curiosity: the degree to which it is stimulus bound.

Second, curiosity tends to be associated with impulsive behavior. People who are curious not only desire information intensely but desire it immediately and even seek it out "against their better judgment." Curiosity's connection to impulsivity is illustrated compellingly by the fact that curiosity has been used as an impulsivity induction method in experimental research comparing the effectiveness of alternative self-control techniques. Hartig and Kanfer (1973; see also Kanfer & Zich, 1974) instructed children in the use of alternative self-control techniques, told them not to turn around and look at an attractive toy display behind them, and then observed whether they were able to resist the temptation to do so. Such studies are premised on, and thus give additional support to, the notion of a link between curiosity and impulsivity.

The fact that curiosity can cause one to act knowingly against one's own self-interest is vividly illustrated in the confessions of St. Augustine (1943, p. 13) in a passage describing the experience of his law student friend Alypius in Rome. Alypius was "utterly opposed to and detesting" of gladiatorial shows. However, "one day [he] met by chance diverse acquaintances [who], with a friendly violence drew him, vehemently objecting and resisting, into the amphitheater, on a day of these cruel and deadly shows." He protested that "though you drag my body to that place, and there place me, can you force me to give my mind and lend my eyes to these shows?" and closed his eyes. However, after sitting there for a period, "upon the fall of one in the fight, a mighty cry from the whole audience stirring him strongly [and] he, overcome by curiosity, . . . opened his eyes, and was struck with a deeper wound in his soul than the other . . . on whose fall that mighty clamor was raised."

Finally, and not unrelated to curiosity's association with impulsivity, when curiosity is satisfied, the result is generally disappointing. For example, Felcher, Petrison, and Wang (1993) interviewed 30 people about their attitudes toward mail and found that although the daily mail delivery is looked forward to with anxious anticipation and impatience, most respondents reported almost always being disappointed by the actual mail they received. Likewise, the pleasure people obtain from a glimpse of the person they have been trailing on the sidewalk, or the satisfaction my colleague derives from learning who is calling him, is typically meager in comparison with the intensity of the curiosity that preceded these acts. Indeed, there are situations, such as Alypius's desire to know what the crowd was shouting about, in which people recognize from the start that the information curiosity impels them to obtain will bring no pleasure or even pain.

6.6. An Integrative Interpretation of Specific Epistemic Curiosity

In an attempt to address the issues raised in the previous sections. I propose an integrative interpretation of curiosity—an "information-gap" perspective—that combines insights from the theories just reviewed with ideas borrowed from Gestalt psychology, social psychology, and behavioral decision theory. Consistent with the conclusion of the section on the definition and dimensionality of curiosity, the theory deals exclusively with specific state curiosity (an intrinsically motivated desire for specific information). After presenting the basic components of the new perspective, I show how it addresses three of the questions considered earlier: the explanation for voluntary exposure to curiosity, curiosity's situational determinants, and the explanation for curiosity's intensity, transience, association with impulsivity, and tendency to disappoint. As noted earlier, the remaining question—the cause of curiosity—is inherently unanswerable. Nevertheless, I believe that the need for sense making discussed by Kagan and others provides a plausible account of the underlying cause of curiosity. Although somewhat vague, the appeal of such an account is that it draws a connection between curiosity and a wide range of other phenomena that involve information seeking.

Like virtually every idea in contemporary psychology, an early rendition of the information-gap perspective can be found in the work of William James. James (1890/1950) proposed that "scientific curiosity"—the type of curiosity that most closely corresponds to specific epistemic curiosity—arises from "an inconsistency or a gap in . . . knowledge, just as the musical brain responds to a discord in what it hears" (p. 429). Consistent with this view, the information-gap theory views curiosity as arising when attention becomes focused on a gap in one's knowledge. Such information gaps produce the feeling of deprivation labeled *curiosity*. The curious individual is motivated to obtain the missing information to reduce or eliminate the feeling of deprivation.

6.6.1. *Curiosity as a Reference-Point Phenomenon*

Like other types of gaps in attainments, an information gap can be defined by two quantities: what one knows and what one wants to know. What one knows is relatively objective (although people may misestimate their own degree of knowledge in different domains), but what one wants to know is highly subjective. In decision-theoretic terms, what one wants to know can be thought of as one's informational "reference point." The most developed application of the reference-point concept is in decision making under uncertainty. New reference-point theories of decision making under uncertainty, most prominently Kahneman and Tversky's (1979) prospect theory, underscore the subjective nature of attainments; the same absolute level can be viewed positively or negatively depending on the decision maker's reference point.

Curiosity, in this view, arises when one's informational reference point in a particular domain becomes elevated above one's current level of knowledge. The central insight gained by applying such a formulation to curiosity is that the same degree of knowledge can evoke or not evoke curiosity depending on the level of one's reference point.

Application of the reference-point concept to curiosity suggests an analogy between curiosity and other reference-point phenomena in which dissatisfaction depends on the discrepancy between one's actual level of attainment and a goal or aspiration level. For example, relative deprivation theories posit that negative feelings result from a comparison of one's own material position against that of people who have more. Of course, most people are surrounded by countless others who have more than they do. But people generally do not feel globally deprived; rather, they feel deprived only when they compare themselves with specific others. Similarly, in the case of curiosity, people are not always curious, even though they are surrounded by vast regions of ignorance. Dissatisfaction with one's state of knowledge, like dissatisfaction with one's material condition, depends on a contrast between one's objective situation and a subjective reference point.[12]

The informational reference point and information level concepts imply that quantity of information is a unidimensional concept that can be expressed as a single number. But information is inherently multidimensional. This creates an analytical problem that recurs in numerous domains that have been analyzed in terms of reference points. For example, an individual's feeling of material deprivation may result from comparing her or his own fancy car with the neighbor's swimming pool. Although it is possible, in theory, to treat such a problem multidimensionally, the wide range of possible possessions makes such an approach extremely cumbersome. To facilitate comparisons between people with heterogeneous possessions, relative deprivation researchers often collapse multidimensional material possessions into a unidimensional quantity by describing individuals' possessions in terms of dollar values.

The equivalent practice in regard to information is to use principles of information theory (e.g. see Attneave, 1959) to quantify an individual's level of information in a particular domain. Information theory interprets level of knowledge in terms of the fineness of "partitions" a person is able to draw. For example, early in a presidential campaign, there may be a wide range of candidates who cannot be ruled out as eventual victors. This can be viewed as a coarse partition, because many candidates are included in the same partition—the set of potential victors—and because there is little reason to favor one over another probabilistically. Clearly, the informational reference point—the goal—in this situation is to find out who gets elected to the presidency. As the campaign proceeds, with primaries weeding out candidates and public opinion polls providing further information, the range of possible victors decreases, probability estimates for those who remain become more varied, and the gap between what one knows and what one wants to know decreases.

Information theory's entropy coefficient provides a potential measure of the degree of one's information (actually one's ignorance) in situations such as a

---

[12] This connection between curiosity and relative comparison in the material realm reinforces Abelson's (1986) view that people treat beliefs (or knowledge, in this case) as if they were material possessions.

presidential election. Entropy is defined as

$$-\sum_{i=1}^{n} p_i \log_2 p_i, \qquad (1)$$

where, in this example, n is the total number of candidates and p_i refers to the assessed probability that a particular candidate (subscripted by i) will prevail.[13]

Consider a race with 10 initial candidates. Let $w_i = 0$, 1 indicate a particular candidate's eventual success ($w = 1$) or failure ($w = 0$). If initially one has no idea who will win, then the best guess of the likelihood that any one candidate will win is $p = 1/10$, which can be written as $p(w_i = 1) = .1$ for $i = 1$, 10. The entropy coefficient in this situation is equal to 3.3 $[-10^*.1^*\log_2(.1)]$ and would drop to 2.3 $[-5^*.2^*\log_2(.2)]$ if primaries eliminated half of the candidates from the race [creating a new partition with $p(w_i = 1) = 0$ for $i = 1$ to 5 and $p(w_i = 1) = .2$ for $i = 6$ to 10]. The entropy coefficient can be applied to a wide range of curiosity-inducing informational settings (e.g. the possible solutions to a puzzle, the lineup of potential murderers in a "whodunit," or the range of frontal appearances one might anticipate for a person viewed from the back).

Quantifying the magnitude of an information gap requires entropy measures of (1) the individual's current situation, (2) the individual's informational goal, and, possibly, (3) a situation of total ignorance. The absolute magnitude of the information gap can be expressed as (2) – (1), and a common measure of the relative magnitude of the gap is [(2) – (1)]/[(2) – (3)]. In the case of a race that has been reduced to five equiprobable candidates, the individual's current level of information is equal to 2.3, the goal is to achieve a level of 0, and total ignorance (10 equiprobable candidates) equals 3.3. Thus, the absolute magnitude of the gap is –2.3 [0 – (2.3)], and the relative magnitude is 0.7.

Based on findings from other domains, it is likely that people are sensitive to both the absolute and relative magnitude of the information gap (Prelec & Loewenstein, 1991). For example, in decision making under uncertainty, the contrast between a .1 and .2 chance of winning a prize is seen as greater than the contrast between 0.8 and 0.9 because the ratio between the former is greater than that of the latter, even though the difference is the same. However, the contrast between 0.45 and 0.9 is seen as greater than that between 0.1 and 0.2 (even though the ratios are equivalent) because the difference is greater in the former. Applied to curiosity, the same reasoning suggests that the perceived magnitude of an information gap will depend on both the absolute and relative magnitude of the gap. Thus, the information gap when one knows 4 of the 5 states bordering the Pacific Ocean is likely to

---

[13] This formula applies to situations in which information is in binary form (e.g. candidates can either win or lose) It is easily generalized to more complex informational settings.

be perceived as larger than the gap inherent in knowing 49 of the 50 states in the country. However, the gap inherent in knowing 40 of the 50 United States will be seen as larger than that associated with knowing 4 of the 5 states bordering the Pacific.

Entropy values should be treated as crude proxies rather than as precise measures of the magnitude of information gaps. Entropy is typically difficult to measure in real-world settings, and its calculation often requires numerous simplifying assumptions that are of dubious validity. Furthermore, as Kreitler, Zigler, and Kreitler (1974) argued, there are forms of information that powerfully affect curiosity but are not captured by entropy. For example, in murder mysteries there are numerous facts about the characters and the overall situation that may not help to resolve the "whodunit" question but that nevertheless promote curiosity by bringing the characters and plot to life. These facts constitute real information but do not affect the entropy coefficient when it is defined as in the preceding illustration.

Fortunately, for research purposes it is frequently unnecessary to measure the precise magnitude of an information gap. Often, one makes only ordinal predictions (e.g. that curiosity will increase with information), in which case it is sufficient to establish experimental situations with more or less information. For example, in an experiment discussed later, subjects were shown from zero to three photographs of parts of a person's body. Although it is difficult to measure their level of information contingent on viewing a certain number of photographs, the amount of information is clearly an increasing function of the number of photographs viewed.

Furthermore, information gaps can be measured without recourse to entropy by eliciting from subjects subjective ratings of knowledge or ignorance. This is a common procedure in research involving constructs such as feeling-of-knowing, which are well understood at an intuitive level but are difficult to quantify. Subjects generally seem to have no problem coming up with a single number that represents their feeling-of-knowing, even though this judgment requires expressing inherently multidimensional quantities as a single number.

6.6.2. *The Situational Determinants of Curiosity*

Among the implications of the information-gap perspective, two are particularly fundamental. First, the intensity of curiosity directed at a particular item of information should be related positively to its ability to resolve uncertainty (i.e., to close the information gap). Because curiosity reflects a desire to close information gaps, it is natural to assume that curiosity will be greater toward information that more nearly accomplishes this task.

Support for this prediction was obtained in an experiment reported in Loewenstein, Adler, Behrens, and Gillis (1992). Subjects were exposed to two lists of states and were asked to guess the rule that had generated each list. One list was always twice as large as the other (10 states as opposed to 5), but list length was crossed with the actual rule. After guessing the rule for each list, subjects were asked to choose the rule they would like to learn. The prediction was that subjects would want to learn the rule that would shed light on the relationship between a larger number of states (i.e. the rule associated with the longer list). As predicted, approximately 70% of subjects chose to learn whichever rule was associated with the longer list even after controlling for the subjects' perceived and actual accuracy of guesses.

The ability of information to close a gap will also depend on other characteristics of the information set. Specifically, with insight problems there is a possibility that a single piece of information (i.e. the insight) can throw light on the entire problem. With incremental problems, in contrast, any single piece of information is unlikely to yield a sudden solution. Thus, the information-gap perspective predicts that, all else equal, curiosity should be greater for insight than for incremental problems.

A study reported in Loewenstein et al. (1992) tested this prediction. Although it is difficult to compare curiosity toward incremental and insight problems without varying the problem itself, an attempt was made to hold the problem essentially constant while varying its character (insight vs. incremental). This was done by allowing subjects to explore a visual matrix consisting of either pictures of different animals or a single enlarged picture of a single animal chosen randomly from the larger set. The former was intended as an incremental problem because subjects would learn a new animal each time they exposed a picture; the latter was more of an insight problem because subjects would be unable to determine which animal they were viewing at first but would eventually figure it out. Subjects recruited for a computer-controlled experiment were presented with what they were told was a "practice screen" that consisted of a 5 (wide) × 9 (high) grid of blank squares. They were told that they should click the mouse on at least 5 of the 45 squares to familiarize themselves with the operation of the mouse. Thus, subjects had no idea that the experiment had anything to do with curiosity. Clicking the mouse on a square revealed an image that was hidden behind the square. A 4-s delay was introduced to make information acquisition costly in terms of time. In one condition (multiple animals), each square contained a picture of a different animal; in the other (single animal), the entire screen contained a picture of a single animal that was randomly selected for each subject from the set of animals included in the multiple-animal condition. Curiosity was measured by how many squares a subject exposed over and above the required 5. The prediction was that subjects in the single-animal condition would become curious to solve the gestalt—to determine what image was contained on the screen—whereas those in the multiple-animal condition would be less curious to learn the full range of concealed animals. As predicted, subjects in the single-animal condition exposed a significantly larger number of squares.

A second and less intuitively obvious implication of the information-gap perspective is that curiosity should be positively related to one's knowledge in a particular domain. There are two reasons for anticipating such a relationship. First, as one gains information about a particular topic, there is an ever-increasing likelihood that one will focus on what one does not know rather than on what one knows. According to the information-gap perspective, such a focus on missing information is a necessary condition for curiosity. To illustrate, consider an individual who knows the capitals of only 3 of the 50 states. Such a person is likely to frame her or his knowledge as such (i.e. that she or he knows 3 state capitals). However, a person who knows the capitals of 47 states is more likely to frame her or his situation as one of not knowing 3 state capitals. Thus, as information about a topic increases, one's attention is more likely to be attracted to the gap in one's knowledge.

As a visual analogy, imagine a piece of paper (representing a coherent information set), one contiguous part of which is colored red (information possessed) and the rest of which is colored white (missing information). When the red area is small, it will be the focus of attention; the white area will be perceived as background. However, as the size of the red area increases relative to the white, a point will be reached at which attention will be drawn toward the white part. Such a shift of focus is characteristic of numerous gestalt illusions in which different images arise from the same visual display depending on what part one perceives as the "figure" and what part one perceives as the "ground."

A similar attention-shift phenomenon is observed in decision making under uncertainty. Consider a gamble that offers a p chance of winning $1,000. Initially an individual offered the gamble is likely to frame it as such: a p chance of winning $1,000. As p increases, however, at some point an abrupt reframing is likely to occur to a focus on what can be lost. Thus, a person with a 0.9 chance of winning $1,000 is likely to frame it as $1,000 with a 0.1 chance of losing the money (Elster & Loewenstein, 1992).

The implication for curiosity is that an individual is likely to focus on the information that is present when most of the information from a set is missing. At this point, the informational reference set is effectively zero. As information is acquired, however, at some point a qualitative shift of attention is likely to occur from a focus on what is known to one on what is not known. This shift is the genesis of curiosity because, at that moment, the individual suddenly becomes focused on the gap in his or her knowledge. This suggests that curiosity is unlikely to arise in the absence of an existing knowledge base and that the likelihood of experiencing curiosity should increase as an individual obtains information about a particular topic. Marcel Proust (1924/1982) captured this tendency when he described his protagonist Swann as lacking "even the tiny, initial clue which, by allowing us to imagine what we do not know, stimulates a desire for knowledge" (p. 261).

There is a second reason for anticipating a positive relationship between curiosity and information. In numerous domains, such as animal behavior (N. E. Miller, 1944), social comparison (Messick & Sentis, 1989), and decision making under uncertainty (Kahneman & Tversky, 1979), researchers have found that motivation tends to increase at the margin as an individual approaches a reference state from below. The approach gradient estimated from animal studies exhibits an accelerating form; motivation increases as an organism physically approaches a goal. Applied to information, such an accelerating function would imply that the marginal value of information should increase as the individual accumulates information toward the goal of completing the reference set. Whereas the attention-shift effect discussed earlier is discontinuous, this effect is continuous. Thus, as information is accumulated, the information-gap perspective predicts a sudden increase in curiosity when the individual becomes focused on the missing information and then a more gradual increase as he or she approaches the goal of closing the information gap.

Although a positive relationship between curiosity and knowledge is a central prediction of the information-gap perspective, in practice, the relationship between information and curiosity may not be so simple because new information can change the perceived size of the information set, causing the reference point to shift. New information provides an ever-changing idea of what there is to be known. For example, when one sets out to learn a new language, the relevant information set may initially seem small, and curiosity should be commensurately strong. But as one begins to learn the language and becomes aware of its complexities, the perceived information set—what there is to know—is likely to increase. Thus, curiosity may well decline early on rather than increase, even as one gains proficiency in the language.

There is a second reason why curiosity may not increase with knowledge. Sometimes, as one gains information, the objective value of a particular item of information declines, even though it remains unknown. For example, when one is completing a jigsaw puzzle of an unknown picture, there may be a particular moment at which one guesses with confidence the content of the picture (e.g. the Mona Lisa). At this point, one's curiosity to see a particular piece of the puzzle completed is likely to decline because one can infer its content with some accuracy. Similarly, in reading a murder mystery, one's curiosity to learn the identity of the murderer is likely to decline if one becomes extremely confident that one already knows the answer. The prediction that curiosity increases with knowledge, therefore, assumes that the objective value of the missing information remains constant as related information is acquired.

157

The general prediction that curiosity should increase with knowledge has already received some empirical support. In Berlyne's (1954b) experiment reviewed earlier, for example, questions about more familiar animals evoked greater curiosity. A similar finding was obtained by S. Jones (1979), who had subjects rate how curious they were to see the answers to questions and also tested them on their knowledge related to the questions. Jones anticipated that subjects who were more generally knowledgeable would also be more curious as individuals; however, he failed to find the correlation he hypothesized between overall knowledge and trait curiosity. Instead, and consistent with the relationship predicted here between knowledge in a particular domain and curiosity in that domain, Jones did observe a significant correlation (0.51) between self-evaluated knowledge of a particular item and curiosity about that item. He concluded that "subjects were more curious toward items about which they already had some knowledge than toward those about which they had little or no knowledge" (S. Jones, 1979, p. 640).

A positive relationship between curiosity and knowledge was also found in two studies conducted by Loewenstein et al. (1992). In one study, subjects were shown, one by one, from zero to three photographs of different body parts (hands, feet, and torso) of a man or a woman. After all of the selected photographs had been turned over, subjects completed a form that elicited their self-reported curiosity to see the photograph of the whole person and were given a choice between seeing the photograph or getting a $.50 bonus payment. As predicted curiosity increased significantly with the number of body parts viewed. In the second study (discussed in more detail later), they found a positive relationship between feelings of knowing and curiosity, consistent with the view that curiosity increases with perceived knowledge.

6.6.3. *Voluntary Exposure to Curiosity*

Like the drive theories but contrary to Hebb's perspective the interpretation of curiosity proposed here assumes that curiosity is always aversive. The key to understanding curiosity seeking lies in recognizing that the process of satisfying curiosity is itself pleasurable. As William James commented in an autobiographical essay, movement from a "state of puzzle and perplexity to rational comprehension is full of lively relief and pleasure" (cited in Posnock, 1991, p. 39). Similarly, Piaget (1969) noted (but did not relate to curiosity) that, after an attempt at problem solving, "there follows, sometimes abruptly, a feeling of coherence and of necessity, the satisfaction of arriving at a system which is both complete in itself and indefinitely extensible" (p. 139). As an illustration, consider how unsatisfying is the information that the wife was the murderer in Turow's *Presumed Innocent* if one is not immersed in the book. However, figuring out or learning the identity of the killer is intensely satisfying when one is reading the book.

The pleasure derived from satisfying curiosity provides a simple explanation for voluntary curiosity seeking. It is perfectly sensible for people to expose themselves to curiosity-inducing situations if the expected incremental pleasure from obtaining the information compensates for the aversiveness of the curiosity itself. People often intentionally exacerbate aversive states such as hunger and thirst to heighten the pleasure they will derive subsequently from eating or drinking. In such situations, it is not hunger and thirst that are pleasurable, as earlier explanations of curiosity seeking implied by analogy, but their elimination. Fasting before a fancy meal and denying oneself water after exercising so as to better appreciate the customary post-jog beer are just two examples of a ubiquitous pattern of behavior. Likewise, it makes sense for people to expose themselves to curiosity-inducing stimuli if, by doing so, they enhance the pleasure subsequently derived from obtaining information.

Voluntary exposure to curiosity can be viewed as a type of gamble. Before exposing oneself to a particular curiosity-inducing situation, one must estimate the likelihood that one's curiosity will be ultimately satisfied and, if so, how long such satisfaction is likely to take. When the protability of satisfying the curiosity is low, or if it is likely that one will be left in a state of aversive curiosity for a long period, exposing oneself to curiosity will generally not be worth the gamble. By analogy, imagine that one was virtually certain of eating a large, delicious dinner in the evening. In such a case, fasting during the day would make sense. However, if there were only a small chance of such a dinner materializing, fasting would be a mistake. Therefore, one strong prediction that emerges from the information-gap perspective is that people will not expose themselves to curiosity-inducing situations in which there is only a slim chance of satisfying the curiosity or in which there would be a long delay before the information is received. As Feuerbach commented, "man only wants to know what *man* can know. What lies beyond this region has no existence whatever for him; so for him it is also the object of no drive or wish whatsoever" (cited in Blumenberg, 1966/1983, p. 442).

Several closely related phenomena have been observed in the domain of social comparison. A frequent observation in the social comparison literature is that people tend to compare themselves with others who are only marginally better off on some dimension than they are: most people do not make themselves miserable by comparing themselves with the rich and famous (Festinger, 1954; Wheeler, 1966). Similarly, Davies's (1962) work on revolutions that are caused by rising expectations argued that people become discontent and likely to rebel when they not only perceive that others possess what they do not but also perceive what they do not have as potentially attainable. The idea that people tend not to be attracted to things that are out of their reach is also reflected in research (cited in Schelling, 1984) showing that addicts experience less painful withdrawal symptoms in detoxification institutions that have a reputation for inviolability. Perhaps for evolutionary reasons, people do not focus their feelings of deprivation on things that are impossible to attain. There is no reason to expect curiosity to be an exception to this rule.

6.6.4. *Involuntary Curiosity*

Although people sometimes expose themselves voluntarily to situations that they know will make them curious, it is probably more common for curiosity to arise spontaneously as a result of unintentional exposure to curiosity-inducing stimuli. The information-gap perspective predicts that curiosity will arise spontaneously when situational factors alert an individual to the existence of an information gap in a particular domain. This can occur either because the gap itself becomes salient or because the information set as a whole becomes salient and the individual recognizes that information is missing from the set. Situational factors that produce these effects include the following:

1. The posing of a question or presentation of a riddle or puzzle confronts the individual directly with missing information and is therefore perhaps the most straightforward curiosity inducer. Berlyne (1960) referred to curiosity-inducing questions as "thematic probes."

2. Exposure to a sequence of events with an anticipated but unknown resolution will almost inevitably create curiosity to know the outcome. This class of situations is exemplified by the desire to find out who wins an election or athletic event or to learn the identity of the murderer in a mystery novel. In Schank and Abelson's (1977) terms, curiosity arises from the desire to complete a "script." Such curiosity is exacerbated when an individual generates a prediction or forecast of the outcome, in which case curiosity about the outcome itself is combined with a desire to know whether the prediction was correct. The desire to know whether one's prediction was correct is closely related to White's competence motive.

3. The violation of expectations often triggers a search for an explanation (Hastie, 1984), and curiosity is frequently a major factor motivating the search. In addition to the work showing that violated expectations trigger causal attributions, recent research has shown that people tend to engage in effortful systematic, as opposed to heuristic, processing when presented with information incongruent with expectations, even when the resultant inferences have little practical importance to them (Maheswaran & Chaiken, 1991).

4. Possession of information by someone else also causes curiosity. Here, curiosity and social comparison are linked directly rather than by analogy.

In some cases, another person's information set may become sufficiently salient to establish an informational reference point for oneself. Consider, for example, parents' curiosity to know the sex of a fetus when the information is known to their doctor or the burgeoning numbers of "900" telephone lines in which callers are promised that they will be the recipients of intimate secrets. Similarly, watching someone chuckle as he or she reads a news article is likely to make one curious to see the article.

5. Past attainments can serve as a reference point against which current attainments are compared. This has been shown in a number of studies of saving behavior and life satisfaction (e.g. Duesenberry, 1952). It is likely that past knowledge sets have a similar effect. Consider the enormous curiosity that is evoked by the recognition that one knew a piece of information but has forgotten it. In keeping with this prediction, Loewenstein et al. (1992) found that subjects were more curious about information that was reported to be "on the tip of the tongue" than about information that was not. Subjects were presented with a series of definitions and asked to guess the words to which the definitions applied. For words they were unable to identify, they were asked whether the word was on the tip of their tongue and to rate their feeling of knowing. The central prediction, that curiosity would be related positively to tip-of-the-tongue perceptions and feeling of knowing, was strongly confirmed.

6.6.5. *Guessing and Feedback*

The information-gap perspective implies that awareness of an information gap is a necessary precondition for experiencing curiosity. Thus, a failure to appreciate what one does not know would constitute an absolute barrier to curiosity. There is good reason to believe that such barriers are pervasive. Decision researchers have documented an "overconfidence" phenomenon (e.g. Lichtenstein, Fischhoff, & Phillips, 1982) whereby people underestimate the magnitude of gaps in their knowledge. In a slightly different vein, Charles Gettys and coauthors (Gettys, Pliske, Manning, & Casey, 1987) argued that people generally believe they have much more information about a topic than they actually do. He had subjects generate as many solutions as they could to various problems (e.g. solving the parking problem at the University of Oklahoma) and then asked them to guess how many additional good solutions to the problem existed. The typical subject generated a relatively small number of solutions but believed that he or she had come fairly close to exhausting the set of possible good solutions. Gettys et al. referred to this effect as the "fat but happy" hypothesis: Subjects have major knowledge gaps but are not aware of them. Convinced that they have generated most of the good solutions, they are unlikely to be curious about other potential ideas.

One way for people to gain an accurate perception of what they do not know is to have them make guesses and receive accuracy feedback. It is difficult to ignore or deny a gap in one's knowledge when one has guessed the answer to a question and been told that it is wrong. Without accuracy feedback, people may believe that they have guessed correctly when they have not, thus eliminating curiosity. Guessing with feedback not only may increase the salience of the gap but may create a type of Zeigarnik effect (Zeigarnik, 1927): an urge to complete successfully the task of guessing.

Consistent with this reasoning, Loewenstein et al. (1992) found that guessing combined with accuracy feedback increased curiosity. In one experiment, subjects rated their curiosity to learn the easternmost state of the United States. Half of the subjects first guessed which states were most southern, northern, and western, whereas half did not, and half of the subjects were given the correct answer to each of these questions, whereas half were not. Neither manipulation alone had a significant effect, but the combination of guessing and feedback increased curiosity substantially. Although this study did not show a main effect for either guessing or feedback alone, a subsequent experiment did show a main effect for feedback. Subjects guessed the easternmost state three times and were told "right" or "wrong" either after each guess or after guessing all three. Few people gave the correct answer (which is Alaska; it crosses the international date line). Subjects who received feedback after each guess were significantly more curious to know the answer to the question than subjects who received feedback only after making all three guesses.

6.6.6. Curiosity's Combination of Intensity, Transience, and Impulsivity

Although they have not been discussed in the psychology literature, the four qualities of curiosity alluded to by Burke (1757/1958)—its intensity, transience, and association with impulsivity and the tendency for its satisfaction to disappoint—are easily explained by the information-gap perspective.

Curiosity's intensity is explained by the fact that it is a loss phenomenon; information seeking is motivated by the aversiveness of not possessing the information more than it is by the anticipation of pleasure from obtaining it. Considerable research has shown that losses have greater motivational impact than gains of comparable objective value (e.g. see Kahneman & Tversky, 1979). Theories such as White's competence perspective, which view curiosity as motivated by a desire for positive affect (e.g. a feeling of competence), naturally imply that curiosity is a relatively weak force. In contrast, drive theories and the information-gap perspective, which view curiosity as driven by the pain of not having information rather than by the pleasure of obtaining it, can account for the observed motivating power of curiosity.

Curiosity's transience is explained by the fact that curiosity requires attention, which is a limited cognitive resource (Kahneman, 1973; Treisman & Gelade, 1980). Because curiosity results from attention to an information gap, it will typically end when attention is distracted. This feature of curiosity differs from homeostatic drives such as hunger and thirst. Although one can be distracted temporarily from hunger and thirst, they will ultimately intensify if not satisfied.

Curiosity's association with impulsivity is also easily accommodated by the information-gap perspective. Research on delay of gratification has shown that people are more likely to behave impulsively—to opt for inferior immediate rewards—when failing to select the immediate reward exposes them to deprivation. For example, Walter Mischel (1974) found that when young subjects were placed in immediate proximity to candy, they were more likely to take a small piece of candy immediately instead of waiting for a large piece of candy. Presumably, seeing and smelling the candy produced a feeling of deprivation that made it difficult for them to wait. In a recent article, Steve Hoch and I presented diverse evidence supporting a link between impulsivity and deprivation and argued that this association results from the fact that delay of gratification in a given situation depends in large part on the pain one would experience if consumption were deferred (Hoch & Loewenstein, 1991). The association of curiosity with impulsivity, therefore, like the explanation for curiosity's intensity, follows naturally from the view of curiosity as a form of cognitively induced deprivation.

Finally, the disappointment often experienced when curiosity is satisfied can also be explained by the fact that curiosity is driven by deprivation. Eliminating curiosity eliminates the deprivation but leaves one in a neutral hedonic state. A similar pattern seems to be characteristic of other drives, such as hunger, that leave one in a neutral state when satisfied. But assimilating food is a more drawn out process than assimilating information; thus, with food, there is a period of pleasure when hunger is slowly diminishing. Information, in contrast, is typically assimilated almost instantly, so the transition from aversive deprivation to a neutral state is exceedingly fleeting.

Curiosity has much in common with the sex drive, which is also a powerful motivator, highly stimulus bound, and associated with impulsive behavior and disappointment. Indeed, for men, the disappointment is recognized to the point of possessing its own label: *postcoitus triste*. The sex drive also shares other characteristics with curiosity. As is true for curiosity, people sometimes put off having sex, even when it makes them feel deprived in the present, because they think it will enhance future pleasure. However, people also expose themselves to sexually stimulating materials, such as pornography, without the prospect of imminent sexual release. This raises the question of whether, contrary to the theory espoused here, there are situations in which people derive pleasure from curiosity even when they have no hope of satisfying it.

6.7. Discussion

Despite widespread recognition of its importance for education, scientific progress, and other domains of human activity, a century of research and theorizing has left large gaps in our understanding of curiosity. This is particularly true of its epistemic, specific state variant. As Kakar (1976, p. 185) noted, "epistemic behavior, or intellectual activity in search of knowledge, is a form of curiosity which is of utmost importance in the process and planning of education. Yet this is a field where our knowledge is quite scanty." Educational attainment and scientific exploration both involve specific epistemic curiosity, but most curiosity research has focused on its diversive and perceptual variants. Likewise, policies designed to stimulate curiosity in students require an understanding of state curiosity, but most recent curiosity research has investigated issues relating to trait curiosity.

In this article, I have addressed the gap in our understanding of curiosity by proposing a new account of specific epistemic state curiosity that starts with existing theoretical accounts of curiosity and integrates insights from Gestalt psychology, behavioral decision theory, and other subdisciplines in psychology. Like drive theories, the new account views curiosity as aversive; it incorporates elements of homeostatic and stimulus-based theories by assuming that curiosity is stimulated by both external and internal factors.

The new account is also consistent with the incongruity theorists' position that cognition can provide its own motivation even in the absence of any physiological tissue needs and with the assumption that curiosity can arise from violated expectations. However, the information-gap interpretation of curiosity parts ways with Hebb, Piaget, and Hunt when it comes to their claim that information seeking is connected to a search for an optimal level of incongruity. An information gap refers to a discrepancy between what one knows and what one wishes to know. Incongruity, on the other hand, as used by these researchers, refers to violated expectations (i.e. a discrepancy between what one perceives and what one expected to perceive). Although violated expectations are an important factor leading to the identification of knowledge gaps and, thus, to curiosity, they do not represent the only source of such gaps.

Finally, filling information gaps is an important aspect of achieving competence (White, 1959), and curiosity is certainly particularly strong when it comes to knowledge pertaining to one's own competence. However, not all curiosity can be understood as a desire to feel competent, even if one adopts the broadest possible meaning of the term.

6.7.1. *Limitations of the Proposed Theory*

The proposed theory views curiosity as occurring when an individual's informational reference point becomes elevated in a certain domain, drawing attention to an information gap. Curiosity is the feeling of deprivation that results from an awareness of the gap. However, it must be acknowledged that people often seek information in the absence of curiosity. In some situations, external rewards motivate information search, as in the case of a student who studies solely to obtain a high grade. Even more commonly, people seek information because they believe they will find it interesting, even though its absence is not viewed as a deficiency. Such a situation would not be classified as curiosity according to the theoretical position proposed here. Although both extrinsic rewards and intrinsic interest are important determinants of information seeking, in neither case would one expect to observe the most salient symptoms of curiosity: the intensity of motivation, transience, association with impulsivity, and disappointment when information is successfully assimilated.

Curiosity arises from the landscape of an individual's preexisting interests when one's informational reference point becomes elevated in a particular domain. Preexisting interests, by focusing attention, play an important role in determining what information is salient to an individual and, thus, which informational reference points become elevated. Interest can also provide a weak motive contributing to the accumulation of information. Because curiosity is more likely to occur and will tend to be stronger as information is accumulated, interest, in effect, primes the pump of curiosity. Therefore, a comprehensive theory of curiosity will need to explain why certain people become interested in certain topics and why certain topics (e.g. anything having to do with the self) are almost universally interesting. However, the goal of constructing such a theory is extremely ambitious. No theory that I know of provides much insight into individual differences in interests. The one area of research that one might expect to deal with this problem—that of intrinsic motivation—has been preoccupied with a single narrow issue: the effect of extrinsic rewards on intrinsic motivation. There has been a prevailing belief that extrinsic rewards tend to diminish intrinsic motivation, although a recent meta-analysis of the literature casts doubt on the validity of this central assumption (Wiersma, 1992).

Interests arise from a number of situational and dispositional factors associated with culture, socialization, age, sex, and genes. Some people are fascinated by brain teasers or physics problems, whereas others are interested in what makes people tick or in world events. The current theory does not attempt to delineate these factors but, rather, seeks to identify some situational determinants that will influence the onset and magnitude of curiosity—all else held constant—and to shed light on some of curiosity's salient characteristics.

6.7.2. Potential Research Directions

The information-gap interpretation of curiosity suggests several natural directions for future research. First, the notion that curiosity is a reference-point phenomenon suggests numerous predictions that have yet to be tested. For example, one important reference point for individuals is the attainments of others. If individuals adopt other people's information sets as their own informational reference points, then they should often become curious to know what others know. It would be easy to test whether an individual's curiosity increases with the knowledge that another person possesses a piece of information, all else held equal. Another untested prediction of the theory is that people will be more curious to know something if they think it is knowable or if they expect to know it in the future. Ruderman (1986) found that dieters who had previously resisted eating began to eat when they were told that they would be served food in an hour, as if knowing that they would eat in the future made them hungry in the present. It would be interesting to test whether a similar pattern would hold for curiosity.

A second potentially fruitful focus for empirical research involves the characteristics of curiosity—its transience, intensity, association with impulsivity, and tendency to disappoint—that have heretofore been ignored, and thus not examined critically, by psychologists. Transience could be examined by determining how rapidly curiosity subsides when a curiosity-inducing stimulus is removed. Impulsivity could be researched by looking at the difference between what people will pay to obtain curiosity-satisfying information immediately or at some point in the future. Finally, the disappointment hypothesis could be tested by asking people how they feel after their curiosity has been satisfied. Although the satisfaction one obtains from satisfying curiosity will undoubtedly occasionally exceed one's expectations, the prediction is that these cases will be outnumbered by those in which the information one receives is seen as disappointing.

6.7.3. Practical and Social Implications of the Proposed Theory

The information-gap perspective has significant implications for education. Educators know much more about educating motivated students than they do about motivating them in the first place. As Engelhard and Monsaas (1988, p. 22) stated, "historically, education research has focused primarily on the cognitive outcomes of schooling" rather than on motivational factors. The theoretical framework proposed here has several implications for curiosity stimulation in educational settings. First, it implies that curiosity requires a preexisting knowledge base. Simply encouraging students to ask questions— a technique often prescribed in the pedagogical literature—will not, in this view, go very far toward stimulating curiosity. To induce curiosity about a particular topic, it may be necessary to "prime the pump" to stimulate information acquisition in the initial absence of curiosity. The new research showing that extrinsic rewards do not quell intrinsic motivation suggests that such rewards may be able to serve this function without drastically negative side effects.

Second, to stimulate curiosity, it is necessary to make students aware of manageable gaps in their knowledge. The importance of knowing what one does not know may explain the success of the "Socratic method" of teaching, which, according to Malone (1981), has the effect of "systematically exposing incompleteness, inconsistencies, and unparsimoniousness in the learner's knowledge structures" (p. 364).

The finding that curiosity increases with knowledge has several ramifications that go beyond the realm of education. First, the positive relationship between curiosity and knowledge creates a powerful impetus toward specialization. As people gain knowledge in a particular area, they are not only likely to perceive gaps in their knowledge, but those gaps will become smaller relative to what they already know. Thus, people are likely to become progressively more curious about the topics that they know the most about. The seeming ever-increasing drive toward specialization in academia may therefore reflect intrinsic as well as extrinsic incentives. Moreover, such specialization may have its origin in relatively minor and often chance differences in initial knowledge accumulation. As Arthur (1989) has pointed out, systems exhibiting increasing returns (in this case, the positive relationship between curiosity and knowledge) tend to have unstable properties whereby small perturbations in early periods produce large long-run effects.[14]

The relationship between curiosity and information gaps also has implications for social stereotyping. It is well established that people possess well-articulated social schemata and that they use these schemata to infer missing information about individuals whom they meet (Fiske, 1982; Gilovich, 1981). Thus, for example, one might assume that a Native American on a reservation is unemployed. The failure to perceive a gap in one's information, because one has filled in the gap automatically with a social stereotype, is likely to reduce

---

[14] The same mechanism could lead to significant individual differences in curiosity as a result of small initial environmental or dispositional differences. As McDougall (1918) commented, "these differences [in curiosity] are apt to be increased during the course of life, the impulse growing weaker for lack of use in those in whom it is innately weak, stronger through exercise in those in whom it is innately strong" (p. 61).

or negate the amount of curiosity one experiences about the individual's actual occupational status. Lack of curiosity about others as a result of the failure to recognize information gaps may be a contributing factor to the well-documented resistance of stereotypes to change. At the same time, however, the information-gap theory suggests a possible solution to the problem. If people are made aware of their stereotypes and of the predictions they make on the basis of them, they may become curious to know whether their predictions are correct.

Finally, the proposed theoretical framework may help to explain why certain nonsanctioned exploratory behaviors (e.g. experimentation with drugs, sex, and cigarettes) are so difficult to discourage. In all of these cases, numerous factors conspire to increase the salience of the information gap for those who fail to experiment: The information set (the experience itself) is well defined, the information is relatively easy to obtain, and the individual is typically surrounded by others who already possess the information. The information-gap perspective predicts that all of these factors will strengthen the intensity of curiosity. Unfortunately, it is far easier to create such conditions than to eliminate them.

6.8. Concluding Comments

As I have attempted to highlight in this review, research and theorizing about curiosity has been largely moribund during the past two decades. Although the research on scale creation has shed light on the issue of curiosity's definition and dimensionality, other fundamental questions such as curiosity's underlying cause and its situational determinants have not been addressed. This state of affairs can be attributed to the triumph of the cognitive paradigm in psychology and to the general loss of interest in motivational phenomena such as curiosity.

The extremity of this shift in focus is evident in the substantial literature on problem solving, which has extensive applications both to cognitive development and learning and to scientific discovery. Virtually all of this research has examined the cognitive strategies that people use to solve problems (e.g. see Duncker, 1945; Mayer, 1983). Amazingly, there has been almost no research on why people are so powerfully driven to solve such problems, even though many researchers studying problem solving in the laboratory and in naturalistic settings have been struck by the intensity of individuals' efforts to solve problems in the absence of material rewards.

Although theoretical accounts of creativity, problem solving, and scientific discovery tend to emphasize the cognitive dimension, personal accounts of the scientific process often betray an important motivational component. For example, in reflecting on his discovery of shock waves. Mach wrote that "the first questions are formed upon the intention of the inquirer by practical considerations; the subsequent ones are not. An irresistible attraction draws him to these; a nobler interest which far transcends the mere needs of life" (cited in Seeger, 1970, p. 60). In a similar vein, Herbert Simon (1992) stated that through scientific inquiry, "scientists are relieved of the itch of curiosity that constantly torments them"[15] (p. 3).

Curiosity involves an indissoluble mixture of cognition and motivation. As Hunt (1963) expressed it, curiosity refers to a "motivation inherent in information processing" (p. 35). Curiosity is influenced by cognitive variables such as the state of one's knowledge structures but may, in turn, be one of the most important motives encouraging their formation in the first place. Positioned at the junction of motivation and cognition, the investigation of curiosity has the potential to bridge the historical gulf between the two paradigms.

References

Abelson, R. P. (1986). Beliefs as possessions. *Journal for the Theory of Social Behavior, 16*, 223–250.

Aristotle. (1933). *Metaphysics*. Cambridge, MA: Harvard University Press.

Aronoff, J. (1962). Freud's conception of the origin of curiosity. *Journal of Psychology, 54*, 39–45.

Arthur, W. B. (1989). Competing technologies, increasing returns, and lock-in by historical events. *Economic Journal, 99*, 116–131.

Asch, D. A., Patton, J. P., & Hershey, J. C. (1990). Knowing for the sake of knowing. *Medical Decision Making, 10*, 47–57.

Attneave, F. (1959). *Applications of information theory to psychology*. New York: Holt, Rinehart & Winston.

Beiser, H. R. (1984). On curiosity: A developmental approach. *Journal of the American Academy of Child Psychiatry, 23*, 517–526.

Bentham, J. (1948). *Principles of morals and legislation*. New York: Macmillan. (Original work published 1789)

Berg, C. A., & Sternberg, R. J. (1985). Response to novelty: Continuity versus discontinuity in the developmental course of intelligence. In H. W. Reese (Ed.), *Advances in child development and behavior* (Vol. 19, pp. 1–47). New York, Academic Press.

Berlyne, D. E. (1954a). A theory of human curiosity. *British Journal of Psychology, 45*, 180–191.

Berlyne, D. E. (1954b). An experimental study of human curiosity. *British Journal of Psychology, 45*, 256–265.

---

[15] Curiosity manifests itself at all levels of cognitive and emotional life. For example, the *Philadelphia Inquirer* (Rozansky, 1993) reported the predicament of a secretary who was given a mobile phone and could not muster the willpower to turn it off, even for a brief period. The *Inquirer* reported that she "hoped no one would flush while she answered a call in a stall in the second floor ladies room in Porter Hall. 'I could turn it off in there. I could. It's two minutes,' she said 'but I'm afraid I will miss something good'" (p. D12).

Berlyne, D. E. (1955). The arousal and satiation of perceptual curiosity in the rat. *Journal of Comparative and Physiological Psychology, 48*, 238–246.

Berlyne, D. E. (1960). *Conflict, arousal, and curiosity*. New York: McGraw-Hill.

Berlyne, D. E. (1974). *Studies in the new experimental aesthetics*. Washington. DC: Hemisphere.

Berlyne, D. E. (1978). Curiosity and learning. *Motivation and Emotion, 2*, 97–175.

Berlyne, D. E., & Parham, L. C. C. (1968). Determinants of subjective novelty. *Perception and Psychophysics, 3*, 415–423.

Blumenberg, H. (1983). *The legitimacy of the modern age*. (R. M. Wallace, Trans.). Cambridge, MA: MIT Press. (Original work published 1966)

Boyle, G. J. (1983). Critical review of state-trait curiosity test development. *Motivation and Emotion, 4*, 377–397.

Boyle, G. J. (1989). Breadth-depth or state-trait curiosity? A factor analysis of state-trait curiosity and state anxiety scales. *Personality and Individual Differences, 10*, 175–183.

Brown, J. S. (1953). Comments on Professor Harlow's paper. In *Current theory and research in motivation* (pp. 1–21). Lincoln: University of Nebraska Press.

Bühler, C., Hetzer, H., & Mabel, F. (1928). Die affecktwirksamkeit von fremdheitsein-drücken im ersten lebensjahr [The emotional impact of alien impressions in the first year of life]. *Zeitschrift für Psychologie, 107*, 30–49.

Burke, E. (1958). *A philosophical enquiry into the origin of our ideas of the sublime and beautiful*. London: Routledge & Kegan Paul. (Original work published 1757)

Butler, R. A. (1953). Discrimination learning by rhesus monkeys to visual exploration motivation. *Journal of Comparative and Physiological Psychology, 46*, 95–98.

Butler, R. A. (1957). The effect of deprivation of visual incentives on visual exploration motivation in monkeys. *Journal of Comparative and Physiological Psychology, 50*, 177–179.

Butler, R. A., & Alexander, H. M. (1955). Daily patterns of visual exploratory behavior in the monkey. *Journal of Comparative and Physiological Psychology, 48*, 247–249.

Cacioppo, J. T., & Petty, R. E. (1982). The need for cognition. *Journal of Personality and Social Psychology, 42*, 116–131.

Camp, C. J., Rodrigue, J. R., & Olson, K. R. (1984). Curiosity in young, middle-aged, and older adults. *Educational Gerontology, 10*, 387–400.

Cicero. (1914). *De finibus bonorum et malorum* (H. Rackham, Trans.). Cambridge, MA: Harvard Press.

Cofer, C. N., & Appley, M. H. (1964). *Motivation: Theory and research*. New York: Wiley.

Cohen, A. R., Stotland, E., & Wolfe, D. M. (1955). An experimental investigation of need for cognition. *Journal of Abnormal and Social Psychology, 51*, 291–294.

Coie, J. D. (1974). An evaluation of the cross-situational stability of children's curiosity. *Journal of Personality, 42*, 93–117.

Cullari, S., & Mikus, R. (1990). Correlates of adolescent sexual behavior. *Psychological Reports, 66*, 1179–1184.

Darchen, R. (1957). Sur le comportement d'exploration de *Batella germancia*. Exploration d'un plan [On the exploratory behavior of cockroaches. Exploration of a plane]. *Journal de Psychologie Normale et Pathologiqué, 54*, 190–205.

Dashiell, J. F. (1925). A quantitative demonstration of animal drive. *Comparative Psychology, 5*, 205–208.

Davies, J. C. (1962). Toward a theory of revolution. *American Sociological Review, 27*, 5–19.

Day, H. I. (1971). The measurement of specific curiosity. In H. I. Day, D. E. Berlyne, & D. E. Hunt (Eds.), *Intrinsic motivation: A new direction in education.* New York: Holt, Rinehart & Winston.

Day, H. I. (1982). Curiosity and the interested explorer. *Performance and Instruction, 21*, 19–22.

Deci, E. L. (1975). *Intrinsic motivation.* New York: Plenum.

Dember, W. N. (1956). Response by the rat to environmental change. *Journal of Comparative and Physiological Psychology, 49*, 93–95.

Duesenberry, J. (1952). *Income, saving, and the theory of consumer behavior.* Cambridge, MA: Harvard University Press.

Duncker, K. (1945). On problem solving. *Psychological Monographs, 58* (Whole No. 270).

Ellsberg, D. (1961). Risk, ambiguity, and the savage axioms. *Quarterly Journal of Economics, 75*, 643–699.

Elster, J., & Loewenstein, G. (1992). Utility from memory and anticipation. In G. Loewenstein & J. Elster (Eds.), *Choice over time* (pp. 213–234). New York: Russell Sage Foundation.

Engelhard, G., & Monsaas, J. A. (1988). Grade level, gender and school-related curiosity in urban elementary schools. *Journal of Educational Research, 82*, 22–26.

Fazio, R. H., Herr, P. M., & Powell, M. C. (1992). On the development and strength of category-brand associations in memory: The case of mystery ads. *Journal of Consumer Psychology, 1*, 1–13.

Felcher, M., Petrison, L., & Wang, D. (1993, October). *Towards an understanding of consumer feelings toward mail.* Paper presented at the Direct Marketing Association annual meeting, Toronto, Ontario, Canada.

Feldman, M. S., & March, J. G. (1981). Information in organizations as signal and symbol. *Administrative Science Quarterly, 26*, 171–186.

Festinger, L. (1954). A theory of social comparison processes. *Human Relations, 7*, 117–140.

Festinger, L. (1957). *A theory of cognitive dissonance.* Evanston, Il.: Row, Peterson.

Fiske, S. T. (1982). Schema-triggered affect: Applications to social perception. In M. S. Clark & S. T. Fiske (Eds.), *Affect and cognition: The 17th Annual Carnegie Symposium on Cognition* (pp. 55–78). Hills-dale, NJ: Erlbaum.

Fowler, H. (1965). *Curiosity and exploratory behavior.* New York: Macmillan.

Frenkel-Brunswik, E. (1949). Intolerance of ambiguity as an emotional and perceptual personality variable. *Journal of Personality, 18*, 108–143.

Freud, S. (1915). Analysis of a phobia in a five-year-old boy. In *Collected papers* (vol. 3, pp. 149–289). New York: Basic Books.

Frisch, D., & Baron, J. (1988). Ambiguity and rationality. *Journal of Behavioral Decision Making, 1*, 149–157.

Gettys, C. F., Pliske, R. M., Manning, C., & Casey, J. T. (1987). An evaluation of human act generation performance. *Organizational Behavior and Human Decision Processes, 39*, 23–51.

Gilovich, T. (1981). Seeing the past in the present: The effect of associations to familiar events on judgments and decisions. *Journal of Personality and Social Psychology, 40*, 797–808.

Gilovich, T. (1991). *How we know what isn't so: The fallibility of human reason in everyday life*. New York: Free Press.

Glanzer, M. (1953). Stimulus satiation: An explanation of spontaneous alternation and related phenomena. *Psychological Review, 60*, 257–268.

Glanzer, M. (1961). Changes and interrelations in exploratory behavior. *Journal of Comparative and Physiological Psychology, 54*, 433–438.

Green, D. (1990). Instrument for the measurement of individual and societal attitudes toward drugs. *International Journal of the Addictions, 25*, 141–157.

Harlow, H. F., Harlow, M. K., & Meyer, D. R. (1950). Learning motivated by a manipulation drive. *Journal of Experimental Psychology, 40*, 228–234.

Hartig, M., & Kanfer, F. H. (1973). The role of verbal self-instructions in children's resistance to temptation. *Journal of Personality and Social Psychology, 25*, 259–267.

Hastie, R. (1984). Causes and effects of causal attribution. *Journal of Personality and Social Psychology, 46*, 44–56.

Hebb, D. O. (1949). *The organization of behavior*. New York: Wiley.

Hebb, D. O. (1955). Drives and the C.N.S. (conceptual nervous system). *Psychological Review, 62*, 243–254.

Hebb, D. O. (1958). The motivating effects of exteroceptive stimulation. *American Psychologist, 13*, 109–113.

Heider, F. (1960). The gestalt theory of motivation. In D. Rapaport (Ed.), *Nebraska Symposium on Motivation* (pp. 145–172). Lincoln: University of Nebraska Press.

Helson, H. (1947). Adaptation-level as frame of reference for prediction of psychophysical data. *American Journal of Psychology: 60*, 1–29.

Helson, H. (1948). Adaptation-level as a basis for a quantitative theory of frames of reference. *Psychological Review, 55*, 297–313.

Hoch, S., & Loewenstein, G. (1991). Time-inconsistent preferences and consumer self-control. *Journal of Consumer Research, 17*, 492–507.

Holmes, D. A., & Holmes, C. B. (1991). Curiosity as portrayed in young children's literature. *Psychological Reports, 68*, 695–700.

Hume, D. (1888). *Treatise of human nature*. Oxford, England: Clarendon Press. (Original work published 1777)

Hunt, J. M. (1963). Motivation inherent in information processing and action. In O. J. Harvey (Ed.), *Motivation and social interaction* (pp. 35–94). New York: Ronald Press.

Hunt, J. M. (1965). Intrinsic motivation and its role in psychological development. In D. Levine (Ed.), *Nebraska Symposium on Motivation* (Vol. 13, pp. 189–282). Lincoln: University of Nebraska Press.

James, W. (1950). *Principles of psychology* (Vol. 2). New York: Holt. (Original work published 1890)

Jones, A. (1966). Information deprivation in humans. In B. A. Maher (Ed.), *Progress in experimental personality research* (pp. 241–307). San Diego, CA: Academic Press. 241–307.

Jones, A., Wilkinson, J. J., & Braden, I. (1961). Information deprivation as a motivational variable. *Journal of Experimental Psychology, 62*, 126–137.

Jones, S. (1979). Curiosity and knowledge. *Psychological Reports, 45*, 639–642.

Kagan, J. (1972). Motives and development. *Journal of Personality and Social Psychology, 22*, 51–66.

Kahneman, D. (1973). *Attention and effort*. Englewood Cliffs, NJ: Prentice Hall.

Kahneman, D., & Tversky, A. (1979). Prospect theory: An analysis of decision under risk. *Econometrica, 47*, 263–291.

Kakar, S. (1976). Curiosity in children and adults: A review essay. *Indian Journal of Psychology, 51*, 181–201.

Kanfer, F. H., & Zich, J. (1974). Self-control training: The effects of external control on children's resistance to temptation. *Developmental Psychology, 10*, 108–115.

King, T. R. (1991, October 17). Advertising: Putting forth the art of holding back. *Wall Street Journal*, p. 4.

Kivy, P. N., Earl, R. W., & Walker, E. L. (1956). Stimulus context and satiation. *Journal of Comparative and Physiological Psychology, 49*, 90–92.

Koestler, A. (1973). *The act of creation*. New York: Dell.

Kolko, D. J., & Kazdin, A. E. (1989). Assessment of dimensions of childhood firesetting among patients and nonpatients: The firesetting risk interview. *Journal of Abnormal Child Psychology, 17*, 157–176.

Kreitler, H., & Kreitler, S. (1972). *Psychology of the arts*. Durham, NC: Duke University Press.

Kreitler, S., Kreitler, H., & Zigler, E. (1974). Cognitive orientation and curiosity. *British Journal of Psychology, 65*, 43–52.

Kreitler, S., Zigler, E., & Kreitler, H. (1974). The complexity of complexity. *Human Development, 17*, 54–73.

Kreitler, S., Zigler, E., & Kreitler, H. (1975). The nature of curiosity in children. *Journal of School Psychology, 13*, 185–200.

Kreitler, S., Zigler, E., & Kreitler, H. (1984). Curiosity and demographic factors as determinants of children's probability learning strategies. *Journal of Genetic Psychology, 145*, 61–75.

Laffont, J. (1989). *The economics of uncertainty and information*. Cambridge. MA: MIT Press.

Langevin, R. (1971). Is curiosity a unitary construct? *Canadian Journal of Psychology, 25*, 360–374.

Leherissey, B. L. (1972). Validation of a measure of state epistemic curiosity in a computer-assisted learning situation. *Proceedings of the 80th Annual Convention of the American Psychological Association, 7*, 523–524.

Leherissey-McCombs, B. (1971). *The development of a measure of state epistemic curiosity* (Tech. Memorandum No. 34). Tallahassee: Florida State University.

Lichtenstein, S., Fischhoff, B., & Phillips, L. D. (1982). Calibration of probabilities: The state of the art to 1980. In D. Kahneman. P. Slovic, & A. Tversky (Eds.), *Judgment under uncertainty: Heuristics and biases* (pp. 306–334). Cambridge, England: Cambridge University Press.

Loewenstein, G., Adler, D., Behrens, D., & Gillis, J. (1992). *Why Pandora opened the box: Curiosity as a desire for missing information*. Working paper. Department of Social and Decision Sciences, Carnegie Mellon University, Pittsburgh, PA.

Lowry, N., & Johnson, D. W. (1981). Effects of controversy on epistemic curiosity, achievement, and attitudes. *Journal of Social Psychology, 115*, 31–43.

McCall, R. B., & McGhee, P. E. (1977). "The discrepancy hypotheses of attention and affect in infants." In I. C. Uzgiris & F. Weizmann (Eds.), *The structuring of experience* (pp. 179–210). New York: Plenum.

McClelland, D. C., Atkinson, J. W., Clark, R. W., & Lowell, E. L. (1953). *The achievement motive*. New York: Appleton-Century-Crofts.

McDougall, W. (1918). *An introduction to social psychology*. Boston: Luce.

McNay, M. (1985). Science: All the wonder things. *Childhood Education, 61*, 375–378.

Maheswaran, D., & Chaiken, S. (1991). Promoting systematic processing in low-motivation settings: Effect of incongruent information on processing and judgment. *Journal of Personality and Social Psychology, 61*, 13–25.

Malone, T. W. (1981). Toward a theory of intrinsically motivating instruction. *Cognitive Science, 4*, 333–369.

Maw, W. H., & Magoon, A. J. (1971). The curiosity dimension of fifth-grade children: A factorial discriminant analysis. *Child Development, 42*, 2023–2031.

Maw, W. H., & Maw, E. W. (1964). *An exploratory study into the measurement of curiosity in elementary school children* (CRP No. 801). Newark: University of Delaware.

Maw, W. H., & Maw, E. W. (1968). Self-appraisal of curiosity. *Journal of Educational Research, 61*, 462–465.

Maw, W. H., & Maw, E. W. (1972). Differences between high- and low-curiosity fifth-grade children in their recognition of verbal absurdities. *Journal of Educational Psychology, 63*, 558–562.

Mayer, R. E. (1983). *Thinking, problem solving, cognition*. New York: Freeman.

Messick, D. M., & Sentis, K. (1989). Estimating social and nonsocial utility functions from ordinal data. *European Journal of Social Psychology, 15*, 389–399.

Miller, G. A., Galanter, E., & Pribram, K. H. (1960). *Plans and the structure of behavior*. New York: Holt, Rinehart & Winston.

Miller, N. E. (1944). Experimental studies of conflict. In J. M. Hunt (Ed.), *Personality and the behavior disorders* (pp. 431–465). New York: Ronald Press.

Mischel, W. (1974). Processes in delay of gratification. In D. Berkowitz (Ed.), *Advances in experimental social psychology* (Vol. 7, pp. 249–292). New York: Academic Press.

Miyake, N., & Norman, D. (1979). To ask a question, one must know enough to know what is not known. *Journal of Verbal Learning and Verbal Behavior, 18*, 357–364.

Montgomery, K. C. (1952). Exploratory behavior and its relation to spontaneous alternation in a series of maze exposures. *Journal of Comparative and Physiological Psychology, 45*, 50–57.

Munsinger, H., & Kessen, W. (1964). Uncertainty, structure and preference. *Psychological Monographs, 78*, 1–24.

Munsinger, H., Kessen, W., & Kessen, M. L. (1964). Age and uncertainty: Developmental variations in preference for variability. *Journal of Experimental Child Psychology, 1*, 1–15.

Myers, A. K., & Miller, N. E. (1954). Failure to find a learned drive based on hunger; evidence for learning motivated by "exploration." *Journal of Comparative and Physiological Psychology, 47*, 428–436.

Naylor, F. D. (1981). A state-trait curiosity inventory. *Australian Psychologist, 16*, 172–183.

Nissen, H. W. (1930). A study of exploratory behavior in the white rat by means of the obstruction method. *Journal of Genetic Psychology, 37*, 361–376.

Nissen, H. W. (1954). The nature of the drive as innate determinant of behavioral organization. In M. R. Jones (Ed.), *Nebraska Symposium on Motivation* (Vol. 2, pp. 281–320). Lincoln: University of Nebraska Press.

Nunnally, J. C. (1971). Determinants of visual exploratory behavior: A human tropism for resolving informational conflicts. In H. I. Day, D. E. Berlyne, & D. E. Hunt (Eds.), *Intrinsic motivation: A new direction in education* (pp. 73–82). New York: Holt, Rinehart & Winston.

Olson, K. R., & Camp, C. J. (1984a). Analysis of curiosity measures in adults. *Psychological Reports, 54*, 491–497.

Olson, K. R., & Camp, C. J. (1984b). Curiosity and need for cognition. *Psychological Reports, 54*, 71–74.

Otis, A. (1939). *Otis Quick-Sorting Mental Abilities Test. Manual of Directions for Beta test Forms A and B*. New York: Harcourt Brace.

Pavlov, I. P. (1927). *Conditioned reflexes*. Oxford, England: Clarendon Press.

Penney, R. K., & McCann, B. (1964). The children's reactive curiosity scale. *Psychological Reports, 15*, 323–334.

Piaget, J. (1969). *Psychology of intelligence*. New York: Littlefield, Adams.

Posnock, R. (1991). *The trial of curiosity: Henry James, William James, and the challenge of modernity*. New York: Oxford University Press.

Prelec, D., & Loewenstein, G. (1991). Decision making over time and under uncertainty: A common approach. *Management Science, 37*, 770–786.

Premack, D., Collier, G., & Roberts, C. L. (1957). Frequency of light-contingent bar pressing as a function of the amount of deprivation of light. *American Psychologist, 12*, 411.

Proust, M. (1982). *Remembrance of things past* (Vol. 1). New York: Vintage Books. (Original work published 1924).

Pyszcynski, T. A., & Greenberg, J. (1981). The role of disconfirmed expectancies in the instigation of attributional processing. *Journal of Personality and Social Psychology, 40*, 31–38.

Raven, J. (1960). *Guide to the Standard Progressive Matrices Sets A, B, C, D, and E*. London: H. K. Lewis.

Reiser, O. L. (1931). The logic of Gestalt psychology. *Psychological Review, 38*, 359–368.

Rozansky, M. (1993, May 9). With this ring, I thee locate. *Philadelphia Inquirer,* p. D12.

Ruderman, A. J. (1986). Dietary restraint: A theoretical and empirical review. *Psychological Bulletin, 99*, 247–262.

St. Augustine. (1943). *The confessions of St. Augustine* (J. G. Pilkington, Trans.). New York: Liveright.

Schank, R. C., & Abelson, R. P. (1977). *Scripts, plans, goals, and understanding*. Hillsdale, NJ: Erlbaum.

Schelling, T. (1984). Self-command in practice, in policy, and in a theory of rational choice. *American Economic Review, 74*, 1–11.

Seeger, R. J. (1970). On Mach's curiosity about shockwaves. *Boston Studies in the Philosophy of Science, 6*, 60–67.

Simon, H. (1992). *The cat that curiosity couldn't kill*. Working paper, Department of Psychology, Carnegie Mellon University, Pittsburgh, PA.

Smith, A. A., Malmo, R. B., & Shagass, C. (1954). An electromyographic study of listening and talking. *Canadian Journal of Psychology, 8*, 219–227.

Stern, D. N. (1973). *The interpersonal world of the child*. New York: Basic Books.

Stoner, S. B., & Spencer, W. B. (1986). Age and sex differences on the State-Trait Personality Inventory. *Psychological Reports, 59*, 1315–1319.

Strull, W. M., Lo, B., & Charles, G. (1984). Do patients want to participate in medical decision making? *Journal of the American Medical Association, 252*, 2990–2994.

Suchman, J. R. (1971). Motivation inherent in the pursuit of meaning: Or the desire to inquire. In H. I. Day, D. E. Berlyne, & D. E. Hunt (Eds.), *Intrinsic motivation: A new direction in education* (pp. 61–72). New York: Holt, Rinehart & Winston.

Swann, W. B., Jr., Stephenson, B., & Pittman, T. S. (1981). Curiosity and control: On the determinants of the search for social knowledge. *Journal of Personality and Social Psychology, 40*, 635–642.

Tomkins, G. E., & Tway, E. (1985). Keeping language curiosity alive in elementary school children: Adventuring with words. *Childhood Education, 62*, 361–365.

Torrance, E. P. (1965). *Rewarding creative behavior: Experiments in classroom creative behavior*. Englewood Cliffs, NJ: Prentice Hall.

Treisman, A. M., & Gelade, G. (1980). A feature-integration theory of attention. *Cognitive Psychology, 12*, 97–136.

Turow, S. (1987). *Presumed Innocent*. New York: Farrar, Straus, Giroux.

Vidler, D. C. (1974). The use of contradiction to stimulate curiosity. *Educational Technology, 14*, 41–43.

Vidler, D. C. (1977). Curiosity. In S. Ball (Ed.), *Motivation in education*. San Diego, CA: Academic Press.

Voss, H. G., & Keller, H. (1983). *Curiosity and exploration: Theory and results*. San Diego, CA: Academic Press.

Wachs, T. D. (1977). The optimal stimulation hypothesis and early development: Anybody got a match? In I. C. Uzgiris & F. Weizmann (Eds.), *The structuring of experience* (pp. 153–177). New York: Plenum.

Wallerstein, H. (1954). An electromyographic study of attentive listening. *Canadian Journal of Psychology, 8*, 228–238.

Wheeler, L. (1966). Motivation as a determinant of upward comparison. *Journal of Experimental Social Psychology, 1* (Suppl.), 27–31.

White, R. W. (1959). Motivation reconsidered: The concept of competence. *Psychological Review, 66*, 297–333.

Wiersma, U. J. (1992). The effects of extrinsic rewards in intrinsic motivation: A meta-analysis. *Journal of Occupational and Organizational Psychology, 65*, 101–114.

Williams, C. D., & Kuchta, J. C. (1957). Exploratory behavior into mazes with dissimilar alternatives. *Journal of Comparative and Physiological Psychology, 50*, 509–513.

Wohlwill, J. F. (1987). Introduction. In D. Görlitz & J. F. Wohlwill (Eds.), *Curiosity, imagination, and play* (pp. 1–21). Hillsdale, NJ: Erlbaum.

Wong, P. T. P., & Weiner, B. (1981). When people ask "why" questions, and the heuristics of attributional search. *Journal of Personality and Social Psychology, 40*, 650–663.

Zeigarnik, B. (1927). Über das Behalten von erledigten und unerledigten Handlungen [On the memory for finished and unfinished tasks]. *Psychologische Forschung, 9,* 1–85.

Zubek, J. P. (1973). Behavioral and physiological effects of prolonged sensory and perceptual deprivation: A review. In J. E. Rasmussen (Ed.), *Man in isolation and confinement* (pp. 9–83). Chicago: Aldine.

Zuckerman, M. (1971). Dimensions of sensation seeking. *Journal of Consulting and Clinical Psychology, 36,* 45–52.

Received January 2, 1993
Revision received November 4, 1993
Accepted November 4, 1993

Part II

Social Preferences

7

Social Utility and Decision Making in Interpersonal Contexts

George F. Loewenstein, Leigh Thompson, and Max H. Bazerman

The origin of this paper, at least for me, dates back to when I became embroiled in a dispute over a condominium that my wife and I bought in Chicago in 1986. Unbeknownst to us, the people who sold us the condo kept a key and, after the closing and also right after we had sanded and polyurethaned the floor, reentered and destroyed the finish on the still-wet floor. I was livid, and, dissatisfied with what I saw as a paltry offer of monetary compensation, determined to take them to small claims court. I was rescued by the lawyer who had helped us with the purchase. She explained that it simply wasn't worth my time or the filing fee to bring the case to court, and recommended that I negotiate with the sellers a bit longer, and then accept their offer. She also told me to think about reasons why the judge might not rule in our favor were we to take the case to court.

Perhaps due to the lawyer's prodding, it dawned on me that I was not behaving strategically or trying to maximize my own gains, as economic logic would have dictated. Rather, I felt that I hadn't been treated fairly, and wanted to restore a situation of fairness. It was this incident, I believe, that sparked my interest in the role played by fairness in negotiations.

In discussions with my collaborators, Max Bazerman and Leigh Thompson (who was at that time Max's graduate student) we came to the conclusion that researchers had not come to terms with the negative feelings, such as my feeling of having been treated unjustly, that can arise in negotiations. The project on social utility was an attempt to come up with a theoretical framework for understanding the role of such negative emotions.

There are three major interrelated findings in the paper. The first is that, in situations in which an equal split of resources is the norm, people *hate* coming out behind—a situation we labeled "disadvantageous inequality." The second is that how people feel about coming out ahead—whether they like or dislike it—depends on a wide range of factors, such as the nature of the parties' relationship (whether they like the other person) and the nature of the situation (e.g. whether it is a business transaction or personal interaction). The third is that a major difference between *people*, when it comes to social preferences is their attitudes toward advantageous inequality. Almost everyone dislikes disadvantageous inequality, but there are some people who like advantageous inequality regardless of the situation, some who dislike it regardless, and some who sometimes like and sometimes dislike it, depending on the situation and who they are interacting with. All three of these findings have been supported by subsequent research.[1]

Although this paper has had a fair amount of influence, judging from how often it has been cited, I have several regrets about it. One is that I never wrote a version for economists, despite having received strong advice from Mark Machina, a prominent economic theorist, that I do so. I neglected to follow his advice and ended up regretting it all the more so because of the forceful way in which he delivered it.[2] Indeed, social utility functions of almost exactly the form we propose in the paper have become ubiquitous in economics.

Another regret about the paper is that our theory is wrong in one important respect. It is not so much *inequality* that people care about, whether advantageous or disadvantageous, but departures from *fairness*. People hate getting less than what they view as a fair distribution, but their attitudes toward more than what they view as fair are much more complex. Our model of inequality aversion is only applicable to situations in which an equal split is the norm; but such situations are rare. A model based on departures from

---

[1] See, e.g., Fehr, E. and Schmidt, K. (1999). 'A Theory of Fairness, Competition, and Cooperation,' *The Quarterly Journal of Economics*, 114(3): 817–68.

[2] Research on group decision-making shows that groups don't always make better decisions than individuals, in part because the people who are the most confident, and most vociferous in expressing an opinion are often not the most knowledgeable. My own experience has been, however, that when someone confidently gives advice, I should usually follow it. That's how I came to be an economist. After graduating from college, I worked in a boatyard north of Seattle for a while, got hired and then fired from a job as the electronics specialist in an underground station in Antarctica (my employer decided quite correctly that I didn't have the right personality to spend nine months underground in close quarters with five other people), then moved to New York and spun my wheels for a few years doing statistical and computer work at a hospital in the Bronx. I had no idea about what to do with my life, so I took a few courses in biostatistics with the idea of becoming a biostatistician—a profession that I had no facility for and which didn't especially interest me. For some reason that I no longer recall, one of my bosses at the hospital, seeing that I seemed at loose ends, suggested that I get career advice from a medical researcher at Columbia Medical School. I hadn't spent ten minutes in his office when he started yelling at me that I was wasting my time and that I should go and get a Ph.D. in economics, an idea that had not occurred to me. Since he seemed to know what I should do, and I didn't have a clue, I decided to take his advice, enrolling first in the economics PhD program at Columbia, then transferring to the program at Yale.

fairness rather than equality would have been far more general (applicable to a wider range of situations), more psychologically realistic, and would have allowed for easier integration of our findings with those from the next research project that I worked on involving negotiation—on self-serving biases in assessing fairness. More about that in Chapter 8.

Social Utility and Decision Making in Interpersonal Contexts[*]

George F. Loewenstein, Leigh Thompson, and Max H. Bazerman

People care about the outcomes of others. We sacrifice our own interests to help loved ones or harm adversaries. Participants withdraw from profitable participation in a laboratory experiment if they perceive inequity in remuneration (Schmitt & Marwell, 1972). Players in two-person ultimatum games (in which one player proposes a distribution of a fixed amount of money that the other has the option of either accepting or rejecting) frequently reject a positive but inequitable offer even though the alternative is no gain at all (Guth, Schmittberger, & Schwarze, 1982). Negotiations between parties often collapse when one party becomes incensed with the other and attempts to "maximize his opponent's displeasure rather than his own satisfaction" (Seigel & Fouraker, 1960, p. 100). In general, disputants are concerned not only with the outcomes they receive, but also with the outcomes of their opponents (Pruitt & Rubin, 1986).

The importance of interpersonal comparisons has long been recognized by social psychologists. Equity theorists (Adams, 1963, 1965; Homans, 1961; Walster, Walster, & Berscheid, 1978) have argued that people attempt to maintain proportionality between inputs and outcomes to themselves and comparison others. Research on relative deprivation has enumerated preconditions for experiencing deprivation as a result of adverse social comparison

[*] This chapter was originally published as Loewenstein, G., Thompson, L., and Bazerman, M. (1989). 'Social Utility and Decision Making in Interpersonal Contexts', Journal of Personality and Social Psychology, 57(3): 426–441. Published by APA and reprinted with permission.

The research reported in this article was supported by grants from the Dispute Resolution Research Center in Northwestern University's Kellogg Graduate School of Management, the Russell Sage Foundation, the Alfred P. Sloan Foundation, and the IBM Faculty Research Fund at the University of Chicago.

We gratefully acknowledge comments and suggestions from Colin Camerer, Steve Hoch, Norbert Kerr, and Dave Messick and statistical advice from Dawn Iacobucci.

(Crosby, 1976). Social comparison theory (Festinger, 1954) has focused mainly on the question of with whom people choose to compare themselves.

Recently, a number of researchers have experimented with different ways of graphically or mathematically encoding individuals' concern for others' outcomes. The main focus of this work has been on decomposing individuals' concern for the outcomes of others into underlying primary motives and graphically depicting these motives using indifference curves, a tool widely used by economists. One of the earliest of these analyses (Scott, 1972) distinguished between three motives underlying concern for other people's outcomes: avarice, altruism, and egalitarianism, each with its own characteristically shaped pattern of indifference curves. Later, MacCrimmon and Messick (1976) proposed that concern for others' payoff could be decomposed into six basic motives, consisting of self-interest (choosing so as to increase own payoffs), self-sacrifice (choosing so as to decrease your own payoffs), altruism (choosing so as to increase the payoffs to the other party), aggression (choosing so as to decrease the payoffs to the other party), cooperation (choosing so as to increase the sum of your payoff and the other's payoff), and competition (choosing so as to increase the difference between your payoffs; see also Griesinger & Livingston, 1973). MacCrimmon and Messick also identified a series of supplementary motives that reflected the assumption of equity theory that concern about the other party depends on the ratio of, rather than the difference between, the parties' attainments. Most recently, Lurie (1987) has developed an indifference curve analysis based on the idea that people are concerned with both the difference and the ratio between their own and another party's outcomes.

The indifference curve approach is basically a theory-free tool that permits free expression of preferences. It is useful as a tool for studying preferences, but it has two major limitations. First, it is difficult to make specific behavioral predictions using indifference curves, especially in situations different from those in which the indifference curves were estimated. Second, it is difficult to compare indifference curves to the utility models that have formed the main thrust of work on decision making under uncertainty. An alternative approach that avoids these problems encodes interpersonal preferences using *social utility functions*. Social utility functions specify level of satisfaction as a function of outcome to self and other. Although more restrictive than indifference curves because they impose a specific functional form on preferences, social utility functions permit easier comparison with other decision models such as prospect theory (Kahneman & Tversky, 1979) and make specific behavioral predictions in a wide range of situations.

Although less developed than the work on indifference curves, there has been limited research on social utility. Conrath and Deci (1969) conjectured about different shapes that social utility functions could assume and explored how different basic social motives would manifest themselves in utility

185

function curvature. Other research has empirically estimated social utility functions in different contexts (e.g. Messick & Sentis, 1985). Our research extends the work on social utility in a number of directions.

First, we estimate a separate utility function for each subject. Earlier estimates of social utility functions have fitted a single, aggregate, utility function to all subjects (e.g. Messick & Sentis, 1985). Individual-level estimates permit an examination of the consistency of preferences across decision makers as well as the identification of individual differences in social utility functions.

Second, we examine social and contextual factors that may affect decision making in interpersonal contexts. Although the importance of these factors has been demonstrated in research on social dilemmas (e.g. Orbell & Dawes, 1981), their impact on social utility functions has not been examined systematically.[1] Two important factors that may influence decision making in interpersonal contexts are the nature of the relationship between the individual and the comparison other and the nature of the dispute (dispute type), for example, a business or personal matter. At a simple level, relationships may be dichotomously characterized as positive and harmonious or as negative and disruptive (Heider, 1958; Kelley, 1979). On the basis of prior research (e.g. Walster et al., 1978), one might expect individuals in positive or neutral relationships to value equity. In negative relationships, people may prefer to receive more than the other party (advantageous inequality) and be particularly averse to situations in which the other party receives more than the self (disadvantageous inequality).

The dispute type refers to the issue being negotiated (e.g. a business or personal matter). Lewicki and Litterer (1985) suggested that the norms of a situation affect decision making. For example, with friends and neighbors, the equality norm is expected to prevail (Austin, 1980). However, business transactions often dictate a greater concern for self, with the implicit value being that individuals should maximize their own outcomes. Business disputes generally occur in the context of exchange relationships, whereas personal disputes occur in communal relationships (Clark & Mills, 1979). Exchange relationships are characterized by strict norms of reciprocity, which is expected to be overt, immediate, and typically in kind. Although reciprocity is also important in communal relationships (Thibaut & Kelley, 1959), it is generally less overt and occurs over longer time intervals.

Third, we compare the goodness of fit of a variety of functional forms reflecting different social motives. Earlier research on social utility functions assumed a particular functional form, without testing alternatives.

---

[1] A recent exception is Lurie (1987). Lurie included a relationship condition comparable to ours in his empirical indifference curve analysis. However, his study used too few subjects to systematically compare the different conditions.

186

The functional form that we ultimately estimated has properties that permit a direct comparison to Kahneman and Tversky's prospect theory (1979). A central idea of prospect theory is that people evaluate the utility of alternative courses of action relative to a reference point. Outcomes below the reference point are viewed as losses; outcomes above the reference point are perceived as gains. The reference point represents a state to which individuals have adapted and is usually assumed to correspond to the status quo. However, in an interpersonal context the outcomes of another person may emerge as an alternative (or additional), potentially salient reference point. The prospect theory value function is concave in the region of gains, indicating risk aversion, and convex in the region of losses, indicating risk seeking. A major interest of ours is whether the typical social utility function has a similar shape.

Our studies examined social utility in a dispute context. We were interested in estimating social utility functions that could be used to predict individual behavior in situations, such as negotiations, in which decisions have consequences not only for the self, but also for another party. In Study 1, we performed multiple regressions to estimate a separate utility function for each subject. We examined the impact of the relationship between the disputants and the environmental context on the shape of the utility function. Study 2 extended and replicated the findings from the first study using a separate data set. In Study 3, we used the model specifications from the first two studies to contrast decision making in individual and interpersonal contexts. The primary question addressed in Study 3 is whether the introduction of interpersonal concerns leads to consistent departures from the predictions of prospect theory in competitive decision-making tasks.

7.1. Study 1

7.1.1. *Method*

Subjects and procedure. A total of 148 subjects participated in the study; 98 were undergraduate students and participated in partial fulfillment of an introductory psychology course requirement; 50 were students in a graduate management program in a business school.[2]

Materials and procedure. The experimenter told participants that the purpose of the study was to examine individuals' reactions to situations involving disputes between two people. Participants were each given a booklet consisting of 10 pages. The 1st page instructed participants to assume the role of the disputant described in each situation. The 2nd page described a dispute

---

[2] There were no significant differences between the two groups on any of the analyses. Therefore, the analyses reported in this study are based on the total sample.

between two people. On the 3rd and 4th pages, participants indicated their satisfaction with each of 42 possible outcomes of the dispute by making a slash mark on a scale with endpoints labeled *very unsatisfied* (−5) and *very satisfied* (5). The outcomes described exact dollar payoffs to the self and the other party. The 5th page described a different dispute, and participants rated their satisfaction with outcomes on Pages 6 and 7. The 8th page described a third dispute, and participants rated their satisfaction with outcomes on Pages 9 and 10.

Design. Our design included two within-subjects variables: relationship between disputants (positive, negative, or neutral) and dispute type. Dispute type included three conditions, two occurring between people of the same status in a nonbusiness setting and one occurring between a customer and salesperson in a business setting. In one nonbusiness dispute ("invention") two students were faced with the task of splitting the proceeds or costs resulting from a joint invention:

One day while eating lunch, a student who lives in your dorm, Pat, mentioned to you an idea for a new product: cross-country water skis. They are similar to conventional cross-country skis except that they are floatable pontoons that permit you to "ski" over water. Pat thought of the idea several years ago, but had not done anything with it and had not been able to interest anyone in it.

You find the idea of whisking over the water in a standing position exciting. You suggest to Pat that the two of you work together on the project.

Over the next month you spend long hours together constructing a prototype of the water skis in the basement of your dorm. Since it was Pat's idea, you agree to pay for the materials you use to construct the prototype. After extensively testing and refining the skis at the university pool, you decide that you are ready to patent the invention. You hire a patent lawyer to determine whether there is an existing patent on the invention. At your first meeting with the lawyer, he draws up a patent application document for the two of you to examine.

[relationship manipulation goes here]

Loss: Several weeks after your meeting with the patent lawyer, he returns with the news that cross-country water skis have already been patented. Nevertheless, you are responsible for paying him for his services. Both you and Pat receive copies of his bill and negotiate how to split the cost.

Gain: Several weeks after your meeting with the patent lawyer, he returns with the news that cross-country water skis have already been patented. However, he has contacted the current holder of the patent, who is interested in buying one of the innovative features incorporated in your design. You and Pat agree that the amount offered seems reasonable. The two of you negotiate how to split the profit.

In the other nonbusiness scenario ("lot"), two neighbors split revenue or tax payments from a vacant lot located between their houses. The business dispute scenario ("business") described a conflict between a customer and a sales manager at a computer retail outlet in which the disputants split either the revenue from a retroactive rebate or the cost of repairs. The stimuli for the lot and business disputes are presented in the appendix.

We manipulated the relationship between the two disputants by including details about prior encounters with the other disputant. In the positive relationship condition, participants read a description of a positive, harmonious relationship between the parties. In the invention dispute, this description read as follows: "In perusing the patent application at home later that day, you find that Pat has listed your name as the primary inventor of the skis. You are pleased, but believe that he really deserves this designation." In the negative relationship condition, participants read a description of a negative, acrimonious relationship between the parties. The text for the invention condition read as follows: "In perusing the patent application at home later that day, you find that Pat has not listed your name on the patent. You feel snubbed since, although it was his initial idea, he had taken it nowhere without your assistance." In the neutral relationship condition, the participants were not provided with any information about the disputants' prior relationship.

We combined the three dispute situations (two personal and one business) with the three relationship conditions using a Latin square design. If we label the dispute situations as *A, B,* and *C* and the relationship conditions as *1, 2,* and *3,* then the three sets of stimuli were composed as follows: (A1, B2, C3), (A2, B3, C1), and (A3, B1, C2). These were randomly assigned to participants.

We constructed 21 positive outcomes by combining 3 outcomes to self ($300, $500, and $600) with 7 outcomes to the other party determined by adding one of seven dollar amounts (−$300, −$200, −$100, 0, $100, $200, and $300) to the amount received by self. As a result, the outcomes to the other party ranged from $0 to $900. We constructed 21 negative outcome combinations by expressing the same dollar values as amounts to be paid rather than received. Participants rated their satisfaction with the 21 outcomes involving gains to the self and the other party and then with the 21 outcomes involving losses to the self and the other party for each of the disputes. Because subjects completed these 42 judgments in three different relationship–dispute-type conditions, each subject made a total of 126 judgments. To avoid response set and automatic responding, outcome pairs were randomly ordered on the page; however, all subjects received the same order.

7.1.2. Results

Specification of the model. The first stage of our analysis involved selecting a functional form for the social utility function. We considered three criteria in evaluating different functional specifications: (a) goodness of fit across subjects—the selected functional form should explain a large amount of the variation in an individual subject's ratings; (b) simplicity—it should incorporate a minimum number of explanatory variables; and (c) flexibility—it should be capable of depicting qualitative differences between subjects' patterns of responses. We experimented with several functional forms, each of which included terms for the individual's own payoff and own payoff squared, permitting estimation of both slope and curvature.[3]

The first functional form we examined assumes that people are concerned with absolute level of payments both to self and other. Defining U as utility, SELF as payoff to self, and OTHER as the opponent's payoff, the regression equation is as follows:

$$U = c + B_1 \text{SELF} + B_2 \text{SELF}^2 + B_3 \text{OTHER} + B_4 \text{OTHER}^2. \tag{1}$$

Equation 1 is appropriate if the utility one obtains from the other person's payoff does not depend on the payoff to oneself.

An alternative formulation includes the difference between the payment to the other party and one's own payment rather than the absolute payment to the other party. Defining DIFF as the difference between own and other's payoff,

$$U = c + B_1 \text{SELF} + B_2 \text{SELF}^2 + B_3 \text{DIFF} + B_4 \text{DIFF}^2. \tag{2}$$

Equation 2 is the bivariate utility function proposed by Conrath and Deci (1969). Note that by suitable manipulation, Equation 2 can be rewritten as Equation 1 plus an interaction term. Thus, we would expect Equation 2 to outperform Equation 1 if preferences for own payoff are not independent of the payoff to the other party.

A third form, suggested by equity theory, incorporates the absolute difference between self and other and the absolute difference squared. This formulation is applicable if people dislike disparity in either direction between own and other payoff. Let $|\text{DIFF}|$ represent the absolute difference between own and other payoff. Then,

$$U = c + B_1 \text{SELF} + B_2 \text{SELF}^2 + B_3 |\text{DIFF}| + B_4 |\text{DIFF}|^2. \tag{3}$$

Finally, we tested a formulation based on the social motive that MacCrimmon and Messick (1976) defined as *proportionate competition*. This involves "choosing so as to increase the ratio of your payoff to the other's payoff" (MacCrimmon & Messick, 1976, p. 90). Defining PROP as payments to self divided by total payoffs,

$$U = c + B_1 \text{SELF} + B_2 \text{SELF}^2 + B_3 \text{PROP}^+ + B_4 \text{PROP}^-. \tag{4}$$

---

[3] Although there is no reason to assume that a power function expresses the curvature of the utility function better than any other functional form, the amount of data collected and the limited number of values of own payoff that were collected made it impractical to compare the relative fit of alternative second-order terms.

Table 1. Adjusted R ^{2} by Relationship and Dispute Type: Study 1

Condition		Equation								
Relationship	Dispute type	1		2		3		4		5	
		R^2	SD	R^2	SD	R^2	SD	R^2	SD	R^2	SD
Positive	Invention	.41	.33	.52	.24	.35	.32	.25	.27	.66	.26
Neutral	Invention	.46	.33	.55	.25	.30	.32	.31	.25	.65	.25
Negative	Invention	.59	.31	.63	.23	.41	.30	.47	.31	.70	.20
Positive	Lot	.43	.34	.55	.27	.33	.33	.17	.18	.74	.23
Neutral	Lot	.33	.31	.51	.21	.40	.32	.15	.23	.72	.22
Negative	Lot	.60	.30	.65	.25	.18	.30	.25	.22	.79	.21
Positive	Business	.70	.25	.70	.24	.18	.30	.39	.27	.73	.22
Neutral	Business	.75	.16	.71	.15	.27	.30	.55	.25	.72	.16
Negative	Business	.75	.17	.72	.17	.31	.33	.53	.28	.73	.17
All conditions		.56	.32	.62	.24	.30	.32	.34	.29	.72	.32

Because a higher proportion of payments may be desirable when payoffs are gains, but undesirable when payments are losses, we included separate PROP terms for losses and gains.

To compare the goodness of fit of the four specifications, we performed separate regressions for each subject, and within subjects, for each disputant relationship condition (positive, neutral, or negative) and dispute-type (personal or business) combination. Goodness of fit across the four equations was compared on the basis of adjusted R^2s. The Equation 1–4 columns of Table 1 present the means of the adjusted R^2s for each of the four specifications in each of the relationship and dispute-type conditions.[4] Equations 1 and 2 provided systematically higher R^2s than did Equations 3 and 4, all $ts(725)$ > 141, p < .0001, and Equation 2 also significantly outperformed Equation 1 in terms of R^2, $t(725) = 13.8$, p < .0002.[5] Looking across the nine relationship–dispute-type combinations in Table 1, it can be seen that Equation 2 is superior to Equation 1 in six combinations, equal in one, and inferior in two.

[4] The interpretations of the differences between adjusted R^2s is questionable, due both to the problematic nature of the adjusted R^2 statistic and to the fact that the different adjusted R^2s were estimated from the same population. Nevertheless, we believe the differences between the adjusted R^2s, and the significance of these differences looking across subjects, permits a reasonable qualitative comparison of goodness of fit across equations.

[5] We estimated all t statistics from an analysis of variance (ANOVA) in which the adjusted R^2 of the regression equations served as the dependent variable and the equation type (1–5) served as the independent variable. All comparisons that were significant on the basis of the conventional t test were also significant at the .05 level, using Scheffé's test, which controls for experimentwise error. Each pairwise comparison is based on 888 regressions (148 subjects × 3 conditions × 2 equations); however, this number was reduced to 871 because of missing data. Correcting for the repeated measures nature of the design absorbed 145 degrees of freedom, leaving 725 degrees of freedom.

In a second round of estimation, we compared Equation 2 with a modified function that permitted a different slope and curvature for positive and
negative values of DIFF. We also dropped the self-squared term because it failed
to achieve significance in a majority of the regression equations.

$$U = c + B_1 \text{SELF} + B_2 \text{NEGDIFF} + B_3 \text{NEGDIFF}^2 + B_4 \text{POSDIFF} + B_5 \text{POSDIFF}^2. \qquad (5)$$

The prefixes NEG and POS act as binary switches that activate the terms for
negative and positive values of DIFF respectively.

The mean adjusted R^2 for Equation 5 under each relationship and dispute
type is presented in the last column of Table 1. Across the nine relationship–
dispute-type conditions, the mean adjusted R^2 for Equation 5 was .72, a
significant improvement over the average adjusted R^2 of .62 for Equation 2,
$t(725) = 58.6$, $p < .0001$. The fact that the inclusion of separate terms for
positive and negative differences leads to such a great improvement in R^2
suggests that in interpersonal, as in individual, decision making, there is a
discontinuity in the treatment of positive and negative departures from one's
reference level (Kahneman & Tversky, 1979; Walster et al., 1978).

The functional form represented by Equation 5 has several desirable qualities. First, it allows one to assess the relative importance of intrapersonal and
interpersonal concerns by comparing the parameter values applied to SELF
and to the various DIFF terms. Second, and as noted previously, it makes it
possible to separate subjects' attitudes toward advantageous and disadvantageous inequality. Finally, the functional form is sufficiently flexible to permit
comparison with individual-level models of decision making such as prospect
theory.

The estimated utility function is illustrated in Figure 1, averaging across the
three relationship conditions and three dispute types. Three different curves
correspond to different levels of SELF (payoff to self). The predominant shape
is upward sloping and convex for negative values of DIFF. For positive values
of DIFF, the curve slopes downward and is also convex.

Relationship and dispute type. Table 2 summarizes the results of the regression
analysis in tabular form, disaggregating the data by disputant relationship
and dispute type. Each estimate is the mean of individual subjects' parameter
estimates. To facilitate comparisons of parameter estimates across different
relationship–dispute-type conditions, we performed separate analyses of variance (ANOVAS) with the regression parameters SELF, NEGDIFF, and POSDIFF serving as dependent variables and the relationship and dispute-type conditions
as independent variables.

Concern for own payoff (as indicated by the parameter value for SELF)
differed across the three types of disputes, $F(2, 284) = 36.9$, $p < .0001$. Subjects
displayed greatest concern for their own payoff in the invention and business
disputes, whereas concern for own payoff in the lot scenario was significantly

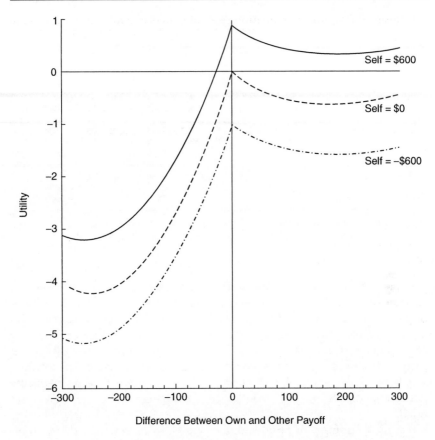

Figure 1. Utility as a function of difference between own and other payoff and payoff to self: Study 1.

lower, all $ts(284) > 40.7$, $p < .0001$.[6] The disputant relationship also had a significant effect on concern for self, $F(2, 284) = 19.4$, $p < .0001$. Concern for own payment was highest in the negative relationship condition, followed by the neutral condition, and lowest in the positive relationship condition, with all three conditions significantly different from one another, all $ts(284) > 9.1$, $p < .003$. The interaction between relationship and dispute type was also significant, $F(2, 284) = 3.18$, $p < .02$; in the invention and business dispute settings, the value of SELF was substantially greater in the negative than in the positive relationship condition, but the effect was less pronounced in the lot condition.

[6] The between-conditions comparisons reported were based on conventional t tests. All pairwise comparisons reported in Studies 1 and 2 were also evaluated using the more conservative Scheffé multiple-comparison procedure; the results were qualitatively indistinguishable.

Table 2. Mean Parameter Estimates by Relationship and Dispute Type: Study 1

Condition		Independent variables								
Relationship	Dispute type	SELF		NEGDIFF		NEGDIFF^2		POSDIFF		POSDIFF^2	
		M	SD	M	SD	M	SD	M	SD	M	SD
Positive	Invention	.12	.16	3.5	2.8	.0065	.0065	−1.2	2.9	.0012	.0073
Neutral	Invention	.13	.20	3.3	2.2	.0059	.0052	−0.87	2.6	.0013	.0048
Negative	Invention	.30	.25	2.2	2.2	.0037	.0055	−0.28	2.5	−.0004	.0065
Positive	Lot	.043	.12	4.4	3.0	.0082	.0081	−2.1	3.2	.0048	.0072
Neutral	Lot	.068	.15	5.1	3.0	.0100	.0075	−2.5	2.6	.0053	.0055
Negative	Lot	.064	.16	4.3	2.9	.0087	.0070	−0.17	2.8	.0006	.0065
Positive	Business	.11	.23	2.3	1.8	.0037	.0046	0.41	1.6	−.0001	.0051
Neutral	Business	.26	.20	1.6	1.4	.0029	.0037	0.73	1.2	−.0004	.0037
Negative	Business	.29	.25	1.6	1.7	.0026	.0043	0.71	1.5	−.0003	.0035

Note. All parameter values and standard deviations multiplied by 100.

NEGDIFF = negative difference between own and other payoff, POSDIFF = positive difference between own and other payoff.

Figure 2 compares the shape of the social utility function on the basis of mean parameter values for the positive, neutral, and negative relationship conditions.[7] The utility functions for all three conditions are positively sloped and convex for negative differences between own and other payoff (disadvantageous inequality); people do not like to do worse than the other party regardless of the relationship between the parties. However, the relationship between disputants did affect preference for disadvantageous inequality (NEGDIFF), $F(2, 284) = 6.5$, $p < .001$, although the magnitude of the effect was small.

It is in the domain of positive differences between self and other (advantageous inequality) that the most striking differences between relationship conditions were observed. The effect of relationship on POSDIFF was significant, $F(2, 284) = 11.6$, $p < .0001$. Averaging across the three dispute types, the slope of POSDIFF was positive under all relationship conditions, although it was much smaller in the negative relationship condition than in the positive and neutral conditions, $ts(284) > 16$, $p < .0001$.

In general, subjects were much more concerned with disadvantageous inequality than with advantageous inequality. The mean parameter estimate for POSDIFF given a positive or neutral relationship was approximately one-third the magnitude of that for NEGDIFF; subjects did not like to obtain a higher payoff than their opponent, but they much preferred a positive discrepancy between their own and the other party's payoff to a negative discrepancy of equal magnitude.

[7] Figures 2, 3, and 5 are all based on a value of own outcome equal to 0.

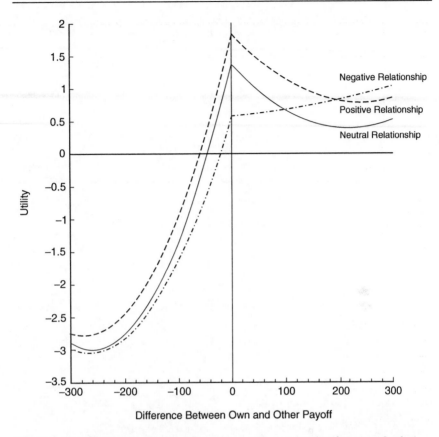

Figure 2. The effect of disputant relationship on the social utility function: Study 1.

Figure 3 depicts the shape of the social utility function for each of the three dispute-type conditions. Again, the utility functions are all positively sloped and convex for negative differences between own and other payoff, although the slope of the utility function in the region of disadvantageous inequality was affected by dispute type, $F(2, 284) = 76.3$, $p < .0001$. Subjects were most concerned about falling below the other party in the lot dispute, were less concerned in the invention dispute, and were least concerned in the business condition, all $ts(284) > 26.8$, $p < .0001$. The effect of dispute type on utility for advantageous inequality is again more striking than that for disadvantageous inequality, $F(2, 284) = 42.2$, $p < .0001$. Subjects were most resistant to receiving a higher payoff in the lot dispute, were next most resistant in the invention dispute, and actually preferred a higher payoff in the business dispute condition, with all $ts(284) > 11.4$, $p < .001$. The interactions

195

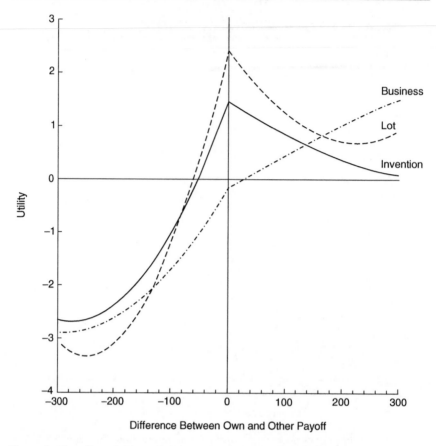

Figure 3. The effect of dispute type on the social utility function: Study 1.

between relationship and dispute type for both POSDIFF and NEGDIFF were not significant, $Fs(4, 284) < 1.45$, $p > .2$.

Individual differences. One advantage to estimating a separate equation for each subject is that it permits classification of qualitatively different patterns of behavior. Table 3 shows the percentage of subjects in each of the relationship–dispute-type conditions who had positive parameter estimates for NEGDIFF and negative parameter estimates for POSDIFF, the modal response pattern. As noted earlier, a negative parameter value for NEGDIFF would mean that the subject preferred to obtain a lower payoff than his opponent. A positive value for POSDIFF would indicate that the subject receives satisfaction from obtaining a superior outcome than his opponent.

Looking down the Dislike disadvantageous inequality column, it is evident that very few subjects in any condition obtained positive satisfaction from receiving an inferior payoff. On the other hand, there is considerable diversity

Table 3. Proportions of Subjects Who Disliked Advantageous and Disadvantageous Inequality: Study 1

Condition		Dislike disadvantageous inequality (%)	Dislike advantageous inequality (%)
Relationship	Dispute type		
Positive	Invention	92	61
Neutral	Invention	92	55
Negative	Invention	94	42
Positive	Lot	98	68
Neutral	Lot	100	80
Negative	Lot	98	40
Positive	Business	94	26
Neutral	Business	96	27
Negative	Business	91	27

among subjects and across conditions in preferences for obtaining a higher payoff than the other player. For the invention and lot disputes, a majority of subjects in the positive and neutral relationship conditions (66%) disliked getting a higher payoff than the other player. On the other hand, in the negative relationship condition a majority (59%) preferred to come out ahead. In the business dispute, the relationship between disputants had little impact on preferences; in all conditions, approximately 73% of subjects increased their level of satisfaction by increasing advantageous inequality.

7.1.3. Discussion

In general, subjects were very concerned with the comparison of their own payoffs to those of the other party. This was true in all of the dispute settings and in each relationship condition. In fact, subjects were more concerned with the comparison of their own outcomes with those of the other party than they were with the value of their own outcomes. Most subjects preferred that rewards or costs be equitably shared, although they were more averse to disadvantageous inequality than to advantageous inequality. Similar results were obtained by Messick and Sentis (1985) in examining individuals' preferences for payoffs to the self and to the other party in an employment situation. Messick and Sentis found that when inputs were equal (students worked the same amount of hours), individuals preferred equal payments. When equality was not possible, however, subjects preferred that the other party be at a disadvantage relative to the self. We had expected the effect to be stronger when there was a negative relationship between disputants, but this was not observed. Instead, the relationship between the disputants had a significant effect on concern with own payoff in two of the three negotiating settings. In both the lot and business disputes, we observed what could be called a "selfish shift"—a move toward greater concern for own payoff as the relationship shifted from positive to negative—that was mediated by dispute type.

The most significant impact of the two conditions was on subjects' preferences for advantageous inequality. In the two personal dispute settings (invention and lot), subjects generally preferred equal payoffs over advantageous inequality. However, in the business setting, subjects obtained positive utility from receiving a higher payoff. With a positive or neutral relationship between disputants, people disliked advantageous inequality. However, in a negative relationship, subjects became relatively unconcerned about the other party's payoff as long as it was less than or equal to their own payoff.

As the vast majority of subjects preferred higher payoffs to themselves (SELF > 0) and disliked disadvantageous inequality (NEGDIFF < 0), subjects' utility functions could be grouped into three qualitatively distinct patterns based on the sign of POSDIFF. One group we labeled *saints;* saints consistently prefer equality, and they do not like to receive higher payoffs than the other party (POSDIFF < 0) even when they are in a negative relationship with the opponent. People in the second group, labeled *loyalists,* do not like to receive higher payoffs (POSDIFF < 0) in positive or neutral relationships, but do seek advantageous inequality (POSDIFF > 0) when they are involved in negative relationships. People in the third group, labeled *ruthless competitors,* consistently prefer to come out ahead of the other party (POSDIFF > 0) regardless of the type of relationship. In our sample, the proportions of saints, loyalists, and ruthless competitors were 24%, 27%, and 36%, respectively. The remaining 18% of subjects could not be neatly classified into any of the three categories. We suspect that the proportions of loyalists and ruthless competitors were elevated by the inclusion of the business condition, in which most subjects derived positive satisfaction from advantageous inequality, regardless of the nature of the relationship.

7.2. Study 2

Some of the results of the first study surprised us. We had expected that people would prefer to receive superior outcomes to the other except, perhaps, in the positive relationship condition. Instead, even in the negative relationship condition subjects were relatively indifferent to advantageous inequality. Given the unexpectedness of this result, and the notorious instability of regression coefficients, we wanted to replicate our results on a different data set. At the same time, we suspected that the general indifference toward advantageous inequality in the negative relationship condition might be due to the subtlety of the relationship manipulation. Therefore, we wanted to estimate social utility functions under a strengthened negative relationship condition. Finally, we were interested in estimating the proportions of saints, loyalists, and ruthless competitors in a different sample. In the first study, our estimate of these groups was affected by the inclusion of the business dispute in which most subjects weakly preferred advantageous inequality but were mainly concerned with their own payoff, regardless of the relationship condition. We conducted the second study, which included a strengthened relationship manipulation and which dropped the business dispute-type condition, to accomplish these goals. The two personal (i.e. nonbusiness) disputes provided a more uniform backdrop against which to observe the effect of the relationship between disputants on preferences for outcomes.

7.2.1. Method

Forty-four graduate students of management participated in the study. The materials and procedures were the same as those used in Study 1. Our design included two within-subjects variables, relationship between disputants and dispute type. Subjects responded to two dispute situations, the lot and invention scenarios from Study 1. Half the subjects received the lot scenario first; the other half completed the invention scenario first. The relationship manipulations were similar to those in the Study 1, but were more detailed and explicit. For example, in the lot scenario, the positive relationship manipulation read as follows:

The Smiths are your neighbors. You like the Smiths a lot, and other neighbors consider the Smiths to be very nice as well. The Smiths always help out others. The Smiths are more than happy to take care of pets, water plants, and collect mail. Last week, the Smiths baby-sat for your children on very short notice, loaned you some very expensive tools for a repair project, and offered their guest bedroom for one of your out-of-town guests. In short, the Smiths are kind, friendly, sincere, responsible, and dependable.

The negative relationship manipulation was as follows:

The Smiths are your neighbors. You have had many unpleasant personal experiences with the Smiths. Your other neighbors also consider the Smiths to be obnoxious. The Smiths complain about others' lawn and house maintenance, yet they do not do any work on their own home. The Smiths borrow tools, but they do not say *thank you* and often fail to return items. Last week, the Smiths threatened to call the police on a small party you were having, damaged your lawn furniture after borrowing it for a larger party, and failed to pick up after their dog had been in your yard. In short, the Smiths are selfish, irresponsible, argumentative, demanding, and insincere.

The relationship manipulations for the invention dispute are included in the appendix. Following each dispute description, participants indicated their satisfaction with the same 42 outcomes for each of the two scenarios that were evaluated in Study 1.

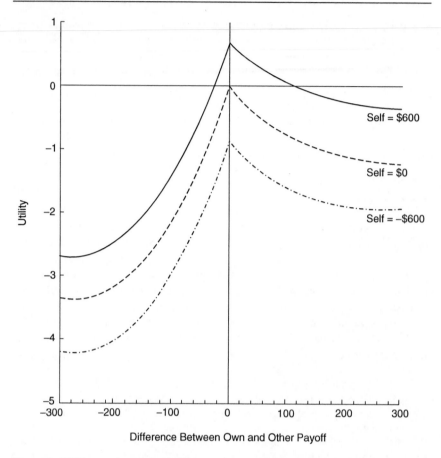

Figure 4. Utility as a function of difference between own and other payoff and payoff to self: Study 2.

7.2.2. Results

Equation 5 was estimated again for all subjects and all relationship–dispute-type conditions. A total of 44 subjects each completed two relationship–dispute-type combinations, so a total of 88 regressions was run. The mean adjusted R^2 for these regressions was .66.

Figure 4 depicts the functional form for the regression, aggregating across the two relationship conditions and negotiating settings. Again the curve displays a tentlike form, upward sloping and convex for negative differences between the subject and the other party, downward sloping and convex for positive differences. Also evident is the steeper slope for negative differences (relative losses hurt more than relative gains) and the substantially

Table 4. Mean Parameter Estimates by Disputant Relationship and Dispute Type: Study 2

Condition		Independent variables								
Relationship	Dispute type	SELF		NEGDIFF		NEGDIFF^2		POSDIFF		POSDIFF^2	
		M	SD	M	SD	M	SD	M	SD	M	SD
Positive	Invention	.060	0.12	2.7	3.0	.0044	.0075	−2.0	3.1	.0034	.0072
Negative	Invention	0.31	0.32	1.8	1.6	.0034	.0040	0.44	1.3	−.0011	.0034
Positive	Lot	0.081	0.15	2.8	2.7	.0052	.0063	−1.7	2.6	.0034	.0060
Negative	Lot	0.081	0.12	2.6	2.5	.0052	.0060	0.067	1.9	.0004	.0038

Note. All parameter values and standard deviations multiplied by 100.

NEGDIFF = negative difference between own and other payoff, POSDIFF = positive difference between own and other payoff.

greater effect on satisfaction of relative payoffs than of absolute payments to self.

Table 4 summarizes the results of the regression analysis, disaggregating the data by relationship and dispute type. We performed separate ANOVAS with regression parameter estimates for the variables SELF, NEGDIFF, and POSDIFF serving as dependent variables and relationship and dispute type serving as independent variables.

Concern for own payoff differed between the two negotiating settings, $F(1, 42) = 8.6$, $p < .005$, and across the two relationship conditions, $F(1, 42) = 12.3$, $p < .001$, but these effects were qualified by a significant interaction, $F(1, 84) = 8.9$, $p < .004$.[8] In the invention scenario, subjects again displayed a selfish shift; they were almost three times as concerned with their own payoff in the negative relationship condition as they were in the positive relationship condition. However, no such effect was observed in the lot dispute type.

Figure 5 depicts the shape of the social utility functions based on mean parameter values given a positive and negative disputant relationship. Again, the relationship had little effect on the utility function in the domain of disadvantageous inequality, $F(1, 42) = 1.7$, $p > .2$. The slope of the function in this region was also not affected by the dispute type, $F(1, 42) = 1.27$, $p > .25$, and the interaction was nonsignificant, $F(1, 84) = 0.3$, $p > .5$. Subjects disliked obtaining a lower payment than the other party received, regardless of the dispute type.

---

[8] Because subjects were always run in diagonal within-subjects cells, it was impossible to simultaneously examine interactions and take account of the repeated measures nature of the design. Therefore, the reported interaction effects are based on a simple ANOVA that treats the same subject in different conditions as two independent observations. It seems unlikely to us that this had much of an impact on the results. When we examined the main effects, both taking and not taking account of the repeated measures nature of the design, the results from the two analyses were virtually indistinguishable.

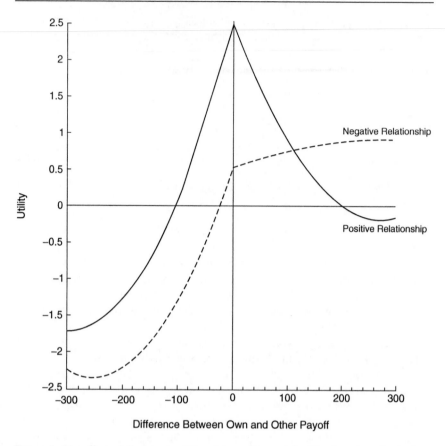

Figure 5. The effect of disputant relationship on the social utility function: Study 2.

The slope of the function in the region of advantageous inequality, however, was affected by the relationship, $F(1, 42) = 26.6$, $p < .0001$. Subjects, on average, disliked advantageous inequality in the positive relationship condition and actually exhibited a weak taste for advantageous inequality in the negative relationship condition. Echoing the results for the lot and invention conditions in Study 1, preferences for advantageous inequality were unrelated to dispute type, $F(1, 42) = 0.04$, $p > .8$, and the interaction effect was not significant, $F(1, 84) = 0.36$, $p > .5$.

We again examined individual differences in outcome preferences among subjects. Table 5 indicates the frequency of subjects in each of the relationship–dispute-type conditions who had positive parameter estimates for NEGDIFF and negative estimates for POSDIFF.

Table 5. Proportions of Subjects Who Disliked Advantageous and Disadvantageous Inequality: Study 2

Relationship	Dispute type	Dislike disadvantageous inequality (%)	Dislike advantageous inequality (%)
Positive	Invention	86	78
Negative	Invention	96	27
Positive	Lot	82	77
Negative	Lot	82	42

Again, few subjects in any condition obtained positive satisfaction from obtaining an inferior payoff, whereas considerable diversity was evident between subjects concerning preferences for a superior payoff. Averaging across the two disputes, a majority of subjects (77%) in the positive relationship condition disliked getting a higher payoff than the other party. In the negative relationship condition, a majority (68%) preferred obtaining a higher payoff. The proportions of saints, loyalists, and ruthless competitors were 20%, 52%, and 22%, respectively. The remaining 6% of subjects could not be classified into any of these three groups.

7.2.3. Discussion

The purpose of Study 2 was to replicate the results of Study 1 and to explore the effects of relationships characterized by strong negative and positive affect on interpersonal decision making. Overall, the results of Study 2 closely parallel those of Study 1. Although the strengthened relationship condition did cause subjects, on average, to seek out advantageous inequality in the negative relationship condition, the social utility functions estimated in Study 2 were similar to those derived in Study 1, and the impact of the manipulations was comparable. Again, relationship conditions (i.e. positive, negative) strongly influenced preferences for advantageous inequality, but did not affect concern for disadvantageous inequality. Also, individuals showed a selfish shift (e.g., greater concern for own payoff) in the invention dispute as interpersonal relationships became more negative.

As in Study 1, most individuals could be classified into one of three groups, reflecting desires for advantageous equality in interpersonal contexts. There was a larger fraction of loyalists in the present study, which may reflect the more explicit relationship manipulations. Subjects were generally more favorably disposed to the opponent in the positive relationship condition and more hostile in the negative relationship condition.

Table 6. Payoffs to Self and Other: Study 3

Choice	Individual choice condition			Interpersonal choice condition				
	Sure thing, payoff to self	Risky choice		Sure thing		Risky choice		
		Probability	Payoff to self	Payoff to self	Payoff to opponent	Probability	Payoff to self	Payoff to opponent
1	$5,000	.3	$4,000	$5,000	$5,000	.3	$4,000	$6,000
		.7	$6,000			.7	$6,000	$4,000
2	$4,000	.5	$3,000	$4,000	$6,000	.5	$3,000	$7,000
		.5	$5,000			.5	$5,000	$5,000
3	−$5,000	.5	−$10,000	−$5,000	−$5,000	.5	−$10,000	$0
			$0			.5	$0	−$10,000

7.3. Study 3

The striking correspondence between the results from Studies 1 and 2 increases our confidence in the reliability of the findings. However, the validity of the estimated social utility functions—whether they accurately predict choice behavior in dispute settings—is uncertain. To assess the predictive accuracy of the estimated social utility functions, we conducted a third study that compared choice behavior in individual and interpersonal decision tasks. Subjects in this study made three hypothetical choices in an individual choice setting and three choices—between arbitrating or accepting a certain offer—in an interpersonal setting. The two sets of choices were matched in terms of payoffs to self, but the interpersonal choice task introduced consequences for another decision maker. The three choices in the individual choice condition are summarized on the left-hand side of Table 6; the three interpersonal choices are summarized on the right-hand side. Disputant relationship (positive or negative) was manipulated between subjects.

The three choices were designed to test implications of the specific features of the social utility functions estimated in the first two studies. The first presented a choice between a sure $5,000 and a risky alternative offering a .7 chance of $6,000 and a .3 chance of $4,000. In the interpersonal choice condition, the payoffs to self were identical, but the other party received the balance of $10,000, that is, $5,000 if the sure settlement was chosen and $4,000 or $6,000 under arbitration. On the basis of its relatively low level of risk and significantly higher expected value ($5,400 vs. $5,000), we expected subjects to prefer the risky option in the individual choice setting. In the interpersonal choice condition, however, we predicted that preferences would depend on the relationship between the disputants. In the positive relationship condition, most subjects dislike either form of inequality, making the arbitration option, which results in either advantageous or disadvantageous inequality, especially unattractive. In the negative relationship condition, people dislike disadvantageous inequality but are relatively indifferent to advantageous inequality. Hence, we expected a larger proportion of subjects in the negative relationship condition to opt for arbitration. Furthermore, we anticipated a greater preference for the sure thing in both interpersonal settings than in the individual decision setting, as aversion to either type of inequality tends to favor the $5,000–$5,000 split.

The second choice offered subjects in both settings (individual or interpersonal) a choice between a sure $4,000 and a .5 chance at $3,000 and at $5,000. In the interpersonal setting, the other party received the balance of $10,000. We expected subjects to prefer the sure thing in the individual choice condition, given the general tendency toward risk aversion for gains. However, we anticipated that subjects would opt for arbitration in the interpersonal condition. First, one of the outcomes involved a $5,000–$5,000 split, which is especially attractive, particularly given a positive relationship between disputants. Second, the slope of the utility function in the region of disadvantageous inequality is convex, so the potential negative discrepancy of $4,000 under the arbitration option is not twice as bad as the negative discrepancy of $2,000 under the sure-thing option. We did not anticipate that preferences would be significantly affected by disputant relationship, which has little impact on preferences for disadvantageous inequality.

The third item involved losses rather than gains. In the individual choice condition, subjects were offered a choice between losing $5,000 for sure or a .5 chance of losing $10,000. On the basis of the tendency toward risk seeking in the domain of losses (Kahneman & Tversky, 1979), we expected subjects to prefer the risky outcome in the individual choice condition. However, in the interpersonal choice condition, because of the attractiveness of the equal-split option, we hypothesized that subjects would prefer the equal split of − $5,000: − $5,000 over equal chances of −$10,000–$0 and $0–$10,000. Furthermore, we predicted that subjects in the positive relationship condition would exhibit a greater preference for the equal split owing to their aversion to both types of inequality.

7.3.1. Method

A total of 111 graduate students of management participated in the study. The experimenter explained that the purpose of the study was to examine decision making under different conditions. There were two phases, each conducted on different days separated by a 1-week interval. In Phase 1, half the participants completed individual choice questionnaires and half completed interpersonal choice questionnaires. In Phase 2, each group completed the questionnaire that they had not previously encountered. The individual choice questionnaire contained three hypothetical choices on a single page, with the instructions: "Below you are given choices between a SURE THING and a GAMBLE. Decide which option you prefer and indicate your choice to each question by circling either A or B." The interpersonal choice questionnaire was based on the lot condition from Studies 1 and 2. The questionnaire began with these instructions: "Below you are given a description of an incident involving you and a neighbor. Please read the description and then answer each question." It then introduced the lot scenario and the disputant relationship manipulation (positive or negative), which was adopted verbatim from Study 2 (see Appendix). The questionnaire described three situations in which the subject and neighbor either jointly owed or were to be paid $10,000. Subjects were then given a choice between accepting a settlement proposed by the neighbor or taking the risky option of arbitrating.

7.3.2. Results and Discussion

Table 7 summarizes the results from Study 3. In general, they conformed to predictions. On the first item, the disputant relationship had a significant impact on preferences. In the positive relationship condition, 15% opted for arbitration, whereas in the negative relationship condition 73% of subjects preferred the risky alternative, $\chi^2(1, N = 67) = 32.7, p < .0001$. Generally, in the interpersonal relationship condition subjects were likely to select the risky alternative. Averaging across the two relationship conditions, 38% of subjects chose the risky alternative in

Table 7. Response Proportions: Individual Versus Interpersonal Choice: Study 3

Question	Individual choice ($n = 67$)	Interpersonal choice	
		Positive relationship ($n = 35$)	Negative relationship ($n = 32$)
Question 1			
Sure thing	19%	85%	27%
Gamble–arbitrate	81%	15%	73%
	100%	100%	100%
Question 2			
Sure thing	73%	56%	33%
Gamble–arbitrate	27%	44%	67%
	100%	100%	100%
Question 3			
Sure thing	25%	85%	82%
Gamble–arbitrate	75%	15%	18%
	100%	100%	100%

the interpersonal choice condition, and 81% did so in the individual choice condition—a significant difference, Cochran $Q(1) = 27$, $p < .0001$.

On the second item there was, as predicted, a greater tendency to select the sure thing in the individual choice than in the interpersonal choice condition. In the individual choice condition, a majority of subjects (73%) preferred the sure $4,000 over the 50–50 chance at $3,000 and $5,000. In the interpersonal condition, 55% preferred the risky option of arbitration, $Q(1) = 10.8$, $p < .001$. However, contrary to our prediction, we observed a significant effect of disputant relationship on preference for arbitration. Subjects in the negative relationship condition were more likely to opt for arbitration (67%) than were subjects in the positive relationship condition (44%), $\chi^2(1, N = 67) = 4.9$, $p < .05$. The effect of disputant relationship may reflect a generally negative attitude toward arbitrating a dispute against a friend.

Finally, the results for the third item were largely as predicted. In the individual decision condition, a majority (75%) of subjects selected the risky option, whereas in the interpersonal choice condition 85% preferred the sure $5,000–$5,000 split, $Q(1) = 38.1$, $p < .0001$. The difference between the positive and negative relationship conditions was not significant, $\chi^2(1, N = 67) = 0.67$, $p > .15$, although, as predicted, a higher proportion in the positive relationship condition opted for the equal split. It is possible that the nonsignificance of the relationship manipulation was due to ceiling effects; even in the negative relationship condition a full 82% chose the equal split.

7.4. General Discussion

Our goal was to estimate social utility functions in a dispute context. We were especially interested in the effect of the relationship between disputants on preferences for own and other outcomes. The following conclusions summarize our main findings.

First, individuals' utilities for disputed outcomes depended on the magnitude of their own outcomes and on the difference between their own and the other party's outcomes. This finding is consistent with earlier research (e.g. Messick & Sentis, 1985), indicating that individuals' concern with own and others' payoffs is well captured by an additive function of nonsocial utility (own payment) and social utility (difference between own and other's payment). Second, most disputants preferred equal payoffs over either advantageous or disadvantageous inequality. The modal utility function was tentshaped: increasing and convex for disadvantageous inequality, decreasing and convex for advantageous inequality. Third, if inequality was unavoidable, people preferred advantageous over disadvantageous inequality. Fourth, the disputant relationship and negotiation context exerted their main impact on concern with own payoff and attitude toward advantageous inequality, but had little impact on attitudes toward disadvantageous inequality. Fifth, as the disputant relationship shifted from positive to negative, subjects displayed a selfish shift: They became more concerned with their own payoff, independent of the other party's, and more tolerant of advantageous inequality. Sixth, we found that subjects could be neatly categorized according to their preferences toward advantageous inequality. We labeled as saints those subjects who preferred equality over inequality, regardless of the relationship between disputants. Loyalists preferred equality when involved in a positive relationship, but preferred advantageous inequality under conditions of a negative relationship. Ruthless competitors sought advantageous inequality under all conditions, even in the positive relationship condition. Averaged across the first two studies, the proportions of saints, loyalists, and ruthless competitors in our samples were, respectively, 22%, 39%, and 29%.

In general, interpersonal concerns overshadowed concern for own outcome independent of the other's outcome, thus providing further evidence for the importance of relative comparisons in decision making, a prominence that has already been recognized in research on decision making under uncertainty (see, e.g., Bell, 1982; Fishburn, 1977; Loomes & Sugden, 1982). Most prominent among theories of decision making under uncertainty that incorporate relative concerns is prospect theory (Kahneman & Tversky, 1979). Prospect theory examines decision making in individual contexts in which decision outcomes affect only the decision maker; the reference point is most frequently modeled as the current state of the decision maker, although it can also assume other psychologically relevant values. One such value, particularly relevant in interpersonal negotiations, is the payoff to another party. If this payoff is adopted as a reference point, then the x-axis will correspond to the difference between the two parties' payoffs as in the social utility functions illustrated in Figures 1–5.

Although further underscoring the importance of relative comparisons, the current findings challenge the generalizability of prospect theory's specific qualitative features to an interpersonal setting. The predominant shape of the social utility function we estimated resembles the prospect theory value function in the domain of losses; it is upward sloping and convex. However, for positive differences in payoffs, the curve slopes downward and is also convex. Prospect theory's value function is upward sloped and concave for gains. We found that prospect theory makes accurate predictions of decision behavior in the individual decision contexts we examined, but that decision making departs systematically from these predictions in an interpersonal context—in ways predicted by a tent-shaped social utility function.

An important question concerns the generalizability of the present results to decision making in real-world disputes. Although having subjects rate their satisfaction with, or choose between, hypothetical outcomes is a common practice in psychological research, the problem of generalizability may be especially significant in interpersonal contexts for several reasons. First, emotions are likely to play a more important role in interpersonal decision making than in other situations, and hypothetical questions are unlikely to evoke the same intensity of emotions as real-world situations. We cannot predict whether or how the emotions that often arise during negotiations would influence social utility functions. Our analysis, however, provides a framework within which to examine such effects. Would concern for own payoff be greater or smaller in a real dispute than in our study? Would the slope of the utility function in the domain of advantageous inequality slope more steeply downward? These questions could be addressed by interrupting an actual dispute, asking disputants to confidentially rate their satisfaction with different outcomes, and using these ratings to estimate individual-level social utility functions. We suspect that emotions would intensify the effects we observed, but not change them qualitatively. Answers to these questions await further research.

A second concern in this, and in most experimental and observational research, is that subjects' responses may be influenced by considerations of social desirability. Norms of behavior for social situations are better established than are those applying to, for example, decision making under uncertainty. However, it is difficult to assess, a priori, the direction of the bias that social desirability considerations introduce. Behavior in real-world settings is also influenced by norms of behavior, and it is unclear whether norms exert a greater impact in real or experimental settings.

A final concern is that the outcomes in our studies were presented to the subjects without any account of how they were arrived at. In real negotiations, any settlement has a history that may influence participants' satisfaction. For example disputants are generally more satisfied with outcomes when they feel personally responsible in the sense of having obtained concessions from the other party. Earlier research has examined the effects of concession rates and other variables relating to settlement history on negotiator attitudes and behavior (e.g. Pruitt & Drews, 1969). We chose to abstract away from historical variables and to focus instead on the effect of the relationship between negotiators and the nature of the dispute on social utility. Again, our estimation methodology would provide an excellent structure for assessing the impact of settlement history on negotiator preferences.

The social utility functions we estimated paint a rather benevolent picture of disputant preferences in a wide range of situations. Most of our subjects either disliked or exhibited only a weak preference for advantageous inequality. Even for ruthless competitors, parameter estimates for advantageous inequality were, if positive, close to zero. In contrast, the negotiation literature (e.g. Raiffa, 1982; Seigel & Fouraker, 1960) highlights the fact that negotiators often fail to reach agreements because of invidious social comparisons. What factors might explain why individuals in our experiments focused on clearly equitable agreements, but individuals in real-world contexts have difficulty reaching mutually acceptable decisions and often appear to be trying to beat the other party?

One possible explanation stems from the great complexity of most interpersonal decision tasks. Most disputes involve a number of issues and often call into play competing norms of distributive justice. Furthermore, disputants are often ignorant of the other party's interests. Complexity and imperfect information permit subjective interpretations of equity. Faced with ambiguous information, egocentric biases (Ross & Sicoly, 1979) may pervade individuals' judgments regarding the fairness of different potential settlements (see, e.g., Raiffa, 1982, p. 75, p. 94). When faced with the task of dividing scarce resources, disputants may invoke norms and reasoning that favor the self, causing both parties to simultaneously perceive themselves as being in the domain of disadvantageous inequality. In this region, most subjects can enhance their utility by decreasing the payoff to the other party, even at the expense of some decrement to their own payoff. Each party is likely to see its own attempts to decrease the other party's relative payoff as an attempt to restore equity, whereas the other party's efforts are seen as efforts to gain an unfair advantage. The likely outcome of these combined efforts to restore equity will be a destructive downward spiral of recriminations and joint losses.

The preceding discussion suggests that one interesting direction for future research would be to examine interpersonal decision making under different levels of complexity and uncertainty regarding the parties' inputs and interests and in situations in which multiple norms of distributive justice are operative. In our study, the neutral dispute situation was relatively unambiguous, and individuals probably focused on a single criterion of equity: equal payoffs or payments by both parties. Thus, we were unable to observe self-serving interpretations of equity and their effect on social utility and decision making. It would be informative to explore whether breakdowns in negotiations are typically due to individual factors, such as the presence of ruthless competitors on one or more sides, or to environmental factors, such as complexity and imperfect information, that permit egocentric interpretations of equity.

References

Adams, J. S. (1963). Toward an understanding of inequity. *Journal of Abnormal and Social Psychology, 67*, 422–436.

Adams, J. S. (1965). Inequity in social exchange. In L. Berkowitz (Ed.), *Advances in experimental social psychology* (Vol. 2, pp. 267–299). New York: Academic Press.

Austin, W. (1980). Friendship and fairness: Effects of type of relationship and task performance on choice of distribution rules. *Personality and Social Psychology Bulletin, 6*, 402–408.

Bell, D. E. (1982). Regret in decision making under uncertainty. *Operations Research, 30*, 961–981.

Clark, M. S., & Mills, J. (1979). Interpersonal attraction in exchange and communal relationships. *Journal of Personality and Social Psychology, 37*, 12–24.

Conrath, D. W., & Deci, E. L. (1969). The determination and scaling of a bivariate utility function. *Behavioral Science, 14*, 316–327.

Crosby, F. (1976). A model of egoistical relative deprivation. *Psychological Review, 83*, 85–113.

Festinger, L. (1954). A theory of social comparison processes. *Human Relations, 7*, 117–140.

Fishburn, P. C. (1977). Mean-risk analysis with risk associated with below-target returns. *American Economic Review, 67*, 116–126.

Griesinger, D. W., & Livingston, J. W., Jr. (1973). Toward a model of interpersonal motivation in experimental games. *Behavioral Science, 18*, 173–188.

Guth, W., Schmittberger, R., & Schwarze, B. (1982). An experimental analysis of ultimatum bargaining. *Journal of Economic Behavior and Organization, 3*, 367–388.

Heider, F. (1958). *The psychology of interpersonal relations.* New York: Wiley.

Homans, G. C. (1961). *Social behavior: Its elementary forms.* New York: Harcourt, Brace & World.

Kahneman, D., & Tversky, A. (1979). Prospect theory: An analysis of decision under risk. *Econometrica, 47*, 263–291.

Kelley, H. (1979). *Personal relationships: Their structures and processes.* Hillsdale, NJ: Erlbaum.

Lewicki, R. J., & Litterer, J. A. (1985). *Negotiation.* Homewood, IL: Irwin.

Loomes, G., & Sugden, R. (1982). Regret theory: An alternative theory of rational choice under uncertainty. *Economic Journal, 92*, 805–824.

Lurie, S. (1987). A parametric model of utility for two-person distributions. *Psychological Review, 94*, 42–60.

MacCrimmon, K. R., & Messick, D. M. (1976). A framework for social motives. *Behavioral Science, 21*, 86–100.

Messick, D. M., & Sentis, K. P. (1985). Estimating social and nonsocial utility functions from ordinal data. *European Journal of Social Psychology, 15*, 389–399.

Orbell, J. M., & Dawes, R. M. (1981). Social dilemmas. In G. M. Stephenson & J. H. Davis (Eds.), *Progress in applied social psychology* (Vol. 1, pp. 37–65). Chichester, England: Wiley.

Pruitt, D. G., & Drews, J. L. (1969). The effect of time pressure, time elapsed, and the opponent's concession rate on behavior in negotiation. *Journal of Experimental and Social Psychology, 31*, 553–60.

Pruitt, D. G., & Rubin, J. Z. (1986). *Social conflict.* New York: Random House.

Raiffa, H. (1982). *The art and science of negotiation.* Cambridge, MA: Harvard University Press.

Ross, M., & Sicoly, F. (1979). Egocentric biases in availability and attribution. *Journal of Personality and Social Psychology, 37*, 322–336.

Schmitt, D. R., & Marwell, G. (1972). Withdrawal and reward reallocation in response to inequity. *Journal of Experimental Social Psychology, 8*, 207–221.

Scott, R. H. (1972). Avarice, altruism, and second party preferences. *Quarterly Journal of Economics, 86*, 1–18.

Seigel, S., & Fouraker, L. E. (1960). *Bargaining and group decision making: Experiments in bilateral monopoly.* New York: McGraw-Hill.

Thibaut, J. W., & Kelley, H. H. (1959). *The social psychology of groups.* New York: Wiley.

Walster, E., Walster, G. W., & Berscheid, E. (1978). *Equity: Theory and research.* Boston: Allyn and Bacon.

Appendix

Stimuli: Experiment 1, Lot Scenario

You live adjacent to an empty lot separating you from your next-door neighbor to your left. No one knows who owns the lot, despite the fact that you and your next-door neighbor have lived there for more than 2 years. However, the city recently informed you that the lot actually belongs to both you and your neighbor, but the percentage owned by each of you has to be negotiated.

POSITIVE RELATIONSHIP

You have always been fond of your neighbors: They take care of your pets when you are out of town, and they always invite you to their parties.

NEGATIVE RELATIONSHIP

You have never been fond of your neighbors: they let their dogs roam in your yard and you frequently have to pick up after the dogs. Adding insult to injury, last New Year's Eve they called the police a few minutes after midnight to disrupt your party.

LOSS

The lot is too small to sell. However, the city has assessed taxes on the property that you and your neighbor must pay. You and your neighbor need to decide how to split the costs of the taxes.

GAIN

A third neighbor who lacks a backyard has agreed to buy the property for gardening purposes. You and your neighbor would both be happy to have a garden between your houses. You and your neighbor need to decide how to split the profit.

Stimuli: Experiment 1, Business Scenario

You bought a new computer system for word processing. Having a computer system has been a major advantage in your life. With each new year of college, you have found that the amount of writing required has increased. You do not know how you would get the work done without the computer.

POSITIVE RELATIONSHIP

During your visit to the computer store, the salesperson gave you excellent information and personal attention. When it appeared that delivery of your computer would be delayed, he personally drove to the warehouse to get the computer in time for your final exams.

NEGATIVE RELATIONSHIP

During your visit to the computer store, the salesperson treated you in a rude manner. Moreover, he tried to sell you an inferior brand. Clearly, he was trying to take advantage of your lack of knowledge.

LOSS

Your computer had a warranty of only 30 days. On the 29th day, a Saturday, the computer broke down. You called the store, but they could not be reached until Monday—2 days after the warranty ended. The manufacturer would not give the extension. The dealer arranged for the computer to be repaired. However, the bill has to be divided between you and the dealer. You and the dealer need to decide how to split the cost.

GAIN

After buying the computer, you and the dealer found out that the manufacturer was offering a rebate. The rebate was a negotiated rebate, meaning that it can be divided between the dealer and customer as the two parties choose. You and the dealer must decide how to split the rebate.

Study 2: Strengthened Relationship Manipulations (Invention Dispute Type)

NEGATIVE RELATIONSHIP

Pat is a student who lives in your dorm. You have had many unpleasant personal experiences with Pat, and other people in the dorm also consider Pat to be obnoxious. Pat complains about others' living habits, yet does not do any work. Pat borrows notes and copies assignments, but does not say *thank you* and often fails to return items. Last week, Pat failed to pick up some party supplies after promising to do so, did not show up for an important intramurals playoff game, and insulted one of your friends. In short, Pat is selfish, irresponsible, argumentative, demanding, and insincere.

Positive Relationship

Pat is a student in your dorm. You like Pat a lot, and other people in the dorm also consider Pat to be very nice. Pat always helps out when others need help in everyday dorm activities. Pat takes notes and picks up assignments for people who miss classes. Last week, Pat made all the arrangements for a small dorm party, gathered everyone together to visit a sick friend in the health center, and offered his room to you for your out-of-town guest. In short, Pat is kind, friendly, sincere, responsible, and dependable.

8

Explaining the Bargaining Impasse: The Role of Self-Serving Biases

Linda Babcock and George Loewenstein

The purpose of the social utility paper (Chapter 7) was to uncover some of the major psychological causes of failures to resolve disputes. I went into that project thinking that the major source of nonsettlement of disputes was the great antagonism that arises between negotiators. However, the social utility functions we observed were seemingly quite benign. As long as their payoffs didn't fall below those of the other side—as long as they stayed clear of the region of disadvantageous inequity—people seemed to be quite content to get what was coming to them in fact, even willing to give part of their payoffs to the other side. Based on that paper alone, one might think that most disputes would settle amicably (and perhaps most do). The caveat about not falling below the other party, however, turns out to be important because, as a result of self-serving perceptions of fairness, it often happens that there is no possible settlement that both parties view as fair. Prior research, most notably by David Messick (who had also made valuable contributions to the social utility research) and Keith Sentis, had observed a self-serving bias when it came to judgments of fairness. Linda Babcock,[1]

---

[1] A professional dancer turned labor economist, Linda's first contribution to the research was to figure out how to demonstrate the causal impact of the self-serving bias. I was presenting the first study we conducted on the topic—a collaboration with Issacharoff and Camerer—at an internal CMU seminar that Linda attended. The study demonstrated the existence of the self-serving bias using a simulated legal dispute and showed that nonsettlement was strongly related to the combined magnitude of the self-serving bias exhibited by a pair of negotiators. But, of course, correlation does not necessarily imply causation, and in the seminar I lamented that we hadn't figured out a way to demonstrate causality. Linda's hand shot up: "Oh, that would be easy; just vary whether you tell them their role before or after they read the case materials." A few weeks later, we had run the study Linda proposed (which worked like a charm and was published in the *American Economic Review*), and Linda became an integral part of, and eventually the de facto leader of, the team.

Sam Issacharoff,[2] Colin Camerer, and I set out to test whether this 'self-serving bias' in the assessment of fairness might be playing a role in negotiation impasse. In a series of studies, both in the laboratory and in the field, we discovered that it does. We not only find that the self-serving bias is strong, but that it predicts nonsettlement of disputes both in the lab and the field, and that various manipulations designed to reduce or eliminate the magnitude of the bias have the effect of increasing settlement rates. Our research also suggests that self-interest doesn't affect people's assessments of fairness directly as much as exerting an unconscious and unintentional influence on how people process information, with evidence and arguments that support self-interest receiving greater weight, and being judged as more credible, than those that oppose it.

I think that I've found this research more useful in my personal life than any other research that I've been involved with. Most obviously, whenever I get involved in a dispute, I automatically ask myself whether—or really how *much*—I am biased. Not that I claim any ability to be impartial, but knowing

---

[2] I count myself lucky to have worked with the brilliant Sam Issacharoff, who is a lawyer and law professor at NYU. I've seen his intelligence on display on numerous occasions, such as when he brought me along as a consultant to two depositions of opposing expert witness statisticians on a voting rights case he was litigating in Peoria Illinois. One of the experts was the head of the statistics department at the University of Illinois Urbana/Champaign and the other was head of the statistics department at Stanford. The night before the first deposition, Sam and I had gone through the statistical output of the U.I. statistician and discovered a minor flaw in the analysis—a coefficient that logically should have had a value between 0 and 1, but had a value closer to 1,000 in the output (because they had not standardized the weights in their analysis to sum to 1). At the first deposition, through a remarkably brilliant sequence of questions, Sam managed, to get the first statistician to vouch for the perfection of his analysis. Though his mistake was in fact quite trivial, his emphatic assertion that there were no mistakes in his work destroyed his credibility when, subsequently confronted with the nonsensical coefficient, he had to eat his words. A few weeks later, Sam knocked out the second witness by getting him to vouch for the quality of the work performed by the first (one wonders why the opposing side didn't communicate more effectively with their experts). With both of their experts discredited, the city of Peoria settled the case, agreeing to change the system by which they elected representatives.

Peoria got a new system of voting, I got a—somewhat arbitrary—consulting fee of $250 (my first) which Sam paid me by check when we returned from Chicago from the second deposition, and Sam and I ended up getting the inspiration for a new research project. The source of the inspiration was my behavior. Before I'd even made it home, I had spent the $250 on a VCR, and months later commented to Sam that I was getting disproportionate pleasure from it because it was not just a VCR to me but a consulting VCR. Later, we wrote a paper titled "Source Dependence in the Valuation of Objects" that is about the idea that how much you enjoy and value an object can depend on how you obtained it. In one of the experiments reported in that paper, subjects played a game, the winner received a coffee mug, and we elicited selling prices from the winner and buying prices from the loser. We observed a robust endowment effect (see Chapter 5). In another, somewhat perverse, condition, we gave the mug to the loser of the contest instead of to the winner. In this condition there was no endowment effect whatsoever: losers were extremely anxious to rid themselves of the mug, which just served to remind them of their failure. (Loewenstein, G. and Issacharoff, S. (1994). 'Source-Dependence in the Valuation of Objects', *Journal of Behavioral Decision Making*, 7: 157–168.)

about this systematic bias, and looking for evidence of it in one's own perceptions, can make one less confident about the righteousness of one's own positions. I've also found some of the research on fairness biases strategically useful when it comes to disputes with my wife. One of the first studies to document the self-serving bias measured student perceptions of a contentious football game between Princeton and Dartmouth, universities that, at the time, had a fierce rivalry. Students from both schools watched a film of the game and rated the number of penalties committed by both teams. The main finding was that Princeton students saw the Dartmouth team commit twice as many flagrant penalties and three times as many mild penalties as their own team, whereas Dartmouth students recorded an approximately equal number of penalties by both teams. Clearly, the Dartmouth team committed many more penalties, but the worst that the Dartmouth fans could admit to was an equal number. When my wife and I argue about the distribution of childcare or housework, and one of us claims that we contribute about equally in some domain, the other has a ready-made single-word response: "Dartmouth."

Explaining the Bargaining Impasse:
The Role of Self-Serving Biases*

Linda Babcock and George Loewenstein

A major unsolved riddle facing the social sciences is the cause of impasse in negotiations. The consequences of impasse are evident in the amount of private and public resources spent on civil litigation, the costs of labor unrest, the psychic and pecuniary wounds of domestic strife, and in clashes among religious, ethnic and regional groups. Impasses in these settings are not only pernicious, but somewhat paradoxical since negotiations typically unfold over long periods of time, offering ample opportunities for interaction between the parties.

Economists, and more specifically game theorists, typically attribute delays in settlement to incomplete information. Bargainers possess private information about factors such as their alternatives to negotiated agreements and costs to delay, causing them to be mutually uncertain about the other side's reservation value. Uncertainty produces impasse because bargainers use costly delays to signal to the other party information about their own reservation value (Kennan and Wilson, 1989; Cramton, 1992). However, this account of impasse is difficult to test because satisfactory measures of uncertainty are rare. With only a few exceptions (Tracy, 1986, 1987), most field research in this area has been limited to testing secondary hypotheses, such as the relationship between wages and strike duration (Farber, 1978; Card, 1990; McConnell, 1989; Kennan, 1985, 1986). Experimental tests of incomplete information accounts of impasse have been hindered by the difficulty of completely controlling important aspects of the experimental environment, such as the beliefs maintained by the

---

* This chapter was originally published as Babcock, L. and Loewenstein, G. (1997) "Explaining Bargaing Impasse". Journal of Economic Perspectives. 11(1): 109–126. Reproduced by kind permission of the AEA.

subjects (Roth, 1995), and those that have been conducted have generally not provided strong support for the specific models under examination.

This paper identifies a different and relatively simple psychological mechanism as a major cause of bargaining impasse. This is the tendency for parties to arrive at judgments that reflect a self-serving bias—to conflate what is fair with what benefits oneself. Such self-serving assessments of fairness can impede negotiations and promote impasse in at least three ways. First, if negotiators estimate the value of the alternatives to negotiated settlements in self-serving ways, this could rule out any chance of settlement by eliminating the contract zone (the set of agreements that both sides prefer to their reservation values). Second, if disputants believe that their notion of fairness is impartial and shared by both sides, then they will interpret the other party's aggressive bargaining not as an attempt to get what they perceive of as fair, but as a cynical and exploitative attempt to gain an unfair strategic advantage. Research in psychology and economics has shown that bargainers care not only about what the other party offers, but also about the other party's motives.[1] Third, negotiators are strongly averse to settling even slightly below the point they view as fair (Loewenstein, Thompson and Bazerman, 1989). If disputants are willing to make economic sacrifices to avoid a settlement perceived as unfair and their ideas of fairness are biased in directions that favor themselves, then bargainers who are "only trying to get what is fair" may not be able to settle their dispute.

The evidence we review shows that the self-serving bias, and the impasses it causes, occurs even when disputants possess identical information, which suggests that private and incomplete information may not be as critical for nonsettlement as is commonly believed. The bias is also present when bargainers have incentives to evaluate the situation impartially, which implies that the bias does not appear to be deliberate or strategic.

We begin by reviewing some evidence from the psychology literature that demonstrates the existence of the self-serving bias in different domains. We then present results from experimental and field research, conducted by ourselves and several coauthors (Colin Camerer, Samuel Issacharoff, and Xianghong Wang), which establishes the connection between self-serving bias and impasse, and helps to pinpoint the cognitive and motivational mechanisms underlying the bias. Finally, we review previous experimental economics research on bargaining and show that some of the results can be interpreted as manifestations of the self-serving bias.

---

[1] Blount (1995) offers an empirical investigation of this point, while Rabin (1993) provides a literature review and a theoretical analysis. See also Kagel, Kim and Moser (1996).

8.1. Psychological Research on the Self-Serving Bias

Although psychologists debate the underlying cause of the self-serving bias, its existence is rarely questioned. The self-serving bias is evident in the "above average" effect, whereby well over half of survey respondents typically rate themselves in the top 50 percent of drivers (Svenson, 1981), ethics (Baumhart, 1968), managerial prowess (Larwood and Whittaker, 1977), productivity (Cross, 1977), health (Weinstein, 1980) and a variety of desirable skills. It is also evident in the large body of research showing that people overestimate their own contribution to joint tasks. For example, when married couples estimate the fraction of various household tasks they are responsible for, their estimates typically add to more than 100 percent (Ross and Sicoly, 1979). People also tend to attribute their successes to ability and skill, but their failures to bad luck (Zuckerman, 1979).

The self-serving bias affects not only individuals' evaluations of themselves, but also of groups they are affiliated with. For example, in one early study, Hastorf and Cantril (1954) examined individuals' judgments of penalties committed during a football game between Princeton and Dartmouth. Students at these schools viewed a film of the game and counted the number of penalties committed by both teams. Princeton students saw the Dartmouth team commit twice as many flagrant penalties and three times as many mild penalties as their own team. Dartmouth students, on the other hand, recorded an approximately equal number of penalties by both teams. While the truth probably lies somewhere in between, the researchers concluded that it was as if the two groups of students "saw a different game."

A subset of research on the self-serving bias has shown that people tend to arrive at judgments of what is fair or right that are biased in the direction of their own self-interests. For example, Messick and Sentis (1979) divided subjects into two groups: one group was told to imagine that they had worked seven hours at a task while another person had worked 10 hours. For the other group, the hours were reversed. It was specified that the person who worked seven hours was paid $25. Subjects were asked how much the subjects who had worked 10 hours should be paid. Seven-hour subjects, on average, thought the 10-hour subject should be paid $30.29. However, the 10-hour subjects thought they should be paid $35.24. The difference between $30.29 and $35.24—$4.95—was cited as evidence of a self-serving bias in perceptions of fairness.

This experiment also yielded insights about the underlying cause of the bias. The perceived fair wage for the 10-hour workers was bimodal: some people thought it was fair to pay both parties equally, regardless of hours worked; others thought it was fair to pay both an equal hourly wage (which would mean paying the 10-hour workers approximately $35.70). The difference between the seven-hour and 10-hour subjects resulted from the higher fraction of

10-hour subjects who believed that an equal hourly wage was fair. This research suggests that self-serving assessments of fairness are likely to occur in morally ambiguous settings in which there are competing "focal points"— that is, settlements that could plausibly be viewed as fair (Schelling, 1960).

8.2. An Experimental Investigation: A Texas Tort Case

To investigate the role of self-serving assessments in bargaining, we designed an experimental paradigm, which we then used in a number of experimental studies. We developed a tort case based on a trial that occurred in Texas, in which an injured motorcyclist sued the driver of the automobile that collided with him, requesting $100,000. Subjects are randomly assigned to the role of plaintiff or defendant and attempt to negotiate a settlement. Subjects first receive a page explaining the experiment, the sequence of events, rules for negotiating and the costs they face if they failed to reach an agreement. Both subjects then receive the same 27 pages of materials from the original legal case in Texas. The materials included witness testimony, police reports, maps and the testimony of the parties.[2] Subjects are informed that we gave the identical case materials to a judge in Texas, who reached a judgment between $0 and $100,000 concerning compensation to the plaintiff.

Before negotiating, subjects are asked to write down their guesses of what the judge awarded. They are told they will receive a bonus of $1 at the end of the session if their prediction is within $5,000 (plus or minus) of the actual judge's award. They are also asked what they considered a fair amount for the plaintiff to receive in an out-of-court settlement "from the vantage point of a neutral third party." Subjects are told that none of this information will be shown to the other party. The two subjects are then allowed to negotiate for 30 minutes. Delays in settlement are made costly to the subjects by imposing "court costs" that accumulate in each period in which the subjects fail to settle. If they fail to reach a voluntary settlement within 30 minutes, then the judge's decision determines the defendant's payment.

At the beginning of a session, both subjects are paid a fixed fee for participating (for example, $4) and the defendant is given an extra $10. Ten thousand dollars is equivalent to $1 for the subjects. For example, if the subjects reach a $60,000 settlement and each side owes court costs of $10,000, the defendant keeps $4 and gives $6 to the plaintiff, and both parties give $1 to the experimenter in court costs. If the parties fail to settle, the defendant pays the plaintiff $3.06, representing the judgment of $30,560 actually awarded by the judge (which was unknown to the subjects during the negotiation), and both parties pay legal costs of $2.50 for not settling.

[2] In some of the experiments, subjects were given a week to read the case and in other experiments, they were given 30 minutes.

The experiment was designed to test for the effect of the self-serving bias in a contextually rich and controlled experimental setting. Since both parties are given the same case information and neither party has private information about the judge, differences in estimates between defendant and plaintiff cannot be attributed to differences in information.

Our first experiment with this framework found strong evidence that the negotiators formed self-serving assessments of the judge's award and that the discrepancy between the plaintiffs' and defendants' assessments was correlated with the parties' ability to reach voluntary settlements (Loewenstein, Issacharoff, Camerer and Babcock, 1993). The subjects were 80 undergraduates from the University of Chicago and 80 law students at the University of Texas at Austin. Subjects were assigned randomly to roles as either the defendant or plaintiff immediately upon entering the experiment.

The self-serving bias was clear in that plaintiffs' predictions of the judge averaged \$14,527 higher than defendants', and plaintiffs' fair settlement values averaged \$17,709 higher than defendants', with both differences statistically different from zero (p < .0001). Table 1 presents a median split of the discrepancy in the parties' assessments of the judge and summarizes the percentage of pairs that reached an impasse for each group. The first row of the table shows that in this experiment, nonsettlement was strongly related to the discrepancy between the plaintiffs' and defendants' predictions of what the judge would award.

One limitation of this study is that it does not necessarily demonstrate that the self-serving bias *causes* impasse. It is possible, for example, that there is a third factor, perhaps some element of personality such as aggressiveness, that causes certain subjects to misestimate the judge and to be unwilling to settle. To avoid this problem, in a new study we introduced a manipulation to diminish the magnitude of the discrepancy in expectations without changing other key features of the experiment. The manipulation involved changing the order of the events in the experiment. In the control condition, the participants learned whether their role would be defendant or plaintiff *before* they

Table 1. Probability of Impasse by Discrepancy Between Plaintiffs' and Defendants' Assessments of the Judge

	Pairs in which the discrepancy is:	
	Below the Median	Above the Median
Loewenstein, Issacharoff, Camerer, and Babcock (1993)	.03	.30
(n = 80)	(.03)	(.09)
Babcock, Loewenstein, Issacharoff, and Camerer (1995)	.05	.28
(n = 94)	(.03)	(.06)
Babcock, Loewenstein, and Issacharoff (1996)	.04	.36
(n = 49)	(.04)	(.10)

Notes: Standard errors are in parentheses. All differences are significant at the .01 level.

read the case materials and offered their anonymous assessments of the judge and a fair settlement; in the experimental condition, they learned which role they would play *after* reading the case materials and offering their estimates of the judge and a fair settlement. Our prediction was that the discrepancy between the plaintiffs' and defendants' assessments would be smaller for those who learned their role after reading the case, because, not knowing their role when they read through the case, they would process the information in an unbiased fashion.

The experiment was run with 38 public policy students at Carnegie Mellon University, 120 law students from the University of Texas and 30 business students from the University of Pennsylvania (Babcock, Loewenstein, Issacharoff and Camerer, 1995). Consistent with a causal relationship running from the self-serving bias to impasse, when the subjects did not learn their roles until after they read the case and made their assessments of the judge and fairness, only 6 percent of the negotiations were resolved by the judge; however, when the subjects knew their roles initially, 28 percent of negotiations had to be resolved by the judge (this statistically significant difference is shown in the first section of Table 2). As in the previous experiment, the discrepancy in the parties' assessments of the judge's decision was related to settlement; only 4 percent of the negotiations in which the discrepancy was below the median ended in impasse while 28 percent of pairs above the median discrepancy failed to settle (see the second row of Table 1).

Prior research on self-serving biases (Dunning, Meyerowitz and Holzberg, 1989), and on biased processing of information in general (Darley and Gross, 1983), suggests that the bias results from selective information processing. As Danitioso, Kunda and Fong (1990, p. 229) argue, "[P]eople attempt to construct a rational justification for the conclusions that they want to draw.

Table 2. Discrepancy in Assessments of the Judge and Rates of Impasse by Condition

Babcock, Loewenstein, Issacharoff and Camerer (1995)	Learned Roles Before Read Case	Learned Roles After Read Case
Discrepancy in Assessment of the Judge	$18,555 (3,787) .28	$6,936 (4,179) .06
Impasse Rate	(.07)	(.03)
Babcock, Loewenstein and Issacharoff (1996)	Control	Learned about Bias and Listed Weaknesses
Discrepancy in Assessments of the Judge	$21,783 (3,956) .36	$4,674 (6,091) .04
Impasse Rate	(.10)	(.04)

Notes: Standard errors are in parentheses. All differences are significant at the .05 level.

To that end, they search through memory for relevant information, but the search is biased in favor of information that is consistent with the desired conclusions. If they succeed in finding a preponderance of such consistent information, they are able to draw the desired conclusion while maintaining an illusion of objectivity." We explored this explanation by giving subjects a questionnaire at the end of the bargaining session in which they were asked to rate the importance of a series of eight arguments favoring the plaintiff and eight favoring the defendant (Babcock, Loewenstein, Issacharoff and Camerer, 1995). Consistent with the psychology research, plaintiffs tended to weight arguments favoring the plaintiff as much more compelling than those favoring the defendant, and vice versa. This provides evidence that the self-serving bias results from role-dependant evaluation of information.

Might other experimental manipulations offer suggestions for practical ways of reducing the discrepancy in the parties' expectations and thus avoid impasse? Obviously, our experiment that gave subjects their role after reading the case materials has no practical implication, since parties to a dispute usually know their own roles from the outset.

We experimented with several interventions that were designed to "debias" the disputants' judgments as a way to promote settlement. In one experimental treatment, subjects read a paragraph describing the extent and consequences of the self-serving bias after they were assigned their roles and read the case, but before they recorded their assessments of fairness and their predictions of the judge's decision. They also took a short test to make sure that they had understood the paragraph explaining the bias. However, being informed of the bias had no effect on the discrepancy in the parties' expectations, nor on the likelihood of settlement. One interesting result, however, did emerge from this study. In addition to asking their perceptions of fairness and the judge, we asked subjects to guess their opponent's prediction of the judge. Our results indicate that informing subjects of the bias made them more realistic about the predictions of the other party. However, it did not cause them to modify their own predictions of the judge. When they learned about the bias, subjects apparently assumed that the other person would succumb to it, but did not think it applied to themselves.

In another treatment, before they negotiated, subjects were instructed to write an essay arguing the opponent's case as convincingly as possible. This intervention was inspired by research that has suggested that people with better perspective-taking ability resolve disputes more efficiently (Bazerman and Neale, 1982). This did change the discrepancy in expectations, and in a way that was marginally statistically significant, but opposite to the intended direction. Again, there was no significant impact on the settlement rate.

Finally, we turned to research in psychology showing that biases are diminished when subjects question their own judgment. Slovic and Fischhoff (1977), for example, found that the "hindsight bias" (the tendency to view the past as having been more predictable than it actually was) was reduced when subjects were instructed to give reasons for why outcomes other than the one that actually occurred could have occurred. Koriat, Lichtenstein and Fischhoff (1980) found that a bias called "overconfidence" was reduced by having subjects list counterarguments to their beliefs. They conclude (p. 113) that "overconfidence derives in part from the tendency to neglect contradicting evidence and that calibration may be improved by making such evidence more salient." Research on other biases has produced similar debiasing success stories when subjects are instructed to "consider the opposite" (Lord, Lepper and Preston, 1984; Anderson, 1982, 1983).

Based on this common finding, we designed an intervention in which subjects, after being assigned their role and reading the case materials, were informed of the self-serving bias (as in the previous experiment) and told that it could arise from the failure to think about the weaknesses in their own case (Babcock, Loewenstein and Issacharoff, 1996). They were then asked to list the weaknesses in their own case. The effect of this intervention was to diminish the discrepancy in the parties' expectations about the judge (see the second section of Table 2): the discrepancy averaged $21,783 in the control condition, in which neither party received this intervention, but only $4,674 when the subjects received the debiasing procedure (p < .05). The debiasing treatment also reduced the rate of impasse from 35 percent to 4 percent (p < .01). Notice that this intervention can be implemented after an individual realizes that he or she is involved in a dispute. It thus holds the potential for serving as a practical tool in mediation.

Our research on debiasing begs the question of whether the self-serving bias is indeed "self-serving." In fact, one reviewer commented that it was more of a "self-defeating" bias since it caused individuals to make systematic errors that made them worse off. However, psychologists have argued that these biases are clearly beneficial to well-being in some domains. For example, Taylor and Brown (1988) argue that unrealistically positive self-evaluations promote happiness as well as other aspects of mental health. Furthermore, they suggest that individuals that have more accurate self-evaluations are either low in self-esteem, moderately depressed, or both. However, it is clear from our research that, in negotiations where the costs of impasse are high, the self-serving bias hurts both parties economically. An unresolved issue, which we are exploring in our current research, is whether it benefits a party to be less biased, holding constant the beliefs of the other party. While this will help to reduce impasse, it may also cause that party to be less persuasive in a negotiation, leading to an inferior outcome should a settlement be reached.

8.3. A Field Study: Public School Teacher Negotiations

In presenting these findings at seminars and conferences, we are often questioned as to whether experienced negotiators would succumb to the self-serving bias. To address this point, we conducted a study to examine the bias and its impact on bargaining in a real-world setting—public school teacher contract negotiations in Pennsylvania (Babcock, Wang and Loewenstein, 1996). Since 1971, approximately 8 percent of all teacher contract negotiations have ended in a strike, with an average strike duration of 16.4 days.

In public sector contract negotiations, it is commonplace for both sides to make references to agreements in "comparable" communities. We hypothesized that both sides would have self-serving beliefs about which communities were comparable and that impasses would be more likely as the gap between their beliefs widened. To explore this hypothesis, we surveyed union and school board presidents from all school districts in Pennsylvania to obtain a list of districts that they viewed as comparable for purposes of salary negotiations.[3] We linked the survey data to a data set that included district-level information about strikes, teachers' salaries, community salary levels, and other demographic and financial information. The combination of survey and field data allows us to examine the relationship between strike activity and the subjective perceptions of the respondents.

Considering only the districts in which both the union and school board returned the survey, we found that both sides listed about the same number of districts as being comparable (about 4.5). However, the actual districts listed by the two sides differed in a way that reflected a self-serving bias. The average salary in districts listed by the union was $27,633, while the average salary in districts listed by the board was $26,922. The mean difference of $711 is statistically and economically significant; it is equivalent to about 2.4 percent of average teacher salary at a time when salary increases averaged less than 5 percent per year.

To test for the effect of the self-serving bias on strikes, we regressed the percentage of previous contract negotiations that ended in a strike against the difference in the average salaries of the two parties' lists of comparables. The regression also included variables controlling for district wealth and local labor market conditions. This regression produced a significant effect of differences in the list of comparables on strike activity. The point estimate suggests that a district where the average salary of the union's list is $1000 greater than the board's list will be approximately 49 percent more likely to

---

[3] The response rate for returning the survey was 57 percent for the union presidents and 35 percent for the school board presidents. See Babcock, Wang and Loewenstein (1996) for details on the response rate and issues of selectivity bias.

strike than a district where the average salaries of the union's and board's lists are the same.

We also found that the difference in the list of comparables was correlated with the variance in the salaries of teachers in the neighboring districts. Apparently, larger variation in neighboring salaries provides more opportunity for each side to choose self-serving comparison groups. However, the difference in the list of comparables was unrelated to the level of experience of either the union or board president. Experience with bargaining does not seem to inoculate one against the self-serving bias.

8.4. Reinterpreting Findings from Previous Bargaining Experiments

The existence of the self-serving bias offers a useful tool for reinterpreting a number of past findings in the research on bargaining. In one study, for example, two subjects bargained over how to distribute 100 tickets for a lottery (Roth and Murnighan, 1982). One subject would receive $5 for winning the lottery, while the other would receive $20. Given this setup, there were two focal points for splitting the chips: 50 chips to each (equal chance of winning) or 20 chips to the $20-prize player and 80 chips to the $5-prize player (equal expected value). When neither player knew who would receive which payoff, subjects generally agreed to divide the chips about equally and only 12 percent of pairs failed to reach an agreement and ended up with no payoff. However, when both subjects knew who was assigned to which payoff, 22 percent failed to reach agreement. A likely interpretation is that both sides viewed as fair the focal settlement that benefitted themselves, so the $20-prize player was likely to hold out for half of the chips, while the $5-prize player demanded equal expected values.

Another well-known bargaining framework is the so-called "shrinking pie" game, in which one subject (the "proposer") is presented with a sum of money and asked to divide it with another subject (the "responder"). If the responder rejects the offer, the amount of money to be divided (the "pie") shrinks, the players switch roles, and the game continues either until an offer is accepted, or until a specified number of rounds have been played. In this game, it is common to see a responder reject a lopsided offer and then propose a counteroffer that gives that player less than the offer rejected but is more equitable because the other side's amount has been reduced by even more. In one investigation of this game, Weg, Rapoport and Felsenthal (1990) found that when the pie shrunk at the same rate for both individuals, the rejection rate was only 12 percent in the first round, but when the pie shrunk at different rates for each subject, the rejection rate was 57 percent in the first round. Again, consistent with the self-serving bias, perhaps subjects whose pies shrank relatively slowly viewed this as justification for requesting a large fraction of the pie, but subjects whose pies shrunk quickly rejected the rate of pie-shrinkage as a criterion for allocating the pie.

A special case of the shrinking pie game is the "ultimatum" game in which there is only a single round. In this case, if the responder rejects the proposer's offer in the first round, the pie shrinks to zero and neither side gets any payoff. If proposers only care about self-interest, and if they believe responders do too, the proposer should offer a trivial amount (like one cent) and it should be accepted. But in practice, the modal offer is typically half the pie, and smaller offers are often rejected.[4]

Although ultimatum experiments have been used by economists to illustrate the importance of fairness considerations, rejections in these experiments can be explained by self-serving biases. Proposers, who view themselves in a powerful role, believe that they deserve more than half of the pie, whereas responders do not believe that role should affect the division of the pie. Beyond the simple fact of nonsettlement, certain variants of the standard ultimatum game have produced results that provide more direct evidence of the role of self-serving biases. In one variant of the game, the roles of proposer and responder were determined either randomly or by the outcome of a trivia contest with the winner playing the role of proposer (Hoffman, McCabe, Shachat and Smith, 1994). Offers in the contest condition were lower than in the chance condition, and the rejection rate was substantially higher. It seems that proposers in the contest condition felt self-servingly entitled to a higher payoff, but responders did not view the contest as relevant to the fair division of the pie.

In another variant of the ultimatum game, Knez and Camerer (1995) conducted experiments in which players earned a known dollar amount if the responder rejected the proposer's ultimatum offer. For example, if the amount to be divided is $10, and, if the offer was rejected, proposers earned $4 and responders earned $3. There are two obvious fair divisions: to divide the $10.00 evenly, giving both parties an equal payoff of $5.00 or to divide the surplus over the outside offers evenly; in this example, an offer of $4.50 would give the responder a surplus of $1.50 ($4.50-$3.00) and the proposer an equal surplus of $1.50 ($5.50-$4.00). These alternative definitions create scope for self-serving assessments of fairness, and indeed, respondents in this situation consistently demanded more than half the "pie," and about half of the offers were rejected—a rate of disagreement much higher than previous ultimatum studies.

Two studies of labor negotiations have produced similar evidence that can be interpreted as showing self-serving biases. In an experimental study of

---

[4] For a brief discussion of the game in this journal, and an overview of findings from various permutations, see Camerer and Thaler (1995).

labor-management negotiations, Thompson and Loewenstein (1992) found that management estimates of a fair settlement were significantly lower than those provided by the union and observed a significant positive correlation between the difference in assessments of fairness and the length of strikes. They also manipulated the complexity of information provided to the two sides and found that complexity had a small but significant effect in increasing the discrepancy between the union and management's self-serving perceptions of the fair wage.

In a field study examining the use of arbitration in contract negotiations for public school teachers in Wisconsin, Babcock, and Olson (1992) found that increases in the variation of wage settlements within a district's athletic conference increased the probability that the district failed to negotiate a contract and ended up using arbitration. This evidence can be interpreted in the same way as our field study of Pennsylvania teachers mentioned earlier; when there are numerous potential comparison groups to assess fairness, the parties focus on those that favor themselves.

8.5. Discussion

Taken as a body, the research discussed here presents strong evidence that the self-serving bias is an important determinant of bargaining impasse. As a general lesson, the research suggests that, for the bias to occur, there needs to be some form of asymmetry in how the negotiation environment is viewed. This should not be taken to mean that the bias comes from asymmetric information. Instead, what we have in mind is that the parties—even with complete information—interpret the situation in different ways. Few subjects placed in a symmetric bargaining setting in which they are instructed to divide $10 with another party will believe that anything other than an even split is fair. However, even in a very simple setting like this, as soon as asymmetries are introduced between the parties—for example, different nonagreement values or costs of nonsettlement, or subtle differences in roles—both parties' notions of fairness will tend to gravitate toward settlements that favor themselves. They will not only view these settlements as fair, but believe that their personal conception of fairness is impartial.

We have attempted to show that the self-serving bias provides an account of impasse that has greater explanatory power than models based on incomplete information. Moreover, the self-serving bias may also help explain other important economic phenomena, such as unemployment. If job searchers have inflated evaluations of their productivity, they will have unrealistically high reservation wages, leading to longer unemployment spells. Research has found that job search assistance programs lead unemployed workers to find jobs more quickly. One reason these programs are successful may be that, like our debiasing treatment described above, they deflate expectations, causing individuals to be more objective about their alternatives. Self-serving biases may also help to explain the low take-up rate for unemployment insurance (the percentage of eligible individuals that use the program). Again, if workers have inflated expectations regarding their job search, they will believe that they will quickly find a good job, reducing the incentive to apply for assistance. Other research has found that self-serving biases contribute to the "tragedy of the commons" problems. When individuals evaluate their "fair share" of the scarce resource in a self-serving way, they will deplete the resource at a faster rate (Wade-Benzoni, Tenbrunsel, and Bazerman, 1996). A closely related bias, overconfidence, may help to explain what some researchers view as excessive trading in foreign exchange markets and on the New York Stock Exchange. Odean (1996) develops a financial market model in which traders are overconfident about the precision of their private information. This leads to a quasi-rational expectations equilibria where there is excessive trading volume.

The self-serving bias has other wide-ranging ramifications. Whenever individuals face tradeoffs between what is best for themselves and what is morally correct, their perceptions of moral correctness are likely to be biased in the direction of what is best for themselves (Loewenstein, 1996). In making the tradeoff, then, self-interest enters twice—directly, when it is traded off against moral correctness, and indirectly, via its impact on perceptions of moral correctness. Transplant surgeons, for example, must often decide how to allocate scarce organs between potential recipients. To maintain favorable statistics, their self-interest may not be to transplant those who would benefit most in terms of *increased* survival, but instead those where the probability of a successful operation is highest. Based on the research we have reviewed, it seems likely that transplant surgeons' views of who benefits most from the transplant will be distorted by their interest in "cream skimming." Similarly, we suspect, doctors who change to a remuneration system that compensates them less for conducting medical tests are likely to alter their views concerning the medical value of testing. In a different domain, it seems likely that the judgments of auditors, who ostensibly represent the interests of shareholders but are hired (and fired) by the people they audit, are likely to be blinded to some degree by the incentive for client retention.

8.5.1. Will Experience and Learning Minimize the Bias?

When we have presented this work, three issues are commonly raised, all relating to the importance of the self-serving bias in the real world. First, it is suggested that while naive experimental subjects might exhibit such a bias, trained professionals, such as lawyers, would be resistant. Besides the evidence from our field study of Pennsylvania teachers, which shows that seasoned negotiators are subject to the bias, other evidence also shows that professionals are not immune. For another example, Eisenberg (1994) analyzed a survey conducted with 205 experienced bankruptcy lawyers and 150 judges involved in bankruptcy cases that asked a series of questions about lawyers' fees, such as how long it takes judges to rule on fee applications and the fairness of fees. Comparisons of judges' and lawyers' responses revealed a self-serving bias in virtually every question in the survey. For example, 78 percent of judges reported that they rule on interim fee applications at the fee hearing, but only 46 percent of lawyers report that the judges rule so quickly. Thirty-seven percent of judges reported that they most frequently allow reimbursement at the "value of the services," while only 15 percent of lawyers reported that judges reimburse at such rates. Sixty percent of lawyers report that they always comply with fee guidelines, but judges reported that only 18 percent of attorneys always comply. Whether the lawyers or judges or, most likely, both, are responsible for these discrepancies, this evidence certainly does not suggest that professionals are immune to the self-serving bias.

A second criticism raised is that the stakes involved in our experiments are too low—that our subjects are insufficiently motivated to process the information in an unbiased way. This criticism fails on several grounds. First, these biases are observed in real-world settings in which the stakes are extremely high, such as the teacher contract negotiations described above. Second, individuals are unlikely to be conscious of their biased processing of information so that increases in incentives will not cause them to be more conscientious. Third, "high-stakes" experiments, such as those conducted by Hoffman, McCabe and Smith (1996), have not produced substantively different behavior than those with lower stakes.

A third criticism of the experiments is that they fail to allow for learning. While our experiments were "one-shot," in most economics experiments it is common to run subjects through the same procedure multiple times to allow for learning. It is not at all obvious, however, that the real world allows for anything like the opportunities for learning that are present in economics laboratory experiments. Most people find themselves only sporadically involved in bargaining, and each bargaining situation differs from past situations on numerous dimensions. Undoubtedly, all of our experimental subjects, especially the law and business school students, had numerous experiences with bargaining prior to participating in our experiment, but this experience did not seem to alert them even to the existence of the self-serving bias, let alone actually give them the capacity to counteract it. We should also note that our results from the Pennsylvania field study are not consistent with the notion that experience will eliminate the bias.

In fact, there is reason to be concerned that experience and real history almost always contain the kind of ambiguous information and competing claims that are breeding grounds for self-serving assessments of fairness. In a study by Camerer and Loewenstein (1993), subjects bargained over the sale of a piece of land, knowing only their reservation value. All pairs agreed on a sale price. In a second phase, the same pairs of students negotiated the identical situation again, after learning their partners' reservation value. Twenty percent of pairs failed to settle on this second round, despite the fact that they possessed more information. Students who did poorly in the first round felt that they deserved to be compensated for the previous bad outcome. Those who did well in the first round viewed the first round as irrelevant to the second. One important implication of these results for mediation is that recriminations about the past should be excluded from negotiations to the greatest extent possible. If the adage "let bygones be bygones" applies to economic decision making, it applies doubly to negotiations.

8.5.2. *Methods: Psychology and Economics*

Experimental economists find several features of the studies discussed in this paper to be unusual. The first is the inclusion of a rich legal context in the experiment. Experiments in economics often deliberately limit the context of the interaction, with generic labeling of roles and rigidly controlled communications between the parties. As Cox and Isaac (1986) write, experiments in economics do not normally involve "role playing" by subjects—that is, "experiments in which the instructions, context, and/or motivation of the experimental design draw upon subjects' knowledge of economic agents or institutions outside the laboratory." In contrast, in our Texas tort experiments subjects took the role of a party in a realistic law case with unstructured face-to-face communication. As our choice of method implies, we think the emphasis among economists on expunging context in experiments is a mistake. Human thinking, problem solving and choice are highly context dependent. Psychologists have found that there are many problems that people are unable to solve in the abstract, but are able to solve when placed in a real-world context (Goldstein and Weber, 1995).

One classical illustration is the Wason "four-card problem." Subjects are shown a deck of cards, each deck with a number on one side and a letter on the other. The exposed sides they see are: X, Y, 1, and 2. They are asked which cards need to be turned over to test the rule that "if there is an X on one side there is a 2 on the other." When the problem is given to people in the abstract form just described, very few people give the correct answer, which is "X" and "1." However, when the task is put into a familiar context, almost everyone answers correctly. For example, when the rule is, "If a student is to be assigned to Grover High School, then that student must live in Grover City," and students are shown cards that read "lives in Grover city," "doesn't live in Grover city," "assigned to Grover High School," and "not assigned to Grover High School" (with the relevant information on the other side of the card), 89 percent of subjects state correctly which cards need to be turned over (Cosmides, 1989).

The notion of a "context-free" experiment is, in any case, illusory. Experiments using the ultimatum game have shown that seemingly subtle variations in procedure that should not matter from a strictly economic point of view—for example, the mechanism that determines the roles, whether the game is framed as an offer game or a demand game, and the timing and method of eliciting an offer—all have powerful effects on how people play the game (Blount, 1995; Hoffman, McCabe, Shachat, and Smith, 1994). Researchers who subscribe to the illusion that their particular experiment is "context free" are likely to come away with an exaggerated sense of the generalizability of their findings.

A second nonstandard feature of the Texas tort experiments and the Pennsylvania teachers field study is that we measured subjects' perceptions. Economists, like behaviorist psychologists, sometimes pride themselves on measuring behavior, rather than perceptions. As a practical matter, we often delude ourselves by this distinction. Much of the data on "behavior" used in economic analyses comes from surveys, such as the National Longitudinal Survey and Current Population Survey, in which respondents provide information on such things as jobs, wages, spells of unemployment, and so on. However, such self-reports of behavior are highly fallible because of biases, limitations in memory and deliberate misreporting. Indeed, Akerlof and Yellen (1985) have shown that people do not even seem able to remember with any great accuracy whether they were employed or unemployed during the past year.

Moreover, failure to collect data on psychological constructs robs us of information that can contribute to more nuanced tests of theory. For example, Tracy (1986, 1987) finds a positive relationship between investor uncertainty (a proxy for the union's uncertainty about the firm) and strike activity and cites this as evidence consistent with an asymmetric information model of impasse. However, there are undoubtedly many theories that could predict this positive correlation. Only by actually collecting data on the unions' perceptions of firm profitability before and after contract negotiations can one directly test the notion that firms are using delay in settlement to signal information about their profitability to unions. Because of the reluctance to collect and analyze data on intervening variables, economists have sometimes been forced into very coarse tests of their models' predictions.

Some economists are concerned that incorporating psychology would complicate economic analysis or force an abandonment of the traditional tools of constrained maximization. Nothing could be further from the truth. Models that incorporate individuals' preferences for "fair" outcomes still use traditional methods, yet lead to predictions with more empirical support than conventional models (Bolton, 1991; Rabin, 1993). Recent attempts to model self-serving interpretations of fairness (Rabin, 1995), we hope, will help to persuade more economists that psychological factors can be incorporated into formal economic analyses.

All economics involves psychology. Bayes' rule, the rational expectations assumption and the theory of revealed preference are all psychological assumptions about how people form expectations and what motivates them. The question for economics is not whether to include or exclude psychology, but rather what type of psychology to include.

References

Akerlof, George, and Janet L. Yellen, "Unemployment Through the Filter of Memory," *Quarterly Journal of Economics*, August 1985, *100*, 747–73.

Anderson, Craig, "Inoculation and Counter-explanation: Debiasing Techniques in the Perseverance of Social Theories," *Social Cognition*, 1982, *1*:2, 126–39.

Anderson, Craig, "Abstract and Concrete Data in the Perseverance of Social Theories: When Weak Data Lead to Unshakeable Beliefs," *Journal of Experimental Social Psychology*, March 1983, *19*, 93–108.

Babcock, Linda, and Craig Olson, "The Causes of Impasses in Labor Disputes," *Industrial Relations*, 1992, *31*:2, 348–360.

Babcock, Linda, George Loewenstein, and Samuel Issacharoff, "Debiasing Litigation Impasse," unpublished paper, 1996.

Babcock, Linda, Xianghong Wang, and George Loewenstein, "Choosing the Wrong Pond: Social Comparisons that Reflect a Self-Serving Bias," *Quarterly Journal of Economics*, February 1996, *111*, 1–19.

Babcock, Linda, George Loewenstein, Samuel Issacharoff, and Colin Camerer, "Biased Judgments of Fairness in Bargaining," *American Economic Review*, 1995, *85*:5, 1337–1343.

Baumhart, R., *An Honest Profit*. New York: Prentice-Hall, 1968.

Bazerman, Max, and Margaret Neale, "Improving Negotiation Effectiveness Under Final Offer Arbitration: The Role of Selection and Training," *Journal of Applied Psychology*, 1982, *67*:5, 543–548.

Blount, Sally, "When Social Outcomes aren't Fair: The Effect of Causal Attributions on Preferences," *Organizational Behavior and Human Decision Processes*, August 1995, *63*, 131–144.

Bolton, Gary, "A Comparative Model of Bargaining: Theory and Evidence," *American Economic Review*, December 1991, *81*, 1096–1136.

Camerer, Colin, and George Loewenstein, "Information, Fairness, and Efficiency in Bargaining." In Mellers, Barbara, and Jonathan Baron, eds., *Psychological Perspectives on Justice*. Cambridge, Engl.: Cambridge University Press, 1993, pp. 155–79.

Camerer, Colin, and Richard Thaler, "Ultimatums, Dictators and Manner," *Journal of Economic Perspectives*, Spring 1995, *9*:2, 209–219.

Card, David, "Strikes and Wages: A Test of an Asymmetric Information Model," *Quarterly Journal of Economics*, August 1990, *105*, 625–659.

Cosmides, Leda, "The Logic of Social Exchange: Has Natural Selection Shaped How Humans Reason? Studies with the Wason Selection Task," *Cognition*, April 1989, *31*, 187–276.

Cox, James C., and R. Mark Isaac, "Experimental Economics and Experimental Psychology: Ever the Twain Shall Meet?" In MacFadyen, A. J., and H. W. MacFadyen, *Economic Psychology: Intersections in Theory and Application*. Amsterdam: North-Holland, 1986, pp. 647–669.

Cramton, Peter, "Strategic Delay in Bargaining with Two-Sided Uncertainty," *Review of Economic Studies*, January 1992, *59*, 205–225.

Cross, K. Patricia, "Not Can, But Will College Teaching be Improved?," *New Directions for Higher Education*, Spring 1977, *17*, 1–15.

Danitioso, R., Z. Kunda, and G. T. Fong, "Motivated Recruitment of Autobiographical Memories," *Journal of Personality and Social Psychology*, August 1990, *59*, 229–241.

Darley, J. M., and P. H. Gross, "A Hypothesis-Confirming Bias in Labeling Effects," *Journal of Personality and Social Psychology*, January 1983, *44*, 20–33.

Dunning, D., J. A. Meyerowitz, and A. D. Holzberg, "Ambiguity and Self-Evaluation: The Role of Idiosyncratic Trait Definitions in Self-Serving Assessments of Ability," *Journal of Personality and Social Psychology*, December 1989, *57*, 1082–1090.

Eisenberg, Theodore, "Differing Perceptions of Attorney Fees in Bankruptcy Cases," *Washington University Law Quarterly*, Fall 1994, *72*, 979–995.

Farber, Henry, "Bargaining Theory, Wage Outcomes, and the Occurrence of Strikes: An Econometric Analysis," *American Economic Review*, June 1978, *68*, 262–284.

Goldstein, William M., and Elke U. Weber, "Content and Discontent: Indications and Implications of Domain Specificity in Preferential Decision Making." In Busemeyer, J. R., R. Hastei, and D. L. Medin, eds., *The Psychology of Learning and Motivation*. Vol. 32, New York, Academic Press, 1995, pp. 83–136.

Hastorf, Albert, and Hadley Cantril, "They Saw a Game: A Case Study," *Journal of Abnormal and Social Psychology*, 1954, *49*:1, 129–134.

Hoffman, Elizabeth, Kevin McCabe, and Vernon Smith, "On Expectations and the Monetary Stakes in Ultimatum Games," *International Journal of Game Theory*, 1996, *25*:3, 289–301.

Hoffman, Elizabeth, Kevin McCabe, Keith Shachat, and Vernon Smith, "Preferences, Property Rights and Anonymity in Bargaining Games," *Games and Economic Behavior*, November 1994, *7*, 346–380.

Kagel, John, Chung Kim, and Donald Moser, "Fairness in Ultimatum Games with Asymmetric Information and Asymmetric Payoffs," *Games and Economic Behavior*, March 1996, *13*:1, 100–110.

Kennan, John, "The Duration of Contract Strikes in U.S. Manufacturing," *Journal of Econometrics*, April 1985, *28*, 5–28.

Kennan, John, "The Economics of Strikes." In Ashenfelter, O., and R. Layard, eds., *Handbook of Labor Economics*. Vol. 2, Amsterdam: Elsevier, 1986, pp. 1091–1237.

Kennan, John, and Robert Wilson, "Strategic Bargaining Models and Interpretation of Strike Data," *Journal of Applied Econometrics*, December 1989, *4*, 87–130.

Knez, Marc, and Colin Camerer, "Outside Options and Social Comparison in Three-Player Ultimatum Game Experiments," *Games and Economic Behavior*, July 1995, *10*, 65–94.

Koriat, Asher, Sarah Lichtenstein, and Baruch Fischhoff, "Reasons for Confidence," *Journal of Experimental Psychology: Human Learning and Memory*, 1980, *6*:2, 107–118.

Larwood, L., and W. Whittaker, "Managerial Myopia: Self-Serving Biases in Organizational Planning," *Journal of Applied Psychology*, April 1977, *62*, 194–198.

Loewenstein, George, "Behavioral Decision Theory and Business Ethics: Skewed Trade-offs Between Self and Other." In Messick, D., and A. Tenbrunsel, eds., *Codes of Conduct: Behavioral Research into Business Ethics*. New York: Russell Sage Foundation, 1996, pp. 214–227.

Loewenstein, George, Leigh Thompson, and Max Bazerman, "Social Utility and Decision Making in Interpersonal Context," *Journal of Personality and Social Psychology*, September 1989, *57*, 426–441.

Loewenstein, George, Samuel Issacharoff, Colin Camerer, and Linda Babcock, "Self-Serving Assessments of Fairness and Pretrial Bargaining," *Journal of Legal Studies*, January 1993, *22*, 135–159.

Lord, Charles, Mark Lepper, and Elizabeth Preston, "Considering the Opposite: A Corrective Strategy for Social Judgment," *Journal of Personality and Social Psychology*, December 1984, *47*, 1231–1243.

McConnell, Sheena, "Strikes, Wages, and Private Information," *American Economic Review*, September 1989, *79*, 801–815.

Messick, David, and Keith Sentis, "Fairness and Preference," *Journal of Experimental Social Psychology*, 1979, *15*: 4, 418–434.

Odean, Terrance, "Volume, Volatility, Price, and Profit When All Traders are Above Average," unpublished paper, 1996.

Rabin, Matthew, "Incorporating Fairness into Game Theory and Economics," *American Economic Review*, December 1993, *83*, 1281–1302.

Rabin, Matthew, "Moral Ambiguity, Moral Constraints, and Self-Serving Biases," unpublished paper, 1995.

Ross, Michael, and Fiore Sicoly, "Egocentric Biases in Availability and Attribution," *Journal of Personality and Social Psychology*, March 1979, *37*, 322–336.

Roth, Alvin E., "Bargaining Experiments." In Kagel, John, and Alvin E. Roth, eds., *Handbook of Experimental Economics*. Princeton: Princeton University Press, 1995, pp. 253–348.

Roth, Alvin E., and J. Keith Murnighan, "The Role of Information in Bargaining: An Experimental Study," *Econometrica*, September 1982, *50*, 1123–1142.

Schelling, Thomas, *Strategy of Conflict*. Cambridge: Harvard University Press, 1960.

Slovic, Paul, and Baruch Fischhoff, "On the Psychology of Experimental Surprises," *Journal of Experimental Psychology: Human Perception and Performance*, 1977, *3*:4, 544–551.

Svenson, Ola, "Are We all Less Risky and More Skillful Than Our Fellow Drivers?," *Acta Psychologica*, February 1981, *94*, 143–148.

Taylor, Shelley, and Jonathon D. Brown, "Illusion and Well-Being: A Social Psychological Perspective on Mental Health," *Psychological Bulletin*, 1988, *103*:2, 193–210.

Thompson, Leigh, and George Loewenstein, "Egocentric Interpretations of Fairness in Interpersonal Conflict," *Organizational Behavior and Human Decision Processes*, March 1992, *51*, 176–197.

Tracy, Joseph, "An Investigation into the Determinants of U.S. Strike Activity," *American Economic Review*, June 1986, *76*, 423–436.

Tracy, Joseph, "An Empirical Test of an Asymmetric Information," *Journal of Labor Economics*, 1987, *5*:2, 149–173.

Wade-Benzoni, Kimberly, Ann Tenbrunsel, and Max Bazerman, "Egocentric Interpretations of Fairness in Asymmetric, Environmental Social Dilemmas: Explaining Harvesting Behavior and the Role of Communication," *Organizational Behavior and Human Decision Processes*, August 1996, *67*:2, 111–126.

Weg, Eythan, Amnon Rapoport, and Dan S. Felsenthal, "Two-Person Bargaining Behavior in Fixed Discounting Games with Infinite Horizon," *Games and Economic Behavior*, March 1990, *2*, 76–95.

Weinstein, N. D., "Unrealistic Optimism about Future Life Events," *Journal of Personality and Social Psychology*, November 1980, *39*, 806–820.

Zuckerman, M., "Attributions of Success and Failure Revisited, Or: The Motivational Bias is Alive and Well in Attribution Theory," *Journal of Personality*, June 1979, *47*, 245–287.

Part III

Basic Research on Preferences

9

Preference Reversals Between Joint and Separate Evaluations of Options: A Review and Theoretical Analysis

Christopher K. Hsee, George F. Loewenstein, Sally Blount, and Max H. Bazerman

The origin of this paper was a hiring dispute that took place in Max Bazerman's department in the early 1990s. Max is a remarkable person, who manages the tricky balancing act of being extraordinarily strategic (before his academic career he played Bridge professionally) and extraordinarily nice at the same time. Max has been a major supporter of mine ever since he heard me give an academic talk very early in my career that, he later admitted, "was horrible, but revealed some kind of spark." He once wrote a promotion letter for me and asked me whether I wanted to read it , an offer which I vehemently declined. He sent it anyway, and of course I read it (consistent with the ideas discussed in Chapter 6). It said nice things, but my initial inclination was the right one: it took me years thereafter not to feel self-conscious in Max's presence.

In the incident that eventually led to this paper, Max wanted to hire a prominent academic into his department, but the salary it would take to attract the individual would have pierced the ceiling of the department's pay scale, and the reaction from his colleagues was negative. Max was exasperated, and attributed his colleagues' resistance to their failure to think about the issue in systematic terms. He decided that they were emotionally reacting to the pay difference rather than thinking about the underlying trade-offs. When framed as a trade-off between a mediocre department with roughly even salaries or an excellent department in which some people were paid a bit more, the choice seemed obvious to him.[1] And, in the tradition of academia, we translated his frustration into a research project.

---

[1] Moreover, raising the top of the salary scale tends, over time, to shift all salaries upward.

Building on our prior work on social utility functions (see Chapter 7), and adding his graduate student Sally Blount (now Sally Blount Lyons) as a collaborator, we presented people with scenarios involving a dispute with another individual, and with specific possible resolutions of the dispute involving payoffs to (or in some scenarios payments made by) both parties. Some of the resolutions were equitable, but involved lower payoffs to both parties—for example, $500 for you and $500 for the other person—and others involved greater individual payoffs, but at the expense of some inequity—for example, $600 for you and $700 for the other party.

The critical experimental manipulation was that in some conditions subjects rated each possible resolution separately—one at a time—using response scales such as "how acceptable would this settlement be to you?," whereas in other conditions subjects were presented with more than one possible resolution, and specified which they preferred. Much as Max observed in his colleagues, people reacted very negatively to inequitable settlements when they were presented with them one at a time, but more positively when they were faced with explicit trade-offs between inequity and personal gain. In a series of papers, we published these findings and offered an explanation for them in terms of what we called 'attribute uncertainty'.

Meanwhile, Chris Hsee at the University of Chicago was doing research on almost the same phenomenon, though applied to very different domains. In a paradigmatic experiment, Chris presented people with two hypothetical music dictionaries, one with more entries but a frayed dustcover and the other in immaculate condition but with fewer entries. Chris also compared preferences when people evaluated objects, such as the dictionaries, either one at a time or comparatively, and also obtaining dramatic differences between the two elicitation modes. Moreover, Chris figured out a simple solution to a problem that had plagued our research team. In our research, when switching from joint to separate evaluation, we also changed elicitation *scales* (e.g., asking for preference when comparing salaries but acceptability when evaluating salaries one at a time), which created a perfect confound. Chris solved this problem by having all subjects price the objects in dollars, with some subjects pricing one object at a time and others pricing multiple objects presented side by side. In the music dictionary case, for example, subjects would put a lower price on the frayed dictionary when they evaluated the dictionaries one at a time, but would price it higher when they priced the two dictionaries comparatively. Evaluated together, people realized that it was worth sacrificing a frayed cover for more entries.

Recognizing the overlap between our research, I contacted Chris and suggested that we join forces on a review paper. And, despite some differences in perspective that turned out to be more significant than we anticipated when the four of us agreed to team up, I think we came up with a coherent explanation for the phenomenon and wrote a decent paper explaining the theory. The gist of the explanation is that the values of certain attributes are inherently difficult to evaluate unless they are compared to other values of the same attribute, and such attributes tend to receive relatively little weight when such comparisons are not possible because alternatives are evaluated one at a time.

Working on this project helped to crystallize in my mind two themes that I have pursued in subsequent research. The first is the idea that many mistakes result from making decisions evaluating in an overly 'narrow' fashion—for example, viewing decisions in isolation of other relevant decisions or (as in the current paper) evaluating outcomes without considering the alternatives. In a paper with Daniel Read and Matthew Rabin, on "choice bracketing," we review a wide range of decision-making phenomena that can be understood in such terms.[2] The second point is that while alternatives or attributes of alternatives may be difficult to evaluate, we still feel the need to make decisions in an at least plausibly sensible fashion. How we do so is the topic of the next chapter.

---

[2] Read, D., Loewenstein, G., and Rabin, M. (1999) 'Choice Bracketing', *Journal of Risk and Uncertainty*, 19: 171–97.

Preference Reversals Between Joint and Separate Evaluations of Options: A Review and Theoretical Analysis*

Christopher K. Hsee, George F. Loewenstein, Sally Blount, and Max H. Bazerman

In normative accounts of decision making, all decisions are viewed as choices between alternatives. Even when decision makers appear to be evaluating single options, such as whether to buy a particular car or to go to a certain movie, they are seen as making implicit trade-offs. The potential car owner must trade off the benefits of car ownership against the best alternative uses of the money. The potential moviegoer is not just deciding whether to go to a movie but also between going to a movie and the next best use of her time, such as staying home and watching television.

At a descriptive level, however, there is an important distinction between situations in which multiple options are presented simultaneously and can be easily compared and situations in which alternatives are presented one at a time and evaluated in isolation. We refer to the former as the joint evaluation (JE) mode and to the latter as the separate evaluation (SE) mode. We review results from a large number of studies that document systematic changes in preferences between alternatives when those alternatives are evaluated jointly

* This chapter was originally published as Hsee, C., Loewenstein, G., Blount, S. and Bazerman, M. (1999) 'Preference Reversals Between Joint and Separate Evaluations of Options: A Review and Theoretical Analysis', Psychological Bulletin, 125(5): 576–590. Published by APA and reprinted with permission.

Christopher K. Hsee and Sally Blount, Graduate School of Business, University of Chicago; George F. Loewenstein, Department of Social and Decision Sciences, Carnegie Mellon University; and Max H. Bazerman, Kellogg School, Northwestern University, and Harvard Business School.

This article has benefitted from our discussions with the following people (in alphabetical order of their last names): Donna Dreier, Scott Jeffrey, Danny Kahneman, Josh Klayman, Rick Larrick, Joe Nunes, Itamar Simonson, Ann Tenbrunsel, Kimberly Wade-Benzoni, and Frank Yates.

or separately. We show that these JE/SE reversals can be explained by a simple theoretical account, which we refer to as the *evaluability hypothesis*.

JE/SE reversals have important ramifications for decision making in real life. Arguably, all judgments and decisions are made in joint evaluation mode, in separate evaluation mode, or in some combination of the two. For example, most people in the market for a new car engage in joint evaluation; they assemble a number of options before deciding between them. In contrast, academic researchers typically select the research projects they work on sequentially—that is, one at a time. Very few academics, at least of our acquaintance, collect multiple research project options before deciding between them. Sometimes, the same decision is made in both modes. For example, a prospective home purchaser might initially be shown a series of houses that are on the market (JE), but, if she rejects all of these options, she will subsequently confront a series of accept/reject decisions as houses come on the market (SE). The research we review shows that preferences elicited in JE may be dramatically different from those elicited in SE. Thus, for instance, the type of house that the prospective homeowner would buy in the JE phase of the search may be quite different from what she would buy in the SE phase.

In fact, most decisions and judgments fall somewhere between the extremes of JE and SE. For example, even when the prospective home buyer is in the second phase of the search—being presented with homes one at a time as they come on the market—she is likely to make comparisons between the current house being evaluated and previous houses she has seen. Strictly speaking, therefore, the distinction between JE and SE should be viewed as a continuum.[1] Most of the studies reviewed in this article involve the two extremes of the continuum.

At a theoretical level, JE/SE reversals constitute a new type of preference reversal that is different from those that have traditionally been studied in the field of judgment and decision making. To appreciate the difference, one needs to distinguish between evaluation scale and evaluation mode, a distinction originally made by Goldstein and Einhorn (1987).[2] Evaluation scale refers to the nature of the response that participants are asked to make. For example, people can be asked which option they would prefer to accept or reject, for which they would pay a higher price, with which they would be happier, and so forth. Evaluation mode, on the other hand, refers to joint versus separate evaluations, as defined earlier. In the traditionally studied

---

[1] SE refers both to (1) situations where different options are presented to and evaluated by different individuals so that each individual sees and evaluates only one option, and to (2) situations where different options are presented to and evaluated by the same individuals at different times so that each individual evaluates only one option *at a given time*. The former situations are pure SE conditions. The latter situations involve a JE flavor because individuals evaluating a later option may recall the previous option and make a comparison.

[2] Goldstein and Einhorn (1987) refer to the evaluation mode as the response method and to the evaluation scale as the worth scale.

preference reversals, the tasks that produce the reversal always involve different evaluation scales; they may or may not involve different evaluation modes. Of those reversals, the most commonly studied is between choosing (which is about selecting the more acceptable option) and pricing (which is about determining a selling price for each option; e.g. Lichtenstein & Slovic, 1971; Tversky, Sattath, & Slovic, 1988). Other preference reversals that involve different evaluation scales include, but are not limited to, those between rating attractiveness and pricing (e.g. Mellers, Chang, Birnbaum, & Ordonez, 1992), choosing and assessing happiness (Tversky & Griffin, 1991), selling prices and buying prices (e.g. Irwin, 1994; Kahneman, Knetsch, & Thaler, 1990; Knetsch & Sinden, 1984; see also Coursey, Hovis, & Schulze, 1987), and accepting and rejecting (e.g. Shafir, 1993; see Birnbaum, 1992; Payne, Bettman, & Johnson, 1992, for reviews).

Unlike those conventionally studied preference reversals, the JE/SE reversal occurs between tasks that take place in different evaluation modes—joint versus separate. They may or may not involve different evaluation scales. The original demonstration of JE/SE reversal was provided by Bazerman, Loewenstein, and White (1992). Participants read a description of a dispute between two neighbors and then evaluated different potential resolutions of the dispute. The dispute involved splitting either sales revenue or a tax liability associated with the ownership of a vacant lot between the neighbors' houses. Participants were asked to take the perspective of one homeowner and to evaluate various possible settlements. Each settlement was expressed in terms of both a payoff (or liability) to oneself and a payoff (or liability) to the neighbor. Across outcomes, the authors varied both the absolute payoff to oneself and whether the neighbor would be receiving the same as or more than the respondent. As an example, consider the following two options:

Option J: $600 for self and $800 for neighbor
Option S: $500 for self and $500 for neighbor

(For ease of exposition, we consistently use the letter *J* to denote the option that is valued more positively in JE and the letter *S* to denote the other option.) In JE, participants were presented with pairs of options, such as the one listed above, and asked to indicate which was more acceptable. In SE, participants were presented with these options one at a time and asked to indicate on a rating scale how acceptable each option was. These two modes of evaluation resulted in strikingly different patterns of preference. For example, of the two options listed above, 75% of the participants judged J to be more acceptable than S in JE, but 71% rated S as more acceptable than J in SE.

In a study reported in Hsee (1996a), participants were asked to assume that as the owner of a consulting firm, they were looking for a computer programmer who could write in a special computer language named KY. The two candidates, who were both new graduates, differed on two attributes: experience with the KY language and undergraduate grade point average (GPA). Specifically,

	Experience	GPA
Candidate J:	Has written 70 KY programs in last 2 years	3.0
Candidate S:	Has written 10 KY programs in last 2 years	4.9

The study was conducted at a public university in the Midwest where GPA is given on a 5-point scale. In the JE condition, participants were presented with the information on both candidates. In the SE condition, participants were presented with the information on only one of the candidates. In all conditions, respondents were asked how much salary they would be willing to pay the candidate(s). Thus, the evaluation scale in this study was held constant across the conditions, that is, willingness to pay (WTP), and the only difference lay in evaluation mode. The results revealed a significant JE/SE reversal ($t = 4.92$, $p < .01$): In JE, WTP values were higher for Candidate J ($Ms = $33.2K for J and $31.2K for S); in SE, WTP values were higher for Candidate S ($Ms = $32.7K for S and $26.8K for J). Because the evaluation scale was identical in both conditions, the reversal could only have resulted from the difference in evaluation mode.

Although other types of preference reversal have attracted substantial attention in both the psychology and economics literature, JE/SE reversals, which are as robust a phenomenon and probably more important in the real world, have received much less attention to date. The studies documenting JE/SE reversals have not been reviewed systematically. Our article attempts to fill that gap.

In the next section of the article, we propose a theoretical account of JE/SE reversals that we call the evaluability hypothesis and present empirical evidence for this hypothesis. Then, in the third section, we review other studies in the literature that have documented JE/SE reversals in diverse domains and show that the evaluability hypothesis can account for all of these findings. In the section that follows, we examine how our explanation differs from explanations for conventional preference reversals. We conclude with a discussion of implications of the evaluability hypothesis beyond preference reversals.

9.1. Theoretical Analysis

In this section, we present a general theoretical proposition called the evaluability hypothesis and apply it to explain JE/SE reversal findings, including those discussed above, and many others that are reviewed in the next section. This hypothesis was first proposed by Hsee (1996a) and has also been presented in somewhat different forms by Loewenstein, Blount, and Bazerman (1993) in terms of attribute ambiguity, by Hsee (1993) in terms of reference dependency of attributes, and by Nowlis and Simonson (1994) in terms of context dependency of attributes.

The basic idea of the evaluability hypothesis can be summarized as follows. Some attributes (such as one's GPA) are easy to evaluate independently, whereas other attributes (such as how many programs a candidate has written) are more difficult to evaluate independently. In SE, difficult-to-evaluate attributes have little impact in differentiating the evaluations of the target options, so that easy-to-evaluate attributes are the primary determinants of the evaluations of the target options. In JE, people can compare one option to the other. Through this comparison, difficult-to-evaluate attributes become easier to evaluate and hence exert a greater influence. Easy-to-evaluate attributes do not benefit as much from JE because they are easy to evaluate even in SE. This shift in the relative impact of the two attributes, if sufficiently large, will result in a JE/SE reversal.

Below we provide a detailed account of the evaluability hypothesis. We first discuss what we mean by evaluability and show how it affects the evaluations of options varying on only one attribute. Then we extend our analysis to JE/SE reversals.

9.1.1. *The Evaluability of an Attribute*

Suppose that there are two options, A and B, to be evaluated, that they vary on only one attribute, and that their values on the attribute are *a* and *b*, respectively. Assume here, and in all of the subsequent examples in this article, that people care about the attribute on which A and B vary, that the attribute has a monotonic function (i.e. either larger values are always better or smaller values are always better), and that people know which direction of the attribute is more desirable (i.e. know whether larger values or smaller values are better). For example, consider two applicants to an MBA (master of business administration) program who are identical on all relevant dimensions except that Applicant A has a Graduate Management Admission Test (GMAT) score of 610 and Applicant B has a GMAT score of 590.

Will Applicant A be evaluated more favorably than Applicant B? Let us first consider JE and then consider SE. In JE, the applicants are presented side by side to the same evaluators. In this case, we propose that Applicant A will always be favored over Applicant B. The reason is simple: In JE people compare one option against the other, and, given that people know which direction of the attribute is more desirable, they can easily tell which candidate is better.

In SE, each of the two applicants is evaluated by a group of evaluators who are not aware of the other applicant. Will Applicant A also be favored over Applicant B in SE? The answer is more complex; it depends on the *evaluability* of the attribute—whether the attribute is difficult or easy to evaluate independently. The evaluability of an attribute further depends on the type and the amount of information the evaluators have about the attribute. Such information, which we call the *evaluability information*, refers to the evaluator's knowledge about which value on the attribute is evaluatively neutral, which value is the best possible, which is the worst possible, what the value distribution of the attribute is, and any other information that helps the evaluator map a given value of the attribute onto the evaluation scale.

The crux of the evaluability hypothesis is that the shape of the evaluability function of an attribute is determined by the evaluability information that evaluators have about the attribute. The evaluability function can vary from a flat line to a fine-grained monotonic function. Depending on the shape of the function, one can predict whether two given values on the attribute (say a GMAT score of 610 and one of 590) will result in reliably different evaluations. There are many types of evaluability information people may have about an attribute. For illustrative purposes, below we examine three alternative scenarios.

Scenario 1: When the evaluators have no evaluability information (except that greater numbers on the attribute are better). In SE of this case, any value on the attribute is extremely difficult or impossible to evaluate. That is, people have no idea whether a particular value is good or bad, let alone how good or how bad it is. We assume that the value will be evaluated, on average, as neutral, although it may be accompanied by a large variance. The evaluation function for the attribute will then be a flat line, as in Figure 1 In other words, those who see one option will give it roughly the same evaluation as those evaluating the other option. For example, suppose that the two applicants mentioned above are evaluated in SE by individuals who know nothing about GMAT scores other than greater numbers are better. Then those evaluating Applicant A will have about the same impression of that applicant as those evaluating Applicant B.

We should note in passing that, in reality, people rarely possess no evaluability information about an attribute. For example, even people who know nothing about the range or distribution of GMAT scores may assume, on the basis of their knowledge of other tests, that GMAT scores should not be negative and that a score of 0 must be bad. As a result, the evaluation function is seldom absolutely flat.

Scenario 2: When the evaluators know the neutral reference point (i.e., the evaluative zero-point) of the attribute. In this case, the evaluation function of the attribute in SE approximates a step function, as depicted in Figure 2 Any

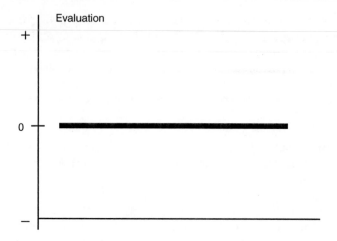

Figure 1. The evaluation function of an attribute when there is no evaluability information.

values above the reference point are considered good, and any values below the reference are considered bad.

In this case, whether two attribute values will result in different evaluations in SE depends on whether they lie on the same side of the neutral reference point or straddle it. If the attribute values lie on the same side of the reference point, they will receive similar evaluations. If the attribute values are on

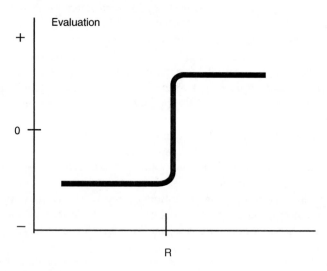

Figure 2. The evaluation function of an attribute when there is neutral reference point information (R).

opposite sides of the reference point (or one of the values coincides with the reference point), then the one above the reference point will be evaluated more favorably than the other. For example, suppose that the individuals who evaluate the two applicants are told that the average GMAT score of applicants is 500, which they interpret as the neutral reference point (i.e., neither good nor bad). Then the two candidates will both be evaluated as good and will not be differentiated. On the other hand, if the evaluators are told that the average GMAT score is 600, then Applicant A (scored 610) will be evaluated as good and Applicant B (scored 590) as bad.[3]

Again, the above analysis is oversimplified. In reality, even if the evaluators only know the neutral reference point of the attribute, they will make speculations about the size and the meaning of the unit on the attribute. For example, people who are told that the average GMAT score is 600 may assume that a score like 601 is not very much different from 600 and not very good and that a score like 700 is quite different from 600 and must be quite good. As a result, the evaluation function is more likely to be S-shaped, rather than a strict step function.

Scenario 3: When the evaluators are aware of the best possible and worst possible values of the attribute. In this scenario, the attribute is relatively easy to evaluate. The evaluation function will be monotonically increasing, as depicted in Figure 3. The general slope of the evaluation function, however, will be inversely related to the size of the range between the best and the worst values (e.g. Beattie & Baron, 1991; Mellers & Cook, 1994).

In this condition, any two values on the attribute will create different impressions and result in different evaluations. The size of the difference depends on the size of the range between the best and the worst values. For example, Applicant A (with a score of 610) and Applicant B (with a score of 590) will be evaluated more differently if the evaluators are told that GMAT scores range from 550 to 650 than if they are told that GMAT scores range from 400 to 800. Qualifying the range effect, Beattie and Baron (1991) found that the range manipulation only affected the evaluations of unfamiliar stimuli. Consistent with the evaluability hypothesis, this finding suggests that providing or varying range information only affects the evaluation of attributes that would otherwise be hard to evaluate, namely, those for which the evaluators do not already have clear knowledge about the range or other evaluability information.

Again, in reality, the evaluation function in this condition will not be as linear as the one depicted in Figure 3. For example, people who are told that most applicants' GMAT scores range from 400 to 800 may treat the

---

[3] Unless otherwise specified, we assume in this article that people evaluating Option A and people evaluating Option B in SE have the same evaluability information. For example, we assume that those evaluating Applicant A and those evaluating Applicant B have the same knowledge about GMAT scores.

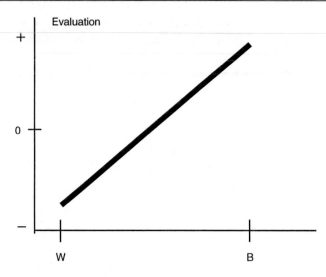

Figure 3. The evaluation function of an attribute when there is information about its worst value (W) and best value (B).

midpoint of the range, 600, as the neutral reference point. As a consequence, the evaluation function will be somewhat S-shaped, with its slope particularly steep around 600.

9.1.2. Evidence for the Preceding Analysis: The Score Study

According to the preceding analysis, the evaluation function of an attribute varies predictably, depending on the evaluability information that people have. To test this proposition, we asked college students ($N = 294$) recruited from a large midwestern university to evaluate a hypothetical applicant to a university. In different experimental conditions, we varied evaluability information to see whether different applicant test scores would lead to different evaluations as a function of evaluability information.

The questionnaire for this study included 12 between-subject versions. They constituted 3 Evaluability Conditions × 4 Score Conditions. In all versions, respondents were asked to imagine that they worked for the admissions office of a university, that their job was to evaluate prospective students' potential to succeed in college, and that they had just received the application of a foreign student named Jane. Participants were further told that Jane had taken an Academic Potential Exam (APE) in her country, that students in Jane's country are on average as intelligent as American students, that APE is a good measure of one's potential to succeed in college, and that the higher an APE score, the better.

Corresponding to the three scenarios discussed in the previous section, the three evaluability versions for this study were (a) no information, (b) average score information, and (c) score range (i.e. best and worst score) information. The no-information version read

You have no idea of the distribution of APE scores. You don't know what the average APE score, what the best APE score, or what the worst APE score is.

The average-score version read

You don't have a clear idea of the distribution of APE scores. You know that the average APE score is 1,250, but you don't know what the best APE score or what the worst APE score is.

The score-range version read

You don't have a clear idea of the distribution of APE scores. You know that the best APE score is 1,400 and the worst APE score is 1,100, but you don't know what the average APE score is.

Each of the three evaluability versions was crossed with four versions of Jane's APE score: 1,100, 1,200, 1,300, and 1,400, respectively. For example, the 1,100-version read

Jane scored 1,100 on APE. The admissions office requires that you give a rating to each applicant even if you don't have all the information. Given what you know, how would you rate Jane's potential to succeed in college? Circle a number below:

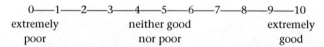

	0—1—2—3—4—5—6—7—8—9—10	
extremely	neither good	extremely
poor	nor poor	good

The results, summarized in Table 1 lend support to the preceding analysis. In the no-information condition, the four scores formed almost a flat line, $F(3, 96) = 1.51$, *ns*. Planned comparisons indicate that the difference between any two score conditions was insignificant, suggesting that different scores created similar impressions. There is, however, a statistically insignificant yet distinctively positive slope across the four scores. This arises probably because

Table 1. Mean Evaluations of the Applicant in the Score Study

Evaluability	Score of applicant			
	1,100	1,200	1,300	1,400
No information	5.13$_a$	5.20$_a$	5.54$_a$	5.84$_a$
Average score information only	4.56$_a$	4.71$_a$	6.40$_b$	6.84$_b$
Score range information	3.04$_a$	3.98$_b$	6.52$_c$	8.30$_d$

Note. The ratings were made on a scale ranging from 0 (*extremely poor*) to 10 (*extremely good*). Means in the same row that do not share subscripts are significantly different from each other.

253

even without any explicitly given evaluability information, the respondents used their knowledge about other tests to speculate on the missing information.

In the average-score condition, the four scores formed an S-shaped function, with a steeper slope around the neutral reference point (the average score of 1,250). An F test across the four score conditions revealed a significant effect, $F(3, 96) = 15.55$, $p < .01$. Planned comparisons indicate that score 1,100 and score 1,200 were not evaluated significantly different, nor were scores 1,300 and 1,400, but either of the first two scores was judged significantly different from either of the latter two.

In the score-range condition, the four scores formed a steep upward slope, $F(3, 97) = 73.83$, $p < .001$. Planned comparisons show that each score was evaluated as significantly different from every other score in the predicted ordering. Note that the data are also indicative of an S-shape, suggesting that the respondents may have treated the midpoint of the range as a reference point and considered scores above this point to be generally good and scores below that point to be bad.

In sum, the findings of this study show that the evaluation function of an attribute can migrate from a flat line to a steeply sloped function depending on the evaluability information the evaluators have.

9.1.3. *Elaboration*

Several points deserve elaboration here. First, whether an attribute is easy or difficult to evaluate is not an intrinsic characteristic of the attribute. It is determined by the evaluability information the evaluators have about the attribute. Thus, the same attribute can be easy to evaluate in one context and for one group of evaluators but difficult to evaluate in another context or for other evaluators. For example, GMAT score is an easy-to-evaluate attribute for people familiar with the meaning of the score, its distribution, etc., but a difficult-to-evaluate attribute for other people.

Second, an attribute can be difficult to evaluate even if its values are precisely given and people perfectly understand its meanings. For example, everybody knows what money is and how much a dollar is worth, but the monetary attribute of an option can be difficult to evaluate if the decision maker does not know the evaluability information for that attribute in the given context. Suppose, for instance, that a person on a trip to a foreign country has learned that a particular hotel room costs $50 a night and needs to judge the desirability of this price. If the person is not familiar with the hotel prices of that country, it will be difficult for him to evaluate whether $50 is a good or bad price. To say that an attribute is difficult to evaluate does not imply that the decision maker does not know its value but means that the decision maker has difficulty determining the *desirability* of its value in the given decision context.

Finally, attributes with dichotomous values—such as whether a job candidate for an accountant position has a certified public accountant (CPA) license or not, or whether a vase being sold at a flea market is broken or not—are often easy to evaluate independently. People often know that these attributes have only two alternative values, and, even in SE when evaluators see only one value of the attribute (e.g. either with or without a CPA license), they know whether the value is the better or worse of the two. This is a special case of the situation where the evaluator has full knowledge of the evaluability information about the attribute. In several of the studies to be reviewed below, the easy-to-evaluate attribute is of this type.

9.1.4. *Evaluability and JE/SE Reversals*

So far, we have only discussed the evaluability of a single attribute. In this section, we extend our analysis to options involving a trade-off across two attributes and explore how the evaluation hypothesis explains JE/SE reversals of these options.

Consider two options, J and S, that involve a trade-off across Attribute x and Attribute y:

	Attribute x	Attribute y
Option J:	x_J	y_J
Option S:	x_S	y_S

where $x_J > x_S$ and $y_J < y_S$ ($>$ denotes better than and $<$ denotes worse than).

According to the evaluability hypothesis, JE/SE reversals occur because one of the attributes is more difficult to evaluate than the other, and the relative impact of the difficult-to-evaluate attribute increases from SE to JE. Specifically, suppose that Attribute x is relatively difficult to evaluate independently and Attribute y is easy to evaluate independently. In SE, because Attribute x is difficult to evaluate, x_J and x_S will receive similar evaluations; as a result, this attribute will have little or no impact in differentiating the desirability of one option from that of the other. Because Attribute y is easy to evaluate, y_J and y_S will be evaluated differently; consequently, the evaluations of J and S in SE will be determined mainly by the values of Attribute y. Because $y_S > y_J$, S will tend to be evaluated more favorably than J. In JE, in contrast, people can easily compare the two options on an attribute-by-attribute basis (e.g., Russo & Dosher, 1983; Tversky, 1969). Through this comparison, people can easily tell which option is better on which attribute, regardless of whether the attribute is difficult or easy to evaluate in SE. Thus, both attributes will affect the evaluations of the target options.

The above analysis indicates that, compared with SE, the impact of the difficult-to-evaluate attribute relative to that of the easy-to-evaluate attribute increases in JE. In other words, the difficult-to-evaluate attribute (x) benefits more from JE than the easy-to-evaluate attribute (y). If Option S is favored in SE, and if Attribute x is important enough and/or the difference between x_J and x_S is large enough, then a JE/SE reversal will emerge, such that Option J will be favored over Option S in JE.

9.1.5. Evidence for the Preceding Analysis: Hiring Study and CD Changer Study

Consider the hiring study (Hsee, 1996a) discussed earlier, involving a candidate with more KY programming experience and one with a higher GPA. Participants in this experiment were all college students, who knew which GPA values are good and which are bad, but they were unfamiliar with the criterion of KY programming experience. Thus, these participants had clear evaluability information for the GPA attribute but not for the KY-programming-experience attribute. By definition, GPA was an easy-to-evaluate attribute, and KY programming experience was a relatively difficult-to-evaluate attribute.

To assess whether our judgment of evaluability concurred with participants' own judgment, Hsee (1996a) asked those in each separate-evaluation condition, after they had made the WTP judgment, to indicate (a) whether they had any idea of how good the GPA of the candidate they had evaluated was and (b) whether they had any idea of how experienced with KY programming the candidate was. Their answers to each question could range from 1 (*I don't have any idea*) to 4 (*I have a clear idea*). The results confirmed our judgment that GPA was easier to evaluate than KY experience. The mean rating for GPA, 3.7, was significantly higher than the mean rating of 2.1 for KY experience ($t = 11.79$, $p < .001$).

According to the evaluability hypothesis, the difficult-to-evaluate attribute has a greater impact relative to the easy-to-evaluate attribute in JE than in SE. This is indeed what happened in the hiring study. As summarized earlier, the results indicate that the evaluations of the candidates in SE were determined primarily by the GPA attribute, and the evaluations in JE were influenced more heavily by the KY-experience attribute. It suggests that JE enabled the participants to compare the two candidates directly and thereby realize that the lower-GPA candidate had in fact completed many more programs than had the higher-GPA candidate.[4]

---

[4] It should be noted that the distinction between difficult-to-evaluate and easy-to-evaluate attributes is different from that between proxy and fundamental attributes in decision analysis (e.g. Fischer, Damodaran, Laskey, & Lincoln, 1987). A proxy attribute is an indirect measure of a fundamental attribute—a factor that the decision maker is ultimately concerned about; for example, cholesterol level is a proxy attribute of one's health. A proxy attribute can be

In most studies that demonstrate JE/SE reversals, whether an attribute is difficult or easy to evaluate independently is assumed. In the CD changer study described below, the evaluability of an attribute was manipulated empirically.[5] As mentioned earlier, the evaluability hypothesis asserts that JE/SE reversals occur because one of the attributes of the stimulus objects is difficult to evaluate in SE, whereas the other attribute is relatively easy to evaluate. If this is correct, then a JE/SE reversal can be turned on or off by varying the relative evaluability of the attributes.

To test this intuition, the CD changer study was designed as follows: It involved the evaluations of two CD changers (i.e. multiple compact disc players):

	CD capacity	THD
CD Changer J:	Holds 5 CDs	.003%
CD Changer S:	Holds 20 CDs	.01%

It was explained to every participant that THD (total harmonic distortion) was an index of sound quality. The smaller the THD, the better the sound quality.

The study consisted of two evaluability conditions: difficult/easy and easy/easy. In the difficult/easy condition, participants received no other information about THD than described previously. As verified in subsequent questions (see below), THD was a difficult-to-evaluate attribute, and CD capacity was a relatively easy-to-evaluate attribute. Although most people know that less distortion is better, few know whether a given THD rating (e.g. .01%) is good or bad. On the other hand, most have some idea of how many CDs a CD changer could hold and whether a CD changer that can hold 5 CDs (or 20 CDs) is good or not. In the easy/easy condition, participants were provided with information about the effective range of the THD attribute. They were told, "For most CD changers on the market, THD ratings range from .002% (best) to .012% (worst)." This information was designed to make THD easier to evaluate independently. With this information, participants in the separate-evaluation conditions would have some idea where the given THD rating fell in the range and hence whether the rating was good or bad.

In each of the evaluability conditions, participants (202 students from a large public university in the Midwest) were either presented with the information about both CD changers and evaluated both of them (JE), or presented with the information about one of the options and evaluated it alone (SE). In all conditions, the dependent variable was willingness-to-pay price.

either easier or more difficult to evaluate than its fundamental attribute. For example, for people familiar with the meaning and the value distribution of cholesterol readings, the cholesterol attribute can be easier to evaluate than its fundamental attribute health; for people unfamiliar with cholesterol numbers, it can be very difficult to evaluate.

[5] This study was originally reported in Hsee (1996a).

Table 2. Mean Willingness-to-Pay Values in the CD Changer Study

Evaluability and evaluation mode	CD changer J	CD changer S
Difficult/easy		
Joint	$228	$204
Separate	$212	$256
Easy/easy		
Joint	$222	$186
Separate	$222	$177

Note. CD = compact disc.

To ensure that the evaluability manipulation was effective, Hsee asked participants in the two separate-evaluation conditions, after they had indicated their WTP prices, (a) whether they had any idea of how good the THD rating of the CD changer was and (b) whether they had any idea of how large its CD capacity was. Answers to those questions ranged from 1 to 4, greater numbers indicating greater evaluability. The results confirmed the effectiveness of the evaluability manipulation. Mean evaluability scores for THD and CD capacity in the difficult/easy condition were 1.98 and 3.25, respectively, and in the easy/easy condition were 2.53 and 3.22. Planned comparisons revealed that evaluability scores for THD increased significantly from the difficult/easy condition to the easy/easy condition ($t = 2.92$, $p < .01$), but those for CD capacity remained the same.

The main prediction for the study is that a JE/SE reversal was more likely to emerge in the difficult/easy condition than in the easy/easy condition. The results, summarized in Table 2 confirmed this prediction: In the difficult/easy condition, there was a significant JE/SE reversal ($t = 3.32$, $p < .01$), and the direction of the reversal was consistent with the evaluability hypothesis, implying that the difficult-to-evaluate attribute (THD) had a lesser relative impact in SE than in JE, and the easy-to-evaluate attribute (CD capacity) had a greater relative impact. In the easy/easy condition, the reversal disappeared ($t < 1$, ns).

The fact that increasing the evaluability of the difficult-to-evaluate attribute could eliminate the JE/SE reversal supports the evaluability hypothesis. It suggests that what drives this type of preference reversal is differential evaluability between the attributes.

9.1.6. Summary

In this section, we first introduced the notion of evaluability and then used it to account for JE/SE reversals. The evaluability hypothesis, as our analysis shows, is not a post hoc speculation but a testable theory. First of all, the concept of evaluability was defined independently of the JE/SE-reversal effect, which it subsequently explained. Moreover, we presented evidence of independent measures of evaluability and showed that participants' judgments of evaluability coincided with ours and predicted the observed reversals. Finally, in one study we empirically manipulated evaluability and demonstrated that this manipulation could turn the JE/SE reversal on or off in the direction predicted by the evaluability hypothesis.

9.2. Review and Explanation of JE/SE Reversals

JE/SE reversals have been documented in diverse contexts. All of the findings involve pairs of options where one option is favored in JE and the other is favored in SE. Within this shared structure, JE/SE reversals can be classified into three types. In one type, the two options belong to the same category (e.g., both options are CD players), they share well-defined attributes (e.g. sound quality and CD capacity), and they involve explicit trade-offs along those attributes. All of the examples shown so far are of this type. In the second type of JE/SE reversal, the options also belong to the same category (just as in the first type), but they do not share well-defined attributes and do not involve explicit trade-offs. In the third type of JE/SE reversal, the options are from different categories. In what follows, we provide examples of each type of reversal and show how the evaluability hypothesis can be used to explain the finding.

9.2.1. JE/SE Reversals for Options From the Same Category and With Explicit Trade-Offs

All of the JE/SE reversals discussed so far belong to this type. Here, the two options are from the same category (e.g. both are job candidates for a programmer position), and they involve an explicit trade-off along two attributes (e.g. GPA and programming experience). For this type of reversal, the evaluability hypothesis provides a straightforward explanation. In the previous section, we already examined how the evaluability hypothesis explains the result of the programmer-hiring study.

The same analysis can be applied to Bazerman et al.'s (1992) self-neighbor study. Recall that in JE of this study the option that would give $600 to oneself and $800 to the neighbor (Option J) was favored over the option that would give $500 to both oneself and the neighbor (Option S), but in SE the pattern was reversed. The two options can be interpreted as involving a trade-off across the following two attributes:

	Payoff to self	Equality between self and neighbor
Option J:	$600	Unequal
Option S:	$500	Equal

Payoffs to self, we believe, were difficult to evaluate in SE because, lacking a comparison, respondents would not know how good a given settlement was. In contrast, whether or not the amount awarded to self was equal to the amount awarded to the neighbor was easy to evaluate. Most people, we surmise, would find an unequal treatment (especially when it is in favor of the other party) highly unattractive and would find an equal treatment neutral or positive. That is why the rank order of the two options in SE was determined primarily by the equality (equal versus unequal treatment) attribute. In JE, the payoff-to-self attribute was made easier to evaluate by the fact that the decision maker could compare the two values directly. On the other hand, the equality attribute, which was already easy to evaluate in SE, would not benefit as much from JE. That is why the payoff-to-self attribute loomed larger and led to a reversal in JE.

Bazerman, Schroth, Shah, Diekmann, and Tenbrunsel (1994) obtained similar preference reversals with hypothetical job offers for MBA students that differed in terms of payoffs to oneself and equality or procedural justice in the company.[6] Blount and Bazerman (1996) showed inconsistent evaluations of absolute versus comparative payoffs in recruiting participants for an experiment. These findings can be analyzed in the same way as Bazerman et al.'s (1992) preference reversal findings.[7]

Interested in trade-offs between absolute amount of income and temporal trend of income, Hsee (1993) solicited joint and separate evaluations of two hypothetical salary options, one with a higher absolute amount but a decreasing trend over a fixed 4-year period (Option J) and the other with a lower absolute amount but an increasing trend (Option S). The results revealed a JE/SE reversal: In JE, respondents slightly preferred the higher absolute-salary option, but in SE, the increasing-trend option was favored. Again, this result can be explained by evaluability. In SE, the absolute amount of earnings was difficult to evaluate, but whether the salary increased or decreased over time would elicit distinct feelings: People feel happy with improving trends and feel dejected with worsening trends, as shown in numerous recent studies (e.g. Ariely, 1998; Hsee & Abelson, 1991; Hsee, Salovey, & Abelson, 1994; Kahneman, Fredrickson, Schreiber, & Redelmeier, 1993; Loewenstein & Prelec, 1993; Loewenstein & Sicherman, 1991). In JE, the difference in absolute amount of earnings between the options became transparent and therefore loomed larger.

---

[6] Even in SE of these studies, the participants (who were MBA students) should have some idea of the distribution information for the salary attribute, and therefore, the salaries were not difficult to evaluate in its absolute sense. However, we suggest that JE provided more information about the salary attribute than SE, and, consequently, the salaries may have been even *more easy* to evaluate in JE than in SE.

[7] Bazerman et al. (1998) had an alternative explanation for these results, which we discuss later.

In a more recent study, Hsee (1996a) observed a JE/SE reversal in WTP for two consumer products. Participants were asked to assume that they were a music major looking for a music dictionary in a used book store. They were provided the information about and indicated their WTP for either both or one of the following dictionaries:

	# of entries	Any defects?
Dictionary J:	20,000	Yes, the cover is torn; otherwise it's like new.
Dictionary S:	10,000	No, it's like new.

In JE, Dictionary J received higher WTP values, but in SE, Dictionary S enjoyed higher WTP values. The evaluability hypothesis also provides a ready explanation for the results. In SE, most respondents, who were not familiar with the evaluability information of music dictionary entries, would not know how to evaluate the desirability of a dictionary with 20,000 (or 10,000) entries. In contrast, even without something to compare it to, people would find a defective dictionary unappealing and a new-looking dictionary appealing. Therefore, we believe that the entry attribute was difficult to evaluate in SE and the defect attribute relatively easy to evaluate. This explains why in SE the rank order of WTPs for the two dictionaries was determined by the defect attribute. In JE, it was easy for people to realize that Dictionary J was twice as comprehensive, thus prompting them to assign a higher value to that dictionary.

Lowenthal (1993) documented a similar JE/SE reversal in a rather different context. Interested in voting behavior, she created hypothetical congressional races between candidates who were similar except for two dimensions. For example, consider the following two candidates:

	Jobs to be created	Personal history
Candidate J:	5000 jobs	Convicted of misdemeanor
Candidate S:	1000 jobs	Clean

In JE, participants voted for Candidate J, but, when asked to evaluate the candidates separately, participants rated Candidate S more favorably. For most respondents, who knew little about employment statistics, whether a candidate could bring 5,000 jobs or 1,000 jobs would be difficult to evaluate in isolation, but a candidate convicted of a misdemeanor would easily be perceived as unappealing and a candidate with a clean history as good. The direction of the reversal observed in the study is consistent with the evaluability hypothesis, suggesting that the personal history attribute had a greater impact in SE, and the job attribute loomed larger in JE.

9.2.2. JE/SE Reversals for Options From the Same Category but Without Explicit Trade-Offs

Sometimes, JE/SE reversals occur with options that do not present explicit trade-offs between attributes. Instead, one option apparently dominates the other.

In a recent study, Hsee (1998) asked students to imagine that they were relaxing on a beach by Lake Michigan and were in the mood for some ice cream. They were assigned to either the joint-evaluation or the separate-evaluation condition. Those in the joint-evaluation condition were told that there were two vendors selling Haagen Dazs ice cream by the cup on the beach. Vendor J used a 10 oz. cup and put 8 oz. of ice cream in it, and Vendor S used a 5 oz. cup and put 7 oz. of ice cream in it. Respondents saw drawings of the two servings and were asked how much they were willing to pay for a serving by each vendor. Respondents in each separate evaluation condition were told about and saw the drawing of only one vendor's serving, and they indicated how much they were willing to pay for a serving by that vendor.

Note that, objectively speaking, Vendor J's serving dominated Vendor S's, because it had more ice cream (and also offered a larger cup). However, J's serving was underfilled, and S's serving was overfilled. The results revealed a JE/SE reversal: In JE, people were willing to pay more for Vendor J's serving, but in SE, they were willing to pay more for Vendor S's serving.

In another experiment, Hsee (1998) asked participants to indicate their WTP prices for one or both of the following dinnerware sets being sold as a clearance item in a store:

	Set J (includes 40 pcs)	Set S (includes 24 pcs)
Dinner plates:	8, in good condition	8, in good condition
Soup/salad bowls:	8, in good condition	8, in good condition
Dessert plates:	8, in good condition	8, in good condition
Cups:	8, 2 of which are broken	
Saucers:	8, 7 of which are broken	

Note that Set J contained all the pieces contained in Set S, plus 6 more intact cups and 1 more intact saucer. Again, there was a JE/SE reversal. In JE, respondents were willing to pay more for Set J. In SE, they were willing to pay more for Set S, although it was the inferior option.

Although the options in these studies do not involve explicit trade-offs along well-defined attributes, the findings can still be accounted for by the evaluability hypothesis. In the ice cream study, the difference between the two servings can be reinterpreted as varying on two attributes: the absolute amount of ice cream a serving contained and whether the serving was over-filled or underfilled. Thus, the two servings can be described as follows:

	Amount of ice cream	Filling
Serving J:	8 oz.	Underfilled
Serving S:	7 oz.	Overfilled

In SE, it was probably difficult to evaluate the desirability of a given amount of ice cream (7 oz. or 8 oz.), but the filling attribute was easier to evaluate: An underfilled serving was certainly bad and an overfilled serving good. According to the evaluability hypothesis, the filling attribute would be the primary factor to differentiate the evaluations of the two servings in SE, but in JE, people could see that Serving J contained more ice cream than Serving S and make their judgments accordingly. The results are consistent with these predictions.

To see how the evaluability hypothesis applies to the dinnerware study, let us rewrite the differences between the dinnerware sets as follows:

	# of intact pieces	Integrity of the set
Set J:	31	Incomplete
Set S:	24	Complete

In SE, the desirability of a certain number of intact pieces (31 or 24) was probably rather difficult to evaluate (especially for students who were unfamiliar with dinnerware). On the other hand, the integrity of a set was probably much easier to evaluate: A set with broken pieces was certainly undesirable, and a complete set was desirable. Thus, the evaluability hypothesis would expect the intact set (S) to be favored in SE. In JE, the respondents could easily compare the sets and thereby would realize that Set J dominated Set S. Again, the results are consistent with these expectations.

9.2.3. JE/SE Reversals for Options From Different Categories

In the studies reviewed so far, the options to be evaluated are always from the same category. JE/SE reversals have also been found between the evaluations of apparently unrelated options.

Kahneman and Ritov (1994) observed a JE/SE reversal in an investigation of what they called the headline method. They presented participants with headlines describing problems from different categories and asked them how much they were willing to contribute to solving these problems. Consider the following, for example:

Problem J:	Skin cancer from sun exposure common among farm workers.
Problem S:	Several Australian mammal species nearly wiped out by hunters.

It was found that in JE, respondents were willing to make a greater contribution to Problem J, and in SE, they were willing to make a greater contribution to Problem S.

In a more recent study, Kahneman, Ritov, and Schkade (in press) studied people's reactions to two problems:

Problem J: Multiple myeloma among the elderly.
Problem S: Cyanide fishing in coral reefs around Asia.

Again, there was a JE/SE reversal: In JE, people considered the disease issue (J) to be more important and also expected greater satisfaction from making a contribution to that issue. In SE, however, the reverse was true.

In an experiment conducted by Irwin, Slovic, Lichtenstein, and McClell and (1993), respondents were asked to evaluate problems such as:

Problem J: Improving the air quality in Denver.
Problem S: Adding a VCR to your TV.

When asked to select in pairwise comparisons between those options (JE), respondents overwhelmingly opted for improving the air quality. When those options were presented separately (SE), most respondents were willing to pay more for upgrading their TV.

The main difference between these effects and the JE/SE reversals reviewed previously is that in these studies, the stimulus options are from unrelated categories. For example, in Kahneman et al.'s (in press) study, multiple myeloma is a human health problem, and cyanide fishing is an ecological problem.

Our explanation of these results requires both norm theory (Kahneman & Miller, 1986) and the evaluability hypothesis. Take Kahneman et al.'s (in press) study, for example. In SE, the absolute importance of either problem is difficult to evaluate independently. People do not have much preexisting evaluability information for either multiple myeloma or cyanide fishing. According to norm theory, when evaluating an object, people often think about the norm of the category to which the object belongs and judge the importance of that object relative to the category norm. More specifically, norm theory suggests that, when evaluating multiple myeloma, participants would evoke the norm of the human-health-problem category, and, when evaluating cyanide fishing, they would evoke the norm of the ecological-problem category. These evoked category norms essentially served as the evaluability information for judging the importance of each problem in SE. According to Kahneman et al., multiple myeloma is unimportant relative to the typical or normative human health problem, and cyanide fishing is important relative to the typical or normative ecological problem.

In summary, the differences between Problems J (multiple myeloma) and S (cyanide fishing) in Kahneman et al.'s (in press) study can be considered as varying on two attributes: their absolute importance and their relative importance within their respective category.

	Absolute importance	Relative importance within category
Problem J:	Hard to evaluate	Unimportant
Problem S:	Hard to evaluate	Important

The absolute importance of each problem is difficult to judge independently, but the relative importance of each problem within its given category (i.e., relative to the category norm) is easy to evaluate. That explains why cyanide fishing was considered more important in SE.

In JE, people could compare one problem with the other, and, through this comparison, they would recognize that a human health problem (J) must be more important than an ecological problem (S), hence assigning a higher WTP value to multiple myeloma.

A similar analysis can be applied to Kahneman and Ritov's (1994) farmer/mammal study and Irwin et al.'s (1993) VCR/air quality study.[8]

The evaluability hypothesis and norm theory are not rival explanations. Instead, they complement each other to explain the above findings. Norm theory describes how category norms are evoked. The evaluability hypothesis describes how differential evaluability information can lead to JE/SE reversals. The linkage between the two theories is that, in all of the studies discussed in this section, the evaluability information is the category norm of the option under evaluation.

Note that the structure of the problems discussed above is indeed quite similar to that of the ice cream study analyzed in the previous section. In the ice cream study, the absolute amount of ice cream is difficult to evaluate independently, but the amount of ice cream relative to the cup size is easy to evaluate. In Kahneman et al.'s (in press) health/ecological problem study, the absolute importance of each problem is difficult to evaluate independently, but the importance of each problem relative to the norm of its given category is easy to evaluate. More generally, the absolute value of an option is often hard to evaluate independently, but its relative position within a given category is usually easier to evaluate because the category serves as the evaluability information. As a result, a high-position member in a low category is often valued more favorably than a low-position member in a high category.

---

[8] There is another possible interpretation of Irwin et al.'s (1993) results. When making a choice between worse air pollution in Denver and upgrading their own appliance, people may have felt it would be selfish to benefit themselves trivially at the expense of *all* Denver residents. When they were asked to put a monetary value of clean air, no such direct tradeoff is implied, and they may have thought about the benefit of clean air to only themselves.

Another study pertinent to the above proposition is reported in Hsee (1998). Students were asked to assume that they had received a graduation gift from a friend and to judge the generosity of the gift giver. For half of the students, the gift was a $45 wool scarf from a department store that carried wool scarves ranging in price from $5 to $50. For the other half of the students, the gift was a $55 wool coat from a department store that carried wool coats ranging in price from $50 to $500. Even though the $55 coat was certainly more expensive, those receiving the scarf considered their gift giver to be significantly more generous. These results can be explained in the same way as the ice cream study and the health/ecological problem study. The absolute price of a gift ($45 or $55) is difficult to evaluate in SE. However, whether the given gift is at the low end or high end of its respective product category is easy to evaluate in SE. The $45 scarf is at the top of the scarf category, and the $55 coat is near the bottom of the coat category. Therefore, the scarf appears more expensive and its giver more generous.

9.2.4. Summary

In this section, we have reviewed recent research findings that document JE/SE reversals in diverse domains of decision making. They include JE/SE reversals between options that involve explicit trade-offs along well-defined attributes (e.g. the programmer-hiring study), between options that belong to the same category but do not involve explicit trade-offs (e.g. the ice cream study), and between options that come from unrelated categories (e.g. the health/ecological problem study). We have shown that the evaluability hypothesis provides a simple and unifying explanation for all of these seemingly unrelated findings.

In the next section, we discuss how the evaluability hypothesis differs from existing explanations of conventionally studied preference reversals.

9.3. Evaluability and Other Explanations for Preference Reversals

Although the term *preference reversal* can be used to describe many documented violations of normative axioms, such as Allais's Paradox (Allais, 1953) and intransitivity (e.g. May, 1954; Tversky, 1969), the concept of preference reversal gained its recognition in decision research with the P-bet/$-bet research of Lichtenstein and Slovic (1971) and subsequently of Grether and Plott (1979). The P-bet offers a high likelihood of winning a small amount of money, whereas the $-bet offers a low probability of winning a larger amount of money. The P-bet is often preferred when participants are asked to make a choice between the two bets, and the $-bet is favored when participants are asked to indicate a minimum selling price for each bet. The standard explanation for this type of preference reversal is the compatibility principle (Slovic, Griffin, & Tversky, 1990). According to this principle, the weight given to an attribute is greater when it matches the evaluation scale than when it does not. For example, attributes involving monetary values, such as monetary payoff, loom larger if preferences are elicited in terms of price than in terms of choice. This principle serves as a compelling explanation for the choice–pricing preference reversal and many other related choice–judgment reversals (see Schkade & Johnson, 1989, for process data that supports the scale compatibility explanation of choice–pricing reversals). The compatibility principle is concerned with preference reversals involving different evaluation scales as opposed to those with different evaluation modes.

Another type of commonly studied preference reversal occurs between choice and matching (Tversky et al., 1988; for more recent studies, see Coupey, Irwin, & Payne, 1998). For example, consider a study by Tversky et al. (1988) involving two hypothetical job candidates for a production engineer position: Candidate A had a technical score of 86 and a human relations score of 76; Candidate B had a technical score of 78 and a human relations score of 91. In choice, participants were asked to choose between the two candidates, and most chose Candidate A. In matching, participants were presented with the same alternatives, but some information about one of the candidates was missing. The participants' task was to fill in that information to make the two alternatives equally attractive. Typically, the values respondents filled in implied that they would have preferred Candidate B had the information not been missing. To explain the preference reversal between choice and matching, Tversky et al. proposed the prominence principle, which states that the most prominent attribute in a multiattribute choice set is weighted more heavily in choice than in matching. In the example above, technical score was apparently the more important attribute, and, according to the prominence principle, it loomed larger in choice than in matching. Fischer and Hawkins (1993) extended the prominence principle by contending that the most prominent attribute looms larger in qualitative tasks (e.g. choice and strength-of-preference judgment) than in quantitative tasks (e.g. value-matching and monetary-equivalent value judgments).

Although the prominence principle provides a good explanation for the standard choice–matching preference reversal, it does not readily apply to JE/SE reversals studied in the present research. In the choice–matching paradigm, both the choice task and the matching task are carried out in the JE mode, and the prominence principle explains how the relative weight of the attributes varies between tasks that involve different evaluation scales. JE/SE reversals, on the other hand, can take place even if the evaluation scale is held constant (e.g. about willingness to pay), and therefore they cannot be explained by theories that focus on differential evaluation scales. In addition, the prominence principle relies on difference in attribute prominence for preference reversals to occur. However, our research shows that a JE/SE reversal can be turned on or off even if the relative prominence of the attributes remains constant (e.g. in the CD-changer experiment previously reviewed). It suggests that for tasks that differ in evaluation modes, differential evaluability alone is sufficient to induce a preference reversal. The evaluability hypothesis is not, therefore, an alternative explanation to the prominence or compatibility principle; instead, they seek to explain different phenomena.

Mellers and her associates (Mellers et al., 1992; Mellers, Ordonez, & Birnbaum, 1992) have a change-of-process theory to account for preference reversals between tasks involving different evaluation scales. It asserts that people using different evaluation scales (e.g. ratings versus prices) adopt different cognitive models when evaluating alternative risky options, thus leading to preference reversals between those options. Like the compatibility and the prominence principles, the change-of-process theory also relies on difference in evaluation scales to explain preference reversals and hence does not apply to the JE/SE reversals explored in the present research.

Recently, Bazerman, Tenbrunsel, and Wade-Benzoni (1998) provided another explanation for some of the JE/SE reversals reviewed earlier, which they termed the want/should proposition. In the series of studies involving options varying on payoffs to self and equality or fairness (e.g. Bazerman et al., 1992, 1994), Bazerman et al. (1998) suggest that the payoff attribute is a should attribute (i.e. a factor the respondents think they should consider) and the equality attribute is a want attribute (i.e. a factor that the respondents want to consider). They then explain these JE/SE reversals by proposing that should attributes loom larger in JE and want attributes loom larger in SE. That is presumably because SE gives decision makers greater leeway to do what they are motivated to do rather than what they feel they should do; this proposition is consistent with the elastic justification notion posited in Hsee (1995, 1996b).

We agree with Bazerman et al. (1998) that the want/should proposition is an appealing alternative explanation for the JE/SE reversals in those studies. However, it lacks several ingredients of a general explanation for JE/SE reversals. First, it is often difficult to know a priori which attributes are should attributes and which are want attributes. For example, in the programmer-hiring study, it is difficult to identify a priori whether GPA is the should attribute and programming experience is the want attribute, or vice versa. Further, the want/should proposition is silent about why a JE/SE reversal can be turned on or off by evaluability manipulation. Nevertheless, the want/should proposition provides a possible explanation for JE/SE reversals involving trade-offs between monetary payoffs and fairness. Further research is needed to determine whether those findings are caused by the want/should difference, by differential attribute evaluability, or by a combination of the two.

Nowlis and Simonson (1997) documented robust preference reversals between a choice task and a rating task. In one experiment, for example, participants in the choice condition were presented with multiple products varying in price and brand and asked to choose one. Participants in the rating condition were also presented with those multiple products simultaneously and asked to rate their purchase intention on a rating scale. For the choice group, low-price/low-quality products (e.g. a $139 Goldstar microwave oven) were preferred; in the rating group, high-price/high-quality products (e.g. a $179 Panasonic microwave oven) were favored. These observations resemble the traditional choice–judgment reversal where the main difference between choice and judgment lies in evaluation scale, not evaluation mode. Nowlis and Simonson also showed that the preference reversal was not mitigated even when the participants were given information about the price range of the product, e.g., that the prices of microwaves range from $99 to $299. This result is not inconsistent with our research. Unlike attributes such as total harmonic distortion, which are extremely difficult to evaluate, the price of a microwave is familiar to most people. Adding range information to an already-familiar attribute, especially when the range is very large ($99 to $299) relative to the difference between the original stimulus values ($139 and $179), may in fact decrease, rather than increase, the impact of the attribute (e.g. Mellers & Cook, 1994).

Nowlis and Simonson's work is complementary to our research. Their findings corroborate most traditional choice–judgment preference reversal studies by showing that a difference in evaluation scale alone is sufficient to produce preference reversals. Their work further indicates that evaluation-scale-based preference reversals are different from JE/SE reversals and cannot be readily explained by the evaluability hypothesis. Nowlis and Simonson explained their results in terms of compatibility between type of response (choice versus rating) and type of attribute (comparative versus enriched). Their explanation is an extension of the compatibility principle (Slovic et al., 1990).

We conclude this section with two caveats. First, we have made a clear distinction between evaluation mode and evaluation scale and have shown that a JE/SE reversal can occur even if the evaluation scale is held constant. However, evaluation mode and evaluation scale are often naturally confounded in real-world decision making. When people are called on to decide which of two options to accept (i.e. a choice task), they are inevitably in the JE mode, comparing the two options side by side. In other words, choice is a special case of JE. On the other hand, when people consider how much they are willing to sell an item for, they are typically in the SE mode, focusing primarily on the target item alone (although they need not be). In this example, choice is confounded with JE, and pricing is confounded with SE. As a result, explanations for these reversals require a combination of the evaluability hypothesis and traditional theories for the evaluation scale effect, such as compatibility and prominence.

Second, the present article focuses only on one type of inconsistency between JE and SE—preference reversal. In a JE/SE reversal, the desirability of one option *relative* to the other changes between the evaluation modes. Hsee and Leclerc (1998) recently explored another type of JE/SE inconsistency where the desirability of *both* options changes between the evaluation modes, although their relative desirability remains unchanged, so there is no preference reversal. Specifically, they found that the desirability of low-quality products increased from SE to JE, whereas the desirability of high-quality products decreased from SE to JE. Those findings are not driven by differential attribute evaluability and are beyond the realm of this article (see Hsee & Leclerc, 1998, for details).

9.4. Implications of the Evaluability Hypothesis

Although the evaluability hypothesis is proposed originally to explain JE/SE reversals, it is potentially a more general theory. It describes how people make judgments and decisions when they do or do not have sufficient evaluability information. As such, the evaluability hypothesis has implications for phenomena beyond preference reversals. To illustrate, let us examine how this hypothesis explains why people are sometimes grossly insensitive to normatively important variables.

In a dramatic demonstration of this insensitivity, Desvousges et al. (1992; cited in Kahneman et al., in press) asked respondents how much they were willing to pay to save x number of migrating birds dying in uncovered oil ponds every year. x varied across different groups of respondents; it was either 2,000, 20,000, or 200,000. Normatively speaking, the number of bird deaths (x) should be an important determinant of respondents' WTP, but it had little effect. Mean WTP was about the same ($80, $78, and $88, respectively) for saving 2,000 birds, 20,000 birds, or 200,000 birds. This apparent anomalous result is highly consistent with the evaluability hypothesis. In the Desvousges et al. (1992) study, respondents had no evaluability information about bird death tolls, making this attribute extremely difficult to evaluate independently. According to the evaluability hypothesis, an attribute would have no power to differentiate the evaluations of the target options if the evaluators have no evaluability information about the attribute; the evaluation function in this condition resembles a flat line. That is why WTP values were virtually the same for the different bird-death conditions. This result is very similar to the finding in the no-information condition of the previously described score study, whereas ratings for the foreign student were virtually the same among the different score conditions.

Although it was not tested in the Desvousges et al. (1992) study, the evaluability hypothesis would predict that if the three bird-death conditions had been evaluated by the same group of participants in a JE mode, or if the respondents had received more evaluability information about endangered birds, then the bird death numbers would have had a greater effect on WTP. Consistent with this prediction, Frederick and Fischhoff (1998) observed much greater scale sensitivity in a within-subject study, in which respondents were asked to evaluate several goods that differed in scale, than in a between-subject design, in which different participants evaluated each of the goods.

The evaluability hypothesis can also explain why people in SE are often insensitive to variation in the value they are actually concerned about and sensitive only to variation in the proportion of that value to a certain base number. For example, suppose that there are two environmental protection programs:

Program J is designed to save birds in a forest where there are 50,000 endangered birds; it can save 20% of these birds.
Program S is designed to save birds in a forest where there are 5,000 endangered birds; it can save 80% of these birds.

Although Program J can save 10,000 birds (i.e. 20% × 50,000), whereas Program S can save only 4,000 birds (i.e. 80% × 5,000), chances are that Program S will be favored in SE. This example is a variant of Fetherstonhaugh, Slovic, Johnson, and Friedrich's (1997) finding that programs expected to save a given number of lives received greater support if the number of lives at risk was small than if it was large (see also Baron, 1997, and Jenni & Loewenstein, 1997, for similar results). Baron (1997) showed that the high sensitivity to relative (rather than absolute) risk was most pronounced in studies using a between-subject (SE) design and was mitigated in a study using a JE mode. This finding is consistent with the evaluability hypothesis.

Note that the structure of the options in the example above is parallel to that in the ice cream study. The actual number of birds the program can save is like the actual amount of ice cream; it is the main value of concern. The size of the forest is like the size of the cup; it is a base number. The proportion of birds a program can save is like the filling attribute; it reflects the relationship between the value of concern and the base number. As in the ice cream study, the evaluability hypothesis predicts that, in SE, Program S would be considered more favorably than Program J. The reason is simple: The actual value of concern—in this case, how many birds the program can save—is difficult to evaluate independently. In contrast, the proportion attribute—whether a program can save 20% or 80% of the birds in a forest—is relatively easy to evaluate; 20% seems small and 80% seems large.

Another finding that may be related to evaluability is the observation by Fox and Tversky (1995) that the ambiguity aversion effect (the tendency to prefer gambles with known probabilities to those with unknown probabilities) occurred only in JE and not in SE. Fox and Tversky interpreted their results as showing that ambiguity aversion is an inherently comparative phenomenon, a hypothesis they called comparative ignorance. However, their findings can also be explained in terms of evaluability. Like many other attributes reviewed earlier, whether a gamble is ambiguous or not may be easier to evaluate in JE than in SE. Fox and Tversky sought to demonstrate that the effect was specific to ambiguity by showing (in their Study 5) that such a reversal did not occur with two gambles that differed in their probability of winning rather than ambiguity (one had a high probability of winning and the other had a small probability of winning). However, this result is consistent with an evaluability interpretation because there is no reason to think that probability was particularly difficult to evaluate even in SE. Ambiguity aversion may, in fact, be an inherently comparative phenomenon, but it is only one of many attributes that receive greater weight in JE than in SE.

Marsh (1984) summarizes a variety of findings from Dr. Fox studies of student evaluation in which students gave higher teaching ratings to slick lecturers who presented little substance than to duller lecturers who covered material in depth. Marsh argues that the findings may reflect a process that is quite analogous to the evaluability hypothesis:

Finally, I would like to suggest a counter-explanation for some of the Dr. Fox findings.... Some instructor characteristics such as expressiveness and speech clarity can be judged in isolation because a frame of reference has probably been established through prior experience, and these characteristics do influence student ratings. For other characteristics such as content coverage, external frames of reference are not so well defined.... If students were asked to compare high and low content lectures... I predict that their responses would more accurately reflect the content manipulation. (1984, p. 745)

Let us conclude this article with a discussion of a rather meta-physical question: Which evaluation mode is better—joint or separate?

The long-standing advice for people to always consider the alternatives in decision making (e.g. Baron, 1988; Janis & Mann, 1977) implies that JE is always better than SE. However, we believe that the answer is not that simple. We agree that, in most cases, JE is better because it makes explicit the trade-offs underlying the options. This point is particularly evident if we consider the ice cream and the dinnerware studies (Hsee, 1998), where JE led to a preference for the objectively dominant option, and SE led to a preference for the objectively inferior option.

The idea that JE is better than SE is consistent with previous findings, showing that people often arrive at better decisions if they have considered alternatives than if they have not. For example, Frisch and Jones (1993) conducted a retrospective study in which participants reported a recent decision that resulted in either a very bad outcome or a very good outcome. Participants then responded to a battery of questions about the decision processes that had led to each of these decisions. Although acknowledging that good decisions can result in bad outcomes and vice versa, their study was premised on the idea that, on average, good decisions tend to result in better outcomes than do bad decisions. The single strongest difference in process between decisions that turned out well and decisions that turned out badly was whether participants had considered alternative courses of action before deciding.

However, JE is not unconditionally better than SE. In JE, people may be overly sensitive to the difference between the alternative options on a certain attribute, whereas this difference may not even be detectable in SE. If the ultimate consumption of an option is in the SE mode, then the preference elicited in JE may be inconsistent with one's actual consumption experience.

The preceding point has important implications for discrepancies between decision and experience utilities (e.g. Kahneman & Snell, 1990, 1992). It is probably not difficult for us to recall times when we decided to choose one option over another, but we ended up being unhappy with the option we chose and would probably be happier had we chosen the forgone option. Such decision–experience inconsistencies permeate consumer decisions, career decisions, and marital decisions, to name just a few. There have been a number of explanations for these inconsistencies, including, for example, changing tastes (March, 1978), inability to predict adaptation (Loewenstein & Frederick, 1997), differential arousal states (Loewenstein, 1996), and the prominence and the compatibility principles (Tversky & Griffin, 1991).

We believe that JE/SE reversals should be added to the list of important sources of discrepancies between decision utility and experience utility. At the time of the decision, an individual is typically exposed to all possible alternatives, and so the evaluation mode is JE. At the time of experiencing the consequence of the option one has chosen, the individual is usually in SE. For example, when a person buys a piano in a musical instrument store, there are typically myriad models for her to compare and choose from (JE). However, after she buys a piano, and when she uses it at home—that is, plays it, looks at it, etc., she is exposed mostly to that particular piano alone (SE). Just as different attributes have different relative impact in JE than in SE, so will these attributes have different relative impact in the decision phase than in the consumption phase.

To illustrate, consider an audio store that carries two models of loudspeakers of equal price. One model looks attractive and the other looks ugly. The ugly-looking model has a slightly lower distortion level and thus sounds slightly better. For most nonaudiophile consumers, the appearance of a

273

speaker is easy to evaluate independently, and its sound quality is not. The sound quality of a speaker can only be appreciated when it is compared directly with another speaker. When consumers are in the store and are making a purchase decision, they are typically in JE; they can easily compare one model against the other. Through the comparison, the difference in sound quality becomes salient. In this situation, many people may end up buying the better-sounding but ugly-looking model. However, once people have purchased a set of speakers and brought them home, they are usually in the SE mode; they enjoy (or suffer with) whatever they have bought and do not actively compare it with the forgone alternative. In SE, the difference in sound quality between the ugly and the attractive models may not make any difference in one's consumption experience, but the difference in appearance may. Thus, people who bought the ugly model may not enjoy its sound quality any more than those who bought the good-looking model, but the former group of consumers may be constantly bothered by the ugly appearance of the speakers they bought.[9] The moral of this example is that when making decisions, people may put too much weight on difficult-to-evaluate attributes and be too concerned with differences between options on those attributes that will make little or no difference in SE, hence little or no difference in actual consumption experience.

Shafir (in press) argues that the distinction between joint and separate evaluation has even wider implications. He proposes that guidelines and policies arise from joint evaluation of alternative scenarios, but events in the real world, to which these guidelines and policies are supposed to apply, usually present themselves one at a time. Because of inconsistencies between joint and separate evaluation, these guidelines and policies may not optimally serve these events in the real world.

In short, people make judgments and decisions in one of two primary evaluation modes—joint or separate. Our research shows that evaluations in these modes can yield inconsistent preferences. In addition, as just discussed, people do not always evaluate objects in the mode that is most likely to result in the best consumption experience. Which mode people use depends on whether they have a ready alternative with which to compare. When there is an available alternative option, people often naturally engage in JE. When no

---

[9] Two qualifications about this example: First, sometimes people may also find themselves in JE during the consumption phase, when, for example, their neighbor happens to have bought the alternative model and they can easily compare theirs with their neighbor's. However, we believe that in most circumstances, the evaluation mode at the consumption phase is much closer to the SE end on the JE-SE continuum than is the evaluation mode at the purchase phase. Second, our analysis here applies mainly to decisions whose main purpose is to optimize consumption experience. However, sometimes the decision maker has other goals in mind, and/or the construct of consumption experience does not capture the whole scope of costs and benefits of an option. Under those circumstances, our analysis may not apply.

alternatives are present, people do not automatically think of alternatives (e.g. Gettys, Pliske, Manning, & Casey, 1987; Legrenzi, Girotto, & Johnson-Laird, 1993), and they engage in SE. Which mode is better for the consumer is a different issue. It depends on the goal people intend to achieve through the decision. If the goal is to choose the objectively most valuable option, then JE is probably better. If the goal is to choose the option that will optimize one's consumption experience, and if consumption takes place in SE, then SE may prove better.

References

Allais, P. M. (1953). The behavior of rational man in risk situations—A critique of the axioms and postulates of the American School. *Econometrica, 21,* 503–546.

Ariely, D. (1998). Combining experiences over time: The effects of duration, intensity changes and on-papers line measurements on retrospective pain evaluation. *Journal of Behavioral Decision Making, 11,* 19–45.

Baron, J. (1988). *Thinking and deciding.* New York: Cambridge University Press.

Baron, J. (1997). Confusion of relative and absolute risk in valuation. *Journal of Risk and Uncertainty, 14,* 301–309.

Bazerman, M. H., Loewenstein, G. F., & White, S. B. (1992). Reversals of preference in allocation decisions: Judging an alternative versus choosing among alternatives. *Administrative Science Quarterly, 37,* 220–240.

Bazerman, M. H., Schroth, H. A., Shah, P. P., Diekmann, K. A., & Tenbrunsel, A. E. (1994). The inconsistent role of comparison others and procedural justice in reactions to hypothetical job descriptions: Implications for job acceptance decisions. *Organizational Behavior and Human Decision Processes, 60,* 326–352.

Bazerman, M. H., Tenbrunsel, A., & Wade-Benzoni, K. (1998). Negotiating with yourself and losing: Understanding and managing competing internal preferences. *Academy of Management Review, 23,* 225–241.

Beattie, J., & Baron, J. (1991). Investigating the effect of stimulus range on attribute. *Journal of Experimental Psychology: Human Perception and Performance, 17,* 571–585.

Bimbaum, M. H. (1992). Issues in utility measurement. *Organizational Behavior and Human Decision Processes, 52,* 319–330.

Blount, S., & Bazerman, M. H. (1996). The inconsistent evaluation of absolute versus comparative payoffs in labor supply and bargaining. *Journal of Economic Behavior & Organization, 30,* 227–240.

Coupey, E., Irwin, J. R., & Payne, J. W. (1998). Product category familiarity and preference construction. *Journal of Consumer Research, 24,* 459–467.

Coursey, D. L., Hovis, J. J., & Schulze, W. D. (1987). The disparity between willingness to accept and willing to pay measures of value. *Quarterly Journal of Economics, 102,* 679–690.

Desvousges, W., Johnson, R., Dunford, R., Boyle, K. J., Hudson, S., & Wilson, K. N. (1992). Measuring non-use damages using contingent valuation: An experimental evaluation accuracy. *Research Triangle Institute Monograph, 92–1.*

Fetherstonhaugh, D., Slovic, P., Johnson, S. M., & Friedrich, J. (1997). Insensitivity to the value of human life: A study of psychophysical numbing. *Journal of Risk and Uncertainty, 14*, 283–300.

Fischer, G. W., Damodaran, N., Laskey, K. B., & Lincoln, D. (1987). Preferences for proxy attributes. *Management Science, 33*, 198–214.

Fischer, G. W., & Hawkins, S. A. (1993). Strategy compatibility, scale compatibility, and the prominence effect. *Journal of Experimental Psychology: Human Perception and and Performance, 19*, 580–597.

Fox, C. R., & Tversky, A. (1995). Ambiguity aversion and comparative ignorance. *The Quarterly Journal of Economics, 110*, 585–603.

Frederick, S., & Fischoff, B. (1998). Scope (in)sensitivity in elicited valuations. *Risk Decision and Policy, 3*, 109–123.

Frisch, D., & Jones, S. K. (1993). Assessing the accuracy of decisions. *Theory and Psychology, 3*, 115–135.

Gettys, C. F., Pliske, R. M., Manning, C., & Casey, J. T. (1987). An evaluation of human act generation performance. *Organizational Behavior and Human Decision Processes, 39*, 23–51.

Goldstein, W. M., & Einhorn, H. J. (1987). Expression theory and the preference reversal phenomena. *Psychological Review, 94*, 236–254.

Grether, D. M., & Plott, C. R. (1979). Economic theory of choice and the preference reversal phenomenon. *American Economic Review, 69*, 623–638.

Hsee, C. K. (1993). *When trend of monetary outcomes matters: Separate versus joint evaluation and judgment of feelings versus choice.* Unpublished manuscript, The University of Chicago.

Hsee, C. K. (1995). Elastic justification: How tempting but task-irrelevant factors influence decisions. *Organizational Behavioral and Human Decision Process, 62*, 330–337.

Hsee, C. K. (1996a). The evaluability hypothesis: An explanation of preference reversals between joint and separate evaluations of alternatives. *Organizational Behavior and Human Decision Processes, 46*, 247–257.

Hsee, C. K. (1996b). Elastic justification: How unjustifiable factors influence judgments. *Organizational Behavior and Human Decision Processes, 66*, 122–129.

Hsee, C. K. (1998). Less is better: When low-value options are valued more highly than high-value options. *Journal of Behavioral Decision Making, 11*, 107–121.

Hsee, C. K., & Abelson, R. P. (1991). The velocity relation: Satisfaction as a function of the first derivative of outcome over time. *Journal of Personality and Social Psychology, 60*, 341–347.

Hsee, C. K., & Leclerc, F. (1998). Will products look more attractive when evaluated jointly or when evaluated separately? *Journal of Consumer Research, 25*, 175–186.

Hsee, C. K., Salovey, P., & Abelson, R. P. (1994). The quasi-acceleration relation: Satisfaction as a function of the change in velocity of outcome over time. *Journal of Experimental Social Psychology, 30*, 96–111.

Irwin, J. R. (1994). Buying/selling price preference reversals: Preference for environmental changes in buying versus selling modes. *Organizational Behavior and Human Decision Processes, 60*, 431–457.

Irwin, J. R. Slovic, P., Lichtenstein, S., & McClelland, G. H. (1993). Preference reversals and the measurement of environmental values. *Journal of Risk and Uncertainty, 6,* 5–18.

Janis, I. L., & Mann, L. (1977). *Decision making: A psychological analysis of conflict, choice, and commitment.* New York: Free Press.

Jenni, K., & Loewenstein, G. (1997). Explaining the "identifiable victim effect." *Journal of Risk and Uncertainty, 14,* 235–257.

Kahneman, D., Fredrickson, B. L., Schreiber, C. A., & Redelmeier, D. A. (1993). When more pain is preferred to less: Adding a better end. *Psychological Science, 4,* 401–405.

Kahneman, D., Knetsch, J. L., & Thaler, R. H. (1990). Experimental tests of the endowment effect and the Coase theorem. *Journal of Political Economy, 98,* 1325–1348.

Kahneman, D., & Miller, D. T. (1986). Norm theory: Comparing reality with its alternatives. *Psychological Review, 93,* 136–153.

Kahneman, D., & Ritov, I. (1994). Determinants of stated willingness to pay for public goods: A study in the headline method. *Journal of Risk and Uncertainty, 9,* 5–38.

Kahneman, D., Ritov, I., & Schkade, D. (in press). Economists have preferences; psychologists have attitudes: An analysis of dollar responses to public issues. In D. Kahneman & A. Tversky (Eds.), *Choices, values and frames.* New York: Cambridge University Press.

Kahneman, D., & Snell, J. (1990). Predicting utility. In R. M. Hogarth (Ed.), *Insights in decision making* (pp. 295–311). Chicago: University of Chicago Press.

Kahneman, D., & Snell, J. (1992). Predicting a changing taste: Do people know what they will like? *Journal of Behavioral Decision Making, 5,* 187–200.

Knetsch, J. L., & Sinden, J. A. (1984). Willingness to pay and compensation demanded—Experimental evidence of an unexpected disparity in measures of value. *Quarterly Journal of Economics, 99,* 507–521.

Legrenzi, P., Girotto, V., & Johnson-Laird, P. N. (1993). Focusing in reasoning and decision making. *Cognition, 49,* 37–66.

Lichtenstein, S., & Slovic, P. (1971). Reversal of preferences between bids and choices in gambling decisions. *Journal of Experimental Psychology, 89,* 46–55.

Loewenstein, G. (1996). Out of control: Visceral influences on behavior. *Organizational Behavior and Human Decision Processes, 65,* 272–292.

Loewenstein, G., Blount, S., & Bazerman, M. H. (1993). *Reversals of Preference Between Independent and Simultaneous Evaluation of Alternatives.* Unpublished manuscript, Carnegie Mellon University, Pittsburgh, Pennsylvania.

Loewenstein, G., & Frederick, S. (1997). Predicting reactions to environmental change. In M. Bazerman, D. Messick, A. Tenbrunsel, & K. Wade-Benzoni (Eds.), *Psychological perspectives on the environment.* San Francisco: New Lexington Press.

Loewenstein, G., & Prelec, D. (1993). Preferences for sequences of outcomes. *Psychological Review, 100,* 91–108.

Loewenstein, G., & Sicherman, N. (1991). Do workers prefer increasing wage profile? *Journal of Labor Economics, 9,* 67–84.

Lowenthal, D. (1993). *Preference reversals in candidate evaluation.* Working paper. Carnegie Mellon University, Pittsburgh, Pennsylvania.

March, J. (1978). Bounded rationality, ambiguity and the engineering of choice. *Bell Journal of Economics, 9,* 587–608.

Marsh, H. W. (1984). Students' evaluations of university teaching: Dimensionality, reliability, validity, potential biases, and utility. *Journal of Educational Psychology, 76,* 707–754.

May, K. O. (1954). Intransitivity, utility and the aggregation of preference patterns. *Econometrica, 22,* 1–13.

Mellers, B. A., Chang, S., Birnbaum, M. H., & Ordonez, L. D. (1992). Preferences, prices and ratings in risky decision making. *Journal of Experimental Psychology: Human Perception and Performance, 18,* 347–361.

Mellers, B. A., & Cook, D. J. (1994). Tradeoffs depend on attribute range. *Journal of Experimental Psychology: Human Perception and Performance, 20,* 1055–1067.

Mellers, B. A., Ordonez, L. D., & Birnbaum, M. H. (1992). A change-of-process theory for contextual effects and preference reversals in risky decision making. *Organizational Behavior and Human Decision Processes, 52,* 331–369.

Nowlis, S. M., & Simonson, I. (1994). *The context-dependency of attributes as a determinant of preference reversals between choices and judgments of purchase likelihood.* Working paper. Stanford University, Palo Alto, California.

Nowlis, S. M., & Simonson, I. (1997). Attribute-task compatibility as a determinant of consumer preference reversals. *Journal of Marketing Research, 34,* 205–218.

Payne, J. W., Bettman, J. R., & Johnson, E. J. (1992). Behavioral decision research: A constructive processing perspective. *Annual Review of Psychology, 43,* 87–131.

Russo, J. E., & Dosher, B. A. (1983). Strategies for multiattribute binary choice. *Journal of Experimental Psychology: Learning, Memory, and Cognition, 9,* 676–696.

Schkade, D. A., & Johnson, E. J. (1989). Cognitive processes in preference reversals. *Organizational Behavior and Human Decision Processes, 44,* 203–231.

Shafir, E. (1993). Choosing versus rejecting: Why some options are both better and worse than others. *Memory & Cognition, 21,* 546–556.

Shafir, E. (in press). Cognition, intuition and policy guidelines. In R. Gowda & J. Fox (Eds.), *Judgments, decisions and public policy.* New York: Cambridge University Press.

Slovic, P., Griffin, D., & Tversky, A. (1990). Compatibility effects in judgment and choice. In R. M. Hogarth (Ed.), *Insights in decision making: Theory and applications* (pp. 5–27). Chicago: University of Chicago.

Tversky, A. (1969). Intransitivity of preferences. *Psychological Review, 76,* 31–48.

Tversky, A., & Griffin, D. (1991). Endowment and contrast in judgments of well-being. In F. Strack, M. Argyle, & N. Schwartz (Eds.), *Subjective well-being: An Interdisciplinary perspective* (Vol. 21, pp. 101–118). Oxford, England: Pergamon Press.

Tversky, A., Sattath, S., & Slovic, P. (1988). Contingent weighting in judgment and choice. *Psychological Review, 95,* 371–384.

10

"Coherent Arbitrariness": Stable Demand Curves without Stable Preferences

Dan Ariely, George Loewenstein, and Drazen Prelec

Months into this project, I suddenly realized that I had been studying coherent arbitrariness starting with the very first study I ever ran—a survey I did of students in the Yale library (see Chapter 14). In that study I asked the students to specify the most they would pay to receive a kiss from the movie star of their choice at various points in time. Suppose that the idea of a kiss from the movie star of your choice is appealing (as seems to be almost universally true of men but much less consistently for women). How much should you be willing to pay for such a kiss? Three dollars?; after all, it only lasts a very short time. But it could be a very fulfilling short time. Ten dollars? One hundred? Think of what an amazingly unique and unusual experience it would be— something you would no doubt remember for the remainder of your life. One thousand? Ten thousand? For me, the answer is indeterminate within several orders of magnitude.

However, suppose you were forced to come up with an amount, however arbitrary, and you somehow decided that $100 was the right amount to pay for a kiss from Michelle Pfeiffer. Now, you are asked how much you would pay for the kiss if it were delayed by one week ($90), or if it were two kisses instead of one ($210) or a kiss from your second-most-preferred movie star ($30). Although you may have incredibly ill-defined preferences when it comes to the simple kiss, as I do, if you are asked subsequent questions that modify the kiss in various ways, you are likely to provide answers that seem very reasonable relative to your initial answer, and this reasonableness is likely to disguise the underlying uncertainty of your original response.

This is the basic insight of the paper. Economists generally assume that people have well-defined preferences, but this is obviously a heroic simplification of reality. It may not be surprising that our preferences will not be well defined for things we have yet to experience, but uncertainty can persist even after considerable experience. The most ambiguous experiences I know of are family vacations, which typically involve a string of miserable events, such as waking up early to catch a plane and dealing with complaining kids, but also, hopefully, some beautiful events such as seeing wonderful sights or connecting with the kids in a way that often doesn't happen at home. Overall, is a vacation a good thing or a bad thing? I believe that many people would find it difficult to assess whether the pleasures adequately compensate for the pains. Perhaps it is because they are becoming more rational, rather than insecure about their jobs, that more and more Americans aren't taking the full amount of vacation times to which their jobs entitle them.

Despite my lousy memory, I have a vivid memory of the genesis of this project. Once again, it was hatched at the Center for Advanced Study in the Behavioral Sciences (see Chapter 1). On the day when we cooked up the project, Drazen and I were sitting on the bench outside my office with Dan Ariely, who was visiting us for the month. Dan and I had been doing research on preferences toward sequences of outcomes (see Chapters 16 and 17), in which we had been blasting people with unpleasant noises over headphones. But we were getting somewhat tired of the topic. I'm not really sure how the idea emerged from our conversation, but I do know that by the end of the conversation we had not only come up with the basic idea, but actually planned out several of the experiments that we report in the paper. Academic ferment as it's supposed to happen.

Unfortunately, the paper also generated the opposite. The idea is very close to a wide range of other ideas, including joint–separate preference reversals, and somehow an incredible number of people ended up conveying to us, usually gently, that they felt ripped off. The biggest potential for a train wreck was when David Schkade and I attended the same meeting a few years later where I presented the first experiments and Schkade reported that he and Daniel Kahneman were exploring the implications for law of a strikingly similar phenomenon, which they had labeled "coherently arbitrary judgments." There was some talk of joining forces, but in the end we decided to move forward in parallel. Ultimately, they published their piece in law, and we published ours in economics, in the same year. Thankfully, judging from the lack of interruption of Schkade's annual Christmastime box of homemade chocolates, the competition doesn't seem to have created hard feelings.

While on the topic of coherent arbitrariness, I should mention another paper that did not make it into this book. Coauthored with my former graduate student Uri Simonsohn and published in *Economic Journal*, the paper is titled "Mistake #37: The Effect of Previously Faced Prices on Current Housing Demand." The paper applies insights from the coherent arbitrariness paper to an important economic domain: housing.

Housing is especially important at present because there is widely perceived to be a bubble in the American housing market (as well as in some markets elsewhere). One of the necessary ingredients of a bubble is that there be some uncertainty about the *correct* price for the item/commodity exhibiting the bubble. Thus, one of the central messages of this paper, that housing prices have a large arbitrary component, may shed some light on how housing bubbles can occur.

Like most of my papers (with Chapter 18 as a notable exception), the Mistake #37 paper had an autobiographical component. The "mistake" in the title is one I made myself, though, consistent with coherent arbitrariness, I'm not sure it actually *was* a mistake. After returning from the year in California, we sold our small house in Pittsburgh and bought a much larger one. During the year in California, we lived in a wonderful but dilapidated house in Menlo Park during what we now know was only the early stages of the housing boom there. Since the housing boom (and the stock-market boom that helped finance it) was all anyone seemed to talk about that year, it was impossible not to notice that houses down the street that were often little more than converted garages—were selling for prices in the million-dollar range. When we got back to Pittsburgh, we realized that we could buy a mansion for less than half of what a converted garage would cost in Menlo Park. So we did.

Mistake #37 refers to one of the "106 Common Mistakes Homebuyers Make," which is the title of a book by Gary Eldred (2002). Eldred's description of the mistake (and how to avoid it) is, "when moving from a high-cost area to a low-cost area, recalibrate your sights...put the home prices of Boston and San Francisco out of your mind." In the paper, we show that both homebuyers and homerenters do not, in fact, follow Eldred's advice. People moving from more expensive areas tend to rent and purchase more expensive residences than those moving to the same place from less expensive areas, even after controlling for all sorts of plausible confounding variables, such as differences in wealth and tastes. As I discovered firsthand, housing in Pittsburgh seems incredibly cheap when you move from San Francisco, and, as the executives at Costco understand well, when something is a deal, it's tempting to buy a lot of it.

"Coherent Arbitrariness": Stable Demand Curves without Stable Preferences*

Dan Ariely, George Loewenstein, and Drazen Prelec

Economic theories of valuation generally assume that prices of commodities and assets are derived from underlying "fundamental" values. For example, in finance theory, asset prices are believed to reflect the market estimate of the discounted present value of the asset's payoff stream. In labor theory, the supply of labor is established by the trade-off between the desire for consumption and the displeasure of work. Finally, and most importantly for this paper, consumer microeconomics assumes that the demand curves for consumer products—chocolates, CDs, movies, vacations, drugs, etc.—can be ultimately traced to the valuation of pleasures that consumers anticipate receiving from these products.

Because it is difficult, as a rule, to measure fundamental values directly, empirical tests of economic theory typically examine whether the effects of *changes* in circumstances on valuations are consistent with theoretical prediction—for example, whether labor supply responds appropriately to a change in the wage rate, whether (compensated) demand curves for commodities are downward sloping, or whether stock prices respond in the predicted way to share repurchases. However, such "comparative static" relationships are a necessary but not sufficient condition for fundamental valuation (e.g. Summers [1986]). Becker [1962] was perhaps the first to make this

* We thank Colin Camerer, Shane Frederick, John Lynch, James Bettman, and Birger Wernerfelt for helpful comments and suggestions. We are also grateful for financial support to Ariely and Prelec from the Sloan School of Management, to Loewenstein from the Integrated Study of the Human Dimensions of Global Change at Carnegie Mellon University (NSF grant No. SBR-9521914), and to Loewenstein and Prelec from the Center for Advanced Study in the Behavioral Sciences (NSF grant No. SBR-960123 to the Center, 1996–1997).

This chapter was originally published as Ariely, D., Loewenstein, G., and Prelec, D. (2003) "Coherent Arbitrariness: Stable Demand Curves without Stable Preferences". The Quarterly Journal of Economics, 118(1): 73–105. © 2003 by the President and Fellows of Harvard College and the Massachusetts Institute of Technology.

point explicitly when he observed that consumers choosing commodity bundles randomly from their budget set would nevertheless produce downward sloping demand curves.

In spite of this ambiguity in the interpretation of demand curves, the intuition that prices must in some way derive from fundamental values is still strongly entrenched. Psychological evidence that preferences can be manipulated by normatively irrelevant factors, such as option "framing," changes in the "choice context," or the presence of prior cues or "anchors," is often rationalized by appealing to consumers' lack of information about the options at stake and the weak incentives operating in the experimental setting. From the standpoint of economic theory, it is easy to admit that consumers might not be very good at predicting the pleasures and pains produced by a purchase, especially if the purchase option is complex and the choice hypothetical. It is harder to accept that consumers might have difficulty establishing how much they value each individual bit of pleasure or pain in a situation where they can experience the full extent of this pleasure or pain just before the pricing decision.

In this paper we show that consumers' absolute valuation of experience goods is surprisingly arbitrary, even under "full information" conditions. However, we also show that consumers' *relative* valuations of different amounts of the good appear orderly, as if supported by demand curves derived from fundamental preferences. Valuations therefore display a combination of arbitrariness and coherence that we refer to as "coherent arbitrariness."

Our findings are consistent with an account of revealed preference which posits that valuations are initially malleable but become "imprinted" (i.e. precisely defined and largely invariant), after the individual is called upon to make an initial decision.[1] Prior to imprinting, valuations have a large arbitrary component, meaning that they are highly responsive to both normative and nonnormative influences. Following imprinting, valuations become locally coherent, as the consumer attempts to reconcile future decisions of a "similar kind" with the initial one. This creates an illusion of order, because consumers' coherent responses to subsequent *changes* in conditions disguise the arbitrary nature of the initial, foundational, choice.

10.1. Experiment 1: Coherently Arbitrary Valuation of Ordinary Products

Our experiments take an old trick from the experimental psychologists' arsenal—the anchoring manipulation—and use it to influence valuation of

---

[1] The idea that preferences are not well defined, but become articulated in the process of making a decision is consistent with a large body of research on what decision researchers refer to as "constructed preferences" (e.g. Slovic [1995] and Hoeffler and Ariely [1999]).

products and hedonic experiences with normatively irrelevant factors. In a famous early demonstration of anchoring, Tversky and Kahneman [1974] spun a wheel of fortune with numbers that ranged from 0 to 100, asked subjects whether the number of African nations in the United Nations was greater than or less than that number, and then instructed subjects to estimate the actual figure. Estimates were significantly related to the number spun on the wheel (the "anchor"), even though subjects could clearly see that the number had been generated by a purely chance process.[2] This, and many other anchoring studies seemed to show that people lack preexisting subjective probability distributions over unknown quantities.

The vast majority of anchoring experiments in the psychological literature have focused on how anchoring corrupts subjective judgment, not subjective valuation or preference. Because valuation typically involves judgment, however, it is not surprising that valuation, too, can be moved up or down by the anchoring manipulation. Johnson and Schkade [1989] were the first to demonstrate this experimentally. They showed that asking subjects whether their certainty equivalent for a lottery is above or below an anchor value influences subsequently stated certainty equivalents. Green, Jacowitz, Kahneman, and McFadden [1998], and Kahneman and Knetsch [1993], found the same effect with judgments of willingness-to-pay for public goods; higher values in the initial Yes/No question led to higher subsequent willingness-to-pay.

Our first experiment replicates these results with ordinary consumer products. The first class meeting of a market research course in the Sloan School MBA program provided the setting for the study. Fifty-five students were shown six products (computer accessories, wine bottles, luxury chocolates, and books), which were briefly described without mentioning market price. The average retail price of the items was about $70. After introducing the products, subjects were asked whether they would buy each good for a dollar figure equal to the last two digits of their social security number. After this Accept/Reject response, they stated their dollar maximum willingness-to-pay (WTP) for the product. A random device determined whether the product would in fact be sold on the basis of the first, Accept/Reject response, or the second, WTP response (via the incentive-compatible Becker-Degroot-Marschak procedure [1963]). Subjects understood that both their Accept/Reject response and their WTP response had some chance of being decisive for the purchase, and that they were eligible to purchase at most one product.

In spite of the realism of the products and transaction, the impact of the social security number on stated WTP was significant in every product category. Subjects with above-median social security numbers stated values

---

[2] For recent studies of anchoring, see, e.g., Chapman and Johnson [1999], Jacowitz and Kahneman [1995], Strack and Mussweiler [1997] and Epley and Gilovitch [2001].

Table I. Average Stated Willingness-to-Pay Sorted by Quintile of the Sample's Social Security Number Distribution

Quintile of SS# distribution	Cordless trackball	Cordless keyboard	Average wine	Rare wine	Design book	Belgian chocolates
1	$8.64	$16.09	$8.64	$11.73	$12.82	$9.55
2	$11.82	$26.82	$14.45	$22.45	$16.18	$10.64
3	$13.45	$29.27	$12.55	$18.09	$15.82	$12.45
4	$21.18	$34.55	$15.45	$24.55	$19.27	$13.27
5	$26.18	$55.64	$27.91	$37.55	$30.00	$20.64
Correlations	.415	.516	0.328	.328	0.319	.419
	$p = .0015$	$p < .0001$	$p = .014$	$p = .0153$	$p = .0172$	$p = .0013$

The last row indicates the correlations between Social Security numbers and WTP (and their significance levels).

from 57 percent to 107 percent greater than did subjects with below-median numbers. The effect is even more striking when examining the valuations by quintiles of the social security number distribution, as shown in Table I. The valuations of the top quintile subjects were typically greater by a factor of *three*. For example, subjects with social security numbers in the top quintile were willing to pay $56 on average for a cordless computer keyboard, compared with $16 on average for subjects with bottom quintile numbers. Evidently, these subjects did not have, or were unable to retrieve personal values for ordinary products.

Alongside this volatility of absolute preference we also observed a marked stability of relative preference. For example, the vast majority of subjects (>95 percent) valued a cordless keyboard more than a trackball, and the highly rated wine more than the lower-rated wine. Subjects, it seems, did not know how much they valued these items, but they did know the relative ordering within the categories of wine and computer accessories.

10.2. Coherent Arbitrariness

The sensitivity of WTP to anchors suggests that consumers do not arrive at a choice or at a pricing task with an inventory of preexisting preferences and probability distributions, which is consistent with a great deal of other psychological evidence [Kahneman and Miller 1986; Payne, Bettman, and Johnson 1993; Drolet, Simonson, and Tversky 2000]. Rather than specific WTP values for products, consumers probably have some range of acceptable values. If a give-or-take price for a product falls outside this range, then the purchase decision is straightforward: "Don't Buy" if the price is above the range, and "Buy" if the price is below the range. But, what if the stated price falls within the WTP range, so that the range does not determine the decision, one way or the other? We do not know much about how a choice in such a case might be made. We do know that if the situation demands a choice, then the person will in fact choose, i.e. will either purchase or not purchase. We assume that this "foundational" choice then becomes a part of that person's stock of decisional precedents, ready to be invoked the next time a similar choice situation arises [Gilboa and Schmeidler 1995].

To relate this discussion to our actual experiment, suppose that a subject with a social security number ending with 25 has an a priori WTP range of $5 to $30 for wine described as "average," and $10 to $50 for the "rare" wine. Both wines, therefore, might or might not be purchased for the $25 price. Suppose that the subject indicates, for whatever reason, that she would be willing to purchase the average bottle for $25. If we were to ask her a moment later whether she would be willing to purchase the "rare" bottle for $25, the answer would obviously be "yes," because from her perspective this particular "choice problem" has been solved and its solution is known: if an average wine is worth at least $25, then a rare wine must be worth more than $25! Moreover, when the subject is subsequently asked to provide WTP values for the wines, then that problem, too, is now substantially constrained: the prices will have to be ordered so that both prices are above $25 and the rare wine is valued more.

There are many psychological details that we are not specifying. We do not say much about how the choice is made if the price falls within the range, nor do we propose a psychological mechanism for the anchoring effect itself. There are several psychological accounts of anchoring, and for our purposes it is not necessary to decide between them [Epley and Gilovich 2001; Mussweiler and Strack 2001]. The substantive claims we do make are the following: first, in situations in which valuations are not constrained by prior precedents, choices will be highly sensitive to normatively irrelevant influences and considerations such as anchoring. Second, because decisions at the earlier stages are used as inputs for future decisions, an initial choice will exert a normatively inappropriate influence over subsequent choices and values. Third, if we look at a series of choices by a single individual, they will exhibit an orderly pattern (coherence) with respect to numerical parameters like price, quantity, quality, and so on.[3]

---

[3] Another research literature, on "evaluability," is also relevant here. "Evaluability" has been identified as the cause of preference reversals that arise when options are evaluated either jointly (within subject) or separately (between subject). Hsee, Loewenstein, Blount, and Bazerman [1999] explain these reversals by assuming that it is more difficult to evaluate some attributes separately than jointly, depending on whether the attributes have well-established standards. For example, subjects in one study were asked to assess two political candidates, one who would bring 1000 jobs to the district and the other who would bring 5000 jobs to the district but had a DUI conviction. When the candidates were evaluated separately, the first candidate was judged more favorably, presumably because the employment figure was hard to evaluate. However, when the candidates were compared side-by-side, people indicated that

Behaviorally then, consumers in the marketplace may largely obey the axioms of revealed preference; indeed, according to this account, a person who remembered all previous choices and accepted the transitivity axiom would never violate transitivity. However, we cannot infer from this that these choices reveal true preferences. Transitivity may only reflect the fact that consumers *remember* earlier choices and make subsequent choices in a fashion that is consistent with them, not that these choices are generated from preexisting preferences.

10.3. Valuation of Novel Pain Experiences

If preferences and valuations at a moment in time are largely inferences that a person draws from the history of his or her own previous decisions, a natural question that arises is whether the inference has a narrow scope (restricted only to very similar previous choices) or whether the scope is more general. For example, if I go on record as being willing to pay $25 for a wine, will that only influence my subsequent willingness-to-pay for wine, for a broader range of items or experiences, or even for pleasures generally? The broader the scope of inferences, the more will previous choices constrain any future choice. If purchases of specific products and services function as precedents not just for those same items but also for the general valuation of pleasure (including here the avoidance of discomfort), then an adult consumer should have accumulated an inventory of previous choices sufficient to stabilize his or her dollar valuation of hedonic experiences.

In the next five experiments, we address the question of whether consumers do indeed enter the laboratory with a stable, preexisting valuation of pleasure and pain. In each experiment, subjects stated their willingness to accept (WTA) pains of different durations (induced by a loud noise played over headphones)—in exchange for payment. Subjects were initially exposed to a sample of the noise, and then asked whether—hypothetically—they would be willing to experience the same noise again in exchange for a payment of magnitude X (with X varied across subjects). Their actual WTAs were then elicited for different noise durations.

We used this artificial hedonic "product" for several reasons. First, we were able to provide subjects with a sample of the experience before they made subsequent decisions about whether to experience it again in exchange for payment. They therefore entered the pricing phase of the experiment with full information about the experience they were pricing. Second, we wanted to avoid a situation in which subjects could solve the pricing problem

the employment difference more than compensated for the DUI conviction, and gave their preference to the second candidate.

intellectually, without drawing on their own sensory experience. Annoying sounds have no clear market price, so our subjects could not refer to similar decisions made outside the laboratory as a basis for their valuations. Third, we wanted to make the money stakes in this decision comparable to the stakes in routine consumer expenditures. The plausible range of values for avoiding the annoying sounds in our experiments ranges from a few cents, to several dollars. Fourth, with annoying sounds it is possible to re-create the same hedonic experience repeatedly, permitting an experiment with repeated trials. Prior research shows that with annoying sounds, unlike many other types of pleasures and pains, there is little or no satiation or sensitization to repeated presentations of annoying sounds [Ariely and Zauberman 2000].

10.4. Experiment 2: Coherently Arbitrary Valuation of Pain

The goal of Experiment 2 was to test (1) whether valuation of annoying sounds was susceptible to an anchoring manipulation; (2) whether additional experience with the sounds would erode the influence of the anchor; and (3) whether valuation would be sensitive to a within-subject manipulation of the duration of the annoying sound, thus demonstrating coherence with respect to this attribute.

One hundred and thirty-two students from the Massachusetts Institute of Technology participated in the experiment. Approximately half were undergraduates, and the rest were MBA students or, in a few cases, recruiters from large investment banks. Subjects were randomly assigned to six experimental conditions. The experiment lasted about 25 minutes, and subjects were paid according to their performance as described below.

At the beginning of the experiment, all subjects listened to an annoying, 30-second sound, delivered through headphones. The sound was a high-pitched scream (a triangular wave with frequency of 3,000 Hz), similar to the broadcasting warning signal.

The main experimental manipulation was the anchor price, which was manipulated between-subject at three levels: an anchor price of 10¢ (**low-anchor**), and anchor price of 50¢ (**high-anchor**), and no anchor (**no-anchor**). Subjects in the low-anchor [high-anchor] condition first encountered a screen that read:[4]

In a few moments we are going to play you a new unpleasant tone over your headset. We are interested in how annoying you find it to be. Immediately after you hear the tone, we are going to ask you whether you would be willing to repeat the same experience in exchange for a payment of 10¢ [50¢].

---

[4] In a different study [Ariely, Loewenstein, and Prelec 2002] we tested whether the order in which subjects received the sample and the anchor made a difference. It did not.

Subjects in the no-anchor condition listened to the sound but were not given any external price and were not asked to answer any hypothetical question.

Before the main part of the experiment started, subjects were told that they would be asked to indicate the amount of payment they required to listen to sounds that differed in duration but were identical in quality and intensity to the one they had just heard. Subjects were further told that on each trial the computer would randomly pick a price from a given price distribution. If the computer's price was higher than their price, the subject would hear the sound and also receive a payment corresponding to the price that the computer had randomly drawn. If the computer's price was lower than their price, they would neither hear the sound nor receive payment for that trial. Subjects were told that this procedure ensured that the best strategy is to pick the minimum price for which they would be willing to listen to the sound, not a few pennies more and not a few pennies less. The prices picked by the computer were drawn from a triangle-distribution ranging from 5¢ to 100¢, with the lower numbers being more frequent than the higher numbers. The distribution was displayed on the screen for subjects to study and, importantly, the distribution was the same for all subjects.

After learning about the procedure, subjects engaged in a sequence of nine trials. On each trial, they were informed of the duration of the sound they were valuing (10, 30, or 60 seconds) and were asked to indicate their WTA for the sound. The three durations were presented either in an increasing (10 seconds, 30 seconds, 60 seconds) or decreasing order (60 seconds, 30 seconds, 10 seconds). In both cases, each ordered sequence repeated itself three times, one after the other. After each WTA entry, the computer asked subjects whether they were willing to experience the sound for that price minus 5¢, and whether they would experience it for that price plus 5¢. If subjects did not answer "no" to the first question and "yes" to the second, the computer drew their attention to the fact that their WTA was not consistent with their responses, and asked to them to reconsider their WTA price.

After finalizing a WTA value, subjects were shown their price along with the random price drawn from the distribution. If the price specified by the subject was higher than the computer's price, the subject did not receive any payment for that trial and continued directly to the next trial. If the price set by the subject was lower than the computer's price, the subject heard the sound over the headphones, was reminded that the payment for the trial would be given to them at the end of the experiment, and then continued to the next trial. At the end of the nine trials, all subjects were paid according to the payment rule.

Results. A set of simple effect comparisons revealed that average WTA in the high-anchor condition [$M = 59.60$] was significantly higher than average WTA in either the low-anchor condition [$M = 39.82$; $F(1,126) = 19.25$, $p < 0.001$] or the no-anchor condition [$M = 43.87$; $F(1,126) = 12.17$, $p < 0.001$].[5] WTA in the low-anchor condition was not significantly different from WTA in the no-anchor condition [$p = 0.37$]. Because subjects in the high-anchor condition specified higher WTAs, they naturally listened to fewer sounds [$M = 2.8$] than subjects in the low-anchor and no-anchor conditions [$Ms = $ 4.5 and 4.1; $F(1,126) = 14.26$, $p < 0.001$]. High-anchor subjects also earned significantly less money on average [$M = \$1.53$] than those in the no-anchor condition and the low-anchor condition [$Ms = \$2.06$, and $\$2.16$; $F(1,126) = 7.99$, $p < 0.005$].

Although there was a significant drop in WTA values from the first to the second replication [$F(1,252) = 17.54$, $p < 0.001$], there was no evidence of convergence of WTA among the different anchor conditions. Such convergence would have produced a significant interaction between the repetition factor and the anchoring manipulation, but this interaction was not significant.[6]

WTA values were highly sensitive to duration in the expected direction [$F(2,252) = 294.46$, $p < 0.001$] (for more discussion of sensitivity to duration see Ariely and Loewenstein [2000] and Kahneman, Wakker, and Sarin [1997]). The mean price for the 10 second sound [$M = 28.35$] was significantly lower than the mean price for the 30 second sound [$M = 48.69$; $F(1,252) = 169.46$, $p < 0.001$], and the mean price for the 30 second sound was lower than the mean price for the 60 second sound [$M = 66.25$; $F(1,252) = 126.06$, $p < 0.001$].

Figure I provides a graphical illustration of the results thus far. First, the vertical displacement between the lines shows the powerful effect of the anchoring manipulation. Second, despite the arbitrariness revealed by the effect of the anchoring manipulation, there is a strong and almost linear relationship between WTA and duration. Finally, there is no evidence of convergence between the different conditions across the nine trials.

Figure II provides additional support for the tight connection between WTA and duration. For each subject, we calculated the ratio of WTA in each of the durations to each of the other durations, and plotted these separately for the three conditions. As can be seen in the figure, the ratios of WTAs are

[5] For the purpose of statistical analysis, responses above 100¢ (7.7 percent) were truncated to 101¢ (the highest random price selected by computer was 100¢, so responses above 101¢ were strategically equivalent). Repeating the analyses using untruncated values did not qualify any of the findings.

[6] A variety of different tests of convergence produced similar results. First, we carried out an ANOVA analysis in which we took only the first and last trial as the repeated measure dependent variable. Again, the interaction between trial (first versus last) and the anchoring manipulation was nonsignificant. We also estimated the linear trend of WTA over time for each subject. The estimated trends were decreasing, but the rate of decline did not differ significantly between the two anchoring conditions.

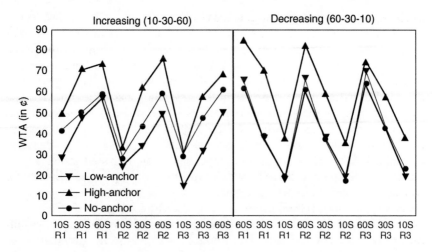

Figure I. Mean WTA for the Nine Trials in the Three Anchor Conditions

The panel on the left shows the increasing condition (duration order of 10, 30, and 60 seconds). The panel on the right shows the decreasing condition (duration order of 60, 30, and 10 seconds).

stable, and independent of condition (there are no significant differences by condition).

In summary, Experiment 2 demonstrates arbitrary but coherent pricing of painful experiences, even when there is no uncertainty about the nature or duration of the experience. Neither repeated experience with the event, nor confrontation with the same price distribution, overrode the impact of the initial anchor.

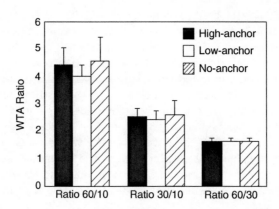

Figure II. Mean of Individual WTA Ratios for the Different Durations across the Different Conditions

Error bars are based on standard errors.

10.5. Experiment 3: Raising the Stakes

Experiment 3 was designed to address two possible objections to the previous procedure. First, it could be argued that subjects might have somehow believed that the anchor was informative, even though they had experienced the sound for themselves. For example, they might have thought that the sound posed some small risk to their hearing, and might have believed that the anchor roughly corresponded to the monetary value of this risk. To eliminate this possibility, Experiment 3 used subjects' own social security numbers as anchors. Second, one might be concerned that the small stakes in the previous experiment provided minimal incentives for accurate responding, which may have increased the arbitrariness of subjects' responses and their sensitivity to the anchor. Experiment 3, therefore, raised the stakes by a factor of ten. In addition, at the end of the experiment, we added a question designed to test whether the anchor-induced changes in valuation carry over to trade-offs involving other experiences.

Ninety students from the Massachusetts Institute of Technology participated in the experiment. The procedure closely followed that of Experiment 2, except that the stimuli were ten times as long: the shortest stimulus lasted 100 seconds; the next lasted 300 seconds, and longest lasted 600 seconds. The manipulation of the anchor in this experiment was also different. At the onset of the experiment, subjects were asked to provide the first three digits of their social security number and were instructed to turn these digits into a money amount (e.g. 678 translates into $6.78). Subjects were then asked whether, hypothetically, they would listen again to the sound they just experienced (for 300 seconds) if they were paid the money amount they had generated from their social security number.

In the main part of the experiment, subjects had three opportunities to listen to sounds in exchange for payment. The three different durations were again ordered in either an increasing set (100 seconds, 300 seconds, 600 seconds) or a decreasing set (600 seconds, 300 seconds, 100 seconds). In each trial, after they indicated their WTA, subjects were shown both their own price and the random price drawn from the distribution (which was the distribution used in Experiment 2 but multiplied by 10). If the price set by the subject was higher than the computer's price, subjects continued directly to the next trial. If the price set by the subjects was lower than the computer's price, subjects received the sound and the money associated with it (the amount set by the randomly drawn number), and then continued to the next trial. This process repeated itself three times, once for each of the three durations.

After completing the three trials, subjects were asked to rank-order a list of events in terms of how annoying they found them (for a list of the different

Table II.

The event	Mean rank
1 Missing your bus by a few seconds	4.3
2 Experiencing 300 seconds of the same sound you experienced	5.1
3 Discovering you purchased a spoiled carton of milk	5.2
4 Forgetting to return a video and having to pay a fine	5.4
5 Experiencing a blackout for an hour	5.8
6 Having a blood test	6.0
7 Having your ice cream fall on the floor	6.0
8 Having to wait 30 minutes in line for your favorite restaurant	6.2
9 Going to a movie theater and having to watch it from the second row	6.7
10 Losing your phone bill and having to call to get another copy	7.3
11 Running out of toothpaste at night	8.1

The different events that subjects were asked to order-rank in terms of their annoyance, at the end of Experiment 3. The items are ordered by their overall mean ranked annoyance from the most annoying (lower numbers) to the least annoying (high numbers).

tasks, see Table II). At the end of the experiment, subjects were paid according to the payment rule.

Results. The three digits entered ranged from 041 (translated to $0.41) to 997 (translated to $9.97), with a mean of 523 and a median of 505. Figure III compares the prices demanded by subjects with social security numbers above and below the median. It is evident that subjects with lower social security numbers required substantially less payment than subjects with higher numbers [Ms = $3.55, and $5.76; $F(1,88)$ = 28.45, $p < 0.001$). Both groups

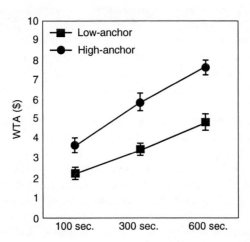

Figure III. Mean WTA (in Dollars) for the Three Annoying Sounds

The data are plotted separately for subjects whose three-digit anchor was below the median (low anchor) and above the median (high anchor). Error bars are based on standard errors.

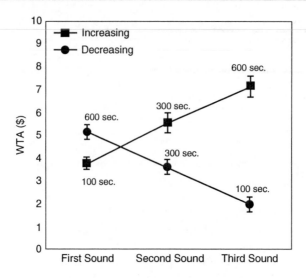

Figure IV. Mean WTA (in Dollars) for the Three Annoying Sounds

The data are plotted separately for the increasing (100 seconds, 300 seconds, 600 seconds) and the decreasing (600 seconds, 300 seconds, 100 seconds) conditions. Error bars are based on standard errors.

were coherent with respect to duration, demanding more payment for longer sounds [$F(2,176) = 92.53$, $p < 0.001$]. As in the previous experiment, there was also a small but significant interaction between anchor and duration [$F(2,176) = 4.17$, $p = 0.017$].

If subjects have little idea about how to price the sounds initially, and hence rely on the random anchor in coming up with a value, we would expect responses to the initial question to be relatively close to the anchor, regardless of whether the duration was 100 seconds or 600 seconds. However, having committed themselves to a particular value for the initial sound, we would expect the increasing duration group to then adjust their values upward while the decreasing group should adjust their anchor downward. This would create a much larger discrepancy between the two groups' valuations of the final sound than existed for the initial sound. Figure IV shows that the prediction is supported. Initial valuations of the 600 second tone in the decreasing order condition [$M = \$5.16$] were significantly larger than initial valuations of the 100 second tone in the increasing order condition [$M = \$3.78$; $t(88) = 3.1$, $p < .01$], but the difference of $1.38 is not very large. In the second period, both groups evaluated the same 300 second tone, and the valuation in the increasing condition was greater than that of the decreasing condition [$Ms = \$5.56$, and $\$3.65$; $t(88) = 3.5$, $p < .001$]. By the final period, the two conditions diverged dramatically with WTA being much higher in the increasing condition compared with the decreasing condition [Ms = $7.15, and $2.01; $t(88) = 9.4$, $p < .0001$].

We now turn to the rank-ordering of the different events in terms of their annoyance (see Table II). Recall that we wanted to see whether the same anchor that influenced subjects' pricing would also influence the way they evaluated the sounds independently of the pricing task. The results showed that the rank-ordering of the annoyance of the sound was not influenced by either the anchor [$F(1,86) = 1.33$, $p = 0.25$], or the order [$F(1,86) = 0.221$, $p = 0.64$]. In fact, when we examined the correlation between the rank-ordering of the annoyance of the sound and the initial anchor, the correlation was slightly negative (-0.096), although this finding was not significant ($p = 0.37$).

In summary, Experiment 3 demonstrates that coherent arbitrariness persists even with randomly generated anchors and larger stakes. In addition, the last part of Experiment 3 provides some evidence that the effect of the anchor on pricing does not influence the evaluation of the experience relative to other experiences.

10.6. Experiment 4: Coherently Arbitrary Valuations in the Market

We now consider the possibility that the presence of market forces could reduce the degree of initial arbitrariness or facilitate learning over time. Earlier research that compared judgments made by individuals who were isolated or who interacted in a market found that market forces did reduce the magnitude of a cognitive bias called the "curse of knowledge" by approximately 50 percent [Camerer, Loewenstein, and Weber 1989].

To test whether market forces would reduce the magnitude of the bias, we exposed subjects to an arbitrary anchor (as in the second experiment), but then elicited the WTA values through a multiperson auction, rather than using the Becker-Degroot-Marschak [1963] procedure. Our conjecture was that the market would not reduce the bias, but would lead to a convergence of prices within specific markets. Earlier research found that subjects who had bid on gambles in an auction similar to ours, adjusted their own bids in response to the market price, which carried information about the bids of other market participants [Cox and Grether 1996]. Relying on others' values can be informative in some purchase settings, but in these markets other participants had been exposed to the same arbitrary anchor. Moreover, having experienced a sample of the noise, subjects had full information about the consumption experience, which makes the valuations of others prescriptively irrelevant.

Fifty-three students from the Massachusetts Institute of Technology participated in the experiment, in exchange for a payment of $5 and earnings from the experiment. Subjects were told that they would participate in a marketplace for annoying sounds, and that they would bid for the opportunity to earn money by listening to annoying sounds. They participated in the experiment in groups, varying in size from six to eight subjects. The experiment lasted approximately 25 minutes.

The design and procedure were very similar to Experiment 2, but we increased the high anchor to $1.00 (instead of 50¢ and used an auction, rather than individual-level pricing procedure. As in the second experiment, the sound durations were 10, 30, or 60 seconds, subjects were given three opportunities to listen to each of these sounds and the order of the durations was manipulated between subjects. In the increasing condition, durations were presented in the order 10, 30, 60 seconds (repeated three times), and in the decreasing condition the durations were in the order 60, 30, 10 seconds (also repeated three times). All subjects first experienced 30 seconds of the same annoying sound that was used in the second experiment. Next, the bidding procedure was explained to the subjects as follows:

On each trial, the experimenter will announce the duration of the sound to be auctioned. At this stage every one of you will be asked to write down and submit your bid. Once all the bids are submitted, they will be written on the board by the experimenter, and the three people with the lowest bids will get the sound they bid for and get paid the amount set by the bid of the fourth lowest person.

Subjects were then asked to write down whether, in a hypothetical choice, a sum of X (10¢ or 100¢ depending on their condition) would be sufficient compensation for them to listen to the sound again. At this point the main part of the experiment started. On each of the nine trials, the experimenter announced the duration of the sound that was being auctioned; each of the subjects wrote a bid on a piece of paper and passed it to the experimenter, who wrote the bids on a large board. At that point, the three lowest bidders were announced, and they were asked to put on their headphones, and listen to the sound. After the sound ended the subjects who "won" the sound received the amount set by the fourth lowest bid.

Results. The general findings paralleled those from the previous experiments. In the low-anchor condition, the average bids were 24¢, 38¢, and 67¢ for the 10, 30, and 60 second sounds, respectively (all differences between sound durations are significant within a condition), and in the high-anchor condition, the corresponding average bids were 47¢, $1.32, and $2.11. Overall, mean WTA in the low-anchor condition was significantly lower than WTA in the high-anchor condition [$F(1,49) = 20.38$, $p < 0.001$]. The difference in the amount of money earned by subjects in the two conditions was quite stunning: the mean payment per sound in the high-anchor condition was $.59, while the mean payment in the low-anchor condition was only $.08.

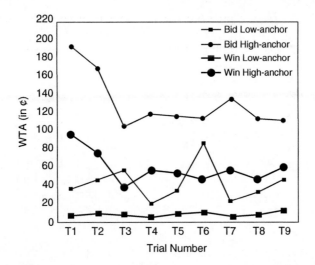

Figure V. Mean Bids (WTA) and Mean Payment as a Function of Trial and the Two Anchor Conditions

The main question that Experiment 4 was designed to address is whether the WTA prices for the low and high anchor conditions would converge over time. As can be seen from Figure V, there is no evidence of convergence, whether one looks at mean bids or the mean of the prices that emerged from the auction.

Although the bids and auction prices in the different conditions did not converge to a common value, bids *within* each group did converge toward that group's arbitrary value. Figure VI, which plots the mean standard deviation of bids in the eight different markets for each of the nine trials, provides visual support for such convergence. To test whether convergence was significant, we first estimated the linear trend in standard deviations across the nine rounds separately for each group. Only one of the eight within-group trends was positive (0.25), and the rest were negative (ranging from -0.76 to -14.89). A two-tailed t-test of these eight estimates showed that they were significantly negative [$t(7) = 2.44$, $p < 0.05$].

In summary, Experiment 4 demonstrates that coherent arbitrariness is robust to market forces. Indeed, by exposing people to others who were exposed to the same arbitrary influences, markets can strengthen the impact of arbitrary stimuli, such as anchors, on valuation.

10.7. Experiment 5: The Impact of Multiple Anchors

According to our account of preference formation, the very first valuation in a given domain has an arbitrary component that makes it vulnerable

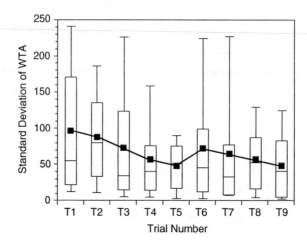

Figure VI. The within-Group Standard Deviations of the Bids (WTA), Plotted as a Function of Trial

to anchoring and similar manipulations. However, once individuals express these somewhat arbitrary values, they later behave in a fashion that is consistent with them, which constrains the range of subsequent choices and renders them less subject to nonnormative influences. To test this, Experiment 5 exposed subjects to three different anchors instead of only one. If the imprinting account is correct, then the first anchor should have a much greater impact on valuations compared with later ones. On the other hand, if subjects are paying attention to anchors because they believe they carry information, then all anchors would have the same impact as the initial one (similarly, Bayesian updating predicts that the order in which information arrives is irrelevant).

At the end of the pricing part of the experiment, we gave subjects a direct-choice between an annoying sound and a completely different unpleasant stimulus. We did this to see whether the influence of the anchor extends beyond prices to qualitative judgments of relative aversiveness.

Forty-four students from the Massachusetts Institute of Technology participated in the experiment, which lasted about 25 minutes. The experiment followed a procedure similar to the one used in Experiment 2, with the following adjustments. First, there were only three trials, each lasting 30 seconds. Second, and most important, in each of the three trials subjects were introduced to a new sound with different characteristics: a constant high-pitched sound (the same as in Experiment 2), a fluctuating high-pitched sound (which oscillated around the volume of the high-pitched sound), or white noise (a broad spectrum sound). The important aspect of these sounds is that they are qualitatively different from each other, but similarly aversive.

After hearing each sound, subjects were asked if, hypothetically, they would listen to it again for 30 seconds in exchange for 10¢, 50¢, or 90¢ (depending on the condition and the trial number). Subjects in the increasing conditions answered the hypothetical questions in increasing order (10¢, 50¢, 90¢), and subjects in the decreasing conditions answered the hypothetical questions in decreasing order (90¢, 50¢, 10¢). Each of these hypothetical questions was coupled with a different sound. After answering each hypothetical question, subjects went on to specify the smallest amount of compensation they would require to listen to 30 seconds of that sound (WTA). The same Becker–Degroot–Marschak [1963] procedure used in Experiment 2 determined whether subjects heard each sound again and how much they were paid for listening to it.

After the three trials, subjects were asked to place their finger in a vise (see Ariely [1998]). The experimenter closed the vise slowly until the subject indicated that he/she just began to experience the pressure as painful—a point called the "pain threshold." After the pain threshold was established, the experimenter tightened the vise an additional 1 mm (a quarter-turn in the handle) and instructed the subject to remember the level of pain. Subjects then experienced the same sound, and answered the same anchoring question that they had been asked, in the first trial. They were then asked if they would prefer to experience the same sound for 30 seconds or the vise for 30 seconds.

Results. Figure VII displays mean WTAs for the three annoying sounds, and the two anchoring orders. With respect to the first bid, the low anchor

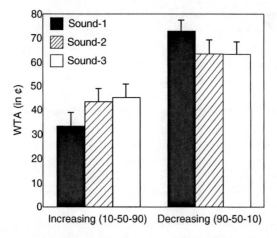

Figure VII. Mean WTA (in Cents) for the Three Annoying Sounds

In the Increasing condition the order of the hypothetical questions was 10¢, 50¢, and 90¢, respectively. In the Decreasing condition the order of the hypothetical questions was 90¢, 50¢, and 10¢, respectively. Error bars are based on standard errors.

generated significantly lower bids [$M = 33.5¢$] than the high anchor [$M = 72.8¢$; $F(1,42) = 30.96$, $p < 0.001$]. More interesting is the way subjects reacted to the second bid, which had the same anchor (50¢) for both conditions. In this case, we can see that there was a carryover effect from the first bid, so that the mean WTA price for the sound in the increasing condition [$M = 43.5¢$] was lower than the sound in the decreasing condition [$M = 63.2¢$; $F(1,42) = 6.03$, $p < 0.02$]. The most interesting comparison, however, is the WTA associated with the third sound. For this sound, subjects in both conditions had been exposed to the same three anchors, but the effects of the initial anchor and the most recent anchor (preceding the final stimulus) were in opposition to each other. In the increasing condition, the initial anchor was 10¢, and the most recent anchor was 90¢. In the decreasing condition, the initial anchor was 90¢, and the most recent anchor was 10¢. If the most recent anchor is stronger than the initial anchor, then WTA in the increasing condition should be higher than the one in the decreasing condition. If the initial anchor is stronger than the most recent anchor, as predicted by the imprinting account, then WTA in the decreasing condition should be higher than WTA in the increasing condition. In fact, WTA was higher in the decreasing condition compared with the increasing condition [$Ms = 63.1¢$, and $45.3¢$; $F(1,42) = 5.82$, $p < 0.03$]. Thus, the initial anchor has a stronger effect on WTA than the anchor that immediately preceded the WTA judgment, even though the initial anchor had been associated with a qualitatively different sound.

Another way to examine the results of Experiment 5 is to look at the binary responses to the hypothetical questions (the anchoring manipulation). In the first trial, the proportion of subjects who stated that they would be willing to listen to the sound they had just heard for $X¢$ was different, but not significantly so, across the two anchor values (55 percent for 10¢, and 73 percent for 90¢; $p > .20$ by x^2 test). The small differences in responses to these two radically different values supports the idea that subjects did not have firm internal values for the sounds before they encountered the first hypothetical question. On the third trial, however, the difference was highly significant (41 percent for 10¢, and 82 percent for 90¢, $p < .001$ by x^2 test). Subjects who were in the increasing-anchor condition were much more willing to listen to the sound, compared with subjects in the decreasing-anchor condition, indicating that they were sensitive to the change in money amounts across the three hypothetical questions. Consistent with the imprinting account proposed earlier, subjects acquired a stable internal reservation price for the sounds.

The response to the choice between the sound and vise pain revealed that subjects in the increasing-anchor condition had a higher tendency to pick the sound (72 percent), compared with the decreasing-anchor condition (64 percent), but this difference was not statistically significant ($p = 0.52$).

These results again fail to support the idea that the anchor affects subjects' evaluations of the sound relative to other stimuli.

10.8. Experiment 6: Money Only?

The previous experiments demonstrated arbitrariness in money valuations. Neither of the follow-up studies (in Experiments 3 and 5), however, found that the anchoring manipulation affected subsequent choices between the unpleasant sounds and other experiences. This raises the question of whether these null results reflect the fact that the effects of the anchor are narrow, or rather that the coherent arbitrariness phenomenon arises only with a relatively abstract response dimension, like money. To address this issue, we conducted an experiment that employed a design similar to that of Experiments 2–4 but which did not involve money. Because Experiments 2–4 had all demonstrated coherence on the dimension of duration, in Experiment 6 we attempted to demonstrate arbitrariness with respect to duration.

Fifty-nine subjects were recruited on the campus of the University of California at Berkeley with the promise of receiving $5.00 in exchange for a few minutes of their time and for experiencing some mildly noxious stimuli. After consenting to participate, they were first exposed to the two unpleasant stimuli used in the experiment: a small sample of an unpleasant-tasting liquid composed of equal parts Gatorade and vinegar, and an aversive sound (the same as used in Experiments 2–4). They were then shown three containers of different sizes (1 oz., 2 oz., and 4 oz.), each filled with the liquid they had just tasted and were asked to "please answer the following hypothetical question: would you prefer the middle size drink or X minutes of the sound," where X was one minute for half the subjects and three minutes for the other half (the anchor manipulation). After the initial anchoring question, subjects were shown three transparent bottles with different drink quantities in each (1 oz., 2 oz., and 4 oz.). For each of the three drink quantities, subjects indicated whether they would prefer to drink that quantity of liquid or endure a sound of duration equal to 10 seconds, 20 seconds, 30 seconds, etc. up to eight minutes. (The specific instructions were: "On each line, please indicate if you prefer that duration of the sound to the amount of the drink. Once you have answered all the questions the experimenter will pick one of the lines at random, and you will be asked to experience the sound described on that line or the drink depending on your preference in that line.") To simplify the task, the choices were arranged in separate blocks for each drink size, and were arranged in order of duration.

Results. Revealing arbitrariness with respect to tone duration, the anchoring manipulation had a significant impact on trade-offs between the sound's

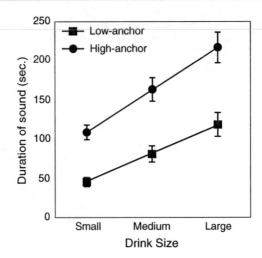

Figure VIII. Mean Maximum Duration at Which Subjects Prefers Tone to Drink

Error bars are based on standard errors.

duration and drink quantity [$F(1,57) = 24.7$, $p < .0001$]. The mean maximum tone duration at which subjects preferred the tone to the drink (averaging over the three drink sizes) was 82 seconds in the one minute anchor condition, and 162 seconds in the three minute anchor condition. Revealing consistency with respect to tone duration, however, subjects were willing to tolerate longer sound durations when the other option involved larger drink size [$F(2,114) = 90.4$, $p < .0001$] (see Figure VIII).

The experiment demonstrates that arbitrariness is not limited to monetary valuations (and, less importantly, that coherence is not an inherent property of duration).[7] In combination with the results of the add-on components of

[7] In a discussion of the arbitrary nature of judgments in "contingent valuation" research, Kahneman, Schkade, and Sunstein [1998] and Kaheman, Ritov, and Schkade [1999] point out a similarity to some classical results in psychophysical scaling of sensory magnitude. The well-known "ratio scaling" procedure [Stevens 1975] asks subjects to assign positive numbers to physical stimuli (e.g. tones of different loudness) in such a manner that the ratio of numbers matches the ratio of subjectively perceived magnitudes. Sometimes the subjects are told that a reference tone has a certain numerical value (e.g. 100) which is also called "the modulus," while in other procedural variants, subjects have no reference tone and are left to assign numbers as they please. In the latter case, one finds typically that the absolute numbers assigned to a given physical stimulus have little significance (are extremely variable across subjects), but the ratios of numbers are relatively stable (across subjects). Kahneman et al. [1998, 1999] point out that the money scale used in WTP is formally an unbounded ratio scale, like the number scale used in psychophysics, and hence should inherit the same combination of arbitrary absolute but stable relative levels. However, unlike the psychophysical setting in which the response modulus is truly arbitrary (the subjects do not come to the experiment knowing what a 100-point loudness level is), the WTP response scale is not at all arbitrary. Subjects should know what a dollar is worth in terms of other small pleasures and conveniences. If we had asked subjects to evaluate the sounds in terms of uninterpreted

Experiments 3 and 5, it suggests that the web of consistency that people draw from their own choices may be narrow. Thus, for example, a subject in our first experiment with a high social security number who priced the average wine at $25, would almost surely price the higher quality wine above $25. However, the same individual's subsequent choice of whether to trade the higher quality wine for a different type of good might be relatively unaffected by her pricing of the wine, and hence by the social security number anchoring manipulation.

10.9. General Discussion

The main experiments presented here (Experiments 2–4) show that when people assess their own willingness to listen to an unpleasant noise in exchange for payment, the money amounts they specify display the pattern that we call "coherent arbitrariness." Experiment 1 demonstrated the pattern with familiar consumer products, and Experiment 6 showed that the pattern is not restricted to judgments about money. Coherent arbitrariness has two aspects: coherence, whereby people respond in a robust and sensible fashion to noticeable changes or differences in relevant variables, and arbitrariness, whereby these responses occur around a base-level that is normatively arbitrary.

Our main focus up to this point was to demonstrate the coherent arbitrariness phenomenon, and test whether it is reduced or eliminated by repeated experience, market forces, or higher stakes. Next, we discuss a variety of other phenomena that may be interpreted as manifestations of coherent arbitrariness.

10.10. A. Contingent Valuation

The clearest analogy to our research comes from research on contingent valuation, in which people indicate the most they would be willing to pay (WTP) for a public benefit (e.g. environmental improvement). Of particular relevance to coherent arbitrariness is the finding that people's willingness to pay for environmental amenities is remarkably unresponsive to the scope or scale of the amenity being provided [Kahneman and Knetsch 1992]. For example, one study found that willingness to pay to clean one polluted lake

"points" rather than dollars, then we would have duplicated the psychophysical procedure of scaling without a modulus, but in that case, of course, the results would be predictable and uninteresting. In any case, the results of Experiment 6 show that exactly the same pattern of coherent arbitrariness can be obtained with well-defined attributes such as duration and drink size.

in Ontario was statistically indistinguishable from willingness to pay to clean all polluted lakes in Ontario [Kahneman and Knetsch 1992].

Importantly, insensitivity to scale is most dramatic in studies that employ between-subjects designs. When scope or scale is varied within-subject, so that a single person is making judgments for different values, the valuations are far more responsive to scale (see Kahneman, Ritov, and Schkade [1999] and Kahneman, Schkade, and Sunstein [1998]).

This effect has even been observed in a study that examined intuitive pricing of common household items. Frederick and Fischhoff [1998] elicited WTPs for two different quantities of common market goods (e.g. toilet paper, applesauce, and tuna fish) using both a between-subjects design (in which respondents valued either the small or large quantity of each good) and a within-subjects design (in which respondents valued both the small and large quantity of each good). The difference in WTP was in the right direction in both designs, but it was much greater (2.5 times as large) in the within-subjects condition, which explicitly manipulated quantity. This held true even for goods such as toilet paper, for which the meaning of the quantity description (number of rolls) should have been easy to evaluate. Frederick and Fischhoff [p. 116] suggest that this would be a common finding for valuation studies generally—that "valuations of any particular quantity [of good] would be sensitive to its relative position within the range selected for valuation, but insensitive to which range is chosen, resulting in insensitive (or incoherent) values across studies using different quantity ranges." In fact, the tendency for within-subject manipulations to produce larger effects than between subject manipulations is a common phenomenon (e.g. Fox and Tversky [1995], Kahneman and Ritov [1994], and Keren and Raaijmakers [1988]).

10.11. B. Financial Markets

Like the price one should ask to listen to an aversive tone, the value of a particular stock is inherently ambiguous. As Shiller [1998] comments, "Who would know what the value of the Dow Jones Industrial Average should be? Is it really "worth" 6,000 today? Or 5,000 or 7,000? or 2,000 or 10,000? There is no agreed-upon economic theory that would answer these questions." In the absence of better information, past prices (asking prices, prices of similar objects, or other simple comparisons) are likely to be important determinants of prices today. In a similar vein, Summers [1986] notes that it is remarkably difficult to demonstrate that asset markets reflect fundamental valuation. It is possible to show that one or more prediction of the strong markets theory are supported, but "the verification of one of the theory's predictions cannot be taken to prove or establish a theory" [p. 594]. Thus, studies showing that the market follows a random walk are consistent with fundamental valuation, but are insufficient to demonstrate it; indeed, Summers presents a simple model in which asset prices have a large arbitrary component, but are nevertheless serially uncorrelated, as predicted by fundamental valuation.

While the overall value of the market or of any particular company is inherently unknowable, the impact of particular pieces of news is often quite straightforward. If Apple was expected to earn $x in a particular year but instead earned $2x, this would almost unquestionably be very good news. If IBM buys back a certain percentage of its own outstanding shares, this has straightforward implications for the value of the remaining shares. As Summers [1986] points out, the market may respond in a coherent, sensible fashion to such developments even when the absolute level of individual stocks, and of the overall market, is arbitrary.

10.12. C. Labor Markets

In the standard account of labor supply, workers intertemporally substitute labor and leisure with the goal of maximizing utility from lifetime labor, leisure, and consumption. To do so optimally, they must have some notion of how much they value these three activities, or at least of how much they value them relative to one another. Although it is difficult to ascertain whether labor supply decisions have an element of arbitrariness, due to the absence of any agreed-upon benchmark, there is some evidence of abnormalities in labor markets that could be attributed to arbitrariness. Summarizing results from a large-scale survey of pay-setting practices by employees, Bewley [1998, p. 485] observes that "Non-union companies seemed to be isolated islands, with most workers having little systematic knowledge of pay rates at other firms. Pay rates in different nonunion companies were loosely linked by the forces of supply and demand, but these allowed a good deal of latitude in setting pay." Wage earners, we suspect, do not have a good idea of what their time is worth when it comes to a trade-off between consumption and leisure, and do not even have a very accurate idea of what they could earn at other firms. Like players in the stock market, the most concrete datum that workers have with which to judge the correctness of their current wage rate is the rate they were paid in the past. Consistent with this reasoning, Bewley continues, "though concern about worker reaction and morale curbed pay cutting, the reaction was to reduction in pay relative to its former level. The fall relative to levels at other firms was believed to have little impact on morale, though it might increase turnover." In other words, workers care about changes in salary but are relatively insensitive to absolute levels or levels relative to what comparable workers make in other firms. This insensitivity may help to explain the maintenance of substantial interindustry wage differentials (see

Dickens and Katz [1987], Krueger and Summers [1988], and Thaler [1989]). Similarly, coherent arbitrariness is supported by the quip that a wealthy man is one who earns $100 more than his wife's sister's husband.

10.13. D. Criminal Deterrence

Imagine an individual who is contemplating committing a crime, whether something as minor as speeding on a freeway, or something as major as a robbery. To what extent will such an individual be deterred by the prospect of apprehension? Research on criminal deterrence has produced mixed answers to this question, with some studies finding significant negative effects of probability or severity of punishment on crime, and others reaching more equivocal conclusions. These studies have employed different methodologies, with some examining cross-sectional differences in crime and punishment across states, and others examining changes over time. Coherent arbitrariness has important implications for these studies. Like many other types of cost-benefit calculations, assessing the probabilities and likely consequences of apprehension is difficult, as is factoring such calculations into one's decision-making calculus. Thus, this is a domain characterized by value uncertainty where one might expect to observe the coherent arbitrariness pattern. Coherent arbitrariness, in this case, would mean that people would respond sensibly to well-publicized *changes* in deterrence levels but much less to absolute levels of deterrence (for a discussion of similar results in civil judgments see Sunstein, Kahneman, Schkade, and Ritov [2002]). We would predict, therefore, that one should find short-term deterrence effects in narrowly focused studies that examine the impact of policy changes, but little or no deterrence effects in cross-sectional studies. This is, indeed, the observed pattern. Interrupted time series studies have measured sizable reactions in criminal behavior to sudden, well-publicized, increases in deterrence [Ross 1973; Sherman 1990], but these effects tend to diminish over time. The implication that we draw is that the prevailing level of criminal activity does not reflect any underlying fundamental trade-off between the gains from crime and the costs of punishment.

10.14. E. Final Comments

Our experiments highlight the general hazards of inferring fundamental valuation by examining individuals' responses to change. If all one observed from our experiment was the relationship between valuation and duration, one might easily conclude that people were basing their WTA values on their fundamental valuation for the different stimuli. However, the effect of the arbitrary anchor shows that, while people are adjusting their valuations in a coherent, seemingly sensible, fashion to account for duration, they are doing so around an arbitrary base value. Moreover, this effect does not diminish as subjects gain more experience with the stimulus or when they provide valuations in a market context.

A key economic implication of coherent arbitrariness is that some economic variables will have a much greater impact than others. When people recognize that a particular economic variable, such as a price, has changed, they will respond robustly but when the change is not drawn to their attention, they will respond more weakly, if at all. This point was recognized early on by the economist John Rae who, [1834] noted that:

When any article rises suddenly and greatly in price, when in their power, they are prone to adopt some substitute and relinquish the use of it. Hence, were a duty at once imposed on any particular wine, or any particular sort of cotton fabric, it might have the effect of diminishing the consumption very greatly, or stopping it entirely. Whereas, were the tax at first slight, and then slowly augmented, the reasoning powers not being startled, vanity, instead of flying off to some other objects, would be apt to apply itself to them as affording a convenient means of gratification [page 374].

The speed at which an economic variable changes is only one of many factors that will determine whether it is visible to individuals—whether it "startles" the reasoning powers, as Rae expressed it. Other factors that can make a difference are how the information is presented, e.g., whether prices of alternative products are listed in a comparative fashion or are encountered sequentially (see Russo and Leclerc [1991]), and whether prices are known privately or discussed. Thus, for example, large salary differentials may be easier to sustain in a work environment in which salary information is not discussed. In sum, changes or differences in prices or other economic conditions will have a much greater impact on behavior when people are made aware of the change or difference than when they are only aware of the prevailing levels at a particular point in time.

These results challenge the central premise of welfare economics that choices reveal true preferences—that the choice of A over B indicates that the individual will in fact be better off with A rather than with B. It is hard to make sense of our results without drawing a distinction between "revealed" and "true" preferences. How, for example, can a pricing decision that is strongly correlated with an individual's social security number reveal a true preference in any meaningful sense of the term? If consumers' choices do not necessarily reflect true preferences, but are to a large extent arbitrary, then the claims of revealed preferences as a guide to public policy and the organization of economic exchange are weakened. Market institutions that maximize consumer sovereignty need not maximize consumer welfare.

As many economists have pointed out (e.g. Sen [1982]), the sole psychological assumption underlying ordinal utility is that people will behave consistently. Our work suggests that ordinal utility may, in fact, be a valid representation of choices under specific, albeit narrow, circumstances, without revealing underlying preferences, in any nonvacuous sense of "preference." When people are aware of changes in conditions, such as the change in price in the example just given, they will respond in a coherent fashion that mimics the behavior of individuals with fixed, well-defined, preferences. However, they will often not respond reasonably to new opportunities or to hidden changes in old variables, such as price or quality. The equilibrium states of the economy may therefore contain a large arbitrary component, created by historical accident or deliberate manipulation.

SLOAN SCHOOL OF MANAGEMENT, MASSACHUSETTS INSTITUTE OF TECHNOLOGY
DEPARTMENT OF SOCIAL AND DECISION SCIENCES, CARNEGIE MELLON
UNIVERSITY
SLOAN SCHOOL OF MANAGEMENT, MASSACHUSETTS INSTITUTE OF TECHNOLOGY

References

Ariely, Dan, "Combining Experiences over Time: The Effects of Duration, Intensity Changes and On-Papers Line Measurements on Retrospective Pain Evaluations," *Journal of Behavioral Decision Making*, XI (1998), 19–45.

Ariely, Dan, and George Loewenstein, "The Importance of Duration in Ratings of, and Choices between, Sequences of Outcomes," *Journal of Experimental Psychology: General*, CXXIX (2000), 508–523.

Ariely, Dan, and G. Zauberman, "On the Making of an Experience: The Effects of Breaking and Combining Experiences on their Overall Evaluation," *Journal of Behavioral Decision Making*, XIII (2000), 219–232.

Ariely, Dan, George Loewenstein, and Drazen Prelec, "Determinants of Anchoring Effects," Working Paper, 2002.

Becker, Gary, "Irrational Behavior and Economic Theory," *Journal of Political Economy*, LXX (1962), 1–13.

Becker, Gary M., Morris H. DeGroot, and Jacob Marschak, "An Experimental Study of Some Stochastic Models for Wagers," *Behavioral Science*, VIII (1963), 199–202.

Bewley, Truman F., "Why Not Cut Pay?" *European Economic Review*, XLII (1998), 459–490.

Camerer, Colin, George Loewenstein, and Martin Weber, "The Curse of Knowledge in Economic Settings: An Experimental Analysis," *Journal of Political Economy*, XCVII (1989), 1232–1254.

Chapman, Gretchen B., and Eric J. Johnson, "Anchoring, Activation, and the Construction of Values," *Organizational Behavior and Human Decision Processes*, LXXIX (1999), 115–153.

Cox, James C., and David M. Grether, "The Preference Reversal Phenomenon: Response Mode, Markets and Incentives," *Economic Theory*, VII (1996), 381–405.

Dickens, William T., and Lawrence F. Katz, "Inter-industry Wage Differences and Industry Characteristics," in K. Lang and J. S. Leonard, eds., *Unemployment and the Structure of Labor Markets* (Oxford: Basil Blackwell, 1987).

Drolet, Aimee L., Itamar Simonson, and Amos Tversky, "Indifference Curves That Travel with the Choice Set," *Marketing Letters,* XI (2000), 199–209.

Epley, Nicholas, and Thomas Gilovich, "Putting Adjustment Back in the Anchoring and Adjustment Heuristic: Differential Processing of Self-Generated and Experimenter-Provided Anchors," *Psychological Science,* XII (2001), 391–396.

Fox, Craig R., and Amos Tversky, "Ambiguity Aversion and Comparative Ignorance," *Quarterly Journal of Economics*, CX (1995), 585–603.

Frederick, Shane, and Baruch Fischhoff, "Scope (in)sensitivity in Elicited Valuations," *Risk Decision and Policy*, III (1998), 109–123.

Gilboa, Itzhak, and David Schmeidler, "Case-Based Decision Theory," *Quarterly Journal of Economics*, CX (1995), 605–639.

Green, Donald, Karen E. Jacowitz, Daniel Kahneman, and Daniel McFadden, "Referendum Contingent Valuation, Anchoring, and Willingness to Pay for Public Goods," *Resources and Energy Economics*, XX (1998), 85–116.

Hoeffler, Steve, and Dan Ariely, "Constructing Stable Preferences: A Look into Dimensions of Experience and their Impact on Preference Stability," *Journal of Consumer Psychology*, XI (1999), 113–139.

Hsee, Christopher K., George Loewenstein, Sally Blount, and Max H. Bazerman, "Preference Reversals between Joint and Separate Evaluations of Options: A Theoretical Analysis," *Psychological Bulletin*, CXXV (1999), 576–590.

Jacowitz, Karen E., and Daniel Kahneman, "Measures of Anchoring in Estimation Tasks," *Personality and Social Psychology Bulletin*, XXI (1995), 1161–1166.

Johnson, Eric J., and David A. Schkade, "Bias in Utility Assessments: Further Evidence and Explanations," *Management Science*, XXXV (1989), 406–424.

Kahneman, Daniel, and Jack Knetsch, "Valuing Public Goods: The Purchase of Moral Satisfaction," *Journal of Environmental Economics and Management*, XXII (1992), 57–70.

Kahneman, Daniel, and Jack Knetsch, "Anchoring or Shallow Inferences: The Effect of Format," unpublished manuscript, University of California, Berkeley, 1993.

Kahneman, Daniel, and Dale T. Miller, "Norm Theory: Comparing Reality to its Alternatives," *Psychological Review*, XCIII (1986), 136–153.

Kahneman, Daniel, and Ilana Ritov, "Determinants of Stated Willingness to Pay for Public Goods. A Study in the Headline Method," *Journal of Risk and Uncertainty*, IX (1994), 5–38.

Kahneman, Daniel, Ilana Ritov, and David Schkade, "Economic Preferences or Attitude Expressions? An Analysis of Dollar Responses to Public Issues," *Journal of Risk and Uncertainty*, XIX (1999), 220–242.

Kahneman, Daniel, David A. Schkade, and Cass R. Sunstein, "Shared Outrage and Erratic Awards: The Psychology of Punitive Damages," *Journal of Risk and Uncertainty*, XVI (1998), 49–86.

Kahneman, Daniel, Peter P. Wakker, and Rakesh Sarin, "Back to Bentham? Explorations of Experienced Utility," *Quarterly Journal of Economics*, CXII (1997), 375–405.

Keren, Gideon, and Jeroen B. Raaijmakers, "On Between-Subjects Versus Within-Subjects Comparisons in Testing Utility Theory," *Organizational-Behavior-and-Human-Decision-Processes*, IV (1988), 233–247.

Krueger, Alan B., and Lawrence H. Summers, "Efficiency Wages and the Inter-Industry Wage Structure," *Econometrica*, LVI (1988), 259–293.

Mussweiler, Thomas, and Fritz Strack, "Considering the Impossible: Explaining the Effects of Implausible Anchors," *Social Cognition*, XIX (2001), 145–160.

Payne, John W., James R. Bettman, and Erik J. Johnson, *The Adaptive Decision Maker* (New York: Cambridge University Press, 1993).

Rae, John, *The Sociological Theory of Capital* (London: Macmillan, (1834), 1905).

Ross, H. Laurence, "Law, Science, and Accidents: The British Road Safety Act of 1967," *Journal of Legal Studies*, II (1973), 1–78.

Russo, J. Edward, and France Leclerc, "Characteristics of Successful Product Information Programs," *Journal of Social Issues*, XLVII (1991), 73–92.

Sen, Amartya Kumar, *Choice, Welfare, and Measurement* (Cambridge, MA: MIT Press, 1982).

Sherman, Lawrence, "Police Crackdowns: Initial and Residual Deterrence," in Michael Tonry and Norval Morris, eds., *Crime and Justice: A Review of Research* (Chicago: University of Chicago Press, 1990).

Shiller, Robert J., "Human Behavior and the Efficiency of the Financial System," in John B. Taylor and Michael Woodford, eds., *Handbook of Macroeconomics*, (Amsterdam: North-Holland, Elsevier: 1998).

Slovic, Paul, "The Construction of Preferences," *American Psychologist*, L (1995), 364–371.

Stevens, S. S. *Psychophysics. Introduction to Its Perceptual, Neural, and Social Prospects* (New York, NY: Wiley, 1975).

Strack, Fritz, and Thomas Mussweiler, "Explaining the Enigmatic Anchoring Effect: Mechanisms of Selective Accessibility," *Journal of Personality and Social Psychology*, LXXIII (1997), 437–446.

Summers, Lawrence H., "Does the Stock Market Rationally Reflect Fundamental Values?" *Journal of Finance*, XLI (1986), 591–602.

Sunstein, Cass R., Daniel Kahneman, David Schkade, and Ilana Ritov, "Predictably Incoherent Judgments," Working paper, University of Chicago Law School, 2002.

Thaler, Richard H. "Inter-Industry Wage Differentials," *Journal of Economic Perspectives*, III (1989), 181–193.

Tversky, Amos, and Daniel Kahneman, "Judgment under Uncertainty: Heuristics and Biases," *Science*, CLXXXV (1974), 1124–1131.

Part IV

Predicting Tastes and Feelings

11

A Bias in the Prediction of Tastes

George Loewenstein and Daniel Adler

I have never been very good at predicting my feelings when it comes to economic affairs. When I buy something nice, I almost inevitably regret having spent too much money, but when I go for the budget model, I end up regretting not having gone for deluxe. My friend, Jonathan Schooler (who is similarly constituted emotionally) and I briefly contemplated establishing a club for regret maximizers, but abandoned the idea because a higher joint priority was to start a club for people who can't say no to research projects.[1]

One of the most dramatic experiences of mispredicting myself occurred the last time I purchased a house. Despite having experienced buyer's remorse in the past, even, as just noted, in connection with small purchases, I was caught by surprise by the transformation of my own feelings before and after I had signed on the dotted line. Before signing on the dotted line, I knew that I was in love with the house, that we could afford it, and that the whole deal made perfect sense. Moments *after* signing, however, my feelings could not have been more different. I experienced a kind of *post emptio triste* so intense and prolonged that I spent several days walking around the neighborhood we were leaving, nauseous from the feeling of having made what, at that moment, I was convinced was the worst, most self-destructive, decision of my life.

House purchases, I believe, often reveal another kind of misprediction. When people come into a sizeable amount of money, whether by their own devices, an inheritance or by any other means, there is a natural tendency to upgrade the residence, which often means moving to a house with more land that is typically further from neighbors. My experience has always been, however, that having neighbors one is close to, both physically and socially, is one of the things that makes the greatest difference for quality of life. So,

---

[1] Maybe there's a connection between the two problems we share; maybe we take on new research projects because we fear the regret we will experience if we don't research the topic and someone else does.

buying the grand house seems like one of a number of domains in which the human tendency is to do with money exactly the opposite of what will make us happy.[2]

This paper is not, in fact, about buyer's remorse, but is actually more closely related to the fact that we eventually got used to the new house; it is about the failure to anticipate adaptation. Research on the endowment effect (mentioned in the introduction to Chapter 5) shows that when people are endowed with an object they become attached to the object and tend to ask very high selling prices in order to part with it. Adler and I were interested in whether people could predict changes in their own tastes, and the best way we knew to produce a dramatic, rapid, and reliable, taste change was via the endowment effect.

As the title indicates, we found that people did not predict that being endowed with an object would cause them to become attached to it. Subsequent research, including the two chapters that follow, has pursued this insight in a number of directions. Some research has shown that people not only mispredict their own future preferences, but also their own future feelings.[3] Other work (see Chapter 13) has sought to formalize these insights mathematically, and to draw out implications for economic behavior.

---

[2] My wife and I had received the most direct feedback we could have received on this point. During the year when we were in California, in typically disorganized fashion, we sublet the house we owned in Pittsburgh a month too early—a month before our departure date. The apartment we managed to find for that month was the small, run-down, second floor of a private house crammed between a series of similar subdivided houses in a very marginal neighborhood. As it turned out, however, it was one of our best months in Pittsburgh. Our son Max was in heaven. There were throngs of kids roaming the crowded streets, bicycling and staging impromptu performances of music or theater. My wife and I were in heaven as well, surrounded by human drama erupting from the cramped, hot, apartments onto the street. We set up lawn chairs on the front stoop and took in the lively scenes swirling around us. So why, when we returned from sabbatical, did we promptly buy a house removed from the neighbors by a large plot of land? What's the benefit of all this research if we don't live by it ourselves?

[3] e.g. Wilson, T. D. and Gilbert, D. T. (2003). 'Affective Forecasting', in M. Zanna (ed.), *Advances in Experimental Social Psychology*. New York: Elsevier, 35: 345–411.

A Bias in the Prediction of Tastes*

George Loewenstein and Daniel Adler

Although the standard economic theory of consumer preference assumes fixed tastes, the idea that tastes change over time is not controversial. Numerous 'habit formation' models have been proposed which assume that current consumption influences future tastes (Duesenberry, 1952; Pollak, 1970; Stigler and Becker, 1977). These models have been applied to such diverse phenomena as the development of tastes for music and food, substance addiction (Becker and Murphy, 1990), and the surprisingly high rate of return on equities relative to fixed-income securities (e.g. Constantinedes, 1990).

Although it is more complicated to model than fixed tastes, there is nothing intrinsically irrational about habit formation as long as economic agents can predict without bias the effect of their current behaviour on their own future tastes. If people are aware of the effect of their actions on their own future tastes, they can adjust their consumption in a rational manner – e.g. by desisting from crack based on anticipation of future disutility from addiction.

There is some evidence, however, pointing to situations in which people systematically mispredict their own tastes. For example Ausubel (1991) noted that large numbers of credit card users expect to maintain a zero credit balance but fail to do so – apparently underestimating their own future desire for spending. This self-forecasting error can explain the downward stickiness of credit card interest rates since consumers who expect to maintain zero card balances will not care about credit card interest rates. A similar pattern occurs in connection with consumer rebate programmes; consumer purchase

* We thank Max Bazerman, Baruch Fischhoff, Colin Camerer, Drazen Prelec, and Shane Frederick for helpful comments and suggestions, and Tina Diekman for assistance in running the experiments. The idea for the first experiments arose in a discussion with Daniel Kahneman.

This chapter was originally published as Loewenstein, G. and Adler, D. (1995) "A Bias in the Prediction of Tastes". The Economic Journal. 105 (July): 929–937. Reproduced by kind permission of Blackwell Publishing.

decisions are quite sensitive to rebate offers, but very few consumers ultimately send in the forms required to obtain the rebate (Tat et al. 1988).

Our specific focus is on whether people are able to predict changes in their own tastes caused by the 'endowment effect' (Thaler, 1980). The endowment effect refers to the tendency for people to value an object more highly if they possess it than they would value the same object if they did not. In the typical demonstration of the endowment effect (see, e.g., Kahneman et al. 1990), one group of subjects (sellers) are endowed with an object and are given the option of trading it for various amounts of cash; another group (choosers) are not given the object but are given a series of choices between getting the object or getting various amounts of cash. Although the objective wealth position of the two groups is identical, as are the choices they face, endowed subjects hold out for significantly more money than those who are not endowed. As Tversky and Kahneman (1991) have shown, the endowment effect implies that indifference curves shift in a systematic manner when individuals acquire goods – increasing the valuation of the endowed good relative to all other goods. Thus, the endowment effect can be viewed as a type of endogenous taste-change.

Tversky and Kahneman analyse the effect of endowments on preferences with a 'reference-dependent preference structure' that indexes the standard preference relations ($\succ$, $\sim$, etc.) according to the individual's point of reference (typically the current asset position). For example, $x \sim_r y$ indicates that an individual with reference position r is indifferent between alternatives x and y. The selling price (s) and choice value (c) estimated in the experimental setup just described are represented in equations 1 and 2 respectively, where the first argument of each pair indicates the individual's level of wealth, the second designates possession (1) or nonpossession (0) of the object, and the preference relation is subscripted according to whether the decision maker is in possession of the object.

$$(w, 1) \sim_1 (w + s, 0) \tag{1}$$

$$(w, 1) \sim_0 (w + c, 0) \tag{2}$$

The endowment effect implies $s \gg c$.

To accommodate predictions of preferences within this framework, we generalise the notation by subscripting the preference relation by the asset position which the individual is attempting to predict, and superscripting it by the individual's current reference level. Thus, for an individual with asset position s, $\sim_r^s$ represents the indifference relations she would expect to prevail if her asset position were r instead of s.[1]

---

[1] Under the generalized notation, the conventional endowment effect can be expressed as: $(w, 1) \sim_1^1 (w + s, 0)$, and $(w, 1) \sim_0^0 (w + c, 0)$, with $s > c$.

In the experiments presented below, we asked subjects to predict their own selling price for an object they did not have – i.e. to predict a selling price, s', as defined by,

$$(w, 1) \sim_1^0 (w + s', 0) \tag{3}$$

If subjects predict their own selling prices without bias, then, on average, $s' = s$. Our prediction is that subjects will underestimate s – i.e. $s' \ll s$.

The endowment effect has several advantages as the focus of a study of taste-change prediction. First, the effect operates very rapidly so that, unlike, for example, changes in the taste for classical music, it can be studied in a single experimental session. Second, discovery of a bias in predicting the impact of the endowment effect would have far-reaching implications for economics. The endowment effect refers to the impact on tastes of merely acquiring a good. Since many economic decisions, including most decisions involving consumer choice, involve acquisitions, documentation of a bias in the prediction of the endowment effect would call into question the rationality of a wide range of economic behaviour. Finally, we believed that there was a high likelihood of observing a prediction bias in this particular domain. This intuition is based on, first, the surprisingly long time it has taken social scientists to discover the effect, given its magnitude and robustness; second, the fact that the endowment effect disappears when people make valuation decisions on behalf of another person, as if they are not aware that others will get attached to objects in their possession (Marshall *et al.* 1987); and third, the fact that other studies have found that people tend to underestimate how quickly they will adapt to changed circumstances such as winning a lottery or becoming paraplegic (Brickman *et al.* 1978) – i.e. that they underestimate the impact of reference point shifts.

11.1. EXPERIMENT 1

The first experiment was designed to test whether subjects without an object could predict how attached they would become if they were endowed with it. We first elicited hypothetical selling prices for an object from unendowed subjects then endowed them with the object and elicited an actual selling price.

Subjects were 27 undergraduates enrolled in a core humanities class at Carnegie Mellon University and 42 adults enrolled in two evening classes in finance at the University of Pittsburgh. In each class, the experimenter held up a mug engraved with the school logo for the students to see. A different style of mug was used at Carnegie Mellon and at the University of Pittsburgh. A form was then randomly distributed to approximately half of the students in each class. The form asked the students to imagine that they possessed the mug on display and to predict whether they would be willing to exchange the mug for various amounts of money. It was worded as follows:

We are interested in your opinion about the mug displayed at the front of the room. Imagine that we gave you a mug exactly like the one you can see, and that we gave you the opportunity to keep it or trade it for some money. Below are a series of lines marked 'Keep mug___ Trade it for $ amount___.' On each line check whether you think that you would prefer to keep the mug or to trade it in for the amount of money written on the line. *Check one or the other on every line.*

The remainder of the page consisted of 40 lines each containing a choice between keeping the mug or trading it for an amount of money that ranged from 25 cents to 10 dollars in $0.25 increments. The experimenter waited until all subjects with a form had completed it. Next, *all* subjects were presented with a mug and given a second form which actually provided the opportunity to exchange the mug for cash. The instructions for the second form were directly analogous to those used in the prediction form, but made it clear that one of their choices would count. Subjects were told that they would receive the option they had circled on one of the lines – which line had been determined in advance by the experimenter.

The experimental design creates two groups of subjects, one that completed the prediction form prior to receiving a mug, and the other that did not. It allows us to conduct both a between- and within-subject analysis of prediction accuracy. The within-subject analysis compares the preliminary valuation predictions of the group that completed the first form with their subsequent actual valuations. The between-subject test compares those predictions with the actual valuations of the group that did *not* make initial predictions. The between-subject comparison was included in case making an initial prediction influenced subjects' subsequent choices, in which case any bias would have been attenuated in the within-subject comparison.

11.1.1. *Results*

Results for the two University of Pittsburgh classes were similar, so their data are aggregated. Three University of Pittsburgh subjects gave nonmonotonic responses to both valuation questions, rendering their data uncodable, and two provided useful predictions, but uncodable actual valuations. All five subjects are excluded from the analyses. The mean minimum selling values for the two institutions are shown in Table 1 For each university group, the first line shows the mean predicted and actual selling price of the prediction group. The second line shows the actual selling price for subjects who did not previously predict their own selling price.

Table 1. Predicted and Actual Valuation of the Mug

Group/ condition	Number of subjects	Prediction of valuation	Actual valuation
Carnegie Mellon University			
Prediction	14	$3.73	$5.40
		(0.41)	(0.65)
No prediction	13	—	$6.46
			(0.54)
University of Pittsburgh			
Prediction	22	$3.27	$4.56
		(0.48)	(0.59)
No prediction	17	—	$4.98
			(0.53)

Std. errors in parentheses.

Actual selling prices differed between the two universities, probably because different mugs were used. More interestingly, there was substantial underestimation of selling prices in both university groups, both within and between subjects. Within subjects, those who completed the first form substantially underestimated their own subsequent selling prices. For the Carnegie Mellon group, mean actual valuations were $1.67 greater than predicted valuations $(t(13) = 2.8, p < 0.02)$; for the University of Pittsburgh group they were greater by $1.17 $(t(16) = 3.2, p < 0.01)$.

Underprediction of value is also evident in the between-subjects comparison of the first group's predicted selling price and the second group's actual selling price. The mean difference between the predictions of the first group and the valuations of the second was $2.73 $(t(25) = 4.1, p < 0.0005)$ for the Carnegie Mellon group, and $1.59 $(t(35) = 2\cdot1, p < 0.05)$ for the University of Pittsburgh group. Mug valuations of the group which did not make a prediction were higher, but not significantly so, than those of the group which did make a prediction, suggestive of a weak anchoring effect.

11.2. Experiment 2

A limitation of the first study is that it was not 'incentive compatible' because subjects had no incentive to provide accurate predictions of their own selling prices (although, by the same token, there was no incentive for misrepresentation). The second experiment avoided this problem by informing subjects that they had a 50% chance of getting a mug and eliciting a selling price that would apply if they got a mug. Our prediction was that subjects who only had a 50% chance of getting a mug would not feel endowed and, like the prediction subjects in the previous experiment, would underestimate the selling price that they would want to prevail if they did get a mug.

319

A second limitation of the first study was that it did not elicit choice prices from subjects, so it was impossible to determine where the predicted selling price lay on the continuum between choice values and actual selling prices. If subjects predict their own selling prices perfectly, then we would observe $s' = s$ (as defined in equations (1)–(3)); if they are completely unable to predict the effect of possessing the object on their preferences, then we would anticipate $s' = c$ – i.e. that predicted selling prices will correspond to choice prices. To assess where their predictions lie on this continuum, we can construct an index of prediction bias, β, defined by:

$$\beta = \frac{s - s'}{s - c}. \tag{4}$$

β will equal o for individuals who predict their own selling prices perfectly, and 1 for those who are completely unable to predict the effect of being endowed on their valuation of the object. Note that this index reflects only the degree of prediction bias, and not the magnitude of the endowment effect which some people view as a type of bias in its own right.

11.2.1. *Method*

Two executive education classes at Northwestern University with a total of 106 students were each randomly assigned to two experimental groups which were isolated in separate rooms. In the control condition, a coin was flipped for each subject and subjects who called it correctly were given a mug emblazoned with the school logo. Selling prices were elicited from those who obtained a mug, and choice prices from those who did not, using forms that were analogous to those used to elicit selling prices in the first experiment.

For the experimental group, the identical type of mug was displayed at the front of the room, and subjects were told that there was a 50% chance of receiving one, based on whether they correctly called a coin flip. Prior to the coin flip, selling prices were elicited, which subjects were told would apply if they called the flip correctly and got a mug.[2] After providing selling prices, subjects individually called a coin toss and were given a mug if they called it correctly. Finally, those who received a mug were asked whether they would

---

[2] The exact wording of the form was as follows: 'There is a 50% chance that you will obtain the mug displayed at the front of the room. In a moment we are going to flip a coin to determine if you receive a mug exactly like the one you can see. We are interested in how much you will value the mug if you get it. Below are a series of lines marked 'Keep mug___ Trade it for $amount___.' On each line check whether, if you do get a mug, you would prefer to keep the mug or to trade it in for the amount of money written on the line. Check one or the other on every line. Later we will announce a line number and you will get your choice on that line. Think carefully about each check mark because if you get a mug your choice on one of the lines will count.'

Table 2. Mean Valuation of Mugs

Group	Form	Description	Number of subjects	Prediction of valuation
Control	1	Selling price	24	$5.96 (0.460)
	2	Choice	29	$4.05 (0.329)
Experimental	3	Selling price contingent on getting a mug	53	$4.16 (0.293)
	4	Desired revision of selling price	34	$4.69 (0.329)

Std. errors in parentheses.

like to revise their selling price (although they were not actually allowed to do so).[3]

11.2.2. Results

The standard endowment effect is evident in the mean values presented in Table 2 Subjects given a mug (Form 1) valued it an average of $1.91 higher than those without the mug (Form 2) (t(51) = 3.4, p < 0.002). More importantly, the bias in prediction of selling price is again evident. Subjects with a 50% chance of receiving a mug stated a mean selling price that was $1.80 lower than that for subjects who actually possessed a mug; the mean valuation for subjects prior to flipping the coin was $4.16 compared to $5.96 for subjects already endowed with a mug (t(75) = 3.352, p < 0.002). Selling prices for those who had a 50% chance of receiving a mug were very close to the choosing prices of subjects who did not have a mug ($4.16 vs. $4.05). The prediction bias β is equal to 0.94 measured between-subjects (i.e. 94% of its plausible maximum value).

The desired price revisions of subjects who got a mug provide further evidence of a prediction bias. The mean valuation of subjects endowed with the mug after having already decided on a selling price was $4.69, which is $0.53 higher than their previous valuation, a significant difference (t(34) = 3.3, p < 0.01). If we use $4.69 as a conservative estimate of the correct selling price, then the prediction bias index, β, drops to 0.84, which is still extremely high. Three subjects indicated that they would have liked to revise their price downward, 14 did not want to revise their price, and 17 wanted to revise

---

[3] The exact wording was as follows: 'The form you filled out earlier will determine whether you get a mug or some money. Nevertheless, we are interested in whether, if you had a chance, you would prefer to change your responses on that form. Suppose you could complete FORM 3 again; please check below how you would respond.' The subject then recompleted the form eliciting selling prices.

it upward. However, the remaining $1.27 discrepancy between the revised selling price and the mean selling price for the control condition ($t(56) = 2.3$, $p < 0.03$) indicates that the hypothetical selling prices of the experimental group were lower than they would have been if they had not 'anchored' their final valuations of the mug on their initial decisions.

11.3. General Discussion

Despite the importance of taste prediction for rational choice, the accuracy of such predictions has only recently become a topic of systematic research and inquiry. Perhaps, as Kahneman and Snell (1990) argue, the earlier absence of such research was limited by the circularity of the revealed preference approach, in which tastes are viewed as revealed by behaviour rather than as an independent construct exerting an influence on behaviour. With tastes defined by behaviour there is, as the economists say, 'no arguing with tastes', and no possibility for tastes to be accurate or inaccurate – they simply are what they are.

While there are some prior results that are suggestive of taste-change misestimation, the current study is, to our knowledge, the first to observe a systematic bias in the prediction of taste-change. Moreover, one could argue that it is a surprising domain in which to observe such a bias. Numerous theoretical articles have focused on the process of habit formation in which tastes change as a function of past consumption. With certain important exceptions, such as, reputedly, the drug crack, such processes operate relatively slowly. The endowment effect, in contrast, leads to a much more rapid change in tastes. Our subjects predicted how their tastes would change, not over a matter of months or years, but minutes. Given how quickly the endowment effect operates, it is remarkable that people are unable to anticipate it. The failure to anticipate the endowment effect is also surprising considering the vast experience most people have had acquiring, possessing, and losing objects – experience that should provide ample opportunities for learning how tastes change following the acquisition of goods. Judging from our experiments, such learning is severely limited.

An unpublished experiment conducted by Kahneman and Loewenstein (1991) provides a possible clue as to why such learning does not occur. They found that subjects who were endowed with an object did not change their ranking of the object's desirability relative to other objects. However, when it came to exchanging the endowed object for another item, they displayed a heightened attachment to the endowed object. It thus appears that a person must be threatened with the loss of an object to appreciate his or her heightened attachment to it. Since people are rarely endowed with an object then immediately deprived of it, they may not get feedback about how attached they become to objects in their possession.

Another factor interfering with feedback is that people may forget their initial valuation of the object. Several studies have shown that people tend to forget their past attitudes – to believe that their past views were similar to those held in the present (e.g. Marcus, 1986). If the same bias applies to tastes, then people will remember their past tastes as being similar to their current tastes and erroneously conclude that their tastes have not changed. Thus, feedback about taste-change may be less plentiful than one might expect based on the accumulation of experience with possession.

Nevertheless, people probably receive more feedback about the effect of endowments than they do about a wide range of other taste changes. Their inability to predict the effect of endowment, therefore, raises the possibility that a much wider range of changes in tastes are predicted with bias. Tastes change for a variety of reasons, typically due to processes that act more slowly than the endowment effect. When hungry, can we predict how our tastes will be different when we are satiated? When unafflicted by addiction, can we accurately anticipate the agonies of addiction and withdrawal? Most changes in tastes are also less predictable and systematic than the endowment effect. Whereas most people are affected similarly by the endowment effect, other endogenous taste changes are more variable. For example, one person may learn to love classical music after repeated exposure, whereas another might grow to detest it.

The failure to predict the endowment effect suggests that hypothetical selling prices elicited from subjects who are not in possession of the relevant goods are probably biased downward. To provide a selling price for a good one does not possess requires two stages of introspection: (1) imagining one possesses the object and has adapted to ownership, and (2) imagining how one would feel about parting with it. Buying prices and choice values, in contrast, both involve one stage of introspection, and we know of no compelling evidence that estimates of either value are biased; indeed, Starmer and Sugden (1991) failed to observe a significant difference between probabilistic as compared to deterministic choices.

As a general rule, it seems likely that people will mispredict their own preferences when the superscript and subscript in equation (3) are different – i.e. when people are asked to introspect about how they would feel or behave in a situation different from their own – but not when the subscript and superscript are identical. It would be interesting to test whether people with objects overpredict the buying prices or choice values of those without such objects, as this hypothesis suggests.

The observation that individuals are unaware of the endowment effect presents a novel view of choice. It suggests that people not only become attached to what they have (as implied by the endowment effect), but do so unknowingly. People seem to be unwittingly trapped by their choices; they make choices with an unrealistic sense of their reversibility.

References

Ausubel, L. M. (1991). 'The failure of competition in the credit card market'. *American Economic Review*, vol. 81, pp. 50–81.

Becker, G. S. and Murphy, K. M. (1990). 'A theory of rational addiction.' *Journal of Political Economy*, vol. 96, pp. 675–700.

Brickman, P., Coates, D. and Janoff-Bulman, R. (1978). 'Lottery winners and accident victims: Is happiness relative?' *Journal of Personality and Social Psychology*, vol. 36, pp. 917–927.

Constantinedes, G. M. (1990). 'Habit formation: a resolution of the equity premium puzzle.' *Journal of Political Economy*, vol. 98, pp. 519–543.

Duesenberry, J. (1952). *Income, Saving, and the Theory of Consumer Behavior.* Cambridge, MA: Harvard University Press.

Kahneman, D., Knetsch, J. L. and Thaler, R. H. (1990). 'Experimental tests of the endowment effect and the Coase theorem.' *Journal of Political Economy*, vol. 98, pp. 1325–1348.

Kahneman, D. and Loewenstein, G. (1991). 'Explaining the endowment effect.' Working Paper, Carnegie Mellon University Department of Social and Decision Sciences.

Kahneman, D. and Snell, J. (1990). 'Predicting utility.' In *Insights in Decision Making* (ed. R. Hogarth). Chicago, IL: University of Chicago Press.

Marcus, G. B. (1986). 'Stability and change in political attitudes: observe, recall, and "Explain" '. *Political Behavior*, vol. 8, pp. 21–44.

Marshall, J. D., Knetsch, J. L. and Sinden, J. A. (1987). 'Agents' evaluations of the disparity in measures of economic loss.' *Journal of Economic Behavior and Organization*, vol. 7, pp. 115–127.

Pollak, R. A. (1970). 'Habit formation and dynamic demand functions.' *Journal of Political Economy*, vol. 78, pp. 272–297.

Starmer, C. and Sugden, R. (1991). 'Does the random-lottery incentive system elicit true preferences? An experimental investigation.' *American Economic Review*, vol. 81, pp. 971–978.

Stigler, G. J. and Becker, G. S. (1977). 'De gustibus non est disputandum.' *American Economic Review*, vol. 67, pp. 76–90.

Tat, P., Cunningham, W. A. and Babakus, E. (1988). 'Consumer perception of rebates.' *Journal of Advertising Research*, vol. 28, pp. 45–50.

Thaler, R. (1980). 'Toward a positive theory of consumer choice.' *Journal of Economic Behavior and Organization*, vol. 39, pp. 36–90.

Tversky, A. and Kahneman, D. (1991). 'Loss aversion in riskless choice: a reference-dependent model.' *Quarterly Journal of Economics*, vol. 106, pp. 1039–1061.

12

Mispredicting the Endowment Effect: Underestimation of Owners' Selling Prices by Buyers' Agents

Leaf Van Boven, George Loewenstein, and David Dunning

I first met Leaf Van Boven at a conference at Northwestern University hosted by Max Bazerman and Doug Medin on the topic of "New Directions in Decision Making." I sat next to him at dinner—an Ethiopian restaurant near Wriggly stadium. I drank a lot of beer; he didn't drink any. I talked a lot and he was virtually silent. He is a very controlled, inscrutable, person. Leaf, Don Moore, and my wife's brother, Douglas Harsch and I went on one of the most arduous mountain trips that I've ever taken—in the Talkeetna range of Alaska—and Leaf maintained his imperturbable composure under the most horrendous conditions (which is not to denigrate the stoicism of the other two). I've teased him on numerous occasions that he must be holding something terrible inside to be so restrained, and he doesn't deny it, but I have never picked up any hints of what it might be.

Leaf was a graduate student at Cornell at the time. Several months later, when I was visiting Cornell, Leaf, his adviser David Dunning and I, cooked up the 'buyer's agent's paradigm which we have used in a series of papers, including the one reprinted here. Our narrow goal in this line of research was to show that people do not only fail to predict that they themselves will become attached to objects they are endowed with (see Chapter 11); they make the same error when predicting other people. We also wanted to show that this error in predicting other people can have economic consequences. So, our task that evening was to come up with an experimental setup in which it would be advantageous for a person to accurately predict the price at which another person will sell an object.

In a typical buyer's agent study, half of the subjects (sellers) are given an object such as a coffee mug embossed with their university's logo, and write down the minimum price at which they are willing to sell the object. The other half, playing the role of buyer's agents, are given $10 and paired with a seller. The buyer's agents' task is to name a price at which they think the mug owner will be willing to sell. If the price is higher than that specified by the seller, then the object goes back to the experimenter (who plays the role of 'principal' in the transaction) and the agent gets to keep whatever is left over of the $10. However, if they state a price that is lower than the seller's price, they must give up the $10 and the owner keeps the object. It is therefore in the buyer's agent's interest to intuit the lowest price at which the owner would sell the mug and offer an amount that is slightly higher. If buyers' agents underpredict sellers' minimum selling prices, however, they will make bids that are too low and will fail to earn money as a result.

This is in fact, what we observed when we ran the study. In the first study we ran, agents bid an average of $4.92 for the coffee mugs, but sellers wanted, on average $6.83 for their mugs. As a result, only 25 percent of buyers' agents received any payment, and their earnings averaged $0.75. If they had made the optimal bid, which was $6.50, 62 percent of bids would have been accepted and their average earnings would have been $2.15.

We asked the unsuccessfully bidding buyers' agents to explain the reasons for that failure. Their spontaneous explanations revealed no awareness of the endowment effect. Instead, they tended to blame the owners, who they viewed as greedy. In other studies we found that the underbidding of buyers' agents was caused by their tendency to underestimate what they themselves would sell the mug for if they owned one. For example when, in one study, we gave buyers' agents a mug of their own to keep, this caused them to make much higher, and hence profitable, bids, presumably because owning a mug themselves put them in touch with how reluctant they would be to part with it.

The study reported in this chapter examines whether people can learn about the endowment effect through repeated experience. We brought participants into the laboratory and gave objects to half of them—the owners. The other half played the role of buyers' agents, and made five sequential bids on the mugs of different owners, receiving feedback after each bid about whether their bids had succeeded. Consistent with learning from experience, buyers' agents raised their bid on each successive trial. On the first trial, they made a bid that, on average, was only 75 percent of what owners typically asked for, but by the fifth try their bid was 88 percent of what owners typically asked for.

However, the learning that occurred was rather limited. After the fifth bid, we distributed a new and different object to the sellers, and repeated the experimental sequence to see whether buyers' agents would behave more optimally than they had with the first object. This is not what happened. Buyers' agents once again made initial bids that were only 75 percent of what owners asked for, and, while once again their successive bids moved in the direction of optimality, there was no evidence that learning was more rapid in the second series of bids than it had been for the first. Buyers' agents seemed to learn that mug owners wanted a lot for their mugs, but this did not seem to lead to any more general understanding of the psychology of ownership.

We were not surprised by this finding. As I discuss in Chapter 5, research by psychologists has generally observed very little 'transfer of learning' from one task to another. If the second task differs in almost any respect from the first, people tend to think that what they learned in the first task is irrelevant to the second. Or, worse, they learn the wrong lesson from their experience with the first task, and then apply their flawed learning to the second. In light of the research on learning, it's quite amazing that most of us make it past age 20, and even sometimes manage to achieve a modicum of success in life. But that may be more of a tribute to forgiving social institutions than to our ability to learn to avoid making repeated mistakes.

Mispredicting the Endowment Effect: Underestimation of Owners' Selling Prices by Buyers' Agents[*]

Leaf Van Boven, George Loewenstein, and David Dunning

12.1. Introduction

The *endowment effect* (Knetch, 1989; Thaler, 1980) is among the most robust phenomena in the emerging field of behavioral economics. Contrary to the traditional assumption in economics that preferences are fixed in the short-term, the endowment effect indicates that preferences can change rapidly and systematically because of changes in an individual's transient asset position. Specifically, people become attached to objects that are in their possession and are reluctant to part with them, even if they would not have particularly desired the objects had they not been endowed with them. The endowment effect has been demonstrated in numerous studies, both in the lab (Kahneman et al., 1990, 1991; Knetch and Sinden, 1984) and in the field (Johnson et al., 1992).

Given the importance of the endowment effect for everyday economic behavior, people's *perceptions* of the endowment effect may be similarly important. If people were aware of the endowment effect—if they were aware that they would quickly become attached to objects in their possession— they could at least take these shifting preferences into account when making decisions. For example, when deciding what price they should be willing to pay for an automobile, consumers could properly weigh how much merely owning the vehicle would increase their valuation of it. Prior research, how-ever, indicates that people underestimate the magnitude of the endowment

[*] Reprinted from Journal of Economic Behavior & Organization, Vol. 51, Van Boven, L., Loewenstein, G., and Dunning, D. "Mispredicting the endowment effect", 351–365 (2003), with permission from Elsevier.

effect. Specifically; individuals underestimate how much they will become attached to objects once those objects become part of their endowment (Loewenstein and Adler, 1995; Van Boven et al., 2000). In this paper, we review evidence indicating that people also underestimate the endowment effect when it comes to predicting other people's preferences. We report a study examining whether this underestimation can lead to suboptimal behavior in settings with economic consequences, and, if so, whether people learn from experience.

12.1.1. *Underestimating the Endowment Effect*

Loewenstein and Adler conducted a series of studies in which individuals predicted their own lowest selling price for an object they did not yet possess. In one study, subjects were shown a coffee mug, told that it would be given to them 1 week later, and asked to predict the minimum price for which they would be willing to sell the mug. The mug was subsequently given to them and they stated actual minimum selling prices. Subjects significantly underestimated what their own selling prices would be. In another study, some subjects (potential owners) were told that there was a 50 percent chance that they would receive a coffee mug, and stated the minimum price for which they would sell the mug if they were to receive it (s'). Other subjects (actual owners) were given a mug, and stated their minimum selling price for the mug (s). Potential owners stated much lower selling prices than actual owners ($s' < s$), even though in both cases their stated selling prices determined whether they actually sold their mugs. A third group of subjects (choosers) who did not have mugs were asked to state a "choice price": the lowest price at which they would choose to receive the mug rather than the money (c). Consistent with the endowment effect, choice prices were lower than owners' selling prices ($c < s$).

Loewenstein and Adler constructed an index of non-owners' underestimation of the endowment effect:

$$\beta = \frac{s - s'}{s - c}.$$

If potential owners correctly anticipate the endowment effect and predict their selling prices perfectly (i.e. if $s' = s$), β equals 0. If potential owners anticipate no endowment effect and predict that their selling price will equal the choice price (i.e. if $s' = c$), β equals 1. In fact, β was 0.84; potential owners underestimated the true impact of the endowment effect on their own preferences by approximately 85 percent.

In studies reported elsewhere, we examined owners' and buyers' predictions of one another's reservation prices (Van Boven et al., 2000). We endowed owners with mugs and asked them to state their lowest selling price (s).

We asked buyers to state the maximum price they would be willing to pay to buy a mug (b). We also asked owners to estimate the average buyer's maximum purchase price (b') and we asked buyers to estimate the average owner's minimum selling price (s'). There was, of course, an endowment effect: owners' minimum selling prices were higher than buyers' maximum purchase prices ($s > b$). More important for the present research, both owners and buyers underestimated the endowment effect: owners overestimated buyers' maximum purchase price ($b' > b$) and buyers underestimated owners' minimum selling price ($s' > s$). Thus, people also underestimate the impact of the endowment effect on *other people's* preferences.

We constructed indices of the gap between owners' and buyers' estimates of the endowment effect and the actual endowment effect, γ_o and γ_b, respectively, analogous to Loewenstein and Adler:

$$\gamma_o = \frac{b' - b}{s - b}, \qquad \gamma_b = \frac{s - s'}{s - b}.$$

If owners and buyers estimate the other role's valuation accurately (i.e., if $b' = b$ and $s' = s$), then γ_o and γ_b equal 0, reflecting perfectly accurate perceptions of the magnitude of the endowment effect. If owners and buyers are completely unaware of the endowment effect and estimate the other role's reservation price to be equal to their own reservation price (i.e. if $b' = s$ and $s' = b$), then γ_o and γ_b equal 1.

Across two studies, both γ_o and γ_b equaled 0.39; both owners and buyers underestimated the magnitude of the endowment effect by approximately 40 percent.[1] This underestimation was not significantly reduced when people had recently attended lectures about the endowment effect in one of their psychology classes, when they estimated the valuations of people in the other role (buyer or seller) before they stated their own valuation, or when they were offered a monetary incentive ($2) for estimating the other role's valuation accurately (within ±5 percent). In sum, people underestimate the impact of the endowment effect on both their own and other people's preferences.

12.1.2. Our Study

We conducted a study patterned on a study we report elsewhere (Van Boven, Dunning, and Loewenstein) in which the profits earned by "buyers' agents" were contingent on their ability to accurately estimate owners' selling prices.

---

[1] Notice that γ_b from Van Boven, Dunning, and Loewenstein (0.39) was less than β from Loewenstein and Adler (0.84). The discrepancy is probably because Loewenstein and Adler examined the ratio $\beta = (s - s')/(s - c)$, whereas Van Boven, Dunning, and Loewenstein examined the ratio $\gamma_b = (s - s')/(s - b)$. Because the buying price (b) is naturally lower than the choice price (c) due to loss aversion for money, γ_b will generally be smaller than β.

Buyers' agents offered a portion of money they had received from the experimenter to purchase an owner's commodity. If the offer was accepted, the agent received the difference between the amount received from the experimenter and the amount offered; otherwise, the agent received nothing. Buyers' agents thus had an incentive to make an offer that was equal to or slightly higher than the owner's selling price. This procedure was repeated for five rounds; owners and buyer's agents were randomly paired with each other in each round.

We predicted that because non-owners tend to underestimate the endowment effect (and thus owners' selling prices), buyers' agents would initially make suboptimal offers—offers that were substantially lower than the expected-value maximizing offer. We also predicted that buyer's agents would learn to make increasingly optimal (i.e. higher) offers over time, as they gained information about owners' lowest selling prices. Previous research has found that the magnitude of some anomalous phenomena declines with stationary replication in a market setting (e.g. Camerer, 1987). The critical features of repetition that produce this effect appear to be experience and feedback (see Cox and Grether, 1996, for a general discussion and specific findings involving preference reversals). In the present study, buyers' agents would have learned of four different selling prices by the time they made an offer in the fifth round. We therefore expected agents' offers in round 5 to be significantly more optimal than their offers were in round 1.

After five rounds of buying and selling with the first commodity, we endowed the same owners with a second commodity and repeated the buying and selling procedure. If buyer's agents make increasingly optimal offers during the first five rounds because they learn about the underlying cause of owners' relatively high selling prices (the endowment effect) then agents' learning should generalize to the new commodity. We did not expect that to be the case. Rather, we expected agents' initial offers for the second commodity to once again be too low, corresponding more to their initial, rather than their final, offers for the first commodity.

We based this prediction on psychological research indicating that learning through repetition is often superficial. People learn to adjust their behavior to produce desired outcomes in specific situations, but have difficulty in understanding the psychological processes or the abstract structure of the situation that produce the desired outcomes (Bassok et al., 1995). Such failures of learning to transfer to novel situations have also been observed in experimental economics. In one study, Kagel and Levin (1986) found that subjects who bid on an asset in a 3-person auction initially overbid, exhibiting the winner's curse (Bazerman and Samuelson, 1983). After several rounds, subjects learned to decrease their bids such that they no longer lost money and no longer exhibited the winner's curse. However, when subjects were introduced to a 6-person auction—a novel task with the same underlying structure—instead of decreasing their bids further, as would have been normative given an understanding of the winner's curse, they increased their bids because they thought it was necessary to bid more aggressively in the new situation. Although subjects learned to avoid losses in the first situation, they did not learn about the abstract structure of the winner's curse in a way that they could immediately apply to the new situation. In our study, by analogy, we did not expect agents' learning with the first commodity to transfer immediately to the second commodity. When the new commodity was introduced, we therefore expected buyer's agents' behavior to resemble their initial behavior with the first commodity more than their final behavior with that commodity.

12.2. Method

Students at Cornell University and Carnegie Mellon University ($N = 302$) enrolled in introductory psychology and economics courses participated in one of nine sessions in exchange for the opportunity to earn either goods or cash, depending on what role they were assigned to. After briefly describing the roles, the experimenter randomly assigned subjects within each session to equal numbers of owners and buyer's agents.

Depending on the session, owners were given a mug, pen, poster, or shot glass, all priced at about $6 at the campus store (see Table 1). Owners within a particular session were all given the same commodity.

All subjects were then given packets containing questionnaires and instructions that were identical for subjects in both roles and that described the

Table 1. Number of subjects in each session, order in which commodities were traded in each session, and the ratio of agents' average offer to the optimal offer in the first and final rounds of trading for each commodity in each session

N	First commodity	Ratio of average offer to optimal offer		Second commodity	Ratio of average offer to optimal offer	
		Round 1	Round 5		Round 6	Round 10
12	Mug	0.71	0.86	Shot glass	0.77	1.03
24	Mug	0.62	0.85	Shot glass	0.76	0.82
34	Shot glass	0.71	0.85	Mug	0.76	0.89
34	Mug	0.67	0.90	Pen	0.71	1.03
34	Mug	0.84	1.00	Poster	0.68	0.96
34	Poster	0.89	0.75	Mug	0.89	0.88
36	Pen	0.82	0.84	Mug	0.77	0.93
46	Mug	0.78	1.01	Shot glass	0.77	1.05
48	Mug	0.71	0.87	Pen	0.66	0.76
Average		0.75	0.88		0.75	0.93

general procedure. The experimenter read all three sets of instructions aloud to all subjects while they read along:

General instructions

In this exercise, you have been assigned either to the role of "owner" or "buyer's agent". Please read the instructions for both roles, regardless of which role you will play.

The first part of this exercise consists of five rounds. In each round, a buyer's agent will be randomly paired with an owner. The owner will specify the lowest price he/she will sell his/her [commodity] for and the buyer's agent will specify an offer. At the end of the experiment, one of the five rounds will be randomly selected to count. If the owner ends up keeping the [commodity] in that round, then he/she will keep the [commodity]. If the owner has sold the [commodity] in that round then he/she will return the [commodity] to the experimenter and receive the amount offered by the buyer's agent in that round.

Instructions for owners

You now own a [commodity] that is yours to keep and take home. You will specify the lowest price you will sell your [commodity] for. In each round, you will be randomly paired with one of the other students acting as a "buyer's agent". The buyer's agent will make an offer to purchase your [commodity]. If the offer is higher than or equal to your lowest selling price, then you will return the [commodity] to the experimenter and be paid the price of the offer. If the offer is lower than your lowest selling price, you will keep your [commodity] and get no money.

Instructions for buyer's agents

You now do not own a [commodity] that is yours to keep and take home. You will act on behalf of a buyer (the experimenter) who has given you $10 to purchase a [commodity] for him/her. In each round, you will be randomly paired with one of the owners who has been given a [commodity] to keep and take home. You will make an offer for that person's [commodity]. The owner will specify a minimum selling price. If the amount that you offer is equal to or higher than the owner's minimum selling price, then your offer is accepted: the owner will be paid the price of the offer and will return the [commodity] to the experimenter, and you will keep whatever is left of the $10—that is, $10 minus the amount of the offer. If the offer is less than the owner's minimum selling price, then your offer is not accepted in which case the owner will keep his or her [commodity] and you will get no money.

The instructions varied slightly from one session to another, depending primarily on the commodity given to owners.

Subjects' packets also contained instructions and questionnaires for each round. In round 1, owners stated their lowest selling price by indicating for every price on a list of prices that increased in 50¢ intervals from $0 to $10 whether they would sell their mug for that price or not. Also for round 1, buyer's agents stated their offer on a list of prices that increased in 50¢ intervals from $0 to $10. Owners wrote their lowest selling prices and agents wrote their offers on slips of paper, which the experimenter collected and randomly distributed to one member of the other group. After buyer's agents received a lowest selling price and owners received an offer, subjects recorded in their packets whether the offer was accepted, and, if so, how much money they would receive or keep. Buyer's agents thus received information about the lowest selling price of one owner after each round of the experiment. This process repeated until round 5 was finished, by which time buyer's agents had learned of five different selling prices.

The market for the first commodity was then declared closed. Owners were immediately given a different commodity that sold for a similar price at the campus store (see Table 1). The item was also shown to buyer's agents, who were asked to examine it. The experimenter explained that subjects would complete five additional rounds that would be identical to the first five rounds, except that owners would state lowest selling prices and buyer's agents would make offers for the new commodity.[2] Subjects were given the following written instructions, which the experimenter read aloud:

The second part of this exercise consists of five additional rounds (rounds 6 through 10). Everything will be exactly the same as in the first five rounds, except that the owners have been given a [commodity] for which they will state their lowest selling price and for which the buyer's agents will make offers. In each round, a buyer's agent will be randomly paired with an owner. At the end of the experiment, one of the five rounds from the second set of rounds will be randomly selected to "count". If the owner ends up keeping the [commodity] in that round, then he or she will keep the [commodity]. If the owner has sold the [commodity] in that round then he or she will return the [commodity] to the experimenter and receive the amount offered by the buyer's agent in that round.

After completing the final round, the experimenter randomly selected one of the first five rounds and one of the second five rounds and honored all transactions in those two rounds.

12.3. Results

Because the behavior of buyer's agents and owners within a particular session are not statistically independent, we either used the nine sessions as the unit of analysis or statistically controlled for the fixed effects of experimental session.

To examine the optimality of buyer's agents' behavior, we computed the ratio of the average actual offer to the expected-profit maximizing offer for each round of each session. A ratio of 1 would indicate the actual offers were exactly optimal. If the offers were too high, the ratio would be greater than 1; if they were too low, as we expected them to be, the ratio would be less than 1.

---

[2] Because of time constraints, one group did not complete rounds 9 and 10.

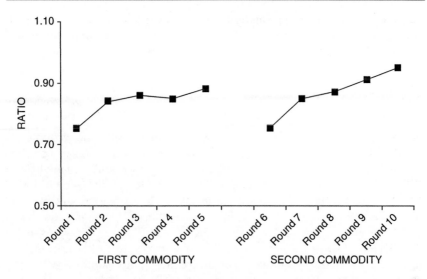

Figure 1. Ratio of average actual offers to optimal offers for each round of interactions with the first and second commodities, averaged across nine sessions.

Note that the ratio of actual to optimal offers is standardized across sessions and commodities.

12.3.1. *Trading the First Commodity*

The average ratio of actual offers to the optimal offer for each round averaged across the nine sessions is displayed in Fig. 1. The ratios of average to optimal offers for the first and final rounds of trading with the first and second commodity for each session are displayed in Table 1. As anticipated, the average ratio in round 1 (0.75) was significantly less than 1 (one-sample $t(8) = 8.53$, $p < 0.01$) indicating that buyer's agents' initial offers were too low.

Buyers' agents also exhibited the anticipated learning (see Fig. 1). In all but one session, the ratio increased by round 5, to an average of 0.88 (see Table 1). To examine the statistical significance of this increase, we conducted two regressions: the first regression predicted the ratio of actual to optimal offers from a variable representing ROUND (coded 1–5); the second regression predicted the ratio from ROUND and ROUND SQUARED.[3] (Both regressions controlled for fixed effects of experimental session.) In the first regression, as predicted, the coefficient associated with ROUND was positive and significant ($\beta = 0.027$, $t(35) = 3.29$, $p < 0.005$). Agents' offers became more optimal as they gathered more information about owners' selling prices. In the second regression, the linear term was significant ($\beta = 0.094$, $t(34) = 2.33$, $p < 0.05$)

---

[3] All linear regressions reported in this paper contain a constant.

and the quadratic term was marginally significant ($\beta = -0.011$, $t(34) = 1.71$, $p < 0.10$), reflecting that agents' offers increased at a somewhat declining rate over time.

12.3.2. Trading the Second Commodity

What happened in round 6, the first round of trading with the second commodity? It is clear in Fig. 1 and Table 1 that the average ratio of actual to optimal offers in round 6 was less than the ratio in round 5 (paired $t(8) = 2.86$, $p < 0.025$). In fact, the average ratio of actual to optimal offers in round 6 (0.75) was the same as in round 1. Indeed, in all but one session, the ratio decreased from rounds 5 to 6. The one exception was the same session in which the ratio in round 5 was less than in round 1. In other words, in all the sessions in which agents learned from rounds 1 to 5 that learning did not transfer to a new commodity. The probability of this pattern occurring by chance is less than 0.0001 (binomial $z = 4.43$).[4] There was thus no observable transfer of learning from rounds 5 to 6.

Over rounds 6–10, as trading with the second commodity progressed, buyer's agents once again increased their offers relative to the optimal offers (see Fig. 1). To examine the statistical significance of this increase, we conducted two regressions: the first regression predicted the ratio of actual to optimal offers from ROUND (coded 1–5 for rounds 6–10, respectively); the second regression predicted the ratio from ROUND and ROUND SQUARED.[5]

In the first regression, as predicted, the coefficient associated with ROUND was positive and significant ($\beta = 0.045$, $t(35) = 5.76$, $p < 0.001$). Agents' offers became more optimal as they (once again) gathered more information about owners' selling prices for the second commodity. In the second regression, the linear term was marginally significant ($\beta = 0.074$, $t(34) = 1.80$, $p = 0.08$) and the quadratic term was not significant ($\beta = -0.0047$, $t < 1$). There was no reliable change in the rate at which relatively optimal offers increased over time. These results indicate that even though buyers' agents' learning with the first commodity did not transfer to the second commodity, agents' did once again learn as they gained experience buying and selling the second commodity.

---

[4] The null probability is 0.25, assuming a null 0.50 probability for each of the two inequalities, i.e. that the ratio in round 5 was higher than in round 1, and that the ratio in round 6 was lower than in round 5.

[5] Because one session did not complete rounds 9 and 10, we used the average ratio of actual to optimal offers from the other eight sessions as an estimate of the shorter session's ratio for those rounds.

12.3.3. *Trading the First Versus Second Commodity*

Was the rate at which the ratio of actual to optimal offers increased during interactions with the second commodity faster than it was during interactions with the first commodity? We examined the possibility of such a "savings in learning" by regressing the ratio of actual to optimal offers on COMMODITY (with 1 representing the second commodity and 0 representing the first commodity), ROUND (coded 1–5 for both rounds 1–5 and for rounds 6–10), and the interaction of ROUND and COMMODITY, again controlling for the fixed effects of session. Our primary interest was in the interaction, which tests whether the linear increase in the ratio over interactions with the second commodity is greater than the linear increase in the ratio over interactions with the first commodity. The coefficient associated with this interaction, although positive ($\beta = 0.019$), was only marginally significant ($t(78) = 1.60$, $p = 0.11$).[6] There was thus no reliable evidence for a savings in learning in interactions with the second commodity relative to the first commodity.

12.3.4. *Alternative Interpretations*

The foregoing analyses indicate that agents' offers are initially too low relative to the expected-payoff maximizing offer and then become increasingly optimal over repeated interactions with an initial commodity. When trading for a novel commodity begins, however, agents' offers are again too low relative to the expected-payoff maximizing offer before increasing over repeated interactions with the second commodity. Our hypothesis is that this pattern stems from agents' underestimation of the endowment effect, their resulting underestimation of selling prices, and their failure to learn about the endowment effect from feedback about owners' selling prices. There are, however, several alternative interpretations for various portions of our results. We consider four alternative interpretations and describe evidence contradicting each.

CHANGING SELLING PRICES?

The first possible alternative is that diminishing selling prices over time caused the offers to be increasingly optimal (see Fig. 2). We examined this possibility by conducting four regressions parallel to those reported earlier, but using offers and selling prices as dependent variables rather than the ratio of actual to optimal offers. For each commodity, we conducted two regressions, one predicting offers and the other predicting selling prices from ROUND (coded

---

[6] We also conducted a regression to compare the quadratic increase in ratios over interactions with the first commodity versus interactions with the second commodity. We estimated the ratio of actual to optimal offers from COMMODITY, ROUND (as defined earlier), ROUND SQUARED, and the product of COMMODITY and ROUND SQUARED, all while controlling for the fixed session effects. This interaction term was not significant ($\beta = 0.0066$, $t < 1$).

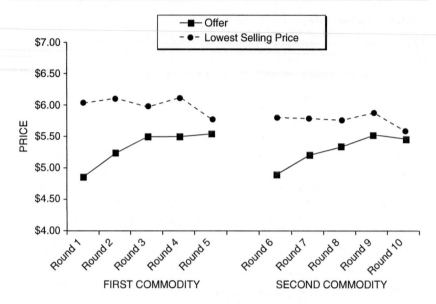

Figure 2. Average offer and lowest selling price for each round of interactions with the first and second commodities, averaged across nine sessions.

1–5 for both rounds 1–5 and for rounds 6–10.[7] For offers, the coefficient associated with ROUND was significant for both the first and second commodities (β's = 0.154 and 0.164, respectively, both p's < 0.01). As we suggested, agents' offers increased over repeated interactions with each commodity. For selling prices, in contrast, the coefficients associated with ROUND, although negative, were not significant for either the first or the second commodity (β's = −0.019 and −0.057, p's > 0.6 and 0.13, respectively). These results indicate that the increasingly optimal offers within each set of rounds were caused more by increases in buyer's agents' offers than by decreases in owners' selling prices.

SIGNALING

Another alternative interpretation is that agents made low offers and owners stated high selling prices in early rounds in an effort to signal or "teach" subjects in the other role to change their behavior. That is, agents may have made especially low offers to entice sellers state lower selling prices while sellers may have stated especially high selling prices to make agents to make

---

[7] To estimate the offers and selling prices for the session that did not complete rounds 9 and 10, we conducted regressions predicting offers and selling prices in round 8 from offers and selling prices, respectively, in rounds 6 and 7. We used the resulting regression equations to estimate what the offers and selling prices would have been if that session had completed all 10 rounds.

338

higher offers. Such a strategy could make sense if the number of subjects were few enough so that the probability of being paired again with a particular owner in later rounds was relatively high. On this analysis, we would expect the ratio of actual to optimal offers in the initial round of trading with a particular commodity to be negatively correlated with the number of subjects in that session. To the contrary, the coefficients associated with number of subjects in a session were not significant in regressions predicting the ratio of actual to optimal offers for either the first or the second commodity (β's = -0.002 and 0.002, respectively, both t's < 1).

FAIRNESS

One reason buyer's agents might have made low offers is that they may have felt that dividing $10 roughly in half was only fair (Kahneman et al., 1986). But such an interpretation neither accounts for the increase in relatively optimal offers from rounds 1 to 5, nor the relative decrease from rounds 5 to 6, nor the subsequent increase from rounds 6 to 10. Concerns about fairness thus do not offer a viable alternative interpretation of our overall pattern of results.

RISKY PREFERENCES

A final alternative interpretation of our results concerns a potential preference by buyers' agents for risky offers. Given the relatively small amounts of money at stake, buyers' agents may have preferred a low probability of a large cash payoff to a high probability of a low cash payoff (Markowtiz, 1952). If so, then agents would have made relatively low, risky offers. Note that this interpretation does not explain why agents' offers would increase over repeated interactions with owners, nor why that increase would not transfer to a new commodity. But it could contribute to agents' relatively low initial offers.

To examine the viability of this risky interpretation, we conducted a small study in which buyers' agents were given full information about owners' lowest selling prices. We divided a group of 12 Carnegie Mellon University students into six owners and six buyer's agents. The instructions and procedure mirrored those described earlier, except that owners were given a Carnegie Mellon key chain rather than a mug and buyer's agents could make offers as high as $5 rather than as high as $10. Before making their offers, buyer's agents were told the distribution of owners' lowest selling prices, which were: $1, $1, $1.5, $2, $3, and $3.5. They were told that they would be randomly paired with one of the sellers who had specified the prices.

If agents' low offers in the main study stem from a preference for risky offers, particularly given the relatively small amount of money at stake, then agents' offers for the key chain should be below the $2 expected-payoff maximizing offer. If, as we hypothesize, agents' low offers stem from their underestimation of the endowment effect and of owners' selling prices, then giving agents full (and accurate) information about owners' selling prices should lead them to make more optimal offers. In line with our interpretation, the average offer ($2.33) was slightly higher than the optimal offer of $2. Four agents made offers of $2 and two made offers of $3. Informed about owners' selling prices, then, buyer's agents came close to maximizing expected value. This casts doubt on the risky interpretation of the buyer's agents' behavior.

12.4. General Discussion

Because buyer's agents underestimated the impact of the endowment effect on owners' selling prices, they made suboptimal offers for an owner's commodity, leaving them with less money than they could have made. Buyer's agents learned to behave more optimally when this procedure was replicated with the same commodity, but this learning did not transfer to interactions with a superficially novel commodity. Rather, agents' initial offers for the second commodity were significantly less optimal than their final offers for the first commodity—they were equivalent, in fact, to agents' initial offers for the first commodity. In short, buyer's agents' underestimation of the endowment effect led them to behave suboptimally in a setting with economic consequences.

12.4.1. *Implications for Everyday Economic Behavior*

Our findings naturally raise the question of whether underestimating the endowment effect might cause similarly suboptimal behavior in settings outside the laboratory. Although the results of our study do not address this question directly, they strongly suggest that it will. Our study was a conservative test of learning among buyer's agents. Less than 5 min elapsed between rounds 5 and 6, and so there was little time for agents to forget what they had learned from their dealings with the first commodity. Furthermore, the instructions for trading with the second commodity explicitly stated the similarity between trading with the two commodities. Subjects read "everything will be *exactly the same* as in the first five rounds, except that the owners have been given a [new commodity] for which they will state their lowest selling price and for which the buyer's agents will make offers" (italics added). Agents nonetheless did not generalize their learning from one commodity to another.

Outside the laboratory, in fact, learning may be more difficult. Buyers are unlikely to receive prompt, unambiguous feedback regarding sellers' reservation prices as they did in our study. Outside the lab, buyers may be informed only that their offer was rejected without learning what the owners' true lowest selling price was. Without such feedback, learning will be slow, if it occurs at all (Einhorn, 1982).

Another reason that learning may be even more difficult outside the laboratory is that the feedback people do receive may be open to many interpretations other than the endowment effect. A potential homebuyer, for example, may make several inferences about a high asking price, only one of which concerns the endowment effect. The buyer may instead infer that the owner is greedy, unintelligent, or misinformed about the value of the home. Evidence we report elsewhere suggests that people are likely to endorse such alternative explanations as these more readily than they endorse explanations based on the endowment effect (Van Boven, Dunning, and Loewenstein, Study 4). In that study, we asked owners and buyer's agents to rate several explanations for the behavior of the person in the other role with whom they were paired. One of the reasons was a simple description of the endowment effect; another reason was that the other person was greedy. People rated the other person's greed as a significantly more likely explanation for the other person's behavior than the endowment effect.

The tendency to misinterpret behaviors that result from the endowment effect can itself have consequences for economic behavior outside the laboratory, in addition to the consequences of underestimating the endowment effect. If an individual interprets someone's behavior as stemming from greed as opposed to the endowment effect, the individual may come to dislike the other person. That dislike, in turn, may increase the individual's willingness to incur losses to hurt the disliked person (Gibbons and Van Boven, 2001; Loewenstein et al., 1989; Levine, 1998; Rabin, 1993). Underestimation of the endowment effect may therefore have both direct and indirect consequences for everyday economic behavior.

12.4.2. *Empathy Gaps in Predictions of Self and Others*

Underestimation of the endowment effect is part of a more general tendency for people to project their current, transient feelings and preferences onto their estimates of what their own and other people's preferences would be in a different role or situation (Loewenstein, 1996; Loewenstein and Adler, 1995; Loewenstein et al., 2001; Van Boven et al., 2002). In one study, for instance, people's current feelings of hunger or satiation influenced their preference for food to be consumed 1 week later (Read and van Leeuwen, 1998; see also Gilbert et al., 2002). In another study, male subjects who viewed sexually arousing photographs reported that they were more likely to engage in sexually aggressive behaviors on a hypothetical date than did male subjects who did not view sexually arousing photographs (Loewenstein et al., 1997).

Because people often use their own preferences as a basis for predicting other people's preferences (Davis et al., 1986; Hoch, 1987; Ross et al., 1977), their biased predictions of their own preferences will lead them to make biased predictions of other people's preferences. In one study, people's current feelings of hunger, thirst, and warmth influenced their predictions of the feelings of a hypothetical group of hikers lost in the woods without food or water (Van Boven and Loewenstein, forthcoming). More directly relevant to underestimation of the endowment effect and the present studies, Van Boven, Dunning, and Loewenstein (Study 5) showed that buyer's agents' offers to owners were closely linked to their predictions of what their own selling price would be if they were an owner. Buyer's agents who did not own a mug underestimated what their own selling price would be if they were an owner and made correspondingly low offers. In contrast, agents who had been endowed with mugs were significantly more accurate in their prediction of what their own selling price would be and they made correspondingly higher offers. Furthermore, the effect of owning a mug on agents' offers was statistically mediated by the effect of owning a mug on agents' predictions of what their selling price would be if they were an owner. In short, people's empathy gaps in self-predictions produce empathy gaps in social predictions.

12.4.3. Conclusion

Given the robustness and ubiquity of the endowment effect, anticipating the endowment effect is an important aspect of everyday economic life. The present studies indicate that people's underestimation of the endowment effect's impact on other people's preferences can lead to behavior that can have costly economic consequences. The implications of this research extend beyond buyers and sellers. Individuals frequently change roles and experience different psychological states, and they are often in different roles or states than the people they interact with. Biased predictions of oneself and of others may therefore be an important source of suboptimal behavior in many aspects of everyday life.

Acknowledgments

This research was funded by NIMH Grant RO1-56072 and by the Center for the Study of Human Dimensions of Global Change at Carnegie Mellon University (NSF Grant SBR-9521914).

References

Bassok, M., Wu, L. L., and Olseth, K. L., 1995. Judging a book by its cover: interpretative effects of content on problem-solving transfer. Memory and Cognition 23, 354–367.
Bazerman, M. H. and Samuelson, W. F., 1983. I won the auction but don't want the prize. Journal of Conflict Resolution 27, 618–634.

Camerer, C., 1987. Do biases in probability judgments matter in markets? Experimental evidence. American Economic Review 77, 981–997.

Cox, J. C. and Grether, D. M., 1996. The preference reversal phenomenon: response mode, markets and incentives. Economic Theory 7, 381–405.

Davis, H. L., Hoch, S. J., and Ragsdale, E. K. E., 1986. An anchoring and adjustment model of spouse predictions. Journal of Consumer Research 13, 25–37.

Einhorn, H. J., 1982. Learning from experience and suboptimal rules in decision making. In: Kahneman, D., Slovic, P., and Tversky, A. (Eds.), Judgment Under Uncertainty: Heuristics and Biases. Cambridge University Press, Cambridge, MA, pp. 268–286.

Gibbons, R., Van Boven, L., 2001. Contingent social utility in the prisoners' dilemma. Journal of Economic Behavior and Organization 45, 1–17.

Gilbert, D. T., Gill, M. J., and Wilson, T. D., 2002. The future is now: temporal correction in affective forecasting. Organizational Behavior and Human Decision Processes 88, 430–444.

Hoch, S. J., 1987. Perceived consensus and predictive accuracy: the pros and cons of projection. Journal of Personality and Social Psychology 53, 221–234.

Johnson, E. J., Hershey, J., Meszaros, J., and Kunrunther, H., 1992. Framing, probability distortions, and insurance decisions. Journal of Risk and Uncertainty 7, 35–51.

Kagel, J., and Levin, D., 1986. The winner's curse and public information in common value auctions. American Economic Review 76, 894–920.

Kahneman, D., Knetch, J., and Thaler, R., 1986. Fairness as a constraint on profit seeking: entitlements in the market. American Economic Review 76, 728–741.

Kahneman, D., Knetch, J., and Thaler, R., 1990. Experimental tests of the endowment effect and the Coase theorem. Journal of Political Economy 98, 1325–1348.

Kahneman, D., Knetch, J., and Thaler, R., 1991. Anomalies: the endowment effect, loss aversion, and status quo bias. Journal of Economic Perspectives 5, 193–206.

Knetch, J. L., 1989. The endowment effect and evidence of nonreversible indifference curves. American Economic Review 79, 1277–1284.

Knetch, J., Sinden, J. A., 1984. Willingness to pay and compensation demanded: experimental evidence of an unexpected disparity in measures of value. Quarterly Journal of Economics 99, 507–521.

Levine, D., 1998. Modeling altruism and spitefulness in experiments. Review of Economic Dynamics 1, 593–622.

Loewenstein, G., 1996. Out of control: visceral influences on behavior. Organizational Behavior and Human Decision Processes 65, 272–292.

Loewenstein, G., and Adler, D., 1995. A bias in the prediction of tastes. Economic Journal 105, 929–937.

Loewenstein, G., Thompson, L., and Bazerman, M., 1989. Social utility and decision making in interpersonal contexts. Journal of Personality and Social Psychology 57, 426–441.

Loewenstein, G., Nagin, D., and Paternoster, R., 1997. The effect of sexual arousal on predictions of sexual forcefulness. Journal of Research in Crime and Delinquency 34, 443–473.

Loewenstein, G., O' Donoghue, T., and Rabin, M., 2001. Projection bias in predicting future utility. Carnegie Mellon University, Pittsburgh, PA. Unpublished manuscript.

Markowtiz, H., 1952. The utility of wealth. Journal of Political Economy 60, 151–158.

Rabin, M., 1993. Incorporating fairness into game theory and economics. American Economic Review 83, 1408–1418.

Read, D., and van Leeuwen, B., 1998. Time and desire: the effects of anticipated and experienced hunger and delay to consumption on the choice between healthy and unhealthy snack food. Organizational Behavior and Human Decision Processes 76, 189–205.

Ross, L., Greene, D., and House, P., 1977. The false consensus effect: an egocentric bias in social perception and attribution processes. Journal of Experimental Social Psychology 13, 279–301.

Thaler, R., 1980. Toward a positive theory of consumer choice. Journal of Economic Behavior and Organization 1, 39–60.

Van Boven, L., and Loewenstein, G., forthcoming. Projection of transient drive states. Personality and Social Psychology Bulletin.

Van Boven, L., Dunning, D., and Loewenstein, G., 2000. Egocentric empathy gaps between owners and buyers: misperceptions of the endowment effect. Journal of Personality and Social Psychology 79, 66–76.

Van Boven, L., Loewenstein, G., Welch, E., and Dunning, D., 2002. The illusion of courage: underestimating social-risk aversion in self and others, submitted for publication.

13

Projection Bias in Predicting Future Utility

George Loewenstein, Ted O'Donoghue, and Matthew Rabin

On the second day of an overnight hike with my son Max on the Laurel Ridge trail in Pennsylvania, I asked him whether, when we got back to our bicycles (which were waiting at the end of the hike so we could bike back to the car), he wanted to take the route we had been planning to take or a longer, more scenic route. Max (who was 10 at the time) knew that I wanted to take the longer, scenic route and informed me that I had made a strategic error: "Daddy: you should have asked me when we were resting back on that rock, not while we are hiking. Of course I won't want to take the long route if you ask me when I'm all tired out". Max's response reflected a deep appreciation for projection bias (though I had never mentioned it to him). While he was hiking, he was feeling tired and couldn't imagine that he would want to put in the extra miles when we got to the bike. When he was rested, however, he intuited, he would 'project' his lack of exhaustion onto his future decision. As it turned out, however, the decision was moot. We got hit by an ice storm about two hours before the end of the hike and by the times we arrived at the bikes they and we were embedded in a thick coat of ice. In a hypothermic state, we abandoned the bikes and slowly and painfully trudged down the road, looking for shelter. We did finally find a house with smoke issuing from the roof, and Max got his first exposure to Appalachian poverty.

I wish I could say that Max's observations inspired the paper, but they didn't. In fact, it was one more idea that hatched in the sunny environment of the Center at Stanford, this time with Ted and Matthew. Ted has an amazing gift when it comes to modeling. On this paper, and on subsequent projects we have worked on, he is able to take complicated ideas and formulate them into simple equations—almost to the point of making me forget my gripes about the excessive mathematization of economics.

Matthew, as the saying goes, 'needs no introduction'; he has won practically every prize there is to win in economics (with one major exception, but I have no doubt that will come in good time). Having worked with him on a number of papers, including this one, and from the many long walks we've taken while attending various conferences and meetings, I can only say that they are all well deserved. And no description of Matthew would be complete without some reference to his attire. Not only have I never seen Matthew don a coat and tie, but I can't recall ever seeing him wearing anything other than shorts and a tie-dyed T-shirt, even in the winter. Based on observing Matthew and others, I have come to the conclusion that there is a strong interaction between one's value in an organization and one's quirks, whether it be dressing strangely or managing punk bands (see introduction to Chapter 4). For someone who is on the 'outs', dressing badly adds one more negative that reinforces the others. However, for someone who is highly valued to begin with, dressing or behaving in an unusual fashion has a positive effect, perhaps because it signals one is so talented that one can wear whatever one likes.

Returning to the paper, in it, we argue that people often mispredict their own future preferences because they underestimate how much they will change; they 'project' their current preferences into the future. Although three years isn't very long, I think that so far the model has withstood the test of time. However, there are at least two ways in which it falls short. The first is that some of the phenomena we discuss in the paper might stem not from people underpredicting how their preferences will change, but instead from their failure to *care* about how they will change. That is, in many cases we act according to our current preferences not because we mispredict our future preferences but because we think that our current preferences are more valid. If, for example, I knew that I was going to be addicted to heroin, become politically conservative or develop a taste for illicit pleasures, I still probably wouldn't make plans to indulge those preferences in the future. In some cases, we may act on our current preferences because we fail to predict how our preferences will change, but in other cases that are often difficult to distinguish on the basis of behavior, we may predict our future preferences accurately but still not act on the prediction.

The second arises from an important phenomenon that our model doesn't easily explain: the "diversification bias" first identified by Itamar Simonson.[1] He found that when people make decisions in the present that apply to the

---

[1] Simonson, I. (1990). 'The effect of Purchase Quantity and Timing on Variety Seeking Behavior', *Journal of Marketing Research*. 32: 150–62. Daniel Read and I followed up on Simonson's research and attempted to determine the cause of the effect. Read, D. and Loewenstein, G. (1995). 'The Diversification Bias: Explaining the Difference Between Prospective and Real-Time Taste for Variety', *Journal of Experimental Psychology: Applied*. 1: 34–49.

future, they tend to seek out greater diversity than they end up wanting. For example, when people choose ahead of time which of six snacks to eat on three occasions each separated by a week, many people opt to consumer different snacks on different days (e.g., Snickers, raisins, and Almond Joy). But if they choose each snack at the time when they will consume it, they tend to want the same snack each time (Snickers, Snickers, and Snickers). Because it implies that people project their own current tastes on the future (in this case favoring Snickers), our model would seem to imply the opposite pattern. In fact, I believe, the model makes the correct prediction: People would not want to eat three Snickers bars in a row, and they project their distaste for eating the second and third onto the future when their Snicker-specific satiation will in fact have dissipated. But, such a prediction does not naturally 'drop out' of the model in the way we have formulated it.

Projection Bias in Predicting Future Utility[*]

George Loewenstein, Ted O'Donoghue, and Matthew Rabin

People exaggerate the degree to which their future tastes will resemble their current tastes. We present evidence from a variety of domains which demonstrates the prevalence of such *projection bias,* develop a formal model of it, and use this model to demonstrate its importance in economic environments. We show that, when people exhibit habit formation, projection bias leads people to consume too much early in life, and to decide, as time passes, to consume more—and save less—than originally planned. Projection bias can also lead to misguided purchases of durable goods. We discuss a number of additional applications and implications.

The great source of both the misery and disorders of human life, seems to arise from over-rating the difference between one permanent situation and another. Avarice over-rates the difference between poverty and riches: ambition, that between a private and a public station: vain-glory, that between obscurity and extensive reputation—Adam Smith, *The Theory of Moral Sentiments* [2002, p. 173; III,iii,31].

* For helpful comments, we are grateful to Erik Eyster, Christopher Harris, and members of the Russell Sage Foundation Behavioral Economics Roundtable; seminar participants at Cornell University, Yale University, Harvard University, University of Michigan, University of Texas, Syracuse University, London School of Economics, University of Zurich, the Toulouse Conference on Psychology and Economics, and the Jerome Levy Institute; and Lawrence Katz, Edward Glaeser, and an anonymous referee. We especially thank Colin Camerer and Drazen Prelec for very helpful discussions at the formative stages of this project. For research assistance, we thank Kitt Carpenter, Erik Eyster, Jeffrey Holman, David Huffman, Christopher Meissner, and Mandar Oak. For financial support, Loewenstein thanks the Center for the Study of Human Dimensions of Global Change at Carnegie Mellon University (NSF Grant SBR-9521914), O'Donoghue and Rabin thank the National Science Foundation (Awards SBR-9709485, SES-0078796, and SES-0079266), and Rabin thanks the Russell Sage, MacArthur, and Sloan Foundations. This research was started while Loewenstein and Rabin were Fellows at the Center for Advanced Study in the Behavioral Sciences, supported by NSF Grant SBR-960123, and they are very grateful for the Center's hospitality and the National Science Foundation's support.

13.1. Introduction

Optimal decision-making often requires a prediction of future tastes, and future tastes may differ from current tastes due to such factors as habit formation, day-to-day mood fluctuations, social influences, maturation, and changes in the environment. When making summer vacation plans during the cold of winter, people must predict what vacations will be most enjoyable during the heat of summer. When ordering food at the beginning of a meal, people must predict how hungry they will be at the end of the meal. When contemplating smoking cigarettes or indulging in other habit-forming substances, people must predict how this consumption will affect their future desire for and enjoyment of these substances.

In this paper we provide evidence for, formalize, and explore the implications of a general bias in the prediction of future tastes: people tend to understand qualitatively the directions in which their tastes will change, but systematically underestimate the magnitudes of these changes. Hence, they tend to exaggerate the degree to which their future tastes will resemble their current tastes. Such *projection bias* may cause people making summer vacation plans in the winter to choose overly warm destinations, diners to order too much food at the beginning of meals, and people unaddicted to cigarettes to underestimate the power of and drawbacks of addiction.

In Section II we review evidence from a variety of domains supporting the existence of projection bias. People underappreciate the effects of long-term changes in tastes, such as those that result from adaptation to a shifting standard of living. People also underappreciate the effects of frequently fluctuating tastes, such as fluctuating hunger. Indeed, virtually all evidence we are familiar with on misprediction of future tastes is consistent with projection bias.

In Section III we develop a formal model of projection bias. To fix ideas, suppose that a person's instantaneous utility can be written as $u(c, s)$, where c is her consumption and s is a "state" that parameterizes her tastes. Suppose further that the person with current state s' must predict her tastes at a time in the future when her state will be s. Consistent with evidence that people tend to understand the qualitative nature of changes in tastes, but underestimate the degree of change, we assume that the person's prediction of her own future preferences, $\tilde{u}(c, s|s')$, lies somewhere "in between" her true future tastes $u(c, s)$ and her current tastes $u(c, s')$. Our formal analysis in this paper assumes that $\tilde{u}(c, s|s')$ is a simple linear combination of $u(c, s)$ and $u(c, s')$, which we refer to as *simple projection bias*.

Because projection bias leads to discrepancies between predicted and subsequently realized utilities, it implies that a person's behavior need not correspond to correct intertemporal utility maximization. For instance, if current consumption has deleterious effects on future well-being, and projection bias leads the person to underappreciate these effects, she may overconsume

349

relative to what would maximize her true intertemporal utility. Moreover, as tastes change over time in ways she does not predict, a person makes plans that she may end up not carrying out; that is, projection bias can lead to dynamic inconsistency. A stressed undergraduate who underappreciates the addictiveness of cigarettes, for instance, might start smoking with the plan of quitting upon graduation, only to continue smoking after graduation once she becomes addicted.

To demonstrate the potential economic importance of projection bias, in Sections IV and V we formally analyze two economic environments. Section IV explores the implications of projection bias in a life-cycle consumption model with habit formation. When consumption is habit-forming, a person should rationally pursue an increasing consumption profile, so that she is always consuming more than she is accustomed to. Projection bias leads a person to underappreciate the impact of current consumption on future utility, and hence to consume too much early in life and too little late in life relative to what would be optimal. More interesting, as time passes and the person habituates to higher consumption levels, she may decide to consume more than she had earlier planned; hence projection bias can cause saving to fall short of intentions. Finally, as the person gets accustomed to higher consumption levels, she also values income more highly, and hence might decide to work more (or retire later) than she had earlier planned.

In Section V we show how projection bias can cause misguided purchases of durable goods. The satisfaction that a person derives from a durable good often fluctuates from day to day, and projection bias leads a person to underappreciate how much her future valuations may differ from her current valuation. As a result, people will overvalue the good on high-value days and undervalue it on low-value days. A person making a one-time buying decision is therefore equally likely to buy when she should not or not to buy when she should. However, if the person has multiple opportunities to buy, and (as is typically the case) un-buying is more difficult than buying, projection bias will lead on average to overpurchasing of durable goods.

We believe that projection bias is important for many economic applications, and that it can provide an intuitive and parsimonious account for many phenomena that are otherwise difficult to explain. In Section VI we extrapolate from our formal analysis in Sections IV and V and discuss some of these additional implications. We conclude in Section VII.

13.2. Evidence of Projection Bias

In this section we review evidence from a variety of domains supporting the existence of projection bias.[1] A common type of taste change is adaptation:

---

[1] See Loewenstein and Schkade [1999] for a summary of much of the evidence presented in this section, as well as for a discussion of the psychological mechanisms that underlie

people have a remarkable ability to adapt to major changes in their life circumstances, such as acquiring serious medical conditions, moving to different climates, and changing occupations (see Helson [1964] and Frederick and Loewenstein [1999] for a recent review).[2] Moreover, there is a great deal of evidence that people underappreciate the extent of such adaptation. Specifically, by comparing a "control" group's predictions for how some major change would affect their lives to the self-reports of people who have actually experienced that change, a number of studies suggest that people overestimate the impact of major changes on their long-run level of happiness.

In the medical domain, cross-sectional studies have consistently found that nonpatients' predictions of the quality of life associated with serious medical conditions are lower than actual patients' self-reported quality of life. For instance, Sackett and Torrance [1978] find that nonpatients predict that chronic dialysis would yield a quality of life of 0.39, whereas dialysis patients report a quality of life of 0.56 (on a 0 to 1 scale on which 0 means as bad as death and 1 means perfect health). Boyd et al. [1990] find analogous cross-sectional results with regard to colostomies. The same pattern also shows up in longitudinal studies. Jepson, Loewenstein, and Ubel [2001] asked people waiting for a kidney transplant to predict what their quality of life would be one year later if they did or did not receive a transplant, and then asked those same people one year later to report their quality of life. Patients who received transplants predicted a higher quality of life than they ended up reporting, and those who did not predicted a lower quality of life than they ended up reporting. Sieff, Dawes, and Loewenstein [1999] find similar longitudinal results for people testing for HIV.

Outside the medical domain, Gilbert et al. [1998] compared (among other things) assistant professors' predictions of the impact of getting or being denied tenure to the self-reports of former assistant professors, and Loewenstein and Frederick [1997] compared the predictions by survey respondents of how various events (e.g. a decline in sport fishing and an increase in the number of coffee shops) would affect their well-being over the next decade to the self-reports of other respondents about how actual events in the past decade had affected their well-being. A clear pattern emerged in both studies: those making prospective predictions expected future changes

projection bias. Also see Loewenstein, O'Donoghue, and Rabin [2002] for a more extensive discussion of this evidence.

[2] There are some exceptions to this rule. First, there are a variety of factors that impede adaptation, such as uncertainty about whether a situation is permanent and repeated reminders of the original situation. Second, some studies have found that people do not seem to adapt to noise; indeed, if anything, they seem to become increasingly irritated by it (for an overview, see Weinstein [1982]). Moreover, noise is the one example we know of that might contradict our assertion that people understand the direction in which tastes change, because people seem to predict that they will adapt when in fact they tend to become more irritated.

to affect their well-being more than those making retrospective evaluations reported that matched changes in the past had affected their well-being.

While there are alternative explanations for the results above, other research suggests that they are driven in large part by underappreciation of adaptation. First, in the medical domain, recent research by Ubel, Loewenstein, and Jepson [2003] shows that it is sometimes possible to "debias" people—to bring nonpatients' predictions closer to patients' self-reports—by inducing them to think more carefully about adaptation, which suggests that underappreciation of adaptation plays a significant role in the discrepancy. Second, a number of ongoing studies are ruling out other explanations. For instance, a commonly mentioned alternative is "response norming"—chronic dialysis patients, for instance, might interpret a 0.8 on a 0-to-1 scale differently from nonpatients— but Baron et al. [forthcoming] found that making the scales more precise only increases the discrepancy.[3] Finally, and perhaps more importantly, analogous results are found in experiments on shorter term changes in tastes, for which these alternative explanations do not hold; we turn to such evidence next.

A prevalent experimental finding is the *endowment effect:* people tend to value an object (such as a coffee mug) more highly if they possess it than if they do not.[4] The usual explanation is that people adapt to owning or not owning the object, and that there is more pain upon parting with the object than there is joy upon obtaining the object. An underappreciation of this adaptation implies that unendowed subjects should underestimate by how much becoming endowed will increase their valuation, and that endowed subjects should underestimate by how much becoming unendowed will decrease their valuation. Van Boven, Dunning, and Loewenstein [2000] find cross-sectional evidence of both predictions. In one experiment the usual endowment effect was replicated by eliciting selling prices from subjects not endowed with coffee mugs and buying prices from subjects not endowed (average selling price = $6.37; average buying price = $1.85). Sellers were then asked to estimate how much buyers would pay, and buyers were asked to estimate how much sellers would charge, with subjects rewarded for accurate predictions. Consistent with projection bias, the average estimate of sellers ($3.93) was less than their own average selling price but more than the average buying price, and the average estimate of buyers ($4.39) was more than their own average buying price but less than the average selling price. Loewenstein and Adler [1995] provide longitudinal evidence of the former prediction.

---

[3] The other main explanation that has been offered is a "focusing illusion"—that people exaggerate the impact of anything their attention is focused on, including disabilities [Schkade and Kahneman 1998; Wilson et al. 2000]. However, Ubel, Loewenstein, and Jepson [2003] also found that a wide range of "defocusing" interventions actually decreased rather than increased nonpatients' estimates of patients' quality of life.

[4] The endowment effect was first discussed by Thaler [1980]; see Kahneman, Knetsch, and Thaler [1991] for a review.

Table I. Percentage of Subjects Choosing Unhealthy Snack (from Read and van Leeuwen [1998])

		Future hunger	
		Hungry	Satiated
Current	Hungry	78%	42%
Hunger	Satiated	56%	26%

In one study, subjects were shown a coffee mug, told to imagine that they had been given one but had the opportunity to exchange it for cash, and then filled out a form that elicited their predicted reservation values. After a delay, they were actually given the mug, and then asked to complete an identical form that elicited their actual reservation values. Again consistent with projection bias, the predicted selling prices were significantly lower than the actual selling prices.

There is also considerable evidence on underappreciation of the effects of hunger. This evidence is particularly valuable because it demonstrates that the same basic pattern of misprediction—understanding the direction of taste changes but underappreciating the magnitude of the changes—shows up for other types of taste changes besides adaptation, and it can show up even for taste changes with which people have ample experience and hence ought to understand well.

Several studies lend support to the folk wisdom that shopping on an empty stomach leads people to buy too much [Nisbett and Kanouse 1968; Gilbert, Gill, and Wilson 2002]. This phenomenon can be interpreted as a manifestation of projection bias: people who are hungry act as if their future taste for food will reflect such hunger. Read and van Leeuwen [1998] provide even sharper evidence of projection bias with respect to hunger. Office workers were asked to choose between healthy snacks and unhealthy snacks that they would receive in one week, either at a time when they should expect to be hungry (late in the afternoon) or satiated (immediately after lunch).[5] Subjects were approached to make the choice either when they were hungry (late in the afternoon) or satiated (immediately after lunch). As depicted in Table I, people who expected to be hungry the next week were more likely to opt for unhealthy snacks, presumably reflecting an increased taste for unhealthy snacks in the hungry state, but in addition, people who were hungry *when they made the choice* were more likely to opt for unhealthy snacks, suggesting that people were projecting their current tastes onto their future tastes.

---

[5] The healthy snacks were apples and bananas; the unhealthy snacks were crisps, borrel-noten, Mars Bars, and Snickers Bars. We adopt the terminology healthy and unhealthy from the experimenters, but none of the snacks were thusly labeled to the subjects.

Indeed, if we interpret the main diagonal—the hungry-hungry and satiated-satiated conditions—as reflecting true preferences, the data fit exactly the pattern of projection bias. For those subjects who are currently hungry but expect to be satiated, they understand the direction in which their tastes will change as they become satiated—fewer choose the unhealthy snack than in the hungry-hungry condition—but they underestimate the magnitude of this change—more choose the unhealthy snack than in the satiated-satiated condition. An analogous conclusion holds for subjects who are currently satiated and expect to be hungry.

While we have limited our detailed discussion to a few realms, there is considerable further evidence that projection bias operates across a broad array of domains. Indeed, virtually all evidence that we are aware of is consistent with projection bias (except possibly noise, as discussed in footnote 3).[6] Our goal in the remainder of this paper is to demonstrate its potential importance for economics.

13.3. The Model

In this section we build a formal model of projection bias. To describe changes in tastes, we use the apparatus of state-dependent utility. Suppose that a person's instantaneous utility in period τ, which captures her tastes, is given by $u(c_\tau, s_\tau)$, where c_τ is her period τ consumption. The variable s_τ, her "state," parameterizes her tastes. The state might reflect past behavior, as when past consumption of a good determines current addiction to that good, or exogenous factors, as when fluctuations in serotonin levels affect mood or when peer pressure affects the benefits and costs of current behavior.[7]

Next consider a person currently with state s' who is attempting to predict her future instantaneous utility from consuming c in state s; that is, she is trying to predict $u(c, s)$. Let $\tilde{u}(c, s|s')$ denote her prediction. If she were accurate, her predicted utility would equal true utility, or $\tilde{u}(c, s|s') = u(c, s)$. But the

[6] Other domains for which there is evidence consistent with projection bias include sexual arousal [Loewenstein, Nagin, and Paternoster 1997], pain [Read and Loewenstein 1999], thirst [Van Boven and Loewenstein 2003], fear [Van Boven et al. 2003], and heroin craving [Giordano et al. 2001]. See also Loewenstein's [1996, 1999] discussion of hot/cold empathy gaps wherein individuals who are in cold visceral states underappreciate the impact of hot visceral states on their own behavior.

[7] By "consumption," we mean any current physical experience that is relevant for current well-being—in addition to literal consumption of goods, this might include experiencing a health outcome, being exposed to noise, or owning an object. Just as the utility from consuming goods might change over time, the utility from these other types of experiences might change over time, and we capture such effects with the "state" variable. For instance, the utility (quality of life) from being a chronic-dialysis patient might depend on how accustomed the person is to being a chronic-dialysis patient; in this case, consumption is being a chronic-dialysis patient, and the state reflects how accustomed the person is to being a chronic-dialysis patient.

evidence in Section II suggests that, while people understand the qualitative nature of changes in their tastes, they underestimate the magnitude of these changes. Roughly speaking, this *projection bias* means that a person's predicted utility $\tilde{u}(c, s|s')$ lies "in between" her true future utility $u(c, s)$ and her utility given her current state $u(c, s')$.[8] In this paper we consider a particularly simple form of projection bias.

DEFINITION 1: Predicted utility exhibits *simple projection bias* if there exists $a \in [0,1]$ such that for all c, s, and s', $\tilde{u}(c, s|s') = (1 - a) u(c, s) + au(c, s')$.

With this formulation, if $a = 0$, the person has no projection bias: she predicts her future instantaneous utility correctly. If $a > 0$, the person has projection bias; the bigger is a, the stronger is the bias. When $a = 1$, the person perceives that her future tastes will be identical to her current tastes.[9]

Our model says nothing about how tastes change; rather, it makes predictions as a function of how tastes change. Hence, it might be that a person's happiness tends to mean-revert over time due to adaptation, in which case projection bias would lead her to expect some but not enough mean reversion. It could be that a person develops a taste for certain types of consumption— e.g. her enjoyment of coffee might grow over time—in which case projection bias would lead her to underappreciate how much her enjoyment will grow. Or it could be that a person's tastes fluctuate from day to day, in which case projection bias would lead her to underappreciate the magnitudes of these fluctuations. Our formulation permits us to analyze the implications of projection bias—of understanding the direction of taste changes but underestimating magnitudes—for these and other possible types of taste changes.[10]

Most economic decisions involve more than merely predicting future tastes; they involve making choices with intertemporal consequences. We next embed our framework above within an intertemporal-choice environment. Suppose that a person must choose a path of consumption $(c_t, \ldots, c_T)$ when

---

[8] Our formal assumption is that people correctly anticipate changes in states but underappreciate how these changes map into changes in utility. But since states are merely a means of parameterizing utility functions, it would make little difference if we assumed instead that people fully appreciate how changes in states map into changes in utility but underappreciate the degree to which the states will change.

[9] While simple projection bias is sufficient for our analysis in this paper, it is too restrictive for use as a general definition. One problem is that, when there are multiple states, it requires that the magnitude of the bias be identical for different types of states; e.g. that a person who is currently not thirsty and currently unaddicted to cocaine be just as bad at predicting her preferences when she is thirsty as she is at predicting her preferences when addicted to cocaine. A second problem is that the magnitude of the bias cannot depend on the current state; e.g. it does not permit that a satiated person can predict well her preferences when hungry whereas a hungry person cannot predict well her preferences when satiated. See Appendix A in Loewenstein, O'Donoghue, and Rabin [2002] for a more general formulation of projection bias.

[10] For a discussion of many different types of taste changes, see Loewenstein and Angner [2003].

her (true) intertemporal preferences are given by

$$U^t(c_t, \ldots, c_T) = \sum_{\tau=t}^{T} \delta^\tau u(c_\tau, s_\tau),$$

where $\delta \leq 1$ is her discount factor. Standard economic models of state-dependent preferences typically assume that people are "rational" in the sense that they correctly anticipate how their behavior influences the evolution of states. Formally, for any period t and initial state s_t, a rational person chooses a path of consumption $(c_t, \ldots, c_T)$, correctly anticipating the associated path of states $(s_t, \ldots, s_T)$, to maximize true intertemporal utility U^t.

A person with projection bias *attempts* to maximize her intertemporal utility, but may fail to do so because she mispredicts her future instantaneous utilities. More precisely, if a person exhibits projection bias and her state in period t is s_t, then she perceives her period t intertemporal preferences to be

$$\tilde{U}^t(c_t, \ldots, c_T|s_t) = \sum_{\tau=t}^{T} \delta^\tau \tilde{u}(c_\tau, s_\tau|s_t).$$

We assume that for any period t and initial state s_t a person with projection bias chooses a path of consumption $(c_t, \ldots, c_T)$, correctly anticipating the associated path of states $(s_t, \ldots, s_T)$, to maximize her perceived intertemporal utility $\tilde{U}^t$. That is, she behaves exactly as a rational person would except that (possibly) $\tilde{U}^t \neq U^t$.

To incorporate uncertainty over future consumption or future states, we make the standard assumption that a person maximizes her expected discounted utility. For instance, suppose that in period t the person expects her period τ consumption-state combination to be (c', s') with probability p and (c'', s'') with probability $1 - p$. Just as true period τ expected utility is $E_t[u(c_\tau, s_\tau)] = pu(c', s') + (1 - p)u(c'', s'')$, a person with projection bias predicts period τ expected utility to be $E_t[\tilde{u}(c_\tau, s_\tau|s_t)] = p\tilde{u}(c', s'|s_t) + (1 - p)\tilde{u}(c'', s''|s_t)$. Similarly, true expected intertemporal utility is $E_t[U^t(c_t, \ldots, c_T)] = E_t[\sum_{\tau=t}^{T} \delta^\tau u(c_\tau, s_\tau)]$, and a person with projection bias perceives her expected intertemporal utility to be $E_t[\tilde{U}^t(c_t, \ldots, c_T|s_t)] = E_t[\sum_{\tau=t}^{T} \delta^\tau \tilde{u}(c_\tau, s_\tau|s_t)]$.[11]

While the person's true intertemporal preferences U^t are time-consistent, because she incorrectly predicts how her tastes change over time, her perceived intertemporal preferences $\tilde{U}^t$ can be time-inconsistent. Because this time inconsistency derives solely from misprediction of future utilities, it

[11] Research has, of course, documented a number of inadequacies of expected-utility theory (for an overview see Starmer [2000]). To the extent that one feels the need to modify expected-utility theory for rational types, one could use the same modifications for people with projection bias.

would make little sense to assume that the person is fully aware of it.[12] We assume throughout the paper that the person is completely unaware of the time inconsistency—that at all times the person perceives her preferences to be time-consistent, and therefore at all times she plans to follow the consumption path that maximizes her current perceived intertemporal preferences. As a result, projection bias can lead to *dynamic inconsistency*: a person may plan to behave a certain way in the future, but later, in the absence of new information, revise this plan.[13]

Given any particular set of state-dependent preferences and particular economic environment, our model of projection bias makes specific predictions about how actual behavior differs from rational behavior. To demonstrate this point, and to highlight the potential importance of projection bias for economics, Sections IV and V formally analyze two economic environments.

13.4. Projection Bias and Habit Formation

For half a century, though most intensively recently, economists have explored life-cycle consumption models with habit formation. Habit formation—wherein increases in current consumption increase future marginal utility—was discussed by Duesenberry [1949], and later formalized by Pollak [1970] and Ryder and Heal [1973]. In recent years, habit-formation models have been used in specific applications: see Becker and Murphy [1988], Constantinides [1990], Abel [1990], Campbell and Cochrane [1999], Jermann [1998], Boldrin, Christiano, and Fisher [2001], Carroll, Overland, and Weil [2000], and Fuhrer [2000]. All of these recent researchers have examined habit formation within the rational-choice framework.[14]

---

[12] Another psychological phenomenon that has received increasing attention in research on intertemporal choice is hyperbolic discounting (see in particular, Laibson [1994, 1997] and O'Donoghue and Rabin [1999a]). Under hyperbolic discounting, true preferences are time-inconsistent, and hence a person could be fully aware of this fact, as much of the literature has assumed.

[13] Given the logic of our model, it is inherent that a person is unaware of her *current* misprediction. But one could imagine a variant of the model where the person is aware of her *future* propensity to mispredict. She could, for instance, be aware of her general propensity to overshop when hungry, while still committing the error on a case-by-case basis. The coexistence of day-to-day mispredictions with a "meta-awareness" of these mispredictions is similar to the discussion in O'Donoghue and Rabin [1999b] of how people can simultaneously be aware of their general tendency to procrastinate and yet still procrastinate on a case-by-case basis. A model of "sophisticated projection bias" could plausibly better describe behavior in some circumstances, such as when sophisticated shoppers know that they should not shop on an empty stomach, but we choose our current formulation as a simple and realistic starting point.

[14] The early literature on habit formation distinguishes between two polar cases: "rational habits" wherein consumers fully account for how current consumption affects future well-being, and "myopic habits" wherein consumers do not account at all for how current

In this section we formally analyze the implications of projection bias over habit formation in a simple "eat-the-cake" model. Suppose that a person has income Y to allocate over consumption in periods $1, \ldots, T$, which we denote by $c_1, \ldots, c_T$. For simplicity, we assume that there is no discounting, and that the person can borrow and save at 0 percent interest; neither of these assumptions is important for our qualitative conclusions. The person's true instantaneous utility in period t is $u(c_t, s_t)$, where the state s_t can be thought of as her "habit stock." The person's initial habit stock, s_1 is exogenous, and her habit stock evolves according to $s_t = (1 - \gamma)s_{t-1} + \gamma c_{t-1}$ for some $\gamma \in (0, 1]$. Hence, the more the person consumes in a given period, the higher is her subsequent habit stock. The parameter γ represents how quickly the person develops (and eliminates) her habit.

We assume that instantaneous utility takes a particularly simple functional form:

$$u(c_t, s_t) = v(c_t - s_t), \qquad \text{where } v' > 0 \text{ and } v'' < 0.$$

This formulation is potentially restrictive, but it captures the key feature of habit formation and is common in the literature.[15] There are actually two key features that play a role in our results below. First, the marginal utility from consumption is increasing in the habit stock ($\partial[\partial u/\partial c]/\partial s > 0$), which implies habit formation—an increase in current consumption increases the future habit stock and therefore increases the marginal utility from future consumption. Second, the level of utility is declining in the habit stock ($\partial u/\partial s < 0$), which implies that an increase in current consumption reduces the utility from future consumption. Although this negative "internality" [Herrnstein et al. 1993] is not an inherent part of habit formation, it is present in most formal analyses, and real-world instances, of habit formation.

In period 1 the person faces the following choice problem, where s_1 is exogenous:

$$\max_{(c_1, \ldots, c_T)} \tilde{U}^1(c_1, \ldots, c_T | s_1) = \sum_{\tau=1}^{T} [(1 - a)v(c_\tau - s_\tau) + av(c_\tau - s_1)]$$

consumption affects future well-being. Of the papers cited in the text, all assume rational habits except for Pollak [1970], which (implicitly) assumes myopic habits. Our model is equivalent to rational habits when $a = 0$ and to myopic habits when $a = 1$. Muellbauer [1988] provides an excellent overview of the two extremes, and concludes that the empirical evidence seems to favor myopic habits. We return to this and other empirical evidence in Section VI.

[15] This formulation is equivalent to that used by Pollak [1970], Constantinides [1990], Jermann [1998], Campbell and Cochrane [1999], and Boldrin, Christiano, and Fisher [2001]; indeed, all these papers except Pollak further assume that v takes a CRRA specification. Another formulation, proposed by Abel [1990] and used by Fuhrer [2000] and Carroll, Overland, and Weil [2000], is $u(c_t, s_t) = (c_t/s_t^\gamma)^{1-\sigma}/(1-\sigma)$. Yet a third formulation, suggested by Kahneman and Tversky's [1979] prospect theory, is to assume that $v''(x) < 0$ for $x > 0$ but $v''(x) > 0$ for $x < 0$; Bowman, Minehart, and Rabin [1999] use a variant of this approach.

such that

$$s_t = (1 - \gamma)s_{t-1} + \gamma c_{t-1} \text{ for } t \in \{2, \ldots, T\} \quad \text{and} \quad \sum_{\tau=1}^{T} c_\tau \leq Y.$$

For ease of presentation, let $(c_1^*, \ldots, c_T^*)$ denote rational behavior, which solves this maximization when $a = 0$, and let $(c_1^A, \ldots, c_T^A)$ denote planned behavior from the period 1 perspective for a person with $a > 0$, with the value of a suppressed in the notation. Our analysis throughout assumes interior solutions for both rational and actual behavior.

A pattern typically emphasized in models of habit formation is that people choose an increasing consumption profile—that is, $c_1 < \ldots < c_T$—so that they are always consuming more than they are accustomed to. This conclusion holds, however, only if the person's initial habit stock s_1 is not too large. Otherwise, it might be optimal to break the initial habit, and the optimal way to do so might involve a declining consumption path that lowers the habit stock gradually over time.[16] But since breaking a habit is both least painful and most beneficial when done early in life, before the habit has been further developed and when the benefits will be spread over a large number of years, a rational person will break a habit only at the beginning of life. Lemma 1 formally establishes this conclusion by demonstrating that once a person starts further developing her habit—by consuming more than her habit stock—she will follow an increasing consumption profile from that period onward.

LEMMA 1: If $c_\tau^* \geq s_\tau^*$ for some $\tau < T$, then $c_\tau^* < c_{\tau+1}^* < \ldots < c_T^*$.

We focus on the implications of projection bias for situations in which rational behavior does not involve early-life habit-breaking episodes: our results below only apply to parameter values such that a rational person would choose an increasing consumption profile. Lemma 1 implies that a sufficient condition for a rational person to choose an increasing consumption profile is $s_1 = 0$; more generally, this outcome will occur as long as the initial habit stock s_1 is small enough.

Projection bias creates two types of distortions in this environment, because the person underappreciates both the negative internality and the habit formation. The implication of projection bias over the negative internality is straightforward. Because it implies that early consumption decreases utility in all later periods, the negative internality motivates a person to delay consumption. Hence, an underappreciation of the negative internality makes the person prone to consume too much early in life and too little late in life relative to rational behavior. The implication of projection bias over habit

---

[16] Indeed, for $s_1 > Y/T$ the person *must* have a habit-breaking episode, and this episode might last her entire life; that is, she might have $c_1^* > c_2^* > \ldots > c_T^*$.

formation is in principle more complicated because the basic effect of habit formation is complicated. But for the case in which rational behavior does not involve a habit-breaking episode, and therefore involves an increasing consumption profile, the person's habit stock will be increasing over time, and therefore habit formation makes her marginal utility increase over time. As a result, habit formation also motivates the person to delay consumption. Hence, an underappreciation of habit formation, like an underappreciation of the negative internality, makes the person prone to consume too much early in life and too little late in life relative to rational behavior. Proposition 1 reflects this intuition, establishing that whenever rational behavior does not involve a habit-breaking episode, projection bias leads a person to (plan to) consume too much early in life and too little late in life relative to what would be optimal.

PROPOSITION 1: If $c_1^* \geq s_1$, then for any $a > 0$, $\Sigma_{t=1}^{\tau} c_t^A > \Sigma_{t=1}^{\tau} c_t^*$ for all $\tau < T$.

Hence, projection bias causes a person to plan a consumption profile that consumes her income too quickly. Perhaps the cleanest illustration is in the extreme case where $a = 1$, where the person will plan to consume the same amount in all periods rather than increase consumption over time as would be optimal.[17]

More interesting is what happens as time passes and the person's tastes change in ways she did not predict. To study such effects, we examine how a person's plans change in period 2. In period 2 the person reoptimizes given her new perceived preferences; that is, she faces the following choice problem, where s_1 and c_1^A are exogenous:

$$\max{}_{(c_2,\ldots,c_T)} \tilde{U}^2(c_2, \ldots, c_T | s_2) = \sum_{\tau=2}^{T} [(1-a)v(c_\tau - s_\tau) + av(c_\tau - s_2)]$$

such that

$$s_2 = (1-\gamma)s_1 + \gamma c_1^A$$

$$s_t = (1-\gamma)s_{t-1} + \gamma c_{t-1} \text{ for } t \in \{3, \ldots, T\}$$

$$\text{and} \quad \sum_{\tau=2}^{T} c_\tau \leq Y - c_1^A.$$

[17] While the assumption that rational behavior does not involve a habit-breaking episode is sufficient for overconsumption, it is not necessary. Proposition 1 might fail because, during a habit-breaking episode, habit formation and a declining habit stock mean the person's marginal utility declines over time, which in turn means that habit formation motivates the person to accelerate consumption, and so projection bias over habit formation leads the person to consume her income too slowly. But Proposition 1 need not fail, because projection bias over the negative internality still motivates the person to consume her income too quickly.

Rational behavior, of course, does not change over time, and hence the solution to this problem for $a = 0$ is $(c_2^*, \ldots, c_T^*)$. For a person with projection bias, the solution for this problem, which we denote by $(c_2^{AA}, \ldots, c_T^{AA})$, may differ from her period 1 plans $(c_2^A, \ldots, c_T^A)$. Proposition 2 characterizes this revision of plans in the case where she is developing a habit and $T = 3$.

PROPOSITION 2: Suppose that $T = 3$ and $c_1^A > s_1$. Then $v''' > 0$ implies that $c_2^{AA} > c_2^A$, $v''' < 0$ implies that $c_2^{AA} < c_2^A$, and $v''' = 0$ implies that $c_2^{AA} < c_2^A$.

As the person's habit stock changes over time, her (perceived) marginal utilities from consumption in each period also change. When the person is developing a habit, these marginal utilities all increase.[18] Hence, the relative magnitudes of these changes in marginal utility determine the revision of plans. If $v''' = 0$, the increase in marginal utility is the same for all periods, which implies that the person's marginal trade-offs have not changed, and hence she does not revise her consumption plan. If $v''' > 0$, the increase in marginal utility is larger for period 2 than period 3, and as a result she revises her period 2 consumption upward. If $v''' < 0$, the increase in marginal utility is smaller for period 2, and she revises her period 2 consumption downward.[19]

Any utility function that satisfies nonincreasing absolute risk aversion, which includes the CARA and CRRA families, must have $v''' > 0$. Because this seems a plausible restriction on the instantaneous utility function, Proposition 2 suggests that projection bias leads people to repeatedly readjust their immediate consumption upwards relative to their most recent plans. Hence, if people experience habit formation in consumption, projection bias represents a possible source for actual saving being smaller than planned saving. Laibson, Repetto, and Tobacman [1998] review considerable evidence that the actual saving of many households falls short of their plans. The authors posit self-control problems and naivete about those self-control problems as primary sources of this shortfall. Our analysis suggests that projection bias, in the form of underappreciation of how increasing consumption in the present will raise one's consumption standard in the future, might also contribute to such mispredictions.

---

[18] Formally, from a period t perspective, the (perceived) marginal utility from period 2 consumption is $(1-a)v'(c_2 - s_2) + av'(c_2 - s_t) + (1-a)\gamma v'(c_3 - s_3)$; and since $s_2 > s_1$ implies that $v'(c_2 - s_2) > v'(c_2 - s_1)$, this marginal utility is larger from a period 2 perspective. Similarly, from a period t perspective, the (perceived) marginal utility from period 3 consumption is $(1-a)v'(c_3 - s_3) + av'(c_3 - s_t)$; and since $s_2 > s_1$ implies that $v'(c_3 - s_2) > v'(c_3 - s_1)$, this marginal utility is also larger from a period 2 perspective.

[19] We conjecture, but have not proved, that this conclusion holds for $T > 3$. The result that $v''' = 0$ yields dynamic consistency is quite general. For the case $v''' > 0$, it is straightforward to show that marginal utility increases most for period 2 and least for period T, and so, perhaps subject to additional regularity conditions, after reoptimization we should expect period 2 consumption to increase and period T consumption to decrease. Analogous conclusions hold for the $v''' < 0$ case.

While our analysis assumes that a person's lifetime income is exogenous, our model suggests implications for how projection bias might influence decisions about how hard to work to increase income. Specifically, let λ^A be the marginal utility of lifetime income as perceived from period 1, and let λ^{AA} be the marginal utility of lifetime income as perceived from period 2. Again limiting ourselves to the case when a person is developing a habit and the horizon is $T = 3$, Proposition 3 establishes that the marginal utility of lifetime income increases over time.

PROPOSITION 3: Suppose that $T = 3$ and $c_1^A > s_1$. Then $\lambda^{AA} > \lambda^A$.

Proposition 3 reflects a simple intuition: as time passes, and the person's real and perceived marginal utilities from consumption increase, income becomes more valuable. Extrapolating beyond our formal framework, this result suggests that projection bias over habit formation might lead people to pursue higher income than planned as time passes. Projection bias might, for instance, create a force toward choosing a later and later planned retirement date as time passes, using the proceeds to increase consumption.[20] Similarly, with endogenous per-period labor-leisure decisions, projection bias might create a tendency to repeatedly increase labor and decrease leisure relative to earlier plans. We are wary of pushing this intuition too far without further theoretical and empirical analysis, however, because the logic of the argument assumes that there is no reference dependence in leisure. But we do note that this intuition parallels the arguments of many previous researchers, such as Scitovsky [1976] and Frank [1999], who have argued that people spend too much time and energy generating wealth and too little time on leisure activities, and that people enjoy increases in their material consumption less than they think they will.

13.5. Projection Bias and Durable Goods

For most durable goods—such as a tent, a golf-swing trainer, or a Johnny Depp video—people experience day-to-day fluctuations in their valuations. For rational consumers, such fluctuations are virtually irrelevant, because they will purchase durable goods based almost exclusively on their expected daily valuations for the goods, and virtually ignore their valuations on the day they happen to be in the store. But for people with projection bias, buying decisions are oversensitive to the momentary feelings they experience when they happen to be in the store, and thus the nature of day-to-day fluctuations

---

[20] There is some evidence, however, that people are somewhat accurate at predicting their retirement dates (see Bernheim [1989]), although this may in part be due to the existence of focal retirement ages.

becomes important. In this section we present a stylized model that identifies some implications of such effects.

Suppose that a person's valuation of a durable good in period τ is given by a random variable μ_τ, where μ_τ is distributed identically and independently across periods, and has finite mean $\bar{\mu}$. The person learns the realization of μ_τ at the start of period τ. For simplicity, we further assume that the durable good lasts for exactly D days, and that the person cannot consume the good on the day she purchases it.[21]

Consider first a consumer who has just one opportunity, on day 1, to purchase the item; if she does not purchase it on day 1, she cannot purchase it at all. We normalize the person's intertemporal utility to be zero when she does not buy the product. If she buys the product at price P, she will enjoy the benefits of ownership, but must forgo the consumption of other goods that she could have financed with wealth P.[22] We assume that the person's utility from the durable good is additively separable from her utility for other goods, and that the price P represents the total utility value of the other goods forgone by purchasing the durable good. The person's state in period τ is her current valuation, or $s_\tau = \mu_\tau$. Finally, we assume that there is no discounting, or $\delta = 1$; none of our conclusions depend on this assumption.

If the person buys the durable good in period 1, then, given the information available, her true expected intertemporal utility is

$$E_1[U^1] = E_1\left[\sum_{k=1}^{D} \mu_{1+k} - P\right] = D\bar{\mu} - P.$$

A person exhibiting simple projection bias perceives her expected intertemporal utility to be

$$E_1[\tilde{U}^1] = E_1\left[\sum_{k=1}^{D} [(1-a)\mu_{1+k} + a\mu_1] - P\right] = D\bar{\mu} + aD(\mu_1 - \bar{\mu}) - P.$$

$\mu_1 > \bar{\mu}$ implies that $E_1[\tilde{U}^1] > E_1[U^1]$, and $\mu_1 < \bar{\mu}$ implies that $E_1[\tilde{U}^1] < E_1[U^1]$. Hence, an underappreciation of day-to-day fluctuations can lead variously to underbuying or overbuying. If her day 1 valuation is larger than average, and she projects this above-average valuation onto the future, the person is prone to overvalue the durable good. If, in contrast, her day 1 valuation is smaller than average, and she projects this below-average valuation onto

---

[21] While it is often unrealistic to assume that the person cannot consume the good on the day she purchases it, none of our qualitative conclusions depend on this assumption, and it vastly simplifies our analysis.

[22] We take the price P to be exogenous. In Loewenstein, O'Donoghue, and Rabin [2000] we formulate a more complicated model that derives a monopolist's pricing and valuation-changing sales-hype policies in the face of projection bias by consumers.

the future, she is prone to undervalue the durable good. In other words, a person with projection bias is too sensitive to her valuation at purchase time.[23]

While projection bias has ambiguous effects in one-shot buying decisions, things change dramatically in the more realistic case where the person has multiple opportunities to buy a durable good. To make this point in a particularly stark way, we suppose that the consumer will purchase the good at most once, and can buy the good in any period $t \in \{1, 2, \ldots\}$. In this situation a rational person either will buy the durable good immediately in period 1 or never buy the durable good, and she buys the durable good if and only if $D_{\bar{\mu}} - P \geq 0$. Intuitively, given our assumption that the person cannot consume the good on the day she purchases it, the net expected value of the durable good is independent of the valuation on the date purchased. Hence, the good is either worth purchasing immediately or not at all.[24]

A person with projection bias, like a rational person, always *perceives* that the good is either worth purchasing immediately or not at all. But her perception of whether it is worth purchasing immediately is influenced by her current valuation. As a result, she ends up purchasing the good in the first period that $D\bar{\mu} + aD(\mu_{\tau} - \bar{\mu}) - P \geq 0$. If we let μ_H denote the largest value that μ_{τ} might possibly take on, then there will eventually be some period in which the person perceives the good to be worth purchasing if and only if $D\bar{\mu} + aD(\mu_H - \bar{\mu}) - P > 0$. Because $\mu_H > \bar{\mu}$, a person with projection bias is unambiguously more prone to buy the durable good than is a rational person: she will always buy when she should buy, and sometimes when she should not.

The intuition behind this conclusion is an inherent asymmetry in purchases of durable goods. A decision not to buy is reversible, so if the person does not buy today when she should, she can still buy in the future. But a decision to buy is irreversible, so if she buys today when she should not, she cannot unbuy in the future. With multiple buying opportunities, a person is prone not to buy when she should only in the unlikely event that she has a particularly low valuation *on every* buying opportunity, whereas she is prone to buy when she should not in the quite likely event that she has a particularly high valuation *on at least one* buying opportunity. Hence, projection bias represents a source of "impulse purchases" wherein people overbuy durable goods in

---

[23] If we allowed immediate consumption, a rational type would also be sensitive to her day 1 valuation. But a projector would still be oversensitive to her day 1 valuation: indeed, the conclusion generalizes that an underappreciation of day-to-day fluctuations leads a person to overvalue the good when $\mu_1 > \bar{\mu}$ and undervalue it when $\mu_1 < \bar{\mu}$.

[24] Formally, we assume that when indifferent between buying now versus buying in the future, people choose to buy now (which would be optimal if we replace $\delta = 1$ with $\delta < 1$ but very close to 1).

response to transitory desire for that good. Many prior theoretical treatments of impulse purchases have attributed the phenomena to hyperbolic discounting. But for durable goods, projection bias is more relevant than hyperbolic discounting. Hyperbolic discounting provides a compelling explanation for overconsumption on cumulative small-scale consumption decisions, such as purchases of potato chips, where the net effects of repeated purchases can be vast overconsumption of potato chips. The purchase of a durable good, however, is by its very nature a long-term-consumption decision. As such, self-control problems are *less* likely to be implicated in the purchase of durable than nondurable goods, whereas projection bias is more likely to be implicated.

Our analysis suggests that certain types of sales tactics might be understood as attempts by businesses to exploit projection bias. If consumers overestimate the longevity of their current feelings, sellers will have an incentive to induce high valuations when people are making buying decisions, via sales hype, enticing displays, or mood-inducing music. Sellers will also have an incentive to pressure people to make purchase decisions when hot, and to facilitate rapid purchases by consumers who are in a hot state that is unlikely to last, such as one-click shopping on the internet. Finally, projection bias might motivate firms to turn nondurable goods into durable goods via "intertemporal bundling," e.g. selling memberships in health clubs, golf clubs, vacation time shares, or season ski passes. Consider, for instance, a person who becomes enthusiastic about exercise and makes a visit to a health club. Rather than making a profit solely on that one visit, the health club may exploit the consumer's tendency to project her current enthusiasm into the future by offering a more expensive "club membership" that entitles the person to additional free (or low-cost) visits in the future. Indeed, Della Vigna and Malmendier [2002] empirically document that people overpay for health club memberships. Using a panel data set that tracks members of three New England health clubs, they find that members who chose a contract with a flat monthly fee paid a price per visit of $17, and members who chose a contract with a flat yearly fee paid a price per visit of $15, even though a $10-per-visit contract was also available. Della Vigna and Malmendier attribute these findings to partially naive self-control problems: people sign up in an attempt to "commit" themselves to future exercise, but then do not have enough self-control to carry out these plans. Our model suggests an additional possible explanation: people plan to attend frequently because they project their current enthusiasm into the future, but then decide not to attend in the future when their enthusiasm has waned.[25]

---

[25] We suspect that another contributory factor is that people dislike paying on the margin for consumption [Prelec and Loewenstein 1998]. Neither this nor projection bias is likely to explain Della Vigna and Malmendier's evidence of procrastination in canceling memberships, which is more consistent with naive self-control problems.

In addition to helping to explain sales tactics, our analysis may also shed light on laws designed to counteract them. Cooling-off laws enacted at both the state and federal level allow consumers to rescind certain types of purchases within a few days of the transaction.[26] Such laws can be viewed as devices for combatting the effects of projection bias. Cooling-off periods that force consumers to reflect on their decisions for several days can decrease the likelihood that they end up owning products that they should not. Cooling-off laws may also have the benefit of reducing sales-persons' incentives to hype. If consumers can return products once they cool down and if such returns are costly for the seller, sellers will have an incentive to put buyers in a long-run average mood rather than an overenthusiastic state.

Although our analysis focuses solely on random fluctuations in tastes, more generally durable goods might involve other types of taste changes. Projection bias over such changes could yield further interesting conclusions. For some durable goods, a person's valuation systematically declines over time as the "novelty" wears off. Projection bias over such taste changes would create a tendency to overbuy, and hence firms might engage in attempts to create increased feelings of novelty. Alternatively, for other durable goods, a person's valuation increases over time as the person develops a taste for the good (or becomes attached to the good). Projection bias over these taste changes would create a tendency to underbuy. In such cases firms might, in fact, engage in behaviors designed to overcome projection bias, such as offering a free-trial period.

13.6. Other Applications

Sections IV and V derive the implications of projection bias in two specific economic environments. These implications highlight two types of errors to which projection bias can give rise. First, the failure to predict future taste changes can lead to misguided choices for current consumption, e.g. overconsumption due to underappreciation of habit formation, and oversensitivity to current valuations as a result of exaggerating the longevity of day-to-day fluctuations in tastes. Second, as perceived tastes change over time in ways that people do not predict, people make plans that they may end up not carrying out; e.g. people may consume more (and save less) than earlier planned. We believe that projection bias is important for many economic applications, and that it can provide an intuitive and parsimonious account for many phenomena that are otherwise difficult to explain. In this section we extrapolate from our formal analysis in Sections IV and V to discuss additional implications of projection bias.

---

[26] For a detailed discussion of such laws, see Camerer et al. [2003].

There are many implications of projection bias for recent models of habit formation beyond the formal analysis in Section IV. In recent years economists have often invoked habit formation in consumption as an explanation for empirical phenomena that are hard to understand within a stationary-utility framework. As we discuss in Section IV, for instance, habit formation is sometimes invoked as an explanation for why people choose consumption profiles that increase over time. In addition, Constantinides [1990] argues that habit formation can provide an explanation for the equity-premium puzzle, because it leads people to expect to maintain high levels of risk aversion even with rising levels of consumption and wealth (see also Abel [1990] and Campbell and Cochrane [1999]). Fuhrer [2000] shows that habit formation might explain the "excess smoothness" of consumption (documented by Campbell and Deaton [1989]) and Carroll, Overland, and Weil [2000] demonstrate that habit formation can explain recent empirical evidence that periods of high aggregate income growth seem to cause periods of high aggregate saving. These explanations derive from the fact that, because people expect to adapt to their changing consumption levels, they adjust slowly to shocks to their permanent income.

Habit formation is a compelling explanation for these phenomena, because it accords well with introspection and common wisdom, and is consistent with psychological evidence on adaptation. Even so, it has been hard to find direct evidence of habit formation in time-series consumption data. Dynan [2000] reviews the mixed results from tests using aggregate consumption data, and describes how such tests might be prone to overstate the degree of habit formation. Dynan then tests for habit formation using household data on food consumption, and finds no evidence of habit formation. Our model suggests an explanation: even if people are characterized by habit formation, projection bias may lead people to not react to that habit formation as strongly as the rational model suggests. Indeed, in our simple eat-the-cake model, we saw exactly this point: whereas introducing habit formation would lead rational consumers to switch from smooth consumption to an increasing consumption profile, projection bias undermines this effect. In fact, for a person with complete projection bias, or $\alpha = 1$, the introduction of habit formation does not change her behavior at all. Muellbauer [1988] makes a similar point when he compares rational versus myopic habits—which is equivalent to $\alpha = 0$ and $\alpha = 1$ in our model. Specifically, he points out that habit formation would show up in cross-sectional evidence under either assumption, but it would show up in time-series evidence only under the assumption of rational habits. Given that it is hard to find evidence of habit formation in time-series evidence, Muellbauer concludes that the evidence supports myopic habits.

Hence, perhaps a better hypothesis is that people are characterized by a combination of habit formation and projection bias. If so, our model suggests where to look for additional evidence. Specifically, it predicts specific patterns of dynamic inconsistency. We already described one such prediction in Section IV: people with projection bias over habit formation will plan to save more in the future than they actually end up saving (under the plausible assumption of nonincreasing absolute risk aversion). Extrapolating from our model, an additional area on which there might be dynamic inconsistency is charitable giving. Charitable giving depends on a trade-off between the benefits of giving and the cost of forgone personal consumption. While the marginal utility of consumption may decline with wealth, habit formation reduces the magnitude of this change. As a result, people with projection bias may plan to increase their charitable giving as their wealth increases by more than they actually end up doing.[27]

An obvious application of projection bias is addiction. Rational-choice models of addiction provide plausible explanations for many different patterns associated with addiction, but often have difficulty accounting for the most central problem: why do people become addicted in the first place? Because habit formation is a natural way to formalize "addictiveness"—indeed most models of addiction use this formulation—our analysis in Section IV suggests two reasons why people with projection bias might be over-prone to develop harmful addictions. First, projection bias may lead people to underappreciate the degree to which current consumption has negative consequences for their future health, employment, and personal lives; that is, they may underappreciate the negative internality associated with addictive products. Second, and perhaps more important, projection bias may lead people to underappreciate the degree to which current consumption changes their future desire for addictive products; that is, they may underappreciate the habit formation associated with addictive products. This second error is particularly pernicious because it can lead people to consume addictive products in the short run, planning not to continue in the long run, but then end up becoming addicted.[28]

---

[27] A difficulty with identifying projection bias via dynamic inconsistency is that there are other sources of dynamic inconsistency, such as naive hyperbolic discounting. Here, saving less than planned and giving less than planned also seem consistent with naive hyperbolic discounting; but in fact one can distinguish the two sources because of the asymmetry in the predictions. Projection bias predicts saving less than planned and giving less than planned when wealth is increasing, but the opposite effects when wealth is declining.

[28] There is, in fact, evidence that unaddicted cigarette smokers significantly underappreciate their own risk of becoming addicted. For instance, only 15 percent of high school students who were occasional smokers (less than one cigarette per day) predicted that they might be smoking in five years, when in fact 42 percent were still smoking five years later, and 28 percent were daily smokers. But there is also evidence that *addicted* cigarette smokers underappreciate their risk of staying addicted. For instance, 68 percent of high school students who were heavy smokers (more than one pack per day) predicted that they would still be smoking in five years, while 80 percent were still smoking at least half a pack per day five years later [U.S. DHHS 1994]. The mispredictions of occasional smokers are arguably larger than those for heavy smokers, and even the mispredictions of heavy smokers could be due to

Our analysis in Section V of day-to-day fluctuations in tastes is also relevant for addiction. In particular, it suggests that people might overreact to transitory changes in the craving for addictive products. When a person's craving is particularly high, projection bias will lead her to overestimate her future craving for the drug, and therefore may discourage her from any efforts to quit. Analogously, when her craving is particularly low, projection bias will lead her to underestimate her future craving for the drug, and therefore may cause her to make repeated painful efforts to quit only to fail in these endeavors when her craving returns to average or high levels. There is, in fact, empirical support for addicts believing that their future craving will be similar to their current craving. Giordano et al. [2001] studied heroin addicts who came to a clinic for a maintenance dose of Buprenorphine (similar to methadone). These addicts were asked to choose between extra BUP or extra cash on a visit scheduled for five days later, where half were given the choice right before receiving the BUP and half were given the choice right after. Those making the choice before receiving the BUP valued the future BUP dose by almost twice as much as those who made the choice after receiving the BUP.

Projection bias over the endowment effect has further implications (beyond those in Section II). The usual explanation for the endowment effect is that people adapt to owning or not owning objects, and that there is more pain upon parting with objects than there is joy upon obtaining objects. Projection bias over this adaptation has several interesting implications. First, because projection bias leads to exaggerated feelings of loss aversion, it magnifies the size of the endowment effect. In other words, while the endowment effect may be caused by valid expectations that losses will hurt more than gains will help, the endowment effect that we observe in experiments may be an exaggerated response to these real preferences.[29] Perhaps more important is that people may fail to predict the endowment effect. At a purely individual level, this failure can lead individuals to make purchases with a false sense of their reversibility, and undoubtedly lowers the cost to retailers of offering money-back guarantees and free returns. In bilateral economic transactions, it can cause distortions or break down in bargaining, because buyers will tend to underestimate owners' reservation prices, and owners will tend to overestimate buyers' reservation prices. Indeed, Van Boven,

---

projection bias if they made predictions while in a nicotine-sated state. Even so, the average mispredictions of heavy smokers suggests that the mispredictions of even the occasional smokers might in part be due to overoptimism about self-control or other factors rather than projection bias.

[29] Kahneman [1991, p. 143] and Tversky and Kahneman [1991] argue that the endowment effect is a "bias" because people's actual pain when losing an object is not commensurate with their unwillingness to part with that object. Evidence from Strahilevitz and Loewenstein [1998] supports this interpretation. Loewenstein, O'Donoghue, and Rabin [2002] present a detailed analysis of the role of projection bias in the endowment effect.

Dunning, and Loewenstein [2000] experimentally demonstrate bargaining inefficiency due to "buyers' agents" underestimating sellers' reservation values.[30]

As highlighted by our analysis in Section V, projection bias predicts sub-optimal patterns of behavior when people make decisions with long-term consequences but experience highly variable day-to-day feelings. While our formal analysis concerned durable goods, more important life decisions such as marriage, divorce, and especially fertility all display such a pattern. For such long-term decisions, momentary fluctuations in feelings should be virtually irrelevant, but projection bias will cause people to exaggerate their longevity and therefore to give them too much weight in their decisions. Hence, projection bias might lead people to get married—or make proposals of marriage that are costly to rescind—in the thralls of love, say things they later wish they had not in a fit of rage, and fail to use birth control or to follow safe sex practices in the heat of passion. There are, in fact, policies that seek to circumvent such tendencies: for example, in many states there are mandatory time delays between filing for marriage or divorce and actual changes in status. And there seems to be a demand for methods of birth control that allow one to control fertility without making decisions in the heat of passion, such as Norplant and the "morning after" pill.

Whereas marriage, divorce, and fertility decisions are difficult to reverse, suicide is totally irreversible. Yet much suicidal behavior seems to occur on impulse, or after only a relatively short period of misery. Projection bias may well contribute to this phenomenon. The literature on depression documents a tendency for people who are depressed to project their depressed feelings not only on the future, but also on the past. As Solomon [1998, p. 49] expresses it, "When you are depressed, the past and the future are absorbed entirely by the present.... You can neither remember feeling better nor imagine that you will feel better." Other research documents that the will to live varies dramatically over time. In a study of 168 cancer patients admitted to a hospital for end-of-life care, the patients' will to live, as measured on a 100-point scale, fluctuated an average of 30 percent over a 12-hour period and more than 60 percent over a 30-day period [Chochinov et al. 1999].

The combination of such fluctuations and projection bias also has important ramifications for end-of-life care, in particular for the use of mechanisms such as "advanced directives" and "living wills" that permit people to make decisions that will apply when they are in a health state that renders them

---

[30] Also see Genesove and Mayer [2001], who find evidence of financial loss aversion in housing markets—of people experiencing "pain" when they realize a nominal loss on their home. In particular, they find that sellers subject to nominal losses set higher asking prices and exhibit a lower hazard rate of sale. Projection bias suggests that the magnitudes of these effects may be larger than justified by any true feelings of pain that people experience if and when they do sell their residence at a loss.

unable to make decisions for themselves. The premise of such tools is that healthy people can make decisions that will reflect their own preferences when sick, but the presence of projection bias would challenge the validity of this assumption (see Coppola et al. [1999] and Druley et al. [1993]). Indeed, in one study [Slevin et al. 1988], respondents were asked whether they would accept a grueling course of chemotherapy if it would extend their lives by three months. While only 10 percent of healthy people said that they would accept the chemotherapy, 42 percent of current cancer patients say they would. A natural interpretation is that the value of a day of life is larger when the prospect of death is close at hand, but projection bias leads people to underappreciate this change.

Projection bias also has further implications in the mundane world of consumer theory. Although economists usually capture satiation with a static model that assumes diminishing marginal utility, we usually have in mind a dynamic notion that the utility of current consumption depends on recent consumption. The satisfaction from eating a pint of ice cream is smaller if one has just consumed another pint of ice cream. The satisfaction from eating salmon is smaller if one has already consumed salmon for several evenings in a row. Projection bias over such effects has diverse consequences. Most straightforwardly, it leads to overconsumption, or at least overordering of appetite-dependent goods. More generally, people may be prone to over-purchase activities that they currently do not engage in. People may plan overly long vacations, believing the ninth day lying on the beach will be nearly as enjoyable as the first; and professionals who have little time for reading or traveling may falsely anticipate the blissfulness of spending their retirement years with nonstop reading and traveling. Firms may, of course, take advantage of such mispredictions, by selling large quantities in advance; restaurants may take advantage of projection bias by offering all-you-can-eat meals to hungry diners who underestimate how quickly they will become satiated.

We conclude with perhaps the broadest implication of projection bias: much as in the opening quotation from Adam Smith, projection bias will lead to a general "over-rating the difference between one permanent situation and another." Projection bias over habit formation, for instance, can lead people to overrate the differences between "poverty and riches." In simple terms, poor people will overestimate how good it would be to become rich, and rich people will overestimate how bad it would be to become poor. Perhaps more important, because projection bias makes people mispredict how they themselves would behave in other situations, it can lead to misunderstandings between these two groups of people. For instance, projection bias can lead low-wealth individuals to find the behavior of wealthy individuals reprehensible because they expect the rich to engage in more charitable giving than they actually do.

371

Although on a smaller scale, there is experimental evidence of such misunderstandings between groups. As mentioned above with regard to projection bias over the endowment effect, Van Boven, Dunning, and Loewenstein [2000] experimentally demonstrate bargaining inefficiency due to "buyers' agents" underestimating sellers' reservation values. They further show that when the buyers' agents were asked to explain the high prices of the sellers, they rejected explanations that resembled the endowment effect in favor of explanations that hinged on greed on the part of the sellers. Much in the same way that the rich might seem greedy to the poor, projection bias over the endowment effect can lead to negative judgments of other people's characters. To the extent that such negative judgments might make people willing to incur losses to hurt others [Gibbons and Van Boven 2001; Loewenstein, Thompson, and Bazerman 1989], projection bias might have both direct and indirect consequences in everyday economic behavior.

Smith also suggests that people are likely to exaggerate the importance between "private and public station," i.e. social status. In recent years, social-comparison theory, which studies the ways a person cares about her status relative to comparison groups, has received increasing attention from economists. When people make decisions that cause their comparison groups to change—such as switching jobs or buying a house in a new neighborhood—projection bias predicts that people will underappreciate the effects of a change in comparison groups and hence, consistent with Smith's assertion, overestimate the long-term satisfaction that would accompany such a change. As a result, people may be too prone to make reference-group-changing decisions that give them a sensation of status relative to their current reference group. If a person buys a small house in a wealthy neighborhood in part because it has a certain status value in her apartment building, she may not fully appreciate that her frame of reference may quickly become the larger houses and bigger cars that her new neighbors have.

13.7. Discussion and Conclusion

Our goal in this paper has been to introduce a formal model that can improve the realism of the economic analysis of intertemporal decision-making by incorporating a common form of misprediction of future preferences. The psychological evidence presented in Section II provides support for the existence of projection bias, and our analysis and discussion in Sections IV, V, and VI demonstrate the potential importance of projection bias for economics. We conclude by putting projection bias in broader economic context, and discussing some shortcomings and potential extensions of our model.

How might one empirically identify projection bias in economic data? According to our model, while people may be wrong in their predicted utility, they still obey the axioms of "rational" choice in one-shot decisions: they have well-defined predicted preferences and make decisions to maximize those preferences.[31] Hence, if all we observe is a single decision by each person, projection bias may be difficult to identify, except insofar as we can find field-data analogues of Read and van Leeuwen's [1998] experiments—instances in which people's current state plays "too large" a role in their decisions. However, if we observe multiple observations for each decision-maker, researchers can identify projection bias through dynamic inconsistency. We might compare directly people's plans and their later behavior, as in the Loewenstein and Adler [1995] experiments. Or we might indirectly infer dynamic inconsistency from intertemporal behavior, as in the health-club evidence from Della Vigna and Malmendier [2002].[32]

Our review of evidence and our analysis in this paper leave a number of open questions. One is the extent to which projection bias diminishes with experience. That projection bias operates on states, such as hunger, with which people should have ample experience suggests that it does not disappear with experience. Moreover, an explicit test of the effect of repeated experience failed to produce any appreciable learning [Van Boven, Loewenstein, and Dunning 2003]. In this study, "buyers' agents"—with incentives to facilitate exchange but at the lowest possible price—made take-it-or-leave-it offers for an object to sellers. There were five rounds of possible trade, with feedback after each round about whether the bids were too high or too low. Bids, which were initially too low due to buyers' agents' underappreciation of sellers' attachments to objects, increased over the five rounds, and converged toward the profit-maximizing level. However, when a new object of similar value was substituted for the original object, the same pattern occurred. Subjects learned to adjust their bids upward, but they did not learn to anticipate the endowment effect.

A related second open question is how aware are people of the bias. The existence of advice such as "count to ten before you respond" or "never shop on an empty stomach" suggests that people are aware of projection bias on a meta-level. In addition, we suspect that many rules people develop are designed to deal with moment-by-moment projection bias. For instance, in the context of our durable-good model, people might develop rules such as never buy a car on a first visit to a dealer. The need for such rules provides

---

[31] Kahneman [1994] distinguishes between "experienced utility," which reflects one's welfare, and "decision utility," which reflects the attractiveness of options as inferred from one's decisions; projection bias represents a reason why decision utility may deviate from experienced utility.

[32] When we observe dynamic inconsistency, the question arises whether the source is projection bias or some other error, such as naive hyperbolic discounting. But as we discuss in footnote 28, it is often possible to find situations where different behavioral errors predict different types of dynamic inconsistency.

further evidence that people suffer from projection bias, but also implies that its damaging effects may be mitigated in many circumstances.

A third open question concerns our treatment of projection bias as a pure error. We believe that perhaps the most important reason to incorporate projection bias into economics is to improve welfare analysis (rather than solely to improve behavioral predictions)—to study, for instance, whether addicts are making an optimal lifetime decision to become addicts. As such, we have emphasized the ways in which people behave suboptimally. There may, however, be reasons to be more cautious about treating all changes in behavior as suboptimal.[33]

As models that reflect the reality of both short-term fluctuations and long-term changes in preferences become more wide-spread in economics, economists must seriously address the question of whether people accurately predict how their preferences will change. We hope our analysis and examples illustrate the potential benefits for both behavioral and welfare economics of incorporating mispredictions of utilities in general, and projection bias in particular, into formal economic analysis.

Appendix: Proofs

Proof of Lemma 1. To ease our notation, we use $v_t^* \equiv v'(c_t^* - s_t^*)$ for all t. Also, for any function $g(i)$, we say $\sum_{i=a}^{b} g(i) = 0$ when $a > b$.

Given $a = 0$, the first-order conditions are $v_t^* - X_t^* = \lambda^*$ for all t, where λ^* is the multiplier on the income constraint, and $X_t^* \equiv \gamma \sum_{\tau=t+1}^{T} (1 - \gamma)^{\tau-(t+1)} v_\tau^*$. Hence, for all t, $v_{t-1}^* - X_{t-1}^* = v_t^* - X_t^*$ or $v_{t-1}^* - v_t^* = X_{t-1}^* - X_t^*$. Because $X_{t-1}^* - X_t^* = \gamma(v_t^* - X_t^*)$, and because $v_t^* - X_t^* = v_T^*$, it follows that for all t, $v_{t-1}^* - v_t^* = \gamma v_T^* > 0$, which in turn implies $v_t^* = (1 + (T - t)\gamma)v_T^*$. Hence, $v_1^* > \ldots > v_T^*$, which given $v'' < 0$ implies $c_1^* - s_1^* < \ldots < c_T^* - s_T^*$.

For any t, $c_t^* \geq s_t^*$ implies that $c_t^* \geq s_{t+1}^* \geq s_t^*$; combining these conditions with $c_{t+1}^* - s_{t+1}^* > c_t^* - s_t^*$ implies that $c_{t+1}^* > c_t^* \geq s_{t+1}^*$. Hence, if $c_\tau^* \geq s_\tau^*$ for some $\tau < T$, then $c_{\tau+1}^* > c_\tau^* \geq s_{\tau+1}^*$, which in turn implies that $c_{\tau+2}^* > c_{\tau+1}^* \geq s_{\tau+2}^*$, and so forth. The result follows.

---

[33] Projection bias might, for instance, serve the interests of the human race to the detriment of the individual; e.g. the failure to appreciate adaptation to paraplegia or blindness may help to limit the number of disabled people in the population. A full normative analysis should, as always, take into account such externalities, and it is possible that projection bias mitigates them. Similarly, at the individual level it is possible that projection bias serves to mitigate other errors; e.g. to work against factors such as self-control problems or underappreciation of risks that might cause people to exert too little effort at avoiding paraplegia. But we see no reason to expect projection bias to more often mitigate externalities and other errors as opposed to exacerbate them, and we believe that in any event full articulation of all errors and externalities, including projection bias, is the appropriate way to conduct welfare analysis.

Proof of Proposition 1. We use v_t^* as in the proof of Lemma 1, and note that $c_t^* \geq s_1$ implies $c_1^* < \ldots < c_T^*$ and also $c_t^* - s_t^* > 0$ for all $t > 1$. We also use $v_t^A \equiv v'(c_t^A - s_t^A)$ and $\hat{v}_t \equiv v'(c_t^A - s_1)$, and note that $\hat{v}_t > \hat{v}_s$ if and only if $c_t^A < c_s^A$. The first-order conditions are $v_t^A - X_t^A + a/(1-a)\hat{v}_t = \lambda^A/(1-a)$, where λ^A is the multiplier on the income constraint, and $X_t^A \equiv \gamma \sum_{\tau=t+1}^{T} (1-\gamma)^{\tau-(t+1)} v_\tau^A$. Hence, for all t, $v_{t-1}^A - v_t^A = X_{t-1}^A - X_t^A + a/(1-a)[\hat{v}_t - \hat{v}_{t-1}]$. Because $X_{t-1}^A - X_t^A = \gamma(v_t^A - X_t^A)$, and because $v_t^A = X_t^A = v_T^A + a/(1-a)[\hat{v}_T - \hat{v}_t]$, it follows that for all t, $v_{t-1}^A - v_t^A = \gamma v_T^A + a/(1-a)[\gamma \hat{v}_T - (\hat{v}_{t-1} - (1-\gamma)\hat{v}_t)]$. By starting with the condition for $t = T$ and iterating backwards, we can derive that for all t,

$$v_t^A = (1 + (T-t)\gamma)v_T^A + \left(\frac{a}{1-a}\right)\left[(1+(T-t)\gamma)\hat{v}_T - \left(\hat{v}_t + \gamma \sum_{i=t+1}^{T} \hat{v}_i\right)\right].$$

It is useful to rewrite this condition as $v_t^A/(1+(T-t)\gamma) + a/(1-a)R_t/(1+(T-t)\gamma) = v_T^A + a/(1-a)\hat{v}_T$, where $R_t = (\hat{v}_t + \gamma \sum_{i=t+1}^{T} \hat{v}_i)$. Also note that for all t and s,

$$\frac{v_t^A - v_t^*}{(1+(T-t)\gamma)} + \frac{a}{1-a}\frac{R_t}{(1+(T-t)\gamma)} = \frac{v_s^A - v_s^*}{(1+(T-s)\gamma)} + \frac{a}{1-a}\frac{R_s}{(1+(T-s)\gamma)}. \quad (1)$$

We next establish two claims.

Claim 1. There exist t and s such that $v_t^A < v_t^*$ and $v_s^A > v_s^*$.

Proof. Suppose otherwise. First, consider the case in which $v_t^A = v_t^*$ for all t, which implies that $c_t^A = c_t^*$ for all t. Applying equation (1), $v_t^A = v_t^*$ for all t implies that $R_t/(1+(T-t)\gamma) = R_s/(1+(T-s)\gamma)$ for all t and s; but this requires that $\hat{v}_t = \hat{v}_s$ and therefore $c_t^A = c_s^A$ for all t and s, which contradicts $c_1^* < \ldots < c_T^*$. Next consider the case in which $v_t^A \leq v_t^*$ and therefore $c_t^A - s_t^A \geq c_t^* - s_t^*$ for all t, where the inequalities are strict for some t. For any t, if $s_t^A \geq s_t^*$, then $c_t^A - s_t^A \geq c_t^* - s_t^*$ implies that $c_t^A \geq c_t^*$ and therefore $s_{t+1}^A \geq s_{t+1}^*$, where either $s_t^A > s_t^*$ or $c_t^A - s_t^A > c_t^* - s_t^*$ implies that $c_t^A > c_t^*$ and $s_{t+1}^A > s_{t+1}^*$. In addition, $c_1^A - s_1^A \geq c_1^* - s_1^*$ implies that $c_1^A \geq c_1^*$ and therefore $s_2^A \geq s_2^*$, where $c_1^A - s_1^A > c_1^* - s_1^*$ implies that $c_1^A > c_1^*$ and $s_2^A > s_2^*$. It follows that $c_t^A \geq c_t^*$ for all t and $c_t^A > c_t^*$ for some t, which contradicts that $\sum_{t=1}^{T} c_t^A = \sum_{t=1}^{T} c_t^* = Y$. Finally, an analogous logic rules out the case in which $v_t^A \geq v_t^*$ for all t and $v_t^A > v_t^*$ for some t.

Claim 2. There exists $\bar{\tau} \in \{1, \ldots, T-1\}$ such that $v_t^A \leq v_t^*$ for $t \in \{1, \ldots, \bar{\tau}\}$ and $v_t^A > v_t^*$ for $t \in \{\bar{\tau}+1, \ldots, T\}$.

Proof. Suppose otherwise. Let $x \equiv \max\{t|v_t^A \leq v_t^*\}$, which exists given Claim 1, and let $z \equiv \max\{t < x|v_t^A > v_t^*\}$, which must exist if the Claim 2 is not true. Applying equation (1), $v_z^A > v_z^*$ and $v_{z+1}^A \leq v_{z+1}^*$ together imply that $R_z/(1+(T-z)\gamma) < R_{z+1}/(1+(T-z-1)\gamma)$, which means $[\hat{v}_z + \gamma\hat{v}_{z+1} + \gamma \sum_{i=z+2}^{T} \hat{v}_i]/(1+(T-z)\gamma) < [\hat{v}_{z+1} + \gamma \sum_{i=z+2}^{T} \hat{v}_i]/(1+(T-z-1)\gamma)$ or

$$[1 + T - z - 1)\gamma]\hat{v}_z - [1 + (T-z-1)\gamma(1-\gamma)]\hat{v}_{z+1} < \gamma^2 \sum_{i=z+2}^{T} \hat{v}_i. \quad (2)$$

We prove that inequality (2) cannot hold, from which Claim 2 follows.

We first establish that $c_t^A > c_z^A$ and therefore $\hat{v}_t < \hat{v}_z$ for all $t \in \{z+1, \ldots, x\}$. Because $v_t^* > v_{t+1}^*$ for all t, it follows that $v_z^* > v_z^* > v_t^* \geq v_t^A$ for all $t \in \{z+1, \ldots, x\}$. Since $v_t^A \leq v_t^*$ implies that $c_t^A - s_t^A \geq c_t^* - s_t^*$, $c_t^* - s_t^* > 0$ implies that $c_t^A > s_t^A$ and therefore $s_{t+1}^A > s_t^A$, and so $s_t^A > s_{z+1}^A$ for all $t \in \{z+2, \ldots, x\}$. If $c_z^A < s_z^A$, then $s_{z+1}^A > c_z^A$, and therefore $c_t^A > s_t^A \geq s_{z+1}^A > c_z^A$. If instead $c_z^A \geq s_z^A$, then $s_{z+1}^A \geq s_z^A$, and since $v_z^A > v_t^A$ implies that $c_z^A - s_z^A < c_t^A - s_t^A$, $s_t^A \geq s_{z+1}^A \geq s_z^A$ implies that $c_t^A > c_z^A$.

If $x = T$, then $\hat{v}_t < \hat{v}_z$ for all $t \in \{z+2, \ldots, T\}$, and therefore $\gamma^2 \sum_{i=z+2}^{T} \hat{v}_i < \gamma^2(T-z-1)\hat{v}_z$. But then $\hat{v}_z > \hat{v}_{z+1}$ implies that $\gamma^2(T-z-1)\hat{v}_z < [1 + (T-z-1)\gamma]\hat{v}_z - [1 + (T-z-1)\gamma(1-\gamma)]\hat{v}_{z+1}$, which contradicts inequality (2).

Consider instead $x < T$. Given $(v_t^A - v_t^*) + a/(1-a)R_t = (1 - (T-t)\gamma)[v_t^A - v_t^* + a/(1-a)\hat{v}_T]$, it follows that for all t and s, $1/(s-t)[(v_t^A - v_t^*) - (v_s^A - v_s^*) + a/(1-a)(R_t - R_s)] = -\gamma[v_t^A - v_T^* + a/(1-a)\hat{v}_T]$. Hence, $(v_z^A - v_z^*) - (v_{z+1}^A - v_{z+1}^*) + a/(1-a)(R_z - R_{z+1}) = 1/n[(v_x^A - v_x^*) - (v_{x+n}^A - v_{x+n}^*) + a/(1-a)(R_x - R_{x+n})]$. Given $v_z^A > v_z^*$, $v_{z+1}^A \leq v_{z+1}^*$, $v_x^A \leq v_x^*$, and $v_{x+n}^A > v_{x+n}^*$, it follows that $(R_x - R_{x+n}) - n(R_z - R_{z+1}) > 0$. Because $R_x - R_{x+n} = \hat{v}_x + \gamma \sum_{i=1}^{n-1} \hat{v}_{x+1} - (1-\gamma)\hat{v}_{x+n}$ and $R_z - R_{z+1} = \hat{v}_z - (1-\gamma)\hat{v}_{z+1}$, this condition becomes $(R_x - R_{x+n}) - n(R_z - R_{z+1}) = (1-\gamma)(\hat{v}_{z+1} - \hat{v}_{x+n}) + [\hat{v}_x + (n-1)\hat{v}_{z+1} - n\hat{v}_z] + \gamma \sum_{i=1}^{n-1} (\hat{v}_{x+i} - \hat{v}_{z+1}) > 0$. Since $\hat{v}_x < \hat{v}_z$ and $\hat{v}_{z+1} < \hat{v}_z$, applying this condition for $n=1$ yields $\hat{v}_{z+1} > \hat{v}_{x+1}$, and then applying it for $n=2$ yields $\hat{v}_{z+1} > \hat{v}_{x+2}$, and so forth. It follows that $\hat{v}_{x+n} < \hat{v}_{z+1} < \hat{v}_z$ for all $n \in \{1, \ldots, T-x\}$, and therefore $\hat{v}_t < \hat{v}_z$ for all $t \in \{z+1, \ldots, T\}$. But then $\gamma^2 \sum_{i=z+2}^{T} \hat{v}_i < \gamma^2(T-z-1)\hat{v}_z < [1 + (T-z-1)\gamma]\hat{v}_z - [1 + (T-z-1)\gamma(1-\gamma)] \hat{v}_{z+1}$, which contradicts inequality (2). Claim 2 follows.

Finally, we prove the main result. Posit otherwise, and define $w \equiv \min\{\tau | \Sigma_{i=1}^{\tau} c_i^A \leq \Sigma_{i=1}^{\tau} c_i^*\}$. Claims 1 and 2 together imply that $v_1^A < v_1^*$, and therefore $c_1^A > c_1^*$. Hence, $w > 1$, and $c_w^A < c_w^*$. Note that if $w \leq \bar{\tau}$ (where $\bar{\tau}$ defined as in Claim 2) then $v_1^A < v_1^*$, and $v_t^A \leq v_t^*$ for all $t \in \{2, \ldots, w-1\}$, which implies that $s_w^A > s_w^*$ (using logic identical to that in proof of Claim 1). But then $c_w^A < c_w^*$ implies that $v_w^A > v_w^*$, which contradicts that $w \leq \bar{\tau}$. It follows that $w > \bar{\tau}$ and therefore $v_w^A > v_w^*$.

Define $y \equiv \min\{\tau > w | c_\tau^A \geq c_\tau^*\}$; such a y must exist. We can write the state s_t as

$$s_t = \gamma c_{t-1} + (1-\gamma)\gamma c_{t-2} + (1-\gamma)^2 \gamma c_{t-3} + \ldots + (1-\gamma)^{t-2}\gamma c_1 + (1-\gamma)^{t-1}s_1$$

$$= \gamma \sum_{i=1}^{t-1} c_i - \gamma^2 \sum_{j=1}^{t=2} \left[(1-\gamma)^{j-1} \sum_{i-1}^{t-1-j} c_i \right] + (1-\gamma)^{t-1}s_1.$$

Then $\Sigma_{i=1}^{w} c_i^* \geq \Sigma_{i=1}^{w} c_i^A$ and $\Sigma_{i=1}^{\tau} c_i^* < \Sigma_{i=1}^{\tau} c_i^A$ for all $\tau < w$ together imply that

$$s_{w+1}^* - s_{w+1}^A = \gamma \left(\sum_{i=1}^{w} c_i^* - \sum_{i=1}^{w} c_i^A \right) - \gamma^2 \sum_{j=1}^{w-1} \left[(1-\gamma)^{j-1} \left(\sum_{i=1}^{w-j} c_i^* - \sum_{i=1}^{w-j} c_i^A \right) \right] > 0.$$

Moreover, when $y > w + 1$, $s^*_{w+1} > s^A_{w+1}$ combined with $c^*_t > c^A_t$ for all $t \in \{w + 1, \ldots, y - 1\}$ implies that $s^*_y > s^A_y$. Since, by the definition of y, $c^A_y \geq c^*_y$, it follows that $c^A_y - s^A_y > c^*_y - s^*_y$ and therefore $v^A_y < v^*_y$. But given $v^A_w > v^*_w$, this contradicts Claim 2. The result follows.

Proof of Proposition 2. As a preliminary step, we prove $c^A_1 < c^A_3$ and $c^A_2 < c^A_3$. Posit otherwise, and suppose that $z \in \arg \max_{t \in \{1,2\}} c^A_t$. Hence, $c^A_z \geq c^A_{z+1}$ and $c^A_z \geq c^A_T$, which implies that $\hat{u}_z \leq \hat{u}_{z+1}$ and $\hat{v}_z \leq \hat{v}_T$. Recall that $v^A_z - v^A_{z-1} = \gamma v^A_T + a/(1 - a)[\gamma \hat{v}_T - (\hat{v}_z - (1 - \gamma)(\hat{v}_{z+1}))]$. Because $\gamma \hat{v}_T - (\hat{v}_z - (1 - \gamma)\hat{v}_{z+1}) = (1 - \gamma)(\hat{v}_{z+1} - \hat{v}_z) + \gamma(\hat{v}_T - \hat{v}_z) \geq 0$, $v^A_z - v^A_{z+1} > 0$. Given $v'' < 0$, this implies that $c^A_z - s^A_z < c^A_{z+1} - s^A_{z+1}$, and given $c^A_z \geq c^A_{z+1}$, this holds only if $s^A_z > s^A_{z+1}$, which in turn holds only if $c^A_z < s^A_z$. But if $z = 1$, this contradicts $c^A_1 > s_1$, and if $z = 2$, this contradicts $c^A_2 > c^A_1 > s^A_2(c^A_1 > s_1$ implies that $c^A_1 > s^A_2)$.

In period 1, true utility is $U^1(c_1, c_2, c_3) = \Sigma^3_{\tau=1} v(c_\tau - s_\tau)$, and perceived utility is

$$\tilde{U}^1(c_1, c_2, c_3 | s_1) = \sum_{\tau=1}^{3} [(1 - a)v(c_\tau - s_\tau) + av(c_\tau - s_1)]$$

$$= (1 - a)U^1(c_1, c_2, c_3) + a \sum_{\tau=1}^{3} v(c_\tau - s_1).$$

Period 1 behavior (c^A_1, c^A_2, c^A_3) must satisfy $\partial \tilde{U}^1(c^A_1, c^A_2, c^A_3 | s_1)/\partial c_1 = \partial \tilde{U}^1(c^A_1, c^A_2, c^A_3 | s_1)/\partial c_2 = \partial \tilde{U}^1(c^A_1, c^A_2, c^A_3 | s_1)/\partial c_3$. Because $\partial \tilde{U}^1(c_1, c_2, c_3 | s_1)/\partial c_t = (1 - a)\partial U^1(c_1, c_2, c_3)/\partial c_t + av'(c_t - s_1)$ for $t \in \{1, 2, 3\}$, $\partial \tilde{U}^1(c^A_1, c^A_2, c^A_3 | s_1)/\partial c_2 = \partial \tilde{U}^1(c^A_1, c^A_2, c^A_3 | s_1)/\partial c_3$ implies that $(1 - a)[\partial U^1(c^A_1, c^A_2, c^A_3)/\partial c_2 - \partial U^1(c^A_1, c^A_2, c^A_3)/\partial c_3] = a[v'(c^A_2 - s_1) - v'(c^A_2 - s_1)]$.

After choosing $c^A_1 > s_1$, in period 2, the state is $s^A_2 = (1 - \gamma)s_1 + \gamma c^A_1$, true utility is $U^2(c_2, c_3 | s^A_2) = \Sigma^3_{\tau=2} v(c_\tau - s_\tau)$, and perceived utility is $\tilde{U}^2(c_2, c_3 | s^A_2) = \Sigma^3_{\tau=2}[(1 - a)v(c_\tau - s_\tau) + av(c_\tau - s^A_2)] = (1 - a)U^2(c_2, c_3 | s^A_2) + a \Sigma^3_{\tau=2} v(c_\tau - s^A_2)$. Period 2 behavior (c^{AA}_2, c^{AA}_3) must satisfy $\partial \tilde{U}^2(c^{AA}_2, c^{AA}_3 | s^A_2)/\partial c_2 = \partial \tilde{U}^2(c^{AA}_2, c^{AA}_3 | s^A_2)/\partial c_3$. Note that for $t \in \{2, 3\}$, $\partial U^1(c_1, c_2, c_3)/\partial c_t = \partial U^2(c_2, c_3 | s^A_2)\partial c_t$ for all c_2 and c_3. Hence, because $\partial \tilde{U}^2(c_2, c_3 | s^A_2)/\partial c_t = (1 - a)\partial U^1(c^A_1, c_2, c_3)/\partial c_t + av'(c_t - s^A_2)$ for $t \in \{2, 3\}$, $\partial \tilde{U}^2(c^A_2, c^A_3 | s^A_2)/\partial c_2 - \partial \tilde{U}^2(c^A_2, c^A_3 | s^A_2)/\partial c_3 = a[v'(c^A_3 - s_1) - v'(c^A_2 - s_1)] + a[v'(c^A_2 - s^A_2) - v'(c^A_3 - s^A_2)]$.

$v''' > 0$, $s^A_2 > s_1$ (which follows from $c^A_1 > s_1$), and $c^A_2 < c^A_3$ together imply $v'(c^A_2 - s^A_2) - v'(c^A_2 - s_1) > v'(c^A_3 - s^A_2) - v'(c^A_3 - s_1)$, which in turn implies that $\partial \tilde{U}^2(c^A_2, c^A_3 | s_2)/\partial c_2 > \partial \tilde{U}^2(c^A_2, c^A_3 | s_2)/\partial c_3$. Given the concavity of $\tilde{U}^2$, we must have $c^{AA}_2 > c^A_2$ and $c^{AA}_3 < c^A_3$.

An analogous argument holds for $v''' < 0$.

$v''' = 0$ implies that $v'(c^A_2 - s^A_2) - v'(c^A_2 - s_1) = v'(c^A_3 - s^A_2) - v'(c^A_3 - s_1) = k(s_2 - s_1)$ for some constant k (i.e., $v''' = 0$ implies that v' is linear and decreasing, so $-k$ is the slope of v'), and so $\partial \tilde{U}^2(c^A_2, c^A_3 | s_2)/\partial c_2 = \partial \tilde{U}^2(c^A_2, c^A_3 | s_2)/\partial c_3$. It follows that $(c_2^{AA}, c_3^{AA}) = (c_2^A, c_3^A)$. (The conclusion that $v''' = 0$ yields dynamic consistency would hold for any T and for any c_1^A.)

Proof of Proposition 3. Using the notation from the proof of Proposition 2,

$$\lambda^A = \frac{\partial \tilde{U}^1(c_1^A, c_2^A, c_3^A | s_1)}{\partial c_1}$$

$$= \frac{\partial \tilde{U}^1(c_1^A, c_2^A, c_3^A | s_1)}{\partial c_2}$$

$$= \frac{\partial \tilde{U}^1(c_1^A, c_2^A, c_3^A | s_1)}{\partial c_3},$$

$$\text{and} \quad \lambda^{AA} = \frac{\partial \tilde{U}^2(c_2^{AA}, c_3^{AA} | s_2^A)}{\partial c_2}$$

$$= \frac{\partial \tilde{U}^2(c_2^{AA}, c_3^{AA} | s_2^A)}{\partial c_3}.$$

The concavity of $\tilde{U}^2$ implies that $\lambda^{AA} \geq \min\{\partial \tilde{U}^2(c_2^A, c_3^A | s_2^A)/\partial c_2, \partial \tilde{U}^2(c_2^A, c_3^A | s_2^A)/\partial c_3\}$. For $t \in \{2, 3\}$ we have $\partial \tilde{U}^2(c_2^A, c_3^A | s_2^A)/\partial c_t = \partial \tilde{U}^1(c_1^A, c_2^A, c_3^A | s_1)/\partial c_t + a[v'(c_t^A - s_2^A) - v'(c_t^A - s_2^A) - v'(c_t^A - s_1)]$. Then $s_2^A > s_1$ (which follows from $c_1^A > s_1$) combined with $v'' < 0$ implies that $v'(c_t^A - s_2^A) > v'(c_t^A - s_1)$. Hence, for $t \in \{2, 3\}$, $\partial \tilde{U}^2(c_2^A, c_3^A | s_2^A)/\partial c_t > \partial \tilde{U}^1(c_1^A, c_2^A, c_3^A | s_1)/\partial c_t = \lambda^A$. The result follows.

Carnegie Mellon University
Cornell University
University of California, Berkeley

References

Abel, Andrew, "Asset Prices under Habit Formation and Catching up with the Jones," *American Economic Review,* LXXX (1990), 38–42.

Baron, Jonathan, David A. Asch, Angela Fagerlin, Christopher Jepson, George Loewenstein, Jason Riis, Margaret G. Stineman, and Peter A. Ubel, "Effect of Assessment Method on the Discrepancy between Judgments of Health Disorders People Have and Do Not Have: A Web Study," *Medical Decision Making,* forthcoming.

Becker, Gary, and Kevin Murphy, "A Theory of Rational Addiction," *Journal of Political Economy,* XCVI (1988), 675–700.

Bernheim, B. Douglas, "The Timing of Retirement: A Comparison of Expectations and Realizations," in David A. Wise, ed., *The Economics of Aging* (Chicago, IL: University of Chicago Press, 1989).

Boldrin, Michele, Lawrence Christiano, and Jonas Fisher, "Habit Persistence, Asset Returns, and the Business Cycle," *American Economic Review,* XCI (2001), 149–166.

Bowman, David, Deborah Minehart, and Matthew Rabin, "Loss Aversion in a Consumption-Savings Model," *Journal of Economic Behavior and Organization,* XXXVIII (1999), 155–178.

Boyd, Norman, Heather J. Sutherland, Karen Z. Heasman, David L. Tritcher, and Bernard Cummings, "Whose Utilities for Decision Analysis?" *Medical Decision Making,* X (1990), 58–67.

Camerer, Colin, Samuel Issacharoff, George Loewenstein, Ted O'Donoghue, and Matthew Rabin, "Regulation for Conservatives: Behavioral Economics and the Case for 'Asymmetric Paternalism,'" *University of Pennsylvania Law Review,* CLI (2003), 1211–1254.

Campbell, John, and John Cochrane, "By Force of Habit: A Consumption-Based Explanation of Aggregate Stock Market Behavior," *Journal of Political Economy,* CVII (1999), 205–251.

Campbell, John, and Angus Deaton, "Why Is Consumption So Smooth?" *Review of Economic Studies,* LVI (1989), 357–374.

Carroll, Christopher, Jody Overland, and David Weil, "Saving and Growth with Habit Formation," *American Economic Review,* XC (2000), 341–355.

Chochinov, Harvey M., Douglas Tataryn, Jennifer J. Clinch, and Deborah Dudgeon, "Will to Live in the Terminally Ill," *The Lancet,* CCCLIV (1999, Issue 9181, September 4), 816–819.

Constantinides, George, "Habit Formation: A Resolution of the Equity Premium Puzzle," *Journal of Political Economy,* XCVIII (1990), 519–543.

Coppola, Kristen M., Jamila Bookwala, Peter H. Ditto, Lisa K. Lockhart, Joseph H. Danks, and William D. Smucker, "Elderly Adults' Preferences for Life-Sustaining Treatments: The Role of Impairment, Prognosis, and Pain," *Death Studies,* XXIII (1999), 617–634.

Della Vigna, Stefano, and Ulrike Malmendier, "Overestimating Self-Control: Evidence from the Health Club Industry," Working Paper, University of California at Berkeley and Stanford University, 2002.

Druley, Jennifer A., Peter H. Ditto, Kathleen A. Moore, Joseph H. Danks, A. Townsend, and William D. Smucker, "Physicians' Predictions of Elderly Out-patients' Preferences for Life-Sustaining Treatment," *Journal of Family Practice,* XXXVII (1993), 469–475.

Duesenberry, James, *Income, Saving, and the Theory of Consumer Behavior* (Cambridge, MA: Harvard University Press, 1949).

Dynan, Karen, "Habit Formation in Consumer Preferences: Evidence from Panel Data," *American Economic Review,* XC (2000), 391–406.

Frank, Robert, *Luxury Fever* (New York, NY: Free Press, 1999).

Frederick, Shane, and George Loewenstein, "Hedonic Adaptation," in Daniel Kahneman, Edward Diener, and Norbert Schwarz, eds., *Well-Being: The Foundations of Hedonic Psychology* (New York, NY: Russell Sage Foundation Press, 1999).

Fuhrer, Jeffrey, "Habit Formation in Consumption and Its Implications for Monetary-Policy Models," *American Economic Review,* XC (2000), 367–390.

Genesove, David, and Christopher Mayer, "Loss Aversion and Seller Behavior: Evidence from the Housing Market," *Quarterly Journal of Economics,* CXVI (2001), 1233–1260.

Gibbons, Robert, and Leaf Van Boven, "Contingent Social Utility in the Prisoners' Dilemma," *Journal of Economic Behavior and Organization,* XLV (2001), 1–17.

Gilbert, Daniel T., Michael J. Gill, and Timothy D. Wilson, "The Future Is Now: Temporal Correction in Affective Forecasting," *Organizational Behavior and Human Decision Processes,* LXXXVIII (2002), 430–444.

Gilbert, Daniel T., Elizabeth C. Pinel, Timothy D. Wilson, Stephen J. Blumberg, and Thalia P. Wheatley, "Immune Neglect: A Source of Durability Bias in Affective Forecasting," *Journal of Personality and Social Psychology,* LXXV (1998), 617–638.

Giordano, Louis A., Warren K. Bickel, George Loewenstein, Eric A. Jacobs, Gary J. Badger, and Lisa A. Marsch, "Mild Opioid Deprivation and Delay to Consequences Affects How Opioid-Dependent Outpatients Value an Extra Maintenance Dose of Buprenorphine," Working Paper, Substance Abuse Treatment Center, Psychiatry Department, University of Vermont, Burlington, 2001.

Helson, Harry, *Adaptation-Level Theory: An Experimental and Systematic Approach to Behavior* (New York, NY: Harper & Row, 1964).

Herrnstein, Richard, George Loewenstein, Drazen Prelec, and William Vaughan, Jr., "Utility Maximization and Melioration: Internalities in Individual Choice," *Journal of Behavioral Decision Making,* VI (1993), 149–185.

Jepson, Christopher, George Loewenstein, and Peter Ubel, "Actual versus Estimated Differences in Quality of Life before and after Renal Transplant," Working Paper, Department of Social and Decision Sciences, Carnegie Mellon University, 2001.

Jermann, Urban, "Asset Pricing in Production Economies," *Journal of Monetary Economics,* XLI (1998), 257–275.

Kahneman, Daniel, "Judgement and Decision-Making: A Personal View," *Psychological Science,* II (1991), 142–145.

———, "New Challenges to the Rationality Assumption," *Journal of Institutional and Theoretical Economics,* CL (1994), 18–36.

Kahneman, Daniel, and Amos Tversky, "Prospect Theory: An Analysis of Decision under Risk," *Econometrica,* XLVII (1979), 263–291.

Kahneman, Daniel, Jack L. Knetsch, and Richard H. Thaler, "Anomalies: The Endowment Effect, Loss Aversion, and Status Quo Bias," *Journal of Economic Perspectives,* V (1991 Winter), 193–206.

Laibson, David, "Essays on Hyperbolic Discounting," Ph.D. thesis, Department of Economics, Massachusetts Institute of Technology, 1994.

———, "Golden Eggs and Hyperbolic Discounting," *Quarterly Journal of Economics,* CXII (1997), 443–477.

Laibson, David, Andrea Repetto, and Jeremy Tobacman, "Self-Control and Saving for Retirement," *Brookings Papers on Economic Activity,* 1 (1998), 91–196.

Loewenstein, George, "Out of Control: Visceral Influences on Behavior," *Organizational Behavior and Human Decision Processes,* LXV (1996), 272–292.

———, "A Visceral Account of Addiction," in Jon Elster and Ole-Jørgen Skog, eds., *Getting Hooked: Rationality and Addiction* (Cambridge, UK: Cambridge University Press, 1999).

Loewenstein, George, and Daniel Adler, "A Bias in the Prediction of Tastes," *Economic Journal,* CV (1995), 929–937.

Loewenstein, George, and Erik Angner, "Predicting and Indulging Changing Preferences," in George Loewenstein, Daniel Read, and Roy Baumeister, eds., *Time and Decision: Economic and Psychological Perspectives on Intertemporal Choice* (New York, NY: Russell Sage Foundation Press, 2003).

Loewenstein, George, and Shane Frederick, "Predicting Reactions to Environmental Change," in Max Bazerman, David Messinck, Ann Tenbrunsel, and Kimberly Wade-Benzoni, eds., *Environment, Ethics, and Behavior* (San Francisco, CA: New Lexington Press, 1997).

Loewenstein, George, and David Schkade, "Wouldn't It Be Nice? Predicting Future Feelings," in Daniel Kahneman, Edward Diener, and Norbert Schwarz, eds., *Well-Being: The Foundations of Hedonic Psychology* (New York, NY: Russell Sage Foundation Press, 1999).

Loewenstein, George, Daniel Nagin, and Raymond Paternoster, "The Effect of Sexual Arousal on Predictions of Sexual Forcefulness," *Journal of Crime and Delinquency,* XXXIV (1997), 443–473.

Loewenstein, George, Ted O'Donoghue, and Matthew Rabin, "Projection Bias in Predicting Future Utility," Department of Economics Working Paper E00-284, University of California at Berkeley, 2000.

Loewenstein, George, Ted O'Donoghue, and Matthew Rabin, "Projection Bias in Predicting Future Utility," Center for Analytic Economics Working Paper 02-11, Cornell University, 2002.

Loewenstein, George, Leigh Thompson, and Max Bazerman, "Social Utility and Decision Making in Interpersonal Contexts," *Journal of Personality and Social Psychology,* LVII (1989), 426–441.

Muellbauer, John, "Habits, Rationality and Myopia in the Life Cycle Consumption Function," *Annales d'Economie et de Statistique,* IX (1988), 47–70.

Nisbett, Richard E., and David E. Kanouse, "Obesity, Hunger, and Supermarket Shopping Behavior," *Proceedings of the Annual Convention of the American Psychological Association,* III (1968), 683–684.

O'Donoghue, Ted, and Matthew Rabin, "Doing It Now or Later," *American Economic Review,* LXXXIX (1999a), 103–124.

O'Donoghue, Ted, and Matthew Rabin, "Incentives for Procrastinators," *Quarterly Journal of Economics,* CXIV (1999b), 769–816.

Pollak, Robert A., "Habit Formation and Dynamic Demand Functions," *Journal of Political Economy,* LXXVIII (1970), 745–763.

Prelec, Drazen, and George Loewenstein, "The Red and the Black: Mental Accounting of Savings and Debt," *Marketing Science,* XVII (1998), 4–28.

Read, Daniel, and George Loewenstein, "Enduring Pain for Money: Decisions Based on the Perception of Memory of Pain," *Journal of Behavioral Decision Making,* XII (1999), 1–17.

Read, Daniel, and Barbara van Leeuwen, "Predicting Hunger: The Effects of Appetite and Delay on Choice," *Organizational Behavior and Human Decision Processes,* LXXVI (1998), 189–205.

Ryder, Harl, and Geoffrey Heal, "Optimal Growth with Intertemporally Dependent Preferences," *Review of Economic Studies,* XL (1973), 1–33.

Sackett, David L., and George W. Torrance, "The Utility of Different Health States as Perceived by the General Public," *Journal of Chronic Diseases,* XXXI (1978), 697–704.

Schkade, David, and Daniel Kahneman, "Does Living in California Make People Happy? A Focusing Illusion in Judgments of Life Satisfaction," *Psychological Science,* IX (1998), 340–346.

Scitovsky, Tibor, *The Joyless Economy: An Inquiry into Human Satisfaction and Consumer Dissatisfaction* (Oxford, UK: Oxford University Press, 1976).

Sieff, Elaine, Robyn Dawes, and George Loewenstein, "Anticipated versus Actual Responses to HIV Test Results," *American Journal of Psychology,* CXII (1999), 297–311.

Slevin, Maurice L., H. Plant, D. Lynch, J. Drinkwater, and W. M. Gregory, "Who Should Measure Quality of Life, the Doctor or the Patient?" *British Journal of Cancer,* LVII (1988), 109–112.

Smith, Adam, *The Theory of Moral Sentiments,* Knud Haakonssen, ed. (Cambridge: Cambridge University Press, 2002).

Solomon, Andrew, "A Personal History: Anatomy of Melancholy," *New Yorker,* LXXIII (January 12, 1998), 46–61.

Starmer, Chris, "Developments in Non-Expected Utility Theory: The Hunt for a Descriptive Theory of Choice under Risk," *Journal of Economic Literature,* XXXVIII (2000), 332–382.

Strahilevitz, Michal, and George Loewenstein, "The Effect of Ownership History on the Valuation of Objects," *Journal of Consumer Research,* XXV (1998), 276–289.

Thaler, Richard, "Toward a Positive Theory of Consumer Choice," *Journal of Economic Behavior and Organization,* I (1980), 39–60.

Tversky, Amos, and Daniel Kahneman, "Loss Aversion in Riskless Choice: A Reference-Dependent Model," *Quarterly Journal of Economics,* CVI (1991), 1039–1061.

Ubel, Peter, George Loewenstein, and Christopher Jepson, "Disability and Sunshine: Can Predictions Be Improved by Drawing Attention to Focusing Illusions or Emotional Adaptation?" Working Paper, University of Michigan Medical Center, 2003.

U. S. Department of Health and Human Services (U. S. DHHS), *Preventing Tobacco Use Among Young People: A Report of the Surgeon General* (Washington, DC: U.S. Government Printing Office, 1994).

Van Boven, Leaf, and George Loewenstein, "Projection of Transient Drive States," *Personality and Social Psychology Bulletin,* XXIX (2003), 1159–1168.

Van Boven, Leaf, David Dunning, and George Loewenstein, "Egocentric Empathy Gaps between Owners and Buyers: Misperceptions of the Endowment Effect," *Journal of Personality and Social Psychology,* LXXIX (2000), 66–76.

Van Boven, Leaf, George Loewenstein, and David Dunning, "Mispredicting the Endowment Effect: Underestimation of Owners' Selling Prices by Buyer's Agents," *Journal of Economic Behavior and Organization,* LI (2003), 351–365.

Van Boven, Leaf, George Loewenstein, Ned Welch, and David Dunning, "The Illusion of Courage: Underestimating Social-Risk Aversion in Self and Others," Working Paper, University of Colorado, Boulder, 2003.

Weinstein, Neil, "Community Noise Problems: Evidence against Adaptation," *Journal of Environmental Psychology,* II (1982), 87–97.

Wilson, Timothy D., Thalia P. Wheatley, Jonathan M. Meyers, Daniel T. Gilbert, and Danny Axsom, "Focalism: A Source of Durability Bias in Affective Forecasting," *Journal of Personality and Social Psychology,* LXXVIII (2000), 821–836.

Part V

Intertemporal Choice

14

Anticipation and the Valuation of Delayed Consumption

George Loewenstein

One day during graduate school I went to Naples Pizza—the second-most famous eating and drinking establishment in New Haven—for lunch, and found there a fellow economics graduate student. He had always struck me as a bit uptight and he seemed particularly so on that day. He reported to me that he was passing the hours at Naples waiting for his girlfriend—perhaps already at that point his fiancé—to meet him after her oral qualifying exam. I commented that the waiting must be stressful, and was surprised when he reacted with a long, quizzical, gaze followed by the statement: "George, you know me better than anyone does." As a behavioral economist, I've always been surprised at how far a tiny sliver of psychology can take one with economists. But, as the saying goes, in the land of the blind.

The sliver of psychology in this paper is no more obvious than the idea that one might be nervous while waiting for someone one cares about to emerge from an important exam; it is that people derive utility not only from consumption, but from anticipation. It doesn't take a clinical psychologist to recognize that people not only think about the future, but that such thoughts are a major source of pleasure and misery. Amazingly, however, when I wrote my dissertation in 1984 (this paper is a revised version of its second chapter), this was a novel insight for economics.

Part of the paper is the primitive study I mentioned earlier in which students were asked how much they would pay for a kiss or to avoid a shock at various points in time. Though the data were noisy, they told a coherent story that was consistent with the theory exposited in the paper: most people wanted to either get the shock over with quickly or to delay it for as long as possible, and most people who valued the kiss at all wanted to delay it by at least a few days.

The paper has had quite a bit of influence. I know this, not because it has been cited so many times, but because I inadvertently planted a kind of radioactive tracer in it that helps me to track its influence. When I refined the dissertation chapter for publication, I was already at my first academic job— at the University of Chicago—which was home to the venerable economist and historian of economic thought, George Stigler, since deceased. Stigler was never much of a friend to behavioral economics. A few years earlier, he had been invited to give the dinner address at a two-day conference on psychology and economics, and the gist of his speech was that psychology had not yet had, and was unlikely to have in the future, much of an influence on economics. So, I suspected that Stigler wouldn't be particularly sympathetic toward the paper's message. But I sent it to him anyway, asking for comments.

Perhaps because he hated the paper so much that he didn't know where to begin, or perhaps to preserve collegiality (U of C-ers tend to be nicer to their colleagues than they are to the outsiders they regularly demolish at seminars), Stigler did not tear the paper apart. However, in his brief and rather friendly commentary he did note that if William Stanley Jevons had written the words I attributed to him in 1932, it would have been "the event of the century" since at that point Jevons had been dead for almost fifty years. When I tracked down the problem I discovered that the statement I quoted was not from the great economist William Stanley Jevons, but his son, *Herbert* Stanley Jevons whose career provides unneeded support for the concept of regression to the mean. Unfortunately, or perhaps fortunately from the perspective of forensic academics, my chapter was published by the time I discovered the error.

Academics are, of course, supposed to attribute the source of their quotes, with a "quoted from.." in cases where they obtain the quote from a secondary source rather than from the original. They (and I) *do* sometimes cite sources in this fashion, but mainly when no one would reasonably believe that they had chanced upon the identical quote on their own. However, in cases where one could have plausibly come across the original source, academics often cite the original source, regardless of where they actually discovered the quote. I am aware of this not only from my own reprehensible behavior, but from the number of people who have attributed exactly the same words as I did to *William* Stanley Jevons, with no mention of my paper. Of course, it is *possible* that they also accidentally chanced upon the book by his son and made the same error as I did....

One final postscript on the paper is that I still believe the story that it tells about *negative* outcomes; people want to experience such outcomes quickly to avoid the dread associated with waiting for them to occur. But I'm not sure if I ever believed the story about positive outcomes—that is, that people delay them to enjoy the anticipation. Part of my skepticism is that I myself (and remember that I'm generic man) get so little pleasure from looking forward to things in the future. In fact, if there's something that I really want, and I expect that it's going to happen in the future, I'm more likely to feel impatience and frustration than pleasurable anticipation. But, even in such situations, I'm still likely to put pleasurable things off. I am motivated, I think, not by wanting to look forward to something pleasant, but by the desire to postpone the sadness of the end of something enjoyable—i.e. to avoid having the experience in my past rather than in my future.

Anticipation and the Valuation of Delayed Consumption*

George Loewenstein

'When calculating the rate at which a future benefit is discounted, we must be careful to make allowance for the pleasures of expectation.' (Marshall, 1891, p. 178)

Of the various assumptions underlying analyses of intertemporal choice, perhaps the assumption of positive discounting is the most widespread and noncontroversial. Empirical work which has sought to estimate individual discount rates (Hausman, 1979; Landsberger, 1971) has provided no grounds for questioning this assumption. In fact, a recent study which explicitly questioned the general applicability of positive discounting concluded that 'the case for positive time preference is absolutely compelling' (Olson and Bailey, 1981).

Yet it requires little effort to think of examples of behaviour in which negative discounting is apparent. The pleasurable deferral of a vacation, the speeding up of a dental appointment, the prolonged storage of a bottle of expensive champagne are all instances of this phenomenon. Indeed, if R. H. Strotz had begun his work thirty years ago with behaviour such as this in mind, he might have developed a critique of Discounted Utility theory (DU) equally as compelling as his work on myopia but pointing towards research very different from what has actually ensued from his work. Instead, in introducing the broad concept of 'time inconsistency', Strotz devoted his attention exclusively to a subdomain of instances in which the economic actor behaves more myopically in the present than he previously had planned. While the focus on impulsivity has offered important theoretical insights it may have

* I thank Robert Abelson, Richard Levin, Sidney Winter, John Geanakoplos, Howard Kunreuther, Colin Camerer, Mark Machina and Robin Pope for their helpful suggestions. The support of the Institute for Advanced Study, in Princeton, is gratefully acknowledged.

This chapter was originally published as Loewenstein, G. (1987) 'Anticipation and the Valuation of Delayed Consumption,' The Economic Journal, 97: 666–684. It has been reproduced here with kind permission of Blackwell Publishing.

impeded recognition of the existence and interest of other phenomena, such as low or negative discounting. A more inclusive theory of intertemporal choice should be able to account for both extremes of behaviour – myopic and far-sighted. Such a model is proposed here.

The model modifies DU by introducing an insight once recognized by economists: that anticipation of the future has an impact on immediate well-being.[1] This observation can be traced to Bentham (1789), who included among the ingredients of utility, pleasures and pains that derive from anticipation. For Bentham, anticipation, like consumption itself, was an important source of pleasure and pain.

Jevons who was one of the first to apply the Benthamite concept of utility to understanding intertemporal trade-offs, wrote: 'Three distinct ways are recognisable in which pleasurable or painful feelings are caused:

(1) By the memory of past events;
(2) By the sensation of present events;
(3) By anticipation of future events.' (1905, p. 3)

The latter, which Jevons termed 'antical pleasure' and 'antical pain' were, if anything, the most important for understanding economic behaviour: 'The science of economics is very largely occupied in studying man's efforts to obtain antical pleasure by the provision of stocks of goods for future use: almost all the complicated practices of production and exchange resolve themselves ultimately into manifestations of these efforts' (1905, p. 65). In what follows, the term 'savouring' refers to positive utility derived from anticipation of future consumption; 'dread' refers to negative utility resulting from contemplation of the future.

14.1. An Illustrative Study

Fig. 1 summarises results from a survey in which 30 undergraduates were asked to specify the 'most you would pay now' to obtain (avoid) each of five outcomes, immediately, and following five different time delays. The outcomes were: (1) obtain four dollars; (2) avoid losing four dollars; (3) avoid losing one thousand dollars; (4) avoid receiving a (non-lethal) one hundred and ten volt shock, and (5) obtain a kiss from the movie star of your choice. Time delays were; (1) immediately (no delay); (2) in twenty-four hours; (3) in three days; (4) in one year; (5) in ten years. Subjects were asked to specify the most they would pay for every combination of outcome and time delay. They

---

[1] In exploring the relationship between anticipation and time discounting, the current paper is akin to the recent work of Pope (1983), who examined the role of anticipation in risk aversion, and Wolf (1970), who discussed the implications for intertemporal choice of utility from memory.

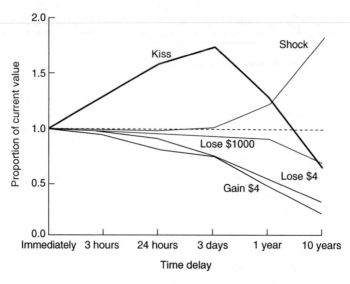

Figure 1. Maximum payment to obtain/avoid outcomes at selected times. Proportion of current value ($N = 30$).

were told to assume that all outcomes were certain to occur at the designated time. Summary statistics for the study are presented in Appendix 1.

It can be seen that the two non-monetary items, the kiss and the shock, both exhibit unusual patterns of devaluation. DU, with positive discounting, predicts that people will prefer to consume desired outcomes as soon as possible. This prediction is contradicted by the kiss item. Subjects on average were willing to pay more to experience a kiss delayed by 3 days than an immediate kiss or one delayed by three hours or one day. Data presented later in this paper show that the hump-shaped pattern of devaluation evident in Fig. 1 is common for desirable consumption that is fleeting.

Likewise, DU asserts that people prefer to delay undesirable outcomes whenever possible. The shock item contrasts sharply with this prediction. Subjects were, on average, willing to pay slightly more to avoid a shock that was delayed for 3 hours to 3 days than to avoid an immediate shock. They were willing to pay substantially more to avoid a shock delayed by one or ten years. In contrast to the patterns of responses for the kiss and shock, the money amounts included in the survey appear to be discounted in the normal fashion.

Why haven't patterns of intertemporal preference such as those exhibited towards the kiss and shock appeared in earlier empirical work on intertemporal choice? Several answers are possible. In some cases, economists have attempted to infer intertemporal preferences from behaviour in which such preferences were irrelevant to behaviour. Hausman's attempt to estimate individual discount rates from air-conditioner purchases provides an example. Air conditioners vary in purchase price and energy efficiency, thus creating a choice between immediate versus deferred payments. Hausman, by observing the price/efficiency rating of a purchased air-conditioner, attempted to impute the discount rate of the purchaser. The problem with this approach is that individual discount rates should be irrelevant to what model is purchased. If consumers are able to save and dissave (or borrow) at established interest rates, they should logically purchase the model of air conditioner that minimises, at the desired level of cooling capacity, the net present value of the time stream of payments.[2] Similar considerations may have caused subjects in the current experiment to discount the money amounts in a conventional manner, in contrast to their behaviour towards the kiss and shock.

In other cases, economists have attempted to estimate discount rate from individual saving behaviour, but such attempts are even more problematic since individuals have little influence on interest rates. The interest rate at which an individual saves or borrows gives no information about his or her own discount rate and hence it is necessary to infer discount rates from level or rate of saving, a process that is extremely sensitive to the specification of the model used to represent the savings decision. Furthermore, savings behaviour depends on so many factors other than discount rates (e.g. expected future income streams, projected needs) that it is exceedingly difficult to isolate the effect of time preference on saving.

In this paper it is argued that patterns of preference such as those exhibited towards the kiss and shock, and other DU anomalies discussed below, can be explained by incorporating Jevons' anticipal pleasure and pain into an otherwise standard model of intertemporal choice. In what follows, such a model is developed in the simplest possible terms, and its implications are discussed.

14.2. The Model

The following model explores the question of how an individual values a single future act of consumption under conditions of certainty. The model depicts a consumer at time t_0 who anticipates consuming x at time $T \geq t_0$. Consumption is assumed to yield a constant stream of utility, $U(x)$, beginning at time T and continuing for duration L, after which it drops to zero. Formally:

$$U_t^c(x, T, L) = U(x) \quad \text{for} \quad T \leq t \leq T + L, \tag{1}$$

$$= 0 \quad \text{otherwise}$$

where U_t^c indicates utility experienced at time t from consumption.

---

[2] His finding of substantial differences in discounting between different income groups suggests either that unobserved economic factors such as liquidity constraints were operative, or that consumers were failing to behave rationally.

At any time t between t_0 and T (when consumption begins) the individual derives utility from anticipation, U_t^A. Utility from anticipation is assumed to be proportional to the integral of utility from consumption discounted at a rate of δ. δ is not the conventional discount rate, but a measure of the degree to which the individual derives immediate utility from anticipated consumption. Thus savouring or dread at each point t is equal to:

$$U_t^A(x, T, L) = a \int_T^{T+L} e^{-\delta(\tau-t)} U(x)\, d\tau \tag{2}$$

$$= \frac{a}{\delta} U(x) e^{-\delta(T-t)} (1 - e^{-\delta L}). \tag{3}$$

This formulation has four desirable properties discussed by Jevons in his enumeration of the laws of anticipal pleasure and pain. Referring to anticipation of a planned vacation, Jevons wrote:

The intensity of the anticipation will be greater the longer the holiday; greater also, the more intensely one expects to enjoy it when the time comes. In other words the amount of pleasure expected is one factor determining the intensity of anticipal pleasure. Again, the nearer the date fixed for leaving home approaches, the greater does the intensity of anticipal pleasure become: at first when the holiday is still many weeks ahead, the intensity increases slowly; then, as the time grows closer, it increases faster and faster, until it culminates on the eve of departure (1905, p. 64).

In the current formulation, as Jevons proposed, utility from anticipation, U_t^A, is a positive function of L, the duration of consumption, a positive function of $U(x)$, the utility that will be derived from consumption, and a negative function of $(T - t)$, the time delay prior to consumption. Also, the second derivative of U^A with respect to $(T - t)$ is positive, yielding the accelerating path of utility from anticipation suggested by Jevons.

Fig. 2 depicts one possible time path of utility from anticipation and consumption.

The individual is assumed to evaluate a delayed act of consumption according to the integral of discounted utility from anticipation and consumption that it yields. Thus, the present value Y (measured in dollars) of a delayed act

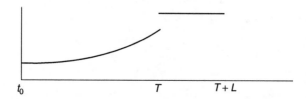

Figure 2. Utility from anticipation and consumption.

of consumption is defined by:

$$U(Y) = \int_{t_0}^{T} \underbrace{\frac{a}{\delta} U(x) e^{-\delta(T-t)}(1 - e^{-\delta L}) \, e^{-r(t-t_0)} \, dt}_{\substack{\text{utility from} \\ \text{anticipation}}} + \underbrace{\int_{T}^{T+L} U(x) \, e^{-r(t-t_0)} \, dt}_{\substack{\text{utility from} \\ \text{consumption}}}, \tag{4}$$

where r is the conventional discount rate used to discount future utility from all sources and $U(Y)$ is a 'ratio scale' utility function[3] with positive first and negative second derivative. Throughout the following, r is assumed to be positive.

Setting $t_0 = 0$ for simplicity, and integrating:

$$U(Y) = U(x) \left[\frac{a}{\delta(\delta - r)} (e^{-rT} - e^{-\delta T}) \, (1 - e^{-\delta L}) + \frac{1}{r} e^{-rT}(1 - e^{-rL}) \right]. \tag{5}$$

δ and a define to the relationship between U^A and U^c. δ is a measure of an individual's preoccupation with the future. Someone with a low δ savours or dreads even those outcomes that will occur in the distant future. a is a measure of the 'imaginability' or 'vividness' of a particular outcome. Factors that raise a or lower δ increase utility from savouring or dread. (A later section discusses attempts on the part of marketers and policy makers to influence a.) Since most people take account of future outcomes (e.g. save for their retirement) even when they do not immediately savour or dread those outcomes, it is assumed that $\delta > r$.

14.3. Implications of the Model

The model, as it stands, suggests the conditions under which people will prefer to delay desired consumption or get undesirable consumption over with quickly. These two cases are explored in turn.

14.3.1. *Delaying of Desired Consumption*

Desired consumption will be delayed when $(\partial Y/\partial T) > 0$ i.e. when the net present value of consumption, taking account of both savouring and consumption itself, increases as a function of time delay. Since $U(Y)$ is monotonically increasing, this condition is equivalent to $\partial U(Y)/\partial T > 0$.

Differentiating (5) with respect to T:

$$\frac{\partial U(Y)}{\partial T} = U(x) \left[\frac{a}{\delta(\delta - r)} (\delta e^{-\delta T} - r e^{-rT})(1 - e^{-\delta L}) - e^{-rT}(1 - e^{-rL}) \right]. \tag{6}$$

---

[3] i.e. invariant with respect to multiplicative transformations.

Anticipation and the Valuation of Delayed Consumption

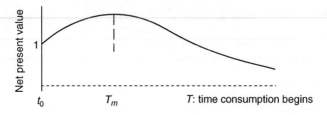

Figure 3. Value at time t_0 of an outcome to be consumed at time T.

The first term in the brackets is the marginal benefit from savouring, that would be gained from delaying. The second term is the marginal cost of delay, in terms of increased discounting of consumption.

Consumption will be deferred when $\partial U(Y)/\partial T$ is positive for $T = 0$. Setting $T = 0$:

$$\left.\frac{\partial U(Y)}{\partial T}\right|_{T=0} = U(x)\frac{a}{\delta}(1 - e^{-\delta L}) - U(x)(1 - e^{-rL}). \tag{7}$$

A necessary and sufficient condition for delaying desired consumption is, therefore,

$$\frac{a}{\delta}(1 - e^{-\delta L}) > 1 - e^{-rL}. \tag{8}$$

As would be expected, delaying is more likely when a is large and δ is small.

Fig. 3 illustrates the relationship between Y, the net present value of consumption and T, the time at which consumption of x begins, for the case when $(\partial Y/\partial T)$ is initially positive.

By reading off the net present value of consumption at any point T on Fig. 3, and subtracting it from one, it is possible to derive a crude measure of the value of consumption of x at time T relative to the value of immediate consumption of x. Note that such 'devaluing' (negative or positive) of consumption as a function of delay must be distinguished from the individual's discounting of future *utility*, which is based only on $r(\cdot)$. To avoid confusion between these concepts a distinction is henceforth drawn between 'discounting', which refers to a preference for early over later *utility*, and 'devaluing', which refers to a decrease in the outcome's *value* at time t_0 as a function of delay. 'Devaluing' is also synonymous with the rate of time discount which would be estimated by an observer who did not take account of utility from anticipation. In Fig. 3, it can be seen, devaluing is initially negative and only eventually becomes positive even though *time* preference is always positive – i.e. $r > 0$.

Point T_m in Fig. 3 has special significance. T_m is, for desirable outcomes, the individual's most preferred time of consumption. T_m will be greater than t_0 if $(\partial Y/\partial T)$ is positive for $T = 0$ (condition 8). When condition 8 is met it will also be the case that $(\partial^2 Y/\partial T^2) < 0$, ensuring that the point T_m is a maximum (see Appendix 2). Under the standard approach (in the absence of planning or scarcity effects), T_m is always equal to t_0. $T_m > t_0$ thus constitutes a sharp distinction between the predictions of the current model and the standard DU approach.

14.3.2. Conditions Conducive to Delaying of Desired Consumption

By totally differentiating (6) (see Appendix 3), it is possible to derive propositions regarding the effect on T_m of changes in the different parameters of the model.

Increasing the duration of consumption, L, raises the marginal cost of deferring at T_m more than it increases the marginal benefit of savouring. Therefore, increasing L discourages delaying behaviour $(\partial T_m/\partial L \leq 0)$. Conversely, *delaying is more likely when consumption is fleeting*. Intuitively this seems plausible. Those forms of consumption that are commonly delayed typically provide brief but intense pleasure. In such cases anticipation (and sometimes memory) serves to extend the otherwise fleeting benefit provided by consumption.

Raising a, as would be expected, also encourages delaying behaviour. a, for desirable outcomes, can be viewed as a measure of the 'savourability' of consumption. Outcomes that can be readily imagined and that are pleasurable to contemplate are therefore more likely to be delayed. The effect of changes in δ on T_m is ambiguous.

The 'kiss from the movie star of your choice' in the study was chosen for its fleeting quality and high degree of 'savourability', characteristics which are predicted to promote delay. It was also chosen to rule out, as much as possible, alternative explanations for delaying behaviour. Two such explanations are worthy of note. The first, the 'planning effect', provides an incentive for delay when, by delaying a desired outcome, preparations can be made that will enhance utility from consumption. This is certainly true of food consumption, in which case fasting (within limits) enhances pleasure from subsequent eating. In the case of the kiss it also seems reasonable to assume that some preparations (such as gargling, or moving to a dimly lit room) could intensify the experience. But it is difficult to see how a delay of three days, which was generally preferred to a single-day delay, could add much to such preparations.

The second alternative explanation for delaying is the 'scarcity effect'. The basis of this argument is that some items are scarcer in the future (e.g. raspberries in winter) than they are in the present and thus should be more highly valued. The kiss from a movie star of your choice, which is a scarce item at any time and certainly as scarce in three days as at the present moment, was chosen to avoid this alternative explanation.

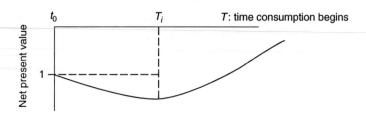

Figure 4. Value at time t_0 of consumption at time T.

14.3.3. *Accelerating Undesirable Consumption*

The shape of $U_{t_0}(T)$ for an undesirable outcome, which is a negative reflection of its shape for desirable outcomes, is shown in Fig. 4. In the case of undesirable outcomes a different point, T_i, has behavioural significance. T_i is the point at which an individual is indifferent between immediate and deferred consumption. If allowed to defer a negative outcome beyond T_i, the individual will do so. If constrained to consume x prior to T_i, however, his preferences will be reversed, and he will prefer to get x over with immediately. A common example of such behaviour is associated with medical or dental treatment. One puts off visiting the doctor or dentist as long as possible, but once a maximum delay is imposed – e.g. when one receives a card in the mail urging a visit – typically one asks for the first available appointment. Under the standard approach T_i always equals t_0.

Equation (9) defines T_i.

$$U(x)\frac{1}{r}(1 - e^{-rL}) = U(x)\frac{a}{\delta(\delta - r)}(e^{-rT_i} - e^{-\delta T_i})(1 - e^{-\delta L})$$

$$+U(x)\frac{1}{r}e^{-rT_i}(1 - e^{-rL}). \tag{9}$$

The left-hand side of (9) represents the (negative) utility that would be experienced if x were consumed beginning immediately. The right-hand side expresses discounted utility (from dread and consumption) when consumption is delayed until $T_i > t_0$. When these expressions are equal, the individual at t_0 is indifferent between consuming immediately or at T_i. If constrained to consume at any point prior to T_i, he would prefer to consume immediately.

Again we are interested in the specific conditions that encourage individuals to get unpleasant outcomes over with quickly – i.e. make $T_i \gg t_0$. These conditions turn out to be analogous to those for T_m (see Appendix 4). The more fleeting an undesirable outcome – i.e. the shorter L – the greater is the tendency to get consumption over with quickly. People should therefore be especially likely to get fleeting outcomes over with quickly and defer those for which consumption is prolonged. This has the sensible implication that people will always defer outcomes whose effects are prolonged or permanent, e.g. loss of a leg. It is also the case that $\partial T_i/\partial a > 0$; people are likely to get those outcomes over with quickly that can be vividly imagined beforehand.

Thus we should expect that the tendency to get unpleasant outcomes over with quickly will be greatest for outcomes that are fleeting and vivid. The shock item in the study was chosen to have these characteristics. Lest the survey results, which involve hypothetical responses, be questioned, it should be noted that several other studies involving real shocks produced similar results (Carlsmith, 1962; Barnes and Barnes, 1964). In fact even rats, in one experiment, when faced with a choice between an immediate or moderately delayed shock, tended to choose the immediate shock (Knapp *et al.* 1959). Furthermore, when rats are exposed to delayed shocks they typically exhibit physiological signs of fear such as elevated heartbeat and blood pressure while they wait, suggesting that fear may be a motivating factor in the choice of the immediate shock.

A problem with the use of the shock item is that it is difficult to generalise the findings to economic behaviour in naturalistic settings. This particular problem is avoided in subsequent research in which subjects were asked among other questions: 'What is the least amount of money you would accept for cleaning 100 hamster cages at the Psychology Department's animal laboratory. You will be paid the money immediately. You should be willing to do the job for the amount you specify but not if you were offered only one dollar less. The job is unpleasant but takes only 3 hours. How much would you need to be paid to clean the cages: (1) once during the next 7 days; (2) once during the week beginning two months from today; (3) once during the week beginning one year from now?'

The mean reservation wage for cage cleaning in the following week was $30 (standard error 3·1). For cleaning the cage in a year respondents required an average of $37 in immediate payment (standard error 3·8). In fact, of 37 respondents only 2 gave a smaller response to question (3) than to question (1)!

14.3.4. *Positive Devaluation*

When condition (8) is not met – i.e. for consumption that is lasting, or if a is small – we should not expect to observe negative devaluing. Nevertheless, utility from anticipation will still affect the devaluation of consumption. Fig. 5 illustrates the effect of variations in L on devaluation of future consumption. Decreasing L will attenuate devaluing, flatten the slope $\partial U_{t_0}/\partial T$ and thus $\partial Y/\partial T$ (see Appendix 5, which demonstrates that $\partial^2 Y/\partial T \partial L < 0$). As L increases, therefore, $Y(T)$ will lose its hump and will begin to take on the reversed '**S**' shape depicted in Fig. 5. Savouring, even when it does not cause devaluing to be negative, attenuates devaluing for small delays, bridging the gap between sporadic or short-lived consumption and pleasure of ownership.

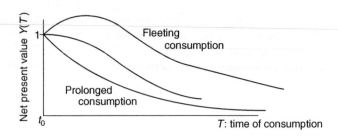

Figure 5.

14.4. Economic Implications

14.4.1. *Attempts to Manipulate* α

The concept of 'vividness' or imaginability embodied in the α term played a central role in historical formulations of intertemporal choice. For example, Böhm-Bawerk cited 'the fragmentary nature of the imaginary picture that we construct of the future state of our works' (1889, p. 269) first in his list of causes for the systematic tendency to undervalue future wants. Marshall noted that a person's willingness . . . to wait depends on his habit of vividly realising the future' (1891, p. 293). Although modern accounts of intertemporal choice have not included discussions of vividness, perhaps because vividness is not directly observable, its meaning is nevertheless intuitively comprehensible, and there are numerous examples of attempts to manipulate it.

Drivers' education films depict the gruesome consequences of car accidents in an effort to make those consequences more vivid to young (and presumably myopic) drivers. But facts and statistics and even photographs of accidents have only a limited impact. Faced with continuing high accident rates among young drivers, several school districts have taken more drastic measures. A device intended to demonstrate the violence of even a low-speed collision has been put into use in several school districts. Students are accelerated down a ramp on a wheeled chair which, after gaining a speed of 5 miles per hour, is abruptly halted. It is difficult to understand this device in purely informational terms. Rather, the intention is to give immediate emotional significance to an otherwise abstract outcome. An analogous attempt to counter youthful myopia through manipulation of vividness is depicted in the documentary movie 'Scared Straight', in which high-school students thought to be at risk of future delinquency toured a maximum security prison, were harassed by inmates, and were given as vivid an image of prison life as is possible without actually being locked up.

While the accident simulator and the visit to the prison were aimed at youth, such efforts are not limited to teenagers. For example, a recent television advertisement for a supplementary retirement plan showed a young couple in the first frame opting not to participate in the plan, and then showed them physically ageing against a backdrop of increasing poverty. Each of these efforts at persuasion can be viewed as attempts to decrease a so as to raise dread and enhance evaluation of the future consequences of current actions.

14.4.2. *Estimation of Discount Rates*

The sensitivity of intertemporal choice behaviour to savouring and dread suggests that the standard model may be mis-specified, leading to systematic bias in the estimation of discount rates. Since DU does not ordinarily incorporate savouring or dread, and since both of these factors attenuate devaluation, conventional estimates of discount rates should be biased downward, especially in situations where savouring or dread significantly affect devaluation. As demonstrated, these include situations in which future outcomes are fleeting or can be vividly imagined. Also, savouring and dread exert their greatest impact at short and moderate time delays, so discount rates estimated from short-term trade-offs will tend to be more biased than rates estimated from long-term trade-offs.

The bias in estimation of discount rates will be especially serious if savouring and dread are different for different categories of consumption. If this were the case, then the general assumption that 'the discount rate is independent of the category of consumption goods for which it is calculated' (Landsberger, 1971, p. 1351) would be invalid. Thus, for example, Hausman, in his 1979 study, implicitly assumed that discount rates imputed from air-conditioner purchases would also apply to other intertemporal trade-offs. What he failed to consider was the possibility that air conditioners or other energy-using appliances have special characteristics that promote steep discounting. Monthly payments for electricity are spread over time and made less salient by being combined with pre-existing electrical charges, leading to the prediction of high devaluing even when time discounting is low. In contrast, purchase cost is immediate and lump-sum. This myopia-inducing quality of fuel- or electricity-consuming durables seems to have been recognised by various agencies of government that require efficiency ratings for appliances, and estimates of fuel consumption and yearly operating costs, to be affixed to new cars.

14.4.3. *Savings Behaviour*

The concepts of savouring and dread may help to explain the anomalous observation that – rather than dissaving following retirement (as is predicted by the permanent income and life-cycle theories of saving) – individuals typically increase their rate of saving following retirement and continue to amass increasing amounts of wealth until they die. A number of explanations have been offered for this phenomenon, including uncertain life expectancy and bequest motives.[4] Another explanation offered by Moore (1978) is that individuals derive utility from wealth itself. The current model bolsters Moore's account by providing a reason why wealth may be a source of utility. Accumulations of wealth can constitute, in effect, a 'licence to savour' – i.e. to imagine and thus derive immediate pleasure from the consumption which the wealth could finance.

But the theory also provides a second, perhaps even more plausible, explanation for the observed failure to dissave following retirement. Retirement for the young is a non-vivid event – perhaps partly because thinking about old age is aversive and tends to be avoided (resulting in a small a). Young middle-aged couples and individuals, possibly for this reason, often 'live like there's no tomorrow'. As retirement approaches, however, the prospect of having inadequate funds for retirement becomes increasingly vivid and causes anxiety, anxiety that can be allayed in part by stepping up savings. The onset of retirement itself, and the sudden loss of wage income, of course, greatly increases this anxiety for the future. This anxiety raises the returns, in terms of anxiety reduction, of saving, and counteracts the savings-discouraging effect of the loss of income upon retirement.

The concept of savouring can also shed light on other anomalous savings phenomena. In a recent series of interviews with family heads that aimed at a preliminary understanding of saving behaviour, one theme that emerged was the apparent need of many individuals for highly specific goals to motivate savings. Such individuals seem incapable of saving for a future retirement in the abstract; they can, however, save for a retirement condominium or other concrete goal that, it is plausible to assume, brings them anticipal pleasure. Also comprehensible in terms of savouring is the behaviour of misers. In this extreme case, anticipated consumption exerts so strong a pull that no present consumption can compete with it.

14.4.4. *Reverse Time Inconsistency*

Since the publication of Strotz's well-known 1955 article, the phenomenon of time inconsistency has attracted the attention of social scientists in a number of disciplines. Time inconsistency occurs when an individual makes a long-term plan at time t but systematically departs from that plan in later periods. As has been said, subsequent departures tend to be myopic in character – i.e. to allocate greater consumption to the immediate period than was originally planned. While not ruling out such forms of time inconsistency, the current

---

[4] For a recent summary of this debate see Modigliani (1986).

model predicts, under certain conditions, a related phenomenon, which could be termed 'reverse time inconsistency'.

Suppose that an individual at time t_0, in the light of the characteristics of a prospective act of consumption, chooses to defer consumption until time $T_m > t_0$ so as to savour his expectations. Logically, it would seem that when he arrives at T_m he has every incentive to defer consumption once again, since he is in the identical situation he was in earlier. One could imagine this situation repeating itself indefinitely. Several factors, however, limit such repeated delaying and savouring of the same object of consumption.

First, concerns about self-credibility may make plans self-reinforcing. Suppose the individual at T_M decides to delay again, until T_{M2}. The problem is, having planned to consume at T_M and then failed to do so, he may not be able to convince himself at T_M that he will follow through on his plan to consume at T_{M2}. Failing to believe that he will consume at T_{M2}, he will be unable to savour the prospect of consumption at T_{M2} and he will have no incentive to defer past T_M. Ultimately, therefore, he will consume at T_M as he had originally planned, without binding himself in any way. Failure to consume as planned may interfere not only with the individual's ability to savour the re-deferred object but also with his ability to savour other forms of delayed consumption, thus adding an additional cost to any act of reverse time inconsistency.

Second, many decisions concerning future consumption carry with them their own enforcement, or at least reinforcement mechanisms – for example, when reservations are made, items are ordered, or plans are made with other people. In addition there are well-known self-control techniques such as the strategy of making 'side bets' that alter future incentives to encourage conformity with current plans. These have received extensive coverage in the literature on self-control and time consistency (Strotz, 1956; Ainslile, 1975; Elster, 1979; Schelling, 1978).

Nevertheless, despite the self-reinforcing character of plans, psychological incentives for adherence to plans, and various types of self-control techniques, people often *do* exhibit time inconsistency of this reverse form – i.e. repeated deferral for the purpose of savouring. This pattern is often observed among children at Hallowe'en when some trick-or-treaters collect then hoard their candy rather than consuming it. Apparently the pleasure derived from savouring future consumption of the candy in some cases outweighs what can be obtained from immediate consumption. Such behaviour often ultimately results in the stale candy being thrown out without having been even partially consumed. Similar behaviour can be seen among adults towards bottles of wine and holidays. Often people profess to need a vacation desperately, yet they keep putting off actually taking one, preferring instead to savour their accumulated vacation days.

14.4.5. *Violations of Independence*

Like axiomatic derivations of the Expected Utility Model, derivations of the Discounted Utility Model (Koopmans, 1960; Meyer, 1976) have centred on some type of independence axiom. Independence, in the context of intertemporal choice, posits that an individual's preference between two time streams or sequences of consumption should not be affected by periods in which the streams share identically valued consumption.

The following study illustrates a common violation of independence in an intertemporal context. Thirty-seven undergraduates were given the following paired choices. They were asked to ignore scheduling considerations.

The first finding of note is that 84% of the respondents chose option *B* over option *A* in question 1. This finding conforms to the prediction made earlier that people will tend to delay desirable and fleeting consumption for purposes of savouring. More interesting is the fact that 57% of the respondents chose option *C* over option *D* in question 2. Note that consumption is equivalent in the third weekend for *A* and *B* and for *C* and *D*. Thus this pattern of responses violates the assumption of independence that has formed the core of axiomatic derivations of DU.

Question 1. Which would you prefer? (circle *A* or *B*)

Alternative	This weekend	Next weekend	Two weekends from now
A	Dinner at a fancy French restaurant	Eat at home	Eat at home
B	Eat at home	Dinner at a fancy French restaurant	Eat at home

Question 2. Which would you prefer? (circle *C* or *D*)

Alternative	This weekend	Next weekend	Two weekends from now
C	Dinner at a fancy French restaurant	Eat at home	Fancy lobster dinner
D	Eat at home	Dinner at a fancy French restaurant	Fancy lobster dinner

These results point to a problem in applying the notion of independence to intertemporal choice. When outcomes are conditional on mutually exclusive and comprehensive states of nature, as is true in decision-making under uncertainty, it follows that one and only one outcome will occur. In this situation the independence axiom seems valid, at least as a normative rule. If the state in which pay-offs are equal is revealed, the individual receives the same pay-off regardless of his choice. Thus the common pay-off should not affect his preference between these alternatives. If any other state occurs, the common pay-off in the state that did not occur would appear to be irrelevant.

In the case of intertemporal choice, however, typically all periods will occur. Hence if consumption of one outcome affects the usefulness or satisfaction associated with another there is no reason to expect independence to hold. The current theory, generalized to accommodate complex patterns of consumption,[5] provides a reason why consumption in a later period may affect utility from consumption in an earlier period, even when there are no interperiod consumption externalities. According to our assumptions, the lobster dinner in week 3 provides greater anticipal pleasure in week 2 than in week 1. This increases the marginal utility of consuming the French dinner in the first week, when utility is low, even at the cost of forestalling the savouring of the French dinner. When no lobster dinner follows, marginal utility in the first two periods is comparable, and the anticipal pleasure preceding the French dinner is sufficient to motivate delay. This effect can account for the general preference for spreading discrete acts of consumption over time, even in the absence of consumption externalities.

14.5. Discussion

The model discussed in this paper modifies DU by recognizing that anticipation, like consumption itself, is a source of utility. That waiting for consumption to occur can often be pleasurable or painful – indeed, that much of our feeling of well-being and despair arise from emotions associated with anticipation – seems self-evident. The behavioural consequences of these feelings have been the subject of this paper.

When anticipation is a source of utility, the effect of delay on the value of an object can diverge from the predictions of existing theories. For consumption

[5] The model can be generalized to deal with complex temporal consumption streams or sequences as follows:

$$\max \int_0^\infty V(U_t^c + U_t^A) r(t) \, dt, \tag{6}$$

where $V' > 0$, $V'' < 0$. U^c and U^A represent the sum of utility from consumption and anticipal pleasure from all sources.

that is fleeting and easy to imagine devaluing will often be initially negative. Even if it is not initially negative, it may display a reversed '**S**' pattern rather than the convex shape suggested by DU.

The dependence of discounting on the characteristics of a waited consumption means that discount rates estimated in specific contexts, such as studies of consumer durable purchases (Hausman, 1979) or of savings behaviour (Landsberger, 1971), cannot be generalised beyond the domain of behavior in which they were derived. The concepts of antical pleasure and pain also provide an explanation for violations of the independence axiom used in axiomatic derivations of DU. Finally, the model draws attention to the phenomenon of 'reverse time inconsistency' that many people at times exhibit.

University of Chicago

References

Ainslie, G. (1975). 'Specious reward: a behavioural theory of impulsiveness and impulse control.' *Psychological Bulletin,* vol. 82, pp. 463–509.

Barnes, O. and Barnes, L. W. (1964). 'Choice of delay of inevitable shock.' *Journal of Abnormal Social Psychology,* vol. 68, pp. 669–672.

Bentham, J. (1970). *Introduction to the Principles and Morals of Legislation* (1789). London: Athlone Press.

Böhm-Bawerk, E. von (1889). *Capital and Interest.* News edition South Holland, Illinois: Libertarian Press, 1970.

Carlsmith, J. M. (1962). 'Strength of Expectancy: its determinants and effects.' Unpublished doctoral dissertation, Harvard.

de Villiers, P. A. and Hernstein, R. J. (1976). 'Toward a law of response strength.' *Psychological Bulletin,* vol. 83, pp. 1131–1153.

Elster, J. (1979). *Ulysses and the Sirens.* Cambridge: Cambridge University Press.

Hausman, J. (1979). 'Individual discount rates and the purchase and utilization of energy-using durables.' *Bell Journal of Economics,* vol. 10, pp. 33–54.

Jevons, W. S. (1905). *Essays on Economics.* London: Macmillan.

Knapp, R. K., Kause, R. H. and Perkins, C. C. (1959). 'Immediate versus delayed shock in T-maze performance.' *Journal of Experimental Psychology,* vol. 58, pp. 357–362.

Koopmans, T. C. (1960). 'Stationary ordinal utility and impatience.' *Econometrica,* vol. 28, pp. 207–309.

Landsberger, M. (1971). 'Consumer discount rate and the horizon: new evidence.' *Journal of Political Economy,* vol. 79, pp. 1346–1359.

Loewenstein, G. (1985). 'Expectations and intertemporal choice.' Economics Dissertation, Yale University.

Marshall, A. (1891). *Principles of Economics,* 2nd edn. London: Macmillan.

Meyer, R. F. (1976). 'Preferences over time.' In *Decisions with Multiple Objectives: Preferences and Value Tradeoffs* (R. L. Keeney and H. Raiffa eds.), New York: John Wiley.

Modigliani, F. (1986). 'Life cycle, individual thrift, and the wealth of nations.' *American Economic Review,* vol. 76 (3), pp. 297–313.

Moore, B. J. (1978). 'Life-cycle saving and bequest behavior.' *Journal of Post-Keynesian Economics,* vol. I, no. 2.

Olson, M. and Bailey, M. (1981). 'Positive time preference.' *Journal of Political Economy,* vol. 89, pp. 1–25.

Pareto, V. (1971). *Manual of Political Economy.* New York: A. M. Kelley (translated from French edition of 1927).

Pope, R. (1983). 'The pre-outcome period and the utility of gambling.' In *Foundations of Utility and Risk Theory with Applications* (ed. B. P. Stigum and F. Wenstop), pp. 137–177. Dordrecht: Reidel.

Rachlin, H. and Green, L. (1972). 'Commitment, choice, and self control.' *Journal of the Experimental Analysis of Behavior,* vol. 17, pp. 15–22.

Schelling, T. C. (1978). Egonomics, or the art of self-management.' *American Economic Review,* vol. 68, pp. 290–294.

Strotz, R. H. (1956). 'Myopia and inconsistency in dynamic utility maximization.' *Review of Economic Studies,* vol. 23, pp. 165–180.

Thaler, R. (1981). 'Some empirical evidence on dynamic inconsistency.' *Economic Letters,* vol. 8, pp. 201–207.

Wolf, C., Jr (1970). 'The present value of the past.' *Journal of Political Economy,* vol. 78, pp. 783–792.

Appendix 1

The following table presents, for each of the five survey outcomes the fraction of the amount that people would pay to obtain or avoid the outcome immediately, that they would pay to obtain or avoid the outcome after each of the five time delays. Numbers are means across subjects. Standard errors are in parentheses.

Fraction of Initial Value

Time delays	Obtain four dollars	Avoid losing four dollars	Avoid losing one thousand dollars	Kiss from movie star	120-volt electric shock
3 hours	0.93	0.97	0.97	1.30	1.0
	(0.028)	(0.023)	(0.016)	(0.155)	(0.015)
24 hours	0.82	0.91	0.96	1.59	0.99
	(0.045)	(0.044)	(0.021)	(0.280)	(0.053)
3 days	0.74	0.75	0.94	1.78	1.01
	(0.057)	(0.072)	(0.031)	(0.487)	(0.11)
1 year	0.46	0.54	0.91	1.31	1.23
	(0.069)	(0.083)	(0.075)	(0.295)	(0.20)
10 years	0.21	0.32	0.68	0.639	1.84
	(0.065)	(0.081)	(0.153)	(0.156)	(0.4)

Appendix 2

This demonstrates that

$$\frac{\partial^2 Y}{\partial T^2} < 0 \quad \text{at point } T_m.$$

Differentiating (6) a second time with respect to T:

$$\frac{\partial^2 U}{\partial T^2} = U(x)\left[\frac{a}{\delta(\delta - r)}(r^2 e^{-rT} - \delta^2 e^{-\delta T})(1 - e^{-\delta L}) + re^{-rT}(1 - e^{-rL})\right] \tag{A 1}$$

at T_m, $\dfrac{\partial U}{\partial T} = 0$ so $\dfrac{a}{\delta(\delta - r)}(\delta e^{-\delta T} - re^{-rT})(1 - e^{-\delta L}) = e^{-rT}(1 - e^{-rL}).$ $\tag{A 2}$

Substituting (A 2) into (A 1):

$$\frac{\partial^2 U}{\partial T^2} = U(x)\left[\frac{a}{\delta(\delta - r)}(r^2 e^{-rT} - \delta^2 e^{-\delta T})(1 - e^{-\delta L})\right.$$

$$\left. + \frac{ra}{\delta(\delta - r)}(\delta e^{-\delta T} - re^{-rT})(1 - e^{-\delta L})\right] \tag{A 3}$$

$$= U(x)\frac{a}{\delta(\delta - r)}(1 - e^{-\delta L})(r^2 e^{-rT} - \delta^2 e^{-\delta T} + r\delta e^{-\delta T} - r^2 e^{-rT}) \tag{A 4}$$

$$= U(x)\frac{a}{\delta(\delta - T)}(1 - e^{-\delta L})e^{-\delta T}(r\delta - \delta^2).$$

Since by assumption, $\delta > r$ it follows that $(\partial^2 U/\partial T^2) < 0$. It remains to be demonstrated that $(\partial^2 U/\partial T^2) < 0$ implies $(\partial^2 Y/\partial T^2) < 0$.

Proof: $Y = U^{-1}[U(Y)]$
so

$$\frac{\partial^2 Y}{\partial T^2} = \frac{\partial^2 U^{-1}[U(Y)]}{\partial U^2(Y)}\left\{\frac{\partial[U(Y)]}{\partial T}\right\}^2 + \frac{\partial U^{-1}[U(Y)]}{\partial U(Y)}\frac{\partial^2 U(Y)}{\partial T^2}. \tag{A 5}$$

But $\partial U(Y)/\partial T$ is equal to zero, by the definition of T_m, so the first term is zero, and $\partial U^{-1}[U(Y)]/\partial U(Y) > 0$ since $U(Y)$ is a motonically increasing function. Since $\partial^2 U(Y)/\partial T^2 < 0$, it follows that $(\partial^2 Y/\partial T^2)$ is also < 0.

Appendix 3

Derivation of the partial derivatives of T_m with respect to L, a, δ and r: T_m is defined by

$$0 = \frac{\partial U(Y)}{\partial T} = U(x)\left[\frac{a}{\delta(\delta - r)}(\delta e^{-\delta T_m} - re^{-rT_m})(1 - e^{-\delta L}) - e^{-rT_m}(1 - e^{-rL})\right]. \tag{A 6}$$

Totally differentiation with respect to T_m, L, a and δ:

$$0 = dT_m \left[\overset{<0}{\frac{a}{\delta(\delta-r)}(r^2 e^{-rT_m} - \delta^2 e^{-\delta T_m})(1 - e^{-\delta L}) + r e^{-rT_m}(1 - e^{-rL})} \right]$$

$$+dL \left[\overset{<0}{\frac{a}{\delta-r}(\delta e^{-\delta T_m} - r e^{-rT_m})e^{-\delta L} - r e^{-r(T_m+L)}} \right] \tag{A 7}$$

$$+da \left[\overset{>0}{\frac{1}{\delta(\delta-r)}(\delta e^{-\delta T_m} - r e^{-rT_m})(1 - e^{-\delta L})} \right].$$

Therefore, $\dfrac{\partial T_m}{\partial L} < 0$ and $\dfrac{\partial T_m}{\partial a} > 0$.

The sign of the first term is derived in Appendix 2. The second term is equal to $(\partial^2 U/\partial T \partial L)$, the sign of which is derived in Appendix 5. The sign of the third term is positive since it is equal to the first term of (A 6) divided by a; the second term of (A 6) is negative, and the first and second term sum to zero.

Appendix 4

Derivation of the partial derivatives of T_i with respect to a and L.
T_i is defined by:

$$0 = \frac{a}{\delta(\delta-r)}(e^{-rT_i} - e^{-\delta T_i})(1 - e^{-\delta L}) - \frac{1}{r}(1 - e^{-rL})(1 - e^{-rT_i}). \tag{A 8}$$

Totally differentiating with respect to T_i, a, L:

$$0 = dT_i \left[\overset{<0}{\frac{a}{\delta(\delta-r)}(1 - e^{-\delta L})(\delta e^{-\delta T_i} - r e^{-rT_i}) - e^{-rT_i}(1 - e^{-rL})} \right]$$

$$+da \left[\overset{>0}{\frac{1}{\delta(\delta-r)}(e^{-rT_i} - e^{-\delta T_i})(1 - e^{-\delta L})} \right] \tag{A 9}$$

$$+dL \left[\overset{<0}{\frac{a}{\delta-r}(e^{-rT_i} - e^{-\delta T_i})e^{-\delta L} - e^{-rL}(1 - e^{-rT_i})} \right].$$

The first term is simply the slope $(\partial U/\partial T)$ at T_i, which will be negative. The sign of the second term is straightforward. The sign of the third term can be derived as follows:

from (A 8),

$$\frac{a}{\delta - r}(e^{-rT_i} - e^{-\delta T_i}) = \frac{\delta}{r}\frac{(1 - e^{-rL})(1 - e^{-rT_i})}{(1 - e^{-\delta L})} \tag{A 10}$$

substituting into the third term of (A 9):

$$\frac{\delta}{r}e^{-\delta L}\frac{(1 - e^{-rL})(1 - e^{rT_i})}{(1 - e^{-\delta L})} - e^{-rL}(1 - e^{-rT_i}) \tag{A 11}$$

$$= \left[\frac{\delta}{r}e^{-\delta L}\frac{(1 - e^{-rL})}{(1 - e^{-\delta L})} - e^{-rL}\right](1 - e^{-rT_i}). \tag{A 12}$$

Multiplying both sides by $r(1 - e^{-\delta L})$ and dividing by $e^{-rL-\delta L}(1 - e^{-rT_i})$ will not change the sign.

$$\text{Sign}\left[\left(\frac{\delta}{r}e^{-\delta L}\frac{(1 - e^{-rL})}{(1 - e^{-\delta L})} - e^{-rL}\right)(1 - e^{-rT_i})\right] = \text{sign}\,[r(1 - e^{\delta L}) - \delta(1 - e^{rL})] < 0 \tag{A 13}$$

for all $\delta > r > 0$.

Appendix 5

Derivation of

$$\frac{\partial^2 Y}{\partial T \partial L} = \frac{\partial}{\partial L}(\partial Y/\partial T)$$

when $\partial U/\partial T$ and $\partial Y/\partial T$ are both negative.

$$\frac{\partial Y}{\partial T} = \frac{\partial U^{-1}[U(Y)]}{\partial T}$$

$$\frac{\partial^2 Y}{\partial T \partial L} = \overset{+}{\frac{\partial^2 U^{-1}[U(Y)]}{\partial U^2(Y)}}\overset{-}{\frac{\partial U(Y)}{\partial T}}\overset{+}{\frac{\partial U(Y)}{\partial L}} + \overset{+}{\frac{\partial U^{-1}[U(Y)]}{\partial U(Y)}}\overset{?}{\frac{\partial^2 U(Y)}{\partial T \partial L}}. \tag{A 14}$$

The signs of each of the terms except the last are self-evident. To demonstrate that $\partial^2 Y/\partial T \partial L < 0$ it is simply necessary to prove that $\partial^2 U(Y)/\partial T \partial L < 0$. Differentiating (6) with respect to L:

$$\frac{\partial^2 U(Y)}{\partial T \partial L} = U(x)\left[\frac{a}{(\delta - r)}(\delta e^{-\delta T} - re^{-rT})e^{-\delta L} - re^{-r(T+L)}\right]. \tag{A 15}$$

Since $\partial U(Y)/\partial T < 0$, from (6):

$$\frac{a}{\delta - r}(\delta e^{-\delta T} - re^{-rT}) < \frac{\delta e^{-rT}(1 - e^{-rL})}{(1 - e^{-\delta L})}. \tag{A 16}$$

Substituting (A 16) into (A 15).

$$\frac{\partial^2 U(Y)}{\partial T \partial L} < \frac{\delta e^{-\delta L} e^{-rT}(1 - e^{-rL})}{(1 - e^{-\delta L})} - r e^{-r(T+L)}$$

multiplying by $(1 - e^{-\delta L})$ and dividing by $e^{-r(T+L)-\delta L}$ leaves the sign unchanged

$$\text{sign} \left[\frac{\delta e^{-\delta L} e^{-rT}(1 - e^{-rL})}{(1 - e^{-\delta L})} - r e^{-r(T+L)} \right] = \text{sign} \left[r(1 - e^{\delta L}) - \delta(1 - e^{rL}) \right] < 0. \quad \text{(Q.E.D.)}$$

15

Anomalies in Intertemporal Choice: Evidence and an Interpretation

George Loewenstein and Dražen Prelec

This paper was written during the academic year 1988/89, when Dražen Prelec and I were both fellows in residence at the Russell Sage Foundation. Before we spent the year there together I had only met Dražen once—at a memorial conference for Hilly Einhorn—and I recall that we didn't hit it off. I think that there was some kind of implicit competition between us because we are similar on so many dimensions. We are both tall and dark-haired, got our PhDs at the same time, and interviewed for the same two jobs, one at Harvard Business School and the other at the University of Chicago Graduate School of Business. Fortunately, we each got one of the jobs, and fortunately for me I got the one I was better suited for.

In 1988, however, Dražen and I were each plucked from our respective business schools and replanted into adjoining one bedroom apartments on the 11th floor of the Royale (a luxury building on East 64th St. in Manhattan in which the Russell Sage Foundation owns several apartments). And, despite the coolness of our initial meeting, Dražen and I hit it off in a big way. We were at Russell Sage as part of a larger group that Richard Herrnstein assembled to spend the year working together.

Much of my best work has been with Dražen, and I'd like to think that he is of the same opinion (with the roles reversed, of course). Dražen has all sorts of amazing skills that I don't have. He's a brilliant mathematician, a superb writer, and a deep thinker. Inspired by my collaborations with Dražen, I always advise my graduate students to pick their collaborators judiciously and to collaborate with people who have skills that complement theirs. The problem is, I'm not exactly sure what skills *I* bring to the table in my collaborations with Dražen.

There is a downside to Dražen's brilliance: he is extremely, notoriously, slow. Dražen is of Croatian, not Montenegrin origin, but nevertheless a joke he once told me about Montenegrins stuck in my mind, perhaps because it somehow came to embody my view of him. Two Montenegrins are walking around on a sunny day, and one keeps looking over his shoulder. Finally, after hours of walking, he pulls out a gun, walks back a few paces and shoots a snail, explaining to his companion that it "serves him right; he's been following us all day."

Another downside of Dražen's brilliance is that he writes very tersely; he assumes that other people are as brilliant as he is and hence that they will not only understand a bunch of stripped down equations with barely any text, but would actually be burdened by the extraneous description and explanation. The result is that each time Dražen edits a paper it gets more and more refined, to the point where, I sometimes fantasize, it will end up as a single distilled sentence followed by a single incredibly elegant equation. So, at least one function I serve in our collaborations is to counteract these tendencies—to make sure that readers other than mathematicians will be able to understand our papers. Unfortunately, at the time when we wrote this paper, I hadn't yet learned that lesson. As a result, though the paper has been cited gratifyingly many times, I fear it has had less real influence than it could have had if its central message were more accessible.

The paper shows that anomalies quite parallel to those that had already been identified for decision-making under risk also occur in intertemporal choice, and that a model similar to Kahneman and Tversky's Prospect Theory (which applies to decision-making under risk) could account for diverse patterns of intertemporal choice behavior. However, its central message relates to the issue of intraindividual variability, mentioned in the introduction to Chapter 4. When it comes to time discounting, as in so many other domains, people tend to be extremely inconsistent. The standard economic account of intertemporal choice assumes that everyone walks around with a 'discount rate' that defines how much they care about the future relative to the present. This implies that someone who smokes cigarettes (because they ignore delayed health consequences) should also be less likely to save money (because they don't care about their well-being in retirement) and more likely to succumb to road rage (because they ignore the delayed consequences). However, the limited research that has examined the consistency of time discounting has not observed such consistency across different domains of behavior.

Prior to the publication of this paper, researchers had identified a number of inconsistencies in people's treatment of the future. For example, people seem to discount small outcomes more steeply than large outcomes, and gains more steeply than losses (e.g. Thaler 1981). My own prior research (Loewenstein 1989) had shown that people seem to have asymmetric attitudes toward speed up and delay of consumption; they dislike delaying positive outcomes that they expect to experience at a specific point in time, but aren't particularly enthusiastic about speeding up the delivery of outcomes they expect to experience in the future. The central point of the paper is that these effects should not be treated as individual differences in time discounting per se, but can be explained by properties of the utility function. For example, most people view $10 as subjectively closer in magnitude to $15 than $1,000 is to $1,500. The reason is that, though both pairs exhibit the same ratios, the absolute difference between $10 and $15 is smaller than the absolute difference between $1,000 and $1,500. A utility function that treats $1,500 as more different from $1,000 than $15 is from $10 can, therefore, explain why an individual would be likely to prefer $10 today over $15 in a year, but would also prefer $1,500 in a year over $1,000 today.

People *are*, in fact, strikingly inconsistent in the intertemporal choices they make. Sometimes they behave as if they only care about the present, and sometimes they seem to care more about the future than they do about the present. However, many of the apparent inconsistencies can be explained by simply taking a more complex and nuanced view of the preferences that drive human behavior.

Anomalies in Intertemporal Choice: Evidence and an Interpretation*

George Loewenstein and Dražen Prelec

15.1. Introduction

Since its introduction by Samuelson in 1937, the discounted utility model (DU) has dominated economic analyses of intertemporal choice. In its most restrictive form, the model states that a sequence of consumption levels, $(c_0, \ldots, c_T)$ will be preferred to sequence $(c'_0, \ldots, c'_T)$, if and only if,

$$\sum_{t=0}^{T} \delta^t u(c_t) > \sum_{t=0}^{T} \delta^t u(c'_t), \tag{1}$$

where $u(c)$ is a concave ratio scale utility function, and δ is the discount factor for one period. DU has been applied to such diverse topics as savings behavior, labor supply, security valuation, education decisions, and crime. It has provided a simple, powerful framework for analyzing a broad range of economic decisions with delayed consequences.

Yet, in spite of its widespread use, the DU model has not received substantial scrutiny—in marked contrast to the expected utility model for choice under uncertainty, which has been extensively criticized on empirical grounds and which has subsequently spawned a great number of variant models (reviewed, for example, by Weber and Camerer [1988]).

* We thank Wayne Ferson, Brian Gibbs, Jerry Green, Richard Herrnstein, Robin Hogarth, Mark Machina, Howard Rachlin, and, especially, Colin Camerer and Joshua Klayman for useful suggestions. The assistance of Eric Wanner, the Russell Sage Foundation, the Alfred P. Sloan Foundation, the IBM Faculty Research Fund at the University of Chicago Graduate School of Business, and the Research Division of the Harvard Business School is also gratefully acknowledged.

This chapter was originally published as George Loewenstein and Dražen Prelec, 'Anomalies in Intertemporal Choice: Evidence and Interpretation', The Quarterly Journal of Economics, 107:2 (May, 1992) pp 573–597. © 1992 by the President and Fellows of Harvard College and the Massachusetts Institute of Technology.

Our first aim in this paper is to remedy this imbalance by enumerating the anomalous empirical findings on time preference that have been reported so far. Taken together, they present a challenge to normative theory that is at least as serious as that posed by the much more familiar EU anomalies. Unlike the EU violations, which in many cases can only be demonstrated with a clever arrangement of multiple choice problems (e.g. the Allais paradox), the counterexamples to DU are simple, robust, and bear directly on central aspects of economic behavior. Our second aim is to construct (in Section III) a descriptive model of intertemporal choice that predicts the anomalous preference patterns. In formal structure the model is closely related to Kahneman and Tversky's "prospect theory" [1979], but the interpretation and shape of the component functions are different. The paper concludes with a discussion of some additional implications of the model for individual behavior and market outcomes.

15.2. Four Anomalies

In this section we present four common preference patterns that create difficulty for the discounted utility model.

15.2.1. *The Common Difference Effect*

Consider an individual who is indifferent between adding x units to consumption at time t and $y > x$ units at a later time t', given a constant baseline consumption level (c) in all time periods:

$$u(c + x)\delta^t + u(c)\delta^{t'} = u(c)\delta^t + u(c + y)\delta^{t'}. \tag{2}$$

Dividing through by δ^t,

$$u(c + x) - u(c) = (u(c + y) - u(c))\delta^{t'-t} \tag{3}$$

shows that preference between the two consumption adjustments depends only on the absolute time interval separating them, or $(t' - t)$ in the example above. This is the *stationarity* property, which plays a critical role in axiomatic derivations of the DU model [Koopmans, 1960; Fishburn and Rubinstein, 1982].

In practice, preferences between two delayed outcomes often switch when both delays are incremented by a given constant amount. An example of Thaler [1981] makes the point crisply: a person might prefer one apple today to two apples tomorrow, but at the same time prefer two apples in 51 days to one apple in 50 days. We shall refer to this pattern as the *common difference effect*.[1]

The common difference effect gives rise to dynamically inconsistent behavior, as noted first by Strotz [1956], and richly elaborated in the papers of the psychologist Ainslie [1975, 1985]. It also implies that discount rates should decrease as a function of the time delay over which they are estimated which has been observed in a number of studies, including one with real money outcomes [Horowitz, 1988].[2] See Figure VI for the results of Benzion et al. [1989], which are representative.

15.2.2. *The Absolute Magnitude Effect*

Empirical studies of time preference have also found that large dollar amounts suffer less proportional discounting than do small ones. Thaler [1981], for example, reported that subjects who were on average indifferent between receiving $15 immediately and $60 in a year, were also indifferent between an immediate $250 and $350 in a year, as well as between $3000 now and $4000 in a year. Similar results were obtained by Holcomb and Nelson [1989] with real money outcomes.

15.2.3. *The Gain–Loss Asymmetry*

A closely related finding is that losses are discounted at a lower rate than gains are. For example, subjects in a study by Loewenstein [1988c] were, on average, indifferent between receiving $10 immediately and receiving $21 in one year, and indifferent between losing $10 immediately and losing $15 in one year. The corresponding figures for $100 were $157 for gains and $133 for losses. Even more dramatic loss–gain asymmetries were obtained by Thaler [1981], who estimated discount rates for gains that were three to ten times greater than those for losses. Several of his subjects actually exhibited negative discounting, in that they preferred an immediate loss over a delayed loss of equal value (also see Loewenstein [1987]).

The magnitude and gain-loss effects are problematic for DU in two senses. First, the predictions that DU makes are sensitive to the baseline consumption profile, since the baseline level at a given time period directly controls the marginal utility of an extra unit of consumption. Experimental subjects

[1] The common difference effect is analogous to the common ratio effect in decision making under uncertainty [Kahneman and Tversky, 1979]. For a discussion of similarities and differences between the EU and DU axioms, see Prelec and Loewenstein [1991].

[2] Horowitz [1988] used a second price sealed bit auction to estimated discount rates for $50 "bonds" of varying maturity. Implicit discount rates were a declining function of time to bond maturity.

represent a diversity of baseline levels of consumption, yet these choice patterns are consistent over a wide range of income (and hence consumption) levels. This pattern evokes the comments of Markowitz [1952] on the Friedman–Savage explanation for simultaneous gambling and insurance purchases. Friedman and Savage argued that simultaneous gambling and insurance could be explained by a doubly inflected utility function defined over levels of wealth. Markowitz pointed out that no single utility function defined over levels of wealth could explain why people at vastly different levels of wealth engage in both activities; a function that predicted simultaneous gambling and insuring for people at one wealth level would make counterintuitive predictions for people at other wealth levels.

Second, even the determinate predictions that DU yields, on the assumption that the baseline consumption level is constant across time periods, are not entirely consistent with the effects just described. Note first that the present value of a consumption change at time t, from c to $c + x$, can be measured in two ways, either by assessing the *equivalent* present value $q(x, t)$ defined implicitly by

$$u(c + q) + \delta^t u(c) = u(c) + \delta^t u(c + x), \tag{4}$$

or by assessing the *compensating* present value $p(x, t)$ that would exactly balance the change at time t:

$$u(c - p) + \delta^t u(c + x) = u(c) + \delta^t u(c). \tag{5}$$

(These are also referred to as the methods of *equivalent* and *compensating* variation.)

The gain-loss asymmetry is obtained by comparing the equivalent variation ratios (q/x) for positive and negative x. Here the DU model makes the correct qualitative prediction, as the following simple calculation shows:

$$
\begin{aligned}
q(x, t) &= u^{-1}\{(1 - \delta^t)u(c) & (6) \\
&\quad + \delta^t u(c + x)\} - c & \text{(solving from (4))} \\
&< (1 - \delta^t)c + \delta^t(c + x) - c & \text{(by concavity of } u(x)) \\
&= \delta^t x.
\end{aligned}
$$

Consequently, the ratio, $q(x, t)/x$, is smaller than δ^t for positive x and greater than δ^t for negative x, which is consistent with the observed greater relative discounting of gains.

The critical weakness of this explanation lies in the prediction it makes about the size of the gain-loss asymmetry at different absolute magnitudes. The normative explanation is driven by the global concavity of the utility function, which creates a gap (analogous to a risk premium) between time discounting and the pure rate of time preference. Since the utility function is approximately linear for small intervals $(c - x, c + x)$, the gain-loss asymmetry should disappear for small x. Indeed, in the limit as x goes to zero (from either side), the predicted devaluation ratio q/x will approach the discount factor δ^t, for both gains and losses. In practice, however, we observe the exact opposite, with the gain-loss asymmetry being most pronounced for small outcomes [Thaler, 1981; Benzion et al., 1989].

With regard to the magnitude effect the DU predictions hinge partly on the method of elicitation. When present values are assessed by the equivalent variation method, DU contradicts the magnitude effect. For compensating variation, DU predicts the effect when x is negative, but predicts the exact opposite (i.e. smaller discounting of *small* amounts) for positive x. We now derive this last result as an illustration; the argument in the other cases is similar.

Suppose that p is the most one would be willing to pay now in order to receive $x > 0$ at time t, as in equation (5), and consider what happens as both p and x are increased by a common factor, $a > 1$:

$$\frac{\partial}{\partial a}\bigg|_{a=1} \{u(c - ap) + \delta^t u(c + ax) - (u(c) + \delta^t u(c))\} \tag{7}$$

$$= -pu'(c - p) + \delta^t xu'(c + x) \quad \text{(from (5))}$$

$$> 0 \quad \text{(if the magnitude effect holds).}$$

After substituting for δ^t from (5), this inequality reduces to

$$pu'(c - p)(u(c + x) - u(c)) < xu'(c + x)((u(c) - u(c - p)). \tag{8}$$

But, since $u(c)$ is concave, we have $u(c + x) - u(c) > xu'(c + x)$ and $u(c) - u(c - p)$, $< pu'(c - p)$, which are jointly incompatible with the stated inequality in (8).

15.2.4. *The Delay-Speedup Asymmetry*

A recent study by Loewenstein [1988a] has documented a fourth anomaly, consisting of an asymmetric preference between speeding up and delaying consumption. In general, the amount required to compensate for delaying receiving a (real) reward by a given interval, from t to $t + s$, was from two to four times greater than the amount subjects were willing to sacrifice to speed consumption up by the same interval, i.e. from $t + s$ to t. Because the two pairs of choices are actually different representations of the same underlying pair of options, the results constitute a classic framing effect, which is inconsistent with any normative theory, including DU.

15.3. A Behavioral Model of Intertemporal Choice

This section presents a model of intertemporal choice that accounts for the anomalies just enumerated. Our model assumes that intertemporal choice is defined with respect to *deviations* from an anticipated status quo (or "reference") consumption plan; this is in explicit contrast to the DU assumption that people integrate new consumption alternatives with existing plans before making a choice. The objects of choice, then, are sequences of dated adjustments to consumption $\{(x_i, t_i); i = 1, \ldots, n\}$, which we shall refer to as *temporal prospects*.

As in the prospect theory for risky choice, we shall represent preference by a doubly separable formula (equation (9) below), which rests on three qualitative properties (see Appendix in Kahneman and Tversky [1979] for details). The first property, also invoked by DU, is that preferences over prospects are intertemporally separable [Debreu, 1959] and can, therefore, be represented by an additive utility function, $\Sigma_i\ u(x_i, t_i)$. This important assumption is psychologically most questionable when the choice is perceived to be between complete alternative sequences of outcomes, e.g. savings plans, or multiyear salary contracts. In these cases, it appears that people care about global sequence properties, most notably whether the sequence improves over time [Loewenstein and Prelec, 1991; Loewenstein and Sicherman, 1991]. The present model is primarily concerned with explaining elementary types of intertemporal choices, involving no more than two or three distinct dated outcomes.

In the absence of any strong contrary evidence, we assume that x and t are separable within a single outcome, so that $u(x,t)$ equals $F(v(x)\phi(t))$, where $v(x)$ is a *value function*, $\phi(t)$ a *discount function*, and F an arbitrary monotonically increasing transformation. To eliminate F, one imposes a distributivity condition: (x,t) is indifferent to $(x, t'x; t'')$ implies that (y, t) is indifferent to $(y, t';$ $y, t'')$, for any outcome y, which essentially states that the equality $\phi(t) = \phi(t') + \phi(t'')$ can be established with any one outcome [Kahneman and Tversky, 1979, p. 290]. The discount function is then uniquely specified, given the standard normalization $\phi(0) = 1$. The final model represents preference by the formula,

$$U(x_1, t_1; \ldots; x_n, t_n) = \sum_i v(x_i)\phi(t_i). \tag{9}$$

The remainder of this section specifies the properties of the two component functions and shows how the model accounts for the anomalies presented in Section II.

15.3.1. Discount Function

The common difference effect reveals that people are more sensitive to a given time delay if it occurs earlier rather than later. Specifically, if a person is indifferent between receiving $x > 0$ immediately, and $y > x$ at some later time s, then he or she will strictly prefer the better outcome if both outcomes are postponed by a common amount t:

$$v(x) = v(y)\phi(s), \quad \text{implies that } v(x)\phi(t) < v(y)\phi(t + s). \quad (10)$$

In order to maintain indifference, the later larger outcome would have to be delayed by some interval s' greater than s. To account for this phenomenon, Ainslie [1975] proposed the discount function, $\phi(t) = 1/t$, which had been found to explain a large body of data on animal time discounting. We now derive a more general functional form, by postulating that the delay that compensates for the larger outcome is a linear function of the time to the smaller, earlier outcome (holding fixed the two outcomes x and y),

$$v(x) = v(y)\phi(s), \quad \text{implies that } v(x)\phi(t) = v(y)\phi(kt + s), \quad (11)$$

for some constant k, which, of course depends on x and y. One can think of this as a more general form of stationarity, in which the "clocks" for the two outcomes being compared run at different speeds. In the normative case, the clocks are identical, and $k = 1$, which yields the exponential discount function [Fishburn and Rubinstein, 1982]. From (11) it follows that

$$v(x)\phi(t') = v(y)\phi(kt' + s), \quad (12)$$

and

$$v(x)\phi(\lambda t + (1 - \lambda)t') = v(y)\phi(k(\lambda t + (1 - \lambda)t') + s) \quad (13)$$

$$= v(y)\phi(\lambda(kt + s) + (1 - \lambda)(kt' + s))$$

$$= v(y)\phi(\lambda\phi^{-1}(v(x)\phi(t)/v(y)) + (1 - \lambda)\pi^{-1}(v(x)\phi(t')/v(y))),$$

after substituting for $(kt + s)$ and $(kt' + s)$ from equations (11) and (12). Letting, $r = v(x)/v(y)$, $w = \phi(t)$, $z = \phi(t')$, and $u = \phi^{-1}$, produces a functional equation,

$$ru^{-1}(\lambda u(w) + (1 - \lambda)u(z)) = u^{-1}(\lambda u(rw) + (1 - \lambda)u(rz)), \quad (14)$$

whose only solutions are the logarithmic and power functions: $u(t) = c\ln(t) + d$, $u(t) = ct^\tau + d$ [Aczel, 1966; p. 152, equation (18)]. As $\phi(t) = u^{-1}(t)$, the discount function must be either exponential or hyperbolic.

D1. The discount function is a generalized hyperbola:

$$\phi(t) = (1 + \alpha t)^{-\beta/\alpha}, \quad \alpha, \beta > 0. \quad (15)$$

The α-coefficient determines how much the function departs from constant discounting; the limiting case, as α goes to zero, is the exponential discount function, $\phi(t) = e^{-\beta t}$. Figure I displays the hyperbolic function for three different values of α, along with the pure exponential which is the least convex

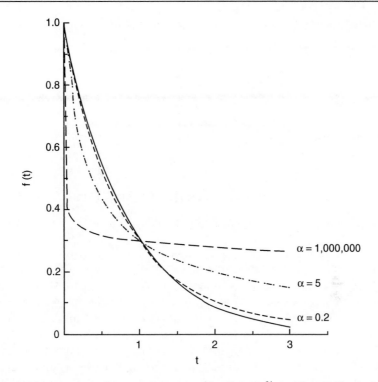

Figure I. The Hyperbolic Discount Function $\phi(t) = (1 + at)^{-\beta/a}$ for Three Different Levels of a. All βs are adjusted so that curves cross at $\phi(1) = 0.3$. The most steeply sloped curve represents conventional exponential discounting.

of the four lines. For each level of a a corresponding β is selected so that the discount function has value 0.3 at $t = 1$. When a is very large, the hyperbola approximates a step function, with value one at $t = 0$, and value 0.3 (in this case) at all other times. This would produce dichotomous time preferences, in which the present outcome has unit weight, and all future events are discounted by a common constant.

As noted already, equation (15) satisfies the empirical "matching law," which integrates a large body of experimental findings pertaining to animal time discounting [Chung and Herrnstein, 1967]; the special case, $(1 + at)^{-1}$, was proposed initially by Herrnstein [1981], and further investigated by Mazur [1987]; the general hyperbola was defined by Harvey [1986], and given an axiomatic derivation by Prelec [1989] along the lines presented here.

15.3.2. Value Function

A distinguishing feature of the current model is the replacement of the utility function with a value function with a reference point, as shown in Figure II.

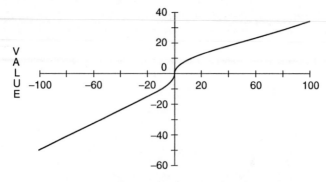

$ CHANGE RELATIVE TO STATUS QUO

Figure II. A Value Function Satisfying the Three Conditions Described in the Text.

The value function is pieced together from two independent segments, one for losses and one for gains, which connect at the reference point. Such functions have previously been applied to decision making under uncertainty [Kahneman and Tversky, 1979], consumer choice [Thaler, 1980], negotiations [Bazerman, 1984], and financial economics [Shefrin and Statman, 1984]. The shape and reference point assumption reflects basic psychophysical considerations: extra attention to negative aspects of the environment, decreasing sensitivity to increments in stimuli of increasing magnitude, and cognitive limitations.

It is assumed that the reference level represents the status quo (i.e., the current level of consumption), and that new consumption alternatives are evaluated without consideration of existing plans. In certain cases, however, the reference point may deviate from the status quo to reflect psychological considerations such as social comparison [Duesenberry, 1949], or the effect of past consumption which sets a standard for the present [Ferson and Constantinides, 1988; Pollak, 1970].

The function in Figure II is representative of a class of functions that is consistent with the behavioral evidence presented earlier in Section II. The first, and most elementary assumption built into the figure is *loss aversion* [Tversky and Kahneman, 1990].

V1. The value function for losses is steeper than the value function for gains:

$$v(x) < -v(-x).$$

This means that the loss in value associated with a given monetary loss exceeds the gain in value produced by a monetary gain of the same absolute size. In this respect, our value function resembles the prospect theory value function [Kahneman and Tversky, 1979], which also places greater weight on losses.

In the context of intertemporal choice, loss aversion specifically penalizes intertemporal exchanges that are framed in compensating variation terms, i.e. as incurring a loss now in exchange for a future gain, or enjoying a current gain in return for a future loss. For instance, a person who is indifferent between receiving $+q$ now, or $+x$ at some later date, would nevertheless not be willing *to pay q* now in order to receive $+x$ at the later date, because the value of $-q$ is greater in absolute magnitude than the value of $+q$.

The remaining two constraints on $v(x)$ are geometrically more subtle and have not been explicitly discussed in the context of prospect theory. Both constraints pertain to the *elasticity* of $v(x)$:

$$\epsilon_v(x) \equiv \frac{\partial \log(v)}{\partial \log(x)} = \frac{xv'(x)}{v(x)}. \tag{16}$$

Our second assumption about the value function is behaviorally determined by the gain-loss asymmetry.

V2. The value function for losses is more elastic than the value function for gains:

$$\epsilon_v(x) < \epsilon_v(-x), \qquad \text{for } x > 0.$$

Suppose that $+q$ is the equivalent present value of $+x$ at time t, so that, $v(q) = \phi(t)\, v(x)$. The gain-loss asymmetry then implies that one would prefer to pay $-q$ now instead of $-x$ at time t: $v(-q) > \phi(t)v\,(-x)$. Equating $\phi(t)$ in both of these expressions, shows that

$$\frac{v(q)}{v(x)} > \frac{v(-q)}{v(-x)}, \qquad \text{for all } 0 < q < x. \tag{17}$$

Consequently, $v(x)$ must "bend over" faster than $v(-x)$, in the precise sense captured by condition V2.[3]

Our third and final assumption about $v(x)$ is dictated by the magnitude effect, in equivalent variation choices. If $+q$ is the equivalent present value for x at time t, $v(q) = \phi(t)v(x)$, then the magnitude effect predicts that a proportional increase in both q and x, to aq and ax, will cause preference to tip in favor of the later positive outcome, $v(aq) < \phi(t)v\,(ax)$. As in the previous paragraph, by eliminating $\phi(t)$, we have

$$\frac{v(q)}{v(x)} < \frac{v(aq)}{v(ax)}, \qquad \text{for all } 0 < q < x; a > 1. \tag{18}$$

The value function is *subproportional,* like the probability weighting function in prospect theory. As Kahneman and Tversky remarked [1979, p. 282], such a function is convex in log-log coordinates, which for our model means that the derivative of $\log(v(x))$ with respect to $\log(x)$ is increasing, or that:

---

[3] Let $u_1(x) \equiv -\ln\{v(x)\}$ and $u_2(x) \equiv -ln\{-v(-x)\}$. Then (17) implies that $u_1(x) - u_1(q) < u_2(x) - u_2(s)$, for all $0 < q < x$, or: $u_1'(x) < u_2'(x)$, for all $x > 0$, which is equivalent to condition V2.

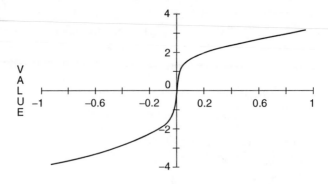

Figure III. The Same Value Function as in Figure II, but Plotted over a Smaller Range of Outcomes.

V3. The value function is more elastic for outcomes that are larger in absolute magnitude:

$$\epsilon_v(x) < \epsilon_v(y), \qquad \text{for } 0 < x < y \text{ or } y < x < 0.$$

The implications of this condition can be visually assessed by comparing Figures II and III. Both figures show the same value function, but plotted over a small (Figure III) or a large (Figure II) range of outcomes. For small outcomes the function is sharply convex, indicating that there is not much perceived value difference between, say, a \$1 gain and a \$2 gain. This property accounts for the high discount rates that apply to small outcomes (i.e. in a choice between \$1 now or \$2 in a year). For large outcomes, however, the function straightens out considerably (Figure II) and, as a result, generates much lower discount rates.

Most probably, the elasticity of the value function does not increase indefinitely, but rather attains a maximum at some large dollar amount, and then begins to decline. When comparing large and unexpected windfalls, it may be reasonable to prefer a million dollars today to several million a few years hence—if drawing on the money in advance was completely prevented. The implausibility of this last requirement makes the interpretation of stated preference over large amounts problematic.

15.4. Further Implications of the Model

15.4.1. *Aversion to Intertemporal Tradeoffs*

It follows from our model that a single individual will reveal not one but several discount factors for future cash outcomes, depending on how the

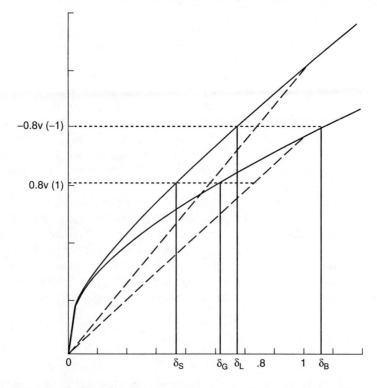

Figure IV. Relationship among Discount Factors for Compensating and Equivalent Variation.

choice is formulated. These discount factors can be geometrically derived, as in Figure IV. In the figure we have overlaid the positive and negative branches of the value function, so that both positive and negative outcomes can be represented along the positive x-axis. Starting with a delayed outcome of absolute magnitude x, and a time interval yielding a discount factor *for utility* of 0.8, we can generate four distinct "present values" for x, depending on whether x is positive or negative, and whether the elicitation method is equivalent or compensating variation. Each present value, divided by x, then yields a specific discount factor.

From equivalent variation, $v(q) = \phi(t)v(x)$, we get the discount factors for gains (G) and losses (L):

$$\delta_{G,L} = \frac{q}{x} = \frac{v^{-1}\{\phi(t)v(x)\}}{x} \qquad (\delta_G \text{ for } x > 0, \ \delta_L \text{ for } x < 0). \qquad (19)$$

While from compensating variation, $v(p) + \phi(t)v(x) = 0$, we have the *borrowing* (B) and *saving* (S) factors:

$$\delta_{S,B} = \frac{p}{x} = \frac{v^{-1}\{-\phi(t)v(x)\}}{x} \qquad (\delta_S \text{ for } x > 0, \delta_B \text{ for } x < 0). \qquad (20)$$

It is apparent from the geometry of the gain and loss value functions in Figure IV, that these discount factors are ordered as $\delta_S < \delta_G < \delta_L < \delta_B$.

A notable aspect of the ranking is the large gap between the savings and borrowing discount factors: a person whose choices are consistent with the value functions in Figure II would require a much more favorable rate in order to borrow than he would to save. The gap between δ_B and δ_S is a measure of how averse a person is to borrowing and savings commitments generally, because it implies a range of risk-free interest rates at which a person will be unwilling to either save or borrow.

The existence of this gap was confirmed by Horowitz [1988], who elicited present and future values for real money payoffs, through a "first-rejected price" auction. According to Horowitz, "The most striking feature of [the] experiment is individuals' apparent aversion to both borrowing and lending." A substantial fraction of subjects revealed discount factors greater than one for borrowing (i.e. they refused zero-interest loans); this, too, is consistent with the model, as we can see from the fact that $\delta_B > 1$ in Figure IV.

15.4.2. *Framing Effects*

As in prospect theory [Kahneman and Tversky, 1979], we assume that the reference level is sensitive to the wording of the questions that elicit the intertemporal tradeoffs. For instance, direct choices between two losses, or two gains, are presumed to be likewise encoded (or "framed") as a pair of positive or negative values. The same would be true of requests for present amounts that create subjective indifference with respect to some future amount of the same sign. In such a context we would interpret the elicited present value q for amount x at time t, according to the equivalent variation formula, $v(q) = \phi(t)v(x)$.

Questions involving delay or speedup of consumption are a clear case where the compensating variation formula is appropriate. A request, for example, for the maximum value that one would be willing to sacrifice in order to speed up some positive amount (x) from time t to the present, suggests that the baseline levels are zero now, and $+x$ at the future time. In this frame the speedup constitutes a loss of x at time t, and a gain of x minus the speedup cost at time zero. The latter value, p, would then be interpreted according to the compensating variation formula, $v(p) + \phi(t)v(x) = 0$, with $x < 0$ and $p > 0$. The same frame covers delay-of-loss judgments, because in that case there is again a positive present benefit (avoiding the immediate loss), and a future cost (absorbing the loss at the later date). The two complementary question formats—delaying a gain, and speeding up a loss—would yield present values

	Speed-up	Delay
Gains	High	High
Losses	Low	Low

Normative Model

	Speed-up	Delay
Gains	High	Low
Losses	Low	High

Reference Point Model

Figure V. Discount Rates When Expediting and Speeding up Gains and Losses: Comparison of DU and Reference Point Model Predictions.

also consistent with equation (20) but for a reversal in the sign of p and x, since there is a negative adjustment to current consumption ($p < 0$), and a positive adjustment to future consumption ($x > 0$).

Figure V compares these predictions with those of the normative model, in which the distinction between a speedup or delay is not recognized. As indicated in the top half of the figure, the discount rates estimated from expediting and delaying gains should be equal, and higher than the devaluation rates estimated from expediting and delaying losses. In contrast, the reference point model predicts that common rates will be observed for the diagonal pairs in the matrix, with the delaying gains/speeding up losses pair producing a higher estimate.

Clear support for the reference point model can be found in the data reported by Benzion et al. [1989]. Figure VI displays implicit discount rates calculated from their data for each of the four elicitation methods. As predicted, discount rates are high and virtually identical for expediting a loss (white diamonds) and delaying a gain (black squares), and lower and again virtually identical for expediting a gain (black triangles) and delaying a loss (white squares).

Our second framing example is produced by the discrepancy between discounting of gains and losses. In this study 85 students in an MBA class on decision making were randomly divided into two groups which each answered one of the following two questions.

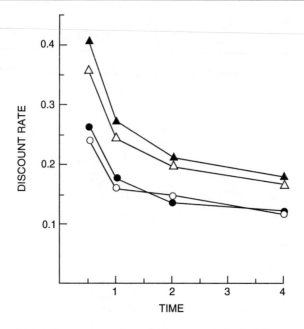

Figure VI. Implicit Discount Rates from Benzion et al. [1989] The rates have been averaged across the four dollar amounts used in their study.

Version 1.

Suppose that you bought a TV on a special installment plan. The plan calls for two payments; one this week and one in six months. You have two options for paying: (circle the one that you would choose)

A. An initial payment of $160 and a later payment of $110.
B. An initial payment of $115 and a later payment of $160.

Version 2.

Suppose that you bought a TV on a special installment plan. The plan calls for two payments of $200; one this week and one in six months. Happily, however, the company has announced a sale which applies retroactively to your purchase. You have two options: (circle the one that you would choose)

C. A rebate of $40 on the initial payment and a rebate of $90 on the later payment.
D. A rebate of $85 on the initial payment and a rebate of $40 on the later payment.

Since options A and C and options B and D are the same in terms of payoffs and delivery times, DU predicts that there will be no systematic difference in responses to the two versions. Nevertheless, a higher fraction of subjects opted for the lower-discount option (the one involving greater earlier payments) when the question was framed as a loss rather than as a gain. Fifty-four percent of subjects exposed to version 1 stated a preference for A over B. However, a significantly different fraction (33 percent) preferred C over D ($X^2(1) = 3.9$, $p < 0.05$). The proposed model explains the observed pattern of responses as follows: in the first frame the large, negative outcomes suffer less discounting, which causes people to decide on the basis of total payments. In the second frame, however, the outcomes are smaller in absolute magnitude and positive. Both of these factors contribute to relatively high discounting of the delayed outcomes, leading to a preference for the second option which offers a greater initial rebate.

The choice of appropriate frame is not always unambiguous. A savings decision, for example, can be viewed as a simple choice between benefits enjoyed now or later (equation (19)) or a postponement of present consumption for the future (equation (20)). Such changes in frame will, according to our theory, affect the range of interest rates that a person considers acceptable.

15.4.3. *Effect of Prior Expectations on Choice*

Consider two people waiting for an object (e.g. a computer): one has been told to expect delivery in two weeks; the other anticipates delivery in four weeks. Two weeks pass, and both are faced with a new choice: the original computer to be delivered immediately, or a superior computer to be delivered in two weeks. Who is more likely to wait? If both parties adapt their reference points to anticipated delivery times, then the reference point model predicts that the person who anticipated delivery in two weeks will be more impatient. This person frames the choice as the status quo versus a loss of a computer immediately and a gain of a slightly superior computer in two weeks. Loss aversion and discounting both mitigate against choice of the delayed, superior, model. On the other hand, the person who anticipated later delivery would frame the choice as a loss of the later computer and gain of an earlier computer. Here loss aversion discourages the choice of the earlier computer, while discounting has an opposing influence. Thus, we predict that the person anticipating two-week delivery would be more likely to accept. In effect, people who are psychologically prepared for delay are more willing to wait.

This prediction was tested in a laboratory experiment conducted with 105 suburban Chicago tenth graders [Loewenstein, 1988b]. All prizes were in the form of nontransferable gift certificates. As a result of an earlier experiment, half the students expected to obtain a $7 gift certificate at an earlier date, half at a later date. When the earlier date arrived, all subjects were given a new choice between getting the $7 certificate immediately or a larger valued certificate at a later date. As predicted, prior expectations had a significant impact on choice. Twenty-seven out of 47 subjects who anticipated getting the prize at the earlier date opted for the immediate $7; only 17 of the 57 who expected late delivery chose not to wait for the larger prize, a statistically significant difference.

15.4.4. *High Discount Rates Estimated from Purchases of Consumer Durables*

Several studies have estimated discount rates from purchases of consumer durables (e.g. air conditioners) [Hausman, 1979; Gately, 1980]. Such purchases typically involve an up-front charge (the purchase price) and a series of delayed charges (e.g. electricity charges). Because more expensive models are generally more energy efficient, it is possible to calculate the discount rate (or range of discount rates) implicit in a particular purchase. A second source of behavioral estimates of discount rates has been the studies of major economic decisions such as saving [Landsberger, 1971] and intertemporal labor-leisure substitution [Hotz, Kydland, and Sedlacek, 1988; Moore and Viscusi, 1988].

The estimates from these two classes of studies have differed sharply. Studies of consumer durable purchases show very high average discount rates (across different income groups), e.g. from 25 percent [Hausman, 1979] to 45–300 percent [Gately, 1980]. Research on savings behavior or labor supply has almost uniformly found much lower discount rates (typically well below 25 percent). How can these estimates be reconciled? The proposed model predicts that the small delayed electricity charges associated with the consumer durables will be substantially devalued due to the dependence of discounting on outcome magnitude. Thus, consumer durable purchases will be insensitive to electricity charges, and discount rates estimated from those purchases will appear to be high. Discount rates estimated from major economic decisions would not be subject to such small-magnitude effects.

15.4.5. *Nonmonotonic Optimal Benefit Plans*

Our model makes certain predictions about the shape of the optimal intertemporal allocation of benefits under a constant market present value constraint. Assuming that consumption at a point in time, $x(t)$, is framed as a positive quantity, the value of the plan, covering the period from 0 to T, is given by the continuous version of the discounted value formula,

$$\int_0^T \phi(t)v(x(t))\,dt. \tag{21}$$

The optimal plan $x^0(t)$, given a market interest rate r and a present value constraint,

$$\int_0^T e^{-rt}x(t)\,dt \leq I,\tag{22}$$

can be calculated by standard techniques [Yaari, 1964]. Yaari showed that if the optimal plan exists, and if the value function is concave and continuously differentiable, then the rate of change in consumption, for the optimal plan, equals [equation (21)]:

$$\frac{\partial x^0}{\partial t} = r - \left(-\frac{\phi'(t)}{\phi(t)}\right)\left(-\frac{v'(x^0(t))}{v''(x^0)}\right).\tag{23}$$

As Yaari observed, the direction of local change in consumption rate is controlled by the sign of the difference between the market interest rate and the rate of time preference $(-\phi'/\phi)$. In view of our hyperbolic discounting assumption, this allows for only three qualitatively distinct possibilities: (1) the rate of time preference is always greater than the market rate, in which case consumption is decreasing throughout the interval; (2) the rate of time preference is always lower than the market rate, in which case consumption increases over the interval; (3) the rate of time preference starts off above the market rate, but eventually drops below it and remains so, in which case consumption will decline to a minimum value (when the two rates equalize) and then increase afterwards.

Relative to normative theory, our model suggests that people may tend to prefer plans that sacrifice the medium-range future for the sake of the short and the long term. There is nothing clearly wrong with this, provided that one can commit to an entire plan at the moment of decision. However, if the optimal plan can be recalculated at later points in time, then the planned sacrifice in midrange consumption will not take effect [Strotz, 1956]. As a result, a bias in favor of the long and short runs may in practice yield behavior that is oriented only to the short run.

This discussion presupposes a concave value function, which—although not explicitly assumed in V1–V3—is certainly true for the function in Figure IV. In the loss domain, however, our working assumption is that the value function is convex, at least initially, which means that the most attractive plan for intertemporal loss allocation consists of concentrating the loss at a single point in time. The (negative) value of the loss, if allowed to accumulate at the market rate to time t, equals $\phi(t)v\,(Ie^{rt})$, which means that it will pay to delay payment whenever $\phi'(t)v\,(Ie^{rt}) + rIe^{rt}\phi\,(t)\,v'\,(Ie^{rt}) > 0$ or, after rearranging, whenever

$$r < \frac{-\phi'(t)/\phi(t)}{\epsilon_v(Ie^{rt})}.\tag{24}$$

The product on the right is decreasing in t, since $-\phi'/\phi$ equals $\beta/(1 + at)$ by Assumption D1, and $\varepsilon_v(Ie^{rt})$ is increasing by Assumption V3. Hence there is a unique point in time—possibly at one or the other endpoint of the interval—at which the loss is absorbed with smallest perceived cost.

15.4.6. *Other Predictions*

Our model has several implications for the behavior of key economic variables during business cycles. First, it predicts that psychological factors will amplify the tendency for businesses to cut back on investment during periods of lower than anticipated profits. In high profit periods the investment project is viewed in terms of equivalent variation, as a choice between two gains: take the excess profit now, or take greater profits from investment later. But in periods of low or negative returns, an identical investment opportunity would be viewed in terms of compensating variation, i.e., as incurring a current loss in exchange for a future gain, which, as shown in the previous section, will induce a higher subjective discount rate. There may, of course, be good economic reasons for reducing investments during economic down-turns; what the model suggests is that psychological factors additionally and independently contribute to the reduction.

For consumers too, an economic downturn should cause an increase in impatience and a consequent decrease in saving. Consumers are likely to frame drops in disposable income, or negative departures from expected gains, as losses, so that saving from income will be viewed in terms of compensating variation: a further loss in the present for a gain in the future.[4] Saving out of an expanding income or out of bonus income is more likely to be viewed in terms of compensating variation, inducing lower discounting and greater saving. Consistent with this prediction, there is evidence that the marginal propensity to save income from bonuses is higher than that from normal income [Ishikawa and Ueda, 1984].

Our model is also possibly relevant to the so-called "disposition effect" in real estate [Case and Shiller, 1989] and financial markets [Shefrin and Statman, 1985; Ferris, Haugen and Makhija, 1988]. This effect refers to the fact that people tend to hold on to losing stocks and to real estate that has dropped in value, which depresses trading volume during market downturns. In such situations people have a choice between taking an immediate loss (by selling) or holding on to the asset with the potential of further loss or potential

---

[4] The low rates of savings and negative real rates of interest in the 1970s [Mishkin, 1981] may reflect the shortfall from expectations induced by economic stagnation following the prolonged economic boom of the 1960s. At a societal level the tax cuts of the early 1980s, which entailed a transfer of income from the future to the present, can be interpreted similarly.

gain. Since the value function is convex in the loss domain, further losses are less than proportionately painful, while gains yield marginally increasing returns. The incentives are thus stacked in favor of holding on to the asset. The incentives are reversed on the gain side, motivating people to quickly sell assets that have gained in value.

In general, the market level implications of the model depend critically on the presence or absence of arbitrage opportunities that exist in a particular economic domain. Arbitrage opportunities are extensive in some markets, such as those for fixed rate financial assets where leveraged short sales are possible. In other markets, e.g., labor markets, arbitrage opportunities are virtually nonexistent. We would expect to see the effects of subjective time discounting manifested more clearly in the latter markets, in the specific case through labor contracts that offer large initial wage increases.

In financial markets the effects of scale and sign, produced by the curvature of the value function, will presumably be arbitraged away. If a particular market were to offer high interest rates on small investments, reflecting the magnitude effect, investors would simply borrow large sums and then invest them in small packages, driving down the rate on small investments.

Hyperbolic discounting is less easily arbitraged, even in financial markets. If most people demanded lower rates of return for long investment periods than for short ones, the yield curve would be downward sloping with no opportunities for arbitrage. Those who discounted the future at a constant rate would tend to invest in short-term securities, and might even short the long-term securities, but they could not do so without risk. Without denying that many purely economic factors influence the yield curve, our model suggests that psychological biases will independently exert pressure toward downward sloping.[5]

15.5. Concluding Remarks

The discounted utility model has played a dominant role in economic analyses of intertemporal choice. Although economists have experimented with alternative formulations, these efforts have typically responded to a single limitation of DU (e.g. increasing consumption postretirement) rather than to a more comprehensive critique. DU's basic assumptions and implications have, for the most part, not been questioned. This paper presents an integrated critique of DU, enumerating a series of intertemporal choice anomalies that run counter to the predictions of DU.

[5] Our analysis may help to explain Fama's [1984] finding that, contrary to the liquidity preference hypothesis, the yield curve tends to drop, on average, past a certain point.

Perhaps most importantly, sensitivity to time delay is not well expressed by compound discounting. A given absolute delay looms larger if it occurs earlier rather than later; people are relatively insensitive to changes in timing for consumption objects that are already substantially delayed. Second, the marginal utility of consumption at different points in time depends not on absolute levels of consumption, but on consumption relative to some standard or point of reference. Generally, the status quo serves as reference point; people conserve on cognitive effort by evaluating new consumption alternatives in isolation, rather than by integrating them with existing plans.

Our model by no means incorporates all important psychological factors that influence intertemporal choice. For example, like any model with non-constant discounting, it yields time-inconsistent behavior or "myopia" as Strotz [1955] called it. However, it cannot explain the high levels of conflict that such myopic behavior often evokes. Intertemporal choice often seems to involve an internal struggle for self-command [Schelling, 1984]. At the very moment of succumbing to the impulse to consume, individuals often recognize at a cognitive level that they are making a decision that is contrary to their long-term self-interest. Mathematical models of choice do not shed much light on such patterns of cognition and behavior (but see Ainslie [1985]).

Such episodes of internal conflict are not entirely random. Certain types of situations, such as when a person comes into direct sensory contact with a choice object, seem to elicit especially high rates of time discounting, while others do not. People exhibit high rates of discounting when driven by appetites such as hunger, thirst, or sexual desire. While not incompatible with the present model, these phenomena are not predicted by it.

Finally, our model does not incorporate preference interactions between periods, despite the fact that our own recent empirical research has shown such interactions to be pervasive when people choose between sequences of outcomes. Preference interactions are revealed through a strong dislike of deteriorating outcome sequences, and through a liking for evenly spreading consumption over time [Loewenstein and Prelec, 1991]. A taste for steady improvement seems to capture the preferences of most subjects, when sequences are being considered. Generally, the present model is more applicable to short-range decisions involving simple outcomes rather than long-term planning of consumption. No simple theory, however, can hope to reflect all motives that influence a particular decision. We have attempted to demonstrate that a theory with only two scaling functions can explain much of the observed deviation in preference from the normative discounted utility model.

References

Aczel, J., *Lectures on Functional Equations and Their Applications* (New York: Academic Press, 1966).

Ainslie, G., "Specious Reward: A Behavioral Theory of Impulsiveness and Impulse Control," *Psychological Bulletin*, LXXXII (1975), 463–509.

——, "Beyond Microeconomics. Conflict among Interests in a Multiple Self as a Determinant of Value," in J. Elster, ed., *The Multiple Self* (Cambridge: Cambridge University Press, 1985).

Bazerman, M., "The Relevance of Kahneman and Tversky's Concept of Framing to Organizational Behavior," *Journal of Management*, X (1984), 333–343.

Benzion, U., A. Rapoport, and J. Yagil, "Discount Rates Inferred from Decisions: An Experimental Study," *Management Science*, XXXV (March, 1989), 270–284.

Case, K. E., and R. J. Shiller, "The Efficiency of the Market for Single Family Homes," *American Economic Review*, LXXIX (March, 1989), 125–137.

Chung, S. H., and R. J. Herrnstein, "Choice and Delay of Reinforcement," *Journal of the Experimental Analysis of Behavior*, X (1967), 67–74.

Debreu, G., "Topological Methods in Cardinal Utility Theory," in K. J. Arrow, S. Karlin, and P. Suppes, eds., *Mathematical Methods in the Social Sciences* (Stanford, CA: Stanford University Press, 1959), pp. 16–26.

Duesenberry, J., *Income, Saving, and the Theory of Consumer Behavior* (Cambridge, MA: Harvard University Press, 1949).

Fama, E. F., "Term Premiums in Bond Returns," *Journal of Financial Economics*, XIII (1984), 529–546.

Ferris, S. P., R. A. Haugen, and A. K. Makhija, "Predicting Contemporary Volume with Historic Volume at Differential Price Levels: Evidence Supporting the Disposition Effect," *Journal of Finance*, XLIII (July 1988), 677–697.

Ferson, W. E., and G. M. Constantinides, "Habit Formation and Durability in Aggregate Consumption: Empirical Tests," paper presented at the American Finance Association meeting, December 1988.

Fishburn, P. C., and A. Rubinstein, "Time Preference," *International Economic Review*, XXIII (1982), 677–694.

Gately, D., "Individual Discount Rates and the Purchase and Utilization of Energy-Using Durables: Comment," *Bell Journal of Economics*, XI (1980), 373–374.

Harvey, C. M., "Value Functions for Infinite-Period Planning," *Management Science*, XXXII (1986), 1123–1139.

Hausman, J., "Individual Discount Rates and the Purchase and Utilization of Energy-Using Durables, *Bell Journal of Economics*, X (1979), 33–54.

Herrnstein, R. J., "Self-Control as Response Strength," in *Quantification of Steady-State Operant Behavior*, C. M. Bradshaw, E. Szabadi, and C. F. Lowe, eds. (Amsterdam: Elsevier/North-Holland, 1981).

Holcomb, J. H., and P. S. Nelson, "An Experimental Investigation of Individual Time Preference," unpublished working paper, 1989.

Horowitz, J. K., "Discounting Money Payoffs: An Experimental Analysis." working paper, Department of Agricultural and Resource Economics, University of Maryland, 1988.

Hotz, V. J., F. E. Kydland, and G. L. Sedlacek, "Intertemporal Preferences and Labor Supply," *Econometrica,* LVI (1988), 335–360.

Ishikawa, T., and K. Ueda, "The Bonus Payment System and Japanese Personal Savings," in *The Economic Analysis of the Japanese Firm,* M. Aoki, ed. (Amsterdam: North-Holland, 1984).

Kahneman, D., and A. Tversky, "Prospect Theory: An Analysis of Decision Under Risk," *Econometrica,* XLVII (1979), 363–391.

Koopmans, T. C., "Stationary Ordinal Utility and Impatience," *Econometrica,* XXVIII (1960), 287–309.

Landsberger, M., "Consumer Discount Rate and the Horizon: New Evidence," *Journal of Political Economy,* LXXIX (1971), 1346–1359.

Loewenstein, G., "Anticipation and the Valuation of Delayed Consumption," *Economic Journal,* XLVII (1987), 666–684.

——, "Frames of Mind in Intertemporal Choice," *Management Science,* XXXIV (1988a), 200–214.

——, "Reference Points in Intertemporal Choice," working paper, Center for Decision Research, University of Chicago, 1988b.

——, "The Weighting of Waiting: Response Mode Effects in Intertemporal Choice," working paper, Center for Decision Research, University of Chicago, 1988c.

——, and D. Prelec, "Preferences over Outcome Sequences," *American Economic Review, Papers and Proceedings,* LXXXI (May 1991), 247–351.

——, and N. Sicherman, "Do Workers Prefer Increasing Wage Profiles?" *Journal of Labor Economics,* IX (January, 1991), 67–84.

Markowitz, H., "The Utility of Wealth," *Journal of Political Economy,* LX (1952), 151–158.

Mazur, J. E., "An Adjustment Procedure for Studying Delayed Reinforcement," Chapter 2 in M. L. Commons, J. E. Mazur, J. A. Nevins, and H. Rachlin, eds., *Quantitative Analysis of Behavior: The Effect of Delay and of Intervening Events on Reinforcement Value* (Hillsdale, NJ: Ballinger, 1987).

Mishkin, F. S., "The Real Interest Rate: An Empirical Investigation," *Carnegie-Rochester Conference Series on Public Policy,* XV (1981), 151–200.

Moore, M. J., and W. K. Viscusi, "Discounting Environmental Health Risks: New Evidence and Policy Implications," paper presented at a session of the American Economic Association, December 1988.

Pollak, R. A., "Habit Formation and Dynamic Demand Functions," *Journal of Political Economy,* LXXVIII (1970), 745–763.

Prelec, D., "Decreasing Impatience: Definition and Consequences," Harvard Business School working paper, 1989.

——, and G. Loewenstein, "Decision Making over Time and under Uncertainty Approach," *Management Science,* XXXIV (1991), 770–786.

Schelling, T., "Self-Command in Practice, in Policy, and in a Theory of Rational Choice," *American Economic Review,* LXXIV (1984), 1–11.

Shefrin, H. M., and M. Statman, "Explaining Investor Preference for Cash Dividends," *Journal of Financial Economics,* XIII (1984), 253–282.

——, and ——, "The Disposition to Sell Winners too Early and Ride Losers too Long: Theory and Evidence," *Journal of Finance,* XL (July, 1985), 777–792.

Strotz, R. H., "Myopia and Inconsistency in Dynamic Utility Maximization," *Review of Economic Studies,* XXIII (1955), 165–180.

Thaler, R., "Toward a Positive Theory of Consumer Choice," *Journal of Economic Behavior and Organization,* I (1980), 39–60.

——, "Some Empirical Evidence on Dynamic Inconsistency," *Economics Letters,* VIII (1981), 201–207.

Tversky, A., and D. Kahneman, "Reference Theory of Choice and Exchange," unpublished working paper, 1990.

Weber, M., and C. F. Camerer, "Recent Developments in Modelling Preferences Under Risk," *OR Spectrum,* IX (1988), 129–151.

Yaari, M. E., "On the Consumer's Lifetime Allocation Process," *International Economic Review,* V (September 1964), 304–317.

16

Preferences for Sequences of Outcomes

George F. Loewenstein and Dražen Prelec

Dražen and I started this paper during our year at the Russell Sage Foundation. Looking back, I realize that when we started working on the project we didn't really know what it was about. I have notebooks full of the diverse, exploratory, questionnaires we administered that year wherever we could find subjects: parks, airports, on the train between Manhattan (where Dražen and I were living) and Stonybrook (where my wife had an academic position), and in one case on a flight to Chicago (where I still had an academic appointment at the time). I passed out questionnaires to everyone in the plane, but when I went to collect them the flight attendant noticed, notified me that I had broken the law, and informed me that that the captain would meet me at the front of the plane when we landed. She then collected the surveys and brought them into the pilot's cabin, and I spent the rest of the flight in trepidation. Before the flight landed, however, something strange happened: The flight attendant, all smiles, walked over to my seat and handed me the pack of (mainly completed) questionnaires, informing me that "the captain still wants to speak to you." When I met him at the front of the plane, the captain, too, was smiling. "You teach at the U of C? I'm getting my MBA there!" (The questionnaire began with the boilerplate "I am a Professor at the University of Chicago doing research on decision-making . . . ".)

When Dražen and I started the project, the main preoccupation of intertemporal choice researchers was with the shape of the time discounting function. As discussed in Chapter 15, there is no doubt that a hyperbolic time discount function explains time discounting behavior better than the exponential function incorporated in most economic analyses. However, there are a variety of possible functions with hyperbolic properties, and many researchers were on the search for the right one, often claiming that some slightly different functional form from that which had been proposed earlier was the right one—as if we would be in a position to make sense of people's intertemporal choice behavior if we could only get the discount function exactly right.

By some lucky quirk, Dražen and I started giving people choices between sequences of outcomes in our questionnaires, and the results we got were surprising. Not only were people not discounting the future hyperbolically when it came to these sequences, they weren't discounting the future at all. Most subjects in fact expressed a strong preference for sequences that improved over those that declined, as if they cared more about the future than they did about the present. All of a sudden, at least to us, the question of which hyperbolic function fit best no longer seemed so interesting.

There's a beautiful (I think) model in this paper, and two systematic tests of the model, but the main thing the paper is known for is the first 'experiment', which is really little more than an illustrative example. We first asked subjects whether they would prefer a fancy French restaurant dinner or a more plebian Greek one (Richard Thaler, a great epicure, once referred to this as a "rationality check"). Then, limiting our interest to those who preferred the fancy French dinner, we asked half of the subjects whether they would prefer to consume the French dinner that week or a week later and the other half whether they would prefer to eat the Greek dinner that week and the French dinner the following week, or the two dinners in the opposite order. Most people presented with the French dinner alone preferred to enjoy it sooner rather than later, but most people presented with the choice between sequences preferred the Greek dinner first, following by the French dinner. Somehow, being presented with a choice between sequences elicited radically different (and seemingly negative) time preferences from subjects than did a choice involving a single outcome. This was one of the first papers to document the pervasive preference for improving sequences, contrary to the usual assumption that people discount (care less about) future gratifications.

However, perhaps the real contribution of the paper was to show that one can't derive the value of a sequence of experiences by adding up the value of its component parts. As we show in the paper, people don't only care about what they get when; they care about the overall pattern of gratifications. This insight, I'd like to believe, gave rise to a large and diverse body of research on the temporal characteristics of sequences that people like and dislike, both when they evaluate them prospectively and retrospectively (in memory).

Preferences for Sequences of Outcomes[*]

George F. Loewenstein and Dražen Prelec

Decisions of importance have delayed consequences. The choice of education, work, spending and saving, exercise, diet, as well as the timing of life events, such as schooling, marriage, and childbearing, all produce costs and benefits that endure over time. Therefore, it is not surprising that the problem of choosing between temporally distributed outcomes has attracted attention in a variety of disciplinary settings, including behavioral psychology, social psychology, decision theory, and economics.

In spite of this disciplinary diversity, empirical research on intertemporal choice has traditionally had a narrow focus. Until a few years ago, virtually all studies of intertemporal choice were concerned with how people evaluate simple prospects consisting of a single outcome obtained at a point in time. The goal was to estimate equations that express the basic relationship between the atemporal value of an outcome and its value when delayed. Although the estimated functional forms would differ from investigation to investigation, there was general agreement on one point: that delayed outcomes are valued less. In economics, this is referred to as "positive time discounting."

Although plausible at first glance, the uniform imposition of positive discounting on all of one's choices has some disturbing and counterintuitive implications. It implies, for instance, that when faced with a decision about how to schedule a set of outcomes, a person should invariably start with the best outcome, followed by the second best outcome, and so on until the worst outcome is reached at the end. Because nothing restricts the generality of this principle, one should find people preferring a declining rather than an increasing standard of living, deteriorating rather than improving health (again, holding lifetime health constant), and so on.

[*] This chapter was originally published as George Loewenstein and Dražen Prelec (1993) 'Preferences for Sequence Outcomes', Psychological Review, 100(1): 91–108. Published by APA and reprinted with permission.

In the last few years, several studies have independently focused on this problem and have shown that with choices of this type, people typically exhibit *negative* time preference (i.e. they prefer an improving series of events, with all other things being equal). In this article we present results that confirm the preference for improvement but qualify it in several respects. First, we found that preference for improvement depends on whether a particular choice is viewed by the decision maker as being embedded in a sequence of outcomes. In other words, when the decision frame draws attention to the sequential nature of choice, negative time discounting typically prevails; however, when the frame draws attention to individual components of the choice, positive time preference predominates.

Second, we examined the validity of a common assumption in theoretical treatments of intertemporal choice: that preferences for outcome sequences are based on a simple aggregation of preferences for their individual components. Separable formulations, such as the discounted utility model, predict that the overall value (i.e. utility) of a sequence is equal to the summed values of its component outcomes. The findings we present challenge this prediction. In general, an individual's valuation of complex sequences cannot be extrapolated in a simple way from his or her valuation of components but responds instead to certain "gestalt" properties of the sequence.

Third, we developed and tested empirically a theoretical model of choice over outcome sequences. The model incorporates two motives that are not part of standard discounted utility formulations: a preference for improvement and a desire to spread consumption evenly over time.

In the next section, we present a series of examples of preference patterns that illustrate preference for improvement and preference for spreading good outcomes evenly over time. We then develop a theoretical model of sequential choice that incorporates these two motives. Finally, we present two studies that were designed to test the model parametrically.

16.1. Basic Motives Underlying Choices Between Sequences

A temporal sequence is a series of outcomes spaced over time. The outcomes could be specific events, such as one's activities over consecutive weekends, or they could be more abstract economic indexes (e.g. income levels over consecutive years). With a few notable exceptions (Bell, 1977; Epstein & Hynes, 1983; Gilboa, 1989; Horowitz, 1988; Meyer, 1976, 1977), most theoretical treatments of intertemporal choice have been conducted within the framework of the general discounting model, which represents the value of a sequence $X = (x_1, \ldots, x_n)$ by the weighted utility formula (Koopmans, 1960;

Koopmans, Diamond, & Williamson, 1964; Samuelson, 1937):

$$V(X) = \sum_t w_t u(x_t). \tag{1}$$

The formula implies that whenever two sequences differ in only two periods, then preference between them does not depend on the common outcomes in the remaining $n = 2$ periods (separability). Economic applications normally make two additional assumptions:

1. *Impatience*. The coefficients, w_1, w_2, and so forth, are declining, which indicates that earlier periods have greater weight in determining preferences.

2. *Constant discounting*. The marginal rate of utility substitution between any two adjacent periods is the same, $w_{t+1}/w_t = \delta$. This produces the compound discounting formula,

$$V(X) = \sum_t \delta^t u(x_t).$$

In the remainder of this section, we describe simple choice patterns that are inconsistent with these properties.

16.1.1. *Preference for Improvement and the Sequence "Frame"*

A number of recent studies have shown that people typically favor sequences that improve over time. Loewenstein and Sicherman (1991) found that a majority of subjects preferred an increasing wage profile to a declining or flat one for an otherwise identical job. Varey and Kahneman (in press) studied preferences over short-term streams of discomfort, lasting from 2 to 20 min. and found that subjects strongly preferred streams of decreasing discomfort even when the overall sum of discomfort over the interval was otherwise identical. A preference for experiences that end well has also been documented by Ross and Simonson (1991). In one study, they presented subjects with a series of hypothetical choices between sequences that ended with a loss (e.g. win $85, then lose $15) or a gain (lose $15, then win $85). Subjects overwhelmingly preferred sequences that ended with a gain.

The preference for improvement appears to depend not only on the amount of improvement but the speed with which it occurs over time—its "velocity"—as Hsee and Abelson (1991) called it (see also Hsee, Abelson, & Salovey, 1991). Subjects in one of their studies played a game in which their probability of winning either decreased or increased over time at one of three rates of change. Those in conditions with increasing probabilities of winning rated the game as more satisfying than those in conditions with decreasing probabilities, and the effect of direction (increase vs. decrease) was amplified by the velocity of the change.

Preference for improvement appears to be an overdetermined phenom-enon, driven in part by savoring and dread (Loewenstein, 1987), adaptation and loss aversion (Kahneman & Tversky, 1979), and recency effects (Miller & Campbell, 1959). Savoring and dread contribute to preference for improve-ment because, for gains, improving sequences allow decision makers to savor the best outcome until the end of the sequence. With losses, getting unde-sirable outcomes over with quickly eliminates dread. Although there is evi-dence that people sometimes like to defer desirable outcomes (Loewenstein, 1987), getting undesirable outcomes over with quickly appears to be more widespread. A number of studies have shown that people prefer immediate rather than delayed electric shocks (Barnes & Barnes, 1964; Carlsmith, 1962). A similar result has been reported by Carson, Horowitz, and Machina (1987) in the context of cigarette smoking. They found that nonsmokers, when asked how much they would need to be paid immediately to smoke a pack of cigarettes either immediately or in 1, 5, or 10 years, specified amounts that increased as a function of time delay.

Adaptation and loss aversion lead to a preference for improving sequences because people tend to adapt to ongoing stimuli over time and to evaluate new stimuli relative to their adaptation level (Helson, 1964). Loss aversion (Kahneman & Tversky, 1979) refers to the observation that people are more sensitive to a loss than to a gain of equal absolute magnitude. It is illustrated by the fact that few people will voluntarily accept a bet that provides an equal chance of winning or losing any given amount. If people adapt to the most recent level of stimuli they experience, then improving sequences will afford a continual series of positive departures (gains) from their adaptation level, whereas declining sequences provide a series of relative losses. Loss aversion implies that the latter will be especially unattractive relative to the former.

The specific psychological mechanisms underlying the adaptation and loss-aversion explanation are somewhat ambiguous. It may be that when faced with a sequence (e.g. a series of increasing or decreasing salary levels), peo-ple imagine themselves experiencing the sequence, adapting to the stan-dard of living that each salary level implies, and reacting to negative or positive deviations from such standards. They would then recognize that upward adjustments from one's standard of living are more pleasurable than downward adjustments, leading them to prefer the increasing sequences. Alternatively, adaptation and loss aversion may not involve any explicit anticipation of future experience but may instead be a simple application of perceptual loss aversion. Just as people treat risky outcomes as gains and losses instead of absolute wealth levels, it is possible that they eval-uate sequences as series of upward and downward shifts rather than as a series of levels. Loss aversion would then imply that downward shifts receive disproportionate weight. The important difference between these two accounts is that in the former case, the evaluation reflects a type of hedonic forecasting, whereas in the latter case, the preference is instead perceptually driven (i.e. based on the tendency to interpret sequences as gains and losses regardless of how they are actually experienced when they unfold).

The adaptation and loss aversion explanation is closely related to the concept of a "contrast effect" (Elster, 1985; Elster & Loewenstein, in press; Tversky & Griffin, 1991). Contrast effects refer to the effect on one's evaluation of the present of comparing the present with the past or future. If backward-looking contrast effects are more potent than forward-looking ones, as seems plausible (Prelec & Loewenstein, 1991), then the net impact of contrast effects will be to augment the preference for improvement over time. This is because inferior early experiences will create a favorable contrast that will enhance the utility of later experiences.

A final psychological mechanism that may contribute to the preference for improvement is the recency effect, which has been observed in recall, attitude formation, and belief updating (Miller & Campbell, 1959). As Ross and Simonson (1991) noted, the final outcome in a sequence is likely to be the most salient to the decision maker after the conclusion of the sequence. If decision makers naturally adopt a retrospective perspective when evaluating outcome streams, as Varey and Kahneman (in press) argued, then recency effects will cause late periods to be overweighted relative to those that occur in the middle of the sequence. Likewise, "primacy effects" would promote an overweighting of early periods.

Savoring and dread apply to single-outcome prospects as well as to out-come sequences. For this reason, they can explain why people who otherwise discount the future sometimes defer pleasurable outcomes and get unpleas-ant outcomes over with quickly. Neither adaptation and loss aversion, nor recency effects, on the other hand, have obvious implications for single-outcome events. Therefore, these latter effects probably do not play a major role in timing preferences for such simple prospects. Adaptation and loss aversion are, however, present as potential factors in outcome sequences. The fact that only one motive for improvement operates for simple outcomes and two operate for sequences suggests that preference for improvement will be stronger in the latter case. Our first example illustrates the pref-erence for improvement and shows that it depends, in part, on whether a particular choice is perceived as being between individual outcomes or sequences.

Ninety-five Harvard University undergraduates were asked the following three questions and were instructed to ignore their own personal scheduling considerations (e.g. preexisting plans) in responding.

Example 1

1. *Which would you prefer if both were free?* $n = 95$

   A. Dinner at a fancy French restaurant   86%

   B. Dinner at a local Greek restaurant   14%

For those who prefer French:

2. *Which would you prefer?* $n = 82$

   C. Dinner at the French restaurant on Friday in 1 month   80%

   D. Dinner at the French restaurant on Friday in 2 months   20%

3. *Which would you prefer?* $n = 82$

   E. Dinner at the French restaurant on Friday in 1 month and
   dinner at the Greek restaurant on Friday in 2 months   43%

   F. Dinner at the Greek restaurant on Friday in 1 month and
   dinner at the French restaurant on Friday in 2 months   57%

Because two of the three motives hypothesized to motivate the preference for improvement operate only for sequences of outcomes, we anticipated that a larger fraction of respondents would prefer to put the fancy French dinner off into the future when it was combined in a sequence with the Greek dinner than when it was expressed as a single-outcome prospect. This was indeed the pattern that we observed. Of the 86% of subjects who preferred the fancy French dinner, 80% preferred a more immediate dinner (Option C) over a more delayed dinner (Option D). Thus, only 20% preferred to delay the French dinner when it was expressed as a single, isolated item. However, when the French dinner was put into a sequence with the Greek dinner, giving subjects the option of having Greek and then French, or French and then Greek, the majority (57%) preferred to defer the French dinner. Even with single-outcome events, there was some motivation to defer the French dinner: Witness the 20% of subjects who opted for the longer delay. However, this tendency was clearly stronger for sequences than for individual items.

We observed the same pattern when we substituted "dinner at home" for the Greek dinner. Because most people eat dinner at home on most nights anyway, the mere embedding of the French dinner in an explicit binary sequence does not introduce any real modification of the problem relative to the single-outcome frame in Question 2. The only thing that happens is that the subject is reminded that the choice is "really" between complete sequences. Like other framing effects, such reminders cause preferences to shift, in this case in favor of the improving sequence.

The pattern of preferences revealed by these choices is incompatible with any discounted utility model, as defined by Equation 1. A preference for a French dinner in 1 month rather than 2 suggests that $w_1 > w_2$; however, a preference for the improving sequence indicates that $w_1u(\text{French}) + w_2u(\text{Greek}) < w_1u(\text{Greek}) + w_2u(\text{French})$, or $w_2 > w_1$, on the assumption that $u(\text{French}) > u(\text{Greek})$, which is confirmed by Question 1.

16.1.2. *Defining a Sequence*

It appears, then, that two distinct motives are relevant to time preference: impatience and a preference for improvement. Which of these two motives dominates appears to depend on whether the objects of choice are single-outcome prospects or sequences. Impatience dominates choices between single outcomes; the preference for improvement most strongly influences choices between sequences.

In many cases, however, it is not clear whether a particular prospect is properly defined as a sequence. For example, when the attributes of outcomes composing a sequence are incommensurable, or when elements in the sequence are themselves brief but separated by long delays, it seems reasonable to evaluate the elements of the sequence independently of one another. However, when outcomes are commensurable and tightly spaced, the logic for treating them as a sequence will be more compelling. In general, the greater the "integrity" of a series of outcomes, the greater should be its likelihood of being evaluated as an integral sequence.

The following examples illustrate that it is possible to vary the integrity of a sequence so as to influence preferences in a predictable manner. The following three questions were asked of 48 visitors to the Museum of Science and Industry in Chicago. Proportions of subjects giving each response are designated in brackets.

Example 2

Imagine you must schedule two weekend outings to a city where you once lived. You do not plan on visiting the city after these two outings.

You must spend one of these weekends with an irritating, abrasive aunt who is a horrendous cook. The other weekend will be spent visiting former work associates whom you like a lot. From the following pairs, please indicate your preference by checking the appropriate line.

Suppose one outing will take place this coming weekend, the other the weekend after.

	This weekend	Next weekend	
A.	friends	abrasive aunt	[10%] (5/48)
B.	abrasive aunt	friends	[90%] (43/48)

Suppose one outing will take place this coming weekend, the other in 6 months (26 weeks).

	This weekend	26 weeks from now	
A.	friends	abrasive aunt	[48%] (23/48)
B.	abrasive aunt	friends	[52%] (25/48)

Suppose one outing will take place in 6 months (26 weeks from now), the other the weekend after (27 weeks from now).

	26 weeks from now	27 weeks from now	
A.	friends	abrasive aunt	[17%] (8/48)
B.	abrasive aunt	friends	[83%] (40/48)

In the first question, the series of outcomes unfold over a fairly short period (2 weeks) so that we would expect discounting to be relatively weak and the preference for improving sequences to be strong. Here, 90% of subjects opted for the improving sequence. In the second set of options, the absolute interval is much longer (26 weeks), reducing the integrity of the sequence. Here, we would expect discounting to have a greater impact relative to the preference for improvement. Indeed, a much smaller fraction of subjects (52%) chose the improving sequence given the long absolute delay. In the third pair, the sequence interval was once again reduced to 1 week, so we would anticipate a greater preference for the increasing sequences than found in the second pair. However, intuitively, we expected that the long delay prior to the beginning of the sequence would reduce its integrity to some degree. This may explain the slight reduction, relative to the first set of alternatives, in the fraction of subjects opting to get the unpleasant visit over with quickly.

It is not possible to interpret the three modal choice patterns in terms of conventional time preference. The first and third question indicates a negative rate of time preference (i.e. $w_0 < w_1$ and $w_{26} < w_{27}$) in the context of a discounted utility model (see Equation 1). It is safe to generalize that the aunt would be scheduled in the earlier of any consecutive two weekends (i.e., $w_t < w_{t+1}$). Yet, the transitive conclusion does not follow because the middle question implies that $w_0 > w_{26}$. We call this pattern the "magnet effect" because preferences for the two outcomes resemble the behavior of magnets. When distant from one another, two magnets interact only weakly; however, when brought into close proximity, they exert a force on one another, which causes them to reverse position.

16.1.3. *Preference for Spreading*

In addition to the desire for improvement over time, preferences also indicate a sensitivity to certain global or "gestalt" properties of sequences having to do with how evenly the good and bad outcomes are arranged over the total time interval. Unlike the question of positive versus negative time preference, which by now has received some attention, there have been few efforts to examine how people like to distribute outcomes over time. Important exceptions are two recent studies examining whether people like to experience two positive, negative, or mixed (positive and negative) events on the same or on different days. Applications of prospect theory imply that people should like to spread gains out across different days and to concentrate losses in a single day, and, although the first of these predictions is generally supported, the evidence for the latter is far more tenuous. Thaler and Johnson (1990) found that people generally expected to be happier when two gains (e.g. winning $25 in an office lottery and winning $50 in another) were separated by an interval but also expected to be less unhappy when two losses were separated. Thaler and Johnson argued that prior losses may sensitize people to subsequent losses, contrary to the prediction of prospect theory. Linville and Fischer (1991) likewise failed to observe a concentration of losses, although the tendency to do so was greater for small losses than for large ones. They explained this shift in terms a model of "coping capacity," which postulates that people have a limited psychological capacity to absorb losses and that they may wish to separate losses in time in order to replenish their coping resources. Thus, for both gains and losses, there does appear to be a preference for spreading outcomes out over time.

Although these results are suggestive, their applicability to the types of sequences we were concerned with is limited. First, all of the choices in these studies involved only two outcomes. This made it possible to examine whether people like to concentrate or spread out outcomes, but not whether they exhibit more complex patterns of preference (e.g. for certain types of patterns of outcomes over time). Second, the choices were all between experiencing outcomes at the same or different points in time. Such a design leaves unanswered, for those who prefer to separate outcomes, the question of how much of a gap is ideal.

The central insight that we took from this research was that, when presented with more than one same-valence outcome, people generally like to spread outcomes over time rather than concentrating them. The following problem presented to 37 Yale University undergraduates (from Loewenstein, 1987) illustrates this desire for spread. Subjects were first given a choice between Options A and B, then between Options C and D; they were instructed to ignore scheduling considerations. Percentages who chose each of the options are presented in the right-hand column.

Example 3

Which would you prefer?

Option	This weekend	Next weekend	Two weekends from now	Choices
A	Fancy French	Eat at home	Eat at home	16%
B	Eat at home	Fancy French	Eat at home	84%
C	Fancy French	Eat at home	Fancy lobster	54%
D	Eat at home	Fancy French	Fancy lobster	46%

Choosing between Options A and B, the majority of subjects preferred to postpone the fancy dinner until the second weekend, consistent with the widespread preference for improvement. However, the insertion of the common lobster dinner in Options C and D caused preference to shift slightly in favor of having the French dinner right away. This pattern violates additive separability (and any model given by Equation 1). Because the third period is identical for Options A and B and for C and D, separability implies that anyone who prefers A (B) should prefer C (D).

We believe that the relative attractiveness of Options B and C stemmed in part from the fact that they "covered" the 3-week interval better than did their alternatives. Option A exposed the decision maker to a 2-week period of eating at home, whereas Option B placed the one pleasurable event at the center of the interval. Option D concentrated all of the pleasure at one extreme of the 3-week period, whereas Option C distributed the fancy dinners more evenly over time.

It is worth noting that loss aversion as traditionally conceived would not predict this type of violation. Of the four sequences in the example, only Option D was strictly increasing. It appears, therefore, that a person who strongly dislikes utility reductions across adjacent periods will have a greater tendency to prefer Option D over C than Option B over A, which is the opposite of the observed pattern of choice.

Another possibility is that people have a net liking for changes in utility between adjacent periods, as permitted in Gilboa's (1989) model. In that case, Option B has more between-period variation than Option A, and Option C more variation than Option D, in accord with the modal preferences. To rule out this explanation, and to show that preferential interactions occur between nonadjacent periods, we modified the original example by inserting additional "eat at home" weekends between the original first two weekends and between the second and third weekends (see Example 4).

Example 4

Imagine that over the next five weekends you must decide how to spend your Saturday nights. From each pair of sequences of dinners below circle the one you would prefer. "Fancy French" refers to dinner at a fancy French restaurant. "Fancy lobster" refers to an exquisite lobster dinner at a four-star restaurant. Ignore scheduling considerations (e.g. your current plans).

Option	First weekend	Second weekend	Third weekend	Fourth weekend	Fifth weekend
A	Fancy French	Eat at home	Eat at home	Eat at home	Eat at home
B	Eat at home	Eat at home	Fancy French	Eat at home	Eat at home
C	Fancy French	Eat at home	Eat at home	Eat at home	Fancy lobster
D	Eat at home	Eat at home	Fancy French	Eat at home	Fancy lobster

In this example, it is not possible to produce an independence violation solely on the basis of adjacent periods. Suppose, for example, that the utility function for sequences has a special set of functions, f_t, that register the impact of adjacent utility levels on preferences:

$$V[(x_1, \ldots, x_n)] = \sum_{t=1}^{n} u_t(x_t) + \sum_{t=1}^{n-1} f_t(x_t, x_{t+1}).$$

In that case, the difference in value between Sequences A and B still equals the difference in value between Sequences C and D because

$$V(A) - V(B) = u_1(F) + u_3(H) + f_1(F, H) + f_2(H, H) + f_3(H, H) - u_1(H) - u_3(F)$$
$$- f_1(H, H) - f_2(H, H) - f_3(F, H)$$
$$= V(C) - V(D),$$

where F, H refer to the French and home dinners. In the survey, visitors to the Museum of Science and Industry in Chicago ($N = 51$) strongly preferred Sequence B to A (88%) and just slightly preferred Sequence C to D (51%). Despite the different subject population (museum visitors vs. undergraduates), and despite the inclusion of two "filler" weekends, the preference pattern was virtually unchanged from Example 3. The violation of independence cannot therefore be attributed to particular feelings about utility changes from one period to the next.

16.1.4. Marking an Interval

How one distributes events over an interval clearly depends on the duration of that interval. However, in the real world the relevant interval is often ambiguous and may vary for different people and for different types of outcomes. For example, the relevant interval for a free dinner is probably shorter than for a free round-trip flight. The final example we present was constructed to test whether manipulation of the implicit interval would influence timing preferences. One hundred one visitors to Chicago's Museum of Science and Industry were asked to schedule two hypothetical free dinners at the restaurant of their choice.

Example 5

Suppose you were given two coupons for fancy dinners for two at the restaurant of your choice. The coupons are worth up to $100 each. When would you choose to use them? Please ignore considerations such as holidays, birthdays, etc.

One third of the subjects were asked to schedule the two dinners without any imposed time constraints (unconstrained group). Another one third, the "4-month constraint group," were told that they could use the coupons any time in the next 4 months. The remaining third, the 2-year constraint group, were told "You can use the coupons at any time between today and 2 years from today." Although the constraints seemingly *limited* the subjects' abilities to delay the dinners, we felt that constrained subjects would prefer to delay the dinners more than would unconstrained subjects because the default interval for unconstrained subjects was actually shorter than the explicit intervals faced by the constrained subjects. Table 1 presents our findings.

Medians were a more representative measure of population preferences here because they attenuated the impact of a few extremely long delays obtained in the unconstrained condition. Considering the medians, the median delay interval for the second dinner was longer under either constrained condition than the median delay in the unconstrained condition. The effect was especially prominent, however, for the 2-year delay, suggesting that the average default interval for subjects might have been close to 4 months. Overall, the

Table 1. Chosen Delay for First and Second Dinner

Condition	First dinner	Second dinner
Unconstrained		
M	3.3	13.1
Mdn	2.0	8.0
Four-month constraint		
M	3.0	10.4
Mdn	2.0	12.0
Two-year constraint		
M	7.7	31.1
Mdn	4.0	26.0

effect of the two constraints on the selected delays was significant, according to a one-way analysis of variance (ANOVA), $F(2, 96) = 3.7$, $p < .03$, for the first dinner, and $F(2, 96) = 13.2$, $p < .0001$, for the second.

These results are inconsistent with the economic axiom of revealed preference, according to which the imposition of a time constraint on an initially unconstrained population should affect only the responses of that fraction of the population whose preferred delays are longer than permitted by the constraint. Therefore, the population averages should be longer in the unconstrained condition.

16.2. A Model for Preferences Over Outcome Sequences

Taken together, these examples confirm that subjects may or may not frame a given intertemporal choice as one involving sequences of outcomes and that whether they do so can significantly influence their behavior. Furthermore, when people do see themselves as choosing between sequences, their preferences are poorly captured by conventional discounting models.

In this section, we develop a nonseparable model that accommodates the anomalous preference patterns presented in the previous section. The guiding idea behind the model is that evaluation of sequences reflects the interaction between two motives: a basic preference for improvement tempered by a desire to spread the better outcomes more or less uniformly over the entire interval.

In the most general sense, these assumptions are not new. A number of recent nonseparable models have added the rate of utility *change*—either discrete (Gilboa, 1989) or continuous (Bordley, 1986; Frank, 1989, in press; Hsee & Abelson, 1991)—as a contributing factor for preference. The distinctive aspect of our approach is that the notions of utility improvement and uniformness are defined with respect to global rather than local sequence properties.

The term *global*, as we use it, refers to comparisons at a given point in time between the set of outcomes that are yet to occur and the set of outcomes that have already occurred. A globally improving sequence would be one in which, at any point in time, the average utility of the remaining periods is greater than the average utility of the periods that have gone by. For example, the sequence (4,2,3,1,2,0) undoubtedly creates a feeling of global decline, even though it includes two increasing transitions along the way. We feel that the enjoyment of the good initial periods, as well as of the positive transitions between Periods 2 and 3, or 4 and 5, would be inhibited by the deteriorating overall pattern.

Similarly, a globally uniform sequence is one in which, at any point in time, the future offers approximately equal average utility as did the past, notwithstanding local fluctuations in utility levels. We posit that such even spreading of good outcomes contributes to the attractiveness of a sequence, with other things being equal.

By contrast, nonseparable rate-of-change models would identify improvement with a positive change in utility between one period and the next and smoothness with small utility fluctuations between adjacent periods. The distinction between the local and global smoothness (or uniformness), for instance, is illustrated by the sequences (0,0,1,1,1,0,0) and (0,1,0,1,0,1,0). The first sequence is more smooth in the local sense because there are only two points (rather than six) at which adjacent utility levels differ; the second sequence achieves a more uniform pattern of outcomes in the global sense, in that the differences between average future utility and average past utility are smaller.

16.2.1. *The Decumulated Utility Graph and the Reference Line*

The relevant global properties to which we have been referring are displayed visually in a *decumulated* utility graph (see Figure 1), which plots total remaining utility as function of period number. This picture can be interpreted as a "utility-budgeting" chart, showing how much utility has been spent up to a point and how much is left over for subsequent periods. The particular pattern in Figure 1 corresponds to a utility series that starts low, peaks around the middle of the interval, and then declines toward the end.

In a decumulated utility graph, a constant series of utility levels is represented by a negatively sloped straight line. Taking our cue from the

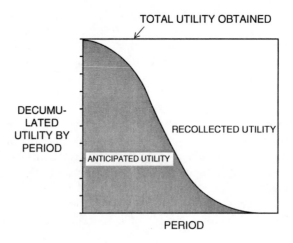

Figure 1. The decumulated utility graph showing remaining utility as a function of time. (The corresponding utility sequence would be bell-shaped.)

well-documented pervasiveness of reference point effects in many different choice domains, we postulate that the decumulated graph of the uniform sequence is the natural global reference point concept for the sequence domain. More precisely, the internal *reference line* for each sequence is the graph of the unique constant sequence that gives the same total utility as the original one.

When the decumulated graph falls below the reference line, utility is being used up at a faster-than-average pace, and leaner periods will necessarily follow; above the reference line, utility is being saved up, and future periods will improve on the previous ones.

In the next section, we develop the formal definition of our model through an accounting scheme for utility derived from anticipation. This simple model captures the essence of the improvement motive, and the motive for uniform spreading of outcomes, and can therefore explain most of the qualitative preference patterns presented earlier. We then show how the separate impact of time discounting can be incorporated into a more generalized version of the model.

16.2.2. *Definition of Improvement and Uniformness*

It is commonplace that events create satisfaction or distress not just while they take place but also before they occur, through anticipation, and after they occur, through recollection. The simplest possible accounting of these two additional sources of value would have the total *anticipated* utility computed as a sum in which each utility level u_1 is multiplied by the number of periods that precede it $(t - 1)$,

$$AU = \sum_t (t - 1)u_t,$$

and total *recollected* utility as a sum in which each utility level is multiplied by the number of subsequent periods $(n - t)$,

$$RU = \sum_t (n - t)u_t.$$

For instance, if a positive event is scheduled on Day 4 of a 5-day sequence, this will yield 3 days of anticipation and 1 day of recollection. (The measures of anticipation and recollection, of course, depend on the framing of the problem, in this case the number of days under consideration.)

In the decumulated utility graph (see Figure 1), anticipated utility is represented by the area to the left and below the curved line, and recollected utility is represented by the area to the right and above the line. The value of the cumulative utility distribution at any point indicates how much of the sequence's overall utility remains to be experienced. We now

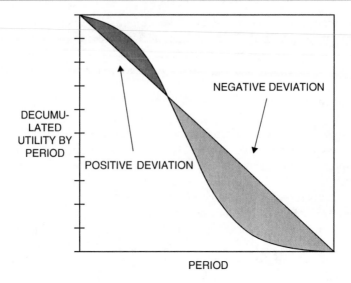

Figure 2. Positive and negative deviations defined as the distance between the decumulated utility function and the negatively sloping reference line.

define the net improvement that a sequence provides as $(AU - RU)/2$, or one half of the excess of anticipated utility over recollected utility. The $^1/_2$ factor makes it possible to read the improvement measure directly from the decumulated graph: It is the difference between the area where the decumulated line falls above the reference line (labeled "positive deviation" in Figure 2) and the area where it falls below it (labeled "negative deviation" in Figure 2).

With regard to the second of the two basic motives, we define the deviation from uniform utility spreading in a particular sequence as the absolute difference between the decumulated graph for that sequence and its reference line, which is to say, the sum of the two shaded areas in Figure 2.

16.2.3. The Model

Expressing the relevant areas formally involves some algebra. For each period t, we first compute the difference, d_t, between the cumulated utility received up to that period and the cumulated utility that *should have been received* had the utility total been allocated in a perfectly uniform manner across the n periods:

$$d_t = \frac{t}{n} \sum_{i=1}^{n} u_t - \sum_{i=1}^{t} u_i. \qquad (2)$$

Geometrically, the value of d_t equals the vertical difference between the decumulated utility line and the reference line. To confirm that the aggregate of all d_ts indeed equals net improvement, we calculate that

$$\sum_{t=1}^{n} d_t = \sum_{t=1}^{n} \left(\frac{t}{n} \sum_{t=1}^{n} u_t - \sum_{t=1}^{t} u_t \right)$$

$$= \frac{\sum t}{n} \sum_{t=1}^{n} u_t - \sum_{t=1}^{n} \sum_{i=1}^{t} u_i$$

$$= \frac{n+1}{2} \sum_{t=1}^{n} u_t - \sum_{t=1}^{n} (n+1-t)u_t$$

$$= \frac{1}{2} [\sum_{t=1}^{n} (t-1)u_t - \sum_{t=1}^{n} (n-1)u_t]$$

$$= \frac{1}{2} (AU - RU).$$

The terms d_t allocate the difference $(AU - RU)/2$ to individual periods, so that positive values are associated with periods at which the future is better than the past and negative values to periods when it is worse than the past.

The value of a sequence is now defined as a weighted sum of three factors: the total utility provided by the sequence, the net improvement, and the deviation from uniform utility spreading:

$$\text{Value} = \sum_{t=1}^{n} u_t + \beta \sum_{t=1}^{n} d_t + \sigma \sum_{t=1}^{n} |d_t|. \tag{3}$$

16.2.4. Interpretation of the Parameters

The parameter β signals whether a person prefers improving ($\beta > 0$) or declining ($\beta < 0$) sequences, whereas σ determines whether he or she prefers uniform ($\sigma < 0$) or nonuniform sequences ($\sigma > 0$). This is a straightforward interpretation of the parameters. However, an alternative and psychologically suggestive set of interpretations can be obtained through a more explicit articulation of the reference point aspect of the model.

We first split the deviation terms into their positive and negative parts:

$$d_t^+ \equiv \frac{|d_t| + d_t}{2}, \quad d_t^- \equiv \frac{|d_t| - d_t}{2}. \tag{4}$$

In words, d_t^+ equals d_t if it is positive, and zero otherwise; d_t^- equals $|d_t|$ if it is negative, and zero otherwise (note that $d_t = d_t^+ - d_t^-$). This allows us to rewrite the model so that the net impact of improvement and deterioration on sequence value is assessed separately:

$$\text{Value}=\sum_{t=1}^{n} u_t + (\beta + \sigma)\sum_{t=1}^{n} d_t^+ + (\beta - \sigma)\sum_{t=1}^{n} d_t^-. \tag{5}$$

If indeed the reference line functions as a reference point, and if improvement (d_t^+) defines the attractive direction away from the reference point, then we would predict the following: $\beta > -\sigma > 0$, that is, $(\beta - \sigma) > (\beta + \sigma) > 0$. The desire for uniform utility levels can be viewed as a consequence of loss aversion, which, in the context of our global variables, implies that the dislike of global deterioration, measured by the coefficient $(\beta - \sigma)$, is stronger than the liking for global improvement, measured by $(\beta + \sigma)$. Without any further assumptions, such global loss aversion would create a motive for interleaving good and bad outcomes more or less evenly over time.

This interpretation covers only one of the eight ordinally distinct sign–magnitude combinations for β and σ. The remaining possibilities have other interpretations, suggested by the labels in Figure 3. The center of the figure is the point $\beta = \sigma = 0$, identifying a person who compares sequences only by total utility; beyond that, all patterns are equally good. The horizontal axis in the figure represents the β coefficient; points along that line identify individuals who have intertemporally additive preferences, favoring either the present ($\beta < 0$) or the future ($\beta > 0$). Points along the vertical axis, which plots the value of the σ coefficient, identify people

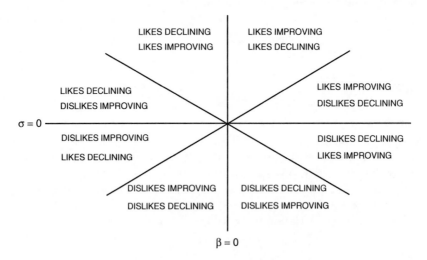

Figure 3. Partitioning of the (β, σ) parameter space into the eight possible sign–magnitude combinations. (The pair of labels in each segment identifies the major [top] and minor [bottom] motive associated with parameter values in that segment.)

without a time orientation who are concerned only with even distribution of utility.

Three of the four corners in Figure 3 have intuitive interpretations. The lower left corner corresponds to the pattern $\beta = \sigma < 0$, which indicates a dislike of improvement but indifference to decline. This describes *impatience* in the nontechnical sense of the term, which is to say, a specific aversion to waiting for good outcomes. The bottom right corner is the pattern $\beta = -\sigma > 0$, which describes the preferences of a person who is indifferent to improvement (as the coefficient for Σd_t^+, $\beta + \sigma = 0$) but is averse to decline; such a person would sacrifice some total utility in order to avoid a declining sequence but would not sacrifice any utility to transform a constant sequence into an increasing one. We label this *dread orientation*. Finally, the complementary pattern is found in the top right corner, where $\beta = \sigma > 0$. This identifies a person who likes improvement but is indifferent to decline (again, in the sense of being willing to sacrifice total utility for one or the other pattern). Such a person derives additional satisfaction from future good outcomes but is not adversely affected by future negative outcomes. A *savoring orientation* would seem to describe this fortunate combination.

16.3. Predictions of the Model and a Generalization

16.3.1. *Separability Violations*

Example 3 induced a violation of independence having the following schematic form: $(1,0,0) < (0,1,0)$, *but* $(1,0,2) > (0,1,2)$, where, 0 = "eat at home," 1 = "fancy French," and 2 = "fancy lobster," as in Loewenstein (1987). We first calculate the deviations (d_1, d_2) for the four sequences:

$$(1,0,0): d_1 = .33 - 1.0 = -.67; \quad d_2 = .67 - 1.0 = -.33;$$

$$(0,1,0): d_1 = .33 - 0.0 = +.33; \quad d_2 = .67 - 1.0 = -.33;$$

$$(1,0,2): d_1 = 1.0 - 1.0 = 0.0; \quad d_2 = 2.0 - 1.0 = +1.0;$$

$$(0,1,2): d_1 = 1.0 - 0.0 = +1.0; \quad d_2 = 2.0 - 1.0 = +1.0.$$

The value of each sequence is then obtained by applying Equation 3:

$$V[(1,0,0)] = 1 - \beta + \sigma;$$

$$V[(0,1,0)] = 1 + \frac{2}{3}\sigma;$$

$$V[(1,0,2)] = 3 + \beta + \sigma;$$

$$V[(0,1,2)] = 3 + 2\beta + 2\sigma.$$

Because σ is negative, it is possible for a person to prefer sequence $(0,1,0)$ to $(1,0,0)$ and sequence $(1,0,2)$ to $(0,1,2)$:

$$V[(1,0,0)] - V[(0,1,0)] = -\beta + .33\sigma < 0,$$

$$V[(1,0,2)] - V[(0,1,2)] = -\beta - \sigma > 0.$$

This formal explanation can be interpreted in two ways, which cannot be discriminated at the level of our model. First, it is possible that a person is fundamentally concerned about even spreading, in which case the sequence $(0,1,0)$ is more uniformly spread then $(1,0,0)$, but $(0,1,2)$ is not as uniformly spread as $(1,0,2)$. The other interpretation would attribute the reversal to a fundamental aversion to declining average utility levels (i.e. negative d_t values). In the first pair, the sequence $(1,0,0)$ is globally declining and is possibly rejected on those grounds alone. In the second pair, however, *both* sequences are globally increasing, so that a person is free to indulge the initial period with the $(1,0,2)$ sequence without disturbing the sense of global improvement.

16.3.2. Scheduling Decisions

The model makes definite predictions about the optimal scheduling of an enjoyable event, when there are n consecutive and otherwise indistinguishable dates available. In general, the optimal period will depend on all of the parameters in the model. However, the net effect of the spreading motive will be to move this period closer to the middle of the interval.

Because utility is represented by an interval scale (see the next section), we can assume without loss of generality that the single enjoyable event in an n-period sequence yields a utility level of exactly n and the background events utility zero. The uniform reference sequence then has a cumulated utility distribution $(1, 2, 3, \ldots, n)$. By scheduling the event in period t^*, one creates deviations $d_t = +t$ for the periods prior to t^* and $d_t = n - t$ for periods later than (and including) t^*. The sum of absolute deviations

$$\left[\sum_{t < t^*} t + \sum_{t \geq t^*} (n - t) \right]$$

is minimized at $t^* = n/2$, the midpoint of the interval.

We feel that this explains the otherwise puzzling results revealed by Example 5. Recall that subjects who were unconstrained in the scheduling of a free meal chose to schedule it sooner, on average, than subjects who were constrained by a long interval. If the explicit interval (2 years) is longer than the implicit one used by unconstrained subjects, then the attraction toward the respective midpoints should further stretch out the optimal scheduling times for the explicitly constrained subjects.

16.3.3. Discounting and the General Model

The model we have just defined represents a radical simplification of intertemporal preferences: Time enters into the picture only in establishing the ordering of events. Whether this is a good approximation to preferences will probably depend on the duration of the entire sequence (the planning interval), as well as on its temporal proximity. Other things being equal, we expect that shorter planning intervals will improve the approximation, whereas temporal proximity will reduce it through a disproportionate weighting of the initial periods.

In this section, we show that the basic model can be readily generalized to incorporate time discounting and other types of differential weighting patterns. We take as a benchmark the most general discounted utility model, restated as follows:

$$V(X) = \sum_t w_t u_t.$$

The model we now introduce retains an additive structure, but, in keeping with the reference point framework developed earlier, it assumes that the sequence value is determined by the positive and negative deviations of the decumulated utility graph from the reference line:

$$V(X) = \sum_{t=1}^{n} u_t + \sum_{t=1}^{n-1} \sigma_t^+ d_t^+ + \sum_{t=1}^{n-1} \sigma_t^- d_t^-. \tag{6}$$

In words, the value of any sequence is a separately weighted sum of the positive and negative deviations from the reference line. As in the basic model, the first term gives weight to the total value of outcomes in the sequence; it cancels out if the sequences being compared are permutations of the same set of outcomes. The remaining two terms add up the psychic costs and benefits of facing rising (d_t^+) or falling (d_t^-) utility levels; what is new here is that these costs and benefits are allowed to differ across periods instead of being applied to the summations Σd_t^+ and Σd_t^-.

This model can also be written in a way that brings out more clearly the relation to the discounting formula:

$$V(X) = \sum_{t=1}^{n} w_t u_t + \sum_{t=1}^{n-1} \sigma_t |d_t|. \tag{7}$$

The first term is the general discounting formula (Equation 1), and the second is the weighted sum of absolute deviations of the cumulated graph from the reference line. The weights, σ_t, are averages of the positive and negative coefficients in Equation 6:

$$\sigma_t = \frac{\sigma_t^+ + \sigma_t^-}{2}, \tag{8}$$

whereas the discounting weights, w_t, have a more complicated relation to the coefficients in Equation 6 (see the Appendix). In the basic model (Equation 3), the coefficients, σ_t, were all identical and presumed negative; the weights, w_t, were linear in period number and presumed increasing, in line with the preference for improvement:

$$w_t = \left(1 + \frac{\beta(n+1)}{2}\right) + \beta t. \tag{9}$$

Discounting enters into the picture when the periods become sufficiently separated in real time or when the first period is close to the present. There is great flexibility in how one could model this through the w_t coefficients. We propose that the relation between $(w_1, \ldots, w_n)$ and the real-time parameters of the sequence $(\tau_1, \ldots, \tau_n)$ be modeled in the following way:

$$w_t = f(\tau_i)(\alpha + \beta t),$$

$$\sigma_t = f(\tau_t)\sigma, \tag{10}$$

where $f(\tau_t)$ is the discount function derived empirically from single-outcome intertemporal choices and applied to the time of the $t - th$ period, τ_t, whereas α, β, and σ play the same role as in the earlier model.

The interplay between discounting and improvement can be seen in Figure 4, which shows how the weights for a five-period sequence depend on the real-time parameters of the sequence. The solid line in the figure is the underlying discount function, $f(\tau)$. The weights for the distant, closely spaced sequence are increasing and nearly linear because the discount function values $f(\tau_1)$ through $f(\tau_5)$ are virtually constant over the five dates; the desire for improvement, which depends on period position rather than absolute time, dominates the discounting effect. Moving that same sequence closer in time to a point at which the hyperbolic discount function is steep produces significant within-sequence discounting, which combines with the linear preference for improvement to produce a U-shaped weighting pattern. Finally, for the widely spaced sequence discounting predominates, and the weights essentially replicate the declining shape of the discount function over time.

This pattern of weights would be consistent with the preference reversal documented in Example 2, in which a visit to an unpleasant relative had to be scheduled in one of two weekends. For adjacent weekends, the values of the discount function at the two weekend dates were not different enough to overwhelm the preference for improvement; however, if the weekends

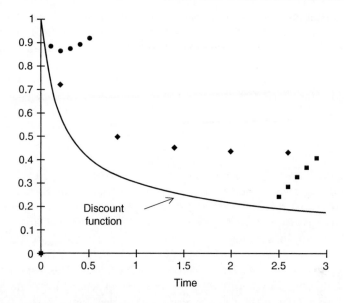

Figure 4. Individual period weights (w_t) for three 5-period sequences that arise when a linear preference for improvement is modulated by a hyperbolic discount function (solid line).

were separated by 6 months, then real-time discounting made it attractive to schedule visiting the aunt in the later slot.

16.3.4. *Three Properties of the General Model*

Notwithstanding the additional complexity, the general model has a number of properties that are either identical or related to the discounting formula.

1. *Interval utility scale.* As in the general discounting formula, preferences are invariant under linear, positive transformations of the utility function (see the Appendix).

2. *Linearity in the small.* Small improvements in the utility of an outcome have a linear impact on sequence value, as if the model were separable. This considerably simplifies the evaluation of certain common scheduling decisions. Consider, for example, whether it is better to schedule some event in period t or in period $t + 1$. In a separable model, this would depend only on the discounting weights w_t and w_{t+1} insofar as it would be desirable to redistribute utility from period t to period $t + 1$ whenever $w_1 < w_{t+1}$:

$$\frac{\partial V}{\partial u_t} - \frac{\partial V}{\partial u_{t+1}} = w_t - w_{t+1} < 0. \tag{11}$$

In our model, one also has to take into account the impact of any such redistribution on the shape of the cumulated utility graph. However, when

463

the redistribution involves the *adjacent* periods t and $t + 1$, the cumulated graph is affected at only one point—at period t. For periods prior to t, and for those later than (and including) $t + 1$, the cumulated utility level does not depend on the division of utility between t and $t + 1$. Hence, the evaluation of the redistribution in the additive case is modified only by the addition of one extra parameter:

$$\frac{\partial V}{\partial u_t} - \frac{\partial V}{\partial u_{t+1}} = w_t - w_{t+1} \pm \sigma_t < 0.$$

The coefficient σ_t is either added or subtracted depending on whether the average utility level in periods $t + 1$ through n is lower or greater than the level in the first t periods. If the future appears worse than the past from the vantage point of period t, then the addition of the (negatively valued) σ_t term creates an additional incentive for later scheduling of high-utility events.

3. *Separability with respect to outcome permutations.* The general model described here is consistent with a weaker form of separability, one that has an intuitive appeal in the context of scheduling decisions. The usual form of separability states that preference between two sequences that have elements in common does not depend on the nature of these common elements. The weaker version is expressed as follows: Suppose that two sequences of length n are permutations of the same set of events (i.e. utility levels) and that they also differ only over the first $m < n$ periods (or, equivalently, over the last m periods). Then, preference between them will not depend on the common ordering of events over the remaining $n - m$ periods.

Here is a concrete example of this type of *permutation separability*. A person is making plans for the next 2 months. At issue for the first month is how to order a fixed set of tasks that have to be completed. For the second month, a vacation month, the issue is how to order a fixed set of leisure activities. The condition we have just defined would imply that the optimal ordering of events for the second month is not affected by how the events are ordered in the first month (and vice versa).

It is not hard to demonstrate that our model generically satisfies this property. Because the two sequences under consideration are permutations of the same set of events, they will share the same reference line. Furthermore, sequences that agree on the scheduling for the first month will have the same decumulated utility graph for that segment. Regardless of the relation of this common segment to the reference line, it will contribute, through the deviation terms, exactly the same amount to the value of either such sequence and hence will have a zero net impact on preference among them. The optimal scheduling of events in the second segment is therefore independent of the schedule imposed in the initial one.

16.4. Two Studies of Preference for Outcome Sequences

In the following two studies, subjects rated the desirability of sequences defined by events occurring over five consecutive weekends. The first study was designed to elicit basic properties of preferences toward sequences and to test the goodness of fit of the model presented in Equation 3. The second study was designed specifically to check for violations of preferential independence across periods.

16.4.1. *Study 1*

METHOD

Subjects. Fifty-two subjects recruited at the Museum of Science and Industry in Chicago were each given a ticket to a multimedia presentation (value $4) in exchange for participating. Subjects represented a wide range of demographic characteristics. Forty-nine percent were male, 55% were married, and the age range was 18–58 years ($M = 32$). Six percent did not have a high school diploma, 11% had graduated from high school, 30% had some college but had not graduated, 36% had a college degree, and 17% possessed an advanced degree. The median yearly family income was approximately $35,000.

Stimuli. Each sequence consisted of five consecutive weekends: one very enjoyable weekend, two moderately enjoyable weekends, and two boring weekends. All permutations of these five events created 30 distinct sequences. Subjects were told first to examine all 30 sequences and locate the best and worst one. The best was given a rating of 10 and the worst a 1. After this, subjects were instructed to go through the remaining 28 sequences and rate them according to their desirability relative to the best and worst. The exact instructions were as follows:

Imagine it is Monday and you are contemplating the next five weekends. Your situation is depicted in the diagram below.

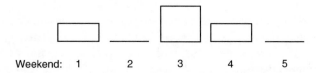

Weekend: 1   2   3   4   5

The tall box represents a very pleasurable way to spend a weekend. Think of who you would like to spend such a weekend with and how you would like to spend it. In the diagram, you are doing the pleasurable thing on the third weekend.

The medium height box represents a moderately pleasurable way of spending a weekend. Think of something you enjoy, but do not love, doing. In the diagram, the first and fourth days are moderately pleasurable.

The flat line represents a boring and not at all fun way to spend a weekend. Think of something you do not enjoy doing. In the diagram, the second and fifth weekends are boring and not at all fun.

On the pages below you will find a series of 30 different sequences consisting of very pleasurable, pleasurable, and boring weekends. In each sequence there is one very pleasurable, two moderately pleasurable, and two boring weekends.

We want you to rate each sequence on a scale from 1 to 10, where 1 is the worst and 10 is the best. First, go through all the sequences and identify the one you like best and the one you like least. For the one you like best, enter a "10" on the blank line. For the one you like least, enter a "1." Then examine each sequence and assign it a rating from 1 to 10. If you like two sequences equally, you should give them the same rating.

The 30 sequences were presented in one of two opposite orderings determined by a random drawing.

RESULTS

Because our sequences involved only three possible outcomes, the underlying utility assignment had only one free parameter, which we could identify with the position of the moderately enjoyable weekend on a 0–2 scale, with 0 and 2 being the values of the boring and very enjoyable weekends, respectively. The descriptions of the outcomes and the height of the vertical bars by which they were visually represented in the survey were intended to suggest a midpoint utility assignment for the moderately enjoyable weekend (i.e. scale value of 1).

We tested the model in Equation 3 by means of a maximum likelihood procedure, which returned for each subject estimates of the coefficients β and σ, as well as the value of the intermediate outcome, constrained to lie between 0 and 2. Positive values of β indicate people who prefer sequences that improve over time; negative values indicate people who discount the future. Negative values of σ designate people who prefer to spread good outcomes over time; people with positive σ values prefer to concentrate them at one point in the sequence.

The estimated value of the middle outcome was fairly close to 1 ($M = 0.81$), indicating that most subjects evaluated the moderately pleasurable weekend as about midway between the very pleasurable and boring weekends. Estimated values of β were positive for 40 of 52 subjects (77%), indicating a preference for improvement. Thirty-five of 52 subjects (67%) exhibited negative values of σ. Of the 52 subjects, 22 (42%) conformed exactly to the conjectured pattern: $\beta > -\sigma > 0$; This corresponds to the segment "dislikes declining, likes improving" in Figure 3. By contrast, we would have expected only 1 of 8, or 6.5 subjects, to reveal this pattern by chance. The mean value of β was .28, and the mean value of σ was $-.13$.

The mean correlation between actual and predicted ratings across all subjects was .60. Forcing the value of the middle-valued outcome exactly equal to 1 and rerunning the analysis lowered the mean correlation between actual and predicted ratings from .60 to .52 and had almost no impact on the other parameters. Therefore, all subsequent analyses were conducted with the value of the intermediate outcome set equal to 1.

To put the goodness-of-fit figures into perspective, we ran two additional analyses in an attempt to fit the standard discounted utility model,

$$\text{Rating} = c + a \sum_{t=1}^{s} \delta^t u_t, \tag{12}$$

to the subjects' ratings. The parameters c and a map the underlying utility scale into the 1–10 rating interval; the parameter δ measures whether a subject places more weight on early periods ($\delta < 1$) or on later ones ($\delta > 1$).

As expected, a large fraction (65%) of the subjects revealed "discount factors" (δ) greater than 1, implying greater weighting for outcomes in later periods. The mean value for δ was 1.23. The mean correlation between predicted and actual ratings was .38, and constraining the δ parameter to be less than or equal to 1 (i.e. ruling out negative time discounting) reduced this correlation to .08. Clearly, our model performs significantly better than the conventional discounted utility model, particularly when positive time discounting is assumed.

A comprehensive picture of intersubject variability is given in Figure 5. Each subject is indicated by a point on the scatterplot, with the direction of each point relative to the origin determined by the relative values of β and σ, and the distance from the origin by the goodness of fit (for that subject). Specifically, the x- and y-coordinates in the scatterplot represent the normalized regression coefficients,

$$\beta' = r \frac{\beta}{\sqrt{\beta^2 + \sigma^2}}, \quad \sigma' = r \frac{\sigma}{\sqrt{\beta^2 + \sigma^2}},$$

where r is the correlation between predicted and actual sequence ratings. If the ratings of all subjects were fit perfectly by the model, then all the points in the central scatterplot would be distributed along the ellipse drawn in the figure that has a fixed radius of 1. Subjects located close to the x-axis care about improvement but are relatively indifferent to spread. Those located close to the y-axis care about spread but not about improvement.

Looking at the scatterplot, one notices a fairly large cluster of subjects in the lower right part of the panel, whose points come close to the ellipse that

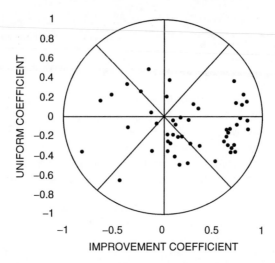

Figure 5. Scatterplot of normalized regression coefficients for all subjects in Study 1. (The *x*-axis plots the normalized coefficient for improvement and the *y*-axis the normalized coefficient for negative spread: $\beta' = r\beta/\sqrt{\beta^2 + \sigma^2}$, $\sigma' = r\sigma/\sqrt{\beta^2 + \sigma^2}$.)

identifies a perfect fit. These subjects have positive coefficients for improvement ($\beta > 0$) and negative coefficients for σ, indicating a preference for spreading outcomes. One *can* find subjects who are motivated by impatience, but such subjects are rare, and their preferences are not well explained by the model. Only 2 subjects' data, located in the lower left quadrant, display impatience and a high goodness of fit.

In general, the model provides reasonable goodness of fit to the data, especially considering that it includes only two free parameters (not including the constant). Inevitably, however, it will fit certain individuals better than others, and certain types of sequences will be predicted more accurately than others. Table 2 presents an analysis of the mean and mean absolute regression residuals for the 30 sequences, averaged across all of the subjects. The mean error indicates the degree of bias in the model's prediction of mean ratings; the mean absolute and squared errors indicate the goodness of fit.

The pattern of residuals across sequences provides clues about aspects of preference that are not picked up by the model. Notably, the model overestimated the attractiveness of every sequence with two consecutive zero periods; among these, the sequence (1,1,2,0,0) was the most overvalued of any of the 30 patterns. This systematic error suggests that subjects may care about the relation between adjacent periods to a degree not captured by our global measure of spreading.

Table 2. Mean and Mean Absolute Regression Residuals by Sequence

Sequence	Mean rating	Mean predicted rating	Mean residual	Mean absolute residual	Mean squared residual
00112	6.11	6.14	−0.03	1.74	4.99
00121	5.74	6.11	−0.38	1.82	5.18
00211	5.57	6.08	−0.52	1.94	5.80
01012	6.81	6.11	0.70	1.69	5.20
01021	6.32	6.08	0.24	1.31	2.62
01102	6.08	6.08	−0.01	1.75	5.06
01120	5.36	5.63	−0.27	1.98	6.09
01201	5.68	5.73	−0.05	1.19	2.22
01210	5.58	5.31	0.28	1.74	4.97
02011	5.36	5.83	−0.47	1.42	3.52
02101	5.72	5.50	0.21	1.39	3.44
02110	5.55	5.08	0.47	1.78	4.53
10012	5.60	5.99	−0.38	1.45	3.27
10021	5.36	5.96	−0.60	1.49	3.98
10102	7.32	5.96	1.36	2.17	6.72
10120	5.51	5.50	0.00	1.50	3.68
10201	6.34	5.60	0.74	2.33	8.18
10210	5.32	5.18	0.14	1.34	3.14
11002	5.34	5.73	−0.39	1.87	5.72
11020	5.06	5.28	−0.22	1.64	4.35
11200	3.55	4.43	−0.88	1.69	4.30
12001	4.26	4.85	−0.60	1.48	3.49
12010	4.85	4.43	0.42	1.29	2.60
12100	3.62	3.91	−0.28	1.39	3.39
20011	4.62	5.18	−0.56	1.79	5.50
20101	5.13	4.85	0.28	1.66	4.48
20110	4.98	4.43	0.55	1.63	4.46
21001	4.11	4.33	−0.22	1.39	2.97
21010	4.43	3.91	0.53	1.43	3.53
21100	3.32	3.38	−0.06	1.29	2.91
M	5.29	5.29	0.0	1.62	4.34

16.4.2. *Study 2*

Because the sequences in the first study were all permutations of a common set of outcomes, the results did not lend themselves to direct tests of separability. It was not possible to directly examine how the attractiveness of sequences changed when a single outcome was altered but all the other outcomes were held constant. The second study addressed this particular question.

In the study, subjects rated two matched blocks of sequences. The first, the *lean* block, consisted of a subset of 18 sequences from the previous study selected to represent the full diversity of the original set of 30. The second, the *rich* block, contained a corresponding set of 18 sequences constructed by applying two operations: (a) inverting the utility of individual outcomes so that very enjoyable weekends occupied the position of the boring ones and vice versa and (b) flipping the order of weekends from last to first. Consequently, each sequence in the rich block contained one boring weekend, two intermediate weekends, and two highly enjoyable weekends. The specific reasons for this construction are explained now further.

For each block we created two orderings, one the reverse of the other. Labeling the two orderings A and B and the blocks L and R, each subject received one of the following four stimulus combinations: (AL, BR), (AR, BL), (BL, AR), and (BR, AL). Subjects were told to independently calibrate the rating scales for the two blocks, with 1 representing the worst and 10 the best sequence in each block.

Separability implies that a person who prefers, for example, the sequence $(1,0,0,1,2)$ to $(2,0,0,1,1)$ in the lean block should prefer the sequence $(1,0,2,1,2)$ to $(2,0,2,1,1)$ in the rich block because the common 0 in the third period has been replaced by the common 2. The two blocks of stimuli provided many equivalent pairs of this type.

The manner in which the two blocks of sequences were constructed also made possible a consistency check for our basic model (Equation 3). The two operations produced for each lean sequence a corresponding rich sequence that had the same amount of total improvement, as measured by Σd_t, and the same total deviation from the reference line, as measured by $\Sigma |d_t|$. For example, starting with the lean sequence $(1,0,0,1,2)$ utility inversion produces a rich sequence $(1,2,2,1,0)$ that has the same deviation terms, d_t, but for a change in sign; formally, utility inversion is a linear transformation of the utility scale, $u(x) \rightarrow au(x) + b$, with $a = -1$, $b = +2$, which, as shown in the Appendix, has the effect of multiplying the deviation terms by the constant a. The second operation, order reversal, then restores the sign of the deviation terms but changes their order, from first to last. Neither operation affects the total absolute deviation of the sequence from its reference line. The effect of these transformations on the deviation terms is summarized as follows:

	(d_1, d_2, d_3, d_4)	Σd_t	$\Sigma |d_t|$
Original lean sequence:			
$(1,0,0,1,2)$	$(-.2, +.6, +1.4, +1.2)$	$+3.0$	$+3.4$
Step 1: Utility inversion:			
$(1,2,2,1,0)$	$(+.2, -.6, -1.4, -1.2)$	-3.0	$+3.4$
Step 2: Order reversal:			
$(0,1,2,2,1)$	$(+1.2, +1.4, +.6, -.2)$	$+3.0$	$+3.4.$

According to the simple model, $\Sigma u_t + \beta\Sigma d_t + a\Sigma |d_t|$, the value of a rich sequence equals the value of its corresponding lean sequence, plus an additive constant, which is the same for all sequences and represents the increase of total utility by two units in the rich set. After recalibration of the rating

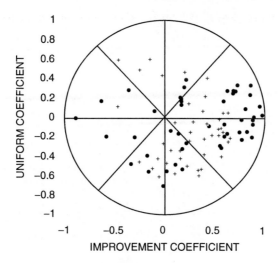

Figure 6. Scatterplot of normalized regression coefficients for all subjects in Study 2.

scale, the nominal ratings assigned to each pair of corresponding lean and rich sequences should therefore be the same.

METHOD

Fifty-seven subjects were recruited at the Museum of Science and Industry in Chicago and were given a ticket to a multimedia presentation (value $4) in exchange for participating. Forty-nine percent of the subjects were male, 55% were married, and the mean age was 33. Four percent did not have a high school diploma, 6% had graduated from high school, 33% had some college, 35% had a college degree, and 20% had earned advanced degrees. The median yearly family income of the sample was again approximately $35,000.

RESULTS

The success of the model and the distribution of parameter estimates were comparable to those obtained in Study 1. Again, most subjects preferred improving sequences (81% and 79% for the lean and rich sets, respectively). The mean goodness of fit, as measured by the correlation between actual and expected values, was .61 for the lean sequence set and .58 for the rich set (i.e. slightly higher than that observed in the first experiment). Figure 6 displays the β and σ values and the goodness of fit for individual subjects in the same format as in Figure 5. The dots represent estimates derived from the lean block of sequences; the plus signs result from the rich block. The correlation between the β coefficient values estimated from the two blocks of data was .64; the correlation for the σ coefficients was .44.

Table 3. Mean Ranks and Ratings for Corresponding Pairs of Sequences in the Lean and Rich Blocks

Lean sequence	Corresponding rich sequence	Mean ranks		Mean ratings	
		Lean	Rich	Lean	Rich
01102	02112	13.3	12.5	7.2	7.1
00112	01122	13.1	11.6	7.2	6.3
01201	12012	12.3	12.4	6.6	6.9
01021	10212	11.7	12.2	6.3	7.0
00211	11022	11.3	11.0	5.9	6.3
02011	11202	10.9	10.1	5.9	5.8
10210	21021	10.3	10.2	5.6	6.1
10012	01221	10.1	10.0	5.5	5.9
11020	20211	10.1	9.1	5.5	5.3
01120	20112	9.7	11.4	5.2	6.4
11002	02211	9.0	8.9	5.0	5.2
12010	21201	8.6	9.2	4.7	5.4
02110	21102	8.5	9.8	4.6	5.8
20110	21120	8.1	7.7	4.6	4.4
20011	11220	6.9	6.5	3.8	3.9
21001	12210	6.5	6.9	3.6	4.1
11200	22011	6.1	6.9	3.4	4.2
21100	22110	4.5	4.6	2.7	2.8

Table 3 presents the mean ranks and ratings for the 18 pairs of corresponding sequences in the two blocks. The results are largely consistent with the simple model. The two best sequences, $(0,1,1,0,2)$ and $(0,2,1,1,2)$, are a corresponding pair, as are the two worst sequences, $(2,1,1,0,0)$ and $(2,2,1,1,0)$. The correlation across corresponding pairs in the two blocks is .95 (for mean ranks) and .92 (for mean ratings). The only two cases in which mean ranks (or ratings) diverge by more than 1.0 involve the two lean sequences $(0,1,1,2,0)$ and $(0,2,1,1,0)$, which both start and end on a bad note. Their corresponding sequences, $(2,0,1,1,2)$ and $(2,1,1,0,2)$, have good outcomes in these salient positions, which may enhance their value.

It is worth noting that the predicted one-to-one relation between the sequences in the lean and rich blocks is not self-evident, outside of the context of our model. For many pairs in the list, for example, $(1,1,0,0,2)$ and $(0,2,2,1,1)$ or $(0,2,0,1,1)$ and $(1,1,2,0,2)$, it is not at all obvious why they should receive similar ratings within their respective blocks. Consequently, the fact that the ratings *do* agree for so many of the pairs is strong evidence in support of the simple model.

Turning now to the separability tests, we examined all pairs of sequences that differed in exactly one period. Given the construction of the lean and rich blocks, each sequence in such a pair would have either a 0 or a 2 in the nonmatching position. It is natural to further divide these pairs into five subgroups, depending on whether the nonmatching weekend occupied the

Table 4. Test of Preferential Independence Mean Rank by Sequence

Residual sequence	Value of first period		Value of second period		Value of third period		Value of fourth period		Value of fifth period	
	0	2	0	2	0	2	0	2	0	2
0112	5.5	**5.9**	4.6	**4.7**			**5.0**	4.1**	**5.3**	4.9
0121					**5.7**	4.8***	**4.7**	3.6***		
0211	4.4	**4.9**	3.9	**3.5***	**5.3**	4.3**			**4.7**	5.1
1012			3.4	**4.6***	5.0	**6.0**				
1021	4.7	**5.4**							**5.5**	4.9
1102	5.6	**5.0***			4.4	**5.0**	3.6	**4.1***	**5.5**	4.1***
1120	**3.7**	3.9			**5.0**	3.3***	2.8	2.5	3.4	**3.8**
1201	**4.8**	4.7							4.7	**4.9**
1210			**3.6**	3.0**	**4.1**	3.5				
2011	**4.2**	3.7*	2.5	**3.1***	3.2	**4.4***			4.3	**4.4**
2101					3.1	**4.5***	3.0	**3.7***		
2110	**3.0**	2.4	**2.9**	2.2**			2.1	**3.0***	2.5	**3.8***

Note. The boldfaced element in each pair should have higher rank according to theory.
* $p < .10$.   ** $p < .05$.   *** $p < .01$.

first, second, third, fourth, or fifth position. The ranks were computed within each of these subdivisions and separately for the lean and the rich blocks.

Separability implies that such matching pairs of sequences should have the same rank within their respective blocks. Violations of independence are thus revealed by a divergence in ranking. This is a conservative test of independence violations because preferential interactions might occur but would not be sufficiently strong to influence ranks.

Table 4 shows the average sequence rankings in a format relevant to our separability tests. (We converted the direct ratings into rankings in an obvious manner, giving sequences with the same rating a tie rank.) The first pair of columns present mean ranks for all sequences that were identical except for the first period, which was either boring (first column) or very enjoyable (second column). The numbers 5.5 and 5.9, for example, represent the mean ranks of sequences $(0,0,1,1,2)$ and $(2,0,1,1,2)$. The mean value of each of these columns is the mean of the ranks 1–8. Likewise, the second pair of columns provides mean ranks for sequences that are identical except in the second period. If independence is satisfied, then the rank of the matched pairs should not be significantly different from one another. The underlined element in each pair is the one that has lower total deviation from its respective reference line (i.e. $\Sigma|d_t|$), and therefore it is also the one that should have higher rank according to our theory.

The data in Table 4 provide strong evidence of preferential interactions of the type predicted by the model. For the 36 pairs of ranks, in 29 cases (or 81%) the difference in ranks has the correct sign, including 13 of the 14 pairs where the difference is significant at the .05 level.

For example, introducing a very pleasurable weekend in the first position of a sequence in which the second weekend is boring, in both cases improves its relative ranking, whereas providing such a weekend when the first weekend is already very enjoyable, lowers its relative ranking. In the second pair of columns, substitution of the high-value outcome in the second period helps the sequence (1,*,0,1,2), which is otherwise very thin in the first four periods, and hurts the sequence (2,*,1,1,0), which adopts a monotonically declining profile when the very enjoyable weekend is inserted. Perhaps the most clear evidence of the importance of spread comes from the third pair of columns, where the middle period is being changed. Independence is violated at the .05 level for six of the eight residual subsequences. Likewise, in the fourth column, there are several sequences that show large interaction effects. For example, the sequence (2,1,1,*,0) becomes maximally declining and poorly spread on the introduction of a boring weekend in the fourth period. The two back-loaded sequences (0,1,1,*,2) and (0,1,2,*,1), however, are both hurt by the introduction of the enjoyable weekend in the fourth position. Finally, in the fifth pair of columns, there are two dramatic interactions, (1,1,0,2,*), which is hurt by the introduction of a very enjoyable weekend in the last period, and (2,1,1,0,*), which is helped.

For a more global test of interaction, we ran five ANOVAs, one for each of the columns summarized in Table 3. The value of the variable period (either 0 or 2) was the first variable, and the pattern of the residual sequence was the second. We also included subject identification as an independent variable, to adjust for differences in subjects' mean ratings.

If independence holds, we would expect to observe main effects for the value of consumption in the first period and for the remaining sequence but should not observe a significant interaction between the two. In other words, a subject's ranking of a sequence should depend on what happens in the first period and what happens in subsequent periods but should not depend on an interaction between the first period and subsequent periods.

The independence hypothesis was, in fact, rejected in every period except the first in which the interaction term bordered on significance, $F(7, 705) = 1.60$, $p < .14$. The interaction effect was strongly significant in the second, $F(5, 517) = 5.34$, $p < .0001$, third, $F(7, 705) = 6.92$, $p < .0001$, fourth, $F(5, 517) = 7.00$, $p < .0001$, and fifth, $F(7, 705) = 3.2$, $p < .003$, periods.

DISCUSSION

Several general conclusions emerge from these analyses. It appears that for sequences of outcomes, negative time preference is the rule rather than the exception. In the two studies just presented, more than 75% of the subjects exhibited a desire for improvement. We also observed strong violations of temporal independence, which indicates that any model that excludes inter-actions, such as an additive utility model, will miss important aspects of preferences.

Finally, we found that our two-parameter model did a good job of explaining individual's preferences toward sequences of outcomes. It did better than the discounting formula, even if the discount rate was allowed to be negative. As shown in the second study, it accurately predicted which sequences would receive the same rank in separate choice sets.

At the same time, however, we acknowledge several limitations in our work. First, there are subjective considerations that may be important to individuals but that are excluded from the model. For example, the fact that our model tended to predict overly high ratings of sequences with two successive boring periods suggests that our spread measure was not sufficiently sensitive to such interactions between adjacent periods. The under-prediction of the sequence (1,0,2,0,1)—compare Table 2—may indicate a premium for symmetry and so forth.

Second, our studies involved outcomes that were all gains; it is an open question how well the model generalizes to sequences involving losses or combinations of gains and losses. It is possible, for example, that people will prefer to isolate a single gain in a sequence of losses or a single loss in a sequence of gains, a pattern that would not be consistent with our model.

Third, our sequences were all permutations of a common set of outcomes over a constant number of periods of equal duration. Varey and Kahneman (in press) argued that preferences tend to be insensitive to the duration of a sequence and observed violations of dominance that stem, in part, from this insensitivity. This important finding needs to be replicated and, if robust, addressed theoretically.

Fourth, we did not address whether individuals would actually stick to the choice of an improving utility sequence when opportunities to change their original choice appeared along the way. The choice of an improving sequence represents a decision to defer gratification, and we know from research and from personal experience that such decisions are easier to entertain than to carry out. Countervailing temptations arise partly from the shape of the psychological discount function, which places disproportionate weight on immediate satisfaction (Ainslie, 1975), and partly from other factors, such as sensory contact with rewards (Mischel, 1974). Mischel drew a useful distinction between *delay choice*—choice between immediate and delayed alternatives—and *delay of gratification*, which refers to the implementation of such delay choices. He showed that implementing an initial decision to delay is not conflict free if the immediate reward remains available during the waiting period. Consequently, although individuals may prefer sequences that improve, in reality they may succumb to the manifold temptations of the moment. Repeated lapses of this type will, of course, in the long run produce a declining utility sequence, precisely the opposite of that which is desired.

However, individuals are not helpless in the face of their urges. They may resort to self-control strategies (Ainslie, 1975; Schelling, 1984), cognitive restructuring (Ainslie, 1975; Mischel, 1974), and raw willpower (Hoch & Loewenstein, 1991). Many social institutions and arrangements provide further support for delay of gratification. These include social security, retirement plans, term insurance, Christmas and dieting clubs (Thaler & Shefrin, 1981), and traditionally increasing wage trajectories (Frank, in press; Loewenstein & Sicherman, 1991). All of these combine to help people avoid declining utility profiles.

16.5. Conclusion

Understanding choice between sequences is important because planning for the future invariably requires one to choose between alternative sequences of outcomes. Taking a vacation now may forestall a future vacation; increasing one's spending in the present may force reductions in future expenditures; and dieting in the present is intended to produce delayed rewards, whereas binge eating entails delayed costs. In each of these cases, a given decision has multiple consequences that are spread out over time.

Previous empirical work on time preference has focused almost entirely on the tradeoff that arises when two outcomes of different values and occurring at different times are compared. The tacit premise has been that such judgments will reveal an individual's "raw" time preference, from which one can then derive preferences over more complex objects (e.g. retirement plans, intertemporal income profiles, etc.). This view we now know is fundamentally incorrect. The empirical evidence presented in this article, in conjunction with the related work of Frank (in press), Loewenstein and Sicherman (1991), Ross and Simonson (1991), and Varey and Kahneman (in press), shows that as soon as an intertemporal tradeoff is embedded in the context of two alternative *sequences* of outcomes, the psychological perspective, or "frame," shifts, and individuals become more farsighted, often wishing to postpone the better outcome until the end. The same person who prefers a good dinner sooner rather than later, if given a choice between two explicitly formulated sequences, one consisting of a good dinner *followed* by an indifferent one, the other of the indifferent dinner *followed* by the good one, may well prefer the latter alternative. Sequences of outcomes that decline in value are greatly disliked, indicating a negative rate of time preference.

The sensitivity of intertemporal decisions to choice representation has important policy implications. Efforts to lengthen time perspectives have generally focused on material inducements. For example, attempts to increase the personal savings of Americans have typically involved tax deductions on certain types of interest income. Although not denigrating such efforts, our research suggests that there may be other, more effective and less costly methods of altering time perspective. Such methods can take the form of media and educational campaigns that express decisions as sequences rather than as individual decisions. Alternatively, policymakers could bolster and expand on the institutions that already exist that implicitly or explicitly present decision makers with choices between sequences.

The significant difference in preferences observed in intertemporal choices involving single outcomes and sequences challenges the claim often made that groups and individuals differ in their fundamental attitude toward the future. It is plausible that such variations are not attributable to any fundamental attitude toward the future but instead reflect differences in the way that options are perceived. Any factor, whether personal or situational, that causes intertemporal choices to fragment and to be perceived as a series of individual decisions will tend to induce high positive time discounting. Likewise, factors that cause such decisions to be internally "framed" as sequences will promote low and even negative time discounting.

References

Ainslie, G. (1975). Specious reward: A behavioral theory of impulsiveness and impulse control. *Psychological Bulletin, 82*, 463–509.

Barnes, O., & Barnes, L. W. (1964). Choice of delay of inevitable shock. *Journal of Abnormal Social Psychology, 68*, 669–672.

Bell, D. E. (1977). A utility function for time streams having inter-period dependencies. *Operations Research, 25*, 448–458.

Bordley, R. F. (1986). Satiation and habit persistence (or the dieter's dilemma). *Journal of Economic Theory, 38*, 178–184.

Carlsmith, J. M. (1962). Strength of expectancy: Its determinants and effects. Unpublished doctoral dissertation, Harvard University, Cambridge, MA.

Carson, R. T., Horowitz, J. K., & Machina, M. J. (1987). Discounting mortality risks. Unpublished manuscript.

Elster, J. (1985). Weakness of the will and the free-rider problem. *Economics and Philosophy, 1*, 231–265.

Elster, J., & Loewenstein, G. (in press). Utility from memory and anticipation. In G. Loewenstein & J. Elster (Eds.), *Choice over time*. New York: Russell Sage Foundation.

Epstein, L. G., & Hynes, J. A. (1983). The rate of time preference and dynamic economic analysis. *Journal of Political Economy, 91*, 611–635.

Frank, R. (1989). Frames of reference and the quality of life. *American Economic Review, 79*, 80–85.

Frank, R. (in press). Frames of reference and the intertemporal wage profile. In G. Loewenstein & J. Elster (Eds.), *Choice over time*. New York: Russell Sage Foundation.

Gilboa, I. (1989). Expectation and variation in multi-period decisions. *Econometrica, 57,* 1153–1169.

Helson, H. (1964). *Adaptation-level theory: An experimental and systematic approach to behavior.* New York: Harper & Row.

Hoch, S., & Loewenstein, G. (1991). Time-inconsistent preferences and consumer self-control. *Journal of Consumer Research, 17,* 1–16.

Horowitz, J. K. (1988). Discounting money payoffs: An experimental analysis. Unpublished manuscript.

Hsee, C. K., & Abelson, R. P. (1991). The velocity relation: Satisfaction as a function of the first derivative of outcome over time. *Journal of Personality and Social Psychology, 60,* 341–347.

Hsee, C. K., Abelson, R. P., & Salovey, P. (1991). The relative weighting of position and velocity in satisfaction. *Psychological Science, 2,* 263–266.

Kahneman, D., & Tversky, A. (1979). Prospect theory: An analysis of decision under risk. *Econometrica, 47,* 363–391.

Koopmans, T. C. (1960). Stationary ordinal utility and impatience. *Econometrica, 28,* 287–309.

Koopmans, T. C., Diamond, P. A., & Williamson, R. E. (1964). Stationary utility and time perspective. *Econometrica, 46,* 82–100.

Linville, P., & Fischer, G. (1991). Preferences for combining or separating events: A social application of prospect theory and mental accounting. *Journal of Personality and Social Psychology, 60,* 5–23.

Loewenstein, G. (1987). Anticipation and the valuation of delayed consumption. *Economic Journal, 97,* 666–684.

Loewenstein, G., & Sicherman, N. (1991). Do workers prefer increasing wage profiles? *Journal of Labor Economics, 9,* 67–84.

Meyer, R. F. (1976). Preferences over time. In R. L. Keeney & H. Raiffa (Eds.), *Decisions with multiple objectives: Preferences and value trade-offs* (pp. 473–485). New York: Wiley.

Meyer, R. F. (1977). State dependent time preference. In D. Bell, R. L. Keeney, & H. Raiffa (Eds.), *Conflicting objectives in decision* (pp. 232–244). New York: Wiley.

Miller, N., & Campbell, D. T. (1959). Recency and primacy in persuasion as a function of the timing of speeches and measurements. *Journal of Abnormal and Social Psychology, 59,* 1–9.

Mischel, W. (1974). Processes in delay of gratification. In L. Berkowitz (Ed.), *Advances in experimental social psychology* (Vol. 7, pp. 249–292). San Diego, CA: Academic Press.

Prelec, D., & Loewenstein, G. (1991). Decision-making over time and under uncertainty: A common approach. *Management Science, 37,* 770–786.

Ross, W. T., Jr., & Simonson, I. (1991). Evaluations of pairs of experiences: A preference for happy endings. *Journal of Behavioral Decision Making, 4,* 273–282.

Samuelson, P. (1937). A note on measurement of utility. *Review of Economic Studies, 4,* 155–161.

Schelling, T. (1984). Self-command in practice, in policy, and in a theory of rational choice. *American Economic Review, 74,* 1–11.

Thaler, R., & Johnson, E. (1990). Gambling with the house money and trying to break even: The effects of prior outcomes on risky choice. *Management Science, 36,* 643–660.

Thaler, R., & Shefrin, H. (1981). An economic theory of self-control. *Journal of Political Economy, 89*, 392–410.

Tversky, A., & Griffin, D. (1991). Endowment and contrast in judgments of well-being. In R. J. Zeckhauser (Ed.), *Strategy and choice* (pp. 297–318). Cambridge, MA: MIT Press.

Varey, C., & Kahneman, D. (in press). The integration of aversive experiences over time: Normative considerations and lay intuitions. *Journal of Behavioral Decision Making.*

Appendix

To show that the two forms of the model are equivalent, we start with Equation 6 and substitute for d_t^+ and d_t^- (from Equation 4):

$$V(X) = \sum_{t=1}^{n} u_t + \sum_{t=1}^{n-1} \sigma_t^+ d_t^+ + \sum_{t=1}^{n-1} \sigma_t^- d_t^-$$

$$= \sum_{t=1}^{n} u_t + \sum_{t=1}^{n-1} \left(\frac{\sigma_t^+ - \sigma_t^-}{2} \right) d_t + \sum_{t=1}^{n-1} \left(\frac{\sigma_t^+ - \sigma_t^-}{2} \right) |d_t| .$$

Substituting for d_t and σ_t,

$$d_t = \frac{t}{n} \sum_{i=1}^{n} u_i - \sum_{i=1}^{t} u_i , \qquad \sigma_t = \frac{\sigma_t^+ + \sigma_t^-}{2},$$

yields the second form of the model (Equation 7),

$$V(X) = \sum_{t=1}^{n} u_t + \sum_{t=1}^{n-1} \left(\frac{\sigma_t^+ - \sigma_t^-}{2} \right) \left(\frac{t}{n} \sum_{i=1}^{n} u_i - \sum_{i=1}^{t} u_i \right) + \sum_{t=1}^{n-1} \sigma_t |d_t|$$

$$= \sum_{t=1}^{n} w_t u_t + \sum_{t=1}^{n-1} \sigma_t |d_t| ,$$

with the weights equal to

$$w_t = 1 + \sum_{t=1}^{n-1} \frac{i}{n} \left(\frac{\sigma_t^+ - \sigma_t^-}{2} \right) + \sum_{i=t}^{n-1} \left(\frac{\sigma_i^+ - \sigma_i^-}{2} \right).$$

The first two terms do not depend on the period t. Therefore, the difference between adjacent weights simplifies to

$$w_t - w_{t+1} = - \sum_{i=t}^{n-1} \left(\frac{\sigma_i^+ - \sigma_i^-}{2} \right) + \sum_{i=t+1}^{n-1} \left(\frac{\sigma_t^+ - \sigma_t^-}{2} \right)$$

$$= \sigma_t^+ - \sigma_t^-$$

To check that $u(x)$ is an interval scale, we first assess the impact of the substitution of $u_t^*(x_i) = au(x_i) + b$ for $u(x_i)$ on the following deviation terms:

$$d_t^* = \frac{t}{n} \sum_{i=1}^{n} (au_i + b) - \sum_{i=1}^{t} (au_t + b)$$

$$= a\frac{t}{n} \sum_{i=1}^{n} u_i + tb - a\sum_{i=1}^{t} u_i - tb$$

$$= a\left(\frac{t}{n} \sum_{i=1}^{n} u_t - \sum_{i=1}^{t} u_i\right)$$

$$= ad_t.$$

After the transformation, the value function (Equation 7) appears as

$$V^*(X) = \sum_{t=1}^{n} w_t(au_t + b) + \sum_{t=1}^{n-1} \sigma_t a\,|d_t|$$

$$= a(\sum_{t=1}^{n} w_t u_t + \sum_{t=1}^{n-1} \sigma_t\,|d_t|) + b\sum_{t=1}^{n} w_t$$

$$= aV(X) + b\sum_{t=1}^{n} w_t,$$

which ranks sequences in the same way as does $V(X)$.

17

The Red and the Black: Mental Accounting of Savings and Debt

Dražen Prelec and George Loewenstein

This was long my favorite of my own papers (displaced only recently by a working paper titled "Animal Spirits"). The paper introduces a variety of ideas that I think are really important for understanding consumer behavior including that people experience pain when they pay for things and that this pain depends on a variety of factors, including most importantly whether payment for an item occurs before, during, or after consumption.

I wish I could take credit for the model, but it's Dražen's brainchild. My main contribution was to reject earlier models that weren't as true to the psychology and to say "that's it" when I felt that Dražen got it right. I may have also contributed the central notion of the pain of paying. Dražen and I often joke that I'm the tightwad in the partnership and he's the spendthrift.

The model we propose in the paper has numerous implications—for why consumers like to prepay for things, why they like zero marginal cost payment plans, why it's often better to pay for things like parks via taxes rather than user fees, and so on. It also provides a novel account of individual differences in spending and saving behavior based on differences in the pain of paying rather than differences in discount rates.

In subsequent work, Dražen and I have been pursuing some of the insights from the paper. In work with Brian Knutson, Scott Rick, and Elliott Wimmer, we scanned people's brains while they make decisions about whether to purchase items (to the best of our knowledge, the first study to examine the neural basis of purchasing).[1] We first expose subjects to the items they can buy, and the "reward centers" of their brains activate in proportion to how much they like the item. Then, they are informed of the price, and, consistent with the Red and Black model, brain systems associated

---

[1] Knutson, B., Rick, S., Wimmer, G. E., Prelec, D., and Loewenstein, G., (2006). 'Neural Predictors of Purchases,' *Neuron* 53(1), 147–156.

with processing of pain light up. Best, we can then predict whether or not they choose to purchase based on the relative strength of these two activation levels.

In other work, Scott Rick, Cynthia Cryder, and I have been exploring in much greater detail the differences in emotions and behavior between spendthrifts and tightwads.[2] We find that tightwads are emotionally driven to not spend, and have to exert willpower to spend, whereas spendthrifts are emotionally driven to spend, and have to exert willpower to not spend. As this account predicts, when we induce both groups to become more deliberative, which we do by playing sad music while they are deciding whether to buy, the tightwads spend more and the spendthrifts spend less.

A depressing dimension of the model is its implications for the effects of poverty. The standard economic model predicts that, while rich people enjoy their consumption more in total, poor people enjoy it more on the margin, because they are consuming things that, on average, they value more highly. The model laid out in the paper, however, suggests that this might not be accurate because, to regulate their spending, low-income individuals need to crank up their pain of paying. If poor people find it especially painful to pay for the things they purchase, then their net pleasure from making a purchase—their pleasure from the purchase minus the pain of paying—may be lower than it would be for a more affluent consumer. If valid, this logic adds yet another argument for substantial redistribution of income: Increasing the incomes of the poor will not only allow them to consume more, but will, by muting the pain of paying, increase their enjoyment of the additional consumption.

[2] Rick, S., Cryder, C., and Loewenstein, G. (2008). 'Spendthrifts and Tightwads,' Journal of Consumer Research.

The Red and the Black: Mental Accounting of Savings and Debt*

Dražen Prelec and George Loewenstein

"Now you can call your loved ones and not think about how much it costs."

Billboard advertisement for long-distance telephone debit card

"Hotels are twice as good when you pay half as much."

Web advertisement for discount hotel rates

17.1. Introduction

We start with a brief story:

Last year, just after his 25th college reunion, Jones bought a slightly used red two-seater, financing the purchase with a standard car loan. Although the car performed well enough, he found that suitable driving occasions were less frequent than he had anticipated, and that the thrill of recreating the college years dissipated quickly. The monthly payments became regular reminders of what was in truth a rather expensive indulgence: It was hard to justify each bill with the pleasures of an occasional weekend drive. After a bout of worrying and procrastination, he decided to pay off the entire loan. Writing the check was painful but produced relief, and restored some of the pleasures of driving. Now that he owned the car, he was no longer concerned with driving a certain amount each month, and let suitable occasions arise spontaneously. He even began to enjoy how the thing looked in the driveway....

In the traditional economic analysis of consumer choice, consumers are assumed to finance expenditures so as to minimize the present value of payments, perhaps making allowance for liquidity and convenience. The

* Reprinted by permission. © 1998 Informs. Prelec, D. and Loewenstein, G. 'The red and the black: mental accounting of savings and debt.' Marketing Science. 17(1): 4–28, the Institute for Operations Research and Management Sciences, 7240 Parkway Drive, Suite 310, Hanover, Maryland 21706, USA.

psychological reality of payment decisions is more complicated, as suggested by our story. The first and perhaps most obvious complication is that debt is unpleasant. It feels good to be rid of debt, and especially good to be rid of debt for a disappointing purchase such as the underused sports car. The rationale for such a feeling is somewhat unclear, since paying off the loan doesn't diminish the real opportunity cost of purchasing the car: However he pays for the car, Jones has less wealth, which will inevitably require some sacrifice in future consumption.

Second, according to the economic view, the costs and benefits of paying off the loan should be a purely financial matter, involving interest rates, liquidity concerns, and so on. In this example, however, a paper transaction—drawing down other accounts to clear a loan—changes Jones' enjoyment of the car, indicating that consumption utility has been affected by the composition of assets on the balance sheet.

Third, it is puzzling why Jones finds it painful to dispose of the entire loan with a single payment if that very action will bring relief. It is almost as if the discontent over the purchase is somehow collected and discharged through the brief but painful action of writing the check.

The feelings described in this example illustrate a systematic interference between the pleasures derived from consumption and the magnitude and timing of payments. Thinking about the cost of a purchase can undermine the pleasure one derives from it. Thinking about the benefits derived from a purchase can blunt the pain of making payments. These two-way hedonic interactions between payments and consumption fall outside the scope of traditional economic models. Nonetheless, they are important for understanding the financial behavior of consumers.

Our objective in this paper is to provide a theoretical account of these payment-consumption interactions that can both explain the observed patterns of behavior and give insights into designing payment mechanisms for products or services. Building on an idea first proposed by Richard Thaler (1980, 1985), we postulate that people establish mental accounts that create symbolic linkages between specific acts of consumption and specific payments. Acts of consumption and financial transactions call mental accounts to mind, which generates pleasure or pain depending on whether the accounts are in the red or in the black. For example, paying off the car in our story provides relief because it puts the "car account" in the black, thus ensuring that subsequent driving experiences are freed from thoughts about payment.

Our model makes a variety of predictions that are at variance with those of standard economic formulations. Contrary to the traditional notion that consumers prefer to consume now and spend later, our model predicts strong *debt aversion*, which supports (in some cases) a preference to pay for consumption in advance. Contrary to notions of economic efficiency, which dictate that consumers should pay for what they consume at the margin, our model predicts a preference for flatrate pricing, such as unlimited Internet access at a fixed monthly price, even if it involves paying more for the same usage. Other predictions deal with differences in spending patterns with cash, charge, or credit purchases, and with preferences for earmarking saving and debt accounts to specific purchases.

17.2. Preferences for Prepayment

What would economic analysis have to say about Jones' dilemmas? In a simple treatment of the purchase decision problem, the sports car purchase would be represented by a sequence of dated utilities (benefits) $\{u_b, b \geq 0\}$, and the loan by a sequence of dated payments (costs), $\{p_c, c \geq 0\}$.[1] The decision whether to purchase the car would rest on whether the discounted present value of the utility stream exceeded the discounted present value of loan payments,

$$\text{Buy if}: \sum_{b \geq 0} \delta^b u_b - \lambda \sum_{c \geq 0} \rho^c p_c > 0. \tag{1}$$

The parameter δ is the discount rate applicable to utility from consumption, ρ is the discount rate that applies to delayed monetary outlays ($0 < \delta, \rho \leq 1$), and λ is a Lagrange multiplier that, when the consumer optimizes, is equal to the marginal utility of money.

Interpreted as a descriptive model, Equation (1) makes a number of predictions about financing preferences. First, consumers should prefer to make payments later rather than sooner, as later payments have lower present value. Second, choice of financing (e.g. saving versus borrowing) should not be influenced by the type of product being purchased but only by the criterion of minimizing the second term in Equation (1). Both predictions have surface plausibility, but one can readily construct choice problems that reveal opposite intuitions. Consider Items 1A and 1B below. In each case, a decision needs to be made whether to finance an expenditure sooner or later, e.g.:

Item 1A
Imagine that you are planning a one-week vacation to the Caribbean, six months from now. The vacation will cost $1,200. You have two options for financing the vacation:

---

[1] For example, if Jones made two $200 payments prior to acquiring the car, three payments of $200 while driving the car, and paid off the car with a final payment of $15,000, then $p = \{200,200,200,200,200,15K,0,0,\ldots\}$, and if he derives one unit of utility per month of car usage, then $u = \{0,0,1,1,1,1,1,1,\ldots\}$.

Table 1. Percentage of Subjects Who Prefer to Pre-pay (Item 1) or to Delay a Salary Payment (Item 2)

Item	Within subjects		Between subjects (first question only)	
	%	N	%	N
Prefer to prepay				
1A Vacation	63*	89	60*	31
1B Washer-dryer	24	89	16	30
1C Misc. expenses	70*	89	67*	30
Prefer to delay salary				
1D Work (brief)	60*	89	57*	45
1E Work (long)	66*	89	76*	46

Note: The order of questions was varied across subjects. The right side of Table 1 reports only the choices of first encounter of a payment question or a salary question (i.e. the data conform to a between-subjects design). The left panel includes all responses.

* Significantly different from the percentages in 1B, $p < .02$.

A. Six monthly payments of $200 each during the six months before the vacation.

B. Six monthly payments of $200 each during the six months beginning after you return.

When this question was posed to 91 visitors to the Phipps Conservatory in Pittsburgh, 60% of respondents opted for the earlier payments, despite an implicit interest penalty of about $50 (results summarized in Table 1).

The preference for prepaying does not hold for all types of expenditures, however:

Item 1B

Imagine that, six months from now, you are planning to purchase a clothes washer and dryer for your new residence. The two machines together will cost $1,200. You have two options for financing the washer/dryer:

A. Six monthly payments of $200 each during the six months before the washer and dryer arrive.

B. Six monthly payments of $200 each during the six months beginning after the washer and dryer arrive.

Here, 84% of subjects prefer to postpone payments until the units arrive (Table 1). Such a reversal of preference in choosing between financing options is a robust phenomenon, holding both between and within subjects.[2] It is also consistent with the findings of Hirst, Joyce, and Schadewald (1992), who describe several studies in which subjects show a preference for matching the duration of a loan with the life of the durable.

---

[2] Forty-three percent of subjects preferred the early vacation and late washer/dryer payments; 3% displayed the opposite pattern.

Table 1 reports two other variations on this question, designed to rule out two possible interpretations of debt aversion. In Item 1C, the six payments of $200 were described as covering miscellaneous living expenses for a brief and fully anticipated period of unemployment. The fact that the majority of subjects still prefer prepayment shows that the debt aversion is not restricted to the category of luxury purchases, such as the vacation in 1A. In Items 1D and 1E, the six $200 transactions were described as salary receipts for an "intensive weekend of work" (Item 1D) or "a few hours of work each weekend for the next six months" (Item 1E). The receipts could be collected before doing the work or afterwards. In both cases, the majority of subjects declined advance payment. This shows that the preferences in 1A and 1C are not caused by a simple desire to expedite financial transactions, whether payments or receipts.

Taken together, the majority choices in Table 1 reveal a form of debt aversion, where debt is construed as either consuming something before paying for it or getting advance payment for future work. Such preferences are consistent with our own earlier research (Loewenstein and Prelec 1993), which showed that people generally like sequences of events that improve over time and dislike sequences that deteriorate (see also Hsee and Abelson 1991; Kahneman et al. 1993; Loewenstein 1987).

Two distinct motives might incline a person to prepay for a product. One might hope to enjoy it unencumbered by payment concerns, or, alternatively, one might want to avoid the unpleasant experience of paying for consumption that has already been enjoyed. When we probe our subjects' intuitions on this matter we find that both motives are recognized, but their force varies according to the nature of the product. In a different survey we asked 60 visitors to the botanical gardens to consider two men who had financed a purchase (a one-week cruise in the Bahamas or a washer-dryer combination package) either with six monthly *pre*payments (Mr. A) or six payments beginning after the purchase (Mr. B). Subjects judged which of the two persons felt better when making the payments, and which felt better while consuming the good or service, in the case of each purchase. There was also an indifference option.

The evaluations in 2A (see Table 2) demonstrate that the attractiveness of vacation prepayment is derived from the consumption experience: People think that a prepaid vacation is more pleasurable than one that must be financed after returning. The washer-dryer unit (2B) yields no significant hedonic differentials, which means that the financial advantages of later payments can become decisive. Apparently, people are able to distinguish between the hedonic impact of payments on consumption and of consumption on payments, and these impacts are not exactly symmetric.[3] The theory

---

[3] Leaving out the indifference option produces more pronounced preferences for prepayment and more symmetric attitudes toward payments and consumption. In a different survey of 60 visitors to the Phipps Conservatory, a large majority (92%) judged that they would enjoy

Table 2. Hedonic Evaluation of Paying for Products Before or Afterward

	Payments	Consumption
2A Vacation	−.26	−.79*
	(.21)	(.12)
2B Washer-Dryer	.19	−.19
	(.21)	(.19)

Note: The answers were encoded −1 (prepayment better), 0 (no difference), +1 (postpayment better). Hence, negative means indicate paying early is better. $n = 19$–21 in all cells.
*Significantly different from zero, $p < .05$

that we develop will therefore have to accommodate both the impact of payment on consumption and the reciprocal impact of consumption on payment.

17.3. A "Double-Entry" Mental Accounting Theory

The purpose of these examples has been to reinforce the intuition that thoughts of payment can undermine the pleasures of consumption and, conversely, that the pain of making payments can be buffered by thoughts of the benefits that these payments finance. We will now introduce a "double-entry" mental accounting theory, in which one set of entries records the "net" utility derived from consumption after subtracting the disutility of associated payments, and the other set records the "net" disutility of payments after subtracting the utility of associated consumption.

Each time a consumer engages in an episode of consumption, we assume she asks herself: "How much is this pleasure costing me?" The answer to this question is the *imputed cost* of consumption. This imputed cost is "real" in the sense that it actually detracts from consumption pleasure. For some types of purchases, these costs may be highly salient, while for others they may only dimly impinge on consciousness.

Figure 1 illustrates the notion of imputed cost with the example of a consumer who finances a one-week vacation with six monthly payments, three before the vacation and three after. The six downward arrows represent the six payments and the upward facing bar represents the utility derived from the vacation. If the vacation were free, then the consumer's enjoyment of the vacation would equal the full size of the bar. However, thinking about the costs reduces the quality of the vacation experience. The top section of the

---

a Caribbean vacation more if the vacation was prepaid, and an almost as large majority (82%) judged that making the payments would also be less unpleasant if done before leaving.

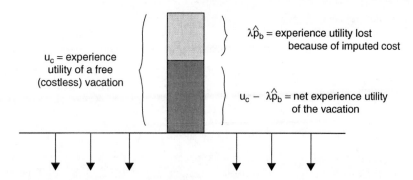

$\lambda \hat{p}_b$ = experience utility lost
because of imputed cost

u_c = experience
utility of a free
(costless) vacation

$u_c - \lambda \hat{p}_b$ = net experience utility
of the vacation

Figure 1. Net Experience Utility Expressed as a Difference Between the Utility of a Costless (Free) Vacation and the Imputed Cost

bar represents the "utility lost" from the imputed vacation cost. The bottom section of the bar represents the utility that remains after subtracting imputed cost, which is the actual, or "experienced," utility derived from the vacation (Kahneman and Varey 1991).

In formal terms, experienced utility is the utility of consumption when free (u_b) minus the imputed cost ($\hat{p}_b$) multiplied by a payment/utility conversion parameter, λ:

$$u_b - \lambda \hat{p}_b. \tag{2a}$$

Like the Lagrange multiplier in the conventional formulation (Equation (1)), λ here reflects the marginal utility of money, which in turn depends on an individual's financial situation. For example, a major economic loss would increase λ, which would diminish subsequent utility from consumption.

The critical difference between λp from Equation (1) and $\lambda \hat{p}$ is that the former is a decision criterion while the latter is the actual psychological burden of payment. In the standard formulation, the consumer should buy if $u - \lambda p > 0$. Provided he does buy, and barring any miscalculation about the quality of the product, his enjoyment of consumption will equal u. The cost—in utility terms—of the purchase is only realized in the future, when some other bit of consumption is canceled. In our model, however, the utility of consumption is actually reduced by its imputed cost, $\lambda \hat{p}$; "net experienced utility" is equal to $u - \lambda \hat{p}$.

The other half of the accounting system records the disutility of making payments. Just as utility from consumption is undermined by the disutility of making payments, the disutility of making payments is buffered by the *imputed benefit* derived from each payment. In this case, the experienced disutility of making payment (p_c) equals the disutility of the payment if there were no associated benefits – λp_c, compensated by the imputed benefits of this particular payment $(\hat{u}_c)$:[4]

$$\hat{u}_c - \lambda p_c. \tag{2b}$$

The consumer's mental accounting rules determine how these imputed costs and benefits depend on the magnitude and timing of consumption.

17.3.1. *The Purchase Criterion*

The decision whether to purchase a product will depend on the antici-pated sequence of net consumption and payment utilities, as defined by Equations (2a) and (2b). We assume that future net utilities are discounted according to some time discount function, which is possibly but not nec-essarily exponential. In the case of exponential (i.e., compound) discount-ing, the time discount factors would be given by: $\delta_b = \delta^b$, and $\rho_c = \rho^c$. We assume also that consumers are *loss averse* with respect to individual con-sumption and payment events, so that events that have negative net utility are given disproportionate weight at the moment of choice (Tversky and Kahneman 1992). Loss aversion is captured by a parameter, $\mu, 0 \le \mu \le 1$, which creates a gap between the decision weights of positive and negative experiences:[5]

Loss-averse decision weights:

$$\begin{cases} (1 - \mu) \text{ if}: u_b - \lambda \hat{p}_b \ge 0, \text{ or}: \hat{u}_c - \lambda p_c \ge 0, \\ (1 + \mu) \text{ if}: u_b - \lambda \hat{p}_b < 0, \text{ or}: \hat{u}_c - \lambda p_c < 0. \end{cases} \tag{3}$$

These two assumptions, loss aversion and discounting, combine to give a decision criterion:

$$\text{Buy if}: \sum_{b \ge 0} (1 + \mu)\delta_b(u_b - \lambda \hat{p}_b) + \sum_{c \ge 0} (1 + \mu)\rho_c(\hat{u}_c - \lambda p_c) > 0. \tag{4}$$

---

[4] The term $(\hat{u}_c - \lambda p_c)$ may be compared to Thaler's (1985) "acquisition utility," which is a function of the difference between the "value equivalent" for the purchased product and the actual price paid (p_c). Because $\hat{u}_c/\lambda$ is a sort of money equivalent of the benefits imputed to payment p_c the term $(\hat{u}_c - \lambda p_c) = \lambda(\hat{u}_c/\lambda - p_c)$ resembles acquisition utility, at least in the special case when the purchase is made with a single payment and the benefits imputed to that payment equal the full utility of the product, $\hat{u} = u$. In Thaler's theory, acquisition utility is one of the two components of the utility of a purchase, the other component being "transactions utility," which is driven by a comparison of actual price paid with a fair or "reference" price.

[5] The loss-averse weights in Equation (3) can be derived from a penalty function on absolute deviations from zero, $f(x) = x - \mu|x|$, applied to the terms $x = (u - \lambda \hat{p})$, and $x = (\hat{u} - \lambda p)$. The impact of loss aversion, holding all else equal, is to increase the attractiveness of consumption-payment schedules for which imputed costs match the utility stream, and for which the imputed benefits match the payment stream. Schedules where the temporal payments profile tracks the temporal consumption profile will generally exhibit this kind of matching.

To briefly review the model: Each term in the Summation (4) refers to an anticipated experience.[6] The experience has a focal event, either consumption or payment, and a hedonic evaluation. Experiences that are further away from the decision point are discounted ($\delta, \rho < 1$), as are positive, relative to negative, experiences ($\mu > 0$). When there is no loss aversion ($\mu = 0$), no mental accounting ($\hat{p} = \hat{u} = 0$), and discounting is exponential, then we are left with the net present value purchase criterion, Equation (1).

17.3.2. Imputed Costs and Benefits

So far we have said nothing about the mental accounting terms, which are at the heart of the model. When both consumption and payment are brief and simultaneous—e.g. when we pay \$75 for a restaurant dinner—then consumption (i.e. of the dinner) is the only benefit that could be imputed to the payment, and the payment (i.e. the \$75) is the only cost that could be imputed to consumption. Few important purchases are this straightforward. What happens in more complex situations, when there are multiple payments and when the purchase benefits extend over time? In the car example, the imputed costs of a weekend drive may depend on any and all costs associated with car ownership: loan payments, operating costs, insurance, and so forth. A general expression for the imputed cost, $\hat{p}_b$, would indicate what fraction, w_{bc}^p, of payment at time c (p_c) is "applied to" consumption at time b:

$$\hat{p}_b = \sum_c w_{bc}^p p_{c'} \tag{5a}$$

A similar sum would indicate what fraction, w_{cb}^u, of consumption utility at $b(u_b)$ is applied to payment at time c:

$$\hat{u}_c = \sum_b w_{cb}^u u_b. \tag{5b}$$

The entire set of coefficients $\{w_{bc}^p, w_{cb}^u\}$ in (5ab) constitutes a person's mental accounting system. It specifies how particular costs are matched with particular benefits, and how this in turn affects anticipated feelings (Equations (2ab)) and choices (Equation (4)).

We now describe three mental accounting assumptions that constrain the general form of (5ab). The first assumption, which we call *prospective accounting*, addresses the question of how imputed costs and benefits depend on the timing of consumption and payments. The second, *prorating* assumption, is a simple amortization rule for dividing up a single payment over multiple consumption events, or a single utility over multiple payments. The third, *coupling* assumption, allows for imperfect (i.e. less than 100%) imputation of costs and benefits.

---

[6] In practice, actual experienced utility may deviate from anticipated (i.e. predicted) utility in systematic ways (Loewenstein and Schkade forthcoming).

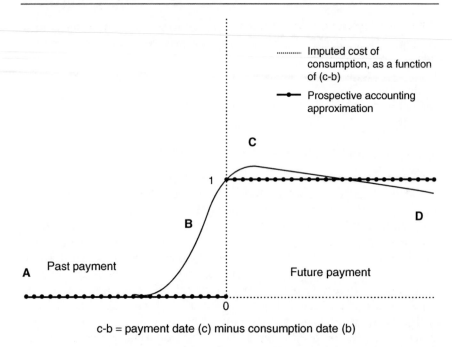

c-b = payment date (c) minus consumption date (b)

Figure 2. Showing How the Imputed Cost of Consumption Depends on the Time of Payment

17.3.3. *Prospective Accounting*

The survey results in Table 2, showing how the enjoyment of a vacation is affected by the timing of payments, would be consistent with a mental accounting rule that fully recognizes future payments $(c > b)$ and largely "writes off" past ones $(c < b)$. The vacation is enjoyed more if prepaid because it feels "free." Likewise, payments would be particularly onerous if the vacation had already taken place, because it would feel as if one were paying for nothing. We believe that the relationship between imputed cost and the time of payment looks like the dotted line in Figure 2. If the vacation has been prepaid a long time in advance (point "A"), then the imputed cost is essentially zero and the vacation feels as if it were free. If the vacation has been recently prepaid (point "B"), then the imputed cost is no longer negligible though it is still relatively small (see Gourville and Soman 1997). The imputed cost is highest if payment is due right after the vacation (point "C"), and then declines gradually as the payment is pushed off into the distant future (point "D").

Although the conjectured relationship in Figure 2 is nonlinear and includes both future and past events, for analytical convenience we will approximate it by a step function, having value zero for past events and a constant value for all future ones (shaded line in the figure). This prospective accounting assumption combines two separate simplifications. First, the impact of past events is zero, as if past events were simply deleted from the mental accounting sheet. Second, the impact of future events is the same irrespective of their date. Consequently, all that matters from a given temporal vantage point is the total sum of residual (i.e. future) utilities and payments.

17.3.4. *Prorating Over Multiple Events*

In many cases the prospective mental account for a particular purchase—the sequence of payments and consumption yet to be realized—will include more than one payment or consumption episode. In such cases we need an accounting rule for assigning payments to consumption, and consumption to payments. While little is known about how consumers perform such assignments (but, see Heath and Soll 1998), a sensible default hypothesis is that they prorate residual payments to residual consumption, and vice versa. For example, if a prospective mental account includes two future payments of $10 and $20 and three consumption episodes, each conferring one unit of utility, then the prorated imputed cost of each consumption episode would be ($10 + $20)/3 = $10, and the prorated imputed benefit of the smaller payment would be: $(1 + 1 + 1)*\$10/(\$10 + \$20) = 1$ util, and of the larger payment: $(1 + 1 + 1)*\$20/(\$10 + \$20) = 2$ utils. Over time, these imputations will change as specific payments and consumption episodes recede into the past and are dropped from the prospective mental account.

17.3.5. *Coupling*

So far, we have assumed a 100% conversion of payments into imputed costs and of consumption utilities into imputed benefits (except as this is qualified by prospective accounting and prorating). As a general hypothesis, this is clearly unrealistic. Consider the dinner example mentioned earlier. If the dinner is a breakeven proposition: $u(\text{dinner}) = \lambda(\$75)$, then a full imputation of costs and benefits, $u = \hat{u}$, $p = \hat{p}$, would imply that the pleasure of the dinner is entirely erased by thoughts of payment: $u(\text{dinner}) - \lambda\hat{p}(\text{dinner}) = 0$, and, likewise, that the pain of paying the $75 is completely erased by thoughts of the dinner: $\hat{u}(\$75) - \lambda(\$75) = 0$. This seems counterintuitive. It is more plausible (in the break-even case) that the person would derive some pleasure from the dinner and some pain from the payment. To accommodate such partial linkages between payments and consumption we introduce two coupling coefficients, α (for "attenuation") and β (for "buffering"), which represent, respectively, the degree to which payments attenuate the pleasure of consumption and the degree to which consumption buffers the pain of payments. As we discuss later in the paper, coupling is likely to differ across situations and as a function of method of payment, e.g. credit card or cash purchase. It is also likely to vary across individuals. Some people tend to think very little about the cost of purchases, which would be represented by a low baseline level of a. Others feel payments acutely because they are unable to derive much solace from the benefits that the payments provide. This would correspond to a low baseline level of β.

17.3.6. Imputations

The imputations that result from our three accounting assumptions are given in Equation (6). The first line in the equation, for example, expresses the imputed cost of consumption at time b as equal to the sum of payments still due at time b, $\Sigma_{t \geq b} p_t$, prorated over consumption remaining at time b, $(u_b / \Sigma_{t \geq b} u_t)$, and adjusted downwards for the degree of coupling, a.

$$
\text{Imputations}: \begin{cases} \hat{p}_b = a \left(\dfrac{u_b}{\displaystyle\sum_{t \geq b} u_t} \right) \displaystyle\sum_{t \geq b} p_t, \\[2em] \hat{u}_c = \beta \left(\dfrac{p_c}{\displaystyle\sum_{t \geq c} p_t} \right) \displaystyle\sum_{t \geq c} u_t. \end{cases} \tag{6}
$$

A prediction of how consumption and payment will actually be experienced is then obtained by substituting these imputed costs and benefits into (2ab):

Consumption experience:

$$
u_b - \lambda \hat{p}_b = u_b - \lambda a \left(\frac{u_b}{\displaystyle\sum_{t \geq b} u_t} \right) \sum_{t \geq b} p_t, \tag{7a}
$$

Payment experience:

$$
\hat{u}_c - \lambda p_c = \beta \left(\frac{p_c}{\displaystyle\sum_{t \geq c} p_t} \right) \sum_{t \geq c} u_t - \lambda p_c. \tag{7b}
$$

When these equations are plotted over time, we obtain a set of predictions about the temporal hedonics of falling into debt, paying off a loan, or saving up for a future good. Figure 3 displays a simple, but representative example— the purchase of a durable product, e.g. a car. The top-left panel in the figure displays the constant utility stream that the car would provide over its lifespan if it was entirely free (e.g. a gift). The car is not free, however, but is instead paid off in seven equal installments, indicated by the seven solid lines in the

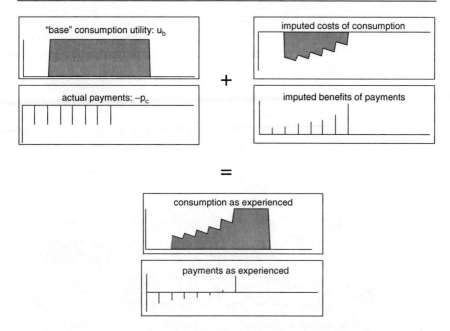

Figure 3. Transformation of Utility and Payment Streams into the Experienced Streams (Explanation in Text)

panel just below. The two panels to the right then show the imputed costs and benefits, calculated according to Equation (6), for $\alpha = \beta = .75$. The bottom two panels, which present the sequences produced by summing the top left and right panels, show how the car and the payments would be experienced according to the model (2ab). The patterns displayed here highlight certain generic predictions of the model: First, debt financing takes some of the glow off consumption, as we can see from the loss in experienced utility in the initial phase of ownership; full consumption pleasure is gradually restored as the car is paid off. Second, on the payment side, the loan payments become progressively less onerous as the debt balance is reduced, with especially sharp improvements observed near the end of the payment series. For example, the next-to-the-last payment in the bottom panel of Figure 3 has a slightly positive hedonic level, because it receives credit for 50% of car utility remaining at that point, and the very last payment is a cause for a celebration because it captures 100% of remaining utility.

17.3.7. Debt Aversion

Under prospective accounting, the experience of consumption and payment is unequivocally enhanced by prepayment. From the vantage point of a

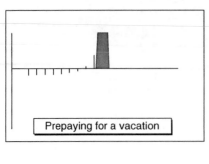

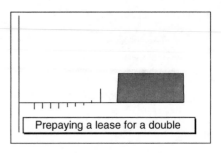

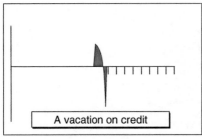

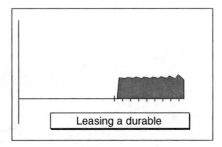

Figure 4. Impact of Prepayment on the Hedonics of Consumption and Payment for a Vacation (Left Panels) and a Durable (Right Panels)

Notes: The shaded area is experienced utility as computed by applying Equation (2a) and the bars are the experienced disutility of the payments as computed by applying Equation (2b). The underlying model parameters are the same in all four panels ($a = \beta = .35$, $\lambda = 1$, $\mu = 0$) as is the total utility integral for the vacation and for the durable (the vacation and the durable are an equally good deal). The utility scale for the durable is larger by a factor of 3 to facilitate comparisons of the utility profiles.

consumption event, prepayment diminishes the sum of residual payments and so increases net enjoyment (Equation (7a)). From the vantage point of a payment transaction, prepayment increases the sum of residual utilities and so diminishes the pain of payment (Equation (7b)).

Although prepayment always provides hedonic benefits, the magnitude of these benefits is not constant for different types of consumption. Figure 4 illustrates the interaction between the magnitude of hedonic benefits and the duration of the utility flow. The top two panels represent prepayment for an item, either a brief, high-utility episode ("vacation," left panels) or longer, lower-utility pattern ("durable," right panels). The bottom two panels maintain the same pair of underlying utility profiles but shift the payment schedule toward the future so that the payments now either follow the "vacation" or coincide with usage of the "durable." As in Figure 3, the shaded area is experienced utility as computed by applying Equation (2a), and the bars are the experienced disutility of the payments, as computed by applying Equation (2b).

The important comparison is between the top and bottom panels. Let's look at the vacation first. In the top left panel the vacation is prepaid, while in the bottom panel it is taken on credit. In the latter case, the model predicts that the start of the vacation will be enjoyable, but as the vacation progresses the residual payments will be no longer covered by residual vacation time and the balance will move into the red. A big hedonic plunge is predicted at the very end of the trip, when one has only the payments to look forward to. This is not the case with the durable, however. There is little cost to delaying payment, because there is always enough residual utility to keep one "out of debt," in terms of Equations (7ab).

The patterns in Figure 4 are consistent with the hedonic intuitions reported in Table 2. According to the judgments in the table, prepayment strongly improves the quality of the vacation experience, but has a negligible impact on the hedonics of payment. This is what happens in the left panels of Figure 4, where the impact on feelings about payment is small. Likewise, Table 2 shows that prepaying for a durable (washer-dryer) may improve the feelings about payment and consumption, but the impact is small relative to the impact on the vacation. This, too, is consistent with the profiles shown in the right panels of Figure 4.

In general, the attractiveness of prepayment will depend on whether a particular account is in the red or in the black. Given the desire to keep accounts in the black, there should be a strong tendency to accelerate payments for items whose utility declines over time.[7] Jones in the story would be more likely to pay off the car loan when a friend whose judgment he respects makes disparaging remarks about the image such a car projects.[8] We would expect to see an increase in mortgage prepayments in areas where property values fall, or when new developments such as an airport extension decrease people's liking of their own homes.[9]

17.3.8. *Impact of Time Discounting*

Does debt aversion imply that consumers will necessarily choose to prepay for consumption? No. Although prepayment always provides future experiential

---

[7] Contrary to the general desirability of prepayment, there are some situations in which deferred payment is desirable even apart from discounting considerations. Recently we were told a (true) anecdote about an Israeli academic who has seen inflation reduce his home mortgage to a trivial sum. Although he could have easily disposed of the mortgage with a single payment, he nevertheless did not do so. The reason? It was a pleasure to write those tiny checks each month. Prolonging payments will be advantageous when the payment account is in the black, because the payments themselves are pleasurable.

[8] This was suggested to us by Brian Gibbs.

[9] Also consistent with this are the results of Hirst, Joyce, and Schadewald (1992) who find that people prefer to first pay off debt for an item that is stolen.

Table 3. Consumption and Payment Experiences, Given Prepayment and Postpayment

	Postpayment Consume at time 0, pay at time 1	Prepayment Pay at time 0, consume at time 1
Consumption experience	$u - \lambda a p$	u
Payment experience	$-\lambda p$	$a u - \lambda p$

benefits, these benefits may not be large enough to overcome the opposing influence of time discounting, which favors the delay of payments.

Consider, for example, the decision whether to prepay or postpay for a single consumption episode. To keep things simple, assume equal coupling of consumption and payment, $a = \beta$, and no loss aversion ($\mu = 0$). The experiences of consumption and payment under the two scenarios (prepay and postpay) are given in Table 3. Comparing the left and right columns, we see that both consumption and payment will feel better under the prepayment option. Such debt aversion is a general implication of prospective accounting, even with more complex sequences of consumption and payment (viz. Equations (7ab)).

To determine whether a consumer would actually prefer prepayment according to the model, one has to compare the present value of the two options, using Equation (4) with the one-period discount factor δ (we assume here a common discount factor for payments and utility, $\delta = \rho$). The present value of the postpayment option equals $(u - \lambda a p) + \delta(-\lambda p)$, while the present value of the prepayment option equals $(a u - \lambda p) + \delta(u)$. Prepayment will therefore be more attractive if $(a u - \lambda p) + \delta(u) > (u - \lambda a p) + \delta(-\lambda p)$, which is to say, if $(1 - a - \delta)(u + \lambda p) > 0$. Because $(u + \lambda p)$ is positive, prepayment is preferred whenever the sum of the discount factor (δ) and the coupling coefficient (a) exceeds one. When impatience is high ($\delta << 1$) and/or coupling is low ($a << 1$), the consumer will choose to consume first and pay later, as predicted by the standard discounting model.

17.3.9. *Planned Versus Unplanned Debt*

In assessing the realism of the debt-aversion prediction, it is also important to distinguish between planned and unplanned debt. Our purchase criterion in Equation (4) predicts a dislike of fully planned borrowing from future income for present consumption. Indeed, there is evidence that young persons with temporarily low incomes, such as those who are educating themselves for lucrative careers, fail to borrow sufficiently against future earnings (Carroll and Summers 1991). This failure to borrow is a well-recognized paradox for the influential "life-cycle" model of spending and saving, which posits that consumers borrow and save so as to maintain a constant consumption profile over their lifetime.

With credit card debt, however, a large share of the debt may be unplanned, in that consumers underestimate their ability or willingness to pay off the monthly balance (Ausubel 1991). Such underestimation is thought to be behind high credit card interest rates, as consumers who expect to pay off their balances regularly will ignore the rate and choose credit cards on other attributes.[10]

What could motivate debt-averse but financially liquid individuals to delay paying off old debts? In our model, this behavior can be explained by nonexponential (e.g. hyperbolic) discounting, which creates an incentive to perpetually keep postponing any painful event, like debt clearing. To take a simple example, suppose that maintaining a debt account of size D requires an interest payment of d per time period, and that there are no imputed benefits, $\hat{u} = 0$ (i.e. this is old debt for past consumption). Consider three options, (a) to pay off the debt immediately, (b) to pay the debt in the next period, and (c) to pay the debt in some distant period $c = t$. If time discounting is hyperbolic, $\rho = 1/(1 + c)$, then the present values of the three options are:

(a) Clear debt immediately (at $c = 0$): $- D$.

(b) Clear debt "tomorrow" (at $c = 1$): $-d - \frac{D}{2}$.

(c) Clear debt at $c = t$: $-d - \frac{d}{3} - \ldots - \frac{d}{t-1} - \frac{D}{t}$.

If the pain of making the interest payments is small relative to the pain of clearing the debt ($d < D/2$), then delaying payment till tomorrow (option b) will be preferred to paying off the full debt today (option a). Of course, when tomorrow comes around, the same evaluation of options will cause another postponement, and so on, so that the debt may never be repaid. At the same time, it is possible that option c has the lowest present value, so that at a conscious level the consumer doesn't want to bear the debt for a long time. This sort of procrastination arises in any situation where a stream of small costs can be cut short with a single large cost (Prelec 1989). After a while, the consumer may become aware of the inconsistency between intentions and actual behavior, and, like Jones in the story, summon up the courage to pay off the entire amount. The point we wish to make is that maintaining a large amount of credit card debt is not inconsistent with debt aversion provided consumers have a hyperbolic time discount function.

---

[10] Ausubel (1994, p. 18) cites a *New York Times* report on the new "Prime Option" MasterCard, issued by Dean Witter, Discover & Co., and Nationsbank: "Under the card's terms, customers pay 9.9% interest for the first two months after a purchase, but then the rate rises to the prime rate plus 9.9%. This structure is meant to take advantage of the gap between the intentions of consumers to pay off their credit card bills quickly, and the reality that most run balances for long periods."

17.4. A Parametric Test of the Mental Accounting Model

According to the interpretation being offered here, the decisions to prepay some purchases and not others reflect basic consumer preferences and are not merely the expression of ad hoc financing habits or customs. The following study was designed to measure these preferences at the level of an individual subject. We created a nonstandard decision situation where conventional financing rules would be less likely to be invoked. Here is how the subjects learned about the problem:

Imagine that you have invested $3,000 into acquiring three weeks of time-share for a luxury apartment suite at a very nice seaside hotel. The hotel has its own private beach and pool and is about half an hour's drive away from a lively harbor town. You are now negotiating how to schedule your five weeks and when to pay the $3,000. One possibility is described in the "time line" diagram.

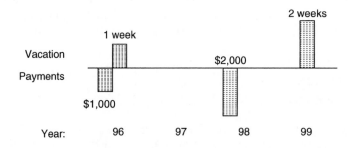

The diagram describes the situation where: (1) in the summer of 1996, you make an initial payment of $1,000 after which you take one week of your vacation time; (2) in the summer of 1997, your neither pay nor take any of your time; (3) in the summer of 1998, you pay off the remaining $2,000; (4) in the summer of 1999, you take the remaining two weeks of your vacation time.

On the next page of the survey, subjects saw a 4 × 4 matrix of 16 such diagrams, each displaying a different schedule with two payments and two vacations times. Subjects were asked to look over the entire set, and then rate each schedule on a scale from 0, for the worst schedule, to 10, for the best schedule. The set of 16 schedules was composed judgmentally by pairing eight distinct vacation schedules and eight distinct payment schedules so as to create variance in the overall timing of payments and vacation times, and in the ordering of payments and vacation times *within* a given summer. (Table 4 contains a list of the 16 schedules; Table 5 gives the pairwise correlations between the key explanatory variables.)

This was only the first of three rating tasks. In the second rating task, subjects were asked to rate the eight distinct vacation time schedules that

Table 4. Mean Ratings (for All Subjects, and by Cluster) for the 16 Schedules Used in the Study

Schedule #	'96	'97	'98	'99	Group A (n = 45)	Group B (n = 23)	Group C (n = 18)	All Subjects
1	$$	$	w	ww	6.8	1.2	0.8	4.0
2	$	$$	ww	w	6.5	1.7	0.7	4.0
3	$	w	$$	ww	7.7	4.3	3.6	5.9
4	$$	ww	w	$	4.7	4.5	3.7	4.5
5	w$$	ww$			5.8	7.3	4.6	5.9
6		$$w	$ww		6.5	5.7	3.6	5.7
7	w	$	$$	ww	5.5	4.1	4.7	5.0
8		$$ww	$w		6.8	8.0	3.4	6.4
9	ww$$	w$			3.9	6.7	6.7	5.2
10	$w	$$ww			7.6	8.4	4.2	7.1
11		w$	ww$$		4.4	6.3	6.1	5.3
12		ww$	w$$		3.0	5.6	6.4	4.4
13	$ww	$$w			4.3	6.8	5.8	5.3
14	ww	$$	w	$	4.0	5.1	7.0	4.9
15	w	ww	$$	$	1.9	3.3	8.7	3.7
16	ww	w	$	$$	0.6	2.7	8.9	2.9

Note: The highest rated pair of schedules in each column is given in boldface $ and $$ indicate the $1K and $2K payment and w and ww the one-week and two-week vacation slots.

Table 5. Summary of the Four Regressions

	Combined regression (all subjects)		Individual subject-level regressions			
	Mean	t value (1,376 obs.)	% signif. pos. coeff. (.1 level)	% signif. neg. coeff. (.1 level)	% signif. regressions (.05 level)	Mean R^2
Mental accounting (8a)					69	0.57
v = Prepayment	0.13	5.18	37	26		
$-\mu$ = Pay as you go	1.11	9.27	57	0		
Discôunting (8b)					42	0.35
d_2 = Discounted utility	−0.54	−1.57	22	30		
$-d_3 = -$ Discounted payments	−1.07	−2.97	16	28		
Ratings regression (8c)					31	0.27
k_2 = Utility stream rating	0.23	7.64	26	3		
k_3 = Payment stream rating	0.15	6.29	31	3		
Combined model (9)					63	0.61
d_2 = Discounted utility	1.36	2.65	21	2		
$-d_3 = -$ Discounted payments	1.42	2.71	22	10		
v = Prepayment	0.25	5.31	29	13		
$-\mu$ = Pay as you go	0.79	9.16	34	1		

Note: The correlations between the explanatory variables (labeled by corresponding coefficients) are $r(v, \mu) = -0.03$, $r(d_2, d_3) = +0.28$, $r(\mu, d_2) = -0.12$, $r(\mu, d_3) = -0.16$, $r(v, d_2) = -0.53$, $r(v, d_3) = +0.46$.

appeared in the original set on the assumption that the vacation time was completely free; in the third task, they were asked to rate the eight distinct payment schedules that appeared in the original set on the assumption that these payments were without any benefit whatsoever. This measured their attitudes to cost-free consumption and utility-free payments.

Surveys were filled out at an MIT student center ($n = 44$) and at a US airport ($n = 42$). We included for analysis only those surveys where the instructions were followed to the letter, i.e., where subjects supplied all 32 (= 16 + 8 + 8) ratings and included at least one "zero" and one "ten" in each of the three rating tasks.

The primary objective of the survey was to distinguish between preferences for the timing of consumption and payment from preferences for debt and savings per se. Pure timing preferences—even if inconsistent with time discounting—could nevertheless be modeled in simpler ways, e.g. by allowing discount factors greater than one in the present value formula (Equation (1)). A step up in complexity would be to represent preferences over consumption and over payment schedules with separate, temporally nonadditive models (e.g. Gilboa 1989, Loewenstein and Prelec 1993). Because these models would still be additive across consumption and payment, they could not capture attitudes to debt or savings, as these concepts refer to the temporal ordering of consumption and payment.

17.4.1. Results

The rightmost column in Table 4 contains the mean schedule ratings across all subjects. The columns for Groups A–C are means for the three groups of subjects who emerged from cluster analysis (Ward's algorithm). The vertical sorting of the patterns in the table corresponds to their ranking as given by Equation (1), assuming a 0.9 discount factor and a utility value of $1,000 per week of vacation time. A present-value maximizing decision maker should tend to prefer schedules near the bottom of the table. This is a pretty good description of the preferences of Group C, but not of the two larger clusters of subjects, A and B.

Let us first look at the ratings of the largest group, A. Their most favored schedules (#3, #10) allow for prepayment but also for some interleaving of payment and consumption. The least attractive schedules put vacation time ahead of payment. Group B agrees with Group A on desirable schedules, but disagrees with respect to the undesirable ones. In particular, these subjects strongly dislike asymmetric patterns where vacation time is entirely prepaid (#1, #2) or postpaid (#15, #16). As noted, Group C approximates the standard discounting model (Equation (1)).

17.4.2. *Comparison Against Two Benchmark Alternatives*

To translate Equation (4) into a simple model that can be applied to individual ratings, we assume that one week of vacation time is priced at $1,000 ($\lambda = 1$, for u and p denominated in weeks and $000) and that $\beta = \alpha = 1$ (see Appendix 1 for analyses supporting these simplifications). We also assume no time discounting ($\delta = \rho = 1$). With these simplifications, the decision criterion in Equation (4) becomes:

$$\left(\sum_{b=0}^{3}(u_b - \hat{p}_b) + \sum_{c=0}^{3}(\hat{u}_c - p_c) \right) - \mu \left(\sum_{b=0}^{3}|u_b - \hat{p}_b| + \sum_{c=0}^{3}|\hat{u}_c - p_c| \right).$$

Assuming that the ratings are a linear function of the purchase criterion, we obtain the following three-parameter *mental accounting* model of ratings:

$$\text{Rating}\{u_t; p_t\} = \kappa + \nu \left(\sum_{t=0}^{2}(u_t - \hat{p}_t) + (\hat{u}_t - p_t) \right) - \mu \left(\sum_{t=0}^{3}|u_t - \hat{p}_t| + |\hat{u}_t - p_t| \right).$$

$$(8a)$$

The accounting terms in (8a), $\hat{p}$ and $\hat{u}$, are computed from Equation (6) and contain no free parameters (as $\beta = \alpha = 1$). Here is how the imputations would go for the schedule diagrammed in the introduction to this section. The utility imputed to the first $1,000 payment in '96 is $\hat{u}_{96} = (1/3)(3) = 1$. Utility imputed to the second $2,000 payment in '98 is $\hat{u}_{98} = (2/2)(2) = 2$. In words, the first $1,000 is interpreted as prepayment for exactly one week of vacation time, and the second $2,000 in '98 as prepayment for the remaining two weeks. The cost imputed to the first week in '96 is $\hat{p}_{96} = (1/3)(2) = 2/3$, i.e., $667, because the $2,000 outstanding balance is prorated over the remaining three weeks. The final two weeks are fully prepaid, and have zero imputed cost, $\hat{p}_{99} = (2/2)(0) = 0$.

Equation (8a) is the model we wish to compare to two benchmark alternatives. The first alternative is the *discounting model*, based on Equation (1), with annual discount factor 0.9:

$$\text{Rating }\{u_t; p_t\} = d_1 + d_2 \sum_{t=0}^{3}(0.9)^t u_t - d_3 \sum_{t=0}^{3}(0.9)^t p_t. \qquad (8b)$$

Changing the value of the discount factor within reasonable limits will not substantially affect the ability of (8b) to explain the ratings of these particular 16 schedules. With $\delta = .9$ this model explains at least 95% of the variance in ratings generated by any δ-value within the interval $\delta = .5$ to $\delta = 1.5$, and 90% of the variance for the interval $\delta = .33$ to $\delta = 2.5$. Therefore, even if the discount factor is misspecified for a particular individual, the model in Equation (8b) will still explain that person's ratings (provided that the discount factor is reasonable, i.e. falling in the range of $\delta = .33$ to $\delta = 2.5$). For example, if the true discount factor for consumption is greater than one, indicating a negative rate of time discount, this will show up as a negative estimate for the d_2 coefficient.

The second benchmark is the *ratings regression model,* which uses the separate ratings of the vacation schedules and of the payment schedules collected in the second and third rating task:

$$\text{Rating } \{u_t : p_t\} = k_1 + k_2 \text{ Rating } \{u_t\} + k_3 \text{ Rating } \{p_t\}. \tag{8c}$$

Whereas the mental accounting and discounting models attempt to explain the subject's overall ratings on the basis of objective variables, this model uses the subject's own ratings of consumption and payment schedules as predictors. A priori, one would expect this to confer a major advantage on (8c).

Each of the models has three parameters. Summarizing, the discounting model assumes that overall preferences for consumption-payment schedules are additive both across consumption and payment and across time periods. The ratings regression model allows for temporally nonadditive preferences for consumption schedules; it only requires that these consumption and payment preferences are additively combined in the end. The mental accounting model is intrinsically nonadditive. Even if the loss aversion coefficient μ is zero, nonadditivity still enters through the $\hat{p}$ and $\hat{u}$ terms, which draw on the entire time profile of payment and consumption.

Comparing regressions for individual subjects, we find that the mental accounting model (8a) does better than the other two in 60% of the cases, ((8b) is best in 29% of the cases, and (8c) in 11%). More than one-half of the subjects show a significantly negative coefficient on loss aversion (μ), which means that—all else equal—they like "pay-as-you-go" schedules where consumption and payment are interleaved. As for prepayment, 35% show a significant preference for prepayment ($\nu > 0$) while 26% show a significant dislike of prepayment ($\nu < 0$). Such debt aversion is also revealed in the test of the discounting model, whose coefficients have the wrong sign (from the normative perspective). More subjects prefer to postpone rather than speed up vacation time (30% versus 22%) and more subjects prefer to accelerate rather than delay payments (28% versus 16%).

17.4.3. *Individual Attitudes to Savings, Debt, and the Timing of Consumption and Payment*

To tease apart the component of preference associated with temporal order from that associated with positive or negative discounting, we now regress each subject's ratings against both the accounting variables (8a) and the discounting variables (8b) simultaneously. In this combined regression,

$$\kappa + \nu \left(\sum_{t=0}^{3} (u_t - \hat{p}_t) + (\hat{u}_t - p_t) \right) - \mu \left(\sum_{t=0}^{3} |u_t - \hat{p}_t| + |\hat{u}_t - p_t| \right)$$

$$+ d_2 \sum_{t=0}^{3} (.9)^t u_t - d_3 \sum_{t=0}^{3} (.9)^t p_t, \tag{8d}$$

the coefficients for the accounting variables (ν, μ) measure preference for the temporal ordering of consumption and payment (i.e. savings and debt), while the coefficients for the present value variables (d_2, d_3) measure pure time preference independent of temporal order.

The results are given in the bottom part of Table 5. Turning first to the discounting variables, we see that the full regression restores the normatively correct positive sign on their coefficients, d_2 and d_3. This is an important finding, because it shows that, controlling for debt aversion, the subjects in the study generally prefer later payments and earlier consumption, i.e. they exhibit a positive rate of time preference.[11] Moreover, the correlation between the individual values of the utility and payment coefficients, d_2 and d_3, is +.79, indicating that subjects are consistent: Those who are most impatient with respect to vacation timing are also the ones most eager to delay payments.

Turning now to the accounting variables, the prevalence of positive ν-coefficients means that people prefer to prepay for consumption, holding time preference constant. However, there are still some subjects (13%) who significantly prefer to postpay; almost all of these subjects are from the present-value maximizing Group C.

The accounting coefficients provide a two-dimensional measure of individual attitudes to savings and debt. Recall that the sum ($\nu + \mu$) is the decision weight of consumption or payment "in the red," while the difference ($\nu - \mu$) is the decision weight "in the black" (see Equations (3) and (4) and footnote 5). Given that most subjects have positive ν, μ coefficients, we can characterize their debt attitude as a relatively strong dislike of borrowing combined with a relatively weak attitude to saving. In other words, they are willing to sacrifice some other desirable schedule attribute in order to stay out of the red, but are less concerned about pushing further out into the black. These preferences would predict selective prepayment for transient consumption but not for durables (viz. Tables 1 and 2 and Figure 2).

---

[11] The fact that controlling for debt aversion restores positive time preference is consistent with the general interpretation that delaying positive outcomes and getting unpleasant outcomes over with quickly is not evidence of negative time preference but rather reflects utility from anticipation and dread (Loewenstein 1987).

17.5. Prepayment and Other Strategies for Pushing Costs Out of Mind

The dislike of debt and the desire to prepay seem to be a robust but largely unrecognized phenomenon. Debt aversion has gone unrecognized partly because of a long-standing prejudice about consumers as myopic, self-indulgent creatures, and partly because the decision to prepay for consumption is often made indirectly—for instance, by choosing to own rather than to rent a product. Perhaps as a result of this prejudice, marketers have been slow in recognizing the appeal of prepayment and seem to have been caught by surprise by the positive reception of debit cards, which offer no fundamental advantage over credit cards except that they eliminate the feeling of being even briefly in debt.[12] In this section, we draw attention to the variety of forms that prepayment can assume, some of which have not previously been viewed in such terms.

17.5.1. Token Payment Systems

Diverse institutional arrangements cater to consumers' desire for prepayment. A clear example is provided by token payment systems, such as casino chips or the "beads" that one uses to pay for drinks at the Club Med. Our model predicts that it is easier to part with the chips than with cash because the cost of the chips is absorbed at the moment when they are purchased. In a similar vein, people often report that spending is easy in foreign countries, where the foreign currency feels like "play money." While the act of converting dollars to Swiss francs may be painful for US tourists, subsequent spending (at Swiss prices!) becomes less painful since all cash purchases are in essence prepaid.

17.5.2. Mental Prepayment

Even in the absence of an actual prepayment mechanism, consumers can capture some of the same hedonic benefits by mentally setting aside the requisite amount. Mental budgets, which are fixed amounts allocated to a particular purpose (e.g. entertainment), have traditionally been interpreted

---

[12] In contrast to the success of debit cards, a recently introduced credit card that allows customers to borrow from retirement saving accounts, and thus pay lower interest rates, has been a resounding flop (*New York Times*, August 27, 1995). Debt aversion may also have contributed to the political failure of ex-President Bush's decision to decrease tax withholdings (without lowering taxes) prior to the 1992 election. Bush may have reasoned that putting money in people's pockets prior to the election would boost his support, but the public reaction was generally negative and large numbers of people increased their own withholding amounts to offset the change.

as a self-control device, designed to prevent overspending on certain categories of expenses (Shefrin and Thaler 1988, 1992; Heath and Soll 1998). They may, however, also play the complementary role of facilitating mental prepayment.

The following true anecdote conveys the distinction nicely. A Manhattan newlywed couple were deciding whether to live on the East side (her preference, on account of the better restaurants) or the West side (his preference, on account of the cheaper rent). The clinching argument put forth in favor of the West side was that the rental savings would easily cover any reasonable number of taxi rides to the East side. However, having moved in, the couple soon realized that the cost of the round-trip ride made dining out on the East side look too expensive. Their solution: On the first of the month they would set aside ("prepay") a certain amount just for the cab rides. The purpose of the mental budget here was not to limit expenditures, but rather to protect the dinner experience from the imputed transportation costs (and to make sure that the dinners would take place as planned).

The mental prepayment tactic can be applied not only to money but to any scarce resource. For example, in dual-career families it is common for certain days or hours of the week to be designated as "family time," or "quality time." Besides ensuring that time is actually put aside for the family, such labeling makes the time more carefree: Instead of deciding whether to work or spend time with the family, the tradeoffs become localized, e.g. go to the zoo versus the children's museum (Beattie and Barias 1993). The supposedly high quality of the time, therefore, results in part from the fact that the harried parent is not distracted by thoughts of alternative work-related uses of the time. New technologies, such as satellite telephones, that make it possible to carry on work in any environment, including the zoo or children's museum, undermine the effectiveness of such strategies.

17.5.3. Fixed-Fee Pricing

To prepay mentally, the consumer must know the size of the bill ahead of time. Therefore, prepayment will be facilitated by pricing schemes that eliminate uncertainty in payment amount. This creates an advantage to the "prix fixe" menu—knowing the cost exactly, the customer can absorb it before the food arrives at the table. The disadvantage, of course, is that such a menu limits the range of choices, which is why prix fixe restaurants allow for a range of substitutions. In effect, the restaurant offers a multi-token budget, with one "token" exchangeable for an appetizer, another "token" for a main course, and so on.

Mental prepayment may also increases the attractiveness of flat-rate over variable-rate payment structures for services. To elicit such preferences, we presented 89 visitors to the Pittsburgh International Airport a series of questions asking them to compare fixed and variable pricing arrangements in a variety of contexts (health club, long-distance telephone calls, public transportation, and meals taken during a one-week Caribbean cruise). In each case, subjects were first asked to imagine two men who had made the same total use of the resource and had paid the same amount at the end of the consumption interval. The only difference was that one person had paid a fixed fee while the other had paid an amount based on his usage of the resource.

For example, the public transportation question asked:

Item 4
Mr. A and Mr. B both joined health clubs. Mr. A's club charged a fixed fee for each month of usage, payable at the end of the month. Mr. B's club charged an hourly fee for using the health club, with the total payable at the end of the month.

By chance, both men used the health club about the same amount, and both ended up getting a bill for the same amount at the end of the month. Who enjoyed himself more while using the health club?

Subjects were also given a "no difference" option. Note that on economic grounds Mr. B—whose marginal cost is higher—reveals a greater intrinsic appetite for exercise (in that month at least) and hence ought to derive greater total utility.

Subjects were then asked, "Which payment method would you personally prefer if they ended up costing you about the same?" and were again given a "no preference" option. Approximately one-half of the subjects ($n = 47$) responded to the public transportation and food during cruise items; the other half ($n = 42$) responded to the health club and phone-call items. A plurality of subjects viewed fixed rate contracts as superior hedonically (Table 6, left), and in three out of four cases a majority preferred such contracts themselves (Table 6, right).

These preferences are consistent with the "flat-rate bias" that has been observed in telecommunications research (Train 1991). The bias refers to the tendency for telephone customers to select flat-rate pricing options that cost

Table 6. Percentage of Subjects Who Think That a Fixed- or Variable-Rate Contract Would Be Better, Either for Another Person (Left Panel) or for Themselves (Right Panel) (Rows Add to 100%)

	Mr. A versus Mr. B			Own preference		
	Fixed	Variable	Same	Fixed	Variable	Indifferent
Public transportation	38	23	38	39	41	20
Food during cruise	49	25	25	55	30	15
Health club	48	14	38	55	21	24
Long-distance phone calls	55	14	31	60	19	21
Average	48	19	33	52	28	20

them more than "measured service" plans (given their calling rate). In one study, approximately 65% of telephone customers who self-select flat-rate service would have saved money by choosing a per-call billing option. In contrast, only 10% of those who selected variable-rate service would have saved by choosing flat-rate service (Kridel et al. 1993). Explanations for the flat-rate bias include biased use forecasts (Nunes 1997) and "consumer lack of information, irrationality, poor telephone company marketing, aversion to being metered and/or an unexplained aversion to bill uncertainty" (Kridel et al. 1993, p. 134). We offer another explanation: Talking on the phone is more pleasurable when you don't have to think about what each call is costing you.

A flat-rate arrangement not only allows for mental prepayment, but also shifts the cost imputations ($\hat{p}_c - s$) away from the actual acts of consumption, because the marginal cost of consumption is zero. In our terminology, consumption is decoupled from payment. On the other hand, payment-per-usage arrangements, like hourly tennis court fees, taxi meter charges, and the cumulating sushi bill, all impose a tight coupling of payment and consumption.[13] In the next section we discuss situational and strategic determinants of coupling.

17.6. Coupling

17.6.1. *Situational Determinants of Coupling*

The method of payment is one of the most important determinants of coupling. There are currently large numbers of payment methods available and the possibilities keep expanding, e.g. with the recent introduction of so-called "smart cards." The impact of some common methods on coupling is displayed in Figure 5, which diagrams the temporal relations for three cases: cash, charge card, and credit card. A single payment for a good or service creates tight coupling because it is obvious what is being paid for and when payment is occurring (top panel). Paying by charge card (middle panel) selectively reduces α because a single bill covers many distinct items, none of which is individually "responsible" for the total. Finally, credit card charging (bottom panel) promotes symmetric reduction in both α and β.

A second source of decoupling is the diversity of benefits that may be generated by one type of expense, and the diversity of payments that may be required to support a single consumption activity. Overhead that no one

---

[13] Here is a 1920s account of one customer's response to metered service on horse-drawn carriages (so-called "fiacres"): "Heinzl [the mayor of Zagreb] forced rubber wheels on the fiacres and by 1924 they all had meters. A friend rode in one with my father. Suddenly he jumped out and started walking alongside the carriage. 'I cannot go on watching the cost go up every few seconds!' he cried. 'But I am paying the fare,' replied my father. 'Yes, I know, but the pain is mine even if the cost is not'" (Ivanovic 1977, p. 35).

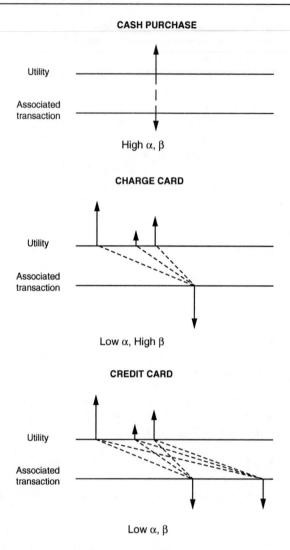

Figure 5. The Temporal Relationship Between Payments and Consumption for Three Payment Methods

wants "to pick up" is a classic example of a decoupled cost in business accounting, and it suggests a number of analogues in the mental accounting domain. At the Club Med vacation, for example, diverse activities are covered by a single comprehensive fee, for which no single activity is uniquely responsible. The decoupled activities can then be enjoyed without thought of payment. A fee-per-use arrangement, on the other hand, highlights the causal connection between a consumption event and the cost, leading to greater coupling and lower net satisfaction with consumption.

The same principle operates on the payment side to explain, for example, the disagreeable nature of payments that are "incidental" to primary consumption (rent, utilities, insurance, gasoline, health maintenance, taxes, etc.). The electricity bill is an almost a perfect example of a decoupled payment, because electricity enables many forms of consumption but provides no unique pleasure on its own.

17.6.2. Credit Cards and the Decoupling of Debt

A puzzling aspect of credit card financing is that it seems to be both a stimulus to spending (Feinberg 1986, Prelec and Simester 1994) as well as an especially disagreeable form of debt. To confirm that credit card payments are exceptionally unpleasant, we asked 88 persons at Pittsburgh airport to judge how good it would feel to have various types of payments offset by an unexpected refund from the IRS. They were told to consider 10 otherwise identical people, each of whom gets a reprieve from an imminent and unavoidable $300 payment via an unexpected $300 refund from the IRS. In Table 7 we see that the $300 refund is most satisfying if it cancels the credit card bill—even more satisfying than if it cancels parking tickets or dental expenses.

Here is how our model might resolve the puzzle. According to the model, payments are painful to the extent that they are not adequately covered by *accounted* benefits, where the latter quantity is represented by $\hat{u}_c$. This can happen for two reasons. The first is when payments are applied to past consumption (prospective accounting). The second is when payments cannot claim any unique benefits (decoupling). For credit card debt both of these unfortunate conditions may hold simultaneously. Imagine a consumer

Table 7. Mean Rank of People According to How Pleasantly Surprised They Were to Receive an Unexpected $300 Rebate

About to pay...	Mean rank	St. error (n = 88)
$300 for miscellaneous credit card bills	3.66	.29
$300 for dental work	4.51	.25
$300 for recent parking tickets	4.72	.30
$300 for installment on student loan	4.94	.31
$300 for monthly car lease	4.98	.28
$300 for a VCR	5.04	.30
$300 for a physical exercise machine	5.31	.29
$300 for a weekend spent at a country inn	5.45	.30
$300 for arnis lessons	5.92	.29
$300 for a fancy sportcoat	6.38	.30

Note: Low ranks mean more pleasantly surprised.

who has maintained a credit card balance for some time, irregularly making payments while simultaneously adding new charges to the account. In theory, the consumer could take each card payment, and deliberately "apply" parts of it to specific charges, e.g. so much for interest, so much for that dinner, etc. More likely, he or she will have no clear idea what purchases account for the debt, nor which items have been paid off. Both coupling coefficients, a and β, will tend to be low, putting consumption "in the black" but leaving the payment transactions "in the red." This means that at the moment of purchase, the consumer can enjoy his acquisitions as if they are paid off. However, the payments for those same acquisitions—when they come due—will be regarded as a loathsome tax, divorced from specific consumption benefits.[14]

17.6.3. *Earmarking of Savings and Debt*

Coupling can also be enhanced by earmarking a single savings or debt account to a particular expenditure or category of expenditures. According to our model, earmarking should be an attractive setup for accounts that are in the black (typically savings accounts) but unattractive for those that are in the red (typically debt accounts). Layaway plans, which involve putting aside an item while a consumer makes payments on it, are probably the most common examples of earmarked savings. Christmas clubs and college tuition funds are other prominent examples of such accounts. A novel college-financing venture that allows consumers to prepay up to four years of college tuition almost instantly subscribed 400,000 participating families.[15] On the other hand, earmarked debt arrangements are relatively uncommon, except in the case of durables (house, car) where ongoing services cover the monthly payments.

A related prediction is that people should prefer to earmark comparatively desirable items when saving but comparatively undesirable items when borrowing. The argument goes like this: When financing by saving, payments are buffered by consideration of future utilities, and the greater such utilities, the more effective is the buffering. On the other hand, when financing by borrowing, the thought of future payments undermines pleasure from consumption. In this case it makes sense to earmark the less desirable item, thus protecting

---

[14] Bingers' attitudes to credit card debt bear a certain resemblance to voter attitudes toward taxes. Like credit card payments, taxes contribute to a varied and complicated array of government services, few of which comes to mind when one writes the check. Voters do not object to the benefits, which they think belong to them as a matter of course, but are mystified at where the "taxpayer dollars" are going. This surely helps to explain the intensity of taxpayer disaffection and the corresponding appeal of "designated taxes" (Page and Shapiro 1992, p. 161).

[15] *New York Times*, August 6, 1995.

the more desirable one from being tainted by thoughts of payments. The following pair of items illustrate this pattern:

Item 5A
Imagine that in six months you will spend $1,000 on assorted expenses for a party for your father, and $1,000 for a variety of one-time miscellaneous expenditures. You plan to cover one set of expenditures from regular savings, and for the other you will set up and contribute to a special earmarked savings account. For which set of expenditures would you like to set up the special savings account? Assume that both options are equivalent in terms of payments, time, and effort.

Item 5B
Imagine that you are about to spend $1,000 on assorted expenses for a party for your father, and $1,000 for a variety of one-time miscellaneous expenditures. You plan to finance one set of expenditures with your credit card, and the other set with a separate loan. For which set of expenditures would you like to take out the separate loan? Assume that both options are equivalent in terms of payments, time, and effort.

The earmarked accounts create high coupling of consumption and expenditures, the general accounts, low coupling. According to the argument, people would be more likely to earmark the party payments when the payments were made beforehand (saving) than afterward (borrowing). As anticipated, a majority of the subjects preferred to earmark the party when saving (26/44 or 59%), but only 39% (17/44) preferred to do so when borrowing, a significant difference ($\chi^2(1) = 3.7$, $p < 0.06$).

17.6.4. Gifts

Gifts provide a direct method of decoupling consumption from payments (i.e., lowering a). The prevalence of gift-giving has long posed an anomaly for economics, according to which money is the perfect gift since presumably people know their own tastes best. A recent paper published in the *American Economic Review* even estimated the efficiency loss to society attributable to people receiving gifts rather than cash (Waldfogel 1993). Among the strangest customs, as Thaler pointed out (1985), is that of couples with joint budgets purchasing expensive gifts for one another. Such gifts clearly serve the purpose of signaling affection and commitment to the relationship (Camerer 1988). In addition, however, gifts may also serve the function of liberating purchases from thoughts of paying. When your spouse buys you the leather jacket you balked at buying for yourself, you know that the money is coming out of your own pocket. But it is one thing to actually write the check or hand over the cash, and another to know that it has already happened at some time in the past.

17.6.5. *Buyers Versus Sellers*

Strong coupling should be generally undesirable for buyers, but desirable for sellers of services or labor.[16] The two perspectives are illustrated by an ad for "The Pocket-Penpoint," a calculator-sized device that accepted automatic teller cards (featured in the May 1994 issue of *California Lawyer Magazine*). According to the description, lawyers, consultants, and other time-rate professionals could slip a client's card into the device, and bill them continuously as they work. Although a careful reader could see in the fine print that the advertisement was an elaborate joke, the "Pocket-Penpoint" nonetheless elicited many real purchase requests. "I thought the idea of having a client's money go instantly into your account was almost too good to be true," commented one disappointed lawyer. The psychological benefits of real-time billing are not hard to deduce. A lawyer working overtime or hand-holding an irritating client might well take comfort in the silent transfers executed by the "Pocket-Penpoint." Of course, the very feature that makes it so attractive to the lawyer makes it unattractive to the client, which explains why the device is "topped with a handkerchief so it can be worn discreetly in a breast pocket."

17.7. Conclusion

17.7.1. *Individual Differences*

In the economic account of intertemporal choice, an individual's rate of spending depends mainly on her discount rate. People with relatively high rates of time discounting should consume more and save less. However, the current empirical evidence seems to contradict the claim that people exhibit a consistent discount rate across different domains—e.g. consumption and health, monetary and nonmonetary outcomes, gains and losses, etc. (Chapman and Elstein 1993, Fuchs 1982).

Despite the lack of evidence for individual differences in discounting, it is easy to recognize strong differences in spending habits between those who seem to spend "as if there is no tomorrow" and the "tightwads" who appear slated to take their ever-accumulating wealth to the grave. The mental accounting concepts developed here offer clues about possible causes of such differences other than variations in rates of subjective time discounting. First, people may vary in their tendency to think about payments when consuming (α) and their tendency to think about consumption when paying (β). A person

---

[16] We note also that our model may be applied to situations involving labor effort by reversing the signs for consumption and for payments in Equations (2) and (3), i.e., "negative consumption" refers to work, and "negative payments" to the earnings. The implications of the model are complementary, e.g. a liking for consumption pre-payment translates into a dislike of salary advances (see examples 1D&E from Table 1).

whose mental accounting style is to impute the full cost of consumption is likely to be a tightwad. For such a person, it may not make sense to splurge on an expensive dinner, as the dinner will in any case be spoiled. Spendthrifts, on the other hand, probably have an exceptional capacity to push costs out of mind.

Second, people may have also different mental conventions for defining the subjective moment of payment. According to our model, people who regard an ATM cash withdrawal as the moment of payment should both spend more freely and derive grater enjoyment from their purchases, because for them all subsequent cash purchases are prepaid. In a similar vein, credit card users who identify payment with the writing of the monthly check, rather than with the signing of the credit card slip, should find consumption more enjoyable because it is decoupled from thoughts about paying.

17.7.2. *Hedonic Efficiency Versus Outcome Efficiency*

In standard economic analysis, consumers decide whether to make a purchase by balancing the anticipated utility against the cost, which is the utility that could have been derived from the best alternative use of the money. In some cases, the best alternative is also immediate consumption, but more typically it is something that the consumer would have purchased in the future. Thus, in the standard formulation, the costs of a purchase (1) are typically incurred in the future, and (2) take the vague form of foregone consumption. In our framework, in contrast, people experience an immediate "pain of paying" for purchases. Since they also sacrifice utility when future consumption must be foregone, one could say that in our model consumers pay twice for all purchases.

If the pain of paying is redundant, from an economic point of view, then why are we psychologically constructed to experience it at all? The functional role of the pain of payment is to counteract biases or "mismatches" in the assessment of costs and benefits at the moment of purchase, biases that would otherwise lead to chronic overspending (Prelec 1991). The most obvious of these mismatches is temporal; Because the benefits of a purchase are typically more immediate than the costs, a consumer who discounts the future steeply may find the mere prospect of future sacrifice an insufficient deterrent to impulsive spending. A second mismatch involves the underweighting of opportunity costs relative to out-of-pocket costs (Thaler 1980). In most cases, it is natural for the consumer to represent foregone future consumption as an opportunity cost rather than as a loss. Because opportunity costs are systematically underweighted, such framing of the purchase decision again skews the decisional balance sheet in favor of immediate consumption. Finally, a third "scale" mismatch arises if the benefit of *not* spending on a given occasion is framed as a tiny contribution to some larger financial goal (e.g. retirement). In that case it may be tempting to ignore the particular expenditure as "too small to matter" and so take one more step along a slippery slope (Herrnstein and Prelec 1991). Just as feelings of guilt or shame shape moral behavior and hunger tells us to eat, the pain of paying is a crude but effective reminder of the sacrifice that even a minor purchase will entail.

This functional interpretation now points to a key dilemma. From a hedonic standpoint, consumers want to minimize thoughts of payment. From a decisional standpoint, however, they definitely need to know "how much it costs." The paradox may be expressed by saying that consumers wish to know how much consumption costs, but do not wish to unduly think about how much it costs.

The poor face an especially harsh version of the dilemma. Low income amplifies the pain of paying, by increasing λ, and so makes more attractive those arrangements that decouple consumption from payment. With low coupling, however, the decisional benefits of mental accounting—the ability to allocate consumption expenditures efficiently based on an accurate imputation of costs—are lost. The poor are likely to be torn between the need for precise accounting and the desire to avoid its hedonic consequences.

The tradeoff between the demands of hedonic and decision efficiency appears at the individual and the societal level (Table 8). At the individual level, practices that promote tight linkage between spending and consumption increase decisional efficiency but diminish hedonic efficiency. The car purchaser, for example, who makes a separate decision about whether to purchase each option (e.g. tinted glass, sunroof, etc.) ends up with a car that may be ideally tailored to his tastes and needs, but also one where he knows the cost of every option. When he rolls down the electric windows he may recall the $300 price tag of this minor convenience, and the feeling of warmth from heated driver's seat may be chilled somewhat by the realization that it cost him $300. These nagging thoughts would not be there if the features came in a standard package.

Table 8.

Arrangements that promote hedonic efficiency	Arrangements that promote decision efficiency
ownership	leasing/renting
prepayment	postpayment
fixed fees	variable fees
few options—"prix fixs"	many options—"a la carte"
disguised opportunity costs	salient opportunity costs
public goods	market goods

The same tradeoff appears at the societal level when we encounter policy choices involving arrangements that increase the salience of costs in return for more efficient distribution. User fees for parks, for example, may limit crowding, reduce taxes, and ensure that the people who value the park most highly are those who will use it, but the fees can also undermine the pleasures of the visit. In general, societies that remove goods and services from the market will be less efficient—people will get less of what they want—but what little those societies provide may well be enjoyed more.

Going down the list on the left side of Table 8, we see that each arrangement is associated with specific inefficiencies relative to the arrangement on the right. Outright ownership of large durables and real estate reduces financial liquidity. Foregone interest is the cost of prepayment. Fixed fees, e.g., for health clubs or telephone services, carry the risk of misjudging true usage rate. Standard offerings without options preclude tailoring the product to each consumer's tastes. Disguised opportunity costs make it more difficult to monitor expenses: as in business, so in mental accounting, the sharing of costs makes it hard to perform a precise accounting of costs and benefits. The very endurance of left-side arrangements testifies to the attraction of keeping costs out of mind. The desire finds its ultimate and comprehensive expression in the socialist fantasy where all goods are "free."

The ideal payment arrangements, for rich and poor alike, will be those that facilitate rational spending while mitigating the pain of paying, that create the illusion of free benefits without sacrificing accountability. In principle, we should be able to enjoy all of our possessions and activities as if they were free: The pain of paying is pure deadweight loss. To design transaction mechanisms and institutions that serve this function, marketing specialists, policy makers, and those who dispense advice to consumers need to understand how people actually feel about payments, not merely how they would feel if feelings complied with economic logic.[17]

Appendix 1

Reviewing Table 4, it seems that heterogeneity is mostly due to different attitudes to prepayment. A simple way of accommodating such heterogeneity is to give each segment a distinct v-parameter while keeping the other

[17] The paper was completed while the authors were Fellows at the Center for Advanced Study in the Behavioral Science. We are grateful for financial support by NSF grants # SBR-9511131 (to the authors) and # SBR-960123 (to the Center). We would also like to acknowledge the efforts of three anonymous reviewers, the editor, and area editor at *Marketing Science*, as well as numerous useful suggestions from friends and colleagues.

Table 9.

	Model I		Model II: $\lambda = 1$		Model III: $\lambda = 1, a = \beta$		Model IV; $\lambda = a = \beta = 1$	
	Coeff.	St. error	Coeff.	St. error	Coeff.	St. error	Coeff.	St. error
κ	6.872	0.287	7.971	0.392	7.310	0.242	7.413	0.233
v_A	0.413	0.100	0.613	0.065	0.586	0.032	0.585	0.032
v_B	−0.192	0.099	−0.001	0.071	−0.028	0.043	−0.029	0.043
v_C	−0.881	0.101	−0.701	0.075	−0.728	0.050	−0.729	0.050
μ	−0.559	0.100	−0.901	0.107	−0.680	0.097	−0.784	0.072
β	1.032	0.168	1.061	0.111	1.125	0.090	1	
a	1.370	0.213	0.840	0.082	1.125	0.090	1	
λ	1.032	0.066	1		1		1	
	Adj. $R^2 = 0.3252$		Adj. $R^2 = 0.3274$		Adj. $R^2 = 0.3276$		Adj. $R^2 = 0.3268$	

parameters constant. The columns for Model I in Table 9 show the results of the nonlinear least-square regression for the equation:

$$\text{Rating}|u_t; p_t| = \kappa + \sum_S I_S v_S \left(\sum_{t=1}^{4} (u_t - a\lambda\hat{p}_t) + (\beta\hat{u}_t - \lambda p_t) \right)$$

$$- \mu \left(\sum_{t=1}^{4} |u_t - a\lambda\hat{p}_t| + |\beta\hat{u}_t - \lambda p_t| \right).$$

where I_S is the segment dummy variable.

R^2 is reasonably high given that all subjects are being fitted with one equation. More importantly, we now have tight estimates of a, β, λ, and for none of the three parameters can we reject the hypothesis that the coefficient equals one. The fit provided by Model IV, which assumes $a = \beta = \lambda = 1$, is essentially as good as that of Model I. This is perhaps not surprising, as the schedule format promoted full coupling ($\beta = a = 1$) and indicated a \$1,000/week cost of vacation time ($\lambda = 1$). The further advantage of Model IV is that it is testable with OLS, as there are no parameters inside the absolute value terms in Equation (4).

References

Ausubel, Lawrence M. (1991). "The Failure of Competition in the Credit Card Market," *American Economic Review*, 81, 50–81.

—— (1994), "The Credit Card Market, Revisited," Working Paper, Department of Economics, University of Maryland, College Park, MD.

Beattie, Jane and Sema Barlas (1993), "Predicting Perceived Differences in Tradeoff Difficulty," Working Paper, Laboratory of Experimental Psychology, University of Sussex, England, U.K.

Carroll, Christopher D. and Lawrence H. Summers (1991), "Consumption Growth Parallels Income Growth: Some New Evidence." in *National Saving and Economic Performance*. B. Douglas Bernheim and John B. Shoven (Eds.), Chicago, IL: University of Chicago Press.

Chapman, Gretchen B. and Arthur S. Elstein (1995), "Valuing the Future: Temporal Discounting of Health and Money," *Medical Decision Making*, 15, 373–386.

Feinberg, Richard A. (1986), "Credit Cards as Spending Facilitating Stimuli: A Conditioning Interpretation," *Journal of Consumer Research*, 12, 304–356.

Fuchs, Victor (1982), "Time Preferences and Health: An Exploratory Study," in *Economic Aspects of Health*, Victor R. Fuchs (Ed.), Chicago, IL: University of Chicago Press.

Gilboa, Itzach (1989), "Expectation and Variation in Multi-period Decisions," *Econometrica*, 57, 1153–1169.

Gourville, John T. and D. Soman (1997), "Payment Depreciation: The Effects of Temporally Separating Payments form Consumption," Working Paper 97-059, Harvard Business School, Boston, MA.

Heath, Chip and Jack Soll (1998), "Mental Budgeting and Consumer Decisions," *Journal of Consumer Research*, in press.

Hermstein, Richard J. and Dražen Prelec (1991), "Melioration: A Theory of Distributed Choice," *Journal of Economic Perspectives*, 5, 137–156.

Hirst, Eric E., Edward J. Joyce, and Michael S. Schadewald (1992), "Mental Accounting and Outcome Contiguity in Consumer Borrowing Decisions," *Organizational Behavior and Human Decision Processes*, 58, 136–52.

Hsee, Christopher K. and Robert P. Abelson (1991), "Velocity Relation: Satisfaction as a Function of the First Derivative Over Time," *Journal of Personality and Social Psychology*, 60, 341–347.

Ivanovic, Vane (1977), *LX: Memoirs of a Jugoslav*, New York: Harcourt Brace Jovanovich.

Kahneman, Daniel, Barbara L. Fredrickson, Charles A. Schereiber, and Donald A. Redelmeier (1993), "When More Pain is Preferred to Less: Adding a Better Ending," *Psychological Science* 4, 6, 401–405.

—— and J. Snell (1990), "Predicting Utility," in *Insights in Decision Making: A Tribute to Hillel J. Einhorn*, R. M. Hogarth (Ed.), Chicago, IL: University of Chicago Press, 295–310.

—— and C. Varey (1991), "Notes on the Psychology of Utility," in *Interpersonal Comparisons of Well-Being*, J. Roemer and J. Elster (Eds.), New York: Cambridge University Press.

Kridel, Donald J., D. E. Lehman, and D. L. Weisman (1993), "Option Value, Telecommunications Demand, and Policy," *Information Economics and Policy*, 5, 125–144.

Loewenstein, George (1987), "Anticipation and the Valuation of Delayed Consumption," *Economic Journal*, 97, 666–684.

—— and Dražen Prelec (1993), "Preferences Over Outcome Sequences," *Psychological Review*, 100, 91–108.

Loewenstein, G. and D. Schkade (forthcoming), "Wouldn't It Be Nice? Predicting Future Feelings," in *Foundations of Hedonic Psychology: Scientific Perspectives on Enjoyment and Suffering*, E. Diener, N. Schwartz, and D. Kahneman (Eds.), New York: Russell Sage Foundation Press.

Nunes, Joseph C. (1997), A Cognitive Model of People's Usage Estimations, Unpublished Ph.D. Dissertation, The University of Chicago, Chicago, IL.

Page, Benjamin I. and Robert Y. Shapiro (1992), *The Rational Public*, Chicago, IL: University of Chicago Press.

Prelec, Dražen (1989), "Decreasing Impatience: Definition and Consequences," Working Paper 90-015, Harvard Business School, Boston, MA.

_____ (1991), "Values and Principles: Some Limitations on Traditional Economic Analysis," in *Socioeconomics: Toward a New Synthesis*, A. Etzioni and P. Lawrence (Eds.), New York: M. E. Sharpe.

_____ and Duncan Simester (1994), "The Credit Card Premium: Evidence from an Experimental Auction," Working Paper, Massachusetts Institute of Technology, Cambridge MA.

Shefrin, Hersh M. and Richard H. Thaler (1988), "The Behavioral Life-Cycle Hypothesis," *Economic Inquiry*, 26, 609–643.

_____ and_____ (1992), "Mental Accounting, Saving, and Self-Control," in *Choice Over Time*, G. Loewenstein and J. Elster (Eds.), New York: Russell Sage Press.

Thaler, Richard (1980), "Toward a Positive Theory of Consumer Choice," *Journal of Economic Behavior and Organization*, 1, 39–60.

_____ (1985), "Mental Accounting and Consumer Choice," *Marketing Science*, 4, 199–214.

Train, K. E. (1991), *Optimal Regulation: The Theory of Natural Monopoly*. Cambridge, MA: MIT Press.

Tversky, Amos and Daniel Kahneman (1992), "Loss Aversion in Riskless Choice: A Reference Dependent Model," *Quarterly Journal of Economics*, 105, 1039–1061.

This paper was received June 5, 1995, and has been with the authors 22 months for 2 revisions; processed by J. Wesley Hutchinson.

Part VI

Emotions

18

Out of Control: Visceral Influences on Behavior

George Loewenstein

In the final game of the World Cup of 2006, between Italy and France, the score had remained at 1–1 since the 19th minute of the game, and the game had gone into a second extra time. At that moment, with over a billion viewers watching on TV, the cameras captured a seemingly remarkable event. Zinedine Zidane, the captain of the French team who had scored the lone goal for France (making him the fourth player in history to score more than one goal in the world cup play-offs), who was playing the last game of an illustrious career, walked up to an Italian player who had, apparently, been taunting him verbally, and violently head-butted him, which led to his expulsion from the game. The French team, although down their most important player, managed to hold the line at 1–1 in the remaining minutes of the game, but lost on penalty kicks, a skill which Zidane was famous for. Everyone wanted to know what it was that the recipient of the head-butt, midfielder Marco Materazzi, had said to Zidane, but it really didn't matter; no one could imagine anything he *could* have said that would justify the response. An article in an Australian newspaper carried the headline: "ZIDANE HEADS A LIST THAT DATES BACK TO THE DINOSAUR" and quoted a Katherine Ralls, senior scientist at the National Zoo in Washington, DC, who observed that "most animals that fight that way have skulls built to take it. We don't appear to be built that way, but I guess when you get so much adrenaline and testosterone going, it's butt first and think later."

How would conventional economics make sense of such an action? If individuals are assumed, as an unquestioned and unquestionable axiom, to maximize well-being, then one would be forced to interpret Zidane's head-butt as a rational utility-maximizing action. One would have to argue that the momentary pleasure of head-butting his opponent exceeded the expected value of its negative consequences—including the cost to his team and country, loss of lucrative product endorsements, and the instantaneous destruction of a reputation that he had spent his entire career developing. Having concluded that the fact that he took the action *revealed* that it was what he wanted to do, one would be further precluded from asking *why* he behaved in such a fashion. Such questions, we are told, lie outside the proper purview of economics.

Despite my own position at the extreme low-end of the emotionality scale, the role of emotions in behavior, including economic behavior, has always fascinated me. Emotions, it seems to me, enter into economic behavior in two ways: they are goals of behavior, and they also exert a more immediate influence.[1] The idea that emotions serve as goals is entirely consistent with the conventional consequentialist perspective of economics. Even if utility is not currently viewed as commensurate with happiness, no economist would object to the idea that people earn money and spend money to make themselves happy—that is, to experience positive emotions. However, the idea that transient immediate emotions that have little or nothing to do with actual economic consequences can influence behavior is far more controversial, and is the subject of this paper.

I wrote the paper during the academic year 1994–5 when I was a fellow at the Wissenschaftskolleg (WIKO)—Berlin's answer to Princeton's Institute for Advanced Study. It was an interesting year, thanks to the lingering history of the Berlin wall, but on the whole a miserable one. Although we made a few close friends among the fellows who were visiting the institute that year, overall I felt intellectually isolated. Most of the other fellows were in the humanities—anthropologists, historians, and philosophers—and most had 'postmodernist' intellectual proclivities. To them, the kind of empirical social science that I did was ridiculous and trivial, and, despite feeling very appreciated among the behavioral decision researchers and behavioral economists back in the USA, it only took a few weeks for me to pick up on the local attitude and to feel totally worthless.[2]

Every Wednesday evening at the WIKO one of the forty 'fellows' would deliver a formal public lecture. After not being able to make sense of the first two or three, in the days leading up to subsequent Wednesdays I would attempt to mentally psych myself up, convinced that if I could only pay proper attention I would understand the lecture. But, time after time, despite this mental preparation, not only would I find myself unable to understand

---

[1] My colleague Jennifer Lerner and I discuss this perspective in detail in Loewenstein, G. and Lerner, J. (2003). 'The Role of Emotion in Decision Making', in R. J. Davidson, H. H., Goldsmith, and K. R. Scherer, (eds.), *Handbook of Affective Science*. Oxford, England: Oxford University Press.

[2] Kalle Moene and I discuss the fragility of self-concept in Loewenstein, G. and Moene, K. (2006). 'On Mattering Maps', in J. Elster, O. Gjelsvik, A. Hylland, and K. Moene (eds.), *Understanding Choice, Explaining Behavior: Essays in Honour of Ole-Jørgen Skog*. Oslo, Norway: Oslo Academic Press.

the point of the lecture, but I could barely even make sense of individual sentences. My lack of comprehension was to the point where there was no incremental loss of clarity when, late in the year, the talks began to be delivered in German instead of English.

I've always been very bad at hiding my feelings, especially negative ones, and I was no more successful at the WIKO than in other aspects of my life. As a result, by the time my Wednesday in the limelight arrived, the audience was not exactly kindly disposed toward me. I was determined to battle the tidal wave of incomprehensibility, and chose to give a particularly straightforward talk—a presentation of a series of studies documenting the role of the self-serving bias in negotiations (see Chapter 8). This was probably a bad strategy. I remember looking up at the audience during my presentation to the unmistakable sight of a sea of hostile, almost exaggeratedly bored, expressions. The first question, delivered by a University of Chicago philosopher who was famous for drinking eighteen cups of coffee a day set the stage for the bloodbath that followed. The question was prefaced with a statement that is still seared in my memory: "Wittgenstein stated that nothing was ever learned from an experiment. And I must say that you have vindicated him." It was downhill from there. Since that moment, I've always had a conditioned negative response when I hear the name Wittgenstein.

The upside of the year was that I had a lot of time to read and a lot of uninterrupted time to think, which is really what one is supposed to do at the WIKO in any case. And, in the course of all this thinking and reading, I gradually hatched the ideas in this paper which have guided much of my thinking and research since that time.

Out of Control: Visceral Influences on Behavior[*]

George Loewenstein

Understanding discrepancies between behavior and perceived self-interest has been one of the major, but largely untackled, theoretical challenges confronting decision theory from its infancy to the present. People often act against their self-interest in full knowledge that they are doing so; they experience a feeling of being "out of control." This paper attributes this phenomenon to the operation of "visceral factors," which include drive states such as hunger, thirst and sexual desire, moods and emotions, physical pain, and craving for a drug one is addicted to. The defining characteristics of visceral factors are, first, a direct hedonic impact (which is usually negative), and second, an effect on the relative desirability of different goods and actions. The largely aversive experience of hunger, for example, affects the desirability of eating, but also of other activities such as sex. Likewise, fear and pain are both aversive, and both increase the desirability of withdrawal behaviors. The visceral factor perspective has two central premises: First, immediately experienced visceral factors have a disproportionate effect on behavior and tend to "crowd out" virtually all goals other than that of mitigating the visceral factor. Second, people underweigh, or even ignore, visceral factors that they will experience in the future, have experienced in the past, or that are experienced by other people. The paper details these two assumptions, then shows how they can help to explain a wide range of phenomena: impulsivity and self-control, drug addiction, various anomalies concerning sexual behavior, the effect of vividness on decision making, and certain phenomena relating to motivation and action.

* The ideas in this essay were stimulated by discussions with Drazen Prelec, and the formal analysis in section III is adapted from our joint grant proposal. I thank Baruch Fischhoff, Chris Hsee, Helmut Jungermann, Daniel Kahneman, Gideon Keren, Sam Issacharoff, Graham Loomes, Daniel Nagin, Fritz Oser, and Peter Ubel for numerous helpful discussions, suggestions, and comments.

Reprinted from Organizational Behavior and Human Decision, Vol. 65, No. 3, George Loewenstein, 'Out of Control: Visceral Influences on Behavior', pp. 272–292, © 1996, with permission from Elsevier.

It is always thus, impelled by a state of mind which is destined not to last, that we make our irrevocable decisions.

Marcel Proust

Das ist eine Versuchung, sagte der Hofprediger und erlag ihr.[1]

Bertolt Brecht, Mutter Courage

18.1. Introduction

Avrum Goldstein, in his instant classic *Addiction*, provides the following account of relapse to drug addiction:

Relapse is, of course, always preceded by a decision to use, however vague and inchoate that decision may be. It is an impulsive decision, not a rational one; and it is provoked by craving—the intense and overwhelming desire to use the drug (1994, p. 220).

Goldstein is anxious to portray relapse as a decision involving personal volition, to bolster his position that drug users should be held personally accountable for their behavior. However, the difficulty of doing so is evident from his resorting to adjectives such as "impulsive" and "inchoate" to describe the decision and his picture of craving as "intense" and "overwhelming." The addict knows, in one sense, that taking the drug is the wrong course of action but is unable to translate this belief into action. Craving, it seems, has the capacity to drive a wedge between perceived self-interest and behavior.

Understanding discrepancies between self-interest and behavior has been one of the major, but largely untackled, theoretical challenges confronting decision theory from its infancy to the present (though, see Beach, 1990; Fishbein & Azjen, 1975; Janis & Mann, 1977; Kuhl & Beckmann, 1994). In 1960, Miller, Galanter, and Pribram lamented that "something is needed to bridge the gap from knowledge to action" (p. 10). Two decades later, Nisbett and Ross were continuing to despair "our field's inability to bridge the gap between cognition and behavior, a gap that in our opinion is the most serious failing of modern cognitive psychology" (1980, p. 11). This essay is an attempt to construct the foundation for a bridge across the gap between perceived self-interest and behavior. I argue that disjunctions between perceived self-interest and behavior result from the action of *visceral factors* such as the cravings associated with drug addiction, drive states (e.g. hunger, thirst, and sexual desire), moods and emotions, and physical pain. At sufficient levels of intensity, these, and most other visceral factors, cause people to behave

---

[1] "This is a temptation, the court priest said, then succumbed."

contrary to their own long-term self-interest, often with full awareness that they are doing so.

The defining characteristics of visceral factors are, first, a direct hedonic impact, and second, an influence on the relative desirability of different goods and actions. Hunger, for example, is an aversive sensation that affects the desirability of eating. Anger is also typically unpleasant and increases one's taste for various types of aggressive actions. Physical pain is, needless to say, painful and enhances the attractiveness of pain killers, food, and sex. Although from a purely formal standpoint one could regard visceral factors as inputs into tastes, such an approach would obscure several crucial qualitative differences between visceral factors and tastes:

(1) Changes in visceral factors have direct hedonic consequences, *holding actual consumption constant*. In that sense, visceral factors resemble consumption, not tastes. Whether I would be better off having one set or preferences or another is an abstract philosophical question; whether I would be better off hungry or satiated, angry or calm, in pain or pain-free, in each case holding consumption constant, is as obvious as whether I would prefer to consume more or less, holding tastes and visceral factors constant.

(2) Changes in visceral factors are predictably correlated with external circumstances (stimulation, deprivation, and such) and do not imply a permanent change in a person's behavioral dispositions. In contrast, changes in preferences are caused by slow experience and reflection, are typically not anticipated, and do imply a permanent change in behavior.

(3) Visceral factors typically change more rapidly than tastes. Tastes also change, but tend to be stable in the short run.

(4) Finally, tastes and visceral factors draw on different neurophysiological mechanisms. As Pribram (1984, p. 2) writes, "the core of the brain...uses chemical regulations to control body functions. The configuration of concentrations of these chemicals, although fluctuating around some set point, is sufficiently stable over periods of time to constitute steady 'states.' These states apparently are experienced as hunger, thirst, sleepiness, elation, depression, effort, comfort, and so on." Their common neurochemical basis may explain why so many behavior disorders associated with visceral factors—e.g. overeating, compulsive shopping, phobias, and drug addictions—appear to be susceptible to moderation by a single drug: Fluoxetine (Messiha, 1993). Tastes, in contrast to visceral factors, consist of information stored in memory concerning the relative desirability of different goods and activities.[2]

---

[2] Although visceral factors are distinct from tastes in underlying mechanisms and effects on well-being and behavior, there are important interdependencies between them. Tastes are importantly shaped by visceral factors. For example, one's taste for barbecued chicken may well underlie one's visceral reaction to the smell of comingled charcoal, grease, and tomato sauce. At the same time, the visceral hunger produced by such smells, and the visceral

Rational choice requires that visceral factors be taken into account. It makes good sense to eat when hungry, to have sex when amorous, and to take pain killers when in pain. However, many classic patterns of self-destructive behavior, such as overeating, sexual misconduct, substance abuse, and crimes of passion, seem to reflect an *excessive* influence of visceral factors on behavior. As the intensity of a specific visceral factor increases, its influence on behavior tends to increase and to change in a characteristic fashion. At low levels of intensity, people seem to be capable of dealing with visceral factors in a relatively optimal fashion. For example, someone who is slightly sleepy might decide to leave work early or to forgo an evening's planned entertainment so as to catch up on sleep. There is nothing obviously self-destructive about these decisions, even though they may not maximize *ex post* utility in every instance. Increases in the intensity of visceral factors, however, often produce clearly suboptimal patterns of behavior. For example, the momentary painfulness of rising early produces "sleeping in"—a behavioral syndrome with wide-ranging negative consequences. It is at intermediate levels of intensity that one observes the classic cases of impulsive behavior and efforts at self-control—e.g. placing the alarm clock across the room (Schelling, 1984). Finally, at even greater levels of intensity, visceral factors can be so powerful as to virtually preclude decision making. No one *decides* to fall asleep at the wheel, but many people do.

The overriding of rational deliberation by the influence of visceral factors is well illustrated by the behavior of phobics who are typically perfectly aware that the object of their fear is objectively nonthreatening, but are prevented by their own fear from acting on this judgment (Epstein, 1994, p. 711). It can also be seen in behaviors commonly associated with addiction, such as that of Charlie T, a former heroin addict whose urine test showed that he had suddenly used heroin after a long hiatus. Charlie was "overwhelmed by an irresistible craving and ... rushed out of his house to find some heroin. . . . It was as though he were driven by some external force he was powerless to resist, *even though he knew while it was happening that it was a disastrous course of action for him*" (Goldstein, 1994, p. 220, emphasis added). Behavior at variance with deliberation, however, is by no means confined to the realm of the "abnormal." Adam Smith, for example, who is widely viewed as a proponent of enlightened self-interest, described his own internal conflict—presumably in the face of sexual desire—as follows:

At the very time of acting, at the moment in which passion mounts the highest, he hesitates and trembles at the thought of what he is about to do: he is secretly conscious to himself that he is breaking through those measures of conduct which, in all his cool hours, he had resolved never to infringe, which he had never seen infringed by

pleasure produced by subsequent consumption, are likely to reinforce one's preexisting taste for barbecued chicken.

529

others without the highest disapprobation, and the infringement of which, his own mind forebodes, must soon render him the object of the same disagreeable sentiments. (1892/1759, p. 227)

Success, in many professions, is achieved through a skillful manipulation of visceral factors. Automobile salespersons, realtors, and other professionals who use "high pressure" sales tactics, for example, are skillful manipulators of emotions. Con men are likewise expert at rapidly invoking greed, pity, and other emotions that can eclipse deliberation and produce an override of normal behavioral restraints. Cults and cult-like groups such as "EST" use food deprivation, forced incontinence, and various forms of social pressure in their efforts to recruit new members (Cinnamon & Farson, 1979; Galanter, 1989). In all of these cases there is a strong emphasis on the importance of immediate action—presumably because influence peddlers recognize that visceral factors tend to subside over time. The car or house one is considering will be "snapped up" if not purchased immediately, and the one-time-only deal on the stereo system will expire. The once-in-a-lifetime opportunity for enrichment will be lost if one doesn't entrust one's bank card to the con artist, and there is an unexplained urgency to the insistence that one signs up for EST in the introductory meeting rather than at home after careful deliberation.

Tactics of this type are not, however, restricted to those involved in the selling professions. Interrogators use hunger, thirst, and sleep deprivation to extract confessions. Like Esau, who sold his birthright for a mess of pottage, prisoners may sacrifice years of freedom for an extra hour of sleep or a glass of water. Lawyers use a similar tactic when taking depositions.[3] The early stages of a deposition, when the witness is fresh, are used to elicit background information. Information that is potentially damaging to the witness or the opposing side is requested only after the witness begins to tire, lose concentration, and is more likely to make mistakes or concessions just for the sake of ending the questioning.[4] Similarly, though by mutual agreement, labor negotiations are commonly structured to go "round the clock" as the strike deadline approaches. Rarely is new information produced in these last sessions, nor is there a discussion of technicalities of agreement. Perhaps, however, both sides recognize that mutual willingness to make concessions will be enhanced when sleep is the reward for speedy reconciliation.

Decision theory, as it is currently practiced, makes no distinction between visceral factors and tastes and thus does not recognize the special impact of visceral factors on behavior. It is best equipped to deal with "cool" or

[3] Personal communication, Sam Issacharoff.

[4] Just as a skillful lawyers strategically manipulate the opposing side's emotions, they must also work to counteract such influences on themselves and their clients. The adage "the lawyer who represents himself has a fool for a client" reflects the dangers to a lawyer of excessive personal—i.e. emotional—involvement in a case.

"dispassionate" settings in which there is typically a very close connection between perceived self-interest and behavior. The decision-making paradigm has much greater difficulty in providing an account of decisions occurring at the "hot" end of the continuum defined by the intensity of visceral factors. The drive mechanism of Freudian and behavioristic psychology provides a better account of behavior at the opposite end of the same continuum. The decline of the behaviorist paradigm in psychology can be attributed to its failure to make sense of volitional, deliberative, behavior. Does the decision-making paradigm face a similar fate if it fails to address the full range of visceral influences? My intent is to show that visceral influences on behavior can, in fact, be expressed in decision-theoretic terms. Section II below addresses the question of why and how visceral factors create discrepancies between perceived self-interest and behavior. Section III enumerates a series of propositions concerning the effect of visceral factors on behavior and perceptions, and shows how these can be expressed in the verbal and mathematical language of decision-theory. Section IV discusses applications of the proposed theoretical perspective.

18.2. Visceral Factors and Behavior

As visceral factors intensify, they focus attention and motivation on activities and forms of consumption that are associated with the visceral factor—e.g. hunger draws attention and motivation to food. Non-associated forms of consumption lose their value (Easterbrook, 1959). At sufficient levels of intensity, individuals will sacrifice almost any quantity of goods not associated with the visceral factor for even a small amount of associated goods, a pattern that is most dramatically evident in the behavior of drug addicts. Frawley (1988, p. 32) describes addicts as progressively "eliminating behavior that interferes with or does not lead to drug or alcohol use... [which] leads to a kind of 'tunnel vision' on the part of the addict." Cocaine addicts, according to Gawin (1991, p. 1581), "report that virtually all thoughts are focused on cocaine during binges; nourishment, sleep, money, loved ones, responsibility, and survival lose all significance." In economic parlance, the marginal rate of substitution between goods associated with the visceral factor and goods that are not so-associated becomes infinitessimal.

Visceral factors also produce a second form of attention-narrowing: a good-specific collapsing of one's time-perspective toward the present. A hungry person, for example, is likely to make short-sighted tradeoffs between immediate and delayed food, even if tomorrow's hunger promises to be as intense as today's. This present-orientation, however, applies only to goods that are associated with the visceral factor, and only to tradeoffs between the present and some other point in time. A hungry person would probably make the

531

same choices as a non-hungry person between immediate and delayed money (assuming that food cannot be purchased) or immediate and delayed sex. A hungry person might also make the same choices as a non-hungry person between food tomorrow versus food on the day after tomorrow.

Yet a third form of attention-narrowing involves the self versus others. Intense visceral factors tend to narrow one's focus inwardly—to undermine altruism. People who are hungry, in pain, angry, or craving drugs tend to be selfish. As interrogators understand all too well, sleep deprivation, hunger, thirst, pain, and indeed most visceral factors, can cause even the most strongly willed individuals to "betray" comrades, friends and family (e.g. Biderman, 1960).

The peremptory nature of immediate visceral factors is generally adaptive. Visceral factors play an important role in regulating behavior, and can be observed in a wide range of animals. Hunger signals the need for nutritional input, pain indicates the impingement of some type of potentially harmful environmental factor, and emotions serve a range of interrupting, prioritizing, and energizing functions (Simon, 1967; Mandler, 1964; Pluchik, 1984; Frank, 1988). The absence of even one of these signalling systems detracts dramatically from an individual's quality of life and chances of survival. Although most people occasionally wish they could eschew pain, one only has to witness the playground behavior of children who are congenitally incapable of experiencing pain (and to observe the perpetual vigilance of their parents) to abandon this fantasy (Fields, 1987, pp. 2–4).

Evolution, however, has its limitations (Gould, 1992). The same visceral factors that serve the individual's interests effectively at moderate levels produce distinctly suboptimal patterns of behavior at higher levels. Extreme fear produces panic and immobilization rather than effective escape (Janis, 1967; Janis & Leventhal, 1967). Uncontrolled anger produces ineffectual, impulsive actions or the opposite, immobilization. Intense visceral factors not only undermine effective behavior, but produce extreme misery. This should not surprise us; the 'goal' of evolution is reproduction, not happiness. If hunger ensures that an organism will eat, the fact that it is an unpleasant sensation is immaterial. As Damasio (1994, p. 264) argues, visceral factors tend to be aversive because "suffering puts us on notice. Suffering offers us the best protection for survival, since it increases the probability that individuals will heed pain signals and act to avert their source or correct their consequences."

Although visceral factors should be and are taken into account in decision making, they also influence behavior more directly. Hunger, thirst, sexual desire, pain, and indeed virtually all visceral factors, can influence behavior without conscious cognitive mediation (Bolles, 1975). To illustrate this point, Pribram (1984) provides the vivid example of a brain surgery patient who ate ravenously with no subjective feeling of hunger:

One patient who had gained more than one hundred pounds in the years since surgery was examined at lunch time. Was she hungry? She answered, "No." Would she like a piece of rare, juicy steak? "No." Would she like a piece of chocolate candy? She answered, "Umhumm," but when no candy was offered she did not pursue the matter. A few minutes later, when the examination was completed, the doors to the common room were opened and she saw the other patients already seated at a long table eating lunch. She rushed to the table, pushed the others aside, and began to stuff food into her mouth with both hands. She was immediately recalled to the examining room and the questions about food were repeated. The same negative answers were obtained again, even after they were pointedly contrasted with her recent behavior at the table. (p. 24).

Further evidence for the direct impact of visceral factors—without deliberative mediation—comes from neuropsychological research. This research shows, for example, that brain lesions in the reward centers of the brain can produce a total lack of interest in eating (Bolles, 1975). Electrical stimulation of the same areas can produce complex sequences of behavior without conscious mediation (Gardner, 1992, p. 71). Many of the sensory organs have direct nerve connections to these pleasure/motivation centers, strongly hinting at the possibility that sensory inputs can have a direct influence on behavior. Electrical stimulation of these same regions is so pleasurable that animals will self-administer such stimulation in preference to food, water, and sex, and will do so until the point of collapse and even death (Olds & Milner, 1954). Similarly self-destructive patterns of behavior are exhibited by both animals and humans towards addictive substances, such as crack cocaine, which have a very similar effect on the reward centers of the brain as electrical stimulation (Pickens & Harris, 1968). It is difficult to imagine that this type of behavior reflects the outcome of a rational decision process, since the rather rapid consequence is to eliminate the capacity to experience pleasure altogether. Again, these findings suggest that there are certain types of influences or incentives that operate independently of, and overwhelm, individual deliberation and volition.

In contrast to this relatively strong evidence that visceral factors can influence behavior directly, there is only weak evidence supporting the standard decision-theoretic assumption that behavior follows automatically from deliberation. In fact, the standard decision-theoretic assumption seems to be supported by little more than introspection. Most people experience their own actions as resulting from decisions (Pettit, 1991), or at least as deliberate. However, it is questionable whether these introspections represent veridical reports of underlying decision processes, or *ex post* rationalizations of behavior. The limitation of verbal reports is well established (Nisbett & Wilson, 1977), as is the fact that "implicit theories" powerfully influence one's perception of the world (Bruner, 1957; Ross, 1989). People process information in a hyper-Bayesian fashion, ignoring or down-playing evidence that is at variance with their implicit theories while placing great weight on data that is supportive (Lord, Lepper & Ross, 1979). Trained to view behavior as the result of attribute-based decisions (Pettit, 1991; Christensen & Turner, 1993), most people in Western culture will almost inevitably interpret their own behavior accordingly.

Such a tendency to make retrospective sense of one's own preferences and behavior can be seen in research by Robert Zajonc and his colleagues on the "mere exposure effect" (e.g. Zajonc, 1968). People are unaware of the effect of "mere" exposure on their preferences, but, when preferences are experimentally influenced through differential exposure, they readily generate attribute-based explanations for their own preferences (Zajonc & Marcus, 1982). A subject might decide that he likes polygon number 3, for example, not because he viewed it 12 times, but due to its geometric symmetry. Likewise, someone suffering from a tic that causes his hand to fly toward his head periodically will, over time, develop a head-itch that requires scratching (Brown, 1988). Recent neuropsychological research shows that, for many actions that are subjectively experienced as purposive by decision makers, electrical impulses associated with the action begin fractions of a second before any conscious awareness of the intention to act (Libet, Gleason, Wright, & Pearl, 1983).

The issue of cognitive versus visceral control of behavior remains unresolved, and some compromise position may well ultimately prevail. At present, however, there is little evidence beyond fallible introspection supporting the standard decision-theoretic assumption of complete volitional control of behavior.

18.3. Seven Propositions and A Mathematical Representation

Much is known, or at least can plausibly be inferred from available evidence, about the relationship between deliberation and action under the influence of visceral factors. The propositions enumerated below can be summarized simply: visceral factors operating on us in the here and now have a disproportionate impact on our behavior. Visceral factors operating in the past or future, or experienced by another individual are, if anything, underweighted. Although these propositions are simple enough to be stated in words, for the interested reader I also indicate how they could be expressed mathematically.

To represent the influence of visceral factors on behavior we need a representation of preferences that includes a new set of variables, a_{ti}, to represent how the fluctuating levels of the visceral factors affect intertemporal utility:

$$U = \Sigma_t u(x_{t1}, \ldots, x_{tn}, a_{t1}, \ldots, a_{tm}, t), \tag{1}$$

where U is the total utility of an intertemporal consumption plan, $(x_{t1}, \ldots, x_{tn})$ is the consumption vector at time t, and $a = (a_{t1}, \ldots, a_{tm})$ is the vector of visceral factors at time t. In a given experiment, the a parameters will be operationally defined, e.g. as the hours of food deprivation, the presence or absence of food stimuli, and so on. We assume that the person knows the values of x, a, and t when choosing between different consumption opportunities.

Equation (1) is the most general temporally separable model, and it allows for the value of any good or activity to be affected by all visceral factors operating at the same point in time. In many instances, however, it is possible to partition visceral factors into subsets that influence only a single consumption variable. In the simplest case, each consumption variable, x_i, is influenced by at most one visceral factor, a_i, as in Eq. (2).

$$U = \Sigma_t u(v_1(x_{t1}, a_{t1}, t), \ldots, v_n(x_{tn}, a_{tn}, t)). \tag{2}$$

In this equation, $v_1(x_{t1}, a_{t1}, t)$ might be, say, the value of consuming meal x_{t1} at time t relative to the present, given that one's hunger will be at level a_{t1} at that time. The separability structure in Eq. (2) implies that the "conditional" preference ordering of triples (x_{ti}, a_{ti}, t), holding all else constant, is independent of the levels of other consumption variables and visceral factors. Stable preferences across different types of consumption are captured by the function $u(v_1, \ldots, v_n)$. The function tells us whether a person prefers dining out to dancing, for instance. The subordinate functions, v_i, tell us how the value of particular dining opportunity hinges on what is offered (x_{it}), the hunger level (a_{it}), and delay (t). Each of the v_i functions is assumed to be increasing in the first variable, decreasing in the third, and possibly increasing or decreasing in the second. Further, x_i and a_i will usually be complements, e.g., hunger will enhance a solid meal, but hurt when no food is forthcoming. I also assume that x_i and a_i have natural zero levels. For x_i, it is the status quo, or reference consumption level (Tversky & Kahneman, 1991). For a_i, it is the level a_i^* such that $v(0, a_i^*, t) = 0$. Intuitively, the natural zero level of a visceral factor is the level at which, in the absence of the relevant form of consumption, the visceral factor neither contributes to nor detracts from utility.

18.3.1. Propositions

The observation that visceral factors influence the desirability of goods and activities is hardly surprising. To provide useful insights into behavior it is necessary to specify the nature of this influence with the greatest detail possible given the available evidence. The following seven propositions, which are summarized in Table 1 and discussed in detail below, encode observations concerning the influence of visceral factors on desired, predicted, recollected, and actual behavior. Although all seven have some support from existing research, I refer to them as propositions to emphasize their tentative status.

Table 1. Propositions Concerning the Actual, Desired, Predicted, and Recollected Influence of Visceral Factors on Behavior

Proposition	Description
1	The discrepancy between the actual and desired value placed on a particular good or activity increases with the intensity of the immediate good-relevant visceral factor.
2	Future visceral factors produce little discrepancy between the value we plan to place on goods in the future and the value we view as desirable.
3	Increasing the level of an immediate and delayed visceral factor simultaneously enhances the actual valuation of immediate relative to delayed consumption of the associated good.
4	Currently experienced visceral factors have a mild effect on decisions for the future, even when those factors will not be operative in the future.
5	People underestimate the impact of visceral factors on their own future behavior.
6	As time passes, people forget the degree of influence that visceral factors had on their own past behavior. As a result, past behavior that occurred under the influence of visceral factors will increasingly be forgotten, or will seem perplexing to the individual.
7	The first six propositions apply to interpersonal as well as intrapersonal comparisons, where other people play the same role vis a vis the self as the delayed self plays relative to the current self:
	i. We tend to become less altruistic than we would like to be when visceral factors intensify.
	ii. When making decisions for another person, we tend to ignore or give little weight to visceral factors they are experiencing
	iii. Increasing the intensity of a visceral factor for ourselves and another person in parallel leads to a decline in altruism.
	iv. When we experience a particular visceral factor, we tend to imagine others experiencing it as well, regardless of whether they actually are.
	v. & vi. People underestimate the impact of visceral factors on other people's behavior.

Proposition 1:
The discrepancy between the actual and desired value placed on a particular good or activity increases with the intensity of the immediate good-relevant visceral factor.[5]

If we define v^d as the desired, as opposed to the actual, value of a particular action or consumption alternative, then proposition 1 implies that

$$\text{If } a' > a > a_i^*, \text{ and } v^d(x', a', 0)$$
$$= v^d(x, a, 0), \text{ then } v(x', a', 0) > v(x, a, 0).$$

This regularity was illustrated in the introduction with the example of sleepiness, which can be dealt with in a reasonable fashion at low levels, but at high levels produces self-destructive patterns of behavior such as falling asleep at the wheel. A similar pattern of initially reasonable, but ultimately excessive, influence can be observed for virtually all visceral factors. Low levels of fear may be dealt with in an optimal fashion (e.g. by taking deliberate protective action), but higher levels of fear often produce panic or, perhaps worse,

---

[5] By "actual value" I mean the value implied by the individual's behavior; by "desired value," I mean the value that the individual views as in his or her self-interest.

immobilization (Janis, 1967). Likewise, low levels of anger can be factored into daily decision making in a reasonable way, but high levels of anger often produce impulsive, self-destructive, behavior.

Proposition 2:
Future visceral factors produce little discrepancy between the value we plan to place on goods in the future and the value we view as desirable.

That is, if $a' > a > a_i^*$, and $v^d(x', a', t) = v^d(x, a, t)$, then $v(x', a', t) \approx v(x, a, t)$, for $t > 0$.

When visceral factors are not having an immediate influence on our behavior, but will be experienced in the future, we are free to give them the weight that we deem appropriate in decision making. Thus, we position the alarm clock across the room to prevent sleeping late only because we are not currently experiencing the pain of rising early. Likewise, we avoid buying sweets when shopping after lunch because the evening's cravings, however predictable, have little reality to our current, unhungry selves. When the future becomes the present, however, and we actually experience the visceral factor, its influence on our behavior is much greater, as implied by proposition 1.

A well-known study of pregnant women's decisions concerning anesthesia illustrates the types of behavioral phenomena associated with proposition 2. Christensen-Szalanski (1984) asked expectant women to make a non-binding decision about whether to use anesthesia during childbirth; a majority stated a desire to eschew anesthesia. However, following the onset of labor, when they began to experience pain, most reversed their decision. Consistent with proposition 2, the women were relatively cavalier with respect to their own future pain. Although Christensen-Szalanski himself explained the reversals in terms of hyperbolic discounting curves, such an account should predict that at least some reversals would occur prior to the onset of labor, but none did. Moreover, the reversal of preference was observed not only for women giving birth for the first time, but also those who had previously experienced the pain of childbirth; experience does not seem to go very far in terms of enhancing one's appreciation for future pain.

A similarly underappreciation of the impact of future visceral states—again by people with considerable experience—can be seen in the relapse behavior of addicts who, after achieving a period of abstinence, believe they can indulge in low level consumption without relapsing. Underestimating the impact of the craving that even small amounts of consumption can produce (Gardner & Lowinson, 1993), such addicts typically find themselves rapidly resuming their original addictive pattern of consumption (Stewart & Wise, 1992). As Seeburger (1993) comments:

Any addict can tell us how long such negative motivation [to stay off the drug] lasts. It lasts as long as the memory of the undesirable consequences stays strong. But the more successful one is at avoiding an addictive practice on the grounds of such motivation, the less strong does that very memory become. Before long, the memory of the pain that one brought on oneself through the addiction begins to pale in comparison to the anticipation of the satisfaction that would immediately attend relapse into the addiction. Sometimes in AA it is said that the farther away one is from one's last drink, the closer one is to the next one. That is surely true for alcoholics and all other addicts whose only reason to stop "using" is to avoid negative consequences that accompany continuing usage. (p. 152)

In a similar vein, Osiatynski refers to the tendency to underestimate the power of alcohol addiction: "After hitting bottom and achieving sobriety, many alcoholics must get drunk again, often not once but a few times, in order to come to believe and never forget about their powerlessness" (1992, p. 128). Osiatynsi argues that a major task of relapse prevention is to sustain the exaddict's appreciation for the force of craving and the miseries of addiction; alcoholics anonymous serves this function by exposing abstinent alcoholics to a continual stream of new inductees who provide graphic reports of their own current or recent miseries.[6]

18.3.2. *Impulsivity*

The disproportionate response to immediately operative visceral factors expressed by proposition 1, and the tendency to give little weight to delayed visceral factors expressed by proposition 2, have important implications for intertemporal choice.[7] Together they point to a novel account of impulsivity—an alternative to the currently dominant account which is based on non-exponential time discounting.

In a seminal article, R. H. Strotz (1955) showed that a discounted utility maximizer who does not discount at a constant rate will systematically depart from his own prior consumption plans. When the deviation from constant discounting involves higher proportionate discounting of shorter time delays than of long ones, this "time inconsistency" takes the form of temporally *myopic* or impulsive behavior: spending in the present but vowing to save in the future, binge-eating in the present while planning future diets, or resolving to quit smoking, but not until tomorrow. A standard non-exponential discounting formulation that predicts impulsive behavior is $U = u(x_0) + \gamma\delta u(x_1) + \gamma\delta^2 u(x_2)$, where δ is the conventional exponential discount factor and $\gamma(<1)$ is a special discount factor applying to all periods other than the immediate present (see Elster, 1977; Akerlof, 1991). The conventional, i.e., constant discounting, approach is identical, except that γ is assumed to equal

---

[6] Personal communication.
[7] For a preliminary rendition of this perspective, see Hoch and Loewenstein (1991).

unity. A person who maximizes a function of this type will choose a larger reward x' at time 2 over a smaller reward x at time 1 if $\delta u(x') > u(x)$, but will opt for the smaller, more immediate reward if the choice is between immediate consumption or consumption at time 1 if $\gamma \delta u(x') < u(x)$.

The non-exponential discounting perspective has been bolstered by findings from hundreds of experiments showing that humans and a wide range of other animals, display hyperbolic discount functions of the type predicted to produce impulsive behavior (see, e.g., Chung & Herrnstein, 1967; Mazur, 1987). Many experiments with animals, and a small number with humans, have also demonstrated the types of temporally based preference reversals that are implied by hyperbolic discounting. Nevertheless, the non-exponential discounting perspective has at least two significant limitations as a general theory of impulsivity.

First, it does not shed light on why certain types of consumption are commonly associated with impulsivity while others are not. People commonly display impulsive behavior while under the influence of visceral factors such as hunger, thirst, or sexual desire or emotional states such as anger or fear. The hyperbolic discounting perspective has difficulty accounting for such situation- and reward-specific variations in impulsivity.

Second, the hyperbolic discounting perspective cannot explain why many situational features other than time delay—for example, physical proximity and sensory contact with a desired object—are commonly associated with impulsive behavior. For example, it is difficult to explain the impulsive behavior evoked by cookie shops that vent baking smells into shopping malls in terms of hyperbolic discounting.

The account of impulsivity embodied in propositions 1 and 2 is consistent with the observed differences in impulsivity across goods and situations. It views impulsivity as resulting not from the disproportionate attractiveness of immediately available rewards but from the disproportionate effect of visceral factors on the desirability of immediate consumption. It predicts, therefore, that impulsive behavior will tend to occur when visceral factors such as hunger, thirst, physical pain, sexual desire, or emotions are intense. In combination, propositions 1 and 2 imply that people will give much greater weight to immediately experienced visceral factors than to delayed visceral factors. Thus, according to proposition 2, the fact that I will be hungry (and dying to eat dessert), in pain (and longing for pain killers), or sexually deprived in the future has little meaning to me in the present. If food, pain killers, or sex have undesirable consequences I will plan to desist from these behaviors. When these visceral factors arise, however, and increase my momentary valuation of these activities, proposition 1 implies that I will deviate from my prior plans. In fact, neither proposition 1 nor 2 are necessary conditions for this account of impulsivity; what is required is a somewhat weaker condition which can be expressed as a third proposition.

Proposition 3:
Increasing the level of an immediate and delayed visceral factor simultaneously enhances the actual valuation of immediate relative to delayed consumption of the associated good.

That is, if $a' > a$ and $v(x, a, 0) = v(x', a, t)$, then $v(x, a', 0) > v(x', a', t)$. Whereas propositions 1 and 2 deal with the effect of visceral factors on the relationship between actual and desired behavior, proposition 3 makes no reference to desired behavior and refers only to the impact of visceral factors on time preference. The absence of the subjective concept of desired behavior renders proposition 3 especially amenable to empirical investigation.

Like the hyperbolic discounting perspective, the visceral factor perspective predicts that impulsivity will often be associated with short time delays to consumption; however, it provides a different rationale for this prediction and does not predict that short time delays will *always* produce impulsive behavior. According to the hyperbolic discounting perspective, desirability increases automatically when rewards become imminently available. The visceral factor perspective, in contrast, assumes that immediate availability produces impulsivity only when physical proximity elicits an appetitive response (influences an a). Many visceral factors, such as hunger and sexual desire, are powerfully influenced by temporal proximity. Neurochemical research on animals shows that the expectation of an imminent reward produces an aversive dopaminic state in the brain that is analogous to the impact of food expectation on hunger (Gratton & Wise, 1994). That is, the mere expectation of an imminent reward seems to trigger appetite-like mechanisms at the most basic level of the brain's reward system. The account of impulsivity proposed here, therefore, predicts that short time delays will elicit impulsivity only when they produce such an appetitive, or other type of visceral, response.

Short time delays, however, are only one factor that can produce such a visceral response. Other forms of proximity, such as physical closeness or sensory contact (the sight, smell, sound, or feeling of a desired object) can elicit visceral cravings. Indeed, as the literature on conditioned craving in animals shows, almost any cue associated with a reward—e.g. time of day, the color of a room, or certain sounds—can produce an appetitive response (Siegel, 1979). Perhaps the strongest cue of all, however, is a small taste, referred to as a "priming dose" in the neuropharmacological literature on drug addiction (Gardner & Lowinson, 1993).

Much of the seminal research of Walter Mischel and associates (summarized in Mischel, 1974; Mischel, Shoda, & Yuichi, 1992) can be interpreted as demonstrating the impact of visceral factors on impulsivity. Mischel's research focused on the determinants of delay of gratification in children and was the first to raise the problem of intraindividual variability in intertemporal choice. In a series of experiments, children were placed in a room by themselves and taught that they could summon the experimenter by ringing a bell. The children would then be shown a superior and inferior prize and told that they would receive the superior prize if they could wait successfully for the experimenter to return.

One major finding was that children found it harder to wait for the delayed reward if they were made to wait in the presence of either one of the reward objects (the immediate inferior or delayed superior). The fact that the presence of either reward had this effect is significant, because conventional analysis of intertemporal choice, including the hyperbolic discounting perspective, would predict that children would be more likely to wait in the presence of the delayed reward. The visceral factor perspective offers a ready explanation for this pattern, since the sight, smell, and physical proximity of either reward would be likely to increase the child's level of hunger and desire.

Other findings from Mischel's research are also consistent with a visceral factor account of impulsivity. For example, showing children a photograph of the delayed reward, rather than the reward itself, increased waiting times. Apparently the photograph provided a "picture" of the benefits of waiting without increasing the child's level of acute hunger or desire. Likewise, and explicable in similar terms, instructing children to ignore the candies or to cognitively restructure them (e.g. by thinking of chocolate bars as little brown logs) also increased waiting times.

18.3.3. *Vividness*

The notion that various dimensions of proximity—temporal, physical, and sensory—can elicit visceral influences that change behavior also provides a somewhat different interpretation of the often noted effect of vividness. Vividness has a powerful impact on behavior that is difficult to reconcile with the standard decision model. Sweepstakes advertise concrete grand prizes such as luxury cars or vacations, even though any normative model would predict that the monetary equivalent of the prize should have higher value to most individuals. When Rock Hudson and Magic Johnson were diagnosed with AIDS, concern for the disease skyrocketed (Loewenstein & Mather, 1990). Well-publicized incidents of "sudden acceleration" and terrorist attacks at airports in Europe squelched Audi sales and travel abroad by Americans, despite the comparative safety of Audis and foreign travel. Behavioral decision researchers have acknowledged the impact of vividness (Tversky & Kahneman, 1973; Nisbett & Ross, 1980), but have argued that vividness affects decision making via its influence on subjective probability. Vividness is assumed to affect the ease with which past instances of the outcome can be remembered or future instances imagined, producing an exaggeration of the outcome's subjective probability via the "availability heuristic."

Vividness, however, has a second, possibly more important, consequence. Immediate emotions arising from future events are inevitably linked to some mental image or representation of those events. There is considerable research demonstrating that the more vivid such images are, and the greater detail with which they are recalled, the greater will be the emotional response (e.g. Miller *et al.*, 1987). Hence, vividness may operate in part by intensifying immediate emotions associated with thinking about the outcome rather than (or in addition to) increasing the subjective likelihood of the outcome.

Many phenomena which have previously been attributed to availability effects on subjective probability could easily be reinterpreted in these terms. It has been shown, for example, that earthquake insurance purchases rise after earthquakes when, if anything, the objective probability is probably at a low-point but anxiety about these hazards is at a peak (Palm, Hodgson, Blanchard, & Lyons, 1990). Similarly, purchases of flood and earthquake insurance are influenced more by whether friends have experienced the event than by the experience of one's immediate neighbors, even though neighbors' experiences would seem to provide a better guide to one's own probability of experiencing a flood or earthquake (Kunreuther *et al.*, 1978). The large increase in the number of women seeking breast exams following the highly publicized mastectomies of Hope Rockefeller and Betty Ford, the tendency for doctors whose specialties are near the lung to stop smoking, and each of the examples of vividness listed earlier could also plausibly be attributed to emotion effects rather than to changes in subjective probabilities. Most doctors have a clear understanding of the dangers of smoking, but daily confrontation with blackened lungs undoubtedly increases the frequency and intensity of negative emotions associated with smoking.

Proposition 4:
Currently experienced visceral factors can have a mild effect on decisions for the future, even when those factors will not be operative in the future.

Proposition 4 is probably a minor effect relative to the other six discussed here, and it cannot be expressed in conditions pertaining to Eq. (2), which assumes that the value of consumption is influenced only by visceral factors operating at the same point in time. To express proposition 4 mathematically we could allow visceral factors operating in the present to influence the value of consumption at other points in time—e.g. $v_i(x_{ti}, a_{ti}, t, a_{0i})$. Proposition 4 would then imply that if $a'_{0i} > a_{0i}$ and $vi(x_{ti}, a_{ti}, t, a_{0i}) = vj(x_{tj}, a_{tj}, t, a_{0j})$, then $vi(x_{ti}, a_{ti}, t, a'_{0i}) \geq vj(x_{tj}, a_{tj}, t, a_{0j})$.

The classic illustration of proposition 4 is the tendency to buy more groceries when shopping on an empty stomach (Nisbett & Kanouse, 1968). Similarly, when sick we are likely to overreact by cancelling appointments later in the week, only to find ourselves recovered on the following day. It also seems likely that an aggrieved person would decide to take delayed revenge if immediate revenge were not an option, even if she knew intellectually that her anger was likely to "blow over."

The same failure of perspective taking can be observed in the interpersonal realm. For example, it is difficult for a parent, who feels hot from carrying a baby, to recognize that his baby might not be as hot. Similarly, it is difficult not to empathize with a wounded person even when they report feeling no pain. The latter phenomenon is illustrated vividly by the case of Edward Gibson, the "human pincushion." A Vaudeville performer who experienced no pain, Gibson would walk onto the stage and ask a man from the audience to stick 50–60 pins into him up to their heads, then would himself pull them out one by one (Morris, 1991). By Morris' description, "it is clear that Gibson's audience, no doubt reflecting a general human response, found themselves incapable of imagining a truly pain-free existence. They instinctively supplied the pain he did not feel" (p. 13).

Proposition 5:
People underestimate the impact of visceral factors on their own future behavior.

Let $\hat{v}$ represent the individual's prediction at time $t < 0$ of the value she will place on consumption at time 0 (when a visceral factor will be operative). Proposition 5 implies that if $a' > a > a_i^*$, and $\hat{v}(x', a', 0) = \hat{v}(x, a, 0)$, then $v(x', a', 0) > v(x, a, 0)$.

Proposition 5 is similar to proposition 2 except that it refers to predictions of future behavior rather than to decisions applying to the future. It implies that we underestimate the influence of future visceral factors on our behavior, whereas proposition 2 implies that we give future visceral factors little weight when making decisions for the future. Although closely related, the two phenomena have somewhat opposite implications for behavior; the failure to *appreciate* future visceral factors (as implied by proposition 2) increases our likelihood of binding our own future behavior—thus contributing to far-sighted decision making. For example, showing little sensitivity to tomorrow morning's self, we experience no qualms in placing the alarm clock across the room. The failure to *predict* our own future behavior (as implied by condition 5), however, decreases the likelihood that we will take such actions, even when they are necessary. Failing to predict the next morning's pain of awakening, we may underestimate the necessity of placing the alarm clock on the other side of the room.

The difficulty of predicting the influence of future visceral factors on our behavior results partly from the fact that visceral factors are themselves difficult to predict. The strength of visceral factors depends on a wide range of influences. Drive states such as sexual desire and hunger depend on how recently the drive was satisfied and on the presence of arousing stimuli such as potential sexual objects or the proximity of food. Moods and emotions depend on the interaction of situational factors and construal processes and on internal psychobiological factors. Physical pain and pleasure often depend on sensory stimulation, although construal processes also play an important role (Chapman, 1994). Because these underlying factors are themselves often erratic, predicting changes in visceral factors is commensurately difficult.

Even when visceral factors change in a regular fashion, however, people will not be able to predict such change if they lack a theory of how they change over time. Thus, Loewenstein and Adler (1995) demonstrated that people are unable to predict that ownership will evoke attachment to objects and aversion to giving them up, presumably because they, like social scientists until recently, are unaware of the endowment effect. They elicited selling prices from subjects actually endowed with an object and others who were told they had a 50% chance of getting the object. Selling prices were substantially higher for the former group, and the valuations of subjects who were not sure of getting the object were indistinguishable from the buying prices of subjects who did not have the object.

Moreover, even in the many cases when we can predict the intensity of a particular visceral factor relatively accurately, we may still have difficulty in predicting its impact on our own future behavior. It is one thing to be intellectually aware that one will be hungry or cold at a certain point in the future and another to truly appreciate the impact of that hunger or cold on one's own future behavior. If a teenager tries crack once for the experience, how difficult will he or she find it to desist from trying it again? How strong will a smoker's desire to smoke be if she goes to a bar where others are smoking, or the ex-alcoholic's desire for a drink if he attends the annual Christmas party at his place of work? Proposition 5 implies that people who are not experiencing these visceral factors will underestimate their impact on their own future behavior.

The difficulty of anticipating the effect of future visceral factors on one's own behavior is also illustrated by a study in which subjects were informed of the Milgram shock experiment findings and were asked to guess what they personally would have done if they had been subjects in the experiment. Most subjects in the piggyback study did not think that they themselves would have succumbed to the pressure to shock. Despite their awareness that a substantial majority of subjects delivered what they believed were powerful shocks, subjects underestimated the likely effect on their own behavior of being exposed to the authoritative and relentless pressure of the experimenter.

Proposition 6:
As time passes, people forget the degree of influence that visceral factors had on their own past behavior. As a result, past behavior that occurred under the influence of visceral factors will seem increasingly perplexing to the individual.

If we define v^r as the individual's recollection at time $t > 0$ of his own past utility, then, if $a' > a > a_i^*$, and $v(x', a', 0) = v(x, a, 0)$, then $v^r(x', a', 0) < v^r(x, a, 0)$.

Human memory is well suited to remembering visual images, words, and semantic meaning, but seems ill-suited to storing information about visceral sensations. Recall of visual images actually activates many of the brain systems that are involved in visual perception (Kosslyn *et al.*, 1993). Thus, it appears that to imagine a visual scene is, in a very real sense, to "see" the scene again, albeit in distorted, incomplete, and less vivid form. The same probably applies to memory for music and words; one can render a tune in one's head, or articulate a word, without producing any externally audible sound.

Except under exceptional circumstances,[8] memory for pain, and probably other visceral factors, appears to be qualitatively different from other forms of memory. As Morley (1993) observes in an insightful paper, we can easily *recognize* pain, but few can *recall* any of these sensations at will, at least in the sense of reexperiencing them at any meaningful level. Morley distinguishes between three possible variants of memory for pain: (1) sensory reexperiencing of the pain; (2) remembering the sensory, intensity, and affective qualities of the pain without re-experiencing it; and (3) remembering the circumstances in which the pain was experienced. Most studies of memory for pain have focussed on the second variant and have obtained mixed results. For example, several studies have examined the accuracy of women's memory of the pain of childbirth—most employing a so-called visual analog scale (basically a mark made on a thermometer scale) (e.g. Rofé & Algom, 1985; Norvell, Gaston-Johansson, & Fridh, 1987). These have been about evenly split in their conclusions, with about half finding accurate recall of pain (or even slight retrospective exaggeration) and the other half finding significant, and in some cases quite substantial, under-remembering of pain.

Morley himself (1993) conducted a study in which subjects completed a two-part survey on pain memories. In the first part they were asked to recall a pain event and in the second they were asked questions designed to measure the extent of the three variants of pain memory dimensions. When asked questions about the second variant type of pain memory, 59% were able to

---

[8] Traumatic injury may be such a case. Katz and Melzack (1990) argue, based on research on amputees experiencing the "phantom limb" phenomenon, that amputees store pain memories in a "neuromatrix" such that they can be retrieved and veridically reexperienced: "The results of the present study suggest that the somatosensory memories described here are not merely images or cognitive recollections (although obviously a cognitive component is involved); they are direct experiences of pain (and other sensations) that resemble an earlier pain in location and quality" (p. 333). They summarize different past studies of phantom limb pain in which 46, 79, 50, 17.5, 37.5, and 12.5% of patients who had lost limbs reported that the pain mimicked the original pain. There are problems with this research, most notably the retrospective methodology which introduces the possibility of recall bias. However, at a minimum, the phantom limb research suggests that some people in some situations may, in fact, be capable of remembering pain.

recall at least some aspect of the pain sensation, while the remaining 41% reported that they had no recall of the pain sensation at all and were thus unable to rate the vividness of their pain experience. For example, one subject reported "I remember the pain getting worse and worse, but I can't remember what the pain felt like at all." Not a single subject reported actually reexperiencing the pain—i.e. Morley's first variant of pain memory. Consistent with these results, Strongman and Kemp (1991) found that spontaneous accounts of pain tended to fit Morley's first variant of pain memory—remembering the circumstances in which the pain was experienced. Their subjects were given a list of 12 emotions and were asked for each to remember a time they had experienced the emotion. They found that, "Overwhelmingly, the descriptions were of 'objective' details of the events rather than of the feelings of the respondents" (p. 195).

Scarry (1985, p. 15) notes a similar phenomenon when it comes to descriptions of pain; these rarely describe the pain itself, but typically focus either on the external agent of pain (e.g. "it feels as though a hammer is coming down on my spine") or on the objective bodily damage associated with the pain ("it feels as if my arm is broken at each joint and the jagged ends are sticking through the skin"). Fienberg, Loftus, and Tanur (1985, p. 592) reached virtually the same conclusion in their review of the literature on memory for pain which concluded with the question: "Is it pain that people recall or is it really the events such as injuries and severe illnesses?"

Whether people can remember the sensory, intensity, and affective qualities of a pain (Morley's second variant), therefore, or only the events that produced the pain, the evidence is strong that most people cannot remember pain in the sense of reexperiencing it in imagination (Morley's first variant). We can recognize pain all too effortlessly when it is experienced, but only in a limited number of cases actually call it to mind spontaneously—i.e. recall them—in the same way that we can recall words or visual images.[9]

There may be certain types of visceral sensations, however, which, if not remembered in Morley's third sense, at least evoke arousal upon recall. For pain, this is true of those for which the pain-causing event can be imagined vividly. Highly imaginable events such as dentist visits, cuts and wounds, and bone breakage produce immediate anxiety and dread, to the point where the recollection of the event may actually be worse than the reality (e.g., Linton, 1991; Rachman & Arntz, 1991). For such events there is evidence that what people remember is what they expected to experience before-hand, rather than what they actually experienced (Kent, 1985).

A similar pattern holds for emotions. Some emotions are associated with straightforward cognitions. For example, anger may arise from a perceived insult, shame or embarrassment from a faux pas. To the extent that the insult

---

[9] Deleted in proof.

or faux pas can be conjured up in the mind, one can reproduce the emotion at any time, not just at the time when the instigating incident occurs (see, Strack, Schwarz & Gschneidinger, 1985, p. 1464).[10] Thus, as for pain, the ability to imagine the impact of future emotions depends on the concreteness and imaginability of the instigating stimuli. Moods or feeling states that have no obvious object, such as sadness or depression, by this reasoning, will be especially prone to anticipatory underestimation, as will pains and discomforts that are not associated with vivid images.

The latter observation may help to explain an observation made by Irena Scherbakowa (personal communication), on the basis of hundreds of interviews conducted with victims of Stalin's terror. She noted that people who had "betrayed" friends or family, or confessed to crimes they didn't commit when they were tortured by such methods as being forced to stand in one position for hours, or prevented from sleeping, may have been particularly haunted by the memory years later because it was difficult to understand, in retrospect, why they had succumbed to such seemingly "mild" methods. A similar observation was made by Biderman (1960) in his analysis of the retrospective reports of 220 repatriated U.S. Air Force prisoners captured during the Korean war. According to Biderman, "the failure of the prisoner to recognize the sources of the compulsion he experiences in interrogation intensifies their effects, particularly the disabling effects of guilt reactions" (p. 145).

Limitations in the memory for visceral sensations may also help to explain the disappointing results that have been obtained by interventions designed to alter behavior by invoking fear. In some such efforts, such as trying to "scare-straight" at-risk youths by exposing them to life in a maximum security penitentiary, the effect seems to have been opposite to what was intended (Finckenauer, 1982; Lewis, 1983). The standard explanation for such an effect is that the fear communication produced a defensive compensatory response. Perhaps, however, the paradoxical effect resulted from the weakness of the evoked response to the memory. If thinking about incarceration fails to evoke affect, even after touring the facility, perhaps the youths in question conclude that "I've experienced the worst, and it must not be that bad since thinking about it leaves me cold." This conjecture is consistent with research on people's response to minimally, moderately, and strongly fear-arousing lectures about dental hygiene (Janis & Feshbach, 1953). Immediately following the communication there appeared to be a monotonic relationship between fear intensity and vigilance; however, 1 week later the effect of the lectures on behavior was inversely related to fear.

In sum, with certain important exceptions, it appears that people can remember visceral sensations at a cognitive level, but cannot reproduce them, even at diminished levels of intensity. It seems that the human brain is not

---

[10] Jon Elster brought this point to my attention.

well equipped for storing information about pain, emotions, or other types of visceral influences, in the same way that visual, verbal, and semantic information is stored. We can recognize visceral sensations often too effortlessly when they occur, but only in a limited number of cases actually call them to mind spontaneously—i.e. recall them—in the same way that we can recall words or visual images. Unable to recall visceral sensations as we can recall other types of information, their power over our behavior is difficult to make sense of retrospectively or to anticipate prospectively.

Proposition 7:
Each of the first six propositions apply to interpersonal as well as intrapersonal comparisons, where other people play the same role visavis the self as the delayed self plays relative to the current self.

Analogous to proposition 1, actual altruism tends to decline relative to desired altruism as visceral factors intensify. A friend related to me the frenzied struggles between passengers that occurred on a transatlantic flight when the plane suddenly dived and only about half the oxygen masks dropped. Although fear caused people to become self-centered, it seems likely that even as they grasped for their neighbor's child's mask, they knew that they were violating their own moral codes. The self-focusing effects of visceral factors is not surprising given the prioritizing and motivating role that visceral factors play in human and nonhuman behavior. Analogous to proposition 2, when making decisions for others, we are likely to ignore or radically underweight the impact of visceral factors on them. Few of the classic tragedies (e.g., Eve and the apple; Macbeth) would have happened if the protagonists had turned over decision-making power to a disinterested party. Combining both of these analogous propositions, the interpersonal equivalent to proposition 3 states that the weight one places on oneself relative to other persons who are experiencing equivalent levels of a visceral factor increases as the common level of the visceral factor intensifies. Hunger, thirst, pain, and fear are all powerful antidotes to altruism (Loewenstein, forthcoming a).

Proposition 4 applied to the interpersonal domain implies that people who are themselves experiencing a visceral factor will be more empathic toward, and more accurate predictors of, others who are experiencing the same visceral factor. One summer, for example, a friend mentioned his back problems to me. I responded sympathetically, but his pain had little reality until, when working in the garden one day, I suddenly felt something "give" in my back. My virtually instant reaction was to think of him and to feel deeply for the first time what he must have been experiencing all along. Despite such occasional examples of "priming," however, in which one's own weak experience of a visceral factor allow us to empathize with another person's stronger one, in general, there seems to be an empathic gulf when it comes to appreciating another person's pain, hunger, fear, etc. As Elaine Scarry writes with respect to pain,

When one speaks about "one's own physical pain" and about "another person's physical pain," one might almost appear to be speaking about two wholly distinct orders of events. For the person whose pain it is, it is "effortlessly" grasped (that is, even with the most heroic effort it cannot *not* be grasped); while for the person outside the sufferer's body, what is "effortless" is *not* grasping it (it is easy to remain wholly unaware of its existence; even with effort, one may remain in doubt about its existence or may retain the astonishing freedom of denying its existence; and, finally, if with the best effort of sustained attention one successfully apprehends it, the aversiveness of the "it" one apprehends will only be a shadowy fraction of the actual 'it'). (1985, p. 4).

Scarry argues that pain, uniquely, possesses such an empathic gulf, and attributes it to the poverty of language when it comes to expressing pain. While agreeing with her that such a gulf exists, I think it applies to a much wider range of feelings than pain, doubt it arises from limitations of linguistic expression, and also believe that virtually the same gulf exists when it comes to remembering or anticipating one's own pain and other visceral factors. Regardless of the source of such an empathic gulf, its existence implies that, analogous to proposition 5, people will have difficulty predicting the behavior of other people who are experiencing intense visceral factors. Just as people underestimated the likelihood that they themselves would have conformed to the modal pattern of behavior in the Milgram experiment, for example, they also underestimated the likelihood that other, superficially described, persons would do so (Nisbett & Ross, 1980). Finally, analogous to proposition 6, the behavior of other people acting under the influence of visceral factors will seem as incomprehensible as one's own past visceral-factor-influenced behavior.

Most of the propositions just enumerated, including the 7th, are illustrated in William Styron's autobiographical treatise on depression. Depression fits the definition of a visceral factor since it has a direct impact on well-being and also influences the relative desirability of different activities. Proposition 1 (the excessive influence of immediately operative visceral factors) is illustrated by the fact that while he was depressed Styron experienced an almost overwhelming desire to commit suicide, but recognized that this was not in his self-interest. This latter awareness induced him to seek psychiatric help. Proposition 2 (the underweighting of future visceral factors), proposition 5 (underestimation of the impact of future visceral factors), and proposition 6 (the minimization in memory of the impact of past visceral factors) are also all vividly described in the book. When Styron was not feeling depressed, he reports, depression had little reality to him; indeed, writing the book was his attempt to come to terms with this lack of intrapersonal empathy. Proposition 4 (the projection of currently experienced visceral factors onto the future) is well illustrated by the feeling he reports, while depressed, that the depression will never end—all the while recognizing intellectually that this is probably false. Finally proposition 7 (the analog between intra- and interpersonal empathy vis-à-vis the effect of visceral factors) is amply illustrated both from his own perspective and that of others. Prior to his own long bout with depression, Styron received a visit from two friends who were suffering from severe depression, but reports that he found their behavior baffling, since their depression had no reality to him in his own nondepressed state. Later, when he became depressed himself, he experienced the same empathic void with respect to the people around him.

18.4. Applications

A major challenge confronting the decision paradigm is the generally poor "fit" achieved in empirical analyses of behavior that are guided by decision theory. In attempts to use decision models to explain or predict such wide-ranging behaviors as job choice, migration, contraception, criminal activity, and self-protective measures against health, home and work-place risks, the fraction of explained variance has generally been low. Although disappointing results are often attributed to measurement error, the poor fit problem persists even when researchers collect their own data, and despite the opportunities for data fitting inherent in the typical retrospective design. Even when applied to gambling—an activity which serves as the central metaphor for the decision making perspective—decision models have been largely unable to account for the "stylized" facts of aggregate behavior, let alone to predict the behavior of individuals. Is it possible that part of the poor fit problem results from the decision making paradigm's failure to take account of visceral factors? In this section I discuss a variety of patterns and domains of behavior in which I believe that visceral factors are likely to play an especially prominent role.

18.4.1. *Drug Addiction*

In the introduction of *Addiction,* Avrum Goldstein expresses the central paradox of addiction as follows:

If you know that a certain addictive drug may give you temporary pleasure but will, in the long run, kill you, damage your health seriously, cause harm to others, and bring you into conflict with the law, the rational response would be to avoid that drug. Why then, do we have a drug addiction problem at all? In our information-rich society, no addict can claim ignorance of the consequences.

Several different solutions to this riddle have been proposed. Becker and Murphy (1988), for example, argue that the addict begins taking the addictive substance with a realistic anticipation of the consequences. Such an account is unsatisfactory not only because it fails to fit the facts (e.g. it implies incorrectly that addicts will buy in bulk to save time and money in satisfying their anticipated long term habit), but also because it is difficult to understand how the rapid downward hedonic spiral associated with many kinds of addictions can be viewed as the outcome of a rational choice. Cocaine addiction, for example, seems to produce a relatively rapid diminution in the overall capacity for pleasure (Gardner & Lowinson, 1993). Herrnstein and Prelec (1992), in contrast, argue that people become addicted because they fail to notice the small incremental negative effects of the addictive substance. However their account fails to explain why people don't get the information from sources other than their own personal experience since, as Goldstein notes, the consequences of addiction are well publicized.

The theoretical perspective proposed here provides a somewhat different answer to this question (see, Loewenstein, forthcoming b, for a more detailed discussion). Research on drug addiction suggests that it is not so much the pleasure of taking the drug that produces dependency, but the pain of not taking the drug after one has become habituated to it (Gardner & Lowinson, 1993). This pain is usually subclassified into two components: the pain of withdrawing from the drug and the cravings for the drug that arise from "conditioned association"—i.e. that result from exposure to persons, places, and other types of stimuli that have become associated with drug taking. Proposition 5 (underestimation of the impact of future visceral factors) implies that people who have not experienced the pains of withdrawal and craving may over- or underestimate the aversiveness of withdrawal and craving, but will almost surely underestimate the likely impact of these visceral factors on their behavior. That is, people will exaggerate their own ability to stop taking a particular drug once they have started. Believing that they can stop taking the drug at will, they are free to indulge their curiosity, which, according to Goldstein (1994, p. 215) is the driving force in most early drug use.

Proposition 2 can also help to explain the prevalence of self-binding behavior among addicts. The alcoholic who takes antabuse (assuring him or herself of horrible withdrawal symptoms), the smoker who ventures off into the wilderness without cigarettes (after a final smoke at the departure point), and the dieter who signs up for a miserable, hungry, vacation at a "fat farm" are all imposing extreme future misery on themselves. To those who view these behaviors as the manifestation of myopic time preferences, such seemingly far-sighted behavior may seem anomalous. Proposition 2, however, suggests that such readiness to impose future pain on oneself has less to do with time preference, and more to do with the unreality of future pain to the currently pain-free self. It seems unlikely that alcoholics, smokers, or overeaters would take any of these actions at a moment when they were experiencing active craving for the substance to which they are addicted.

18.4.2. *Sexual Behavior*

As is true for addiction, volition seems to play an ambiguous and often changing role in sexual behavior. Although we hold people accountable for their behavior as a matter of policy, sexually motivated behavior often seems to fall into the "gray region" between pure volition and pure compulsion. The following three examples illustrate the applicability of the proposed theoretical perspective to sexual behavior.

Teenage contraception. In a recent study of teenage contraceptive behavior, Loewenstein and Furstenberg (1991) found that birth control usage was largely unrelated to the main variables that the decision making perspective would predict they should be correlated with—e.g. belief in birth control's effectiveness or the desire to avoid pregnancy. The most important correlates of birth control usage were embarrassment about using it and perceptions that it interferes with pleasure from sex. Clearly, the emotions associated with unwanted pregnancy are much more powerful or at least long-lasting than those associated with sexual spontaneity and enhanced pleasure; however, and consistent with proposition 1, the immediacy and certainty of embarrassment and discomfort seem to overwhelm the delayed and uncertain consequences of using it or failing to use it.[11] Proposition 7 can, perhaps, help to explain some of the misguided policies in this area—such as the abstinence movement—which leaves teenagers unprepared for their own feelings and behavior because its proponents underestimate the influence of visceral factors on the behavior of others.

Self-protection against sexually transmitted disease. Based on his own extensive and innovative research on the AIDS-related sexual behavior of gay men, Gold (1993, p. 1994) argues that much unprotected sex occurs in the heat of the moment but that people can't remember or predict what the heat felt like and so are unprepared to deal with it. He believes that the poor memory for

---

[11] Immediate affect has been found to be a critical determinant of behavior in numerous analyses of decision making. For example, Grasmick, Bursik, and Kinsey (1990) conducted two surveys on littering in Oklahoma City, one just before and one shortly after the initiation of a successful anti-littering program. The survey asked people whether they littered, obtained demographics, and asked questions about shame (e.g. "Generally, in most situations I would feel guilty if I were to litter the highways, streets, or a public recreation area") and also about the embarrassment the respondents would feel if they littered. The R2 jumped from .076 to .269 when shame and embarrassment variables were added to the equation predicting compliance, and the increase in these variables across the surveys mediated the change in mean compliance, strongly suggesting that the effectiveness of the program was due to its success in attaching an immediate negative emotion to littering. Manstead (1995) found that age and sex (typically the two most powerful explanatory variables) dropped out of regression equations predicting risk taking among drivers after controlling for affective variables. Klatzky and Loewenstein (1995) found that traditional decision making variables (probabilities and outcome severities) explained surprisingly little of the variance in women's breast-self examination behavior relative to subjective reports of anxiety associated with breast cancer and self-examination.

the "heat of the moment" has hampered researchers who "have studied only those cognitions that are present in respondents' minds at the time they are answering the researcher's questions (that is, 'in the cold light of day'), rather than those that are present during actual sexual encounters" (Gold, 1993, p. 4). Based on his view that gay men forget the influence of the heat of the moment (consistent with proposition 6), Gold (1994) ran a study in which he compared the effectiveness of a conventional informational intervention intended to increase the use of condoms during anal intercourse (exposure to didactic posters) to a new "self-justification" intervention. Subjects in the self-justification group were sent a questionnaire which instructed them to recall as vividly as possible a sexual encounter in which they had engaged in unprotected anal intercourse and were asked to indicate which of a given a list of possible self-justifications for having unsafe sex had been in their mind at the moment they had decided not to use a condom. They were then asked to select the self-justifications that had been in their mind most strongly at the time, to indicate how reasonable each of these seemed to them now, looking back on it; and to briefly justify these responses. The men were thus required to recall the thinking they had employed in the heat of the encounter and to reflect on it in the cold light of day. The percentage of men in the three groups who subsequently engaged in two or more acts of unprotected anal intercourse differed dramatically between the three groups—42 and 41% for the control and poster groups, but only 17% for the self-justification group.

Sex lives of married couples. Recent surveys of sexual behavior suggest that the sex lives of married couples tend to be even worse (in terms of frequency) than what most people already suspected. For example, a recent study conducted by the National Opinion Research Center (Michael, Gagnon, Laumann & Kolata, 1994) found that the average frequency of intercourse of married couples declined markedly as a function of years of marriage. Certainly some of this drop-off reflects the combined effects of soured relations, diminished attraction, etc. What is surprising, as reported in the same study, is that many couples enjoy sex quite a lot when it actually occurs. The visceral factor perspective can perhaps shed some additional light on the anomaly posed by the failure to take advantage of an obvious opportunity for gratification.

In the early stages of a relationship, the mere thought of sex, or the physical proximity of the other partner is sufficient to produce significant arousal. It is easy to understand this arousal in evolutionary terms, and indeed research has shown that rats, cattle, and other mammals can be sexually rejuvenated following satiation by the presentation of a new partner—the so-called "Coolidge Effect" (Bowles, 1974). Thus, early in a relationship one initiates sex in a visceral state not unlike that associated with the sex act itself. Repeated presentation of the same sexual partner, however, diminishes initial arousal. Proposition 5 implies that people who are not aroused will have difficulty imagining how they will feel or behave once they become aroused. It can thus explain why couples fail to initiate sex despite ample past experience showing that it will be pleasurable if they do. As in so many cases when people experiencing one level of a visceral factor need to make decisions for themselves when they will be at a different level, rules of thumb, such as "have sex nightly, regardless of immediate desire," may provide a better guide to behavior than momentary feelings.

18.4.3. *Motivation and Effort*

Another area in which the decision making perspective falls short is its treatment of motivation and effort. In the decision paradigm there is no qualitative distinction between choosing, say one car over another, or "deciding" to pick up one's pace in the last mile of a marathon; both are simply decisions. Years after the decline of behaviorism, behaviorists still offer the most coherent theoretical perspective on motivation and the most sophisticated and comprehensive program of research (see, e.g., Bolles, 1975).

Physical effort, and often mental effort as well, often produce an aversive sensation referred to as fatigue or, at higher levels, exhaustion. Like other visceral factors, fatigue and exhaustion are directly aversive, and alter the desirability of different activities; most prominently, they decrease the desirability of further increments of effort. Proposition 1 implies that as exhaustion increases, there will be an ever-increasing gap between actual and desired behavior. Anyone who has engaged in competitive sports, or who has taught for several hours in a row can confirm this prediction; regardless of the importance of performing well, and even with full knowledge that one will recover from the exhaustion virtually immediately after suspending the activity, sustained performance is often impossible to achieve. Proposition 5 implies that people will overestimate their own ability to overcome the effect of fatigue— they will exaggerate the degree to which they can overcome limitations in physical conditioning, concentration, etc. through sheer willpower, and proposition 6 implies that, as time passes, people increasingly come to blame themselves for deficiencies in their own prior effort level because they will forget their own past exhaustion. Proposition 7 predicts that people who are observing the effort output of others will have a difficult time understanding or predicting reductions in effort output. Watching speed-skaters during the Olympics, for example, I found it difficult to understand why they failed to maintain their pace in the face of such over-whelming incentives.

Many of the tactics that people use to motivate themselves in the face of fatigue and exhaustion can be described by the observation that you can only fight visceral factors with other visceral factors. Thus, a common tactic for mustering willpower is to attempt to imagine, as vividly as possible, the potential positive consequences of greater effort output, or the potential negative consequences of insufficient output. When I lived in Boston many years ago, a friend and I would regularly drive to West Virginia to go canoeing, and would typically drive back days later in the middle of the night. During these long drives I would remain awake at the wheel by imagining myself ringing the doorbell of my friend's parents house to announce that he had died in a car crash. The effectiveness of mental imagery in eliciting an emotional response explains not only why it is commonly used as an emotion-induction method in research, but also may also help to explain its prominent role in decision making (cf. Pennington & Hastie, 1988; Oliver, Robertson, & Mitchell, 1993). Not only does imagery provide a tool for deciding between alternative courses of action but, once a resolution has been made, it may also help to stimulate the emotional response needed to implement the decision. Multiattribute analytical evaluation seems unlikely to provide such a motivational impetus.

18.4.4. Self-Control

One of the most difficult patterns of behavior to subsume under a conventional rational choice framework, and one that has received increasing attention in the literature, is the phenomenon of intrapersonal conflict and self-control. People sometimes report feeling as if though there were two selves inside them—one more present- and one more future-oriented—battling for control of their behavior. To express the introspective sensation of intra-individual conflict, a number of people have proposed different types of "multiple self" models that apply to intrapersonal conflict preexisting models that have been developed to describe strategic interactions between different people.

Schelling's multiple self model (1984), for example, constitutes a relatively straightforward application of his pioneering research on commitment tactics in interpersonal bargaining to intrapersonal conflict. In his model a series of far-sighted selves who would prefer to wake up early, eat in moderation, and desist from alcohol, use a variety of precommitment techniques to control the behavior of their more short-sighted counterparts. Elster (1985), somewhat differently, sees intrapersonal conflict as a "collective action problem" involving the succession of one's selves. Such a perspective sheds special light on the phenomenon of unraveling. Just as one person's cutting in line can cause a queue to disintegrate into a state of anarchy, the first cigarette of someone who has quit, or the first drink of an ex-alcoholic, often usher in a resumption of the original self-destructive pattern of behavior. Finally, Thaler and Shefrin's (1981) "planner/doer" model adopts a principal-agent framework in which a farsighted planner (the principal) attempts to reconcile the competing demands of a series of present-oriented doers (the agents).

The strength of multiple self models is that they transfer insights from a highly developed field of research on interpersonal interactions to the less studied topic of intraindividual conflict. However, the usefulness of the multiple self approach is limited by imperfections in the analogy between interpersonal and intrapersonal conflict. There is an inherent asymmetry between temporal selves that does not exist between different people. People often take actions that hurt themselves materially to either reward or punish others who have helped or hurt them. In the intrapersonal domain, however, people cannot take actions for the purpose of rewarding or punishing their past selves. Another form of asymmetry arises from the fact that attempts at self control are almost always made by the far sighted self against the short-sighted one, and almost never in the opposite direction. Consistent only with the planner-doer model, there is little camaraderie between successive short-sighted selves, but much more of a sense of continuity between far-sighted selves. For example, when people "decide" to sleep in, they rarely disable the alarm clock to promote the cause of tomorrow morning's sluggish self; however, when not actually experiencing the misery of premature arousal, we might well make a policy decision to place the alarm clock away from the bed every night.

Perhaps the most significant problem with multiple self models is that they are metaphorical and not descriptions of what we think actually takes place in intrapersonal conflict. Advocates of the multiple self approach do not believe that there are little selves in people with independent motives, cognitive systems, and so on. Thus, it is difficult to draw connections between multiple self models and research on brain neurochemistry or physiology beyond the rather simplistic observation that the brain is not a unitary organism.

The visceral factor perspective, and its key assumption that intense visceral factors cause behavior to depart from perceived self-interest, provides a better fit to the stylized facts than do multiple self models. The introspective feeling of multiple selves, for example, arises from the observation that one is clearly behaving contrary to one's own self interest. Since we are used to interpreting behavior as the outcome of a decision, it is natural to assume that there must be some self—other than the self that identifies one's self-interest—that is responsible for the deviant behavior. The fact that impulsive selves never promote one-another's behavior is not surprising if these selves are not, in fact, coherent entities with consciousness and personal motives, but instead represent the motivational impact of visceral factors. The far-sighted self, in contrast, represented by the individual's assessment of self-interest, is much more constant over time. The far-sighted self can, in a sense, represent the individual's tastes, factoring out as much as possible the effect of visceral factors.

18.5. Concluding Remarks

The decision-making paradigm, as it has developed, is the product of a marriage between cognitive psychology and economics. From economics, decision theory inherited, or was socialized into, the language of preferences and beliefs and the religion of utility maximization that provides a unitary perspective for understanding all behavior. From cognitive psychology, decision theory inherited its descriptive focus, concern with process, and many specific theoretical insights. Decision theory is thus the brilliant child of equally brilliant parents. With all its cleverness, however, decision theory is somewhat crippled emotionally, and thus detached from the emotional and visceral richness of life.

Contrary to the central assumption of decision theory, not all behavior is volitional, and very likely most of it is not. This is not a novel critique, but most recent critiques along these lines have attacked from the opposite angle. A number of researchers have argued that most behavior is relatively "automatic" (Shiffrin, Dumais & Schneider, 1981), "mindless" (Langer, 1989), habitual (Ronis, Yates & Kirscht, 1989; Louis & Sutton, 1991), or rule-guided (Anderson, 1987; Prelec, 1991). While not disputing the importance of habitual behavior, my focus is on the opposite extreme—one that, while perhaps less prevalent than habitual behavior, presents a more daunting challenge to the decision making perspective. My argument is that much behavior is non-volitional or only partly volitional—even in situations characterized by substantial deliberation.

The failure to incorporate the volition-undermining influence of emotions and other visceral factors can be seen not only in the disappointing explanatory power of decision models, but also in two additional significant problems faced by the decision-making perspective. The first is the counterintuitive notion of "irrationality" that has arisen in a field which has irrationality as a central focus. As Daniel Kahneman notes (1993), contemporary decision theorists typically define irrationality as a failure to adhere to certain axioms of choice such as transitivity or independence—a definition that diverges sharply from personal accounts of irrationality. In everyday language, the term irrationality is typically applied to impulsive and self-destructive behavior and to actions that violate generally accepted norms about the relative importance of different goals.

The theoretical perspective proposed here views irrationality not as an objective and well-defined phenomenon, but as a subjective perception that occurs in the mid-range of the continuum defined by the influence of visceral factors. At low levels of visceral factors, people generally experience themselves as behaving in a rational fashion. At extremely high levels, such as the level of sleepiness that causes one to fall asleep at the wheel, decision making is seen as *arational*—that is, people don't perceive themselves as making decisions at all. It is in the middle region of visceral influences, when people observe themselves behaving contrary to their own perceived self-interest, that they tend to define their own behavior as irrational. Expressions such as "I don't know what got into me," or "I must have been crazy when I..."

refer to discrepancies between behavior and perceived self-interest that are produced by the influence of visceral factor. As proposition 7 would imply, moreover, the same expressions are used to refer to the irrational behavior of others that is difficult to comprehend as self-interested. In sum, the visceral factor perspective helps to explain when and why people view their own, and others', behavior as irrational.

The second problem resulting from the failure to take account of the impact of visceral factors, is a widespread skepticism toward the decision making perspective, on the part of both the general public and of academics in the humanities. A commonly heard complain is that decision theory fails to capture what makes people "tick," or what it means to be a person (cf. Epstein, 1994). People who introspectively experience high conflict in their personal lives are unlikely to embrace a theory of behavior that denies such conflict or that, at best, treats it as a matter of balancing competing reasons for behaving in different ways (Tversky & Shafir, 1992). The dismaying consequence of decision theory's lack of general appeal is a widespread tendency for those in the humanities and in the general public to fall back on outmoded theoretical accounts of behavior such as those proposed by Freud and his followers. The task of decision researchers, as I see it, is to try to breathe more life into decision models without losing the rigor and structure that are the main existing strengths of the perspective. Incorporating the influence of visceral factors, I hope, is a step in that direction.

References

Akerlof, G. A. (1991). Procrastination and obedience. *American Economic Review*, **81,** 1–19.

Anderson, J. R. (1987). Skill acquisition: compilation of weak-method problem solutions. *Psychological Review,* **94,** 192–210.

Beach, L. R. (1990). *Image theory: Decision making in personal and organizational contexts.* Chichester: Wiley.

Becker, G., & Murphy, K. M. (1988). A theory of rational addiction. *Journal of Political Economy,* **96,** 675–700.

Biderman, A. D. (1960). Social-psychological needs and 'involuntary' behavior as illustrated by compliance in interrogation. *Sociometry,* **23,** 120–147.

Bolles, R. C. (1975). *The theory of motivation* (2nd edn.). New York: Harper & Row.

Brown, J. W. (1988). *The life of the mind.* Hillsdale, NJ: Erlbaum.

Bruner, J. (1957). Going beyond the information given. In J. Bruner *et al.* (Eds.), *Contemporary approaches to cognition.* Cambridge, MA: Harvard Univ. Press.

Chapman, C. R. (1994). Assessment of pain. In W. Nimo & G. Smith (Eds.), *Anaesthesia.* England: Blackwell.

Christensen, S. M., & Turner, D. R. (1993). *Folk psychology and the philosophy of mind.* Hillsdale, NJ: Erlbaum.

Christensen-Szalanski, J. J. J. (1984). Discount functions and the measurement of patients' values: Women's decisions during childbirth, *Medical Decision Making*, **4**, 47–58.

Chung, S-H., & Herrnstein, R. J. (1967). Choice and delay of reinforcement, *Journal of the Experimental Analysis of Behavior*, **10**, 67–74.

Cinnamon, K., & Farson, D. (1979). *Cults and cons*. Chicago: Nelson-Hall.

Damasio, A. R. (1994). *Descartes' error: Emotion, reason, and the human brain*. New York: Putnam.

Easterbrook, J. A. (1959). The effect of emotion on cue utilization and the organization of behavior. *Psychological Review*, **66**, 183–201.

Elster, J. (1977). *Ulysses and the sirens*. Cambridge, England: Cambridge University Press.

Elster, J. (1985). Weakness of will and the free-rider problem, *Economics and Philosophy*, **1**, 231–265.

Epstein, S. (1994). Integration of the cognitive and the psychodynamic unconscious. *American Psychologist*, **49**, 709–24.

Fields, H. L. (1987). *Pain*. New York: McGraw–Hill.

Fienberg, S. E., Loftus, E. F., & Tanur, J. M. (1985). Recalling pain and other symptoms. *Health and Society*, **63**, 582–97.

Finckenauer, J. O. (1982). *Scared straight! and the panacea phenomenon*. Englewood Cliffs, NJ: Prentice–Hall.

Fishbein, M., and Azjen, I. (1975). *Belief, attitude, intention, and behavior: An introduction to theory and research*. Reading, MA: Addison-Wesley.

Frank, R. H. (1988). *Passions within reason: The strategic role of the emotions*. New York: Norton.

Frawley, P. J. (1988). Neurobehavioral model of addiction: Addiction as a primary disease. In S. Peele (Ed.), *Visions of addiction*. Lexington, MA: Lexington Books.

Galanter, M. (1989). *Cults: faith, healing, and coercion*. New York: Oxford University Press.

Gardner, E. L. (1992). Brain reward mechanisms. In J. H. Lowinson, P. Ruiz, R. B. Millman & J. G. Langrod (Eds.), *Substance abuse: A comprehensive textbook* (2nd edn., pp. 70–99). Baltimore: Williams & Wilkins.

Gardner, E. L., & Lowinson, J. H. (1993). Drug craving and positive/negative hedonic brain substrates activated by addicting drugs. *Seminars in the Neurosciences*, **5**, 359–368.

Gawin, F. H. (1991). Cocaine addiction: Psychology and neurophysiology. *Science*, **251**, 1580–1586.

Gold, R. (1993). On the need to mind the gap: On-line versus off-line cognitions underlying sexual risk-taking. In D. Terry, C. Gallons, & M. McCamish (Eds.), *The theory of reasoned action: Its application to AIDS preventive behavior*. New York: Pergamon Press.

Gold, R. (1994). *Why we need to rethink AIDS education for gay men*. Plenary address to the Second International Conference on AIDS' impact: Biopsychosocial aspects of HIV infection 7–10 July, Brighton, UK.

Goldstein, A. (1994). *Addiction: From biology to drug policy*. New York: Freeman.

Gould, S. J. (1992). *The panda's thumb: More reflections on natural history*. New York: Norton.

Grasmick, H. G., Bursik, R. J., & Kinsey, K. A. (1991). Shame and embarrassment as deterrents to noncompliance with the law—The case of an antilittering campaign. *Environment and Behaviour, 23,* 233–251.

Gratton, A., & Wise, R. A. (1994). Drug- and behavior-associated changes in dopamine-related electrochemical signals during intravenous cocaine self-administration in rats. *The Journal of Neuroscience, 14,* 4130–4146.

Herrnstein, R., & Prelec, D. (1992). Addiction. In G. Loewenstein & J. Elster (Eds.), *Choice over time.* New York: Russell Sage.

Hoch, S. J., & Loewenstein, G. F. (1991). "Time-inconsistent preferences and consumer self-control." *Journal of Consumer Research, 17,* 492–507.

Janis, I. L. (1967). Effects of fear arousal on attitude change. In L. Berkowitz (Ed.), *Advances in experimental social psychology* (Vol. 3, pp. 167–224).

Janis, I. L., & Feshbach, S. (1953). Effects of fear-arousing communications. *Journal of Abnormal and Social Psychology, 48,* 78–92.

Janis, I. L., & Leventhal, H. (1967). Human reactions to stress. In E. Borgatta & W. Lambert (Eds.), *Handbook of personality theory and research.* Chicago: Rand McNally.

Janis, I. L., & Mann, L. (1977). *Decision making: A psychological analysis of conflict, choice, and commitment.* New York: Free Press.

Kahneman, D. (1993). *Presidential address to the society for judgment and decision making.* St. Louis, MO.

Katz, J., & Melzack, R. (1990). Pain 'memories' in phantom limbs: review and clinical observations. *Pain, 43,* 319–336.

Kent, G. (1985). Memory of dental pain. *Pain, 21,* 187–94.

Klatzky, R., & Loewenstein, G. (1995). *Proximate influences and decision analyses as predictors of breast self-examination.* Working paper, Carnegie Mellon University, Department of Psychology.

Kosslyn, S. M., Alpert, N. M., Thompson, W. L., Maljkovic, V., Weise, S. B., Chabris, C. F., Hamilton, S. E., Rauch, S. L., & Buonanno, F. S. (1993). Visual mental imagery activates topographically organized visual cortex: PET investigations. *Journal of Cognitive Neuroscience, 5,* 263–87.

Kuhl, J., & Beckmann, J. (Eds.). (1994). *Volition and personality.* Seattle/Toronto/Bern/Göttingen: Hogrefe & Huber Publishers.

Kunreuther, H., Ginsberg, R., Miller, L., Slovic, P., Borkan, B., & Katz, N. (1978). *Disaster insurance protection: Public policy lessons.* New York: Wiley.

Langer, E. (1989). *Mindfulness.* Reading, MA: Addison-Wesley.

Lewis, R. V. (1983). Scared straight—California style. *Criminal Justice and Behavior, 10,* 209–226.

Libet, B., Gleason, C., Wright, E., & Pearl, D. (1983). Time of conscious intention to act in relation to onset of cerebral activity (readiness-potential). *Brain, 106,* 623–642.

Linton, S. J. (1991). Memory for chronic pain intensity: Correlates of accuracy. *Perceptual and Motor Skills, 72,* 1091–1095.

Loewenstein, G. (forthcoming, a). Behavioral decision theory and business ethics: Skewed tradeoffs between self and other. In D. M. Messick (Ed.), *Business ethics.*

Loewenstein, G. (forthcoming, b). Addiction, choice, and rationality. In J. Elster & O. J. Skog (Eds.), *Getting hooked: Rationality and addiction.* Cambridge, England: Cambridge University Press.

Loewenstein, G., & Adler, D. (1995). A bias in the prediction of tastes. *Economic Journal,* **105,** 929–937.

Loewenstein, G., & Furstenberg, F. (1991). Is teenage sexual behavior rational? *Journal of Applied Psychology,* **21,** 957–986.

Loewenstein, G., & Mather, J. (1990). Dynamic processes in risk perception. *Journal of Risk and Uncertainty,* **3,** 155–175.

Lord, Lepper, & Ross (1979). Biased assimilation and attitude polarization: the effect of prior theories on subsequently considered evidence. *Journal of Personality and Social Psychology,* **37,** 2098–2110.

Louis, M. R., & Sutton, R. I. (1991). Switching cognitive gears: from habits of mind to active thinking. *Human Relations,* **44,** 55–76.

Mandler, G. (1964). The interruption of behavior. In D. Levine (Ed.), *Nebraska symposium on motivation.* Lincoln, Nebraska: University of Nebraska Press.

Manstead, A. S. R. (1995). *The role of affect in behavioural decisions: Integrating emotion into the theory of planned behaviour.* Paper presented at seminar on Affect and Decision Making. Technical University of Eindhoven, March 31, 1995.

Mazur, J. E. (1987). An adjustment procedure for studying delayed reinforcement, In M. L. Commons, J. E. Mazur, J. A. Nevins, & H. Rachlin (Eds.), *Quantitative analysis of behavior: The effect of delay and of intervening events on reinforcement value* (Chapter 2). Hillsdale, NJ: Erlbaum.

Messiha, F. S. (1993). Fluoxetine: A spectrum of clinical applications and postulates of underlying mechanisms, Neuroscience and Biobehavioral Reviews, **17**(4), 385–396.

Michael, R. T., Gagnon, J. H., Laumann, E. O., & Kolata, G. (1994). *Sex in America: A definitive survey.* Boston: Little, Brown.

Miller, G. A., Galanter, E. H., & Pribram, K. H. (1960). *Plans and the structure of behavior.* New York: Henry Holt & Co.

Miller, G. A., Levin, D. N., Kozak, M. J., Cook, E. W. III, McLean, A., Jr., & Lang, P. J. (1987). Individual differences in imagery and the psychophysiology of emotion. *Cognition and Emotion,* **1,** 367–90.

Mischel, W. (1974). Processes in delay of gratification. In D. Berkowitz (Ed.), *Advances in experimental social psychology* (Vol. **7,** pp. 249–292).

Mischel, W., Shoda, Y., & Rodriguez, M. L. (1992). Delay of gratification in children. In G. Loewenstein & J. Elster (Eds.), *Choice Over time.* New York: Russell Sage.

Morley, S. (1993). Vivid memory for 'everyday' pains. *Pain,* **55,** 55–62.

Morris, D. B. (1991). *The culture of pain.* Berkeley: University of California Press.

Nisbett, R. E., & Kanouse, D. E. (1968). *Obesity, hunger, and supermarket shopping behavior.* Proceedings, American Psychological Association Annual Convention.

Nisbett, R. E., & Ross, L. (1980). *Human inference: Strategies and shortcomings of social judgment.* Englewood Cliffs, NJ: Prentice–Hall.

Nisbett, R. E., & Wilson, D. D. (1977). Telling more than we can know: Verbal reports on mental processes. *Psychological Review,* **84,** 231–59.

Norvell, K. T., Gaston-Johansson, F., & Fridh, G. (1987). "Remembrance of labor pain: How valid are retrospective pain measurements?" *Pain,* **31,** 77–86.

Olds, J., & Milner, P. (1954). Positive reinforcement produced by electrical stimulation of septal area and other regions of rat brain. *Journal of Comparative and Physiological Psychology,* **47,** 419–427.

Oliver, R. L., Robertson, T. S., & Mitchell, D. J. (1993). Imaging and analyzing in response to new product advertising. *Journal of Advertising, 22,* 35–50.

Osiatynski, W. (1992). *Choroba kontroli (The disease of control).* Warszawa: Instytut Psychiatrii i Neurologii.

Palm, R., Hodgson, M., Blanchard, D., & Lyons, D. (1990). *Earthquake insurance in California.* Boulder, CO: Westview Press.

Pennington, N., & Hastie, R. (1988). Explanation-based decision making: effects of memory structure on judgment. *Journal of Experimental Psychology: Learning, Memory and Cognition, 14,* 521–533.

Pettit, P. (1991). Decision theory and folk psychology. In M. Bacharach & S. Hurley (Eds.), *Foundations of decision theory.* Oxford: Blackwell.

Pickens, R., & Harris, W. C. (1968). "Self-administration of d-amphetamine by rats." *Psychopharmacologia, 12,* 158–163.

Pluchik, R. (1984). A emotions: A general psychoevolutionary theory. In K. R. Scherer & P. Ekman (Eds.), *Approaches to emotion* (Chapter 8, pp. 197–219). Hillsdale, NJ: Erlbaum.

Prelec, D. (1991). Values and principles: Some limitations on traditional economic analysis. In A. Etzioni & P. Lawrence (Eds.), *Socio-economics: toward a new synthesis.* New York: M. E. Sharpe.

Pribram, K. H. (1984). Emotion: A neurobehavioral analysis, In K. R. Scherer & P. Ekman (Eds.), *Approaches to emotion* (Chapter 1, pp. 13–38). Hillsdale, NJ: Erlbaum.

Rachman, S., & Arntz, A. (1991). The overprediction and underprediction of pain. *Clinical Psychology Review, 11,* 339–355.

Rofé, Y., & Algom, D. (1985). Accuracy of remembering postdelivery pain. *Perceptual and Motor Skills, 60,* 99–105.

Ronis, D. L., Yates, J. F., & Kirscht, J. P. (1989). Attitudes, decisions, and habits as determinants of repeated behavior. In A. R. Pratkanis, S. J. Breckerler, & A. G. Greenwald (Eds.), *Attitude, structure and function.* Hillsdale, NJ: Erlbaum.

Ross, M. (1989). Relation of implicit theories to the construction of personal histories. *Psychological Review, 96,* 341–357.

Scarry, E. (1985). *The body in pain.* Oxford, England: Oxford University Press.

Schelling, T. (1984). Self-command in practice, in policy, and in a theory of rational choice. *American Economic Review, 74,* 1–11.

Seeburger, F. F. (1993). *Addiction and responsibility. An inquiry into the addictive mind.* New York: Crossroads Press.

Shiffrin, R. M., Dumais, S. T., & Schneider, W. (1981). Characteristics of automatism. In J. Long & A. Baddeley (Eds.), *Attention and performance* (Vol. IX, pp. 223–238). Hillsdale, NJ: Erlbaum.

Siegel, S. (1979). The role of conditioning in drug tolerance and addiction. In J. D. Keehn (Ed.), *Psychopathology in animals: Research and treatment implications.* New York: Academic Press.

Simon, H. A. (1967). Motivational and emotional controls of cognition. *Psychological Review, 74,* 29–39.

Smith, A. (1892/1759). *Theory of moral sentiments.* London: George Bell & Sons.

Stewart, J., & Wise, R. A. (1992). Reinstatement of heroin self-administration habits: morphine prompts and naltrexone discourages renewed responding after extinction. *Psychopharmacology, 108,* 779–784.

Strack, F., Schwarz, N., & Gschneidinger, E. (1985). Happiness and reminiscing: The role of time perspective, affect, and mode of thinking. *Journal of Personality and Social Psychology, 49,* 1460–1469.

Strotz, R. H. (1956). Myopia and inconsistency in dynamic utility maximization. *Review of Economic Studies, 23,* 165–180.

Thaler, R. H., & Shefrin, H. M. (1981). An economic theory of self-control. *Journal of Political Economy, 89,* 392–406.

Tversky, A., & Kahneman, D. (1973). Availability: A heuristic for judging frequency and probability. *Cognitive Psychology, 5,* 207–232.

Tversky, A., & Kahneman, D. (1991). Loss aversion in riskless choice: A reference-dependent model. *Quarterly Journal of Economics, 106,* 1039–1061.

Tversky, A., & Shafir. (1992). Choice under conflict: The dynamics of deferred decision. *Psychological Science, 13,* 793–795.

Zajonc, R. B. (1968). Attitudinal effects of mere exposure. *Journal of Personality and Social Psychology Monograph, 9,* 1–28.

Zajonc, R. B., & Markus, H. (1982). Affective and cognitive factors in preferences. *Journal of Consumer Research, 9,* 123–131.

19

Risk as Feelings

George F. Loewenstein, Elke U. Weber, Christopher K. Hsee,
and Ned Welch

People sometimes ask me how it is that I'm so prolific. Being paranoid, I always suspect that the subtext is 'Why don't you go for more quality than quantity?' I do have an answer, albeit perhaps a not very satisfactory one. I'm not very good at judging the quality of my own papers, at least as measured by other people's reactions to them, which makes it very difficult to substitute quality for quantity. Some of the papers that I thought were my best, such as 'The Red and the Black', have had almost no impact. Others, such as the one reprinted in this chapter, have had an impact that has surprised me. The success of papers, like that of any product, has as much to do with timing as with the inherent quality of the papers. The timing was very good on this paper.

In it, we argue that the decisions people make under conditions of risk are powerfully conditioned by their emotional reactions to such risks. This seems a blindingly obvious insight, but when we proposed it, it was actually quite a new insight for economics and even for decision research. Although many innovative new 'generalized expected utility' models have been proposed to account for decisions under risk, economists continue to model risk with what could be called a 'consequentialist' approach. The assumption is that people think about the different possible consequences of a particular action (such as choosing to play a lottery), evaluate the utilities (i.e. how much they would like) each possible consequence, and then weight the different utilities according to some function of their probability of occurring. In such models, individuals are assumed to differ in their utilities for consequences, or in the way that they weight probabilities, but however they do, they are assumed to do so toward all risks. Hence, a major prediction of all consequentialist models is that people should exhibit relatively consistent attitudes toward risk.

Our perspective in this paper is quite different. We argue that decisions under risk depend on people's emotional reactions to those risks, which depend on a variety of factors other than probabilities and utilities—for example, the vividness with which the risks are described, and the ease with which they can be imagined. Moreover, because, for reasons that are not well-understood, different people are scared by different things, and, conversely, find certain types of risks pleasurable, we should expect to find very little cross-situational consistency in risk-taking. Again, not a particularly profound insight, but I think that this paper's usefulness was to give voice to what a lot of academics were already thinking.

Since its publication, a number of academics have done research that they cast as either supporting or refuting the theoretical perspective advanced in the paper. The following chapter reports results from a study that, perhaps not surprisingly, provided support for the risk as feelings perspective.

Risk as Feelings[*]

George F. Loewenstein, Elke U. Weber, Christopher K. Hsee,
and Ned Welch

The worst disease here is not radiation sickness. The truth is that the fear of Chernobyl has done more damage than Chernobyl itself. (Specter, 1996)

Decision making under risk and uncertainty has been one of the most active and interdisciplinary research topics in judgment and decision making (J/DM). Stimulated in part by the existence of a strong normative benchmark, expected utility (EU) theory, both psychologists and economists have made important theoretical and empirical contributions. These include tests of EU and its assumptions, identification of a wide range of deviations from EU predictions, and the development of alternative descriptive models such as prospect theory and other rank- and sign-dependent EU-type models (for recent summaries, see Harless & Camerer, 1994; R. D. Luce & von Winterfeldt, 1994; Starmer, 2000). EU-type theories also have wide currency in social and industrial–organizational psychology; take for example Ajzen and Fishbein's (1980) theory of reasoned action and the health belief model (Becker, 1974). The convergence in the theoretical perspectives of psychologists and economists in this area has been greater than for any other topic of mutual interest to the two disciplines.

Part of this convergence can be traced to a common implicit, and thus largely unquestioned, theoretical orientation. With some important

[*] This chapter was originally published as Loewenstein, G., Weber, E., Hsee, C., and Welch, N. (2001) 'Risk as Feelings', Psychological Bulletin. 127(2): 267–286. Published by APA and reproduced with permission.

We thank David Barlow, Colin Camerer, Gerald Clore, Shane Frederick, Howard Kunreuther, Jennifer Lerner, Graham Loomes, Barbara Mellers, Muriel Niederle, Ellen Peters, and Cass Sunstein for numerous helpful comments and suggestions. The first draft of this article was written while George F. Loewenstein was a Fellow at the Center for Advanced Study in the Behavioral Sciences, which was supported by National Science Foundation Grant SBR-960123. Other support was++ received from the Center for Integrated Study of the Human Dimensions of Global Change, a joint creation of National Science Foundation (Grant SBR-9521914) and Carnegie Mellon University, and the National Science Foundation (Grant SBR-9631860).

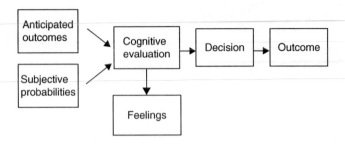

Figure 1. Consequentialist perspective.

exceptions (e.g. Janis & Mann, 1977; Mann, 1992; Slovic, Finucane, Peters, & MacGregor, in press), both psychologists and economists who study risky choice adhere to what could be characterized as a consequentialist perspective. We use the term *consequentialist* in its conventional sense to mean that people make decisions on the basis of an assessment of the consequences of possible choice alternatives.

As illustrated in Figure 1, EU-type theories posit that risky choice can be predicted by assuming that people assess the severity and likelihood of the possible outcomes of choice alternatives, albeit subjectively and possibly with bias or error, and integrate this information through some type of expectation-based calculus to arrive at a decision. Feelings triggered by the decision situation and imminent risky choice are seen as epiphenomenal—that is, not integral to the decision-making process. In this sense J/DM theorists assume (either implicitly or explicitly) that risky decision making is essentially a cognitive activity. Many choice theorists are deliberately agnostic about the psychological processes underlying the patterns of choice that their models predict. However, modelers who are explicit about process (e.g. Lopes, 1995; Payne, Bettman, & Johnson, 1993) typically articulate algebraic accounts of underlying processes that are cognitive in character. Overt or covert cognitive information evaluation and integration are assumed to underlie the full gamut of risk-related decisions, from health and safety decisions such as dieting, seatbelt use, and smoking to choices about recreational and workplace activities.

In this article, we propose a distinction between anticipatory emotions and anticipated emotions. *Anticipatory emotions* are immediate visceral reactions (e.g. fear, anxiety, dread) to risks and uncertainties. *Anticipated emotions* are typically not experienced in the immediate present but are expected to be experienced in the future. To the extent that J/DM research has addressed emotions, the emotions that have been taken into account are anticipated emotions. Several J/DM theories of risky choice provide a prominent role for such emotions, which include the disappointment or regret that might arise from counterfactual comparisons (Bell, 1982, 1985; Loomes & Sugden,

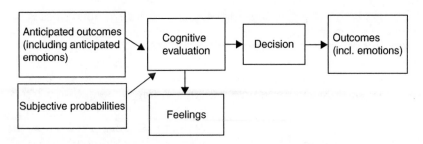

Figure 2. Consequentialist perspective with anticipated emotions.

1982, 1986; Mellers, Schwartz, Ho, & Ritov, 1997; Mellers, Schwartz, & Ritov, 1999). As illustrated in Figure 2, decision makers are assumed to anticipate how they will feel about obtaining different outcomes as the result of various counterfactual comparisons. These anticipated emotions are a component of the expected consequences of the decision; they are emotions that are expected to occur when outcomes are experienced, rather than emotions that are experienced at the time of decision. The decision-making process in these theories is still modeled as the implicitly cognitive task of predicting the nature and strength of future emotions in response to possible decision outcomes and weighting them according to their likelihood of occurring.

Likewise, in Isen's work examining the impact of affect on decision making (e.g. Isen & Geva, 1987; Isen & Patrick, 1983; Nygren, Isen, Taylor, & Dulin, 1996), the assumed role of affect is anticipated rather than anticipatory. Isen and her colleagues have investigated the role of positive affect on risky decision making, presenting research participants with simple decision tasks after inducing positive affect by, for example, giving them a small bag of candy. Although happy decision makers are generally more optimistic about their probability of winning a given lottery (Isen & Patrick, 1983), they are much less willing to gamble than controls. Isen and colleagues (e.g. Isen, Nygren, & Ashby, 1988) explain this effect in terms of what they call a *mood maintenance hypothesis*—that people in a good mood are reluctant to gamble because losing might undermine their good mood. This is inherently consequentialist reasoning.

Whereas decision researchers have focused mainly on anticipated emotions, researchers in fields outside of decision making, such as neuroscience and social psychology, have focused instead on the role of anticipatory emotions in decision making. In contrast to the historical view of emotions (and other "passions") as destructive influences on decision making, much of the new work highlights the role played by emotions as informational inputs into decision making and the negative consequences that result when such inputs are blocked.[1] For example, Damasio's somatic marker hypothesis posits that normal decision making is guided by somatic reactions to deliberations about alternatives that provide information about their relative desirability. In support of this perspective, Damasio and colleagues (Bechara, Damasio, Tranel, & Damasio, 1997; Damasio, 1994) show that certain neurological abnormalities that block such somatic reactions but produce minimal cognitive deficits lead to significant impairments of risky decision making. Other research by Wilson and colleagues (e.g. Wilson et al., 1993; Wilson & Schooler, 1991) shows that the quality of decision making suffers when affective inputs are suppressed by having decision makers think systematically about the pros and cons of a decision.

Research by Zajonc (1980, 1984a, 1984b), Bargh (1984), and LeDoux (1996) likewise shows that affective reactions to stimuli are often more rapid and basic than cognitive evaluations. Such immediate affective responses, the researchers have argued, provide organisms with a fast but crude assessment of the behavioral options they face, which makes it possible to take rapid action. An even more recent interpretation of the evidence, that is consistent with an early argument by Simon (1967), holds that these rapid emotional reactions serve as a mechanism to interrupt and redirect cognitive processing toward potentially high-priority concerns, such as imminent sources of danger (Armony, Servan-Schreiber, Cohen, & LeDoux, 1995, 1997; de Becker, 1997). Armony et al. (1997) commented that

a threatening stimulus occurring outside of the focus of attention may fail to be processed by cortical systems (as its representation is filtered out by a topdown attentional influence). In contrast, the direct pathway is not subject to this type of filtering, and therefore will transmit the information about the threatening stimulus to the amygdala, regardless of whether or not that stimulus occurs in the focus of attention. (p. 33)

A similar argument, with respect to anxiety as opposed to fear, has been advanced by Luu, Tucker, and Derryberry (1998), who argued that "appropriate levels of anxiety reflect the highest level of normal motivational control of working memory, through which the operations of memory in planning and behavioral sequencing are continually linked with adaptive significance" (p. 578).

Clore and Schwarz's affect-as-information hypothesis (Clore, Schwarz, & Conway, 1994; Schwarz & Clore, 1983) draws on very different types of evidence to reach a similar conclusion. As presented in Clore (1992), the affect-as-information hypothesis is a model of how feelings influence (social)

[1] The same pattern can be seen in the popular press and literature. Witness a recent *Newsweek* article titled "Don't Ignore Your Fear" (1997) a Spiegel (1997) article titled "Die Macht der Gefuehle" (The power of feelings), or the recent popular bestseller "The Gift of Fear: Survival Signals That Protect Us From Violence" (de Becker, 1997).

judgments. Judgments of others, for example, are affected by the positive and negative feelings of liking and disliking. The critical difference between the affect-as-information and other social judgment models that address the role of affect is that, according to the affect-as-information perspective, affect has a direct effect (as a sample of experience of the object of judgment) rather than being mediated by affect-congruent memories or concepts. The affect-as-information hypothesis correctly predicts that feelings during the judgment or decision process affect people's judgments or choices in those cases where the feelings are (correctly or through misattributions) experienced as reactions to the imminent judgment or decision. If feelings are attributed to a source that is normatively irrelevant to the decision at hand, their impact is reduced or eliminated (Schwarz & Clore, 1983; but see Winkielman, Zajonc, & Schwarz, 1997).

Most directly relevant to our focus on decision making under risk, and also consistent with the positive view of emotions, Slovic and collaborators (e.g. Finucane et al., 2000; Slovic et al., in press; Slovic, Flynn, & Layman, 1991; Slovic et al., 1991) have proposed an "affect heuristic" that highlights the importance of affect for risk perceptions and risk-related behavior. Over the past 20 years, Slovic, Fischhoff, and Lichtenstein have explored the emotional bases of risk judgments using a range of innovative methods. Adopting a psychometric paradigm (e.g. Fischhoff, Lichtenstein, Slovic, Derby, & Keeney, 1981), these researchers found that people's perceptions of the risks of hazardous technologies or activities are influenced by risk dimensions that have little to do with consequentialist aspects (i.e. possible outcomes and their probabilities).[2] Peters and Slovic (1996) have subsequently found that the "psychological" dimensions of risk can be distilled into two primary factors: *dread*, defined by the extent of perceived lack of control, feelings of dread, and perceived catastrophic potential, and *risk of the unknown*, the extent to which the hazard is judged to be unobservable, unknown, new, or delayed in producing harmful impacts. The first of these dimensions clearly suggests an affective rather than cognitive evaluation of hazards.

Although neither the affect-as-information hypothesis nor the affect heuristic rule out the possibility that affective reactions to decisions can diverge

[2] Holtgrave and Weber (1993) demonstrated that Slovic et al.'s risk dimensions have explanatory power even after controlling for the effect of probabilities and outcomes. They attempted to explain subjective assessments of a wide variety of financial and health and safety risks on the basis of both probabilities and utilities (as captured by a simplified version of R. D. Luce and Weber's 1986 conjoint expected-risk model) and Slovic, Fischhoff, and Lichtenstein's (1986) psychometric risk dimensions. The best fits were obtained by a hybrid model that added Slovic et al.'s three *dread* risk dimensions to the conjoint expected-risk model. These results suggest that even evaluations of the risk of financial investments have emotional components that are not completely described by the objective components of cognitive information-integration models.

from cognitive evaluations, neither perspective draws attention to such divergences or their consequences for behavior. In contrast, other strands of literature in psychology most closely associated with the clinical literature suggest that emotions often conflict with cognitive evaluations and can in some situations produce pathologies of decision making and behavior. Research on anxiety, for example, shows that emotional reactions to a risky situation often diverge from cognitive evaluations of risk severity (Ness & Klaas, 1994). When such departures occur, moreover, the emotional reactions often exert a dominating influence on behavior and frequently produce behavior that does not appear to be adaptive. Fear causes us to slam on the brakes instead of steering into the skid, immobilizes us when we have greatest need for strength, causes sexual dysfunction, insomnia, ulcers, and gives us dry mouth and jitters at the very moment when there is the greatest premium on clarity and eloquence. Most people, therefore, have at least occasionally experienced their own emotions as a destructive influence that they wish they could turn off. As Rolls (1999) wrote,

the puzzle is not only that the emotion is so intense, but also that even with our rational, reasoning capacities, humans still find themselves in these situations, and may find it difficult to produce reasonable and effective behaviour for resolving the situation. (p. 282)

Rolls argues that such divergences between emotional reactions and cognitive evaluations arise because

in humans, the reward and punishment systems may operate implicitly in comparable ways to those in other animals. But in addition to this, humans have the explicit system [closely related to consciousness] which enables us consciously to look and predict many steps ahead. (p. 282)

The divergence of emotional responses from cognitive evaluations of risks, as well as the potency of emotional responses in influencing behavior, are evident in the large numbers of individuals who suffer from often-debilitating fear- and anxiety-related disorders who, in the words of one anxiety researcher, are typically "well aware that there is little or nothing to fear in situations they find so difficult" (Barlow, 1988, p. 13). Even people who are not suffering from full-blown phobias commonly experience powerful fears about outcomes that they recognize as highly unlikely (such as airplane crashes) or not objectively terrible (such as public speaking); in contrast, many experience little fear about hazards that are both more likely and probably more severe (such as car accidents). The divergence between emotional reactions to, and cognitive evaluations of, risk is a common source of the feeling of intrapersonal conflict (see, e.g., Schelling, 1984). As Schelling documented, people often use sophisticated tactics to override their emotional responses to situations—to "conquer their fears."

In other related developments, psychologists from different sub-disciplines (clinical, social, and cognitive) have been drawing similar distinctions between two qualitatively different modes of information processing (e.g. Chaiken & Trope, 1999; Epstein, Lipson, Holstein, & Huh, 1992; Sloman, 1996; Windschitl & Weber, 1999). Sloman, for example, distinguished between rule-based and associative processing. Rule-based processing is a relatively controlled form of processing that operates according to formal rules of logic and evidence and is mediated by conscious appraisal of information. A response driven by *rule-based processing* follows from the execution of one or more rules that are assumed to be relevant to the task (e.g. *modus ponens* or the conjunction rule). *Associative processing* is a more spontaneous form of processing that operates by principles of similarity and temporal contiguity. In associative processing, the situational context influences responses directly, just as associatively based priming influences the recognition of a target word. Pathways and patterns of activation follow principles of similarity and temporal contiguity; the stronger the association between two concepts (which depends on similarity, repeated joint exposure, etc.), the more activation passes from one to another. Because associative processing is not mediated by conscious appraisal it is difficult to suppress its influence on judgments and decisions.

In support of his two-process dichotomy, Sloman (1996) provided examples from reasoning, categorization, and judgment research in which people find two simultaneously contradictory responses—one presumably mediated by associative processing and the other by rule-based processing—to be compelling for a given problem. For example, although people know that a whale does not fit the classification of "fish," statements like "technically a whale is a mammal" suggest that people are influenced by the similarity between whales and fish. Windschitl and Weber (1999) showed that associative processing of contextual information affected judgments of subjective likelihood even in situations where numeric estimates of likelihood were provided by credible experts.

Focusing narrowly on the topic of decision making under risk, we attempt to integrate these two strands of literature, one showing that emotions inform decision making and the other showing that emotional responses to risky decision situations—that is, anticipatory emotions—often diverge from cognitive evaluations. As demonstrated by the many studies that support the somatic marker, affect-as-information, and affect heuristic theories, emotional reactions and cognitive evaluations typically work in concert to guide reasoning and decision making. However, anticipatory emotional reactions sometimes diverge from cognitive evaluations and, when they do, the emotional reactions often exert a dominating influence on behavior. We attempt to explain when and why such emotional reactions diverge from cognitive evaluations of risk and to explain how these responses interact to determine

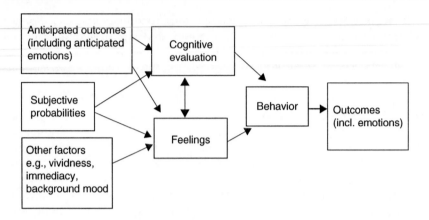

Figure 3. Risk-as-feelings perspective.

behavior. The theoretical framework we propose, which we label the *risk-as-feelings hypothesis*, provides a parsimonious account of a number of risk-related phenomena that are not explained by existing consequentialist models of risky decision making.

The risk-as-feelings hypothesis, illustrated in Figure 3, postulates that responses to risky situations (including decision making) result in part from direct (i.e. not cortically mediated) emotional influences, including feelings such as worry, fear, dread, or anxiety. People are assumed to evaluate risky alternatives at a cognitive level, as in traditional models, based largely on the probability and desirability of associated consequences. Such cognitive evaluations have affective consequences, and feeling states also exert a reciprocal influence on cognitive evaluations. At the same time, however, feelings states are postulated to respond to factors, such as the immediacy of a risk, that do not enter into cognitive evaluations of the risk and also respond to probabilities and outcome values in a fashion that is different from the way in which these variables enter into cognitive evaluations. Because their determinants are different, emotional reactions to risks can diverge from cognitive evaluations of the same risks. As illustrated in Figure 3, behavior is then determined by the interplay between these two, often conflicting, responses to a situation. Note that the term *decision* in Figures 1 and 2 is deliberately replaced with *behavior* in Figure 3. This substitution reflects the observation that many types of emotion-driven risk-related behaviors, ranging from panic reactions (e.g. slamming on the brake when one skids on ice) to the agoraphobic individual's inability to leave the house, do not seem to reflect decisions in the sense that the term is usually used.

The risk-as-feelings hypothesis is similar to the somatic marker hypothesis, the affect-as-information perspective, and the affect heuristic in drawing attention to the important role played by affect in decision making, but the risk-as-feelings hypothesis has a somewhat different focus. Although these approaches do not rule out the possibility that emotional reactions could diverge from cognitive reactions, they focus mainly on the complementary role of the two systems. They assume that affect typically plays an informational role in decision making—that it provides inputs into decision making that help people to evaluate alternative courses of action, albeit not always in a normative fashion. In contrast to these other theories, the risk-as-feelings hypothesis posits that, in addition, emotions often produce behavioral responses that depart from what individuals view as the best course of action. Our intent in this article is to begin to make sense of when and why such divergences occur.

In highlighting the role played by emotions in risk-related decision making, the research we review is representative of an emergent interest in the role played by emotions in decision making more generally. For example, Kahneman and co-authors (Kahneman & Ritov, 1994; Kahneman, Ritov, & Schkade, 1999; Kahneman, Schkade, & Sunstein, 1998) observed that when jurors make decisions or when the public makes contingent valuations of public goods, their judgments are often erratic and cannot be understood from an economic preference perspective. However, these responses can be interpreted as a manifestation of the decision maker's gut feelings toward the target at the time of decision making. M. F. Luce, Bettman, and Payne (1997, 1999) studied another type of decision-moment feeling—tradeoff difficulty emotions. They found that tradeoff difficulty in decision making can evoke negative emotions that bear no relationship to the valence of the consequences but that in turn lead decision makers to alter their coping strategies or avoid the decision altogether. Loewenstein (1996, 1999) has studied the role of emotions and other "visceral factors" such as hunger, sexual arousal, and pain in decision making (see also Loewenstein & Lerner, in press).

The next section lays out the risk-as-feelings hypothesis in detail and presents evidence supporting each of its specific assumptions. The second section discusses the determinants of risk-related feelings to explain why such feelings often diverge from cognitive evaluations of risk severity and reviews a wide range of phenomena that are consistent with the risk-as-feelings perspective but are difficult to explain in terms of standard cognitive–consequentialist approaches. The third section concludes with a discussion of further predictions of the risk-as-feelings hypothesis and implications for public policy.

19.1. Risk-as-Feelings Hypothesis

If risk-related feelings and cognitive evaluations had identical determinants as well as consequences for behavior, the risk-as-feelings hypothesis would be little more than an alternative description of the psychological processes underlying decision making, and anticipatory feelings would not be required as an intervening construct. However, people's emotional reactions to risks depend on a variety of factors that influence cognitive evaluations of risk only weakly or not at all. These include the vividness with which consequences can be imagined, personal exposure to or experience with outcomes, and past history of conditioning. Cognitive assessments of risk, on the other hand, tend to depend on more objective features of the risky situation, such as probabilities of outcomes and assessments of outcome severity. Even when feelings about risk are influenced by these objective features, the functional form of such dependence is different. For example, it has been demonstrated that feelings about risk are largely insensitive to changes in probability, whereas cognitive evaluations do take probability into account. As a result, feelings about risk and cognitive risk perceptions often diverge, sometimes strikingly.

Evidence from different areas of psychology provides support for different aspects of the risk-as-feelings hypothesis, as illustrated in Figure 3. Some elements are not controversial. For example, few would question that cognitive evaluations give rise to affective responses, although there is debate about the relationship between specific cognitions and specific emotions (e.g., Ellsworth & Smith, 1988; Ortony, Clore, & Collins, 1988; Roseman, 1984; Scherer, 1984; C. A. Smith & Ellsworth, 1985).

There is also little disagreement that important influences operate in the reverse direction, from emotion to cognition. From a neurophysiological perspective, the finding that emotions exert a powerful influence on judgments is not surprising. As LeDoux (1996) noted, "emotions can flood consciousness ... because the wiring of the brain at this point in our evolutionary history is such that connections from the emotional systems to the cognitive systems are stronger than connections from the cognitive systems to the emotional systems" (p. 19). Numerous studies have found that people in good moods make optimistic judgments and choices and that people in bad moods make pessimistic judgments and choices (Bower, 1981, 1991; Isen, Shalker, Clark, & Karp, 1978; Johnson & Tversky, 1983; Kavanagh & Bower, 1985; Mayer, Gaschke, Braverman, & Evans, 1992; Mayer & Hanson, 1995; Schwarz & Clore, 1983; Wright & Bower, 1992). For example, Johnson and Tversky found that people who read sad newspaper articles subsequently gave higher risk estimates for a variety of potential causes of death (e.g. floods, disease) than people who read happy newspaper articles. More recent research has gone beyond the valence approach to examine the different effect of different specific emotions of the same valence on judgments and choices. Most relevant to the framework proposed here, many studies have found effects of fear and anxiety on various types of judgments that tend to favor cautious, risk-averse decision making (Lerner & Keltner, 1999, 2000).

Eysenck (1992), for example, proposed that highly anxious individuals attend preferentially to threat-related stimuli and interpret ambiguous stimuli and situations as threatening, and a number of studies have supported these predictions (e.g. Derakshan & Eysenck, 1997; Eysenck, MacLeod, & Matthews, 1987; Vasey, El-Hag, & Daleiden, 1996). Raghunathan and Pham (1999) found that induced anxiety increased individuals' preference for low risk, low reward options, whereas induced sadness had the opposite effect. Lerner and Keltner (2000) found that fearful individuals make relatively pessimistic risk assessments and relatively risk-averse choices.

The two more controversial aspects of the theoretical framework summarized in Figure 3 are (a) that feelings can also arise without cognitive mediation (probabilities, outcomes, and other factors can directly give rise to feelings) and (b) that the impact of cognitive evaluations on behavior is mediated, at least in part, by affective responses (cognitive evaluation gives rise to feelings that in turn affect behavior). We focus on these two points in the remainder of this section.

19.1.1. *Feelings Need Not Be Cognitively Mediated*

There is considerable support for the notion that the pathway from risky stimulus to emotional reaction can be direct, that is, not mediated by any cognitive evaluation of the situation except for the most basic perceptual processing. Evidence for the affect-as-information hypothesis (Clore, Schwarz, & Conway, 1994; Schwarz & Clore, 1983) in social cognition supports the direct effect of feelings on judgments and decisions over indirect (cognitively mediated) effect interpretations that assume that feelings selectively prime semantic concepts (i.e. Bower, 1981, 1992). Clore (1992) provided a summary of two decades of research that shows direct effects of emotions on judgment. The idea that feelings need not be cognitively mediated is also supported by the research of Zajonc (1980, 1984a, 1984b), who first argued for greater speed and automaticity of affective over cognitive reactions and showed that people can have an affective reaction to a stimulus before they know what it is they are reacting to. For example, sudden, unexpected noises can cause fear well before we determine the source of the noise. Zajonc also showed that memory for affective reactions can be dissociated from memory for details of a situation, with the former often being better. An example is that we often remember whether we liked or disliked a particular person, book, or movie without being able to remember any details other than our affective reaction (Bargh, 1984).

Recent research by LeDoux and his colleagues (summarized in LeDoux, 1996) provides the anatomical neurological underpinnings for such direct effects. LeDoux and colleagues have shown that there are direct neural projections from the sensory thalamus (which performs crude signal processing) to the amygdala (which is widely believed to play a critical role in the processing of affective stimuli) that are not mediated by cortical processing. More recently, Servan-Schreiber and Perlstein (1998), in research with humans, have shown that intravenous injections of procaine, which produce powerful emotional responses, also produce amygdal activation. People who receive such injections report experiencing panic sensations and other powerful feelings that are disturbing precisely because they have no obvious cognitive antecedents. Other research has found that when the amygdala and other fear sites are stimulated electrically, people verbally report powerful feelings of foreboding (Panksepp, 1985, 1998). These evoked fears are often described in metaphoric terms; for example, "Somebody is now chasing me," "just like entering into a long, dark tunnel," or "surf coming from all directions," as if the cortex attempts to make sense of these disembodied forebodings (Panksepp, 1998, p. 214). Whatever the reason for these crude, rapid, emotional responses, all of this research suggests that powerful emotional responses can occur with minimal, or possibly no, mediation by higher level cognitive processes.

19.1.2. *Feelings as Determinants of Behavior*

Diverse evidence also supports the proposition that affect mediates, at least in part, the relationship between an individual's cognitive evaluation of risk and his or her behavioral response to it. The idea that emotions exert a direct and powerful influence on behavior receives ample support in the psychological literature on emotions. Zajonc (1998) in his chapter on emotions in the *Handbook of Social Psychology* argued that the defining characteristic of emotions is that they are designed to help people make approach–avoidance distinctions (whereas cognitions help people make true–false distinctions). Frijda (1986) has been a major proponent of the idea that a change in action readiness is the central core of an emotion and has shown that qualitatively distinct emotional states can be distinguished, not only on the basis of the cognitive appraisals that give rise to them, but also in terms of the state of action readiness that they create (Frijda, Kuipers, & ter Schure, 1989).

A number of authors have postulated that emotions play a critical role in rational, risk-averse, forward-looking, decision making. Liddell (cited in Barlow, 1988) referred to anxiety as the "shadow of intelligence." "The capacity to experience anxiety and the capacity to plan," Barlow noted, are "two sides of the same coin" (p. 12). Cottle and Klineberg (1974) argued that people only care about the delayed or uncertain consequences of their decisions to the degree that contemplating such consequences evokes immediate affect. In support of this view, they cited the effects of frontal lobotomies which, they believe, create a deficiency in areas of the brain [that] somehow underlie the capacity for images of absent events to generate experiences of pleasure or discomfort (p. 15). The neurosurgeons who performed these operations wrote of their frontal lobotomy patients that "the capacity for imagination is still present, and certainly not sufficiently reduced to render the patients helpless, and affective responses are often quite lively, [but there is] a separation of one from the other" (Freeman & Watts, 1942, p. 303). Consistent with the notion that such emotions are critical for forward-looking decision making, these surgeons noted that such patients were highly impulsive and risk taking and generally seemed "confined to what is here and now."

More recent work by Damasio lends further support to this perspective. Damasio and colleagues (Bechara et al., 1997; Damasio, 1994) argued that decision makers encode the consequences of alternative courses of action affectively and that such "somatic markers" are an essential input into decision making. Like Cottle and Klineberg (1974), Damasio argued that the prefrontal cortex plays a critical role in translating cognitive inputs from the cortex into terms that the emotional brain can understand. The prefrontal lobe is one terminus for dopaminergic neural pathways that are widely viewed as playing a critical role in volitional behavior.

Damasio and collaborators conducted a study in which patients suffering damage to the prefrontal cortex and non–brain-damaged individuals played a game in which the objective was to win as much money as possible (Bechara et al., 1997). Players earned hypothetical money by turning over cards on which were written either monetary gains or losses. On any given turn, individuals could draw from any of four decks, two of which included high payments ($100) and two of which contained lower payments ($50). The high-paying deck, however, also included occasional very large losses, to the point where these decks had a net negative expected value. Bechara et al. (1997) found that both nonpatients and those with prefrontal damage began by sampling from all four decks, and both groups avoided high-paying decks immediately after penalty cards were encountered. Compared to nonpatients, those with prefrontal damage returned to the high-paying decks more quickly after suffering a loss. As a result of this tendency, they often went "bankrupt" despite a (reportedly) strong desire to win and a thorough understanding of the game. One possible interpretation of the patients' behavior is that even though they "knew" the high-paying deck was risky, their inability to experience fear when contemplating a draw from one of those decks made risky draws more palatable. Consistent with this interpretation, subsequent research using the same task found in a sample of nonpatients that those who were higher in reactivity to negative events (as measured by two standard scales) were more prone to sample from the lower paying but safer decks of cards (Peters & Slovic, in press).

It should be noted that the lack of emotional responses does not necessarily lead to poor decisions. It is the specific design of Damasio's (1994; Bechara et al., 1997) experiment that makes his patients with frontal damage go bankrupt. One could easily design an experiment where the expected value of the high-risk deck (that contains some large losses) is actually higher than that of the low-risk deck. In this case, prefrontal damaged patients would do better in the long run than nonpatients, because the fear in the latter group would hinder them from choosing from the risky but higher expected value deck. Indeed, there may be a real-world analog of such an experiment; because of fear and myopic loss aversion, most employees have historically foregone substantial financial gains by investing their retirement in safe bond or money market funds rather than in equities, even though the long-term return of equities is often many times higher (Benartzi & Thaler, 1995; Gneezy & Potters, 1997; Thaler, Tversky, Kahneman, & Schwartz, 1997).

The anomalous behavior of patients with frontal damage might be consistent with a consequentialist view of decision making if their emotional reaction to losing was simply less intense than that of nonpatients. In this case, their strategy could be seen as a reasonable adaptation to different subjective feedback. However, they did not appear to be operating under different incentives. They were highly engaged in the task and wanted to win. After encountering a penalty card, they avoided the high-risk deck for a few turns (but returned to the high-risk decks more quickly than the nonpatients). Where the patients with frontal damage differed from nonpatients was in the arousal they experienced immediately before cards were turned over. In later phases of the game, when individuals had had experience drawing from all four decks, most of them drew an occasional card from one of the high-risk decks. Contemplating this selection evoked a galvanic skin conductance response in nonpatients in the moments before making their choice, but no such reaction in patients with frontal damage. Damasio concluded from this research that anticipatory emotions—somatic markers—play a critical role in decision making by encoding in a tangible fashion a summary of the likely consequences of a particular action. Lacking such somatic markers, his frontal-lesioned patients did not take account of the future consequences of their choices and, as a result, made bad decisions. They also had difficulty *making* decisions, even trivial ones. Anticipatory emotional reactions thus seem to facilitate the process of risky decision making and to be a crucial input for good decisions.

Damasio's research (Damasio, 1994) derived further support from observations of another abnormal population: criminal psychopathic individuals. Like frontal patients, criminal psychopathic individuals are characterized by insensitivity to the future consequences of their behavior (to themselves as well as other people). Although the neurological bases of this disorder are still not well-understood, there also appears to be a connection to a specific emotional deficit. During the 1940s, researchers speculated that the inability of psychopathic individuals to take account of future consequences of their actions, or the impact of their actions on others, could be due to a defect in their propensity to experience fear (Cleckley, 1941). In support of this hypothesis, Lykken (1957) showed that, compared to controls, sociopathic individuals have less intense physiological reactions to a conditioning stimulus that had been previously paired with a painful electric shock. Hare (1965, 1966) showed that sociopathic individuals have less intense physiological reactions to the prospect of an impending painful shock. Patrick (1994) demonstrated that sociopathic individuals display fewer physiological symptoms of negative affect when exposed to aversive stimuli than controls (see also Fowles & Missel, 1994; Williamson, Harpur, & Hare, 1991).[3]

In summary, consistent with the notion that anticipatory emotions play a critical role in risk aversion and farsighted decision making, several populations who do not feel or fear the future in the same way that others do make decisions that display a profound disregard for future consequences. We acknowledge, however, that none of these studies conclusively demonstrates a causal link, because the observed correlations between affective deficiencies and decision myopia may result from some type of collateral damage to neural systems. However, evidence from a quite different stream of research points to a similar conclusion.

Eisenberg, Baron, and Seligman (1995) asked people who differed in trait anxiety and depression to make a series of choices between pairs of more and less risky options. For some of the choices, the riskier option was the default (it did not involve taking action), whereas the less risky option did involve taking action. For other choice pairs, the riskier option involved taking an action. The researchers found that trait anxiety was strongly and positively correlated with risk aversion, whereas depression was related to a preference for options that did not involve taking an action. In a second study reported in the same article, participants were asked to make these types of decisions not only for themselves, but also for a hypothetical other person. They found that trait anxiety did not correlate with risk aversion for decisions made on behalf of another person.

In a study that produced similar results to those of Eisenberg et al. (1995), Hsee and Weber (1997) examined whether individuals could accurately predict the risk preference of others who were described either in generic (the average student on campus) or specific (another student sitting across the room) terms. Research participants were asked to choose between riskless

[3] More recent research casts some doubt on these earlier results. One study compared psychopathic and nonpsychopathic incarcerated men and found no difference in trait anxiety or fear between the two groups (Schmitt & Newman, 1999). Another study compared psychopathic and nonpsychopathic incarcerees' performance on Damasio's card sort task (Schmitt, Brinkley, & Newman, 1999). Although psychopathic incarcerated men did not perform differently from nonpsychopathic incarcerated men, individuals high in trait anxiety became more risk averse relative to those low in trait anxiety as they gained experience with the cards.

monetary gains and risky monetary gains and also to predict the choices of others who were described in a generic or specific fashion. Participants were generally risk averse in their own choices, and their predictions of risk preference for another specific student (whom they did not know but could observe across the room) were close to their own risk preferences. However, their predictions for the average student on campus were closer to risk neutrality. Hsee and Weber hypothesized that people's personal risk preference is driven at least in part by emotional reactions to risky options, or, as Lopes (1987) put it, that risk preference reflects a compromise between greed and fear. To the extent that risk aversion is the dominant response to risky decisions, negative feelings (i.e., fear, dread, or anxiety) toward risk tend to dominate positive feelings. When people predict the risk preference of another individual, they can base their prediction on their own feelings and reactions to the risky choice situation (i.e. predict by projection), which would be expected to occur when the "other" is a concrete individual. When the prediction is for an abstract "other," people find it more difficult to project and may ignore the impact of positive or negative emotional reactions on the decision, arriving at a prediction much closer to risk neutrality.

In a new study that we conducted for this article, we obtained further support for the idea that the self–other discrepancies in risk preferences are produced by self–other discrepancies in feelings toward risky options. We asked 115 college students to imagine the following scenario: They were riding in a taxi and found out that the driver was drunk. There were no other taxis around or other means of transportation. They could either (a) remain in the taxi (a relatively risky option) or (b) get out of the taxi and walk to their destination 5 miles away (a lower risk option). Participants were asked how worried they would feel if they remained in the taxi cab and to predict how the average student at their university would feel if he or she remained in the cab. Participants were also asked whether they would get out of the cab and to predict the decision of the average student at their university. The results were consistent with the risk-as-feelings hypothesis. With respect to feelings, respondents rated themselves (on a scale from 0 = not worried at all to 5 = extremely worried) as significantly more worried than the average student (Ms = 3.71 and 3.16, t = 4.09, $p < .001$). In decisions, respondents also rated themselves (on a scale from 0 = not likely at all to 5 = extremely likely) as significantly more likely to get out of the cab than the average student (Ms = 2.93 and 2.39, t = 3.45, $p < .001$). Moreover, the self–other difference in decision was highly correlated across respondents with the self–other difference in feelings (r = .58, $p < .001$).

Additional support for the idea that affect plays an important role in behavioral intentions comes from a series of studies conducted by Slovic and his collaborators. In a typical study, participants free-associate about a concept of interest to the experimenters—for example, different states and cities (Slovic, Layman, et al., 1991), a nuclear waste repository (Slovic, Flynn, & Layman, 1991), or health-related behaviors (Benthin et al., 1995)— and then provide affective ratings of these associations. These affective ratings are shown to correlate strongly with attitudes and self-predicted behavior, such as desire to vacation or retire in particular states and cities, willingness to accept a nuclear waste repository in one's state, and the propensity to engage in health-related behaviors. Slovic and coauthors have also shown that, whereas risks and benefits tend to be positively associated in the real world (because high-risk activities are only tolerated to the extent that they provide benefits), they are negatively associated in people's minds (Alhakami & Slovic, 1994; Finucane et al., 2000). This negative relationship, they find, stems from people's reliance on general affective evaluations in making risk and benefit judgments. Through a kind of halo effect, activities that have a negative affective valence are seen as both high in risk and low in benefit.

19.1.3. *Summary*

In this section, we have sought to establish the central role that feelings play in determining people's choices and other responses under conditions of risk and uncertainty. The risk-as-feelings hypothesis suggests that feelings play a much more prominent role in risky decision making than they are given credit for by the cognitive–consequentialist tradition of J/DM research. Behavioral evidence suggests that, to the extent that emotional reactions to, and cognitive evaluations of, risky choice options are dissociated, risk preference is often determined by the former. Emotional reactions guide responses not only at their first occurrence, but also through conditioning and memory at later points in time, serving as somatic markers. Patient populations who lack these markers not only have difficulty making risky decisions, but they also choose in ways that turn their personal and professional lives to shambles. Thus, feelings may be more than just an important input into decision making under uncertainty; they may be necessary and, to a large degree, mediate the connection between cognitive evaluations of risk and risk-related behavior.

19.2. Determinants of Feelings

As we noted in the introduction, the risk-as-feelings hypothesis is only interesting if the addition of feelings as a predictor variable makes risky choice more predictable, both within and across different decision domains and contexts. This can only be the case if emotional reactions have determinants that differ from those that drive cognitive evaluations. In this section we show that divergences between emotional and cognitive reactions occur for two reasons. First, emotions respond to the two central input variables of cognitive consequentialist accounts of risk-related perception and behavior—probabilities and outcomes—in a fashion that is different from cognitive evaluations of riskiness. Second, emotions are influenced by situational variables that play only a minor role in cognitive evaluations. These factors include the time-course of the decision (i.e. the time between the decision and the realization of the outcome of the decision), nonconsequentialist aspects of the decision outcomes (e.g. their vividness or the associations they evoke), and evolutionary preparedness for certain emotional reactions.

In addition to reviewing each of these discrepancies between emotional reactions to, and cognitive evaluations of, risk, we discuss phenomena observed in the laboratory and in natural settings that can be explained by such discrepancies but which are difficult to explain in conventional consequentialist terms. When viewed through the lens of consequentialist models such as the expected utility model, people's risk-taking behavior often appears to be highly variable and inconsistent across domains and situations (Isaac & James, 2000; MacCrimmon & Wehrung, 1986; Schoemaker, 1990). Barsky, Juster, Kimball, and Shapiro (1997), for example, classified respondents to the Health and Retirement Survey (a large-scale panel study of older Americans) into four categories of risk tolerance on the basis of three questions that measured their degree of risk aversion for hypothetical decisions involving a change of job. They found that the resultant measure of risk tolerance correlated only very weakly with other risk-related behaviors such as drinking, smoking, and investment decisions. Weber, Blais, and Betz (1999) similarly found only weak correlations between self-reports of risk taking in decisions involving either financial, health, social, ethical, or recreational risks. To the extent that the risk-as-feelings hypothesis identifies situational factors that can influence risk taking that would not be predicted by consequentialist models, it can help explain the content- and context-specific nature of risk taking.

19.2.1. *Effects of Vividness*

One of the most important determinants of emotional reactions to future outcomes is the vividness with which those outcomes are described or represented mentally (Damasio, 1994). To the extent that anticipatory emotions are generated in response to mental imagery about the experience of decision outcomes, factors that influence the occurrence or vividness of mental images are likely to be important determinants of anticipatory emotions.[4]

[4] In a study that illustrates the importance of mental imagery, Shiv and Huber (2000; see also Shiv & Fedorikhin, 1999) asked individuals to choose between a series of two-choice alternatives. In all cases, one was inferior on a pallid dimension (e.g. a higher price), and the

One such factor is individual differences in mental imagery. Several studies find a correlation between people's self-reported ability to form mental images and visceral responses that are plausibly related to anticipatory emotion. For example, compared with nonvivid imagers, vivid imagers salivate significantly more while thinking about their favorite food (White, 1978), become more sexually aroused in structured fantasy exercises (D. Smith & Over, 1987), and have greater ability to voluntarily increase their heart rate using visual imagery (Carroll, Baker, & Preston, 1979). Consistent with the idea that imagery influences affective response, Miller et al. (1987) reported that enhancing individuals' ability to form vivid images through training increases their visceral response to personalized scripts designed to elicit particular affective reactions, such as anger and fear.

Vividness, and hence the strength of anticipatory emotions, depends not only on individual differences in mental imagery ability, but also on situational factors, such as how an outcome is described. Nisbett and Ross (1980) illustrated this effect by contrasting two descriptions of the same event. In the first description, one learns that "Jack sustained fatal injuries in an auto accident." This description of death evoked weaker emotional reactions than the second description that "Jack was killed by a semi trailer that rolled over on his car and crushed his skull" (p. 47).

The effect of vividness on emotional responses to risk may help explain some common patterns of insurance purchase behavior that are anomalous within the consequentialist framework. Consequentialist models of risky choice (e.g. EU theory) predict that insurance purchases depend exclusively on the magnitude of the loss, its probability, the cost of insurance, and the consumer's wealth and risk tolerance, all variables that are immune to differences in the description of potential losses. Consideration of anticipatory emotions, on the other hand, suggests that the description of the outcomes may matter. Images of losses that evoke vivid negative mental imagery should lead to greater willingness to purchase insurance. Evidence supporting this prediction comes from Johnson, Hershey, Meszaros, and Kunreuther (1993), who found that people were willing to pay more for airline travel insurance covering death from "terrorist acts" (a highly imaginable event) than death from "all possible causes" (which, of course, implicitly subsumes terrorist acts in addition to a range of other causes but does not spontaneously bring fear-provoking mental images to mind). At the opposite extreme, people tend to be

other was inferior on a fear-inducing dimension (e.g. no power protection on a computer). In a 2 × 2 factorial design, some individuals were asked to think about their feelings about each of the products and others were not, and some individuals were instructed to *not* use imagery when they made their choice and others were not. The main finding was that encouraging individuals to think about their feelings about the products increased the weight placed on the fear-inducing dimension, but only when they were not instructed to not use imagery (i.e. when they were, presumably, using it). Asking individuals to not imagine using the product inhibited the impact of feelings on choice.

underinsured against hazards that evoke relatively pallid mental images. Flood insurance is notoriously difficult to sell, even when premiums are heavily subsidized (Insurance Advocate, 1994; Kunreuther, 1976). Consequentialist explanations for this phenomenon would focus on systematic failures to predict the true devastation of a flood or on actuarially optimistic estimates of a flood's likelihood. Slovic, Fischhoff, and Lichtenstein (1980), on the other hand, speculated that people's willingness to insure against small-probability losses may be related to how much these potential losses cause worry or concern. A number of studies have shown that knowing someone who has been in a flood or earthquake, or having been in one oneself, greatly increases the likelihood of purchasing insurance (Browne & Hoyt, 2000). Although these findings could be explained in consequentialist terms as resulting from an increase in individuals' expectations of experiencing a flood or earthquake in the future, the effect remains significant even after controlling for subjective expectations (Kunreuther et al., 1978).

The importance of personal experience has also been noted in other areas. Weinstein (1989) presented evidence showing that the effect of the personal experience of adverse consequences on subsequent precautionary or self-protective behavior goes beyond what one would expect if its main effect is to simply provide "additional information that is inserted into a decision equation" (p. 47). Weinstein documented how personal experience can modify people's emotional reactions to risky situations in complex, situation- and domain-specific ways—for example, increasing feelings of worry, resulting in an increase in self-protective behavior in some domains, but also decreasing feelings of controllability in other situations, with the opposite effect on precautionary responses. In a similar vein, Hendickx, Vlek, and Oppewal (1989) found that warnings are more effective when they are linked to people and anecdotes (and hence emotionally involving) than when they are based on statistics, suggesting that anxiety induction through the use of vividness manipulations can produce desirable changes in risk behaviors.

Anxiety induction is not, however, a panacea when it comes to promoting self-protective behavior. Besides the fact that evoking anxiety saddles people with the hedonic burden of the anxiety itself, it can also induce defensive reactions that undermine efforts at risk mitigation. Thus, for example, Janis and Feshbach (1953) found that high levels of fear induced by a message about dental hygiene led to defensive avoidance, that is, subsequent warding off of exposures to the content of the message. Leventhal and Watts (1966) exposed visitors to a state fair to motion pictures dealing with smoking and lung cancer that were designed to elicit high, medium, or low levels of fear. Consistent with defensive avoidance, the researchers found that higher levels of fear led to less willingness to get an X-ray but did produce a decrease in smoking relative to the other two groups. Thus, high levels of fear led to both information avoidance and some degree of risk mitigation. More recently, Lieberman and

Chaiken (1992) found that defensive processing was heightened when the fear-inducing content of a message was personally relevant, as generally is the case with breast cancer. Indeed, there have been suggestions in the literature on breast self-exams that women's anticipatory anxiety about cancer prevents them from examining themselves (Bernay, Porrath, Golding-Mather, & Murray, 1982; Murray & McMillan, 1993; O'Malley & Fletcher, 1987).

19.2.2. Insensitivity to Probability Variations

In the EU model, the value of a prospect is equal to the sum of the utilities of outcomes that could be experienced, weighted by their likelihood of occurrence. Probabilities and outcomes thus have symmetrical effects on evaluations. This is not the case for emotional reactions. Changes in probability within some broad midrange of values have little effect on anticipatory emotions perhaps because, as just discussed, emotions arise in large part as a reaction to mental images of a decision's outcomes (Damasio, 1994). Because such images are discrete and are not much affected by probabilities, the emotions that arise from them are likewise insensitive to variations in probability. One's mental image of what it would be like to win the state lottery, for example, is likely to be about the same, whether there is a 1 in 10,000,000 chance of winning or a 1 in 10,000 chance of winning. The mental image of winning $10,000,000 or $10,000, on the other hand, is likely to be very different. This is not to say that fear responses are completely unaffected by probabilities, but they are largely unaffected by orders-of-magnitude differences at the extreme (e.g., between a 1 in 100,000,000 chance of winning the lottery and a 1 in 100,000 chance).

Psychophysical studies of anxiety illustrate the relatively small role probability plays in anticipatory emotion. In these experiments, research participants experienced a series of countdown periods of stated length at the end of which they received, with some stated probability, a painful electric shock of varying intensity. Anxiety is operationalized by changes in participants' heart rate and skin conductance during the countdown period. The general finding from this research is that people's physiological responses to the impending shock are correlated with their expectations about the intensity of the shock— that is, bigger shocks elicited greater arousal (Deane, 1969). The probability of receiving the shock, however, does not affect arousal (Bankhart & Elliott, 1974; Elliott, 1975; Monat, Averill, & Lazarus, 1972; Snortum & Wilding, 1971) except for trials in which the probability is stated to be zero. Evidently, the mere thought of receiving a shock is enough to arouse individuals, but the precise likelihood of being shocked has little impact on level of arousal. These results suggest that feelings of fear or worry in the face of decisions under risk or uncertainty have an all-or-none characteristic; they may be sensitive to the possibility rather than the probability of negative consequences.

In a study designed to investigate cross-cultural differences in risky decision making, Weber and Hsee (1998) asked participants to provide maximum buying prices for risky investment options that differed in the probabilities with which gains or losses of different magnitude would be realized. Although not reported in Weber and Hsee, participants were also asked to rate, for each investment option, the degree of worry or concern they would experience between the time they invested in the option and the time they would find out which outcome actually occurred. Whereas maximum buying prices were sensitive to both probability and outcome levels, $F(1, 6634) = 4.64$ and 5.12, respectively, $ps < .05$, reported feelings of worry were far less sensitive to probability levels, $F(1, 6634) = 1.69$, $p > .10$. A similar dissociation between intellectual judgments of risk and emotional reactions expressed by judgments of worry has been reported by Sjöberg (1998) in a study of subjective risk perceptions.

The observation that some changes in probability affect risky decisions more than others has been confirmed by many studies of decision making (for a review, see Camerer, 1989) and has been incorporated into the predictions of many non-EU models as nonlinearities in the probability weighting function (e.g. Kahneman & Tversky, 1979). One of the most robust observations in the domain of decision making under uncertainty is the overweighting of small probabilities, particularly those associated with extreme outcomes (see Prelec, 1998). Many of the famous EU anomalies, such as the Allais paradox and the common ratio effect (see Kahneman & Tversky, 1979, for a description of both), can be explained parsimoniously in such terms (Camerer, 1995, p. 637). A 1% change in the probability of an aversive event seems trivial when there is already a 49% chance, but is likely to cause great concern, and concomitant effort to avert it, if it changes the chances from none at all to 1%, that is, away from the certainty of not being exposed. Viscusi and Magat (1987), for example, found that people were willing to pay considerably more to reduce the risk of inhalation poisoning or skin poisoning from an insect spray from 5 in 10,000 to 0 than from 15 in 10,000 to 5 in 10,000.

Although these nonlinearities in probability weights have been extensively documented and have a well-known label (the *certainty effect*; Kahneman & Tversky, 1979), relatively little work has been done to explain them. Incorporating emotional reactions into the prediction equation helps to explain these phenomena. As the probability of an aversive event passes the zero threshold, a consequence that was previously of no concern now becomes a source of worry. Subsequent increments in probability, however, have little additional emotional impact and, presumably for this reason, have little impact on choice.

In a recent paper, Rottenstreich and Hsee (1999) found not only that people were insensitive to probability variations, but also that such insensitivity depended on the emotional impact of the associated outcomes. This result lends support to the risk-as-feeling hypothesis, according to which people should be more insensitive to probability variations for emotional and vivid outcomes than for pallid outcomes. In one study, Rottenstreich and Hsee asked participants to indicate the largest amount of money they would be willing to pay to avoid an undesirable outcome that occurred with different levels of probability. The undesirable outcome was either a loss of $20 (a relatively pallid outcome) or a brief but painful electric shock (a more emotional–visceral outcome). The results were dramatic. When the outcome was pallid (losing $20), the participants were quite sensitive to probability variations: The dollar value placed on the uncertain outcome changed from $1 (for $p = .01$) to $18 (for $p = .99$). However, when the outcome evoked emotion (receiving an electric shock), participants were extremely insensitive to probability variations: The dollar value changed only from $7 (for $p = .01$) to $10 (for $p = .99$). In other words, when probability increased by a factor of 99 (from 1% to 99%), the value of the uncertain prospect increased by less than a factor of 1.5 (from $7 to $10). Rottenstreich and Hsee (1999) replicated these results using positive outcomes as well. For example, when the outcome was a $500 discount on their tuition (a relatively pallid outcome), students were quite sensitive to probability variations. However, when the outcome was a $500 coupon they could use for their dream trip to Paris and Rome (a more emotion-laden outcome), students were less sensitive to probability variations.

Although most consequentialist decision theories consider probability weighting as independent of the nature of the outcome, the findings of Rottenstreich and Hsee (1999) suggest that the impact of probability depends strongly on the nature of the outcome. The probability weighting function is flatter (i.e. more overweighting of small probabilities) for vivid outcomes that evoke emotions than for pallid outcomes. It seems that the overweighting of small probabilities is a result of feelings of fear and hope—fear in the case of a negative outcome and hope in the case of a positive outcome.

The relationship between probabilities and emotions can help to explain one of the major paradoxes in decision making under uncertainty: the prevalence of simultaneous gambling and purchasing of insurance. According to EU, risk aversion (which motivates insurance purchase) is caused by diminishing marginal utility of wealth (or increasing marginal disutility of poverty). If this is the case, then people who, through purchases of insurance, reveal themselves to be risk averse should not purchase actuarially unfair lottery tickets. Friedman and Savage (1948) argued that the observed pattern of behavior suggests that utility functions take a complicated S-shaped form. H. Markowitz (1952) critiqued Friedman and Savage's explanation by demonstrating that it produced many unrealistic behavioral predictions, and advanced an alternative formulation that assumed (a) that people care about losses and gains relative to some reference point (usually the status quo) rather than about

589

absolute levels of wealth and (b) that they evaluate losses and gains with a value function that is generally risk averse for gains and risk seeking for losses. Kahneman and Tversky (1979) further developed Markowitz's model by adding a nonlinear probability weighting function that overweighted small probabilities of both losses and gains. Prospect theory and similar models explain gambling on the basis of an overweighting of small probabilities of a gain (which is, however, countered by the general tendency toward risk aversion for gains) and insurance purchases on the basis of an overweighting of small probabilities of a loss (which is mitigated by the tendency toward risk seeking for losses).

Although the overweighting of small probabilities may be partly responsible for lottery playing and insurance purchases, the overweighting of small probabilities may, itself, stem from the disproportionate fear and pleasurable anticipation evoked by such prospects, as discussed earlier. Consistent with this prediction, Hogarth and Kunreuther (1995) found that, when people make decisions regarding investment in protective measures such as warranties, they do not think about probabilities of malfunctions unless these figures are given to them. Rather, they use arguments such as peace of mind or sleeping well at night to defend their positions. Only when probabilities are explicitly provided do people include them as part of their reasoning. Marketers of insurance in fact rarely provide probabilities; instead, they tend to emphasize qualitative or emotional considerations. Likewise, lottery marketers highlight the pleasure of anticipation associated with lottery purchases with slogans such as "buy a dream." Middle-class and lower middle-class families who are struggling to make ends meet can savor the possibility that their money problems may come to an instant end when the weekly number is drawn.

The affective response to risks may also help to address another anomaly in the literature on risk taking. For many risky decisions, the moment of uncertainty resolution is different from the time when consequences are actually realized. In some cases, moreover, individuals have some degree of control over when uncertainty is resolved. People can choose whether and when to be tested for diseases such as Huntington's chorea, HIV, or genetic markers associated with increased vulnerability to various types of cancer. Students can decide when to pick up grades, and parents can decide whether and when to learn the sex of a fetus. In some cases, early resolution can only be obtained at a cost. For example, in plea bargaining, early resolution can be achieved at the cost of accepting the prosecutor's offer. In all types of negotiations, the party who can wait longer typically does better; succumbing to the desire for early resolution in the form of a settlement, therefore, usually comes at the expense of a less favorable settlement.

Consequential models of risk taking predict that early resolution will be preferred if other decisions have to be made that depend on the value of the obtained outcome (H. M. Markowitz, 1959; Mossin, 1969; Spence &

Zeckhauser, 1972). For example, knowing the value of one's year-end bonus should help one to make more rational spending decisions during the intervening year. Studies that have tested this prediction have generally found, consistent with consequentialist models, that people do typically prefer early resolution of uncertainty. However, there are important exceptions to this general preference for early resolution. Specifically, people often prefer to delay resolution of uncertainty for gambles with small probabilities of gains or large probabilities of losses (Ahlbrecht & Weber, 1996). Elster and Loewenstein (1992, p. 228) argued that, in these cases, delayed resolution is desirable because it provides utility from anticipation. Small probabilities of large gains provide substantial utility from "savoring" the gamble (Loewenstein, 1987) even when there is actually little likelihood of winning. Large probabilities of losses also provide utility from savoring because they are cognitively reframed as a (virtually) certain loss plus a small probability of a gain. Delaying resolution is desirable in these cases because it prolongs the period of hopeful anticipation. Consistent with this interpretation, Lovallo and Kahneman (2000) found an extremely strong positive correlation between people's evaluations of the attractiveness of a set of gambles and their willingness to delay those gambles. Recent theories that deal with delayed resolution preference have introduced considerations of utility derived from anticipation—hope, fear, and dread (Caplin & Leahy, 1997; Chew & Ho, 1994; Pope, 1985).

19.2.3. *Time Interval Between Decision and Realization of Outcome*

One of the most important determinants of fear that is likely to be relatively uncorrelated with cognitive assessments of risk is the time between the decision and the realization of its outcomes. As the prospect of an uncertain aversive event approaches in time, fear tends to increase, even when cognitive assessments of the probability or likely severity of the event remain constant (Loewenstein, 1987; Paterson & Neufeld, 1987; Roth, Breivik, Jorgensen, & Hofmann, 1996). Breznitz (1971) informed individuals that they would receive a strong electric shock in either 3, 6, or 12 min. The average heart rate was lower for the distant warning group than for either of the other two groups, which did not differ from one another. Monat (1976) threatened individuals with an electric shock that they were told would occur after 1, 3, or 12 min. Heart rate, galvanic skin response, and self-reported anxiety were all inversely related to the duration of the waiting period. Such a temporal pattern of fear is highly adaptive; organisms that experienced similar levels of fear toward distant and immediate risks would be unlikely to survive long in a hostile environment. Indeed, one of the characteristics of certain types of stress disorders is the tendency to ruminate over risks that are remote in time (e.g. Nolen-Hoeksema, 1990; Sapolsky, 1994) or to continue to experience fear toward no longer threatening events that happened in the past (e.g. Barlow, 1988).

The increase in fear just before the "moment of truth" has a range of diverse consequences. Several studies have found that people lower their expectations just prior to receiving important self-relevant information (e.g. Nisan, 1972; Sanna, 1999; Shepperd, Ouellette, & Fernandez, 1996). Welch (1999) showed that the increase in fear before the moment of outcome resolution has behavioral consequences. In one study, students were offered a payment of $1 in exchange for telling a joke in front of a class the following week. When the appointed time arrived, both students who had agreed to tell the joke and those who had declined to do so were given the opportunity to change their minds. As predicted by the risk-as-feelings hypothesis, with the added assumption that fear increases as the moment of taking a risky action draws near, there was substantial "chickening out." Sixty-seven percent of those who initially volunteered to tell a joke (6 out of 9) decided not to when the time came, but none of those who had initially declined the offer (0 out of 49) changed their mind and decided to tell a joke at the last minute ($p < .01$).

Other studies have provided more direct evidence that pessimistic shifts and chickening out are caused by emotional changes. Savitsky, Medvec, Charlton, and Gilovich (1998) found that pessimistic shifts are associated with an increase in arousal. In a different study, Welch (1999) incorporated an explicit test of the hypothesis that chickening out was caused by affective reactions. The design of the study was identical to the study just described except that half of the students watched a fear-inducing film-clip (2 min from Kubrick's *The Shining*) before making their initial choice about whether to tell the joke in front of the class. Table 1 presents the results for the two groups. As can be seen, risk taking was sensitive to both the temporal proximity of the risk and the immediate mood state induced by the film, with less risk taking occurring when fear was aroused by the immediacy of the risky action or the scary film clip. The tendency to chicken out at the last minute undoubtedly overlaps in many situations with the tendency, demonstrated in research by Liberman and Trope (1998), for people to place greater weight on practical

Table 1. Effect of Fear Manipulation on Fear, Choice at Time 1, and Choice at Time 2

Response	No fear induction ($n = 30$)	Fear induction ($n = 32$)	Significance of difference
Self-reported fear about telling the joke[a]	6.1	7.3	$p < .04$
Agree to tell a joke at Time 1 (%)	33	6	$p < .03$
Agree to tell a joke at Time 2 (%)	13	0	ns

Note. Time 1 = 1 week before joke would be told; Time 2 = just before joke would be told.

[a] Measured on a 0–10-point scale.

considerations (e.g. do I really have the time to attend the conference?) relative to more vague dimensions of desirability (the topic matter to be discussed at the conference) as the moment of taking an action draws near. Both effects produce changes in behavior with the passage of time; the increase in fear leads people to change their minds about taking risks, whereas the effect discussed by Liberman and Trope leads people to change their minds about actions that are desirable in a gestalt sense but have practical drawbacks.

19.2.4. *Public Panics*

It is well established that decision makers' emotional states can affect their cognitive evaluations of a risk (e.g. Johnson & Tversky, 1983). These cognitive evaluations, in turn, can affect the individual's emotional states. Because these effects exert reciprocal, self-reinforcing influences, there is a potential for self-reinforcing feedback effects. Fear increases arousal and arousal increases the intensity of new fear responses (Lang, 1995). Feedback processes of this type have the potential to create unstable situations in which relatively mild fears rapidly build into a panic reaction. One prominent theory of panic attacks (at the level of the individual) is precisely based on such a feedback process—namely, the idea that fearful thoughts (induced by a focus on internal bodily sensations) produce further bodily sensations, which intensify fears, which increase physiological reactions, and so on (Beck & Emery, 1985; Clark, 1986).

Attacks of panic can be seen at a societal level (Bartholomew, 1997). Such social panics are characterized by an explosion of public concern about a problem—typically unconnected with any sudden change in the underlying risk—followed by an also-sudden collapse of concern (Weinstein, 1989, p. 37). Well-publicized panics include outbreaks of Koru in Asia (an epidemic of fear in which people believe that their genitals are shrinking; Chakraborty, Das, & Mukherji, 1983; Gwee, 1968), unsubstantiated rumors of mad "slashers" and "gassers" on the loose (Jacobs, 1965), and, recently in the United States, hysterical reactions to herpes and disappearing children (Loewenstein & Mather, 1990).

Panics are typically set off by highly vivid cases, or clusters of cases, that receive concentrated media attention (Weinstein, 1989, p. 46). As with individual-level panics, public panics seem to be fueled, in part, by an interplay between anxiety, fear, and subjective probabilities. Evidence supporting such a dynamic interplay of risk perceptions and anxiety comes from field studies. According to Simon Wessely, who has conducted several case studies of mass panics (see, e.g., David & Wessely, 1995; Wessely, 1987; Wessely & Wardle, 1990), almost all cases fit a common pattern. Someone observes a fear-inducing event or is exposed to a vivid frightening rumor, begins to experience anxiety, displays symptoms such as hyperventilating or collapsing that others see, and those others begin to get anxious themselves. As Wessely (cited in Gladwell, 1999) described it. "before you know it everyone in the room is hyperventilating and collapsing" (p. 24). Feelings clearly play a prominent role in this process.

19.2.5. *Evolutionary Preparedness*

Although cognitive evaluations of the likelihood and magnitude of outcomes are relatively domain independent, the work of Garcia and other researchers in the 1970s (see Seligman, 1971) suggests that the ability of events to evoke fear and other emotional reactions is restricted by biological or evolutionary preparedness. Humans and other animals seem to be preprogrammed to experience certain types of fears. For example, cage-reared rats who have never been exposed to a cat show signs of fear if exposed to the smell of cat fur (Panksepp, 1998). In some cases such preparedness seems to vary over the life course. For example, stranger fear has been observed in humans in a wide range of cultures, usually develops between 4 and 9 months of age, peaks around 12.5 months, and does not require aversive experience with strangers to develop (Menzies, 1995).

Beyond such preprogrammed fears, primates and humans seem to be biologically prepared to become fear-conditioned to certain objects (e.g. snakes, spiders, water, and enclosed spaces) but not to others (but see McNally, 1987). Öhman (1986), for example, found superior conditioning using fear-relevant slides of snakes and spiders as conditional stimuli as compared to fear-irrelevant conditioned stimuli such as slides of flowers and mushrooms or geometric figures. More recent studies have followed up on Lazarus's research on subliminal influences (e.g. Lazarus & McCleary, 1951) by demonstrating that subliminal presentations of fear-relevant, but not of fear-irrelevant, conditioned stimuli are sufficient to elicit conditioned responses. Öhman and Soares (1993) argued that subliminal evocation of fear may help explain the irrationality of fears and phobias "because their origin rests in cognitive structures that are not under the control of conscious intentions" (p. 129; see also Öhman & Soares, 1994).

In many instances of phobias, the inability to uncover any traumatic conditioning history has led to a search for alternative mechanisms. One mechanism, which has received substantial documentation in animal research, has been labeled *vicarious conditioning*. Mineka and colleagues (e.g. Cook & Mineka, 1990; Mineka & Cook, 1993) have demonstrated strong and persistent vicarious conditioning of snake fear in rhesus monkeys. In a prototypical experiment, cage-raised monkeys do not initially show a fear-reaction to snakes but developed one almost instantly after witnessing a fear response from a wild-reared monkey. Subsequent research indicated that vicarious conditioning also exhibits the phenomenon of preparedness. Cage-reared monkeys developed a fear reaction after viewing a tape in which another monkey appeared to react fearfully to a snake, but they did not develop such a reaction when, in a similar tape, the same monkey reacted fearfully to a flower stimulus.

Besides showing very rapid acquisition, certain types of fears also exhibit resistance to extinction. Even when fear conditioning is extinguished through repeated presentation of a conditioned stimulus (e.g. a tone) in the absence of the aversive unconditioned stimulus (e.g. a shock), the fear conditioning of the original association is not lost but remains latent. Such latency has been demonstrated in studies of spontaneous recovery of fear conditioning (Pavlov, 1927) and in studies in which reinstatement of conditioning has been shown to follow presentation of the unconditioned stimulus (Bouton, 1994; Bouton & Swartzentruber, 1991) or as a result of severing connections between the amygdala and the cortex (LeDoux, 1996). The latter finding suggests that the cortex plays an important role in the extinction of fear conditioning and is consistent with the idea that cortical and subcortical processing of fear may often be at odds with one another. The fear is, in a sense, still there, but either the subjective experience of fear or the behavioral response to it is cortically suppressed.

The critical implication of the research on evolutionary preparedness is that people are likely to react with little fear to certain types of objectively dangerous stimuli that evolution has not prepared them for, such as guns, hamburgers, automobiles, smoking, and unsafe sex, even when they recognize the threat at a cognitive level. Types of stimuli that people are evolutionarily prepared to fear, such as caged spiders, snakes, or heights (when adequate safety measures are in place), evoke a visceral response even when, at a cognitive level, they are recognized to be harmless.

It is tempting to draw a connection between such discrepancies in cognitive evaluations and fear reactions and the often-lamented discrepancy between scientists' and the lay public's concern for risks. Just as an animal might be very slow to develop fear toward an unfamiliar poison-emitting flower, there may also be a lag between cognitive and emotional reactions toward risks for which we are not prepared to have emotional reactions. On the one hand, even when environmental policy makers have become convinced that the existing information about the probability and negative consequences of risks such as global warming or radon warrant precautionary action, such sacrifices may require a level of public fear that does not exist. On the other hand, public alarm over risks that experts view as inconsequential, such as Alar or cyanide in Chilean grapes, can force the hand of reluctant policy makers (Gregory, Flynn, & Slovic, 1995; Gregory, Slovic, & Flynn, 1996; Slovic, Flynn, & Gregory, 1994).

19.2.6. *Summary*

The research reviewed in this section can be summarized as follows. First, fear as the emotional response experienced in risky situations reacts to probabilities and outcomes in a manner that is very different from that postulated by EU theory and its generalizations. Second, fear depends on a variety of factors that are not part of such models. Fear typically peaks just before a threat is experienced and is highly dependent on mental imagery (and thus subject to vividness effects). Fear responses also seem to be conditioned, in part, by our evolutionary makeup; we may be prepared to learn very rapidly about some types of risks but much more slowly about others. Fear responses are evoked, often by crude or subliminal cues. Fear conditioning may be permanent, or at least far longer lasting than other kinds of learning. To the extent that these differences exist between the calculus of objective risk and the determinants of fear, and to the extent that fear does, in fact, play an important role in risk-related behaviors, behavior in the face of risk is unlikely to be well-described by traditional consequentialist models.

19.3. Conclusions

Although decision making under risk has been a central topic of decision theory, the decision-theoretic approach to decision making under risk has largely ignored the role played by emotions. Whereas some theorists have considered the effects of emotions experienced after the decision (i.e. emotions elicited by good or bad outcomes), very little attention has been given to the impact of emotions experienced *during* the decision-making process. In contrast, such anticipatory emotions play a prominent role in clinical and social psychological theory and research and have received recent attention from neuroscientists.

People react to the prospect of risk at two levels: they evaluate the risk cognitively, and they react to it emotionally. Although the two reactions are interrelated, with cognitive appraisals giving rise to emotions and emotions influencing appraisals, the two types of reactions have different determinants. Cognitive evaluations of risk are sensitive to the variables identified by decision theory, namely probabilities and outcome valences. Although emotions do respond to cognitive evaluations, they can also arise with minimal cognitive processing (Zajonc, 1980), and people can experience fear reactions without even knowing what they are afraid of. In contrast to cognitive evaluations, emotional reactions are sensitive to the vividness of associated imagery, proximity in time, and a variety of other variables that play a minimal role in cognitive evaluations. Moreover, although emotional reactions are also sensitive to probability and outcome valence, the functional relationships are quite different from those for cognitive evaluations. As a result of these differences, people often experience a discrepancy between the fear they experience in connection with a particular risk and their cognitive evaluation of the threat posed by that risk.

19.3.1. Implications for Research

One important implication of the risk-as-feelings hypothesis is that those doing risk-related research should make it a routine practice to collect information on emotional reactions to risks, in addition to such traditional measures as probabilities and outcome values. Ideally, such measures would include physiological measures as well as self-reports. Two areas in which these measures could provide useful information are gender and age-related changes in risk taking.

When it comes to gender, large numbers of studies have found that male individuals tend to be more risk averse than female individuals (see Byrnes, Miller, & Schafer, 1999, for a recent meta-analysis). These differences are particularly pronounced when it comes to physical, or life-threatening, risks (Hersch, 1997), but have also been observed in other domains such as investment decisions (Bajtelsmit, Bernasek, & Jianakoplos, 1997). Very little of this research has paid explicit attention to the role of risk-related emotions. There is, however, some intriguing evidence suggesting that gender differences in risk taking may be linked to parallel differences in emotional responsiveness. Several studies have found that female individuals report more and better imagery than male individuals (see Harshman & Paivio, 1987, for a review of several studies) and that they experience emotions more intensely than male individuals, on average. When men and women are asked to recall their saddest memory, positron emission tomography scans indicate that brain activity increases significantly more in the female brain than in the male brain (George, 1999). Of greatest relevance to the risk-as-feelings hypothesis, women report experiencing nervousness and fear more intensely than men do (Brody, 1993; Brody, Hay, & Vandewater, 1990; Fujita, Diener, & Sandvik, 1991; Stapley & Haviland, 1989). Further studies are needed to determine whether observed male–female differences in risk taking may be mediated by differences in emotional reactions to risks. If true, it would be interesting to examine whether women are more risk seeking in situations to which they respond less emotionally than men.

There is also a possibility that emotional changes associated with *aging* may help to explain observed age-based differences in risk taking, and specifically adolescents' high risk-taking propensities. One popular explanation for adolescent risk taking is the so-called invulnerability hypothesis according to which adolescent risk taking stems from feelings of invulnerability (see, e.g., Burger & Burns, 1988; Whitley & Hern, 1991). From a decision-making perspective, the invulnerability hypothesis implies that adolescents either do not consider some potentially harmful consequences of risky behavior or underestimate the likelihood of these consequences happening to them. Despite its popularity, however, there is surprisingly little evidence that supports the invulnerability hypothesis and some evidence that conflicts with it. Beyth-Marom, Austin, Fischhoff, Palmgren, and Quadrel (1993) and Quadrel, Fischhoff, and Davis (1993), for example, compared adolescents and adults on their cognitive evaluations of the consequences of engaging or not engaging in various risky behaviors. Contrary to the invulnerability hypothesis, these studies found relatively few differences in the subjective probabilities of negative outcomes. The possibility that age-based differences in risk taking are affectively mediated (and possibly the result of differences in the vividness of mental simulations of behavior), therefore, merits further exploration.

A second pressing need in basic research is to examine the effects of *intense* emotions on risk taking and behavior. Most of the current research on the effects of emotions examines relatively mild emotions that are induced using techniques such as guided imagery. It is exactly at such low levels of intensity that emotions are most likely to play the largely advisory role emphasized by many of the current theories reviewed in the introduction. The clinical literature on fear and anxiety may have been the area in which cognition–emotion conflicts are most prevalent in part because the emotions examined in clinical settings and with clinical populations are much more intense than those elicited in the laboratory with nonclinical populations. Eliciting powerful emotions in normal populations is certainly problematic; perhaps the best opportunities for such research occur in naturalistic settings in which emotions reliably run high (e.g. just before parachuting, or in the courtroom).

19.3.2. *Policy Implications*

Individuals' emotional reactions to risks not only often differ from their cognitive evaluations of those risks; they also often diverge from the evaluations of experts. Public perception of the risks of silicone implants in causing autoimmune diseases, for example, led Dow Corning to stop production of implants in 1992 and file for bankruptcy in 1995, despite two major medical reports that revealed no evidence of silicone-related illnesses and a clean bill of health from the American College of Rheumatology (Cowley, 1995). Controversies about the licensing of technologies such as genetic engineering or the siting of facilities such as landfills, incinerator plants, or halfway houses for the mentally handicapped tend to be fueled primarily by emotional reactions to the risks, rather than by scientific evaluations of objective risk levels. Although the controversy about location of the high-level nuclear waste repository generates powerful emotions, large numbers of people seem amazingly unconcerned about the fact that high-level nuclear waste is currently being stored at nuclear reactors that are in close proximity to major population centers. Referring to the current controversy about the Department of Energy's nuclear waste disposal plans for Yucca Mountain (Nevada), Slovic, Flynn, and Layman (1991) described officials from the Department of Energy, the nuclear industry, and their technical experts as "profoundly puzzled, frustrated, and disturbed by public opposition that many of them consider to be based on irrationality and ignorance" (p. 1603). Whereas business or government experts have clear quantitative definitions of such risks on the basis of objective data or models, members of the general public often seem to evaluate the same options in very different ways. Much of the early work by Slovic, Fischhoff, and Lichtenstein (1986) on psychological risk dimensions was funded by the Nuclear Regulatory Commission (NRC) to explain how public perception of the riskiness of nuclear technology could differ so drastically from the estimates provided by NRC engineers. In the intervening years, these differences in perception have shown no sign of diminishing. Future research should continue to investigate whether these differences in perception are the result of differences in the degree to which risks are processed cognitively versus affectively by different segments of the population.

The divergence between the emotional reactions of the public to risks and professionals' appraisals of risks creates a significant dilemma for policy makers. On the one hand, many policy makers would like to be responsive to public attitudes and opinions. On the other hand, there is a strong rationale for basing public policy on the best scientific assessments of risk severity. Sunstein (in press) justified cost–benefit analysis precisely on the basis that it provides an impartial assessment of programs that are resistant to the influence of public fears. He noted that governments allocate the limited resources for risk mitigation in an inefficient fashion in part because they are responsive to lay judgments about the magnitude of risks. Sunstein then cited results from diverse lines of research showing that a government that could insulate itself from such misinformed judgments could save tens of thousands of lives and tens of billions of dollars annually. Consistent with the risk-as-feelings hypothesis, Sunstein attributed the public's misinformed judgments in part to emotional influences:

Risk-related objections can be a product not so much of thinking as of intense emotions, often produced by extremely vivid images of what might go wrong....The role of cost–benefit analysis is straightforward here. Just as the Senate was designed to have a "cooling effect" on the passions of the House of Representatives, so cost–benefit analysis might ensure that policy is driven not by hysteria or alarm, but by a full appreciation of the effects of relevant risks and their control. (p. 16)

599

Sunstein argued further that cost–benefit analysis could not only act as a check on unwarranted fears (e.g. Alar), but could also serve to introduce regulation of risks that are objectively threatening but that do not elicit visceral reactions in the populace (e.g. lead in gasoline and radon in homes).

Simply disregarding the public's fears and basing policy on the experts, however, is difficult in a democracy and ignores the real costs that fears impose on people, as is well documented in the literatures on stress and anxiety. The best policy, then, would be one that involves mitigating real risks and irrational fears. Although clinical treatment of anxiety disorders "represents one of the great success stories of applied psychological science" (Bouton, Mineka, & Barlow, 2001, p. 4), there is very little research on fear-reduction strategies that might be effective at a societal level.

In this article we have proposed a model of risky choice that highlights the role of anticipatory emotions—immediate visceral reactions (e.g. fear, anxiety, dread) to risks and uncertainties that arise at the time of decision making. The model is fundamentally different from the consequentialist approach that characterizes most existing risky-choice theories. Consequentialist models, to the extent that they include emotions at all, tend to incorporate anticipated emotions—emotions that are expected to result from the consequences of the decision. By taking account of the role of anticipatory emotions that are experienced at the moment of decision making, our model explains a variety of phenomena that have puzzled decision theorists who have attempted to explain them at a purely cognitive level.

Although the focus of this article has been on choices under risk, the basic theme can be applied to any type of decision, whether it involves risks or not. Like theories of risky choice, most theories of riskless choice, including multi-attribute utility theories, also take a consequentialist perspective, assuming that decisions are made to maximize the utility of future consequences. Even theories that do take emotions into consideration typically view emotions as a consequence of one's decision. In contrast, our model, and the substantial body of research on which it is based, suggest that gut feelings experienced at the moment of making a decision, which are often quite independent of the consequences of the decision, can play a critical role in the choice one eventually makes.

References

Ahlbrecht, M., & Weber, M. (1996). The resolution of uncertainty: An experimental study. *Journal of Institutional and Theoretical Economics, 152,* 593–677.

Ajzen, I., & Fishbein, M. (1980). *Understanding attitudes and predicting behavior.* Englewood Cliffs, NJ: Prentice Hall.

Alhakami, A. S., & Slovic, P. (1994). A psychological study of the inverse relationship between perceived risk and perceived benefits. *Risk Analysis, 14,* 1085–1096.

Armony, J. L., Servan-Schreiber, D., Cohen, J. D., & LeDoux, J. E. (1995). An anatomically-constrained neural network model of fear conditioning. *Behavioral Neuroscience, 109*, 246–256.

Armony, J. L., Servan-Schreiber, D., Cohen, J. D., & LeDoux, J. E. (1997). Computational modeling of emotion: Explorations through the anatomy and physiology of fear conditioning. *Trends in Cognitive Sciences, 1*, 28–34.

Bajtelsmit, V. L., Bernasek, A., & Jianakoplos, N. A. (1997). Gender differences in pension investment allocation decisions. *Journal of Risk and Insurance, 16*, 135–147.

Bankhart, C. P., & Elliott, R. (1974). Heart rate and skin conductance in anticipation of shocks with varying probability of occurrence. *Psychophysiology, 11*, 160–174.

Bargh, J. A. (1984). Automatic and conscious processing of social information. In R. S. Wyer & T. K. Srull (Eds.), *Handbook of social cognition* (Vol. 3, pp. 1–43). Hillsdale, NJ: Erlbaum.

Barlow, D. H. (1988). *Anxiety and its disorders: The nature and treatment of anxiety and panic.* New York: Guilford Press.

Barsky, B., Juster, F. T., Kimball, M. S., & Shapiro, M. D. (1997). Preference parameters and behavioral heterogeneity: An experimental approach in the health and retirement study. *Quarterly Journal of Economics, 112*, 537–579.

Bartholomew, R. (1997, May/June). Collective delusions: A skeptic's guide. *Skeptical Inquirer*, pp. 29–33.

Bechara, A., Damasio, H., Tranel, D., & Damasio, A. R. (1997). Deciding advantageously before knowing the advantageous strategy. *Science, 275*, 1293–1295.

Beck, A. T., & Emery, T. (1985). *Anxiety disorders and phobias.* New York: Basic Books.

Becker, M. H. (1974). The health belief model and personal health behavior. *Health Education Monographs, 2*, 324–508.

Bell, D. E. (1982). Regret in decision making under uncertainty. *Operations Research, 30*, 961–981.

Bell, D. E. (1985). Disappointment in decision making under uncertainty. *Operations Research, 33*, 1–27.

Benartzi, S., & Thaler, R. H. (1995). Myopic loss aversion and the equity premium puzzle. *The Quarterly Journal of Economics, 110*, 73–92.

Benthin, A., Slovic, P., Moran, P., Severson, H., Mertz, C. K., & Gerrard, M. (1995). Adolescent health-threatening and health-enhancing behaviors: A study of word association and imagery. *Journal of Adolescent Health, 17*, 143–152.

Bernay, T., Porrath, S., Golding-Mather, J. M., & Murray, J. (1982). The impact of breast cancer screening on feminine identity: Implications for patient education. *Breast, 8*, 2–5.

Beyth-Marom, R., Austin, L., Fischhoff, B., Palmgren, C., & Quadrel, M. (1993). Perceived consequences of risky behavior: Adolescents and adults. *Developmental Psychology, 29*, 549–563.

Bouton, M. E. (1994). Conditioning, remembering, and forgetting. *Journal of Experimental Psychology, 20*, 219–231.

Bouton, M. E., Mineka, S., & Barlow, D. H. (2001). A modern learning theory perspective on the etiology of panic disorder. *Psychological Review, 108*, 4–32.

Bouton, M. E., & Swartzentruber, D. (1991). Sources of relapse after extinction in Pavlovian and instrumental learning. *Clinical Psychology Review, 11*, 123–140.

Bower, G. (1992). How might emotions affect learning. In S.-A. Christianson (Ed.), *The handbook of emotion and memory: Research and theory* (pp. 3–31). Hillsdale, NJ: Erlbaum.

Bower, G. H. (1981). Mood and memory. *American Psychologist, 36*, 129–148.

Bower, G. H. (1991). Mood congruity of social judgment. In J. Forgas (Ed.), *Emotion and social judgment* (pp. 31–54). Oxford, England: Pergamon Press.

Breznitz, S. (1971). A study of worrying. *British Journal of Social and Clinical Psychology, 10*, 271–279.

Brody, L. R. (1993). On understanding gender differences in the expression of emotion. In S. L. Ablon, D. Brown, E. J. Khantzian, & J. E. Mack (Eds.), *Human feelings: Explorations in affect development and meaning* (pp. 87–121). Hillsdale, NJ: Analytic Press.

Brody, L. R., Hay, D., & Vandewater, E. (1990). Gender, gender role identity and children's reported feelings toward the same and opposite sex. *Sex Roles, 21*, 363–387.

Browne, M. J., & Hoyt, R. E. (2000). The demand for flood insurance: Empirical evidence. *Journal of Risk and Uncertainty, 20*, 271–289.

Burger, J. M., & Burns, L. (1988). The illusion of unique invulnerability and the use of effective contraception. *Personality and Social Psychology Bulletin, 14*, 264–270.

Byrnes, J. P., Miller, D. C., & Schafer, W. D. (1999). Gender differences in risk taking: A meta-analysis. *Psychological Bulletin, 125*, 367–383.

Camerer, C. (1989). An experimental test of several generalized utility theories. *Journal of Risk and Uncertainty, 2*, 61–104.

Camerer, C. (1995). Individual decision making. In J. H. Kagel & A. E. Roth (Eds.), *Handbook of experimental economics* (pp. 587–683). Princeton, NJ: Princeton University Press.

Caplin, A., & Leahy, J. (1997). *Psychological expected theory and anticipatory feelings.* Unpublished manuscript, New York University, Department of Economics.

Carroll, D., Baker, J., & Preston, M. (1979). Individual differences in visual imagery and the voluntary control of heart rate. *British Journal of Psychology, 70*, 39–49.

Chaiken, S., & Trope, Y. (Eds.). (1999). *Dual process theories in social psychology.* New York: Guilford Press.

Chakraborty, A., Das, S., & Mukherji, A. (1983). Koro epidemic in India. *Transcultural Psychiatric Research Review, 20*, 150–151.

Chew, S. H., & Ho, J. L. (1994). Hope: An empirical study of attitude toward the timing of uncertainty resolution. *Journal of Risk and Uncertainty, 8*, 267–288.

Clark, D. M. (1986). A cognitive approach to panic. *Behaviour Research and Therapy, 24*, 461–470.

Cleckley, H. (1941). *The mask of sanity.* St. Louis, MO: C. V. Mosby.

Clore, G. L. (1992). Cognitive phenomenology: Feelings and the construction of judgment. In L. L. Martin & A. Tesser (Eds.), *The construction of social judgments* (pp. 133–163). Hillsdale, NJ: Erlbaum.

Clore, G. L., Schwarz, N., & Conway, M. (1994). Affective causes and consequences of social information processing. In R. S. Wyer & T. K. Srull (Eds.), *Handbook of social cognition* (Vol. 1, pp. 323–417). Hillsdale, NJ: Erlbaum.

Cook, M., & Mineka, S. (1990). Selective associations in the observational conditioning of fear in Rhesus monkeys. *Journal of Experimental Psychology: Animal Behavior Processes, 16*, 372–389.

Cottle, T. J., & Klineberg, S. L. (1974). *The present of things future*. New York: Free Press.

Cowley, G. (1995, November 13). Silicone: Juries vs. science. *Newsweek*, p. 75.

Damasio, A. R. (1994). *Descartes' error: Emotion, reason, and the human brain*. New York: Putnam.

David, A. S., & Wessely, S. C. (1995). The legend of Camelford: Medical consequences of a water pollution accident. *Journal of Psychosomatic Research, 39*, 1–9.

Deane, G. (1969). Cardiac activity during experimentally induced anxiety. *Psychophysiology, 6*, 17–30.

de Becker, G. (1997). *The gift of fear: Survival signals that protect us from violence*. Boston: Little, Brown, and Company.

Derakshan, N., & Eysenck, M. W. (1997). Interpretive biases for one's own behavior and physiology in high-trait-anxious individuals and repressors. *Journal of Personality and Social Psychology, 73*, 816–825.

Die Macht der Gefuehle [The power of feelings]. (1997, September 29). *Spiegel, 39*, 244–265.

Don't ignore your fear. (1997, July 21). *Newsweek*, p. 78.

Eisenberg, A. E., Baron, J., & Seligman, M. E. P. (1995). *Individual differences in risk aversion and anxiety* (Working Paper). University of Pennsylvania, Department of Psychology.

Elliott, R. (1975). Heart rate in anticipation of shocks which have different probabilities of occurrences. *Psychological Reports, 36*, 923–931.

Ellsworth, P. C., & Smith, C. A. (1988). From appraisal to emotion: Differences among unpleasant feelings. *Motivation and Emotion, 12*, 271–302.

Elster, J., & Loewenstein, G. (1992). Utility from memory and anticipation. In G. Loewenstein & J. Elster (Eds.), *Choice over time* (pp. 213–234). New York: Russell Sage.

Epstein, S., Lipson, A., Holstein, C., & Huh, E. (1992). Irrational reactions to negative outcomes: Evidence for two conceptual systems. *Journal of Personality and Social Psychology, 62*, 328–339.

Eysenck, M. W. (1992). *Anxiety: The cognitive perspective*. Hove, England: Erlbaum.

Eysenck, M. W., MacLeod, C., & Matthews, A. (1987). Cognitive functioning and anxiety. *Psychological Research, 49*, 189–195.

Finucane, M., Alhakami, A., Slovic, P., & Johnson, S. M. (2000). The affect heuristic in judgments of risks and benefits. *Journal of Behavioral Decision Making, 13*, 1–17.

Fischhoff, B., Lichtenstein, S., Slovic, P., Derby, S. L., & Keeney, R. L. (1981). *Acceptable risk*. Cambridge, England: Cambridge University Press.

Fowles, D. C., & Missel, K. A. (1994). Electrodermal hyporeactivity, motivation, and psychopathy: Theoretical issues. In D. C. Fowles, P. Sutker, & S. Goodman (Eds.), *Progress in experimental personality and psychopathy research 1994: Special focus on psychopathy and antisocial behavior: A developmental perspective* (pp. 263–283). New York: Springer.

Freeman, W., & Watts, J. W. (1942). *Psychosurgery; intelligence, emotion and social behavior following prefrontal lobotomy for mental disorders*. Springfield, IL: Charles C Thomas.

Friedman, M., & Savage, L. (1948). The utility analysis of choices involving risk. *Journal of Political Economy, 56*, 279–304.

Frijda, N. H. (1986). *The emotions*. Cambridge, England: Cambridge University Press.

Frijda, N. H., Kuipers, P., & ter Schure, E. (1989). Relations among emotion, appraisal, and emotional action readiness. *Journal of Personality and Social Psychology, 57,* 212–228.

Fujita, F., Diener, E., & Sandvik, E. (1991). Gender differences in negative affect and well-being: The case for emotional intensity. *Journal of Personality and Social Psychology, 61,* 427–434.

George, M. R. (1999, Spring/Summer). National Institute of Mental Health, Research described in Do Male and Female Brains Respond Differently to Severe Emotional Stress?: In a Flurry of New Research, Scientists are Finding Tantalizing Clues. *Newsweek* (Special Edition: What Every Woman Needs to Know), pp. 68–71.

Gladwell, M. (1999, July 12). Is the Belgian Coca-Cola hysteria the real thing? *New Yorker,* pp. 24–25.

Gneezy, U., & Potters, J. (1997). An experiment on risk taking and evaluation periods. *Quarterly Journal of Economics, 112,* 631–645.

Gregory, R., Flynn, J., & Slovic, P. (1995). Technological stigma. *American Scientist, 83,* 220–223.

Gregory, R., Slovic, P., & Flynn, J. (1996). Risk perceptions, stigma, and health policy. *Health and Place, 2,* 213–220.

Gwee, A. L. (1968). Koro: Its origin and nature as a disease entity. *Singapore Medical Journal, 9,* 3.

Hare, R. D. (1965). Psychopathy, fear arousal and anticipated pain. *Psychological Reports, 16,* 499–502.

Hare, R. D. (1966). Temporal gradient of fear arousal in psychopaths. *Journal of Abnormal and Social Psychology, 70,* 442–445.

Harless, D. W., & Camerer, C. F. (1994). The predictive utility of generalized expected utility theories. *Econometrica, 62,* 1251–1289.

Harshman, R. A., & Paivio, A. (1987). Paradoxical sex differences in self-reported imagery. *Canadian Journal of Psychology, 41,* 303–316.

Hendickx, L., Vlek, C., & Oppewal, H. (1989). Relative importance of scenario and information and frequency information in the judgment of risk. *Acta Psychologica, 72,* 41–63.

Hersch, J. (1997). Smoking, seat belts, and other risky consumer decisions: Differences by gender and race. *Managerial and Decision Economics, 11,* 241–256.

Hogarth, R., & Kunreuther, H. (1995). Decision making under ignorance: Arguing with yourself. *Journal of Risk and Uncertainty, 10,* 1015–1036.

Holtgrave, D., & Weber, E. U. (1993). Dimensions of risk perception for financial and health-and-safety risks. *Risk Analysis, 13,* 553–558.

Hsee, C. K., & Weber, E. U. (1997). A fundamental prediction error: Self–other discrepancies in risk preference. *Journal of Experimental Psychology: General, 126,* 45–53.

Insurance Advocate. (1994). Flood disasters noted by those in jeopardy but they still don't buy flood insurance. *Insurance Advocate, 105,* 17.

Isaac, R. M., & James, D. (2000). "Just who are you calling risk averse?" *Journal of Risk and Uncertainty, 20,* 177–187.

Isen, A. M., & Geva, N. (1987). The influence of positive affect on acceptable level of risk: The person with a large canoe has a large worry. *Organizational Behavior and Human Decision Processes, 39,* 145–154.

Isen, A. M., Nygren, T. E., & Ashby, F. G. (1988). Influence of positive affect on the subjective utility of gains and losses: It is just not worth the risk. *Journal of Personality and Social Psychology, 55*, 710–717.

Isen, A. M., & Patrick, R. (1983). The effect of positive feelings on risk-taking: When the chips are down. *Organizational Behavior and Human Performance, 31*, 194–202.

Isen, A. M., Shalker, T. E., Clark, M., & Karp, L. (1978). Affect, accessibility of material in memory, and behavior: A cognitive loop? *Journal of Personality and Social Psychology, 36*, 1–12.

Jacobs, N. (1965). The phantom slasher of Taipei: Mass hysteria in a non-Western society. *Social Problems, 12*, 318–328.

Janis, I. L., & Feshbach, S. (1953). Effects of fear-arousing communications. *Journal of Abnormal and Social Psychology, 48*, 78–92.

Janis, I. L., & Mann, L. (1977). *Decision making: A psychological analysis of conflict, choice, and commitment.* New York: Free Press.

Johnson, E. J., Hershey, J., Meszaros, J., & Kunreuther, H. (1993). Framing, probability distortions, and insurance decisions. *Journal of Risk and Uncertainty, 7*, 35–51.

Johnson, E. J., & Tversky, A. (1983). Affect, generalization, and the perception of risk. *Journal of Personality and Social Psychology, 45*, 20–31.

Kahneman, D., & Ritov, I. (1994). Determinants of stated willingness to pay for public goods: A study in the headline method. *Journal of Risk and Uncertainty, 9*, 5–38.

Kahneman, D., Ritov, I. & Schkade, D. (1999). Economic preferences or attitude expressions? An analysis of dollar responses to public issues. *Journal of Risk and Uncertainty, 19*, 203–237.

Kahneman, D., Schkade, D. A., & Sunstein, C. R. (1998). Shared outrage and erratic awards: The psychology of punitive damages. *Journal of Risk and Uncertainty, 16*, 49–86.

Kahneman, D., & Tversky, A. (1979). Prospect theory: An analysis of decision under risk. *Econometrica, 47*, 263–291.

Kavanagh, D. J., & Bower, G. H. (1985). Mood and self-efficacy: Impact of joy and sadness on perceived capabilities. *Cognitive Therapy and Research, 9*, 507–525.

Kunreuther, H. (1976). Limited knowledge and insurance protection. *Public Policy, 24*, 227–261.

Kunreuther, H., Ginsburg, R., Miller, L., Sagi, P., Slovic, P., Borkan, B., & Katz, N. (1978). *Disaster insurance protection: Public policy lessons.* New York: Wiley.

Lang, P. J. (1995). The emotion probe: Studies of motivation and attention. *American Psychologist, 50*, 372–385.

Lazarus, R., & McCleary, R. (1951). Autonomic discrimination without awareness: A study of subception. *Psychological Review, 58*, 113–122.

LeDoux, J. (1996). *The emotional brain.* New York: Simon & Schuster.

Lerner, J. S., & Keltner, D. (1999). *Fear, anger, and risk.* Manuscript submitted for publication.

Lerner, J. S., & Keltner, D. (2000). Beyond valence: Toward a model of emotion-specific influences on judgment and choice. *Cognition and Emotion, 14*, 473–494.

Leventhal, H., & Watts, J. (1966). Sources of resistance to fear arousing communications on smoking and lung cancer. *Journal of Personality, 34*, 155–175.

Liberman, N., & Trope, Y. (1998). The role of feasibility and desirability considerations in near and distant future decisions: A test of temporal construal theory. *Journal of Personality and Social Psychology, 75*, 5–18.

Lieberman, A., & Chaiken, S. (1992). Defensive processing of personally relevant health messages. *Personality and Social Psychology Bulletin, 18*, 669–679.

Loewenstein, G. (1987). Anticipation and the valuation of delayed consumption. *Economic Journal, 97*, 666–684.

Loewenstein, G. (1996). Out of control: Visceral influences on behavior. *Organizational Behavior and Human Decision Processes, 65*, 272–292.

Loewenstein, G. (1999). A visceral account of addiction. In J. Elster & O. J. Skog (Eds.), *Getting hooked: Rationality and addiction* (pp. 235–264). Cambridge, England: Cambridge University Press.

Loewenstein, G., & Lerner, J. (in press). The role of emotion in decision making. In R. J. Davidson, H. H. Goldsmith, & K. R. Scherer (Eds.), *The handbook of affective science.* Oxford, England: Oxford University Press.

Loewenstein, G., & Mather, J. (1990). Dynamic processes in risk perception. *Journal of Risk and Uncertainty, 3*, 155–170.

Loomes, G., & Sugden, R. (1982). Regret theory: An alternative theory of rational choice under uncertainty. *Economic Journal, 92*, 805–824.

Loomes, G., & Sugden, R. (1986). Disappointment and dynamic consistency in choice under uncertainty. *Review of Economic Studies, 53*, 271–282.

Lopes, L. L. (1987). Between hope and fear: The psychology of risk. In L. Berkowitz (Ed.), *Advances in experimental social psychology* (Vol. 20, pp. 255–295). San Diego, CA: Academic Press.

Lopes, L. L. (1995). Algebra and process in modeling risky choice. In J. R. Busemeyer, R. Hastie, & D. L. Medin (Eds.), *Decision making from a cognitive perspective. The psychology of learning and motivation* (Vol. 32, pp. 177–220). New York: Academic Press.

Lovallo, D., & Kahneman, D. (2000). Living with uncertainty: Attractiveness and resolution timing. *Journal of Behavioral Decision Making, 13*, 179–190.

Luce, M. F., Bettman, J. R., & Payne, J. W. (1997). Choice processing in emotionally difficult decisions. *Journal of Experimental Psychology: Learning, Memory, and Cognition, 23*, 384–405.

Luce, M. F., Bettman, J. R., & Payne, J. W. (1999). Emotional trade-off difficulty and choice. *Journal of Marketing Research, 36*, 143–159.

Luce, R. D., & von Winterfeldt, D. (1994). What common ground exists for descriptive, prescriptive, and normative utility theories? *Management Science, 40*, 263–279.

Luce, R. D., & Weber, E. U. (1986). An axiomatic theory of conjoint, expected risk. *Journal of Mathematical Psychology, 30*, 188–205.

Luu, P., Tucker, D. M., & Derryberry, D. (1998). Anxiety and the motivational basis of working memory. *Cognitive Therapy and Research, 22*, 577–594.

Lykken, D. T. (1957). A study of anxiety in the sociopathic personality. *Journal of Abnormal and Social Psychology, 55*, 6–10.

MacCrimmon, K. R., & Wehrung, D. A. (1986). *Taking risks: The management of uncertainty.* New York: The Free Press.

McNally, R. J. (1987). Preparedness and phobias: A review. *Psychological Bulletin, 101*, 283–303.

Mann, L. (1992). Stress, affect, and risk taking. In Y. J. Frank (Ed.), *Risk-taking behavior* (Wiley Series in Human Performance and Cognition, pp. 202–230). Chichester, England: John Wiley & Sons.

Markowitz, H. (1952). The utility of wealth. *Journal of Political Economy, 60*, 151–158.

Markowitz. H. M. (1959). *Portfolio selection*. New York: Wiley.

Mayer, J. D., Gaschke, Y. N., Braverman, D. L., & Evans, T. W. (1992). Mood-congruent judgment is a general effect. *Journal of Personality and Social Psychology, 63*, 119–132.

Mayer, J. D., & Hanson, E. (1995). Mood-congruent judgment over time. *Personality and Social Psychology Bulletin, 21*, 237–244.

Mellers, B. A., Schwartz, A., Ho, K., & Ritov, I. (1997). Decision affect theory: Emotional reactions to the outcomes of risky options. *Psychological Science, 8*, 423–429.

Mellers, B., Schwartz, A., & Ritov, I. (1999). Emotion-based choice. *Journal of Experimental Psychology: General, 128*, 332–345.

Menzies, R. G. (1995). The uneven distribution of fears and phobias: A nonassociative account. *Behavioral and Brain Sciences, 18*, 305–306.

Miller, G. A., Levin, D., Kozak, M., Cook, E., McLean, A., & Lang, P. (1987). Individual differences in imagery and the psychophysiology of emotion. *Cognition and Emotion, 1*, 367–390.

Mineka, S., & Cook, M. (1993). Mechanisms involved in the observational conditioning of fear. *Journal of Experimental Psychology: General, 122*, 23–38.

Monat, A. (1976). Temporal uncertainty, anticipation time, and cognitive coping under threat. *Journal of Human Stress, 2*, 32–43.

Monat, A., Averill, J. R., & Lazarus, R. S. (1972). Anticipatory stress and coping reactions under various conditions of uncertainty. *Journal of Personality and Social Psychology, 24*, 237–253.

Mossin, J. (1969). A note on uncertainty and preferences in a temporal context. *American Economic Review, 59*, 172–173.

Murray, M., & McMillan, C. (1993). Social and behavioural predictors of women's cancer screening practices in Northern Ireland. *Journal of Public Health Medicine, 15*, 147–153.

Ness, R. M., & Klaas, R. (1994). Risk perception by patients with anxiety disorders. *Journal of Nervous and Mental Disease, 182*, 466–470.

Nisan, M. (1972). Dimension of time in relation to choice behavior and achievement orientation. *Journal of Personality and Social Psychology, 21*, 175–182.

Nisbett, R., & Ross, L. (1980). *Human inference: Strategies and short-comings of social judgment*. Englewood Cliffs, NJ: Prentice Hall.

Nolen-Hoeksema, S. (1990). *Sex differences in depression*. Stanford, CA: Stanford University Press.

Nygren, T. E., Isen, A. M., Taylor, P. J., & Dulin, J. (1996). The influence of positive affect on the decision rule in risk situations: Focus on outcome (and especially avoidance of loss) rather than probability. *Organizational Behavior and Human Decision Processes, 66*, 59–72.

Öhman, A. (1986). Face the beast and fear the face: Animal and social fears as prototypes for evolutionary analyses of emotion. *Psychophysiology, 23*, 123–145.

Öhman, A., & Soares, J. J. F. (1993). On the automatic nature of phobic fear: Conditioned electrodermal responses to masked fear-relevant stimuli. *Journal of Abnormal Psychology, 102*, 121–132.

Öhman, A., & Soares, J. J. F. (1994). Unconscious anxiety: Phobic responses to masked stimuli. *Journal of Abnormal Psychology, 103*, 231–240.

O'Malley, M. S., & Fletcher, S. W. (1987). Screening for breast cancer with breast self-examination: A critical review. *Journal of the American Medical Association, 257*, 2196–2203.

Ortony, A., Clore, G. L., & Collins, A. (1988). *The cognitive structure of emotions.* Cambridge, England: Cambridge University Press.

Panksepp, J. (1985). Mood changes. In P. J. Vinken, G. W. Buyn, & H. L. Klawans (Eds.), *Handbook of clinical neurology. Revised series:* Vol. 1. *Clinical neuropsychology* (pp. 271–855) Amsterdam: Elsevier Science.

Panksepp, J. (1998). *Affective neuroscience.* New York: Oxford University Press.

Paterson, R. J., & Neufeld, R. W. J. (1987). Clear danger: Situational determinants of the appraisal of threat. *Psychological Bulletin, 101*, 404–416.

Patrick, C. J. (1994). Emotion and psychopathy: Startling new insights. *Psychophysiology, 31*, 415–428.

Pavlov, I. P. (1927). *Conditioned reflexes.* London: Oxford University Press.

Payne, J. W., Bettman, J. R., & Johnson, E. (1993). *The adaptive decisionmaker.* Cambridge, England: Cambridge University Press.

Peters, E., & Slovic, P. (1996). The role of affect and worldviews as orienting dispositions in the perception and acceptance of nuclear power. *Journal of Applied Social Psychology, 26*, 1427–1453.

Peters, E., & Slovic, P. (in press). The springs of action: Affective and analytical information processing in choice. *Personality and Social Psychology Bulletin.*

Pope, R. (1985). Timing contradictions in von Neumann and Morgenstern's axioms and in Savage's "sure thing" proof. *Theory and Decision, 18*, 229–261.

Prelec, D. (1998). The probability weighting function. *Econometric, 66*, 497–529.

Quadrel, M. J., Fischhoff, B., & Davis, W. (1993). Adolescent (in)vulnerability. *American Psychologist, 48*, 102–116.

Raghunathan, R., & Pham, M. T. (1999). All negative moods are not equal: Motivational influences of anxiety and sadness on decision making. *Organizational Behavior and Human Decision Processes. 79*, 56–77.

Rolls, E. T. (1999). *The brain and emotion.* New York: Oxford University Press.

Roseman, I. (1984). Cognitive determinants of emotions: A structural theory. In P. Shaver (Ed.), *Review of personality and social psychology* (Vol. 5, pp. 11–36). Beverly Hills, CA: Sage.

Roth, W. T., Breivik, G., Jorgensen, P. E., & Hofmann, S. (1996). Activation in novice and expert parachutists while jumping. *Psychophysiology, 33*, 63–72.

Rottenstreich, Y., & Hsee, C. K. (1999). *Money, kisses and electric shocks: On the affective psychology of probability weighting.* Working paper, The University of Chicago.

Sanna, L. J. (1999). Mental simulations, affect, and subjective confidence: Timing is everything. *Psychological Science, 10*, 339–345.

Sapolsky, R. M. (1994). *Why zebras don't get ulcers: A guide to stress, stress-related diseases, and coping.* New York: Freeman.

Savitsky, K., Medvec, V. H., Charlton, A. E., & Gilovich, T. (1998). What, me worry?: Arousal, misattribution, and the effect of temporal distance on confidence. *Personality and Social Psychology Bulletin, 24*, 529–536.

Schelling, T. (1984). Self-command in practice, in policy, and in a theory of rational choice. *American Economic Review, 74,* 1–11.

Scherer, K. R. (1984). On the nature and function of emotions: A component process approach. In K. R. Scherer & P. Ekman (Eds.), *Approaches to emotion* (pp. 293–317). Hillsdale, NJ: Erlbaum.

Schmitt, W. A., Brinkley, C. A., & Newman, J. P. (1999). Testing Damasio's somatic marker hypothesis with psychopathic individuals: Risk takers or risk averse? *Journal of Abnormal Psychology, 108,* 538–543.

Schmitt, W. A., & Newman, J. P. (1999). Are all psychopathic individuals low-anxious? *Journal of Abnormal Psychology, 108,* 353–358.

Schoemaker, P. J. H. (1990). Are risk-preferences related across payoff domains and response modes? *Management Science, 36,* 1451–1463.

Schwarz, N., & Clore, G. L. (1983). Mood, misattribution, and judgments of well-being: Information and directive functions of affective states. *Journal of Personality and Social Psychology, 45,* 513–523.

Seligman, M. E. P. (1971). Phobias and preparedness. *Behavior Therapy, 2,* 307–320.

Servan-Schreiber, D., & Perlstein, W. M. (1998). Selective limbic activation and its relevance to emotional disorders. *Cognition & Emotion, 12,* 331–352.

Shepperd, J. A., Ouellette, J. A. & Fernandez, J. K. (1996). Abandoning unrealistic optimism: Performance estimates and the temporal proximity of self-relevant feedback. *Journal of Personality and Social Psychology, 70,* 844–855.

Shiv, B., & Fedorikhin, A. (1999). Heart and mind in conflict: The interplay of affect and cognition in consumer decision making. *Journal of Consumer Research, 26,* 278–292.

Shiv, B., & Huber, J. (2000). The impact of anticipating satisfaction on choice. *Journal of Consumer Research, 27,* 202–216.

Simon, H. A. (1967). Motivational and emotional controls of cognition. *Psychological Review, 57,* 386–420.

Sjöberg, L. (1998). Worry and risk perception. *Risk Analysis, 18,* 85–93.

Sloman, S. A. (1996). The empirical case for two systems of reasoning. *Psychological Bulletin, 119,* 3–22.

Slovic, P., Finucane, M., Peters, E., & MacGregor, D. (in press). The affect heuristic. In T. Gilovich, D. Griffin, & D. Kahneman (Eds.), *Intuitive judgment: Heuristics and biases.* Cambridge, England: Cambridge University Press.

Slovic, P., Fischhoff, B., & Lichtenstein, S. (1980). Facts and fears: Understanding perceived risk. In R. Schwing & W. Albers Jr. (Eds.), *Societal risk assessment: How safe is safe enough?* (pp. 181–216). San Francisco: Jossey-Bass.

Slovic, P., Fischhoff, B., & Lichtenstein, S. (1986). The psychometric study of risk perception. In V. T. Covello, J. Menkes, & J. Mumpower (Eds.), *Risk evaluation and management* (pp. 3–24). New York: Plenum Press.

Slovic, P., Flynn, J., & Gregory, R. (1994). Stigma happens: Social problems in the siting of nuclear waste facilities. *Risk Analysis, 14,* 773.

Slovic, P., Flynn, J. H., & Layman, M. (1991). Perceived risk, trust, and the politics of nuclear waste. *Science, 254,* 1603–1607.

Slovic, P., Layman, M., Kraus, N., Flynn, J., Chalmers, J., & Gesell, G. (1991). Perceived risk, stigma, and potential economic impacts of a high-level nuclear waste repository in Nevada. *Risk Analysis, 11,* 683–696.

Smith, C. A., & Ellsworth, P. C. (1985). Patterns of cognitive appraisal and emotional response related to taking an exam. *Journal of Personality and Social Psychology, 52,* 475–488.

Smith, D., & Over, R. (1987). Male sexual arousal as a function of the content and the vividness of erotic fantasy. *Psychophysiology, 24,* 334–339.

Snortum, J. R., & Wilding, F. W. (1971). Temporal estimation of heart rate as a function of repression-sensitization score and probability of shock. *Journal of Consulting and Clinical Psychology, 37,* 417–422.

Specter, M. (1996, March 31). 10 years later, through fear, Chernobyl still kills in Belarus. *New York Times,* p. 1.

Spence, M., & Zeckhauser, R. (1972). The effect of timing of consumption decisions and the resolution of lotteries on the choice of lotteries. *Econometrica, 40,* 401–403.

Stapley, J. C., & Haviland, J. M. (1989). Beyond depression: Gender differences in normal adolescents' emotional experiences. *Sex Roles, 20,* 295–308.

Starmer, C. (2000). Developments in non-expected utility theory: The hunt for a descriptive theory of choice under risk. *Journal of Economic Literature, 38*(2), 332–383.

Sunstein, C. (in press). Cognition and cost–benefit analysis. *Journal of Legal Studies.*

Thaler, R., Tversky, A., Kahneman, D., & Schwartz, A. (1997). The effect of myopia and loss aversion on risk taking: An experimental test. *Quarterly Journal of Economics, 112,* 647–661.

Vasey, M. W., El-Hag, N., & Daleiden, E. L. (1996). Anxiety and the processing of emotionally threatening stimuli: Distinctive patterns of selective attention among high- and low-test-anxious children. *Child Development, 67,* 1173–1185.

Viscusi, K., & Magat, W. (1987). *Learning about risk.* Cambridge, MA: Harvard University Press.

Weber, E. U., Blais, A.-R., & Betz, N. (1999). A domain-specific risk-attitude scale: Measuring risk perceptions and risk behaviors. Manuscript under review.

Weber, E. U., & Hsee, C. K. (1998). Cross-cultural differences in risk perception but cross-cultural similarities in attitudes towards risk. *Management Science, 44,* 1205–1217.

Weinstein, N. D. (1989). Effects of personal experience on self-protective behavior. *Psychological Bulletin, 105,* 31–50.

Welch, E. (1999). *The heat of the moment.* Doctoral dissertation, Department of Social and Decision Sciences, Carnegie Mellon University.

Wessely, S. (1987). Mass hysteria: Two syndromes? *Psychological Medicine, 17,* 109–120.

Wessely, S., & Wardle, C. J. (1990). Mass sociogenic illness by proxy: Parentally reported epidemic in an elementary school. *British Journal of Psychiatry, 157,* 421–424.

White, K. D. (1978). Salivation: The significance of imagery in its voluntary control. *Psychophysiology, 15,* 196–203.

Whitley, B., & Hern, A. (1991). Perceptions of vulnerability to pregnancy and the use of effective contraception. *Personality and Social Psychology Bulletin, 17,* 104–110.

Williamson, S., Harpur, T. J., & Hare, R. D. (1991). Abnormal processing of affective words by psychopaths. *Psychophysiology, 28,* 260–273.

Wilson, T. D., Lisle, D. J., Schooler, J. W., Hodges, S. D., Klaaren, K. J., & LaFleur, S. J. (1993). Introspecting about reasons can reduce post-choice satisfaction. *Personality and Social Psychology Bulletin, 19,* 331–339.

Wilson, T. D., & Schooler, J. W. (1991). Thinking too much: Introspection can reduce the quality of preferences and decisions. *Journal of Personality and Social Psychology, 60,* 181–192.

Windschitl, P. D., & Weber, E. U. (1999). The interpretation of likely depends on context, but 70% is 70%, right? The influence of associative processes on perceived certainty. *Journal of Experimental Psychology: Learning, Memory, and Cognition, 25,* 1514–1533.

Winkielman, P., Zajonc, R. B., & Schwarz, N. (1997). Subliminal affective priming resists attributional interventions. *Cognition & Emotion, 11,* 433–465.

Wright, W. F., & Bower, G. H. (1992). Mood effects on subjective probability assessment. *Organizational Behavior & Human Decision Processes, 52,* 276–291.

Zajonc, R. B. (1980). Feeling and thinking: Preferences need no inference. *American Psychologist, 35,* 151–175.

Zajonc, R. B. (1984a). The interaction of affect and cognition. In K. R. Scherer & P. Ekman (Eds.), *Approaches to emotion* (pp. 239–246). Hillsdale, NJ: Erlbaum.

Zajonc, R. B. (1984b). On primacy of affect. In K. R. Scherer & P. Ekman (Eds.), *Approaches to emotion* (pp. 259–270). Hillsdale, NJ: Erlbaum.

Zajonc, R. (1998). Emotions. In D. Gilbert, S. Fiske, & G. Lindzey (Eds.), *Handbook of social psychology* (Vol. 1, pp. 591–632). New York: Oxford University Press.

20

Investment Behavior and the Negative Side of Emotion

Baba Shiv, George Loewenstein, Antoine Bechara, Hanna Damasio, and Antonio R. Damasio

The germ for this paper was a suggestion that Chris Hsee made during a phone conversation we had as I was leaving on a trip to Iowa to explore possible collaborations with Baba Shiv and his colleagues. Chris suggested that we might want to examine the dark side of emotions (though I don't think he used that exact language). Historically, the dark side was the main side of emotions that people recognized; emotions were seen as opposed to the rule of reason and as the major cause of self-destructive behavior.

Psychology, for much of the twentieth century, did not adopt this negative view of emotions—or any other for that matter; it ignored emotions altogether. The behaviorists who dominated psychology for the first fifty years of the century ignored emotions because they were not directly observable and hence not a proper topic of study, and the cognitivists who followed in their wake ignored them because they didn't conveniently fit into their perspective. Psychology, seemingly to a greater extent than economics, has a tendency to go to extremes, both in terms of theoretical perspectives and methodological predilections.

When psychologists first trained their sights on emotions in the 1980s, they emphatically did not buy in to the historical view of emotions; much if not most of the work emphasized its functions and benefits. The least controversial, and in my opinion incontrovertible, insight of what became a new perspective on emotion was the idea that emotions play a critical role in human judgment and behavior, a view championed two centuries earlier by David Hume. Thus, for example, people can often function at a surprisingly high level following the disruption of cognitive systems, but damage to emotional systems tends to be devastating.

Although emotions are essential for functioning, my sense from reading the literature when I first became interested in emotions was that psychologists had, to a great extent, lost sight of the "dark side" of emotions—the role they play in self-destructive behavior. Psychologists seemed to be publishing research that almost exclusively highlighted the *benefits* of emotions—in judgment (e.g. intuition) and decision-making. Most prominently, almost all of the research that I read in the burgeoning field of "affective neuroscience" seemed to focus on the functions and benefits of emotion.

A prominent example of affective neuroscience was the work of Antonio Damasio, Antoine Bechara, and their colleagues—the group I was visiting in Iowa (Shiv, although at Iowa and doing research on emotion, was not part of Damasio's laboratory). Their "somatic marker hypothesis" highlighted the important role that emotional signals play in informing decisions about one's own values. Although I endorsed, and continue to endorse, the view that emotions play an essential role in decision making, I was uncomfortable with the main evidence they adduced in support of that position—the so-called "Iowa gambling task." In it, subjects are presented with four decks of cards and, in a series of trials, repeatedly choose cards from the decks. On the back of each card, revealed after they choose it, is an amount of money that, hypothetically, is to be won. However, for some cards, in addition to winning money, participants also lose money. Two of the decks have high gains but periodically also include losses that are sufficiently large such that the expected value of choosing from these decks is negative. The other two decks provide smaller gains, but also smaller losses, and their expected value is positive.

Damasio and his collaborators ran normal subjects and subjects with lesions in regions of the brain associated with the processing of emotions on this task. They found that, while normal subjects quickly learned to avoid the high risk, negative expected value, decks, those with emotion lesions continued to bet on them even after getting 'burned', with many ultimately going broke as a result. They interpreted these findings as providing support for the idea that emotions play an essential role in decision-making.

As I noted, there is ample evidence that brain lesions, and especially those in regions associated with emotion processing, cause serious problems. However, I had long been discontent with this interpretation of the Iowa gambling task results, and Hsee's suggestion gave me the idea of pursuing my misgivings. A problem with the Iowa task is that the riskier decks had higher expected value, whereas in the real world people are generally rewarded for taking risks—for example, stocks have a higher return than bonds, and risky stocks usually have a higher expected return than less risky stocks. It seemed to me that the Iowa gambling task provided evidence that emotion lesion patients were making riskier choices, but not that they were making less advantageous choices. If faced with a choice in which risk taking was rewarded, I conjectured, they might do better.

To their credit, the Iowa researchers (though all have moved to various locations in California since we conducted the research) were game to do research that could potentially challenged their own interpretation of their prior results, and the paper reprinted in this chapter, presents the results of that research. In the study we designed, subjects with emotion lesions, lesions in areas not associated with emotion, and normal subjects engaged in a task in which risk-taking is rewarded. As we predicted, and supportive of the idea (proposed in Chapter 19) that emotions play an important role in risk aversion, the emotion lesion patients took greater risks and, as a result, earned greater profits. To the best of my knowledge, this is the first study to document a situation in which people with brain damage made better decisions than those with intact brains. This does not mean, as Jay Lenno quipped on the Late Show (referring to our findings), that one should hit one's head against the wall before making investment decisions; Damasio and his colleagues are right that emotion brain lesions are generally bad for decision-making. But it does, I believe, call into question their prior interpretation of their findings using the Iowa gambling task and reinforce the historic view that emotions do have a 'dark side'.

Investment Behavior and the Negative Side of Emotion*

Baba Shiv, George Loewenstein, Antoine Bechara, Hanna Damasio, and Antonio R. Damasio

In contrast to the historically dominant view of emotions as a negative influence in human behavior (Peters & Slovic, 2000), recent research in neuroscience and psychology has highlighted the positive roles played by emotions in decision making (Bechara, Damasio, Tranel, & Damasio, 1997; Damasio, 1994; Davidson, Jackson, & Kalin, 2000; Dolan, 2002; LeDoux, 1996; Loewenstein & Lerner, 2003; Peters & Slovic, 2000; Rahman, Sahakian, Rudolph, Rogers, & Robbins, 2001). Notwithstanding the fact that strong negative emotions such as jealousy and anger can lead to destructive patterns of behavior such as crimes of passion and road rage (Loewenstein, 1996), in a series of studies using a gambling task, researchers have shown that individuals with emotional dysfunction tend to perform poorly compared with those who have intact emotional processes (Bechara et al., 1997; Damasio, 1994; Rogers et al., 1999). However, there are reasons to think that individuals deprived of normal emotional reactions might actually make better decisions than normal individuals (Damasio, 1994). For example, consider the case of a patient with ventromedial prefrontal damage who was driving under hazardous road conditions (Damasio, 1994). When other drivers reached an icy patch, they hit their brakes in panic, causing their vehicles to skid out of control, but the patient crossed the icy patch unperturbed, gently pulling away from a tailspin and driving ahead safely. The patient remembered the fact that not hitting the brakes was the appropriate

* This chapter was originally published as Shiv, B., Loewenstein, G., Bechara, A. and Damasio, H. and A. (2005) 'Investment Behavior and the Negative Side of Emotion', Psychological Science. 16(6): 435–439. Reprinted with kind permission of Blackwell Publishing.

behavior, and his lack of fear allowed him to perform optimally. A broad thrust of the current research is to delve into this latter possibility, that individuals deprived of normal emotional reactions might, in certain situations, make more advantageous decisions than those not deprived of such reactions.

Recent evidence suggests that even relatively mild negative emotions that do not result in a loss of self-control can play a counterproductive role among normal individuals in some situations (Benartzi & Thaler, 1995). When gambles that involve some possible loss are presented one at a time, most people display extreme levels of risk aversion toward the gambles, a condition known as *myopic loss aversion* (Benartzi & Thaler, 1995). For example, most people will not voluntarily accept a 50–50 chance to gain $200 or lose $150, despite the gamble's high expected return. Myopic loss aversion has been advanced as an explanation for the large number of individuals who prefer to invest in bonds, even though stocks have historically provided a much higher rate of return, a pattern that economists refer to as the *equity premium puzzle* (Narayana, 1996; Siegel & Thaler, 1997).

On the basis of research showing that patients with neurological disease that impairs their emotional responses take risks even when they result in catastrophic losses (Bechara et al., 1997), as well as anecdotal evidence that such patients may, under certain circumstances, behave more efficiently than normal subjects (Damasio, 1994), we hypothesized that these same patients would make more advantageous decisions than normal subjects (or than patients with neurological lesions that do not impair their emotional responses) when faced with the types of positive-expected-value gambles we have just highlighted. In other words, if myopic loss aversion does indeed have an emotional basis as suggested in the literature (Loewenstein, Weber, Hsee, & Welch, 2001), then any dysfunction in neural systems subserving emotion ought to result in reduced levels of risk aversion and, thus, lead to more advantageous decisions in cases in which risk taking is rewarded.

To test our hypothesis, we developed a risky decision-making task that simulated real-life investment decisions in terms of uncertainties, rewards, and punishments. The task, closely modeled on a paradigm developed by Gneezy (1997) to demonstrate myopic loss aversion, was designed so that it would behoove participants to invest in every round because the expected value on each round was higher if one invested than if one did not. Our goal, then, was to demonstrate that an individual with a deficient emotional circuitry would experience less myopic loss aversion and make more advantageous decisions than an individual with an intact emotional circuitry. Such a finding would provide a new source of support for the idea that emotions play an important role in risk taking and risk aversion.

20.1. Method

20.1.1. *Participants*

We studied 19 normal participants and 15 target patients with chronic and stable focal lesions in specific components of a neural circuitry that has been shown to be critical for the processing of emotions (Damasio, 1994; Davidson et al., 2000; Dolan, 2002; LeDoux, 1996; Rahman et al., 2001; Sanfey, Hastie, Colvin, & Grafman, 2003). Specifically, the target patients' lesions were in the amygdala (bilaterally; 3 patients), the orbitofrontal cortex (bilaterally; 8 patients), or the right insular or somatosensory cortex (4 patients). We also studied 7 control patients with chronic and stable focal lesions in areas of the brain that are not involved in emotion processing. All these patients had a lesion in the right (4 patients) or left (3 patients) dorsolateral sector of the prefrontal cortex.

The patients were drawn from the Division of Cognitive Neuroscience's Patient Registry at the University of Iowa and have been described previously (Bechara et al., 1997). The lesions in the prefrontal cortex are due to stroke or surgical removal of a meningioma, those in the right insular or somatosensory region are due to stroke, and those in the amygdala are due to herpes simplex encephalitis (2 patients) or Urbach Weithe disease (1 patient). (The patients with bilateral amygdala damage due to herpes simplex encephalitis also have damage to the hippocampal system, and consequently have severe antero-grade memory impairment. However, they have normal IQ and intellect. Removing the data for these patients did not affect the results.) The control patients' lesions in the dorsolateral sector of the prefrontal cortex are due to stroke.

All target patients have been shown to perform poorly on the Iowa Gam-bling Task (Bechara, Damasio, & Damasio, 2003) and to have low emotional intelligence as measured by the EQi (Bar-On, Tranel, Denburg, & Bechara, 2003). All control patients have been shown to perform advantageously on the Iowa Gambling Task and to have normal EQi scores (Bar-On et al., 2003; Bechara et al., 2003). The target and control patients had a mean age of 53.6 ($SD = 11$) at the time of this study; they had 14.5 years of education on average ($SD = 3$) and mean verbal and performance IQs of 107.2 ($SD = 11.5$) and 103.4 ($SD = 14.5$), respectively.

The normal participants were recruited from the local community through advertisement in local newspapers. None had any history of neurological or psychiatric disease (assessed by questionnaire). Their mean age was 51.6 years ($SD = 13$); on average, they had 14.6 ($SD = 3$) years of education and verbal and performance IQs of 105.5 ($SD = 7$) and 101.4 ($SD = 10$), respectively.

All participants provided informed consent that was approved by the appro-priate human subject committees at the University of Iowa.

20.1.2. Procedure

At the beginning of the task, all participants were endowed with $20 of play money, which they were told to treat as real because they would receive a gift certificate for the amount they were left with at the end of the study. Participants were told that they would be making several rounds of investment decisions and that, in each round, they had to decide between two options: invest $1 or not invest. On each round, if the participant decided not to invest, he or she would keep the dollar, and the task would advance to the next round. If the participant decided to invest, he or she would hand over a dollar bill to the experimenter. The experimenter would then toss a coin in plain view. If the outcome of the toss were heads (50% chance), then the participant would lose the $1 that was invested; if the outcome of the toss were tails (50% chance), then $2.50 would be added to the participant's account. The task would then advance to the next round.

The task consisted of 20 rounds of investment decisions, and the three groups of participants took roughly the same time on the task. Note that, as indicated earlier, the design of this investment task is such that it would behoove participants to invest in all the rounds because the expected value on each round is higher if one invests ($1.25) than if one does not ($1). In fact, if one invests on each and every round, there is only around a 13% chance of obtaining lower total earnings than if one does not invest in every round and simply keeps the $20.

20.2. Results and Discussion

20.2.1. Overall Investment Decisions and Amounts Earned

Examination of the percentage of the 20 rounds in which participants decided to invest revealed that the target patients made decisions that were closer to a profit-maximizing view-point than the other participants did (see Table 1). Specifically, target patients invested in 83.7% of the rounds on average,

Table 1. Percentages of Decisions to Invest as a Function of Decision and Outcome in the Previous Round

Previous round	Target patients				Normal participants	Control patients
	Orbitofrontal lesion ($n = 8$)	Insular, somatosensory lesion ($n = 4$)	Amygdala lesion ($n = 3$)	Overall		
Did not invest	70.4	70.0	83.3	74.2	64.4	63.4
Invested and lost	79.8	96.8	84.3	85.2	40.5	37.1
Invested and won	79.1	94.4	83.3	84.0	61.7	75.0
Invested overall	79.4	91.3	85.0	83.7	57.6	60.7

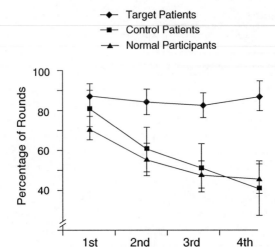

Figure 1. Percentage of rounds in which participants decided to invest $1.

whereas normal participants invested in 57.6% of the rounds (Wilcoxon statistic = 345.0, $p < .002$) and control patients invested in 60.7% of the rounds (Wilcoxon two-sample test statistic = 44.5, $p < .006$). Further, as hypothesized, target patients earned more money over the 20 rounds of the experiment ($25.70, on average) than did normal participants ($22.80; Wilcoxon statistic = 315.5, $p < .03$) or control patients ($20.07; Wilcoxon statistic = 44, $p < .006$); the average amount earned by normal participants did not differ from that earned by control patients (Wilcoxon statistic = 73, n.s.).

Figure 1 shows the percentage of rounds in which participants decided to invest, broken down into four 5-round blocks. The pattern of results suggests that all three groups of participants started close to the normative benchmark. However, unlike target patients, who remained close to the normative benchmark, normal participants and control patients seemed to become more conservative, investing in fewer rounds, as the investment task progressed. One potential account for these findings is that emotional reactions to the outcomes on preceding rounds affected decisions on subsequent rounds for normal participants and control patients, but not for target patients. We examine this potential account in greater detail in the next section.

20.2.2. Impact of Outcomes on Previous Rounds on Decisions in Subsequent Rounds

We conducted a lagged logistic regression analysis to examine whether the decision-outcome combination in preceding rounds (did not invest, invested and won, invested and lost) affected decisions on successive rounds more for control participants (normal participants and control patients) than for target patients. The dependent variable in this analysis was whether the *decision* on a particular round was to invest (coded as 1) or not invest (coded as 0). The independent variables were several dummies that were created for the analysis: *control* (coded as 1 for control participants, 0 otherwise), *invest-won* (coded as 1 if the participant invested on the previous round and won, 0 otherwise), *invest-lost* (coded as 1 if the participant invested on the previous round and lost, 0 otherwise), and participant-specific dummies (e.g., *dummy1*, coded as 1 for Participant 1, 0 otherwise). The overall logit model that was tested was *decision = control invest-won invest-lost control by invest-won control by invest-lost dummy1 dummy2 etc*. Note that any significant interactions would indicate that the effects of the decisions and outcomes in preceding rounds on decisions made in successive rounds were different for target patients and control participants.

Both interactions in the logit model were significant: *control by invest-won*, $\chi^2(1) = 10.27$, $p < .001$; *control by invest-lost*, $\chi^2(1) = 31.98$, $p < .0001$. These results suggest that normal participants and control patients behaved differently from target patients both when they had won on the previous round and when they had lost. As detailed in Table 1, control participants were more likely than target patients to withdraw from risk taking both when they lost on the previous round and when they won. Compared with the target patients, who invested in 85.2% of rounds following losses, normal participants invested in only 40.5% of rounds following losses (Wilcoxon statistic = 350.0, $p < .001$), and control patients invested in only 37.1% of such rounds (Wilcoxon statistic = 45, $p < .006$). Similarly, although target patients invested in 84.0% of rounds following wins, normal participants invested in only 61.7% of rounds following wins (Wilcoxon statistic = 323, $p < .01$), and control patients invested in 75.0% of such rounds (Wilcoxon statistic = 67.5, $p = .16$). These results also suggest that normal participants and control patients were considerably less risk aversive following wins than following losses (normal participants: 61.7% vs. 40.5%, difference = 21.2%; control patients: 75.0% vs. 37.1%, difference = 37.9%); in contrast, target patients invested equally often following wins and following losses (84.0% vs. 85.2%, difference = 1.2%).

20.3. Conclusions

The results of this study support our hypothesis that patients with lesions in specific components of a neural circuitry critical for the processing of emotions will make more advantageous decisions than normal subjects when faced with the types of positive-expected-value gambles that most people routinely shun. Such findings lend support to theoretical accounts of risk-taking behavior that posit a central role for emotions (Loewenstein et al., 2001). Most theoretical models of risk taking assume that risky decision making is largely a cognitive process of integrating the desirability of different possible outcomes with their probabilities. However, researchers have recently argued that emotions play a central role in decision making under risk (Mellers, Schwartz, & Ritov, 1999; Slovic, Finucane, Peters, & MacGregor, 2002). The finding that lack of emotional reactions may lead to more advantageous decisions in certain situations lends further support to such accounts.

Our results raise several issues related to the role of emotions in decision making involving risk. It is apparent that neural systems that subserve human emotions have evolved for survival purposes. The automatic emotions triggered by a given situation help the normal decision-making process by narrowing down the options for action, either by discarding those that are dangerous or by endorsing those that are advantageous. Emotions serve an adaptive role in speeding up the decision-making process. However, there are circumstances in which a naturally occurring emotional response must be inhibited, so that a deliberate and potentially wiser decision can be made. The current study demonstrates this "dark side" of emotions in decision making. Depending on the circumstances, moods and emotions can play useful as well as disruptive roles in decision making. It is important to note that previous experiments demonstrating a positive role of emotion in decision making involved tasks in which decisions were made under ambiguity (i.e. the outcomes were unknown; Bechara et al., 1997). In the present experiment, the patients made decisions under uncertainty (i.e. the outcome involved risk but was defined by some probability distribution). We do not know at this point whether decisions under uncertainty and decisions under ambiguity draw upon different neural processes, so that emotion is disruptive in one case but not the other. Regardless, the issue is not simply whether emotions can be trusted as leading to good or bad decisions. Rather, research needs to determine the circumstances in which emotions can be useful or disruptive, and then the reasoned coupling of circumstances and emotions can be a guide to human behavior.

Acknowledgments

We gratefully acknowledge a suggestion from C. Hsee that sparked the idea for this study. This work was supported by Grant PO1 NS19632 from the National Institutes of Health (National Institute of Neurological Disorders and Stroke) and by Grant SES 03-50984 from the National Science Foundation.

References

Bar-On, R., Tranel, D., Denburg, N., & Bechara, A. (2003). Exploring the neurological substrate of emotional and social intelligence. *Brain, 126,* 1790–1800.

Bechara, A., Damasio, H., & Damasio, A. (2003). The role of the amygdala in decision-making. In P. Shinnick-Gallagher, A. Pitkanen, A. Shekhar, & L. Cahill (Eds.), *The amygdala in brain function: Basic and clinical approaches* (Annals of the New York Academy of Sciences Vol. 985, pp. 356–369). New York: New York Academy of Sciences.

Bechara, A., Damasio, H., Tranel, D., & Damasio, A. R. (1997). Deciding advantageously before knowing the advantageous strategy. *Science, 275,* 1293–1295.

Benartzi, S., & Thaler, R. (1995). Myopic loss aversion and the equity premium puzzle. *Quarterly Journal of Economics, 110,* 73–92.

Damasio, A. R. (1994). *Descartes' error: Emotion, reason, and the human brain.* New York: Grosset/Putnam.

Davidson, R. J., Jackson, D. C., & Kalin, N. H. (2000). Emotion, plasticity, context, and regulation: Perspectives from affective neuroscience. *Psychological Bulletin, 126,* 890–909.

Dolan, R. J. (2002). Emotion, cognition, and behavior. *Science, 298,* 1191–1194.

Gneezy, U. (1997). An experiment on risk taking and evaluation periods. *Quarterly Journal of Economics, 112,* 631–645.

LeDoux, J. (1996). *The emotional brain: The mysterious underpinnings of emotional life.* New York: Simon & Schuster.

Loewenstein, G. (1996). Out of control: Visceral influences on behavior. *Organizational Behavior and Human Decision Processes, 65,* 272–292.

Loewenstein, G., & Lerner, J. (2003). The role of emotion in decision making. In R. J. Davidson, H. H. Goldsmith, & K. R. Scherer (Eds.), *Handbook of affective science* (pp. 619–642). Oxford, England: Oxford University Press.

Loewenstein, G. F., Weber, E. U., Hsee, C. K., & Welch, N. (2001). Risk as feelings. *Psychological Bulletin, 127,* 267–286.

Mellers, B., Schwartz, A., & Ritov, I. (1999). Emotion-based choice. *Journal of Experimental Psychology: General, 128,* 332–345.

Narayana, K. (1996). The equity premium: It is still a puzzle. *Journal of Economics Literature, 34,* 42–71.

Peters, E., & Slovic, P. (2000). The springs of action: Affective and analytical information processing in choice. *Personality and Social Psychology Bulletin, 26,* 1465–1475.

Rahman, S., Sahakian, B. J., Rudolph, N. C., Rogers, R. D., & Robbins, T. W. (2001). Decision making and neuropsychiatry. *Trends in Cognitive Sciences, 6,* 271–277.

Rogers, R. D., Everitt, B. J., Baldacchino, A., Blackshaw, A. J., Swainson, R., Wynne, K., Baker, N. B., Hunter, J., Carthy, T., Booker, E., London, M., Deakin, J. F. W., Sahakian, B. J., & Robbins, T. W. (1999). Dissociable deficits in the decision-making cognition of chronic amphetamine abusers, opiate abusers, patients with focal damage to prefrontal cortex, and tryptophan-depleted normal volunteers: Evidence for monoaminergic mechanisms. *Neuropsychopharmacology, 20,* 322–339.

Rogers, R. D., & Robbins, T. W. (2001). Investigating the neurocognitive deficits associated with chronic drug misuse. *Current Opinion in Neurobiology, 11,* 250–257.

Sanfey, A., Hastie, R., Colvin, M., & Grafman, J. (2003). Phineas gauged: Decision-making and the human prefrontal cortex. *Neuropsychologia, 41*, 1218–1229.

Siegel, J., & Thaler, R. (1997). The equity premium puzzle. *Journal of Economics Perspectives, 11*, 191–200.

Slovic, P., Finucane, M., Peters, E., & MacGregor, D. G. (2002). The affect heuristic. In T. Gilovich, D. Griffin, & D. Kahneman (Eds.), *Heuristics and biases: The psychology of intuitive judgment* (pp. 397–420). New York: Cambridge University Press.

21

Heart Strings and Purse Strings

Carryover Effects of Emotions on Economic Decisions

Jennifer S. Lerner, Deborah A. Small, and George Loewenstein

Jennifer Lerner is one of the most efficient people I know. She arrived in my department about four years ago, and immediately got to work, creating an experimental laboratory for herself, starting a new major in the department, and training a succession of amazing graduate students. I've been the direct beneficiary of the latter, getting the chance to work with them, and in this case also with Jennifer.

I like this study, in part because I think it represents the benefits of interdisciplinary collaboration. Jennifer has a background in psychology, and has specifically done considerable research on the impact of emotions on decision-making. My main background is in economics, and I've done a lot of work on a phenomenon called the endowment effect (see Chapter 11). We put our interests together in the research reported in this paper, which explores the impact of two emotions—sadness and disgust—on the endowment effect.

The other reason why I like the paper is that it provides a good illustration of a point that has become a central theme of my recent research—that emotion transforms people fundamentally, including along lines that are of great interest to economists. As I've become fond of telling seminar audiences, the same person in different emotional states can be altruistic, selfish, or even malevolent, farsighted or shortsighted, risk-taking, or risk-avoiding. In the paper, we show that the same is true of buying and selling: The same person in different emotional states can be very eager or reluctant to buy, and very eager or reluctant to sell. In different emotional states, it seems, it is almost as if we become different people.

Heart Strings and Purse Strings[*]

Carryover Effects of Emotions on Economic Decisions

Jennifer S. Lerner, Deborah A. Small, and George Loewenstein

Two decades of research document the tendency for incidental emotion to color normatively unrelated judgments and decisions (for reviews, see Forgas, 1995; Loewenstein & Lerner, 2002; Schwarz, 1990). Early research found that positive emotions trigger more optimistic assessments than negative emotions, whereas negative emotions trigger more pessimistic assessments than positive emotions, even if the source of the emotion has no relation to the target judgments (Johnson & Tversky, 1983). More recent research has demonstrated the importance of examining specific emotions in addition to global (positive-negative) feelings (Bodenhausen, Sheppard, & Kramer, 1994; DeSteno, Petty, Wegener, & Rucker, 2000). Experiments reveal that emotions not only arise from but also elicit specific appraisals (Keltner, Ellsworth, & Edwards, 1993; Lerner & Keltner, 2001; Tiedens & Linton, 2001), as predicted by appraisal-tendency theory (Lerner & Keltner, 2000). Although tailored to help the individual respond to the event that evoked the emotion, such appraisals persist beyond the eliciting situation, becoming an implicit lens for interpreting subsequent situations. For example, fear arises from and evokes appraisals of uncertainty and lack of individual control, which are two central determinants of risk judgments (Slovic, 1987), whereas anger arises from and evokes appraisals of certainty and individual control (Smith & Ellsworth, 1985). Experimental results are consistent with appraisal-tendency theory in that anger triggered in one situation evokes more optimistic risk estimates and risk-seeking choices in unrelated situations, whereas fear does

[*] This chapter was originally published as Lerner, J., Small, D., and Loewenstein, G. (2004) Heart Strings and Purse Strings' Psychological Science. 15(5): 337–341. Reprinted with kind permission of Blackwell Publishing.

the opposite (Lerner, Gonzalez, Small, & Fischhoff, 2003; Lerner & Keltner, 2001).

Among the many recent studies that document carryover effects of specific emotions, none examined their impact on behavior with financial conse-quences. This gap is significant, for two reasons. First, including financial consequences provides a stronger test of the emotional-carryover hypothesis. It may be that emotions have little impact when real money is at stake. Second, the field of behavioral economics (i.e. the application of psycho-logical insights to economics) has been strongly influenced by cognitively focused research on decision making, but has been largely untouched by decision researchers' recent interest in emotions. The study presented here was intended to bridge this gap.

21.1. Present Study

21.1.1. *Experiment Overview*

A 3 × 2 between-subjects design crossed an emotion manipulation (neutral, disgust, sadness) with an ownership manipulation: Half the participants were endowed with an object and then given the opportunity to sell it back at a range of prices (*sell* condition); the other half were shown, but not given, the object and then asked whether they would prefer to receive the object or to receive various cash amounts (*choice* condition). To reduce potential demand effects, we presented the experiment as two unrelated studies with separate consent forms. In "Study 1" (titled "imagination research"), partici-pants watched a film clip and wrote a response; "Study 2" (titled "asset-pricing research") presented the sell or choice procedures.

This manipulation of ownership status mirrors procedures for testing the *endowment effect*—that is, the tendency for selling prices to exceed buying or "choice" prices for the same object. The endowment effect is one of the most important and robust economic anomalies (see Kahneman, Knetsch, & Thaler, 1991).

21.1.2. *Hypotheses*

On the basis of earlier evidence that emotions often persist beyond the eliciting situation and affect subsequent behavior and cognition, we hypoth-esized that emotions triggered in the first (emotion induction) stage of the experiment would influence valuations in the second. We hypothesized that disgust, which revolves around the appraisal theme of being too close to an indigestible object or idea (Lazarus, 1991), would evoke an implicit action tendency to expel current objects and avoid taking in anything new (Rozin,

627

Haidt, & McCauley, 1993). We therefore expected that, relative to neutral emotion, experimentally induced disgust would reduce both selling prices among participants who owned the experimental object (an "expel" goal) and choice prices among participants who did not (an "avoid taking anything in" goal). Moreover, we predicted greater reduction when the object was already owned (i.e. selling price) than when it was available for purchase because proximity of the object should augment contamination.

Sadness, although also a negative emotion, has distinct appraisal themes. It arises from loss and helplessness (Keltner et al., 1993; Lazarus, 1991) and evokes the implicit goal of changing one's circumstances. We therefore predicted that, relative to neutral emotion, sadness would reduce selling prices but increase buying prices, potentially to the extent of reversing the typical endowment effect. Our rationale was that in the case of selling, getting rid of what one has presents an opportunity for changing one's circumstances, whereas in the case of buying, acquiring new goods presents an opportunity for change.

Whereas three of our hypotheses are consistent with the idea that negative moods simply suppress value, the fourth—that sadness increases buying prices—is not. This latter prediction is, however, consistent with evidence that compulsive shoppers tend to experience depression, that shopping tends to elevate depressed moods of compulsive shoppers, and that antidepressant medication tends to reduce compulsive shopping (Black, Repertinger, Gaffney, & Gabel, 1998; Christenson et al., 1994; Faber & Christenson, 1996).

21.2. Method

21.2.1. *Participants*

One hundred ninety-nine participants (119 males, 80 females) responded to an advertisement offering $7 plus additional cash or prizes in exchange for 45 min of participation. Their ages ranged from 16 to 49 years, with a mean of 21.4; the majority were Carnegie Mellon students.

21.2.2. *Procedure*

Participants were seated in private cubicles (equipped with computers and headsets) with no visual access to other participants. An experimenter explained that two faculty members—a psychologist and an economist—had each contributed a brief study. All participants received two packets of material, one for each study. Participants assigned to the sell condition received, in addition, a highlighter set that they were instructed to hold on to for later use in Study 2.

EMOTION INDUCTIONS

After completing baseline measures of affect (Positive and Negative Affect Scales scores: Watson, Clark, & Tellegen, 1988), each participant put on the headset and pressed a "start" button on the computer, which launched one of three film clips, depending on the experimental condition. The sadness clip (from *The Champ*) portrayed the death of a boy's mentor, the disgust clip (from *Trainspotting*) portrayed a man using an unsanitary toilet, and the neutral clip (from a National Geographic special) portrayed fish at the Great Barrier Reef. Each clip lasted approximately 4 min.

To make the emotional experiences more personally meaningful and intense, we asked participants in the sadness and disgust conditions to write about how they would feel if they were in the situation depicted in the clip. Participants in the neutral condition wrote about their daily activities. Prior research had found that film clips and self-reflective writing provide an effective means of eliciting discrete target emotions (Lerner, Goldberg, & Tetlock, 1998; Lerner & Keltner, 2001). Next, all participants were instructed to take out their second packet of material and begin Study 2.

ELICITING BUYING AND SELLING PRICES

At the start of Study 2, participants assigned to the sell condition, who were already in possession of a highlighter set, received a price-elicitation form that presented them with a series of pair-wise choices. On each of 28 lines, they chose between keeping the highlighter set or trading it for an amount of cash; the amounts ranged from $0.50 to $14.00 in $0.50 increments. So that they would have an incentive to reveal their true values, they were told that one of these choices would be randomly selected to determine what they received at the conclusion of the experiment. Numerous economic experiments (e.g. Kahneman et al., 1991) have employed this procedure, which is formally equivalent to the "Becker, DeGroot, Marschak" (see Becker, DeGroot, & Marschak, 1964) elicitation method.

Participants assigned to the choice condition were shown the highlighter set, then given a series of choices that were equivalent to those in the sell condition but involved getting the highlighter set (which they did not yet own) or getting the various cash amounts. Note that a choice price is somewhat different from a buying price because it involves a choice between an object versus money, rather than deciding whether to give up money to obtain an object. A choice price has three advantages over a buying price: (a) It does not require participants to give up money, and hence is not limited by the amount of money participants bring to a study; (b) it confronts participants with a choice that is formally identical to, but framed differently from, selling; and (c) it holds constant the money side of the equation—both selling and choice involve choices between receiving or not receiving money. Holding the money side of the equation constant ensures that the effects of the emotions are not operating through feelings about gaining or losing money. Indeed, prior research has shown that the endowment effect is driven by attitudes toward the goods rather than the money (Tversky & Kahneman, 1991).

EMOTION-MANIPULATION CHECKS

Next, participants were asked to report their feelings during the video clip. To avoid revealing our interest in specific emotions, we included 27 affective states on the form, although only 5 were of interest.[1] A sadness factor included "blue," "downhearted," and "sad" ($a = .91$), and a disgust factor included "disgust" and "repulsed" ($a = .92$). Response scales ranged from 0 (*did not experience the emotion at all*) to 8 (*experienced the emotion more strongly than ever before*).

Participants then answered a series of questions designed to assess demand awareness, including questions about possible connections between the two studies. No participants guessed that we were interested in whether emotions from Study 1 would influence prices in Study 2. Finally, participants either were given (or kept) the highlighter set or received a cash payment, depending on what they chose for the particular choice (out of 28 choices between cash and highlighter set) that was randomly selected to determine their outcome.

21.3. Results

21.3.1. *Preliminary Analyses*

Individual analyses of variance (ANOVAs) on self-reported experience of disgust, $F(2, 197) = 208.73$, and sadness, $F(2, 197) = 78.94$, revealed strong emotion-induction effects ($ps < .001$). Participants felt significantly more disgusted than sad in the disgust condition, $t(64) = 17.28$, and significantly more sad than disgusted in the sad condition, $t(67) = -10.89$ ($ps < .001$; see Fig. 1). As intended, the emotion inductions produced strong and discrete emotions, not a generalized negativity.

Participants used the full range of pricing options. Values for the highlighter set ranged from \$0.50 to \$14.00, with a mean of \$3.64 ($SD = \$2.20$). Neither age nor gender correlated with assigned price, so these variables were not included in subsequent analyses. Replicating prior research on the endowment effect, a planned comparison in the neutral condition revealed that selling prices exceeded choice prices ($M_{selling} = \$4.80$, $M_{choice} = \$3.70$), $t(63) = -1.73$, $p < .05$ (one-tailed).[2]

---

[1] The full scale is available from the authors.

[2] The selling-price/choice-price ratio of 1.30 is typical in magnitude (e.g. the ratio was 1.46 in Loewenstein & Adler, 1995).

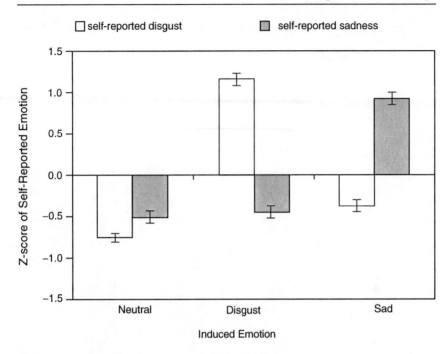

□ self-reported disgust   ■ self-reported sadness

Figure 1. Self-reported emotion in the three emotion conditions. Error bars represent standard errors of the mean.

21.3.2. *Inferential Analyses*

We predicted that (relative to neutral emotion) sadness would reduce selling prices but increase choice prices, and disgust would reduce both selling and choice prices. As recommended by Keppel and Zedeck (1989), the data were analyzed using planned 2 × 2 contrasts.

Results supported the hypotheses; Figure 2 displays means and standard errors.[3] As the "change circumstances" hypothesis predicted, compared with neutral emotion, sadness decreased selling prices, $t(65) = 2.95$, $p < .01$, and increased choice prices, $t(65) = -1.98$, $p = .05$. This pattern reversed the traditional endowment effect, creating significantly higher choice prices than selling prices, $t(67) = 3.67$, $p < .01$. ANOVA revealed the expected crossover interaction, $F(1, 134) = 12.56$, $p < .01$.

As the "expel" hypothesis predicted, compared with neutral emotion, disgust reduced choice and sell prices, $F(1, 131) = 13.29$, $p \leq .01$. A marginally significant interaction between emotion and ownership also emerged, $F(1, 131) = 3.03$, $p = .08$, driven by the fact that disgust had a stronger simple

---

[3] Covarying baseline affect improved the magnitude of the hypothesized effects. Taking a conservative approach, however, we do not report analysis of covariance results.

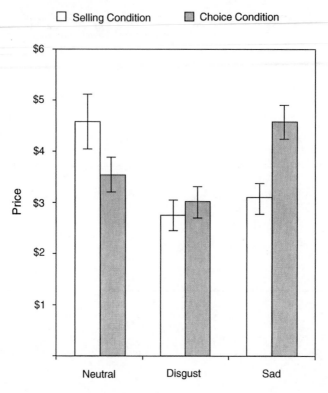

Figure 2. Mean selling and choice prices in the three emotion conditions. Error bars represent standard errors of the mean.

effect on selling prices, $t(63) = -3.40$, $p < .01$, than on choice prices. Moreover, disgust wiped out the traditional endowment effect, creating statistically indistinguishable selling and choice prices ($t < 1$).

The results confirmed the importance of emotion specificity in that sad participants set significantly higher choice prices than did disgusted participants, $t(65) = -3.70$, $p < .01$, yet statistically indistinguishable selling prices ($t < 1$). ANOVA revealed the expected interaction between emotion (disgust, sadness) and ownership, $F(1, 134) = 5.15$, $p < .05$, as well as main effects of emotion, $F(1, 135) = 10.26$, $p < .01$, and ownership, $F(1, 134) = 9.06$, $p < .01$.

21.4. Conclusions

The current results suggest that emotions can have dramatic effects on economic transactions, even when they arise from a prior, irrelevant, situation. Although economists often posit a strong role of emotion in economics

(Krugman, 2001; Loewenstein, 1996) and even find significant correlations between weather (used as a proxy for mood) and stock market returns (Hirshleifer & Shumway, 2003; Kamstra, Kramer, & Levi, 2003), this study demonstrates that emotions of the same valence can have opposing causal effects. Overall, the pattern of results supports the hypotheses that disgust triggers goals to expel, reducing buying and selling prices, whereas sadness triggers the goal of changing one's circumstances, increasing buying prices but reducing selling prices. The effects are sufficiently strong that in one case (disgust) they eliminate the endowment effect, and in the other case (sadness) they actually reverse it. It is worth nothing that a second study focusing on selling prices replicated the results.[4]

Beyond advancing theories of emotion and decision making, these results have practical implications. For example, our findings could have implications for the aggregate economic consequences of emotional events such as the terrorist attacks of September 11; they suggest that, contrary to widespread intuition, such events could actually encourage rather than discourage consumer spending, depending on the specific emotions they evoke in individuals. In sum, the present findings highlight both the powerful effects that emotion can play in everyday economic choices and the need for research on the mechanisms driving such effects.

Acknowledgments

Grants from the National Institute of Mental Health (MH62376), the Fetzer Foundation, and the National Science Foundation (SES-0201525, SES-0239637, and SBR-9521914) supported this research. We thank Stephanie Lesniak, Justin Malakhow, Jonathan Haidt, and Jodut Hashmi for their help.

References

Becker, G. M., DeGroot, M. H., & Marschak, J. (1964). Measuring utility by a single-response sequential method. *Behavioral Science, 9,* 226–232.

Black, D. W., Repertinger, S., Gaffney, G. R., & Gabel, J. (1998). Family history of psychiatric comorbidity in persons with compulsive buying: Preliminary findings. *American Journal of Psychiatry, 155,* 960–963.

Bodenhausen, G., Sheppard, L., & Kramer, G. (1994). Negative affect and social judgment: The different impact of anger and sadness. *European Journal of Social Psychology, 24,* 45–62.

Christenson, G. A., Faber, R. J., de Zwaan, M., Raymond, N. C., Specker, S. M., Ekern, M. D., Mackenzie, T. B., Crosby, R. D., Crow, S. J., Eckert, E. D., Mussell, M. P., &

---

[4] Data from this study can be obtained by contacting the authors.

Mitchell, J. E. (1994). Compulsive buying: Descriptive characteristics and psychiatric comorbidity. *Journal of Clinical Psychiatry, 55*(1), 5–11.

DeSteno, D., Petty, R. E., Wegener, D. T., & Rucker, D. D. (2000). Beyond valence in the perception of likelihood: The role of emotion specificity. *Journal of Personality and Social Psychology, 78*, 397–416.

Faber, R. J., & Christenson, G. A. (1996). In the mood to buy: Differences in the mood states experienced by compulsive buyers and other consumers. *Psychology and Marketing, 13*, 803–819.

Forgas, J. P. (1995). Mood and judgment: The affect infusion model (AIM). *Psychological Bulletin, 117*, 39–66.

Hirshleifer, D., & Shumway, T. (2003). Good day sunshine: Stock returns and the weather. *Journal of Finance, 58*, 1009–1032.

Johnson, E. J., & Tversky, A. (1983). Affect, generalization, and the perception of risk. *Journal of Personality and Social Psychology, 45*, 20–31.

Kahneman, D., Knetsch, J. K., & Thaler, R. H. (1991). Anomalies: The endowment effect, loss aversion, and status quo bias. *Journal of Economic Perspectives, 5*(1), 193–206.

Kamstra, M. J., Kramer, L. A., & Levi, M. D. (2003). Winter blues: Seasonal affective disorder (SAD) and stock market returns. *American Economic Review, 93*, 324–343.

Keltner, D., Ellsworth, P. C., & Edwards, K. (1993). Beyond simple pessimism: Effects of sadness and anger on social perception. *Journal of Personality and Social Psychology, 64*, 740–752.

Keppel, G., & Zedeck, S. (1989). *Data analysis for research designs: Analysis of variance and multiple regression/correlation approaches.* New York: W. H. Freeman & Co.

Krugman, P. (2001, September 30). Fear itself. *New York Times*, Section 6, pp. 36–40.

Lazarus, R. S. (1991). *Emotion and adaptation.* New York: Oxford University Press.

Lerner, J. S., Goldberg, J. H., & Tetlock, P. E. (1998). Sober second thought: The effects of accountability, anger and authoritarianism on attributions of responsibility. *Personality and Social Psychology Bulletin, 24*, 563–574.

Lerner, J. S., Gonzalez, R. M., Small, D. A., & Fischhoff, B. (2003). Effects of fear and anger on perceived risks of terrorism: A national field experiment. *Psychological Science, 14*, 144–150.

Lerner, J. S., & Keltner, D. (2000). Beyond valence: Toward a model of emotion-specific influences on judgment and choice. *Cognition and Emotion, 14*, 473–493.

Lerner, J. S., & Keltner, D. (2001). Fear, anger, and risk. *Journal of Personality and Social Psychology, 81*, 146–159.

Loewenstein, G. (1996). Out of control: Visceral influences on behavior. *Organizational Behavior and Human Decision Processes, 65*, 272–292.

Loewenstein, G., & Adler, D. (1995). A bias in the prediction of tastes. *Economic Journal: The Journal of the Royal Economic Society, 105*, 929–937.

Loewenstein, G., & Lerner, J. S. (2002). The role of affect in decision making. In R. Davidson, K. Scherer, & H. Goldsmith (Eds.), *Handbook of affective science* (pp. 619–642). New York: Oxford University Press.

Rozin, P., Haidt, J., & McCauley, C. R. (1993). Disgust. In M. Lewis & J. M. Haviland (Eds.), *Handbook of emotions* (pp. 575–594). New York: Guilford Press.

Schwarz, N. (1990). Feelings as information: Informational and motivational functions of affective states. In E. T. Higgins & R. M. Sorrentino (Eds.), *Handbook of motivation and cognition: Foundations of social behavior* (Vol. 2, pp. 527–561). New York: Guilford Press.

Slovic, P. (1987). Perception of risk. *Science, 236*, 280–285.

Smith, C. A., & Ellsworth, P. C. (1985). Patterns of cognitive appraisal in emotion. *Journal of Personality and Social Psychology, 48*, 813–838.

Tiedens, L. Z., & Linton, S. (2001). Judgment under emotional certainty and uncertainty: The effects of specific emotions on information processing. *Journal of Personality and Social Psychology, 81*, 973–988.

Tversky, A., & Kahneman, D. (1991). Loss aversion in riskless choice: A Reference-dependent Model. *Quarterly Journal of Economics, 106*, 1039–1061.

Watson, D., Clark, L. A., & Tellegen, A. (1988). Development and validation of brief measures of positive and negative affect: The PANAS scales. *Journal of Personality and Social Psychology, 54*, 1063–1070.

22

Separate Neural Systems Value Immediate and Delayed Monetary Rewards

Samuel M. McClure, David I. Laibson, George Loewenstein, and Jonathan D. Cohen

I had always considered myself *driven* until I got together with this crew. Our weekly hour-long Skype conferences first stretched to an hour and a half, then two hours, then became biweekly calls. And e-mail exchanges could happen seemingly at any time of day or night, typically with all parties weighing in within minutes. Don't these guys ever sleep? (And what was *I* doing on the computer at 3 a.m.?)

When we started the project, McClure, another matured child prodigy, was doing a post-doc with Jonathan Cohen at Princeton. Cohen, who is not only a top neuroscientist but also an award-winning carpenter, I know from his days at CMU, when he and Jonathan Schooler and I used to meet for a weekly lunch. Laibson I've known since he burst on to the behavioral economics scene—the first economist to come out of a mainstream economics PhD program with a dissertation on behavioral economics.

Laibson's dissertation examined the implications of hyperbolic time dis-counting (see Chapter 15) for spending and saving. It assumed that consumers were in every other way hyperrational—for example, that they dealt with their self-control problems in an extremely sophisticated, forward-looking, fashion. While this assumption worked as a strategy for selling hyperbolic time discounting to mainstream economists, it struck me as unrealistic. In fact, I would venture that there is only one individual in the world who is as forward-thinking as the individuals who populate Laibson's models: Laibson himself. For example, when he was still an eligible bachelor in Cambridge some years ago, David confided to me that he rarely got past a first date because, as soon as he could see that a relationship wasn't going to end in marriage, he could no longer justify going out with the woman in question. Similarly, at a conference in Switzerland, David hired a guide to take him on a serious climb in the Alps, but found it difficult to choose between the two options that the guide suggested, despite the fact that—indeed, exactly because—one was obviously much better than the other. Combining psychology (utility from anticipation) with hyperrationality, David was worried that if he took the superior route he wouldn't have it to look forward to in the future. Dick Thaler (also attending the conference) and I teased him mercilessly until he made the obviously right—myopic—decision.

The central topic of the paper is to provide empirical support for an account of impulsivity based on emotion (see Chapter 18). Rather than reflecting a kind of 'hardwired' attitude toward the future, as many researchers have argued, we obtained strong evidence that time discounting reflects the splicing of two systems, an emotional system that is extremely myopic (it responds almost exclusively to immediate costs and benefits) and a more deliberative system that has a more evenhanded attitude toward present and future costs and benefits.

I consider it something of a personal victory to have written this paper with David because, for a long time, he was a staunch defender of the idea that hyperbolic time discounting provided an intellectually sufficient account of impulsivity—a point we once debated quite emotionally in a seminar I gave in his department. David's conversion on the issue is also a victory for the new field of neuroeconomics, because seeing the neural support for the two systems perspective had an impact on his thinking that all of the brilliant points I made in our debate failed to have.

Separate Neural Systems Value Immediate and Delayed Monetary Rewards

Samuel M. McClure, David I. Laibson, George Loewenstein, and Jonathan D. Cohen*

When humans are offered the choice between rewards available at different points in time, the relative values of the options are discounted according to their expected delays until delivery. Using functional magnetic resonance imaging, we examined the neural correlates of time discounting while subjects made a series of choices between monetary reward options that varied by delay to delivery. We demonstrate that two separate systems are involved in such decisions. Parts of the limbic system associated with the midbrain dopamine system, including paralimbic cortex, are preferentially activated by decisions involving immediately available rewards. In contrast, regions of the lateral prefrontal cortex and posterior parietal cortex are engaged uniformly by intertemporal choices irrespective of delay. Furthermore, the relative engagement of the two systems is directly associated with subjects' choices, with greater relative fronto-parietal activity when subjects choose longer term options.

In Aesop's classic fable, the ant and the grasshopper are used to illustrate two familiar, but disparate, approaches to human intertemporal decision making. The grasshopper luxuriates during a warm summer day, inattentive to the future. The ant, in contrast, stores food for the upcoming winter. Human decision makers seem to be torn between an impulse to act like the indulgent grasshopper and an awareness that the patient ant often gets ahead in the long run. An active line of research in both psychology and economics has explored this tension. This research is unified by the idea that consumers behave impatiently today but prefer/plan to act patiently in the future (*1*, *2*). For example, someone offered the choice between $10 today and $11

* Reprinted with permission from McClure, S., Laibson, D., Loewenstein, G. and Cohen, J. (2004) 'Separate Neural Systems Value Immediate and Delayed Monetary Rewards' Science. Vol. 306, 15 Oct. 2004. © 2004 AAAS.

639

tomorrow might be tempted to choose the immediate option. However, if asked today to choose between $10 in a year and $11 in a year and a day, the same person is likely to prefer the slightly delayed but larger amount.

Economists and psychologists have theorized about the underlying cause of these dynamically inconsistent choices. It is well accepted that rationality entails treating each moment of delay equally, thereby discounting according to an exponential function (1–3). Impulsive preference reversals are believed to be indicative of disproportionate valuation of rewards available in the immediate future (4–6). Some authors have argued that such dynamic inconsistency in preference is driven by a single decision-making system that generates the temporal inconsistency (7–9), while other authors have argued that the inconsistency is driven by an interaction between two different decision-making systems (5, 10, 11). We hypothesize that the discrepancy between short-run and long-run preferences reflects the differential activation of distinguishable neural systems. Specifically, we hypothesize that short-run impatience is driven by the limbic system, which responds preferentially to immediate rewards and is less sensitive to the value of future rewards, whereas long-run patience is mediated by the lateral prefrontal cortex and associated structures, which are able to evaluate trade-offs between abstract rewards, including rewards in the more distant future.

A variety of hints in the literature suggest that this might be the case. First, there is the large discrepancy between time discounting in humans and in other species (12, 13). Humans routinely trade off immediate costs/benefits against costs/benefits that are delayed by as much as decades. In contrast, even the most advanced primates, which differ from humans dramatically in the size of their prefrontal cortexes, have not been observed to engage in unpreprogrammed delay of gratification involving more than a few minutes (12, 13). Although some animal behavior appears to weigh trade-offs over longer horizons (e.g. seasonal food storage), such behavior appears invariably to be stereotyped and instinctive, and hence unlike the generalizable nature of human planning. Second, studies of brain damage caused by surgery, accidents, or strokes consistently point to the conclusion that prefrontal damage often leads to behavior that is more heavily influenced by the availability of immediate rewards, as well as failures in the ability to plan (14, 15). Third, a "quasi-hyperbolic" time-discounting function (16) that splices together two different discounting functions—one that distinguishes sharply between present and future and another that discounts exponentially and more shallowly—has been found to provide a good fit to experimental data and to shed light on a wide range of behaviors, such as retirement saving, credit-card borrowing, and procrastination (17, 18). However, despite these and many other hints that time discounting may result from distinct processes, little research to date has attempted to directly identify the source of the tension between short-run and long-run preferences.

The quasi-hyperbolic time-discounting function—sometimes referred to as beta-delta preference—was first proposed by Phelps and Pollack (*19*) to model the planning of wealth transfers across generations and applied to the individual's time scale by Elster (*20*) and Laibson (*16*). It posits that the present discounted value of a reward of value u received at delay t is equal to u for $t = 0$ and to $\beta\delta^t u$ for $t > 0$, where $0 > \beta \leq 1$ and $\delta \leq 1$. The β parameter (actually its inverse) represents the special value placed on immediate rewards relative to rewards received at any other point in time. When $\beta < 1$, all future rewards are uniformly downweighted relative to immediate rewards. The δ parameter is simply the discount rate in the standard exponential formula, which treats a given delay equivalently regardless of when it occurs.

Our key hypothesis is that the pattern of behavior that these two parameters summarize—β, which reflects the special weight placed on outcomes that are immediate, and δ, which reflects a more consistent weighting of time periods—stems from the joint influence of distinct neural processes, with β mediated by limbic structures and δ by the lateral prefrontal cortex and associated structures supporting higher cognitive functions.

To test this hypothesis, we measured the brain activity of participants as they made a series of intertemporal choices between early monetary rewards ($\$R$ available at delay d) and later monetary rewards ($\$R'$ available at delay d'; $d' > d$). The early option always had a lower (undiscounted) value than the later option (i.e., $\$R < \$R'$). The two options were separated by a minimum time delay of 2 weeks. In some choice pairs, the early option was available "immediately" (i.e., at the end of the scanning session; $d = 0$). In other choice pairs, even the early option was available only after a delay ($d > 0$).

Our hypotheses led us to make three critical predictions: (i) choice pairs that include a reward today (i.e. $d = 0$) will preferentially engage limbic structures relative to choice pairs that do not include a reward today (i.e. $d > 0$); (ii) lateral prefrontal areas will exhibit similar activity for all choices, as compared with rest, irrespective of reward delay; (iii) trials in which the later reward is selected will be associated with relatively higher levels of lateral prefrontal activation, reflecting the ability of this system to value greater rewards even when they are delayed.

Participants made a series of binary choices between smaller/earlier and larger/later money amounts while their brains were scanned using functional magnetic resonance imaging. The specific amounts (ranging from \$5 to \$40) and times of availability (ranging from the day of the experiment to 6 weeks later) were varied across choices. At the end of the experiment, one of the participant's choices was randomly selected to count; that is, they received one of the rewards they had selected at the designated time of delivery.

To test our hypotheses, we estimated a general linear model (GLM) using standard regression techniques (*21*). We included two primary regressors in

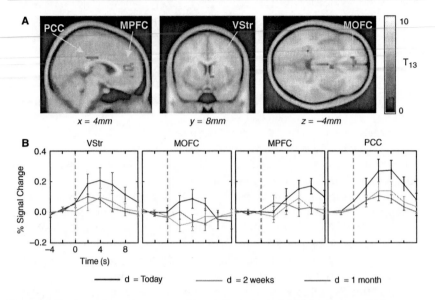

Figure 1. Brain regions that are preferentially activated for choices in which money is available immediately (β areas). **(A)** A random effects general linear model analysis revealed five regions that are significantly more activated by choices with immediate rewards, implying $d = 0$ (at $P < 0.001$, uncorrected; five contiguous voxels). These regions include the ventral striatum (VStr), medial orbitofrontal cortex (MOFC), medial prefrontal cortex (MPFC), posterior cingulate cortex (PCC), and left posterior hippocampus (table S1). **(B)** Mean event-related time courses of β areas (dashed line indicates the time of choice; error bars are SEM; $n = 14$ subjects). BOLD signal changes in the VStr, MOFC, MPFC, and PCC are all significantly greater when choices involve money available today ($d = 0$, red traces) versus when the earliest choice can be obtained only after a 2-week or 1-month delay ($d = 2$ weeks and $d = 1$ month, green and blue traces, respectively).

the model, one that modeled decision epochs with an immediacy option in the choice set (the "immediacy" variable) and another that modeled all decision epochs (the "all decisions" variable).

We defined β areas as voxels that loaded on the "immediacy" variable. These are preferentially activated by experimental choices that included an option for a reward today ($d = 0$) as compared with choices involving only delayed outcomes ($d > 0$). As shown in Fig. 1, brain areas disproportionately activated by choices involving an immediate outcome (β areas) include the ventral striatum, medial orbitofrontal cortex, and medial prefrontal cortex. As predicted, these are classic limbic structures and closely associated par-alimbic cortical projections. These areas are all also heavily innervated by the midbrain dopamine system and have been shown to be responsive to reward expectation and delivery by the use of direct neuronal recordings in

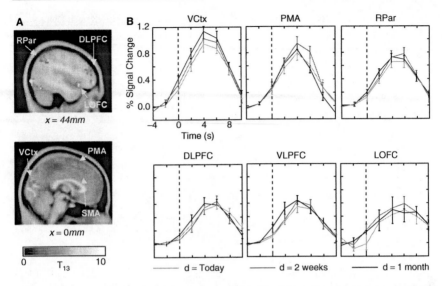

Figure 2. Brain regions that are active while making choices independent of the delay (*d*) until the first available reward (δ areas). **(A)** A random effects general linear model analysis revealed eight regions that are uniformly activated by all decision epochs (at *P* < 0.001, uncorrected; five contiguous voxels). These areas include regions of visual cortex (VCtx), premotor area (PMA), and supplementary motor area (SMA). In addition, areas of the right and left intraparietal cortex (RPar, LPar), right dorsolateral prefrontal cortex (DLPFC), right ventrolateral prefrontal cortex (VLPFC), and right lateral orbitofrontal cortex (LOFC) are also activated (table S2). **(B)** Mean event-related time courses for δ areas (dashed line indicates the time of choice; error bars are SEM; *n* = 14 subjects). A three-way analysis of variance indicated that the brain regions identified by this analysis are differentially affected by delay (*d*) than are those regions identified in Fig. 1 (*P* < 0.0001).

nonhuman species (*22–24*) and brain-imaging techniques in humans (*25–27*) (Fig. 1). The time courses of activity for these areas are shown in Fig. 1B (*28, 29*).

We considered voxels that loaded on the "all decisions" variable in our GLM to be candidate δ areas. These were activated by all decision epochs and were not preferentially activated by experimental choices that included an option for a reward today. This criterion identified several areas (Fig. 2), some of which are consistent with our predictions about the δ system (such as lateral prefrontal cortex). However, others (including primary visual and motor cortices) more likely reflect nonspecific aspects of task performance engaged during the decision-making epoch, such as visual processing and motor response. Therefore, we carried out an additional analysis designed to identify areas among these candidate δ regions that were more specifically associated with the decision process.

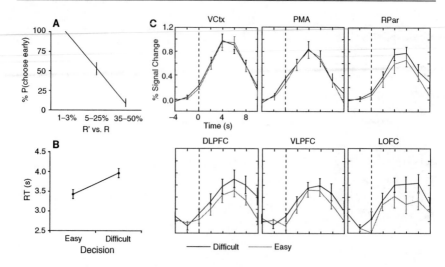

Figure 3. Differences in brain activity while making easy versus difficult decisions separate δ areas associated with decision making from those associated with non–decision-related aspects of task performance. **(A)** Difficult decisions were defined as those for which the difference in dollar amounts was between 5% and 25%. **(B)** Response times (RT) were significantly longer for difficult choices than for easy choices ($P < 0.005$). **(C)** Difficult choices are associated with greater BOLD signal changes in the DLPFC, VLPFC, LOFC, and inferoparietal cortex (time by difficulty interaction significant at $P < 0.05$ for all areas).

Specifically, we examined the relationship of activity to decision difficulty, under the assumption that areas involved in decision making would be engaged to a greater degree (and therefore exhibit greater activity) by more difficult decisions (*30*). As expected, the areas of activity observed in visual, premotor, and supplementary motor cortex were not influenced by difficulty, consistent with their role in non–decision-related processes. In contrast, all of the other regions in prefrontal and parietal cortex identified in our initial screen for δ areas showed a significant effect of difficulty, with greater activity associated with more difficult decisions (Fig. 3) (*31*). These findings are consistent with a large number of neurophysiological and neuroimaging studies that have implicated these areas in higher level cognitive functions (*32, 33*). Furthermore, the areas identified in inferior parietal cortex are similar to those that have been implicated in numerical processing, both in humans and in nonhuman species (*34*). Therefore, our findings are consistent with the hypothesis that lateral prefrontal (and associated parietal) areas are activated by all types of intertemporal choices, not just by those involving immediate rewards.

If this hypothesis is correct, then it makes an additional strong prediction: For choices between immediate and delayed outcomes ($d = 0$), decisions

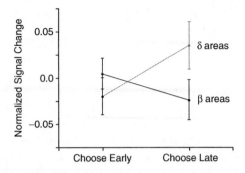

Figure 4. Greater activity in δ than β areas is associated with the choice of later larger rewards. To assess overall activity among β and δ areas and to make appropriate comparisons, we first normalized the percent signal change (using a z-score correction) within each area and each subject, so that the contribution of each brain area was determined relative to its own range of signal variation. Normalized signal change scores were then averaged across areas and subjects separately for the β and δ areas (as identified in Figs. 1 and 2). The average change scores are plotted for each system and each choice outcome. Relative activity in β and δ brain regions correlates with subjects' choices for decisions involving money available today. There was a significant interaction between area and choice ($P < 0.005$), with δ areas showing greater activity when the choice was made for the later option.

should be determined by the relative activation of the β and δ systems (*35*). More specifically, we assume that when the β system is engaged, it almost always favors the earlier option. Therefore, choices for the later option should reflect a greater influence of the δ system. This implies that choices for the later option should be associated with greater activity in the δ system than in the β system. To test this prediction, we examined activity in β and δ areas for all choices involving the opportunity for a reward today ($d = 0$) to ensure some engagement of the β system. Figure 4 shows that our prediction is confirmed: δ areas were significantly more active than were β areas when participants chose the later option, whereas activity was comparable (with a trend toward greater β-system activity) when participants chose the earlier option.

In economics, intertemporal choice has long been recognized as a domain in which "the passions" can have large sway in affecting our choices (*36*). Our findings lend support to this intuition. Our analysis shows that the β areas, which are activated disproportionately when choices involve an opportunity for near-term reward, are associated with limbic and paralimbic cortical structures, known to be rich in dopaminergic innervation. These structures have consistently been implicated in impulsive behavior (*37*), and drug addiction is commonly thought to involve disturbances of dopaminergic neurotransmission in these systems (*38*).

Our results help to explain why many factors other than temporal proximity, such as the sight or smell or touch of a desired object, are associated with impulsive behavior. If impatient behavior is driven by limbic activation, it follows that any factor that produces such activation may have effects similar to that of immediacy (*10*). Thus, for example, heroin addicts temporally discount not only heroin but also money more steeply when they are in a drug-craving state (immediately before receiving treatment with an opioid agonist) than when they are not in a drug-craving state (immediately after treatment) (*39*). Immediacy, it seems, may be only one of many factors that, by producing limbic activation, engenders impatience. An important question for future research will be to consider how the steep discounting exhibited by limbic structures in our study of intertemporal preferences relates to the involvement of these structures (and the striatum in particular) in other time-processing tasks, such as interval timing (*40*) and temporal discounting in reinforcement learning paradigms (*41*).

Our analysis shows that the δ areas, which are activated uniformly during all decision epochs, are associated with lateral prefrontal and parietal areas commonly implicated in higher level deliberative processes and cognitive control, including numerical computation (*34*). Such processes are likely to be engaged by the quantitative analysis of economic options and the valuation of future opportunities for reward. The degree of engagement of the δ areas predicts deferral of gratification, consistent with a key role in future planning (*32, 33, 42*).

More generally, our present results converge with those of a series of recent imaging studies that have examined the role of limbic structures in valuation and decision making (*26, 43, 44*) and interactions between prefrontal cortex and limbic mechanisms in a variety of behavioral contexts, ranging from economic and moral decision making to more visceral responses, such as pain and disgust (*45–48*). Collectively, these studies suggest that human behavior is often governed by a competition between lower level, automatic processes that may reflect evolutionary adaptations to particular environments, and the more recently evolved, uniquely human capacity for abstract, domain-general reasoning and future planning. Within the domain of intertemporal choice, the idiosyncrasies of human preferences seem to reflect a competition between the impetuous limbic grasshopper and the provident prefrontal ant within each of us.

References and Notes

1. G. Ainslie, *Psychol. Bull.* **82**, 463 (1975).
2. S. Frederick, G. Loewenstein, T. O'Donoghue, *J. Econ. Lit.* **40**, 351 (2002).

3. T. C. Koopmans, *Econometrica* **32**, 82 (1960).

4. G. Ainslie, *Picoeconomics* (Cambridge University Press, Cambridge, 1992).

5. H. M. Shefrin, R. H. Thaler, *Econ. Inq.* **26**, 609 (1988).

6. R. Benabou, M. Pycia, *Econ. Lett.* **77**, 419 (2002).

7. R. J. Herrnstein, *The Matching Law: Papers in Psychology and Economics*, H. Rachlin, D. I. Laibson, Eds. (Harvard Univ. Press, Cambridge, MA, 1997).

8. H. Rachlin, *The Science of Self-Control* (Harvard University Press, Cambridge, MA, 2000).

9. P. R. Montague, G. S. Berns, *Neuron* **36**, 265 (2002).

10. G. Loewenstein, *Org. Behav. Hum. Decis. Proc.* **65**, 272 (1996).

11. J. Metcalfe, W. Mischel, *Psychol. Rev.* **106**, 3 (1999).

12. H. Rachlin, *Judgment, Decision and Choice: A Cognitive/Behavioral Synthesis* (Freeman, New York, 1989), chap. 7.

13. J. H. Kagel, R. C. Battalio, L. Green, *Economic Choice Theory: An Experimental Analysis of Animal Behavior* (Cambridge University Press, Cambridge, 1995).

14. M. Macmillan, *Brain Cogn.* **19**, 72 (1992).

15. A. Bechara, A. R. Damasio, H. Damasio, S. W. Anderson, *Cognition* **50**, 7 (1994).

16. D. Laibson, *Q. J. Econ.* **112**, 443 (1997).

17. G. Angeletos, D. Laibson, A. Repetto, J. Tobacman, S. Weinberg, *J. Econ. Perspect.* **15**, 47 (2001).

18. T. O'Donoghue, M. Rabin, *Am. Econ. Rev.* **89**, 103 (1999).

19. E. S. Phelps, R. A. Pollak, *Rev. Econ. Stud.* **35**, 185 (1968).

20. J. Elster, *Ulysses and the Sirens: Studies in Rationality and Irrationality* (Cambridge University Press, Cambridge, 1979).

21. Materials and methods are available as supporting material on *Science* Online.

22. J. Olds, *Science* **127**, 315 (1958).

23. B. G. Hoebel, *Am. J. Clin. Nutr.* **42**, 1133 (1985).

24. W. Schultz, P. Dayan, P. R. Montague, *Science* **275**, 1593 (1997).

25. H. C. Breiter, B. R. Rosen, *Ann. N.Y. Acad. Sci.* **877**, 523 (1999).

26. B. Knutson, G. W. Fong, C. M. Adams, J. L. Varner, D. Hommer, *Neuroreport* **12**, 3683 (2001).

27. S. M. McClure, G. S. Berns, P. R. Montague, *Neuron* **38**, 339 (2003).

28. Our analysis also identified a region in the dorsal hippocampus as responding preferentially in the d = today condition. However, the mean event-related response in these voxels was qualitatively different from that in the other regions identified by the β analysis (fig. S2). To confirm this, for each area we conducted paired t tests comparing d = today with d = 2 weeks and d = 1 month at each time point after the time of choice. All areas showed at least two time points at which activity was significantly greater for d = today ($P < 0.01$; Bonferroni correction for five comparisons) except the hippocampus, which, by contrast, is not significant for any individual time point. For these reasons, we do not include this region in further analyses. Results are available in (*21*) (fig. S2).

29. One possible explanation for increased activity associated with choice sets that contain immediate rewards is that the discounted value for these choice sets is higher than the discounted value of choice sets that contain only delayed rewards.

To rule out this possibility, we estimated discounted value for each choice as the maximum discounted value among the two options. We made the simplifying assumption that subjects maintain a constant weekly discount rate and estimated this value based on expressed preferences (best-fitting value was 7.5% discount rate per week). We then regressed out effects of value from our data with two separate mechanisms. First, we included value as a separate control variable in our baseline GLM model and tested for β and δ effects. Second, we performed a hierarchical analysis in which the effect of value was estimated in a first-stage GLM; this source of variation was then partialed out of the data and the residual data was used to identify β and δ regions in a second-stage GLM. Both of these procedures indicate that value has minimal effects on our results, with all areas of activation remaining significant at $P < 0.001$, uncorrected.

30. Difficulty was assessed by appealing to the variance in preferences indicated by participants. In particular, when the percent difference between dollar amounts of the options in each choice pair was 1% or 3%, subjects invariably opted for the earlier reward, and when the percent difference was 35% or 50%, subjects always selected the later, larger amount. Given this consistency in results, we call these choices "easy." For all other differences, subjects show large variability in preference, and we call these choices "difficult" (Fig. 3A). These designations are further justified by analyzing the mean response time for difficult and easy questions. Subjects required on average 3.95 s to respond to difficult questions and 3.42 s to respond to easy questions (Fig. 3B) ($P < 0.005$). We assume that these differences in response time reflect prolonged decision-making processes for the difficult choices. Based on these designations, we calculated mean blood oxygenation level—dependent (BOLD) responses for easy and difficult choices (Fig. 3C).

31. Because difficulty was associated with longer RT, it was necessary to rule out nonspecific (i.e. non–decision-related) effects of RT as a confound in producing our results. We performed analyses controlling for RT analogous to those performed for discounted value as described above (29). This is a conservative test because, as noted above (30), we hypothesize that at least some of the variance in RT was related to the decision-making processes of interest. Nevertheless, these analyses indicated that removing the effects of RT does not qualitatively affect our results.

32. E. K. Miller, J. D. Cohen, *Annu. Rev. Neurosci.* **24**, 167 (2001).

33. E. E. Smith, J. Jonides, *Science* **283**, 1657 (1999).

34. S. Dehaene, G. Dehaene-Lambertz, L. Cohen, *Trends Neurosci.* **21**, 355 (1998).

35. This prediction requires only that we assume that activity in each system reflects its overall engagement by the decision and, therefore, its contribution to the outcome. Specifically, it does not require that we assume that the level of activity in either system reflects the value assigned to a particular choice.

36. A. Smith, *Theory of Moral Sentiments* (A. Millar, A. Kinkaid, J. Bell, London and Edinburgh, 1759).

37. J. Biederman, S. V. Faraone, *J. Atten. Disord.* **6**, S1 (2002).

38. G. F. Koob, F. E. Bloom, *Science* **242**, 715 (1988).

39. L. A. Giordano *et al.*, *Psychopharmacology (Berl.)* **163**, 174 (2002).

40. W. H. Meck, A. M. Benson, *Brain Cogn.* **48**, 195 (2002).

41. S. C. Tanaka *et al.*, *Nature Rev. Neurosci.* **7**, 887 (2004).

42. Our results are also consistent with the hypothesis that the fronto-parietal system inhibits the impulse to choose more immediate rewards. However, this hypothesis does not easily account for the fact that this system is recruited even when both rewards are substantially delayed (e.g. 1 month versus 1 month and 2 weeks) and the existence of an impulsive response seems unlikely. Therefore, we favor the hypothesis that fronto-parietal regions may project future benefits (through abstract reasoning or possibly "simulation" with imagery), providing top-down support for responses that favor greater long-term reward and allowing them to compete effectively with limbically mediated responses when these are present.

43. I. Aharon *et al.*, *Neuron* **32**, 537 (2001).

44. B. Seymour *et al.*, *Nature* **429**, 664 (2004).

45. J. D. Greene, R. B. Sommerville, L. E. Nystrom, J. M. Darley, J. D. Cohen, *Science* **293**, 2105 (2001).

46. A. G. Sanfey, J. K. Rilling, J. A. Aronson, L. E. Nystrom, J. D. Cohen, *Science* **300**, 1755 (2003).

47. T. D. Wager *et al.*, *Science* **303**, 1162 (2004).

48. K. N. Ochsner, S. A. Bunge, J. J. Gross, J. D. Gabrieli, *J. Cogn. Neurosci.* **14**, 1215 (2002).

49. We thank K. D'Ardenne, L. Nystrom, and J. Lee for help with the experiment and J. Schooler for inspiring discussions in the early planning phases of this work. This work was supported by NIH grants MH132804 (J.D.C.), MH065214 (S.M.M.), National Institute on Aging grant AG05842 (D.I.L.), and NSF grant SES-0099025 (D.I.L.).

Supporting Online Material
www.sciencemag.org/cgi/content/full/306/5695/503/
DC1
Materials and Methods
Figs. S1 and S2
Tables S1 and S2
References

Index

Index

Ashraf, N. 92, 95
Atkinson, J. W. 140
attention-narrowing 531–532
attention-shift 156, 157, 162
Attneave, F. 152
attributes *see* evaluability hypothesis
auctions 296–298, 298**f**, 331–332
    and markets 112–113
Austin, L. 598
Austin, W. 186
Ausubel, L. M. 315, 499**n**
Averill, J. R. 587
aversive curiosity 144, 146, 148, 158, 159; *see*
    also curiosity; diversive curiosity; specific
    curiosity; state curiosity; trait curiosity
Azjen, I. 527, 567

Babakus, E. 316
Babcock, L. 6, 91, 111, 215, 218**n**, 222, 223,
    224, 225, 226, 226**n**, 229
Badger, G. J. 354**n**, 369
Bailey, M. 388
Bajtelsmit, V. L. 597
Baker, J. 585
Baker, N. J. 616
Baldacchino, A. 616
Bankhart, C. P. 587
Bar-On, R. 618
bargaining 223**t**, 369
    impasse 215–237
    inefficiency 370, 373
Bargh, J. A. 570
Barlas, S. 507
Barlow, D. H. 19, 572, 578, 592
Barnes, L. W. 78, 397, 444
Barnes, O. 78, 397, 444
Baron, J. 143, 251, 271, 272, 581
Barsky, B. 584
Bartholomew, R. 593
Bassok, M. 114, 331
Battalio, R. C. 640
Baumeister, R. F. 41, 42, 43, 45, 49
Baumhart, R. 220
Bazerman, M. H. 6, 184**n**, 219, 224, 230, 248,
    259, 260, 268, 286**n**, 331, 341, 372, 422
Beach, L. R. 558
Beattie, J. 251, 507
Because It is There (Loewenstein) 5**n**
Bechara, A. 570, 579, 580, 600, 616, 617, 618,
    622, 640
Beck, A. T. 593
Becker, G. 550
Becker, G. M. 284, 295, 299, 629
Becker, G. S. 282, 315, 357
Becker, M. H. 567
Becker-Degroot-Marschak 284, 295, 299, 629
Beckmann, J. 527

behavior 209, 233, 370, 416, 534, 540, 557, 572
    curiosity 131–133
    decision theory 150, 164
    visceral influences on 526–536, 536**t**,
        537–563; *see also* human behavior
behavioral economics 24, 25, 27, 36, 80, 90,
    99, 328, 527, 627
    disorders 124–125
    experimental 107–120
    modeling 28, 48–49, 50, 359
Behrens, D. 154, 155, 158, 161, 162
Beiser, H. R. 136
Bell, D. E. 208, 442, 568
Bemasek, A. 597
Bénabou, R. 91, 640
Benartzi, S. 580, 617
benefits, nonmonotonic optimal
    plans 430–432
Benhabib, J. 90
Benson, A. M. 646
Bentham, J. 5, 6, 7, 11, 12, 18, 24, 25, 33, 36,
    62, 76, 128, 389
Benthin, A. 583
Benzion, U. 416, 418, 427
bequest motives 74, 75, 99, 400
Berg, C. A. 134
Berg, J. 95
Berlyne, D. E. 127**n**, 129, 130, 131, 138, 139,
    140, 141, 145, 146**n**, 147, 147**n**, 148,
    149, 157, 158, 160
Bernartzi, S. 6, 91
Bernay, T. 587
Bernheim, B. D. 362**n**
Bernheim, D. 25, 90, 92
Berns, G. S. 640, 643
Berridge, K. C. 18, 121, 122
Berscheid, S. 184, 186, 192
Bettman, J. R. 38, 285, 568, 575
Betz, N. 584
Bewley, T. F. 305
Beyth-Maronm, R. 598
Bickel, W. K. 354**n**, 369
Biderman, A. D. 547
Biederman, J. 645
Billig, M. 40
Birnbaum, M. H. 246, 268
Bisin, A. 90
Biswas-Diener, R. 98
Black, D. W. 628
Blackshaw, A. J. 616
Blais, A.-R. 584
Blanchard, D. 542
Bloom, F. E. 645
Blount, S. 219**n**, 233, 248, 260, 286**n**
Blumenberg, H. 127**n**, 128, 159
Blumberg, S. J. 44, 351
Bodenhausen, G. 626

Index